PROPERTY MANAGEMENT HANDBOOK

Real Estate for Professional Practitioners
A Wiley Series

DAVID CLURMAN, Editor

PROPERTY MANAGEMENT HANDBOOK

A PRACTICAL GUIDE TO REAL ESTATE MANAGEMENT

Edited by

ROBERT F. CUSHMAN, ESQUIRE
Partner
Pepper, Hamilton & Scheetz
Philadelphia, Pennsylvania

NEAL I. RODIN
President
Rodin Management, Inc.
Philadelphia, Pennsylvania

A Ronald Press Publication

JOHN WILEY & SONS
NEW YORK   CHICHESTER   BRISBANE   TORONTO   SINGAPORE

Copyright © 1985 by John Wiley & Sons, Inc.

All rights reserved. Published simultaneously in Canada.

This publication is designed to provide accurate and
authoritative information in regard to the subject
matter covered. It is sold with the understanding that
the publisher is not engaged in rendering legal, accounting,
or other professional service. If legal advice or other
expert assistance is required, the services of a competent
professional person should be sought. *From a Declaration
of Principles jointly adopted by a Committee of the
American Bar Association and a Committee of Publishers.*

Library of Congress Cataloging in Publication Data:

Main entry under title:

Property management handbook.

    (Real estate for professional practitioners, ISSN 0190-8375)
    "A Ronald Press publication."
    Includes index.
    1. Real estate management. 2. Real estate investment.
I. Cushman, Robert Fairchild, 1918–   . II. Rodin, Neal I.
III. Series.
HD1394.P76   1984   333.3;068   84-10427
ISBN 0-471-87503-1

Printed in the United States of America

10 9 8 7 6 5 4

This book is dedicated

to

Martha & Rose

Two world-class ladies,
who crystallized the dream
and supplied the love

GARDNER S. MCBRIDE
Executive Vice President
Buildings Owners and
Managers Association International
Washington, D.C.

Gardner S. McBride, a graduate of the Drew University, has been the Executive Vice President of the Building Owners and Managers Association since 1975. BOMA International is a non-profit trade association of commercial office building owners, managers, developers, and investors. It has more than 5,000 members in 75 cities and 10 countries, who control over one billion square feet of office space and look to BOMA International for economic information, industry consulting services, legislative and regulatory monitoring, and book publishing. Mr. McBride is also Secretary of the Building Owners and Managers Institute, a non-profit educational institution that offers programs and professional certification in all aspects of property administration.

FOREWORD

More than at any time in history, private individuals are joining with builders, developers, and brokers in identifying and purchasing property. In recent years, equity participations in real estate by institutional investors such as pension and equity funds, brokerage houses, and other financial investors have increased significantly. Ownership has brought with it the necessity of managing the property responsibly as well as the opportunity to enhance its value.

Often in the past, when investors sought to analyze the value of an acquisition of property, insufficient attention was paid to property management. Today, with future value at stake, sophisticated and knowledgeable property management is the only way to be sure that projections made during the acquisition process are achieved. Good property management creates higher value and property management considerations are now among the first items addressed in the acquisition process.

The new emphasis on property management has raised the level of professionalism throughout the industry and makes it vital for all to be aware of the precise strategies and techniques employed by the most successful industry practitioners in creating and maintaining value. This handbook, written by hands-on experts who approach property management from a number of different angles, documents these state-of-the-art strategies and techniques for all who will manage real estate in the 1980s. It is a unique book in that it is directed to both the private investor on a "roll up your shirt sleeves and do it" practical approach and to the avid professional who will respond to the principles and applications. The editors have chosen their experts wisely and well.

Gardner S. McBride

SERIES PREFACE

Since the end of World War II, tremendous changes have taken place in the business and residential real estate fields throughout the world. This has been evidenced not only be architectural changes, exemplified by the modern shopping center, but also in the many innovative financing responses that have enabled development of new structures and complexes, such as multiuse buildings. It can be expected that real estate development will speed in new directions at an ever increasing pace to match the oncoming needs of our time. With this perspective, the Real Estate for Professional Practitioners Series has been developed in response to professional needs.

As real estate professional activities have become divided into specialties, because of intensive demand for expertise at all stages, so has there developed an increasing need for extensive training and continual education for persons directly involved or dealing in business ventures requiring detailed knowledge of realty procedures.

Perhaps no field of business endeavor is more in need of a series of professional books than real estate. Working in the practical world of business and residential construction and space utilization, or at advanced levels of college training covering these areas, one is constantly aware that too little of existing creative thinking has been transcribed into viable books. Many of the books that have been written do not thoroughly enough encompass both the practical and theoretical aspects of complex subjects. Too often the drive for immediate answers has led to the overlooking of fundamental purposes and technical know-how that might lead to much more favorable results for the persons seeking knowledge.

This series will be made up of books thoroughly and expertly expounding existing procedures in the many fields of real estate, but searching as well for innovative solutions to current and future problems. These books are intended to offer a compendium of each author's wide experience and knowledge to aid the seasoned professional.

The series is addressed to professionals in all walks of realty endeavor. These include business investors and developers, urban affairs specialists, attorneys, accountants, and the many others whose work involves real estate creativity and investment. Just as importantly, the series will present to advanced students in many realty fields the opportunity to review professional thinking that will help to stimulate their own thoughts on modern trends in housing and business construction.

We believe these goals can be achieved by the outstanding group of authors who will create the books in the series.

DAVID CLURMAN

PREFACE

Managing real estate is far more than hiring a good maintenance crew and a competent bookkeeper. Managing real estate is maximizing the profit potential of property through sound planning and financial control. The planning and control process includes the following considerations:

Appropriate management decisions prior to ownership.

The creation of a management plan.

Effective leasing.

The legal and fiduciary aspects of property management.

Tax aspects of asset management.

Record keeping and financial reporting.

The use of the architect engineer and landscape architect.

The use of the interior designer.

Methods to manage a troubled property.

The effective use of insurance.

Reducing energy consumption.

The use of the computer in property management.

That is what Property Management Handbook is about—making the real estate purchase a viable and vibrant investment.

More frequently than not, the most important aspect of buying and owning property—property management—is overlooked, both during the evaluation and, unfortunately, even after the real estate is purchased. *It is in fact only sophisticated and knowledgeable property management which can allow others to achieve their desired projections and keep them viable thereafter.* Property management—creating value by living with the property astutely—increases the equity of an investment.

In reality, property management is the front end of the real estate business.

ROBERT F. CUSHMAN
NEAL I. RODIN

Philadelphia, Pennsylvania
September 1984

ABOUT THE EDITORS

ROBERT F. CUSHMAN, ESQUIRE
Partner
Pepper, Hamilton & Scheetz
Philadelphia, Pennsylvania

Robert F. Cushman is a partner in the national law firm of Pepper, Hamilton & Scheetz and a recognized specialist and lecturer on all phases of real estate and construction and surety law. He serves as legal counsel to numerous trade associations, and construction, development, and bonding companies.

Mr. Cushman is the Editor and Co-Author of

Doing Business in America (Dow Jones-Irwin).

The Construction Management Form Book (McGraw-Hill).

The Construction Business Handbook (McGraw-Hill).

Representing the Owner in Construction Litigation (John Wiley & Sons).

The Businessman's Guide to Construction (Dow Jones-Irwin).

The Construction Industry Formbook (Shepard's Inc.).

The Business Insurance Handbook (Dow Jones-Irwin).

Avoiding Liability in Architecture, Design, and Construction (John Wiley & Sons).

Planning, Financing and Constructing Health Care Facilities (Aspen Systems Corporation).

He is presently editing *Handling Property, Casualty, Fidelity, and Surety Claims* for John Wiley & Sons as well as *Anatomy of a Real Estate Project* for Dow Jones-Irwin.

Mr. Cushman, who is a member of the Bar of the Commonwealth of Pennsylvania and who is admitted to practice before the Supreme Court of the United States and the United States Court of Claims, has served as Executive Vice President and General Counsel to the Construction Industry Foundation as well as Regional Chairman of the Public Contract Law Section of the American Bar Association. He is a member of the International Association of Insurance Counsel.

NEAL I. RODIN, PRESIDENT
Rodin Realty Investment Corporation
Philadelphia, Pennsylvania

Neal I. Rodin is President of Rodin Realty Investment Corporation, Rodin Enterprises, Inc., and Rodin Management, whose companies are correspondent companies for Sun Life Insurance Company of America.

These companies manage over one billion dollars in residential and commercial property. Mr. Rodin, who received his degree in Finance and Economics from Temple University, is on the faculty of the New York Law Journal Real Estate Program.

CONTENTS

H. LELAND WHITFIELD, III
Vice President
Regional Director of Marketing
Coldwell Banker
Atlanta, Georgia

H. Leland Whitfield, III is a graduate of the U.S. Naval Academy, Annapolis, Maryland, where he earned a B.S. in Aerospace Engineering. He is a Vice President and Director of Marketing for Apartment Sales with Coldwell Banker Commercial Real Estate Services. He specializes in analyzing and structuring apartment sale transactions. He has owned, managed, syndicated, and brokered investment properties.

CHAPTER 1

PROPERTY MANAGEMENT BEFORE OWNERSHIP

INTRODUCTION

The key ingredient to the success of an investment in real estate is management. In order to maximize the effectiveness of the investment, considerable thought must be given to the creation of a management plan prior to the acquisition of the property. It is before purchasing an investment property that the investor would be well-advised to both develop a clear understanding of why the purchase is being made and establish the precise goals that the investment is expected to achieve. Determining the "why" to the purchase of real estate is the first step.

Specific objectives should be formulated from the answers to the question "why invest in this particular real estate." For instance, purchasing real estate to generate cash flow or return on the investment may be of particular importance to the investor. Alternatively, the investor might be interested in capital appreciation or in the tax shelter benefits investment property can provide to those who would like to pay the Internal Revenue Service less money at tax time. Because it is impossible to totally isolate these goals from each other, the management plan should strive to weigh each of these components and combine them in proper balance. While there is no guarantee real estate will continue to increase in value, it has faired quite well in the past, even during eras when inflation was eroding the value of other investments.

RETURN ON INVESTMENT

Return on investment is a term that means many things to many people. It is often confused with other similar phrases. Return on investment is frequently referred to as cash flow, pre-tax cash flow, or "yield." In fact, return on investment is simply the ratio of cash flow divided by the amount of the investor's cash that was placed into the property as equity. The definition, however, is not as important as its effect in weighing an investment. It is a means of measuring the performance of a property. For this discussion, cash flows are dollars remaining from the collected rent after the costs of running the property (expenses) are paid and the debt service payments are subtracted. Cash flows can be positive (producing income for the investor) or negative (requiring the investor to supply additional funds to manage the property).

Therefore, if the primary objective is to maximize the immediate return on investment, then the management plan will require the property to produce sufficient cash after expenses and mortgage payments to meet that expected return.

An investor seeking a 10% return on a $100,000 investment in real estate could accomplish his goal in various ways. For example, the investor could purchase an income-producing property with a gross annual income of $20,000 and a vacancy factor and expense deduction totalling $10,000. In this example, there is no loan; therefore, no mortgage payments are required.

$$
\begin{aligned}
\text{Property:} \\
\text{Sale price} &= \$100,000 \\
\text{Cash investment} &= \$100,000 \\
\text{Gross annual income} &= \$20,000 \\
\frac{\text{Vacancy and expenses}}{\text{Cash flow}} &= \frac{-10,000}{\$10,000} \\
\text{Return on investment} &= \frac{\text{Cash flow}}{\text{Cash invested}} \\
\text{Return on investment} &= \frac{\$10,000}{\$100,000} \\
\text{Return on investment} &= 10\%
\end{aligned}
$$

Another way to accomplish a 10% return on a $100,000 investment in real estate is to purchase a $1 million property with a $100,000 down payment, thus creating a $900,000 mortgage. To demonstrate the effect of attaining a 10% return in this way, assume that (1) the mortgage loan has total yearly payments of $72,000, (2) the property produces a gross annual income of $150,000, (3) there are vacancy, and expense deductions totalling $68,000.

Property:		
Sale price	=	$1,000,000
Cash investment	=	$100,000
Gross annual income	=	$150,000
Vacancy and expenses	=	−68,000
Net income before debt service		$82,000
Net income before debt service =		$82,000
Mortgage payment	=	−72,000
Cash flow		$10,000
Return on investment		$10,000
		$100,000
Return on investment	=	10%

These two examples show that an investment in property ranging in price from $100,000 to $1 million—a tenfold difference—could accomplish one of the investor's goals or objectives. Such a major difference in the two potential sale prices should point out that there is more to the ownership of real estate investment, than cash flow.

Real Estate Versus Other Alternatives

This pure cash flow analysis does not demonstrate other important features of real estate ownership. If the 10% return discussed above is to be used as a basis for deciding whether to invest in real estate or whether to invest in a money market fund paying 11%, one must consider several other advantages of real estate ownership which are not present in other investment vehicles. Of major concern are the income tax benefits that are typically enjoyed by the real estate investor. While technical real estate analysts have tried to derive the perfect comparison formula, it is impossible to assign a general formula to compare real estate with other investment alternatives. There is no formula that can generalize each investor's unique circumstances and tax planning needs.

In an attempt to weigh the tax benefits that real estate generates, allow for inflation, and measure the affect of a particular mode and amount of financing in a particular investment situation, the investment community developed the concept or formula of the after-tax discounted yield (also known as the internal rate of return or IRR). The IRR is a calculation encompassing all of the variables influencing the performance of an investment in real estate. The IRR includes inflation, the consequences of financing, and the part that federal and state income tax laws play in the investment picture.

It was hoped that these calculations would yield a figure that would be easily compared to bond yields and stock performance coefficients. Investors would have a way to select the highest ratio.

The IRR is valid in that it is a logical sequence of mathematical computations. However, several of the variables used in the formula are based on assumptions. Allocating amounts for these assumptions is the single most important exercise of the prospective investor. First, the inflation factor causes the largest amount of distortion. Second, the tax laws change. Third, the income tax bracket of the investor may change yearly and can distort the accuracy of the IRR. Consequently, these variables cannot be expected to remain fixed numbers and the assumption of the IRR computation is always subject to forces outside an investor's control.

When comparing investment alternatives, therefore, the choices must be analyzed in a fashion whereby variables correctly portray the unique circumstances that a particular investor will face. An investment selection based purely on return is not valid. Moreover, the risk factor inherent in each investment must also be fully weighed before a specific investment is selected as the "best" alternative.

CAPITAL APPRECIATION

Capital appreciation is the increase in value experienced by a parcel of real estate during the period of ownership. Capital appreciation is synonymous with "equity growth" and "increasing net worth." This increase in value can result from a demand for either the property or its location. If the demand increases and the supply does not increase correspondingly, the value of the property will increase. Capital appreciation can also result from an increase in net income. Typically, an increase in net income will provide for a corresponding increase in value.

Creating capital appreciation by means of increasing the net income can be accomplished by more than one method. Purchasing a property and raising the rent is one obvious way. Investors often look for properties that are out of style or have suffered from lack of maintenance or other factors which have limited the net income. Their management plan encompasses the rehabilitation or modernization of the property. They assume that once the property has been upgraded it will command a higher rent. This potential for increase must be determined by considerable investigation prior to making the commitment of time and money to the property. Certain questions must be answered: What is a reasonable expectation of collectable rent when the property is ready for occupancy? How much will it cost to put the property in condition to attain that rental income? In addition, consultation with those who are active in similar investments and those who have knowledge of the property's location is advised.

Capital appreciation can also be achieved through inflation. Real estate has fared well, and at the very least has maintained its value in the form of purchasing power against a shrinking dollar. In reality, inflation protection is not necessarily an increase in spending power but rather a method of not losing it. For this reason, the "increase" in value and the resulting increase in the owner's equity due to inflation creates a capital appreciation resulting in the retention of dollar value.

LEVERAGE

Investors wishing to maximize the resulting increase in property value caused by inflation have capitalized on the use of leverage. Leverage is a consideration in developing value that should be weighed at the outset of a transaction. The term, frequently used in the real estate business, simply stated means that the purchaser's equity in the property is less than the purchase price. Leverage is achieved by having all or a portion of the funds coming from a source other than the purchaser. The key to leverage is the ability to purchase property without having to provide the entire amount of the purchase price from the buyer's personal funds. The most familiar use of leverage is a purchase where a portion of the purchase price is money borrowed from either a lending institution, the seller, or both.

Leverage is important in the property management plan because the amount of borrowed funds determines both the amount of net income required to make the payments on those borrowed monies and the equity portion needed for a specific transaction.

In the real estate market, it is typical for the purchase price to increase as the amount of equity placed in the property decreases. Initially, this might appear to be contradictory. The market, though, places a premium (normally reflected in the sale price) on reducing the equity required to purchase a property. The typical purchaser considers any return earned from those dollars *not* included in the equity portion. In addition, the increase due to expected appreciation is weighed in determining the desirable amount of leverage.

Assume two adjacent buildings were purchased. Each building had an equal number of units, similar amenities, and no detrimental construction problems. Each is purchased for $1 million. The terms, however, are substantially different. Building A is purchased by an investor who takes the money from his savings account and pays the entire price as equity. After one year the building is sold for $1.1 million. The investor is happy because a 10% "return" on the $1 million investment was realized. Building B, though, was purchased under highly leveraged terms. The purchaser bought the property by making a $100,000 equity payment and received loans for $900,000. This investor also sold Building B after one year for $1.1 million. The investor in this situation doubled his equity or made a 100% return on the invested capital. He is even happier.

Building A gave the investor some return during the year because no loan payments were required. The investor in Building B would have had to pay something for the loan against Building B, thus lowering the overall return. Some of that debt service, however, could have been offset by investing the money not put in Building B into other income producing investments.

The following situations illustrate the debt service versus loan amount aspects of leverage and demonstrate the complexities which leverage introduces to the process of investment evaluating.

Situation A:
Equity	$300,000
Debt	+700,000
Sale price	$1,000,000

$700,000 loan has $6416.67 as a monthly payment.

Situation B:
Equity	$150,000
Debt	+850,000
Sale price	$1,000,000

$850,000 loan has $7791.67 as a monthly payment.

Assume that the $150,000 not used in Situation B can be invested in the stock market or in another investment where it will earn 11%. It will return $16,500 per year or $1,375 per month.

The debt service on $850,000	= $7791.67 per month
The debt service on $700,000	= $6416.67 per month
The difference	= $1375.00 per month

Overall there is no difference. The purchaser is able to earn a sufficient return on the cash not placed in the property to offset the increased debt service. The purchaser can afford to pay more for increased debt service because the dollars not used for equity can be used to earn a return elsewhere.

TAX SHELTER

The term tax shelter is often used to define anything that relates to "write off" against income. All tax shelters are write-offs, but not all write-offs are tax shelters. For example, an amount equal to the paid interest on the money borrowed to complete the purchase of a parcel of real estate may be subtracted from the taxpayer's income. It is a write-off—but it is not a tax shelter.

Tax shelter is the deduction against income provided by the tax laws through the use of depreciation. Depreciation (as it was known until 1981) or cost recovery (the current terminology) is the write-off created by the establishment of an economic life for the property and the annual deduction of a portion of its value from that economic life. It is not something for nothing. The investor has to have an interest in the property before the property can provide the write-off and the write-off is the yearly deduction to recover the cost of the investment.

Consider the following as an example of the effect of depreciation. An investment is made in an apartment property with a purchase price of $1.25 million. The land value is $250,000 and the amount available for cost recovery is $1 million. Assume that the property has a collected annual income of $175,000, a total of fixed and variable expenses of $75,000, and the total of the annual mortgage interest payment is $100,000. The investor has created an income of $175,000 by investing in this apartment project. In order to earn that $175,000, the investor must pay $75,000 to operate the property and $100,000 in interest to make the loan payments on the money borrowed to purchase it. Therefore, the investor has earned $175,000 and had a write-off of $175,000 but hasn't made any money and really has not provided any tax shelter. If the investor is highly motivated to create an additional write-off, then selecting a cost recovery schedule that generates the maximum number of deductions is in order. Thus, the investor might select a 15-year write-off accelerating by 175%. If eligible, the property would create a first-year deduction equal to 12% of the amount available for depreciation or $120,000. (Multiplying 12% times $1 million would furnish a write-off against other income of $120,000.) This write-off is shelter. In effect, the apartment property which was purchased for $1.25 million collected income of $175,000 and generated a write-off of $295,000. Expenses and interest payments totalled $175,000 of this write off; $120,000 represented the depreciation deduction. It should be noted that this example ignores recapture and other relevant tax rules which must be developed by a competent tax specialist.

VALUATION

Arranging the order of an investor's priorities results in the formation of his investment goal. Having defined this investment goal, the investor is better able to focus on the type of property that will best satisfy the requirements of his goal. From this point on, selecting the property is merely a matter of comparing the properties available for purchase. In order to effectively compare alternatives, one must understand how to value a property.

Location

First and foremost in the analysis of value is the location of the property. Many factors make up the location evaluation process, such as the zoning of the area and other governmental regulations. Traffic patterns, proximity to employment, and population trend are other considerations. The advice of an expert who understands both your investment goals and the real estate market should facilitate the task of researching this location analysis.

Net Income Analysis

At the risk of (1) causing a stir among those in the appraisal field, and (2) sounding somewhat arrogant, this author believes that value is in the eye of the beholder and has relatively little to do with sale price. Consider the three investment goals discussed previously. If a property is paid for in cash, its sale price can be quite different than a sale where little or no cash is required. The variables—the sale price, the interest rate, the cash down payments, and other terms of a transaction—must be brought into focus to evaluate value.

Whether the property is a shopping center, office building, apartment, or other income producing property, the basis for value is the net income. Maintaining and increasing net income is the most important function of property management. Before net income can be utilized in an evaluation, it must be verified for accuracy. The first step is to calculate the gross potential rent on an annual basis. The second step is to apply a vacancy factor to it. The third step is to subtract the operating expenses. What is left is the net income. To avoid confusion, the net income is further qualified by naming it "net income before debt service. For this discussion, net income is the remaining cash available after vacancy and expenses are subtracted from the gross income, but before any mortgage payments are made.

To compute the gross income, start with the monthly rent schedule which is derived from the lease or rent agreement. Each tenant's lease or rental agreement must be verified to ascertain the amount of rent expected and what conditions the landlord must meet in order to be reasonably confident that the rent will be paid. The next step is to ascertain whether this is an accurate representation of the rental income that should be collected. The existing tenants should acknowledge that the terms and conditions of the agreement in force are in fact the ones they are observing. Peculiar conditions such as free rent or special improvements promised the tenant will surface at this juncture. Leases and rental agreements are legal contracts and should be reviewed by the investor's legal advisor.

Once the quantity of rent has been established, a quality inspection should be performed. Re-examine the leases or rental agreements. Information pertaining to the quality of the rent can be ascertained from their effective dates and help determine the frequency which the tenants change. Tenant change, referred to as "turnover," can be either favorable or detrimental depending upon the situations. For example, leases in a desirable office location with rent at less than market which may be expiring might be candidates for an increased income. Conversely, an apartment building may have many tenants moving after only brief stays as residents. This may indicate that the rent is too high.

A further review of the quality of the rent can be found in the rent collection ledger. This ledger shows how promptly the tenants pay. The collection ledger should also verify that which is stated in the rental agreement. Analysis of the rental history should help in setting goals for managing the investment and in determining value.

Vacancy and Expense

Once the gross potential rent is developed and is believed to be attainable, the vacancy and expenses affecting the property must be evaluated.

Vacancy, although easy to measure historically, is somewhat harder to project into the future. The basis for vacancy predictions must come from the past performance of the property. "Vacancy" includes the actual time during which the vacant space is marketed as well as the time needed for refurbishing between tenants. Research also helps in forecasting the vacancy. Information obtained from other relatively comparable properties is most valuable, as are the opinions of professional property management organizations. However, these sources of information can be less than accurate, for these organizations will be competing for tenants within the vicinity of the target property. Rent rates also play an important role in a property's expected vacancy. When rents are above market, a larger than average vacancy will normally occur. Conversely, below market rent should permit a property to maintain a lower vacancy factor.

Having determined a dollar amount or percentage estimate, the allowance for vacancy should be subtracted from the gross potential income. Next, the expenses (costs of doing business) are deducted from the gross. The total expense figures are usually broken down into two categories: fixed expenses and variable expenses. In theory, the fixed expenses are those which would be incurred whether or not the property was occupied by tenants. Variable expenses reflect those costs created by tenants occupying the space.

The most obvious fixed expenses, which the owner would have to pay even if the property was vacant, include:

Taxes: Real estate and personal property are subject to assessment by the tax collectors. These should be verified at the county tax office. The tax assessor should be asked if it is customary for the assessed value of the property to increase immediately upon sale.

Insurance: Typically, at least fire and some liability coverage is the responsibility of the owner. More elaborate coverages are available and their cost versus coverage should be examined. If the property has employees, workers compensation insurance is probably included.

Utilities: These include the gas, oil, or electric (energy) costs to heat, cool, and/or illuminate the common areas of the property. The costs for sewer, water, and trash removal should also be included.

Variable expenses generally fall into the following specific cost areas:

Management: This would encompass both the professional company's management fee along with those salaries or concessions paid to employees of the property.

Repairs: Care should be exercised in determining which expenses are capital expenses and which are repairs.

Maintenance: Normally covers redecorating during a turnover and would probably incorporate landscape care and upkeep for the exterior of the property. Loss of rent while redecorating space would not be reflected as maintenance, but should be shown in the vacancy calculation.

Advertising: The cost of the media used.

Reserves for Replacement: The roof, appliances, carpet, and other capital expense items must be replaced periodically. An allowance should be figured yearly to offset the relatively large cost incurred in the year of replacement.

Miscellaneous: Those costs of doing business such as dues to professional organizations, business licenses, telephones, etc.

Market

The basic determinant of value for investment real estate is the net income before debt service. From this number, both as it presently exists and in conjunction with its expected future performance, the value of investment property is established. The key issue in calculating value is the knowledge of what the "market" will pay for an expected net income. The market is not permanent, nor is change in the market easy to predict. Rarely are two similar properties purchased at identical price and terms. Motives for purchasing investment property are not static. In fact, they may change quite frequently. There are times when an investor would be well advised to utilize all his own cash to purchase a net income. There are other times when an investor should use none of his own cash, but should borrow the entire amount of the purchase price to purchase an equal net income.

Sometimes, two investors competing for the same property offer vastly different *prices* for the net income. Both offers, however, may be fundamentally the same. For example, consider a hypothetical property with a net income of $100,000 and no existing mortgage loans. In such a case, each investor will offer 25% of the price as equity and create debt financing for 75% of the purchase price. The investor expects to receive a return on investment equal to 5% of the equity placed into the property.

In the first instance, Investor A offers the seller an all cash price of $800,000 based on a cash down payment of $200,000 and a new loan of $600,000. The total annual debt service on the $600,000 loan is $90,000

Equity	$200,000
Loan	+600,000
Sale price	$800,000
Net income	$100,000
Debt service	−90,000
Cash flow	$ 10,000

$$\text{Return on investment} = \frac{\text{Cash flow}}{\text{Cash equity}}$$

$$\text{Return on investment} = \frac{\$10,000}{\$200,000}$$

$$\text{Return on investment} = 5\%$$

In the second instance, Investor B offers the seller a sale price of $1.25 million with a cash downpayment of $312,500 and gives the seller a note for $937,500 which carries a total annual debt service of $84,375.

Equity	$312,500
Loans	+937,500
Sale price	$1,250,000
Net income	$ 100,000
Debt service	−84,375
Cash flow	$ 15,625

$$\text{Return on investment} = \frac{\text{Cash flow}}{\text{Cash equity}}$$

$$\text{Return on investment} = \frac{\$15,625}{\$312,500}$$

$$\text{Return on investment} = 5\%$$

The above example, illustrates that the value of an investment property is not a direct function of the sale price. The example further illustrates that any given property sold with similar investment criteria can have a sale price variance of $450,000.

Value Is a Function of Net Income. The dollar amount the market will pay for that net income is not a consistent, easily-formulated number. As interest rates and money supply varies, so does value. As tax laws change, so does the value of real estate.

Staying abreast of the market is the most challenging aspect of dealing with investment real estate. Access to that knowledge is imperative to the success of an investment and must be part of the management plan.

SUMMARY

In summary, the property management plan must begin well in advance of the selection of a certain investment property by addressing three important concepts.

First, investment goals must be specified. An acceptable arrangement of the order of investment priorities (a. cash flow, b. capital appreciation, c. tax shelter) must be completed prior to beginning a search for property.

Second, with these items in proper perspective, the importance of net income must be realized. Acknowledging that no matter what the property type, the essence of value is the income stream.

Third, diligent study of the market must take place. Learning the forces at work effecting value are essential to making a sound investment. There is considerable competition for investment property; understanding the market place is required to successfully compete for property.

RICHARD H. KUPCHUNOS
Senior Vice President
CIGNA Capital Advisers, Inc.
Hartford, Connecticut

Richard H. Kupchunos is a Senior Vice President of CIGNA
Capital Advisers, Inc., a subsidiary of the CIGNA Corporation,
which was formed in 1982 through the merger of Connecticut
General and INA Corporations. Mr. Kupchunos is a graduate
of Providence College. His responsibilities at CIGNA include
Asset Management of approximately $6 billion of real estate
investments.

CHAPTER 2

SETTING THE MANAGEMENT PLAN

INTRODUCTION

Why a Plan

When speaking of real estate professionals, we are really talking about a diverse, broad-ranging group of experts, which includes zoning, development, finance, construction, engineering, brokerage, leasing, property management, legal, and asset management experts. Focusing the skills needed to develop and manage real estate effectively is the primary thrust of a management plan. If the needs of each property are not properly identified and the appropriate professionals are not deployed at the appropriate stages, effort, time, and real dollars in the form of lost opportunities, bottom line cash flows, and property values will be wasted.

A properly prepared management plan should be proactive. It should anticipate. In some instances it should create significant opportunities which can impact operations and property values.

The management plan for the 1980s must be more than a document detailing the operations of a property. It must be a dynamic program reflecting the collective best efforts and judgments of a full spectrum of real estate experts focused on a strategic investment direction for each property. This process should challenge and stimulate the participants to rethink all aspects of the development and management of the property. Concepts that were not feasible just two or three years ago may be most attractive today due to changes in technology or to contemporary conservation focus and pressures to contain expenses.

The conductor of this complex process is the asset manager. This asset manager typically works for a financial institution whose organization is a most complicated matrix. It is often comprised of local on-site managers, in-house staff from many areas of involvement, as well as various representatives of the owner. The management plan, properly conceived and documented, can serve as a cohesive bond to this most complicated matrix. This chapter will focus on developing and using a management plan to produce excellent, as well as consistent, results.

The Concept of Real Return/Total Return

There are special types of real estate investment that are short-range in nature and oriented toward specific short-range goals, for example, the conversion of a rental apartment building to condominiums. However, real estate investments should provide attractive long-term rates of return through current income, tax shelter, and appreciation in value. Real estate held for long-term investment has the attractive potential of producing investment return which exceeds the annual compounded rate of inflation and ultimately converts the property to a long-term capital gain as opposed to ordinary income. Simply defined, real return represents the rate of return in excess of inflation. Total return is the summation of the annual return from operations and appreciation in value of the investment.

The specific investment objectives of each owner will determine in large part how the investment must be structured financially, the length of ownership, the current returns, and the capital appreciation potential in the form of residual property value. The management plan must carefully document critical investment decisions and recommend specific courses of action. This process is akin to strategic planning. It provides a foundation for developing and delivering exceptional investment returns on a consistent basis without surprises.

Why Property Selection Alone Is Not Enough

The importance of identifying and selecting attractive real estate that possesses the characteristics required to meet the owner's investment objective cannot be overstated. Historically, property selection was considered to be the *only* important aspect to successful real estate investing. Management of the asset once acquired was relegated to a caretaker mode. The best available talent was directed toward the creation of new properties in expanding markets and was paid the highest compensation for such efforts.

Today, the identification and selection of new investments remain an important part of real estate investment, but this is now balanced with a major emphasis on managing the asset once it is acquired. It is no longer a "given" that location alone will adequately ensure the long-term viability of a real estate project. Increasing pressure on productivity demands that businesses locate in properties that are highly efficient, easily adaptable to tenant needs, and represent good value in their respective markets. This is the exciting challenge facing today's asset managers.

DEVELOPING THE MANAGEMENT PLAN

Evaluating the past performance of an investment and recommending a future course of action to improve investment performance are two important parts of a management plan which are *not* incorporated into a budget. The management plan for a property is similar to the management plan of a business. To all intents and purposes, the property asset manager is operating a business—a business with keen competition in the same market area. The plan must acknowledge this challenge head on.

The two basic elements of the management plan are the investment strategy and the operational budget.

Investment Strategy

The cornerstone of an effective management plan is the investment strategy. For illustrative purposes, assume that the owner is a financial institution committed to real estate as a long-term investment. The investment objectives are high pre-tax earnings and appreciation in value. The investment strategy for each property should be developed after the asset manager has reaffirmed the owner's investment objectives but prior to the finalization of the actual operational plan.

Occasionally, events unfold during the preparation of the management plan which conflict with the investment strategy. When this occurs, it is imperative to vigorously challenge assumptions and modify the strategy to reflect reality. For example, if the strategy is to upgrade a property to a higher use, such as upgrading an industrial building to a laboratory for high-technology research, but market conditions change and auger against this type of improvement, the strategy must respond to this change. The degree of change and its impact on the long-term result may be good reason for an owner to question the suitability of the investment in light of the overall investment objective.

Investment strategy must be developed with a clear understanding of the investment, leasing opportunities, design limitations, local market conditions, general economic conditions, the financial marketplace, and, most important-ly, the owner's investment objectives. The owner's investment objectives should not dictate what the individual property investment strategy will be. Instead, they should complement each other. The owner's investment objec-tives provide a point of reference that does not change frequently, if at all. The investment strategy for each property should support these objectives. A portfolio of one or many properties cannot be effectively managed without this consistent reference point. If a major change does occur in the owner's invest-ment objectives, adequate lead time is needed to revise a strategy and then implement it.

The investment strategy need not be long and detailed, nor should it be a laundry list of to-do items. It is most effective when it is briefly and clearly stated, as, for example:

> The strategy for this investment is to continue ownership over the longer term. In the shorter term (1−2 years) emphasis will be placed on pursuing leasing opportu-nities given the large amount of space becoming available. The property will continue to be positioned as a class A office building fully competitive with new buildings yet offering rental rates below those required in newer, higher cost facilities.

Although changing investment strategies frequently is not advocated, it is important to formally review and reaffirm the strategy yearly. The ideal time for this review is during the development of the annual management plan.

The Operational Plan

It is important to emphasize that an asset manager should not attempt to write the operational plan in a vacuum. Input should be solicited from the on-site manager as well as the leasing staff, brokers, accountants, engineers, and so forth, as needed. If the operational plan has a high degree of development contribution by those involved, it later can serve as a most objective tool in evaluating performance.

The operational plan guidelines which follow are not meant to be all inclu-sive. They are meant to illustrate a basic approach to planning. In many respects, this approach resembles an appraisal since there is a thorough review of the market, the past performance of the property, and a projected perfor-mance. If it is a requirement of the owner that an annual appraisal of value be obtained, it can be incorporated easily into the operational plan.

Operational Plan Outline

1. Market Survey.
2. Property and Investment Description.

3. Financial Review.
4. Current Year Review.
5. Leasing Activity Summary.
6. Retail Sales.
7. Operating Budget.
8. Key Objectives.

Market Survey. The market survey addresses the overall or city-wide market with special attention directed to the subject property's immediate market area. This is an excellent place to identify emerging trends and to evaluate their impact on the subject property. The asset manager must assume the responsibility for developing and updating this market survey from several independent sources. It is generally not necessary to commission a formal study under normal circumstances; however, it is advisable when an expansion or significant releasing activity is planned. The market survey should include a competitive analysis of all existing and proposed projects. Major emphasis should be placed on rental rates, lease structures and terms, operating expenses, real estate taxes, tenant alteration packages, building reputation/image, and advantages and/or disadvantages of the proposed design changes. This is vitally important information which should be used in developing the leasing plan for existing as well as new tenants.

The comparison grid (Table 2.1) helps the asset manager evaluate the relative merits of each competitive building using 10 critieria: building reputation/image, location, tenant parking, condition of common areas (lobbies, hallways, and restrooms), condition of tenant space, life safety features, security, elevators, support facilities (cafeteria, banks, retail, etc.), and hours of operation. Each category is scored using a 1 to 10 point value system with 10 being the highest rating. The total number of points for each building is then related to the current rental rate structure to develop a Rental Value Index (RVI).

$$\text{Rental value index} = \frac{\text{Base rental/Square feet}}{\text{Comparison grid points}}$$

If properly constructed, the RVI should demonstrate that buildings with high comparison grid point totals demand high rental rates. Conversely, buildings with low point totals have low rental rates. The RVI in this scenario supports the adage "you get what you pay for." The paramount value of the index is in identifying properties that are either over- or under-priced at a given point in time.

A comparison grid also can assist the asset manager in pinpointing the strengths and weaknesses of the property he is managing. Once identified, a program can be developed to evaluate the condition including a cost/benefit analysis for improvement or addition to the property.

TABLE 2.1

Comparison Grid.

Building	Reputation/ Image	Location	Parking	Condition Of		Life Safety	Security	Elevators	Facilities	Hours Of Operation	Total
				Tenant Space	Common Areas						
500 North	9	8	10	9	9	8	8	8	8	8	85
Midway	7	6	8	5	6	6	5	5	5	8	61
XYZ	5	8	9	5	4	5	4	4	2	5	51

Property/Investment Description.   The property description is an important tool in comparing the property under consideration with similar properties. It should be detailed enough to support a good understanding of both how the property operates and any positive or negative special features. An important common denominator in most properties is the net rentable area. The property description should include the method used to calculate the net rentable area. In multi-floor buildings the calculation should be done on a floor-by-floor basis.

A site plan and building floor plans showing current tenants may be added as exhibits to the plan. It is nearly impossible to conceptualize a tenant move or space reconfiguration without a current set of floor plans. This is critical when the asset manager is located several thousand miles from the property.

The investment description is a synopsis of the property's financial structure. Mortgages, ground leases, reciprocal easement agreements, deed restriction covenants, partnership agreements, and contracts for various services should be described in enough detail to present a clear understanding of how each can impact investment results. For example, a mortgage might contain a variable interest rate feature, called "kicker interest," that is tied to gross income. The formula for computing the kicker interest should be presented along with the actual kicker interest paid to date by year. This additional interest may be a sum large enough to significantly effect the loan payment constant. At some point in time, it may become attractive to refinance the property. Again, the description of the mortgage should contain information on the period of time during which the loan is closed for prepayment and the prepayment penalty, if any, when the loan opens.

There are two important benefits to documenting the financial structure. First, it establishes the need to fully understand the investment structure and how it may affect the overall investment performance at the beginning of the management plan. Second, it identifies important dates and incorporates them into the plan in a proactive frame of mind. It is much easier to plan for the purchase of a piece of leased land when you are aware of the date upon which a repurchase option becomes effective. It is not inconceivable in a large and complex matrix organization that such dates may come and go unnoticed. Because the asset manager is accountable, he must have access to and fully understand the complete financial structure of each property and be able to achieve the owner's investment objectives within that structure. If legal opinions are needed to clarify ambiguities in documents, they should be obtained as soon as possible—tomorrow may be too late.

Financial Review.   The financial review should be a year-by-year review in summary format of the historical operation of the property from the date it was purchased. The benchmark for comparison should be the original investment underwriting pro forma. This year-by-year analysis should present important factual results in a no frills manner. Emphasis is placed on one or two lines of revenues. Operating expenses are summarized on one line. Real estate taxes and mortgage payments are also shown separately. Admittedly, this is a cursory approach. However, it is important to highlight trends, identify problems with lease terms, quantify the impact of capital expenditures intended to create value, and extrapolate future performance from past experience. This procedure makes this possible. This is an excellent place in the management plan to present historical year-by-year investment return and changes in value. If the review is limited to income and operating expenses, it is of much less value than a review which includes capital expenditure and investment return. If after-tax cash flows are important to the owner, the appropriate changes can be made to include the tax impact. Use the financial review as it best suits the needs of your organization. It will support past actions and create a strong sense of credibility with the owner.

Current Year Review.   Unlike the financial review, the current year review is a detailed comparison of current year operating results with the current year operating budget. Typically, a current year is not over when the management plan is being written for the following year, so that estimating is appropriate for the last month or two included in the review.

The detail of the current year review should be the same as the monthly operating statements. Variances on a line-by-line basis should be explained in a narrative following the comparison. It is recommended that the on-site property manager provide this analysis and narrative. The property manager is accountable for operating results on a day-to-day basis and has the best understanding of monthly operations versus budget. Although not a part of the operating results, capital expenditures should also be included.

It is the owner's prerogative to carry the investment either on a cash or an accrual basis. If the budget and monthly reports are prepared on an accrual basis, the year-by-year comparison as well as the current year review are less subject to the volatility of the timing of large receipts and disbursements. In a cash basis comparison, on the other hand, this volatility must be addressed and carefully documented whenever it occurs or some faulty conclusions might easily be reached.

A current year financial review should conclude with a synopsis of the major events that occurred during the year and their impact on operations. The following section addresses the leasing activity as a separate subject.

Leasing Summary.   The leasing summary should summarize each new lease, renewal or modification negotiated during the year. It should list the tenant's name, building identification number, suite number, square feet occupied, rental rate per square foot, operating expense and real estate tax stops per square foot, the lease commencement and termination dates, tenant finish costs, leasing commissions, special lease provisions, and, for retail tenants only, a retail sales history. The leasing summary should be presented in a table format similar to Table 2.2. Renewed leases should also show the previous rental rates and expense stops.

TABLE 2.2

Leasing Activity.

Tenant	Address/Floor	Sq Ft	New Or Renewal	Commencement/Termination Dates	Lease Term	New Base Rent	New Base Rent/Sq Ft	Operating Expense Base/Sq Ft	Real Estate Tax Base/Sq Ft	Annual Elec./Sq Ft	Previous Base Rent/Sq Ft	Previous Escalation/Sq Ft	Tenant Finish	Leasing Commissions	Options
ABC	22nd	16,000	New	6/1/83 5/31/88	5 yr	$272,000	$17.00	$2.50	$1.00	$0.50	$14.00	$3.50	$80,000	$68,000	None

Retail Sales Report.   In the case of retail properties, the most significant indicator of property performance is the sales results of each tenant. The retail sales report (Table 2.3) should compare each tenant's year-to-date sales and overage rent with that of previous years. Tenants should then be grouped into merchandise categories and the overall performance of each category should be evaluated as well. If the analysis shows that a particular category is enjoying continually increasing sales volumes, it may be concluded that the overall category is undermerchandised, and that additional stores may be needed to compliment and expand this merchandise line. Poorer performing stores represent the most rewarding opportunity. A retail tenant with level or decreasing sales could well be the victim of new competition, change in consumer needs, poor identity, management problems, or a combination of these problems. Every retail facility should be viewed as a dynamic marketplace that must respond to the ever-changing demands of shoppers and competition.

The retail/sales report provides the asset manager with an early indication of emerging trends—a valuable tool for evaluating the overall vitality of the property. However, the retail sales report is not all inclusive. It is only one tool. Periodic traffic surveys and demographic surveys should also be conducted to validate trends and assist retailers with merchandising and advertising.

Operating Budget.   The budget should be prepared on a monthly basis in the same format as the monthly operating statement. Using a zero-base approach demands that each revenue and expense line be constructed intelligently and not based merely on estimated percentage increases over the previous year. The budget format can be most helpful if it shows operating numbers in total and on a per square foot basis for office, industrial, and retail properties and per unit for apartments. Hotel properties are quite different in that revenues and expenses are reported on a departmental basis.

Each revenue and expense line must be supported by a written narrative that clearly explains how the line item was derived, that is, the revenue side should

TABLE 2.3

Retail Sales Report.

			Sales Breakpoint		Historical Sales			
Tenant	Sq Ft	Overage Rent	$'s	$'s/Sq Ft	1979	1980	1981	1982
Name/								
Merchandise								
Group								

include a separate revenue line for each distinct form of revenue. For example, separate revenue lines for an office building might include base rents, metered electric, operating expense escalation, real estate tax escalation, tenant service income, parking income, and miscellaneous income.

Developing the base rental income requires an existing rent roll plus a schedule of all leases scheduled to terminate or renew during the budget period. Each terminating lease requires an estimate of the vacancy period, new rental rate, new expense and real estate tax escalation bases, tenant finish alteration costs, and leasing commissions. In the case of renewals, the on-site manager will have discussed renewal plans with the tenant and can determine fairly accurately if the tenant intends to stay or vacate. The reimbursements from tenants for operating expenses and real estate taxes are only as good as the assumptions used to construct the budgeted operating expenses and real estate taxes. This is perhaps the weakest area of the operating budget. Poorly calculated reimbursements based on faulty expense estimates are a clear case of double jeopardy. Computerization will help greatly, both in limiting computational errors and in speeding the time required to calculate and bill individual tenants. However, the computer cannot determine if the underlying expense estimates were properly forecast.

The on-site property manager should be directly accountable for developing accurate expense forecasts. The asset manager should be accountable for reviewing and challenging the underlying assumptions for each expense line.

When the complete management plan is presented to the owner for approval, the operating budget will be defensible if it supports the investment strategy. An operating budget which is out of synch with the overall investment strategy is more of a liability than an asset.

Key Objectives.   The management plan receives its general direction in the form of a strategy. Key objectives are identified and prioritized in an effort to designate the critical items to be accomplished in a given year. These key objectives should be separate and apart from normal operations. For example, the analysis and evaluation of a building's heating, ventilating and air conditioning system could well be a key objective. This evaluation may require hiring independent consultants to conduct computer simulations, pricing retrofit equipment, and evaluating the payback period. Facing major releasing (with competitive buildings being more cost efficient or where tenant comfort is unsatisfactory), a survey of the existing system with its high energy costs and a thorough feasibility analysis of available options could be the most important key objective.

Highlight the key objectives—no more than three to five major priority items—to be reviewed, evaluated and, if appropriate, implemented in any given year. This key objective identification will position the property to achieve the strategic investment direction and the owner's investment objective.

EVALUATING PROGRESS

While the management plan may be reviewed monthly, a formal quarterly review culminating with the asset manager providing a detailed written explanation of the actual results compared with the planned achievement level is preferable. During these quarterly reviews, it is highly desirable for the asset manager to visit the property and conduct a review of operations with the on-site property manager and leasing staff. This meeting provides important feedback to the on-site staff. It can identify the strengths and weaknesses of the on-site organization in an objective environment. Important issues can be agreed upon and completion dates scheduled. Progress can be evaluated and, if warranted, remedial steps can be taken.

Because the asset manager generally works with a number of properties located throughout a broad territory (sometimes as large as the entire United States), as well as with several different managers, he must standardize his approach in establishing performance targets and evaluating progress. An inconsistent or inattentive approach may confuse on-site personnel and communicate a lack of interest or incompetence.

POCKETS OF OPPORTUNITY

How to Identify Opportunity

Real estate should be managed as though it was a company. Know the product, the market, and the competition. Strive for excellence and innovation where others have not. Create an environment that encourages entrepreneurial enthusiasm and creativity. Be willing to reward good ideas even if they appear futuristic or not immediately cost effective—someday they may be.

The first step in identifying a pocket of opportunity is encouraging everyone involved in the management of a given property to accept nothing at face value. Precedent is important but should not dictate future direction. What was appropriate two years ago may be out-of-date today. On-site staff should be encouraged and, if appropriate, financially rewarded for developing ideas. The asset manager should be concerned if new approaches to operating, marketing, leasing, or improving the investment results of a property are not frequently presented and developed by staff and associates.

The asset manager plays a major role in identifying pockets of opportunity, since he is accountable for understanding the legal and financial structures of each investment. Therefore, he should review and understand all partnership agreements, tenant leases, mortgages, deed restrictions, ground leases, reciprocal easement agreements, management agreements, zoning restrictions, local ordinances, building codes, and any other miscellaneous contracts. Every document has business implications. Understanding these implications is an important first step in being able to improve the property's performance and long-term value.

How to Evaluate Opportunity

Monetary Impact. Each opportunity should be evaluated for financial or monetary and nonmonetary impact. The monetary impact can be analyzed in several different ways. One way is to create a simple model that can measure the incremental return on capital. If the owner's minimum acceptable return on investment is used as a base line or target, then realistic opportunities can be developed. A simple model can use the total capital cost and incremental cash flows generated by the investment.

$$IR = \text{Incremental return}$$
$$C = \text{Capital}$$
$$IC = \text{Incremental cash flow}$$
$$IR = \frac{IC}{C}$$

If a time element is introduced to the formula and full recovery of capital plus a return on capital is expected over that time period, the present value of a stream of future cash flows compared to a cash (capital) outlay today can be determined. The owner's required rate of return can be used as the discount rate. If the present value of the future stream of cash flows exceeds the capital outlay, the opportunity has monetary benefit and should be recommended.

Here is another way to determine monetary impact. Assume the owner desires (1) a pre-tax required rate of return of 15%, (2) an investment proposal requiring $100,000, (3) a projected investment period of five years, (4) no residual value at the end of the five-year period, and (5) a yearly net pre-tax cash flow of $35,000. By using a financial table with a *"present worth of $1 per year"* or a pocket calculator with financial modeling capabilities, the discount rate is found to be 3.352.

The net before tax present value is 3.352 × $35,000	$117,320
Cash outlay	−100,000
Present value in excess of cash invested	$ 17,320

This opportunity exceeds the owner's baseline return on investment and should be recommended.

A third variation to determining the monetary impact involves the introduction of taxes. The approach remains much the same. However, the discount rate used should be an after tax discount rate as determined by the owner's tax position and the particular tax features of the investment. Here, the cash flows will be after tax. If the stream of cash flows are uneven over the analysis period, each year should be discounted separately using a present value/period table and summed to determine the present value.

Most institutional investors rely heavily on the Internal Rate of Return (IRR) analysis. This method of evaluating a proposed investment calculates the interest rate which is equivalent to the projected cash flows from the investment including a return of the original investment. The analysis can be performed either on a pre- or after-tax basis. In some instances it may be necessary to do both.

The final element that may enter into the evaluation is leverage. The owner may wish to finance the capital expenditure in whole or in part. The Present Value Analysis and the IRR will both accommodate leveraging and show any benefits.

Nonmonetary Impact.   The nonmonetary impact is just as important as the monetary analysis. Sometimes, circumstances dictate action that conflicts with the financial evaluation. In every instance, however, the owner should be made aware of all of the ramifications of the proposed investment. This should be disclosed in a "strengths and/or weaknesses" section of the investment analysis.

For illustrative purposes, assume an existing office building constructed in the era of cheap energy is being evaluated for an energy retrofit and that an independent heating ventilating, and air conditioning (HVAC) consultant has been retained to evaluate the system. Assume, too, that specific recommendations requiring a large capital expenditure for significant energy savings have been tendered. Before implementing the recommendations, however, the following questions should be answered:

1. Do the reductions in energy consumption accrue to the benefit of the tenants through reduced escalatable expenses or do they pass through directly to the owner?
2. Will tenant comfort be adversely affected?
3. Will the retrofit improve the building's competitive position?
4. Are there tax benefits to the renovation?
5. Have all of the tenant leases been reviewed in regard to hours of operation, temperature ranges and special uses, i.e., computer rooms?

The question concerning the accounting for energy savings requires a careful and thoughtful approach. If the leases are written so that a reduction in expenses reduces escalatable expenses, the owner will be making a capital improvement for the immediate benefit of the tenants only. A compromise could be to request that the tenants allow the owner to recapture a portion of the actual savings to help defray in part the capital expenditure. A sensitivity analysis demonstrating the payback period and return on the investment should be prepared assuming these variables:

1. No tenant cooperation in sharing savings.
2. Partial tenant cooperation.
3. 100% tenant cooperation.
4. Varying estimates of energy savings using several different inflation assumptions.

The payback period is directly related to the degree of tenant cooperation and the overall success of the retrofit program in reducing energy expenses.

In any analysis of future events an element of risk is present. The purpose of the sensitivity analysis is to evaluate and quantify that risk.

SELECTING A PARTNER

The partnership concept brings together the two most important ingredients for successful real estate development and investing: capital expertise and entrepreneurial expertise.

Historically, the institution provided the capital and the developer provided the expertise. Today, some institutions are assuming both roles. It is critical that the asset manager inventory the strengths and weaknesses of entering into a partnership. Under the best of circumstances, the partnership form of investing is cumbersome and may present difficult problems. It can be a serious mistake to enter into a partnership for the sole purpose of acquiring an investment. While the property itself may be an excellent investment, the partners often have totally different investment objectives and/or management styles. An in-depth study of a proposed partner, including his modus operandi, should be undertaken. The key issues to be investigated include:

1. Investment objectives.
   Term of ownership
   Tax considerations
   Investment returns

2. Control.
   Limited partnership or general partnership
   Decision making

3. Reporting.
   Financial reporting requirements
   Management reports

4. Expertise.
New development
Rehabilitation
Expansion
Conversion
Geographic locations

Ideally, a partnership should combine two or more entities that form a dynamic and capable pool of talent and resources. One and one should equal three.

The partnership will not be long-lived unless honest discussions are held and the management styles of each partner are clearly evident. On the other hand, properly nurtured, the mating can result in a venture that fully avails itself of the unique capabilities of each partner directed toward a mutually agreed upon investment strategy which could involve several properties. It can be the start of a long-term relationship encompassing the development and/or acquisition of properties over an extended period.

If a relationship works on one project and the partners gain mutual respect for each other, the ripple effects can be enormous for it can lead to access to new markets, cross fertilization of ideas, and the ability to respond quickly to opportunities.

SUMMARY

The properly developed management plan can address one of the most important aspects of real estate investing: value creation. Its proactive approach can *identify* and *evaluate* opportunities and recommend those which are consistent with an owner's investment objectives. A high degree of involvement by all of the participants in the plan development process can help to create a strong sense of commitment and accountability.

LARRY C. BAUCOM, Partner
Jones Lang Wootton
Washington, D.C.

Larry C. Baucom is the Senior Partner of Jones Lang Wootton, responsible for the firm's Leasing and Marketing Operation in the United States. A significant part of this responsibility is the developing of marketing strategies and acting as the Leasing Agent for properties purchased by off-shore investors. Mr. Baucom holds a Bachelor's Degree in Engineering, and a Master of Business Administration Degree, with specialties in Finance and Marketing.

BARRY M. NEALON, Partner
Jones Lang Wootton
New York, New York

Barry M. Nealon is the Senior Partner of Jones Lang Wootton, responsible for the firm's Portfolio and Direct Management in the United States. An extensive part of this responsibility relates to the management of U.S. real estate assets for off-shore clients. Educated in England, Mr. Nealon is a qualified Chartered Surveyor. He has served as an Executive Director of the firm's United Kingdom management operations.

CHAPTER 3

EFFECTIVE LEASING

INTRODUCTION

Leasing is often viewed as the simple matching of available space and potential user requirements. Today, however, this process has become one that requires some of the most sophisticated skills in real estate.

Investors compare investment yields in real estate to those that can be achieved in alternative investments. Leasing success is the determinant factor in the yield of any income-producing real estate investment. Investors are not generally buying bricks and mortar. Instead, they are buying an income stream. Critical issues in the quality and durability of that income stream are determined in the leasing process.

From the tenant's point of view, the bottom-line cost of its space and facilities resulting from a poorly negotiated lease can drastically affect its profitability and, in the extreme, even its business survival.

While the usual goal of both the landlord and the tenant in the negotiation process is to achieve the most favorable position possible, it is well to remember that a lease is a long-term arrangement. If either party is seriously disadvantaged, then the relationship may not withstand the test of time. Examples of this include a landlord's reduction in the quantity or quality of services provided to a tenant, poor property management, deferred maintenance, little or no capital improvements to the property, or simply walking away from the property. On the tenant's part, business may not only be adversely affected by the quality of the landlord's services and property management, but also by rents escalating above the level at which the tenant can profitably carry on its business operation. Thus, the landlord may be left with a bankrupt tenant in a period of poor market conditions in which to negotiate a lease with another tenant.

A well-negotiated leasing transaction is one that is ultimately fair to both parties. The relative negotiating strength has frequently favored the landlord. However, due to many changes in our economic environment over the last decade, particularly the inflationary spiral, tenants have had to become much more sophisticated in analyzing real estate decisions affecting their business position over the long term.

The following chapter outlines some of the broad areas that should be considered in developing and implementing marketing strategies to attract the best match of tenants to the space, negotiating the business deal parameters, negotiating the lease and workletter, and discussing issues that affect the negotiation process to achieve an effective leasing transaction.

DEVELOPING MARKETING STRATEGIES

One of the areas most often overlooked or simply given a minimum of attention is that of developing a marketing strategy for an effective leasing program. The usual emphasis is on "flogging" the property to as many potential users as can be reached and on getting deals started as soon as possible. That may not be the best strategy for maximizing the owner's total profit.

Market research is a must for planning an effective leasing campaign. The market, which is made up of users and suppliers of space, must be carefully analyzed. Then, the subject property must be analyzed to determine salient features and amenities that can be used to appeal to this market. From these factors, a marketing strategy can be developed to position the property to this market to achieve the best use and ultimate highest value.

Analyzing the Market

Competition (Supply).   First, the total market must be studied to determine competitive supply and demand conditions.

From a supply viewpoint, the total number of existing competitive buildings in the marketplace should be carefully surveyed. A profile should be prepared of each building. This profile should include

1. space available directly from the owner
2. space available on a sublease from tenants
3. a listing of key tenants
4. size of the building including the size and number of floors
5. age of the property
6. condition of the property
7. parking spaces (this is generally not a factor in cities with mass public transportation systems, but is important in cities dependent on automobiles and locations in suburban areas)
8. quality of the management
9. aggressiveness of the leasing agents
10. flexibility of the offerings.

From this survey, overall current market vacancy factors can be determined, the quality of the competing offerings can be assessed, and a profile of the tenant structure in the marketplace can be compiled. If this survey is continually updated over a prolonged period, take-up rates and market absorption patterns can also be determined.

A thorough survey of buildings under construction, planned for construction, and sites potentially available for construction should also be made. A best case and worst case analysis should be made as to the timing of their completion. These future potential availabilities should then be merged with the current availabilities and average annual absorption rates to forecast the potential supply and demand patterns over future years.

These studies are critical in analyzing the timing of new building construction as well as developing leasing and pricing strategies that will maximize the profitability of a property.

Users of Space (Demand).   From a demand viewpoint, a detailed analysis should be made of the key industries within the market. The survey should include how these industries are doing currently and how they are projected to do in the future. The individual companies in the market within these industries should be studied to determine their relative growth within the industry. From an effective leasing standpoint, it may be advantageous to the owner to make a more competitive deal for a company that is fast growing and may need more space within the property. Higher rents can usually be achieved on additional space requirements since the tenant can avoid the cost of moving its entire operations to another location.

The size of the companies in the marketplace is also important, particularly as to floor-size requirements. For example, if large corporations or institutions are the prevailing users, then floor sizes of 30,000 square feet and greater may be preferred. Horizontal space may allow more efficient use for larger operations than vertically stacked space. On the other hand, if the market is a central business district with a heavy concentration of service firms such as law firms, accounting firms, public relations firms, etc., then there may be a good market for smaller floor sizes. These smaller floors will allow the firm the prestige and image of being located on an entire floor as opposed to a partial floor. If a tenant has an entire floor, its business guests can step off the elevator directly into the firm's lobby area, thus giving an impression of the firm being a larger organization. A full floor user also has a more efficient utilization of space. Even if the price is higher, this utilization factor may make this space more cost effective to the tenant.

Other leasing issues that are highlighted by a study of the users in the market are the relative needs for back office versus front office operations, preference patterns for net versus gross leases, parking requirements, and transportation patterns. Front office needs generally require more services, higher-quality tenant installations, and higher-quality space with a greater window area to floor area ratio. Back office needs may require better mechanical and electrical support facilities for operational efficiencies and good public transportation networks to attract clerical staff.

Larger tenants requiring an entire building may prefer to own or net lease the building. With a net lease, the tenant provides and pays for all operating services and taxes above the net rent. This gives the tenant the operating control of the building which may be preferable for security or special operations. Smaller tenants usually prefer a gross lease where the landlord provides full services.

Analyzing the Property

Having studied the market, it is fundamental to an effective leasing program to carefully analyze the property to determine features that can be highlighted in the leasing campaign. Such special property features include:

Location. If the property is a 100% location, this factor should be a special theme in the campaign. It is hard to get away from the old real estate adage that the three best determinates of property value are "location, location, and location." If it is not a 100% location, the campaign should center on other amenities, such as the quality of the building, key location for back office or other specific use, excellent location to public transportation, shopping, or other public amenities, or excellent rental value.

Quality of the Building. Tenants are attracted to well-maintained, well-managed properties. This applies to both old and new properties. The best leasing programs are achieved in those properties where (1) the facade, lobby area, and structure have been maintained or refurbished to their best condition; (2) the space has been modernized to provide amenities for new office requirements such as (a) central heating, ventilation, and air-conditioning

(HVAC); (b) suspended ceilings with recessed lighting; (c) adequate electrical power for modern computing equipment and capacity for installing modern communications facilities ("smart building") and (3) building services are well-maintained (4) and modern fire and security systems are in place. Capital improvements and modernization programs should be considered as part of an effective leasing campaign. They can provide an excellent return to the owner through increased rents.

Floor Sizes.   Floor sizes of 25,000–35,000 square feet are preferred by the widest range of tenants. If there is a center core area, the floor can be easily divided to accommodate multiple tenants, thus reducing the leasing risks by increasing the number of potential candidates for the space.

   If the floors are smaller than 15,000 square feet, the leasing campaign should focus on smaller tenant-users. For example, if a tenant requires 150,000 square feet in such a building, the tenant would need 10 or more floors of inefficient, vertically-oriented space. In addition, it places more wear and tear on building elevator services and creates inconvenient internal traffic. For a large tenant, this property does not compete well with properties that have larger floor sizes.

Floor Configuration.   In older office buildings, floor configuration can be in various shapes, such as an X, H, L, U, etc., or square, with a courtyard which, before air-conditioning, allowed tenants to be close to windows for ventilation. In many of these older buildings it is ideal to market space in small units with a high proportion of windowed offices on a multi-tenant floor basis. Newer office buildings have square, rectangular, or designed shapes that have modern, more efficient layouts. These layouts can vary substantially in design from center core to side core and differ in column structure, bay size, and window module, all of which can affect a specific tenant's utilization of space. Studies should be made to show the most efficient layout patterns on both a full floor and partial floor basis for varying types of users requiring space designed with open planning to heavy private office density.

Loss Factor.   One of the most important, yet often misunderstood, selling factors from a comparative marketing standpoint is the building's loss factor. The loss factor is the difference between the net rentable square feet on which rent is paid and the usable square feet which the tenant actually occupies for functional purposes. In order to simplify this problem, The Building Owners and Management Association (BOMA) has issued a standard form of measurement, as shown in Exhibit 3.1, to try to establish a common interpretation. (Many local real estate boards have also issued standards for the measurement of space, some of which vary from the BOMA standard.) If a building has a higher efficiency, i.e., more favorable, lower loss factor than other competing buildings within the marketplace, this is a comparative advantage that should be highlighted in the marketing campaign.

EXHIBIT 3.1

STANDARD METHOD OF FLOOR MEASUREMENT
FOR OFFICE BUILDINGS

Effective April 1982

In order to facilitate a comparison of the cost of space among buildings, The Real Estate Board of New York, Inc., recommends that owners use standard definitions of gross area and usable areas, and clearly explain how the definitions are used to calculate rentable area. Architectural plans and calculations should be displayed to the tenant, if requested.

The Real Estate Board of New York, Inc. recommends the following definitions and methods as the Standard Method of Floor Measurement in office buildings.

GROSS AREA OF BUILDING:

The gross area of the building shall be all the floor area within the exterior walls of the building and enclosed by a roof and, in addition, free-standing power plants or other utility structures to the extent that they service the building.

GROSS AREA OF FLOOR:

Determine the gross area by measuring all the space on the floor to the inside finished surface of the exterior walls. Where the exterior walls contain windows, fixed clear glass, or other transparent material, the measurement should be taken to the inside surface of the glass or other transparent material.

USABLE AREA, SINGLE TENANT FLOOR:

Subtract from the gross area of the floor the following, including the finished enclosing wall:

- Public elevator shaft and elevator machines and their enclosing walls.

- Public stairs and their enclosing walls.

- Heating, ventilating, and air-conditioning facilities (including pipes, ducts and shafts) and their enclosing walls, except that shafts serving a floor in question shall not be subtracted.

- Fire tower and fire tower court and their enclosing walls.

- Main telephone equipment rooms and main electric switch gear rooms, except that telephone equipment, and electric switch gear rooms serving the floor exclusively shall not be subtracted.

USABLE AREA, MULTIPLE TENANT FLOOR:

- First, calculate the usable area as if for a single tenant floor.

- Then deduct the corridor area, including toilets, supply rooms, etc., but excluding the enclosing wall of the corridor.

- Measure the net usable area of each space on the floor by measuring each enclosing wall which is a building exterior wall to the inside

finished surface of the exterior wall, or to the inside surface of the glass as the case may be. Measure demising walls to the center and walls which abut corridors to the corridor side of the finished surface of the corridor wall.

- To determine the usable area on a multiple tenant floor, apportion the corridor area to each space by multiplying the corridor area by a fraction, whose numerator is the net usable area of the space and whose denominator is the total of the net usable areas of all the spaces on the floor, and add the result to the net usable area of the space.

BELOW-GRADE,
CELLAR AND SUB-CELLAR SPACE:

To determine the usable area of below grade, cellar and sub-cellar areas, follow the same procedures as is appropriate for single or multiple tenant floors except that, in addition, the following should be omitted from usable area.

- Machine rooms and pump rooms and their enclosing walls.

- Electric switchgear rooms and their enclosing walls.

- Telephone equipment rooms and their enclosing walls.

- Steam and water meter rooms and their enclosing walls.

- All space devoted to servicing the operation of the building, i.e., cleaning contractors, storage, building maintenance shop, building engineer's office, etc.

FULL DISCLOSURE PROVISION:

The variations in location of mechanical equipment, in the zoning regulations under which they were built, and in structural design among buildings of different ages require different methods of calculating rentable space. In view of this, The Real Estate Board of New York, Inc. recommends that owners fully disclose their method of calculating rentable area in a building.

Stores

1. The term "store" as used herein shall mean only that space at ground floor level suitable for commercial use.
2. The rentable area of a store shall be computed by measuring from the building line in the case of street frontages, and from the inside surface of other outer building walls to the finished surface of the corridor side of corridor partition and from the center of the partitions that separate the premises from adjoining rentable area.
3. No deductions shall be made for columns and projections necessary to the building.
4. Rentable area of a store shall include all area within the outside walls, less building stairs, fire towers, elevator shafts, flues, vents, stacks, pipe shafts, vertical ducts with their en-

38

EXHIBIT 3.1 *(continued)*

STANDARD METHOD OF FLOOR MEASUREMENT FOR OFFICE BUILDINGS

For guidance of Owners and Managers, Appraisers, Architects, Lending Institutions and Others.   ©

The purpose of a standard is to permit communication and computation on a clear and understandable basis. Another important purpose is to allow comparison of values on the basis of a generally agreed upon unit of measurement. The Building Owners and Managers Association International has sponsored a Standard Method of Floor Measurement for more than fifty years. The BOMA Standard has also been the one accepted and approved by the American National Standards Institute for many years. The result is a unit of measurement that can be used by owners, managers, tenants, appraisers, architects, lending institutions, among others.

It should also be noted that this standard can and should be used in measuring office space in old as well as new buildings. It is applicable to any architectural design or type of construction because it is based on the premise that the area being measured is that which the tenant may occupy and use for his furnishings and his people.

The Standard Method of measuring office space as described in this publication measures only occupiable space, undistorted by variances in design from one building to another. It measures the area of an office building that actually has rental value and, therefore, as a standard can be used by all parties with confidence and with a clear understanding of what is being measured.

The Building Owners and Managers Association International urges all its members and others in the office building industry to use this method in measuring office space. This publication also includes the approved methods of measuring street-level store space.

The New Standard

Area measurement in office buildings is based in all cases upon the typical floor plans, and barring structural changes which affect materially the typical floor, such measurements stand for the life of the building, regardless of readjustments incident to tenant layouts.

In the case of buildings designed for divided or multiple tenancy, this typical floor plan must permit of subdivisions to accommodate usual tenant requirements with corridors that reach every reasonable office subdivision. The definition of "Rentable Area — Multiple Tenancy Floor" applies to this typical floor, designed for tenant subdivision.

In the case of buildings designed for whole-floor tenancy, where corridors are omitted, the definition of "Rentable Area — Single Tenancy Floor" applies.

BOMA STANDARD

In 1915 the Association adopted the first Standard Method of Floor Measurement for office buildings. This was readily accepted as a "National Standard," serving the industry more than thirty-five years without occasion for amendment. With the advent of "block type" building design, a revised Standard Method was adopted by the Association in 1952. This was further revised (3 years later) to conform to the new "American Standard," of which the Association was co-sponsor. At the Miami Convention in 1971, the Standard was again revised to reflect modern leasing concepts and practices.

AMERICAN STANDARD

The "American Standard" for measuring office areas in buildings is the result of joint action by participating organizations under the auspices of the American National Standards Institute. Our Association, as a sponsoring organization, is represented by the Chairman of our Rental Committee, Leonard J. Adreon of St. Louis, who serves as ANSI Committee Chairman. The new BOMA Standard has been unanimously approved by the ANSI Committee and was submitted on February 18, 1972 to the parent body for adoption as the new "American Standard."

Originally adopted September 15, 1915 — Reissued (without change) December 1, 1925 — Revised and reissued December 8, 1952 — Revised and readopted December 6, 1955, and reissued January 10, 1956 — Reprinted April, 1963; April, 1966; April, 1970. — Revised and readopted June, 1971 and reprinted April, 1972; February, 1973; August, 1976.

AMERICAN NATIONAL STANDARD
Z65.1-1972 Areas in Office Buildings, Method of Determining (revision of ANSI Z65.1-1956 (R 1964) Approved August 14, 1972)

EXHIBIT 3.1 *(continued)*

OFFICE SPACE

RENTABLE AREA — MULTIPLE TENANCY FLOOR

The Net Rentable Area of a multiple tenancy floor, whether above or below grade, shall be the sum of all rentable areas on that floor.

The rentable area of an office on a multiple tenancy floor shall be computed by measuring to the inside finish of permanent outer building walls, or to the glass line if at least 50% of the outer building wall is glass, to the office side of corridors and/or other permanent partitions, and to the center of partitions that separate the premises from adjoining rentable areas.

No deductions shall be made for columns and projections necessary to the building.

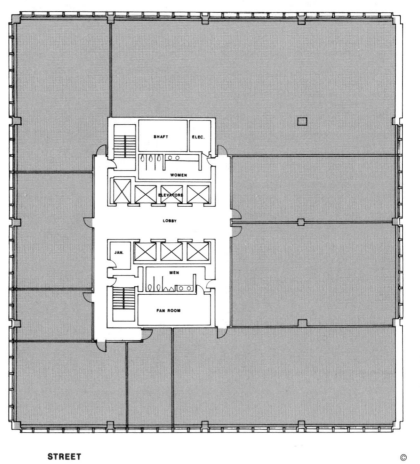

STREET

STREET

©

EXHIBIT 3.1 *(continued)*

RENTABLE AREA — SINGLE TENANCY FLOOR

Rentable area of a single tenancy floor, whether above or below grade, shall be computed by measuring to the inside finish of permanent outer building walls, or from the glass line where at least 50% of the outer building wall is glass. Rentable area shall include all area within outside walls, less stairs, elevator shafts, flues, pipe shafts, vertical ducts, air-conditioning rooms, fan rooms, janitor closets, electrical closets — and such other rooms not actually available to the tenant for his furnishings and personnel — and their enclosing walls. Toilet rooms within and exclusively serving only that floor shall be included in rentable area.

No deductions shall be made for columns and projections necessary to the building.

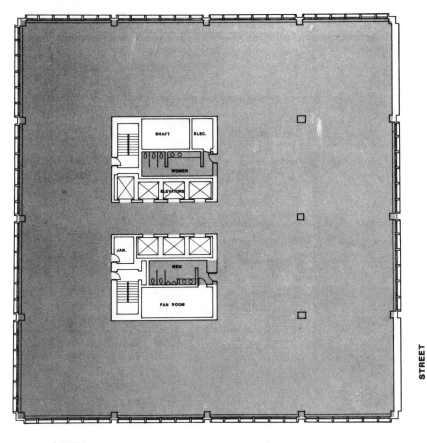

STREET

©   STREET

EXHIBIT 3.1 *(continued)*

STORE SPACE

STORE AREAS IN OFFICE BUILDINGS

To determine the number of square feet in a ground floor rentable store area, measure from the building line in the case of street frontages and from the inner surface of other outer building walls and from the inner surface of corridor and other permanent partitions and to the center of partitions that separate the premises from adjoining rentable areas.

No deduction should be made for vestibules inside the building line or for columns or projections necessary to the building.

No addition should be made for bay windows extending outside the building line.

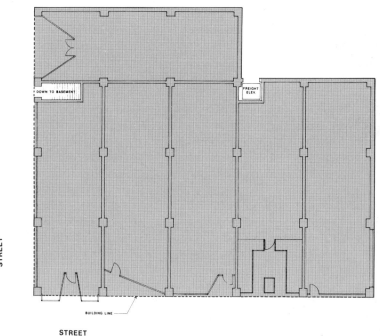

Window Size.   The size of the windows and their perimeter location determine the size of the typical standard windowed office. In buildings where the perimeter wall is substantially glass, the mullions and columns which separate the glass panels are used to locate the walls of the perimeter offices. Generally, window widths are between 4 feet 6 inches and 5 feet. This allows the design of a two-window standard office of between nine and 10 feet in width. Offices of less width cannot easily accommodate standard size desks, chairs, and other office furniture without overly cramping the space. Window widths larger than these dimensions result in standard offices of greater than 10 feet in width which accommodate fewer personnel on the perimeter and reduce the flexibility for efficient layouts of the space.

Ceiling Heights.   Standard building ceiling heights average 8 feet 6 inches in modern office buildings with suspended ceilings, recessed lighting, and air conditioning supply and return duct work in the plennum (area between the suspended ceiling and the floor slab above). If the height between the floor slab of a given floor and the floor slab of the floor above is great enough to give a suspended ceiling height of greater than eight feet six inches, this can be a marketing plus. This feature is particularly important where a raised floor system is needed for computer facilities or to accommodate wiring requirements for heavy communications users.

Floor Loading.   The average floor loading specification for space accommodating standard office use is 50 pounds per square foot live load, with 20 pounds per square foot additional rating for interior partitioning. If the building has a higher floor load specification, that fact should be highlighted in the marketing campaign since it would be an important feature for special uses such as accommodation for library facilities, computer and other equipment requirements, special file storage, etc.

Air Conditioning and Heating Systems.   The efficient functioning of air conditioning and heating systems has become especially important to tenants. Many tenants, particularly law firms, accounting offices, and other professional operations require after-hours facilities. Twenty-four hour tenant control of the air conditioning facilities supporting the tenant space has become very popular in the design of new office buildings. It is an important feature, and should be highlighted in the marketing campaign.

Fire Safety and Security.   Regardless of whether the building is located within the downtown or suburban market, fire safety and security systems are extremely important and are part of the overall selection parameters considered by tenants in today's marketplace. While these features do not have to be highlighted in the marketing campaign, they should be part of any substantive package of promotional materials on the property.

Positioning the Property to the Market

After the market and property are carefully studied, it is important to determine the target group of users to which the property should be presented.

The qualification of the types of users to which the marketing program will be addressed is the concept of market segmentation. For example, if the property is a new, prime property located in the heart of a major city's business district with floor sizes of 5,000 square feet, it will not be well-suited for a tenant who requires a large block of space. Furthermore, it will not be especially attractive for tenants who are looking for a low-priced transaction. Thus, the marketing campaign should be aimed at corporations, banks and financial institutions, law firms, accounting firms, and other prestigious service-oriented businesses requiring a presence in the downtown area. This type of tenant is generally looking for image, address, and quality, as opposed to a low price.

Few properties appeal equally to a wide range of users. Thus, it is important to properly position the property to its market. This can be achieved by a careful analysis of the property and types of users in the market, as discussed above.

IMPLEMENTING MARKETING STRATEGIES

After the conceptual design of the marketing program, an implementation package of promotional materials, support advertising, direct mail, and other solicitation campaigns must be prepared.

Promotional Materials

Rental Brochure.   A quality rental brochure should be printed. It can range from a one-page flyer to a package containing a number of pages, depending upon the size of the project and whether it is a new building under construction or an established, existing building. The brochure for a new building should be more elaborate, since the initial phase of the marketing program will be selling an intangible. Until the building is completed, the brochure has to take the place of an existing product that can be seen and physically reviewed. If an existing property is being extensively modified, a more descriptive brochure would again be a better marketing tool. If the building is well-established, a simple one-page flyer detailing the specific space available for lease may be enough.

In any case, it is important that the brochure sell the property. In order to make a proper sales presentation, the brochure should contain descriptive details of the building's architecture, location, special amenities, overall advantages, and specific space availabilities.

Presentation Folder.   A presentation folder designed to hold all of the promotional materials as well as specific offering proposals should be considered.

This folder should incorporate the same graphic design as that used in the brochure. It is as important to establish the proper image in the marketing campaign as in the completed building being marketed.

Rental Plans.   To aid tenants in visualizing how the space can be utilized, layout studies should be done on typical floors showing various office partitioning configurations. Some of these layout studies should show different ways in which the floor can be subdivided for smaller tenant installations.

In addition, the rental plan package should include one-eighth inch scale plans showing only the perimeter walls, columns, and core areas. The tenant or its space planner will need these plans to develop their own layout studies.

Standard Installation Booklet.   Details of the standard building installation are often not included in the rental brochure, except in summary form. A good technique is to develop a separate booklet describing the details of the building standard installation workletter and interior amenities. This would allow a fairly detailed summary of the workletter. The workletter itself, which is a legal document generally attached to the lease documentation, describes a full legal specification of all of the construction work to be provided for the tenant by the landlord.

Advertising

Some owners rely heavily on advertising in newspapers and other media for their entire rental program. Other owners feel that advertising is not necessary. From a marketing point of view, advertising is a support tool that is helpful in establishing the proper market image for the property being promoted. Even if few direct calls are received from the advertising, it is important in the positioning of the property to the market. It sets the base for property recognition when individual canvassing calls are made.

It is possible to over-advertise, thus giving the image of a property which is having rental problems. Therefore, it is extremely important that the advertising program not be ad hoc. It must be carefully planned and executed to establish the desired image and results.

Direct Mail

If the target markets can be carefully defined, an extensive direct mail campaign can be developed. A high quality rental brochure is usually too expensive to utilize in a mass mailing campaign. An auxiliary one-page rental flyer that is designed to summarize some of the key features in the rental brochure can be used for the mass mailing. In direct mail campaigns, a response level of one to two per 100 mailings is average. When these inquiries are followed-up, the full brochure and presentation packages should be used for maximum impact.

Canvassing

Regardless of how well the marketing program and strategies have been planned, the effective leasing of space requires a strong support program of direct canvassing. This means extensive telephone follow-up of all direct mail campaigns and appointments arranged for personal interviews.

If the direct mail campaign is small, the telephone follow-up program should include calls to each firm that received a mail package. In general, however, the direct mail campaign should cover a large volume of companies. Thus the follow-up telephone campaign can be designed on a sample basis. In the immediate surrounding market where the building is located, a systematic program of direct canvassing of target companies should be implemented through personal interviews.

Agent Versus "Doing It Yourself"

The main issue here is market coverage. Even if the owner has a leasing staff, it may be well to consider hiring a marketing and leasing agent to augment that staff to broaden market coverage.

The key concept is that there is no shelf life on space, for example, a month's rent loss can never be regained. The broadest possible market coverage increases the likelihood that the highest rental values can be achieved by developing more market activity and active candidates vying for space, together with a shorter lease-up period with tenants paying rent in advance of that which might be achieved with a more limited leasing program.

It is important to have a dedicated team of leasing professionals acting on the owner's behalf to generate this extensive market activity and work with the myriad of details necessary to set up and implement an effective leasing program. This task is people-intensive. It is particularly important that the owner or his agent have an effective canvassing team for the implementation and follow-up of the marketing program. Furthermore, in today's environment, with considerably more national and international business being done from both suburban and city locations, an agent having extensive links beyond the local market environment should be considered.

Whether the marketing and leasing program is implemented directly by the owner or through a leasing agent, full cooperation should be extended to outside brokers, thus giving the broadest possible local market coverage.

NEGOTIATING THE LEASE

Nominal Price Versus Effective Price

The first issue generally addressed by most tenants and landlords is the price quoted for the space. The focus for effective leasing transactions, from both the tenant's standpoint and the landlord's, should be the effective price per square foot—not the nominal or quoted price per square foot. For example, the landlord can frequently achieve his quoted price by concentrating on other concessionary points, thus allowing the tenant to achieve an effective price which is lower. By keeping the nominal price higher and by selecting front-end concession patterns, the landlord can still maintain a target asset value for the property which may be advantageous for refinancing, sale, or other disposition of the property.

Issues in Determining the Effective Price

Efficiency of the Space.   Very seldom are two buildings designed entirely alike. As a result, the floor layout patterns, loss factors, floor size, and core factors vary. From a marketing standpoint, a less efficient building with a higher loss factor and lower nominal quoting rent may, upon first inspection by a tenant, be the best transaction to consider. As shown in Exhibit 3.2, it is only later, when proper analysis is done on a comparison basis, that the effective rent is judged.

Thus, to maximize rental levels, the landlord must carefully consider pricing levels. If loss factors are considerably lower than competing buildings, that factor must be clearly highlighted when any pricing is quoted. In that way, the tenant is given more immediate estimate of value and favorable effective price.

EXHIBIT 3.2

COST/EFFICIENCY COMPARISONS

	Building "A"	Building "B"
Rentable area	10,000 Sq Ft	10,000 Sq Ft
Rental rate	$20/Sq Ft	$20/Sq Ft
Total rent	$200,000	$200,000
Usable area	8,200/Sq Ft	7,900/Sq Ft
Rent per sq ft usable area	$24.39/Sq Ft	$25.32/Sq Ft
$\frac{\text{Usable}}{\text{Rentable}}$ (Efficiency)	$\frac{8,200}{10,000} = .82$	$\frac{7,900}{10,000} = .79$
$\frac{\text{Rentable}}{\text{Usable}}$ (Add-on factor)	$\frac{10,000}{8,200} = 1.22$	$\frac{10,000}{7,900} = 1.26$
$\frac{\text{Rentable}-\text{Usable}}{\text{Rentable}}$ (Loss Factor)	$\frac{10,000-8,200}{10,000} = 18\%$	$\frac{10,000-7,900}{10,000} = 21\%$

Space in building "B" costs 93¢ per square foot, (3.8%) more than space in building "A". For 10,000 usable square feet, this would be $9,300 per year.

Escalations.   Most U.S. leases in multi-tenanted office buildings are on a gross rental basis. This gross rental includes a base number for real estate taxes and operating expenses. As real estate taxes and/or operating taxes increase above these base amounts, they are generally passed along to the tenant on a pro-rata basis determined by the total square footage the tenant occupies over the total square footage in the building.

For real estate taxes, it is common for the actual increases in the real estate tax rate and/or assessment value of the property to be passed along to the tenant on a pro-rata basis. For the operating expenses the formulas can vary extensively. The fairest to both tenant and landlord is a formula designed to pass along actual increases in operating expenses on a pro rata basis. However, many other formulas have been designed as an alternative to a direct pass along expense formula.

In some cases, an alternative formula is used because the owner would prefer not to have an open set of books showing all expenses and increases to those expenses for the tenant to review in verifying the charges passed along. Formulas such as the penny-for-penny clause passes along increases in operating expenses using the porter's wage as a proxy variable. This formula is sometimes easier for both the tenant and landlord, since it is tied to a specific verifiable porter's wage rate, generally subject to union contract negotiations. However, most tenants view it with a strong sense of suspicion, even when the ratio can be favorably negotiated. According to this formula, when the porter's wage goes up by one penny, the then price per square foot to the tenant goes up by one penny. Variances on this formula have been 1½−3 cents per square foot per one penny increase in the porter's wage.

It is generally better from a marketing strategy point of view to keep the escalation formula as straightforward as possible, such as the direct pass-along clause.

Rent Concession/Free Rent.   This is a powerful concession to use in closing a lease transaction. It allows a higher nominal rent, yet achieves a lower effective price for the tenant. Particularly in a weak market, if the transaction did not close, it could be a matter of months before another completed transaction could be achieved. Thus, in effect, it may not be as much of a concession as it first appears.

From a tenant's point of view, a move in any one year frequently causes budgetary problems for capital to cover moving and other relocation costs, additional costs for tenant work above building standard, furnishings, and so forth. Many tenants are as concerned about these budget items as they are about the lower term rental patterns. Free rent helps offset these capital budgeting problems. From the owner's point of view frequently, the present value cost of free rent and other up-front concession patterns is the stream of less than the present value of the stream of future benefits created through a higher rental pattern for the term of the lease.

Term. In today's inflationary environment, owners should consider pressing for shorter-term leases, rent reviews every five years, or annual consumer price index adjustments to the rental level. Most larger corporations negotiate hard for 10-year flat deals with fixed price 5 year term options beyond that. Smaller tenants are more willing to consider shorter-term leasing patterns. Where longer-term flat leases are considered, the base rental level should be higher than that in shorter term leases to offset the financial risk associated with time, or step up leases should be considered, with the base rental automatically stepping to a higher rental at the end of each five years of the term. Also from the owner's point of view, shorter term leases, market rent reviews in five years or less increments, CPI escalation clauses, etc., will greatly increase the investment value of the property should sale or refinancing be considered.

Options. Options that protect the tenant from having to relocate because of a lease expiration or requirement for additional space, for example, are a way of making concessions. While options make lease administration more difficult, they can be favorable to the landlord by reducing tenant turnover. The key here is to make sure the options are not at a fixed rent, but subject to a fair market value negotiation. Furthermore, an existing tenant may be willing to pay the landlord a small premium in rent over market in order to save moving costs and disruption of business activities. For the tenant who has an option to expand, even though the tenant is paying a premium rent on the new space in the building, an effective rental package below market levels generally prevails. This is because the high rent level for the additional space is averaged with the low contract rate on the existing space.

Takeovers. Many landlords are unwilling to consider taking over a prospective tenant's current lease obligation. However, this can be an effective marketing ploy since most tenants are not willing to be obligated to two leases. Nor do they want to be in the real estate business of trying to dispose of present facilities.

The financial leasing and legal exposure can be quantified and amortized over the term of the new lease as additional rent which, in many cases, is a much more palatable situation to a prospective tenant.

Services Provided. If special building services such as, tenant electricity, special cleaning after standard hours heating and air conditioning, concierge services, special security and so on are being included in the base price and are provided above those being offered by competing buildings, then they should be quantified into value and presented at the same time that any nominal rental values are discussed.

Construction Work or Allowances Provided. Construction work or allowances for construction may be provided by the landlord in the effective leasing and marketing of a property. Until well along in negotiating, however, many tenants do not take into account the relative values of different work allowances included as part of the price. Therefore, the landlord should quantify the value of any tenant construction work provided as part of the overall lease price.

Tenant Covenant.   Since a lease is a long-term transaction and rental markets can vary considerably, lack of a substantial tenant covenant and/or security deposit can adversely affect lease values. If an owner is considering leasing to a weaker tenant a significant security deposit or letter of credit may be required. Also, a higher pricing level can be justified as a rental risk premium.

Other Major Lease Clauses to Negotiate

Use.   It is important for the owner to carefully define the specific use for which the tenant will be allowed to utilize the space. A tight use clause will not only aide in controlling the prime tenants' activities, but will assist the landlord in controlling the utilization of the space by the sub-tenants as well.

Sublease/Assignment.   The owner should control the tenancy of the entire building as carefully as possible. In addition, since the landlord is in the real estate business and the tenant is generally not, the owner should endeavor to restrict subleasing rights as much as possible.

Even if subleasing is allowed, the lease should contain qualitative factors that allow the landlord to restrict any subtenants to the quality of the tenants originally selected for the building. The landlord should also attempt to require the tenant to first allow the landlord the options of taking the space back or, if a subleasing is approved, to take any profit rents over and above the rent the tenant is paying out.

Alterations.   Again, careful control needs to be designed into any lease clauses allowing the tenant to make alterations to the space. Plans and documentation of any alterations as well as any contractors or subcontractors being used by the tenant for alteration should first be approved by the landlord. Furthermore, all appropriate bonds, insurance, etc. must be supplied by tenant.

Workletter Issues

Value of the Workletter.   In an effective leasing and marketing campaign, the work provided by the landlord for any particular piece of space being marketed should be carefully considered. Where an existing unit of space is small and cannot be configured in any other layouts, in releasing this space the landlord may only want to offer minor alterations to the space. However, in large units, the existing tenant installation generally has to be substantially demolished to suit a new tenant. In such cases, as well as in a new building where a tenant fit out has not been completed, the landlord should consider offering the space with a building standard tenant installation. This building standard specification of work, which is provided as part of the overall pricing of the space, is generally outlined in an addendum (commonly known as a "workletter") attached to the lease document.

In considering the amount of work to be provided, a careful analysis should be given to workletters being offered by competing properties within the marketplace. This workletter will generally include basic air conditioning, floor tile or carpeting, acoustic ceiling tile, venetian blinds, initial painting, and 4 to 5 watts per square foot of power "free" under the lease. Usually, sheet rock partitioning, closets, doors, and basic hardware are included as well, although sometimes there are limits. Usually "free," but always with limits, are thermostats, electrical wall and floor outlets, 2 × 4 flourescent lighting fixtures, some door locks, and some automatic door closers on entry doors.

Substitutions/Credits. If a tenant chooses not to use building standard materials, a credit in the amount of the cost of the building standard materials may be requested to offset the price of new materials to be used. Generally, a landlord can resist any credit for these substitutions since he may have made a quantity buy in order to get economic pricing. Thus, if the tenant does not use the materials, an excess supply will be left on hand. In those cases where substitutions are allowed, care should be taken to assure that the quality of materials substituted are equal to or exceed those specified for the building standard workletter.

Additional Work Over Building Standard. Many tenants require additional tenant work above building standard to fit out their spaces. In these cases, the landlord may want to consider some allowance over building standard as an effective, up-front concession to close the lease transaction. This can be an effective tool since the landlord can generally build at a cheaper cost than the tenant can. Thus, the value passed along to the tenant is greater than the cost to the landlord and can appear to be a greater concession than its cost.

Construction Timing. It is extremely important that the workletter document attached to the lease contains the dates on which tenant plans and construction drawings are to be furnished to the landlord. The landlord has more control over the construction process than over the tenant design and planning process. Generally, rent does not begin until the space is substantially completed and the tenant can take occupancy. Therefore, the landlord should exercise careful monitoring and control throughout this period. Any time beyond the dates which tenant should have delivered completed plans (slippage) should be paid for by the tenant, i.e., if the plans are delivered to the landlord 2 weeks beyond the dates specified, causing the space to be completed for tenant occupancy two weeks beyond schedule, then the tenant pays rent for this two week slippage period.

SUMMARY

In today's market place, the myriad of details associated with an effective lease transaction, including the pricing and promotion of the space, tenant prospecting, and lease negotiation, must be carefully planned and executed through a concentrated professional effort. This emphasis of this effort is on the in design development and implementation of an effective leasing and marketing program that can add significant values to the real estate asset.

ALAN D. SUGARMAN, ESQUIRE
Vice President and Associate General Counsel
Merrill Lynch Realty Inc.
New York, New York

Alan D. Sugarman, Esq., is Vice President and Associate General Counsel for Merrill Lynch Realty Inc., the real estate arm of Merrill Lynch & Co., which is involved in every aspect of commercial and residential real property investment, financing, management, and brokerage. He also served as General Counsel for Merrill Lynch, Hubbard Inc., the Institutional Division of Merrill Lynch Realty Inc., which sponsors various debt and equity real estate financing programs. Formerly in private practice in New York City, he has served as General Counsel, Roosevelt Island Development Corporation, and Senior Staff Counsel, INA Corporation. Mr. Sugarman, who has an undergraduate degree in electrical engineering, is also involved in computers and the law and has lectured on this subject. He currently is editing a book on the impact of the telecommunications industry on real estate.

WILLIAM E. IORIO, ESQUIRE
Director, Senior Vice President and
General Counsel Merrill Lynch Realty Inc.
New York, New York

William E. Iorio, Esq., is a Director, Senior Vice President, and General Counsel of Merrill Lynch Realty Inc. In this position, Mr. Iorio has responsibility for the legal, compliance, and governmental affairs aspects of Merrill Lynch's rapidly expanding role in all areas of real estate, real estate securities, and insurance brokerage. Prior to assuming this position, he served as Director, Vice President, and General Counsel of Merrill Lynch, Hubbard Inc., and as Corporate Counsel for the Diversified Financial Services Group of Merrill Lynch & Co., Inc. Before joining Merrill Lynch in 1980, Mr. Iorio served as Vice President and General Counsel of INA Service Corporation and as the Managing Attorney and Senior Staff Counsel of INA Corporation. Mr. Iorio also served as Deputy General Counsel and Deputy Director of Commercial and Economic Development of the New York State Urban Development Corporation.

CHAPTER 4

LEGAL AND FIDUCIARY ASPECTS OF PROPERTY MANAGEMENT

INTRODUCTION

Strong and effective property management of investment grade real estate is one of the most critical components of a successful, high-yield real estate investment. Nevertheless, it has traditionally been one of the least understood and unjustifiably neglected areas of consideration by legal and business commentators. In most cases, legal and business articles regarding professional property management have been limited to purely financial and accounting matters or to the publication and limited discussion of standardized property management agreements. Little consideration has been given to the legal and fiduciary complexities of professional property management in today's highly regulated financial and real property investment arenas.

The trend toward the ownership of real estate by institutional owners acting in a representative or fiduciary capacity will continue and is likely to accelerate in the 1980s, particularly as a result of the ever increasing amount of pension and retirement fund assets devoted to real estate investment. Accordingly, in the future, property management agreements and arrangements will need to reflect the fiduciary ownership of the property. To the extent that a property interest is held by a pension plan subject to the Employee Retirement Income Security Act of 1974 (ERISA), as amended, institutional or representative owners and professional property managers are likely to find themselves subject to unexpected regulation, potential conflicts of interest, and possible penalties if the governing regulations are ignored.

Many issues raised by the fiduciary ownership of real estate, as applied to property management arrangements, have heretofore received little particularized attention. This lack of attention is principally due to (1) the ability of active property owners generally to control the relationship with property managers, and (2) the ability and willingness of entrepreneurial owners to bear certain business risks. However, the growing number of institutional owners and other fiduciaries holding title to real property in a representative capacity or acting as professional property or real estate investment portfolio managers have a greater, often broader, responsibility that must be considered when a property management relationship is established.

This chapter discusses the critical issues arising out of the legal characteristics of the investment property management relationship, and the relevance of these issues to regulation under ERISA.

THE LEGAL ASPECTS OF THE PROPERTY MANAGEMENT RELATIONSHIP

The nature of the legal relationship between the real property owner and the property manager raises fundamental issues that are frequently ignored. While virtually all property management agreements identify the property manager as either an "agent" or "independent contractor" for the owner, these terms often are not applied with precision. In many instances, these terms inadequately describe the nature of the relationship between an owner and a property manager. In almost all cases, the property manager is an independent contractor, but may not be necessarily an agent.

For example, in some property management arrangements, the property manager has substantial, perhaps even total, discretion over the management of the property, and may be deemed to be an agent with the authority to act for and commit the owner. Such arrangements are, in practical terms, indistinguishable from those resulting under an operating lease, since the manager operates the property, enters into contracts on behalf of the owner, has total control over leasing, retains counsel, and generally carries out a wide variety of similar tasks while receiving an incentive fee based on, for example, a percentage of the gross income. We suggest later that in these situations, if the owner is subject to ERISA, then such a property manager may be deemed to be a fiduciary, and subject to many of the restrictions imposed by ERISA.

On the other hand, where the property owner has a fully staffed department of real estate, financial and legal experts, the on-site property manager may be expected to provide only day-to-day operational management and staff support. In such a case, the manager may be deemed to be an independent contractor with limited authority and discretion, and most likely would not be an agent with authority to act on behalf of or to commit the owner.

The real property owner should recognize and account for these differences in negotiating and drafting the property management agreement. Thus, an owner entering into a property management agreement should carefully consider whether the property manager is to be permitted to act as the owner's agent and the degree of management and control that it wishes, is permitted, or is required to maintain over the property manager and the property. For example, an out-of-town owner with a full-time property management staff, including in-house leasing, maintenance, construction, accounting, and insurance experts, may be engaging the property management company solely to provide on-site management and control, while the owner retains intensive control over the operations. In this situation, an owner would prepare an agreement carefully outlining and limiting in unambiguous language the authority of the manager, and may limit the situations in which the manager acts as an agent.

In contrast, another owner may lack the day-to-day real estate expertise or staff required for reviewing the reports provided by the on-site manager, assisting in the selection of service providers and contractors, reviewing the acceptability of tenants, and reviewing and approving the terms and conditions of proposed leases and lease amendments. In such a case, an absentee owner will be placing substantial reliance on the degree of professionalism and integrity of the property manager. In those situations, the alert owner should be careful to provide legal provisions in the property management agreement to assure that the owner does not lose control of the property, is not exposed to unacceptable risk and liabilities, and is able to meet any fiduciary and regulatory responsibilities that the manager or the owner may have under ERISA or other laws relating to the conduct of fiduciaries.

In determining the nature of the property management relationship, the owner should be concerned with the following issues:

1. Privity of contract between the owner and the property manager or contractors.
2. Controlling the authority of the property manager to bind the owner to unauthorized contracts, amendments and lease approvals.

3. Restrictions and controls on self-dealing.
4. Retention and supervision of counsel, accountants, and other third-party consultants.
5. Establishment of operating, reserve and reimbursement accounts and the budgeting, approval, payment, and reimbursement of the property manager's expenses.
6. Protection of the owner's "soft" assets.

Privity of Contract with Contractors and Service Providers

A property manager entering into a contract for the provision of goods or services to or for the benefit of the real property could be acting either as (1) an agent of the owner, in which case the owner may be deemed to have privity of contract with the outside contractor or provider of goods and services, with the same force and effect as though the owner had entered into the contract directly, or (2) a principal, in which case the owner may look solely to the property manager for the provision of such goods and services and not to the outside contractor or service provider. In this latter case, the owner does not have privity of contract with the actual provider of such goods or services. The property management relationships elected by the owner will have a direct impact on the relationship of the owner and property manager with the service contractors and vendors who provide products and services necessary to operate the property.

For example, it may be necessary to maintain a full-time security force. To meet this need, the owner and the property manager may decide to contract for such services with an outside security services firm. In order to obtain such services two options are available. First, the owner could contract directly with the security firm. As discussed in the next section, the owner need not execute the agreement if the owner has appointed the property manager as an agent to execute contracts on the owner's behalf. The property manager could also be appointed as the owner's agent to manage the security contract.

Second, the owner could request that the property manager provide security services under the property management agreement. Accordingly the property manager, as a principal, rather than the owner would enter directly into the contract with the security company. The security company would then act as the property manager's subcontractor, and would have no privity of contract with the owner. The property manager would be responsible for the overall operation of the security force—and any failure of the security services subcontractor to perform would constitute a failure of the property manager to meet its obligations under the property management agreement. The performance of all the terms of the property manager's obligations under the security services contract would also be the property manager's responsibility.

As a result, the owner (1) would not be as involved in the selection and supervision of the subcontractor security firm, (2) would not need to be as concerned with the terms and conditions of the security agreement (other than the extent of such services) since it is a subcontract, and (3) would have no direct legal involvement with or liability to the subcontractor.

Notwithstanding this general distinction, the owner cannot ignore all of the property manager's subcontracts nor can the owner conclude that a subcontractual arrangement is always preferable to a direct contract for services. For example, when the subcontract is for goods and materials for improvements to the property, the mechanic's lien laws in most states will impose a legal liability on the owner for payment (as well as a possible lien on the property), notwithstanding the lack of privity of contract with the subcontractor. In some states, these protections also are afforded by law to real estate brokers. In a similar regard, if the service provider is providing goods and materials for which the owner may wish to have a warranty, then the owner might wish to review the contract. The owner, in such cases, may opt to contract directly for such goods or services. At the very least the owner should be assured that warranties and representations run directly to, and can be enforced directly by, the owner. Finally, the property manager may have included in the subcontract a provision that in the event of termination of the property management agreement, the subcontractor will not enter into a direct contract with the owner. Such a provision obviously is not in the best interests of the owner, and should be avoided.

In cases where the owner desires the property manager to act as a principal and to provide the services under the property management agreement, then the owner should review the property management agreement to ascertain whether it contains provisions appropriate to the nature of the additional services. Thus, if the property manager is to act as a general contractor and principal for construction related services, the management agreement should contain standard warranties, indemnifications, and insurance and bonding requirements similar to those that are contained in standard forms of construction contracts (such as the American Institute of Architects standard forms of construction contracts and general conditions). In fact, as a general rule, if a property manager is to act as principal in providing the owner with certain goods and services, then the property management agreement should contain the same provisions that otherwise would be contained in a separate agreement with an outside contractor.

Some property owners may choose to disregard these legal niceties. However, a property owner acting in a representative or other fiduciary capacity (such as acting for a private pension plan) should recognize its fiduciary obligations in determining the most appropriate method for handling contracts for services and goods, in view of the realities of the specific situation, including the nature and location of the property, local property management practices, and the track record of the manager.

Controlling the Authority of the Property Manager to Bind the Owner to Unauthorized Contracts and Lease Approvals

The property management agreement may specifically allocate the respective responsibilities of the owner and property manager for the execution and approval of contracts, including leases and lease modifications and waivers. It generally is in the property management agreement that the owner, if it desires, appoints the manager as an agent empowered to execute agreements on behalf of the owner. However, the owner may not wish to delegate unencumbered authority to the manager. The owner must consider the form of execution of such documents so as to avoid being held liable for contracts executed by the property manager where it is intended that the property manager is acting in its own behalf as a principal, or where the property manager has acted outside the authority delegated by the owner. The owner should be aware of the doctrine of apparent authority of an agent to act for and bind a principal even without the consent of the principal. A contract may indicate and in many cases control the intended legal relationship by the manner in which the property manager is described.

The alternatives of execution form include signature by (1) the property manager as principal, (2) the property manager, indicating that it is an agent for owner but not indicating the capacity in which the property manager is acting, (3) the owner itself, or (4) the property manager as agent for the owner.*

Where it is intended that the contract is between the property manager and the outside contractor, then, and only then, should the property manager execute the agreement in its own name as indicated in alternative one. Thus, an employment agreement for an employee of the property manager should be executed in the property manager's name. The owner should not permit the property manager to execute agreements on behalf of the owner (such as a lease) using solely the name of the property manager; to do so may cloak the property manager with the authority to commit the owner in other situations.

The owner should not permit the use of alternative two for it is inherently ambiguous. It may imply, but may not be intended to mean, that the property manager is executing the document on behalf of the owner. Unfortunately, this form is utilized in far too many cases, generally to the regret of the property owner.

Where it is intended that the owner and not the property manager is to be the party to the contract, as is generally the case with a lease, the third alternative, execution by the owner, provides for the best protection of and control by an owner. However, personal execution by the property owner may be impractical for an owner who does not have the time or resources personally to receive, process and execute all agreements, modifications and waivers in a timely

---

*The contracting party may be identified in an agreement in one of the following ways: (1) Property Manager, Inc.; (2) Property Manager, Inc., Managing Agent for Owner, Inc.; (3) Owner, Inc.; (4) Owner, Inc. by Property Manager, Inc., Agent for Owner, Inc.

fashion. As a consequence, the owner may elect to delegate some execution authority to the property manager.

Where it is intended that the owner is to be a party to the contract and the owner has decided to delegate execution authority to the property manager, then the fourth alternative, which discloses that the property manager is the agent for owner, will be preferred. This alternative usually is implemented by an express delegation of authority from the owner to the property manager in the management agreement. This approach does entail some risk to the owner because it provides to the property manager both the apparent and real authority to bind the owner to specific commitments, even commitments that the owner may not wish to make. This is a result of a fundamental concept of the law of agency which holds that a principal is responsible for the acts and commitments of agents who are cloaked with the apparent authority to act on behalf of the principal.

Permitting the property manager to execute any agreements may invest the manager with the apparent authority to act in other respects on behalf of the owner. For example, even if the management agreement prohibits the property manager from entering into certain types of agreements, such as fifteen year (long term) leases, the owner still may be bound if the contracting party has reason to believe that the property manager had general authority to bind the property owner. Permitting tenants to write their rent checks to the order of the property manager also may be construed as cloaking the property manager with apparent authority to act as the owner's agent. If the owner has permitted the property manager to execute agreements on the owner's behalf in some situations, the owner may not be able to deny the agent's authority to bind the owner in other situations unless the contracting party is on notice or would have reason to believe that the property manager is exceeding its authority.

The owner may protect itself from inadvertently cloaking the property manager with excessive authority to bind the owner by reserving the right to review and approve the stationery, cards, leases, contracts, and other forms used by the property manager in connection with management of the property. In such regard the owner should retain the absolute approval authority for all of the foregoing forms that include either the name of the owner or the name of the property.

For example, where the owner retains all signature authority (alternative three) the letterhead for the property manager may state:

The Property
Managed by Property Manager, Inc.
Owned by Owner, Inc.

A legend at the bottom of the letterhead may state:

Property Manager, Inc. is an independent contractor. Owner, Inc. cannot be bound by any agreement, lease, amendment or any modification or amendment thereof unless expressly agreed to in writing by Owner, Inc.

Such a legend may create a difficult administrative problem as discussed previously—and the owner may wish to provide some limited discretion to the property manager. In such cases, the property manager may be permitted to execute minor purchase agreements and service contracts, and the management agreement may provide that the owner will be responsible only when the management agreement authorizes the approval of such service or purchase by the property manager. Where the property manager has been delegated limited authority to execute agreements, the owner may wish to require that the property manager's stationery include both the clause suggested above and a further clause in the legend:

> . . . or unless the aggregate value of the goods or services provided for herein or by any amendment or modification hereof is less than $5,000 or unless the effect of such contract, waiver, or approval does not extend beyond one year.

Such language could also be included in all of the standard lease forms.

Printed lease agreement forms may also state that the property manager can execute only unmodified form leases, and only if the term, including all renewals, does not exceed a stated number of years. Even in such a situation, the owner should recognize the risks of permitting the management to sign any leases or amendments. Some owners give the property manager the discretion to execute leases and amendments that meet certain parameters. If the property manager exceeds or violates these restrictions, then the property manager has defaulted under the agreement and could be terminated—nevertheless, the owner would not be provided with protection from liability to the tenant.

When an owner permits a property manager to execute leases because of administrative convenience (even if limited to cases where the leases meet certain parameters specified in the management agreement), another consequence is that the owner may be deemed to have given the property manager the apparent authority to negotiate and execute subsequent legally binding amendments and modifications to such leases and to provide effective and enforceable approvals and waivers thereunder, even though the property manager may not have had actual authority to do so under the management agreement.

An absentee owner who decides that it has neither the time nor the staff to review, evaluate, and execute each and every lease, amendment, approval, and waiver, as well as each and every contract for goods and services, may, in addition to observing the suggestions above, include the following requirements in the property management agreement to minimize the inherent risks in providing the cloak of apparent authority to the property manager:

1. Provide specific standards limiting the authority of the property manager to execute such documents or otherwise act on behalf of the owner.
2. Obtain written indemnification from the property manager holding the owner harmless from any loss or expense arising out of the execution by

the property manager of a lease or contract or any modification thereof, not made in accordance with the express provisions of the management agreement. Since an indemnity is only as good as the creditworthiness of the indemnitor, the owner also should:

(a)   Use a property manager that has established a good track record and is substantial and well-capitalized, and, if necessary, require that the manager's performance be guaranteed by a creditworthy entity, and/or

(b)   Obtain performance and surety bonds.

3.   Require the property manager to provide to the owner timely copies of all leases, amendments, modifications, waivers, consents and approvals, and periodically summarize for the owner each such lease or modification, and provide other meaningful periodic reports.

4.   Require a periodic certification, representation, and warranty from the officers and controlling owners of the property manager that the copies and summaries are complete and accurate, and are in accordance with the restrictions set forth in the management agreement.

The owner who does not undertake some or all of the foregoing is risking overpaying for goods and services, saddling the property with detrimental leases, and creating confused documentation that could result in unnecessary liabilities for the owner. Again, a fiduciary owner may be duty-bound to include these protections where appropriate.

Restrictions and Controls on Self-Dealing

Another area where the owner should seek contractual protection involves transactions between the property manager and its affiliates (including entities owned and controlled by relatives of such affiliates), such as (1) leasing a portion of the property to an affiliate (2) using an affiliate as the leasing agent, (3) using an affiliate as the insurance broker for the property's insurance, (4) using an affiliated contractor to provide maintenance and tenant fix-up services, (5) using an affiliate to collect wastes, or (6) obtaining other services or supplies from an affiliate.

Not only does the use of a property manager's affiliates increase the owner's risk of either overpaying for goods and services or receiving inferior goods and services, but the owner may find itself paying a double profit and a double supervision fee because the property manager, in using an affiliate, may save supervision and overhead costs that may not be passed on to the owner. And, as discussed later, if the property owner is a pension or profit sharing plan subject to ERISA, the use of affiliates by the property manager may be prohibited, such services by affiliates may need to be performed at cost, or the use may require specific disclosure to or approval by the pension plan, or a fiduciary for the plan. Specific legal guidance is required to manuever freely through the labyrinth of the ERISA regulation maze.

Aside from complying with potential ERISA prohibitions, how does the owner protect itself, and fairly treat a property manager who may, in certain circumstances legitimately wish to use affiliates as the most cost effective method of providing goods and services to the building? One method is to require specific disclosure to and approval by an owner of each instance in which an affiliate of the property manager provides such goods and services. Even in cases where an owner does not reserve the right to approve contracts generally, the owner still may require that it approve affiliate contracts—even if the contract is routine and within the ambit of approved, specific guidelines. In addition, the owner might require (1) a specific periodic report of all affiliate contracts and purchases, and (2) a compliance certification regarding such contracts and purchases by the president of the property manager, the on-site property management supervisor (and where appropriate a controlling share-holder of the property manager). The manager's reports and certifications in this regard will help assure that the affiliate contracts and purchases listed in the disclosure report are complete and accurate and that the transactions were fair and reasonable. At the very least, there will be a basis for auditing compliance with the owner's requirements. In addition, the foregoing may permit a fiduciary-owner to properly discharge some of its fiduciary obligations regarding related party transactions under ERISA.

Finally, the owner should specifically reserve the right to designate any service contractor for the property that the owner may desire to use.

Retention and Supervision of Counsel, Accountants, Engineering, and Other Third-Party Consultants

The relationship among third-party consultants (such as legal counsel, accountants, engineers), the property manager, and the owner is another area where an owner should exercise caution.

When negotiating leases and other contracts, it is not unusual (but not recommended) for an owner to permit the property manager to select legal counsel and to manage the provision of legal services relating to the drafting and negotiation of leases and contracts. However, this practice can be a mistake, since it may be unclear in such cases whether counsel is representing the property manager or acting as counsel for the owner. To avoid the ambiguity of such a situation, the owner should select qualified legal counsel to represent it, and should make it clear that such counsel owes the attorney-client duty to the owner and not the property manager.

Controlling the professional-client relationship can be of particular benefit to an owner, since (1) counsel would then be free to advise the owner of potential conflicts, self-dealing, and other discrepancies in the performance of the property manager, and (2) the owner can be assured of continuity of representation in the event that the property manager is discharged, for whatever reason. To emphasize the nature of the owner's attorney-client relationship with local counsel, the owner should make sure that the legal bills are directed to the owner, and not the property manager.

The same considerations apply to the retention and supervision of other third-party professional consultants such as accountants and engineers: in each case the owner should contractually emphasize that the professional duty is owed to the owner—not the property manager—and should directly retain in the owner's name the third-party consultant.

Establishment of Operating Accounts and Reimbursement of the Property Manager's Expenses

To further clarify the nature of the property manager's relationship to the owner and to outside service providers and contractors, the property manager should be prohibited from paying the manager's expenses from the trust or operating account ordinarily established for income from the property. The trust account, into which all the rents and other property income is usually paid, should be maintained in the owner's name and used only to pay expenses that are the direct legal obligations of the owner such as taxes, insurance premiums, financing costs, building supplies, direct service contracts, and utilities.

The trust account should not be used directly to pay the employees of the property manager or subcontractors of the property manager. For these expenses, a separate and distinct account, which should bear only the name of the property manager, should be used. When reimbursement is permitted, the property manager's account would be reimbursed by the trust or operating account.

All other accounts, such as escrow and reserve accounts, should be similarly analyzed and should be maintained under the proper name. These steps are necessary to emphasize the role of the property manager as an independent contractor of the owner, and not the legal alter ego of the owner.

Protecting the Owner's "Soft" Assets

Commercial or multifamily residential real property should be viewed as an operating business. Accordingly, the property management agreement should require that the books and records relating to the property are properly maintained. The legal relationship to the owner should be made clear: those books and records are the owner's sole property, not the manager's property. The owner also should be sure that the records are maintained separately from the records of other properties that may be under management by the property manager.

The owner should make sure that the following are maintained on a current basis:

1. Lease and contract files.
2. Accounting records.

3. Engineering and architectural records, including current "as built" plans.

4. Computer files and software programs.

The need for the first two items are reasonably clear; the necessity for the second two items is less obvious. The engineering and architectural records regarding the original plans and specifications, construction contracts, and changes to the building and its system are key records. The property manager should maintain them on the owner's behalf. As an alternative to having the property manager maintain these records for the owner, the owner may consider entering into a contract with the original engineer or architect for the building to maintain current "as-built" plans of the building, and to approve and maintain the records of all building changes and tenant alterations.

The property management contract should specify that the computer files of the property records are the owner's sole property, and not the property manager's. The contract should require that the owner be provided with hard copies of all data files and in addition that copies of such files are on magnetic media such as magnetic discs or tape. The owner should have sufficient information about the property manager's computer software to permit these data files to be understood and converted by owner. Indeed, in some cases it may be appropriate for the owner to specify the software that may be used by the property manager. If an outside computer service bureau is used to maintain billing and accounting records, the owner may opt to have the service bureau enter into its agreement directly with the owner, and not with the property manager. For these purposes, an owner could consider retaining a data processing or information services consultant and an experienced computer lawyer to review this aspect of the "assets."

If the owner attends to these details, the property will be better managed, and any future sale or refinancing of the property will be materially facilitated. Much of the delay in consummating many property and financing transactions is the direct result of poorly recorded and maintained leasing, legal, financial, and engineering records. Thus, the prudent owner should consider the enhanced liquidity and value of the property if its books and records are maintained in an accurate and up-to-date fashion.

IMPACT OF ERISA ON PROPERTY MANAGEMENT

As increased pension plan funds are becoming available for investment in real property, it can be assumed that the owners of many investment grade real property will be pension plans or other funds subject to ERISA. Therefore, property managers, joint venturers with pension plans, and other real estate professionals need to become aware of ERISA's regulatory impact on the management of real property. ERISA, in general, applies to privately sponsored pension, profit sharing and other employee benefit plans (collectively "pension plans"), and not to publicly (government) sponsored plans.

ERISA, in its intended effort to cover the breadth of investment and investment management transactions, is an exceedingly complex statute. To add to this complexity, real property owned by an insurance company-pooled separate account, or by a bank-maintained collective investment fund, or by other pooled investment vehicles may also constitute pension plan assets under ERISA, if a pension plan has invested in or contributed to the separate account or fund. They are subject to separate consideration under ERISA. The management of these properties owned by such common funds or pooled vehicles will not be considered in this article. The following overview focuses primarily on the property manager's involvement in the management of real property that is directly owned by a pension plan, either alone or with a joint venture partner, and which may or may not be under the investment management of an investment advisor to such plan.

Definitions under ERISA

In order to better understand and appreciate the potential reach of ERISA, one must understand generally the concepts of " 'fiduciary' plan assets," "party-in-interest," and "prohibited transactions" as used in ERISA. Under ERISA, a "fiduciary" is defined as any person who exercises discretionary authority or control with respect to the management of the plan or its assets ("plan assets") or renders investment advice to the plan for compensation (ERISA Section 3 (21), 29 U.S.C. Section 1002(21)). Although the question of what constitute plan assets is esoteric and complex, at the very least real property directly owned by a pension plan is considered to be a plan asset of the plan.

A "party-in-interest" is defined to include not only fiduciaries for the plan, sponsors of the plan, employees of the sponsor, unions of employees of sponsors of the plan, but also any person providing services (e.g., leasing or property management) to the plan, as well as relatives of any of the foregoing (ERISA Section 3(14)). A property manager for property owned by a pension plan is clearly a party-in-interest because of the property management services provided to the plan. Depending on the extent of discretion delegated to the manager, the property manager also may be deemed to be a fiduciary. A developer-joint venturer with a pension plan, to whom total management authority over the property has been delegated, most likely is a fiduciary with respect to a plan asset, and is certainly a party-in-interest. Trustees and members of an employee-appointed committee are also fiduciaries (as well as parties-in-interest). It is possible that more than one party involved in a particular piece of property which constitutes a plan asset may be deemed to be a fiduciary.

ERISA provides certain specific and general "prohibited transaction" requirements intended to prevent a broad range of transactions between plans and parties-in-interest and fiduciaries. In addition, certain conflict-of-interest restrictions apply only to fiduciaries. Since a property manager is clearly a party-in-interest, and may be deemed to be a fiduciary in some situations, and because of the possibilities of transactions involving the sponsor of the plan and other parties-in-interest, these prohibitions have important ramifications upon property management.

Restrictions on Transactions Involving Parties-In-Interest

Section 406 of ERISA prohibits a fiduciary with respect to an employee benefit plan subject to ERISA to cause such plan to engage in certain transactions (i.e., "prohibited transactions") with a party-in-interest (which includes a fiduciary) with respect to such plan. The prohibited transactions under ERISA Sections 406 (a) (1) (A)–(D) include: (1) the sale or exchange, or leasing, of any property between the pension plan and a party-in-interest; (2) the lending of money or other extension of credit between the pension plan and a party-in-interest; (3) the furnishing of services between the pension plan and a party-in-interest; and (4) the transfer of plan assets to a party-in-interest.

In addition, Section 406 of ERISA prohibits a fiduciary with respect to a pension plan from causing such plan to acquire employer real property in violation of the limitations contained in Section 407 of ERISA, and no fiduciary may permit a plan with respect to which it serves as a fiduciary to hold any employer real property in violation of Section 407 of ERISA (*see* ERISA Section 406(a)(1)(E), 406 (a)(2)).

Fortunately, as explained below, there are available exceptions to this overbroad language.

Property Management Transactions that May Be Prohibited Transactions

Many transactions common in the management of real property may be deemed to be prohibited transactions under Section 406 if a party-in-interest is involved in the transaction.

1. Leasing part of plan asset real property to a plan sponsor.
2. Leasing a part of plan asset real property to the property manager or an affiliate of the property manager.
3. Obtaining building supplies for plan asset real property from an affiliate of the property manager or from the sponsor of the plan.
4. Hiring the sponsor or an affiliate of the property manager or the sponsor to provide services (such as construction) for plan asset real property.
5. Paying a brokerage fee to the property manager or to an affiliate of the property manager for the leasing of space plan asset real property.

Certain exemptions are discussed below which may permit the pension plan or a party-in-interest to engage in some of these transactions when the party-in-interest is not also a fiduciary. If no exemption exists in the statute or the regulations, then an exemption must be obtained from the Labor Department.

Exemptions to Prohibited Transactions

Because of the potentially unreasonable and burdensome breadth of the prohibited transaction provisions, ERISA Sections 408 (b), 408 (c), and 408 (e) contain certain statutory exemptions from the prohibited transaction provisions set forth in Section 406. These exemptions do not apply to transactions involving parties-in-interest who are also fiduciaries (see discussion of Section 406(b) below). In addition, the Secretary of Labor, who administers ERISA, has authority to grant administrative exemptions from the prohibited transaction provisions provided that the Secretary finds that such an exemption is administratively feasible, in the interest of the pension plan, and protective of the rights of plan participants.

One of the statutory exemptions to the prohibited transactions important to real property management is an exemption known as the "service provider exemption," which permits parties-in-interest to receive reasonable compensation for services provided to a plan which is necessary to the establishment or operation of a plan, and are under a contract arrangement that is reasonable (ERISA Section 408 (b)(2)). Section 408(b)(2) does not exempt fiduciary transactions prohibited under Section 406(b) that are discussed below. The Department of Labor has issued regulations applicable to the service provider exemption (29 CFR 2550.4086-2). The provisions of this exemption should be reviewed as to transactions involving the property manager, its affiliates, and the many other parties that may be deemed to be parties-in-interest. Assuming the property manager is not also a fiduciary, the fiduciary for the plan may authorize certain affiliate transaction provided that certain restrictions and requirements are met, if in approving such transactions, the fiduciary meets its other fiduciary obligations. Thus, Section 408(b)(2) provides an exemption that would permit both property management and leasing services to be provided by the same entity, provided certain conditions are satisfied.

It is not the purpose of this article to detail all of the possible transactions that are prohibited transactions, and which transactions have statutory or regulatory exemptions. Pension plan owners of real property should consult with knowledgeable ERISA counsel to review not only the property management arrangements, but to review other real estate related transactions that may run afoul of ERISA. Note that where a pension plan is the owner of the property, there is always at least one fiduciary (the trustees of the plan) and such trustees as fiduciaries may be subject to liability for allowing non-fiduciary property managers to engage in prohibited transactions. Where the property manager is deemed to be a fiduciary, then the property manager is also subject to liability.

Prohibitions Against Fiduciaries (Section 406 (b))

If the party-in-interest is also a fiduciary, stricter rules apply. A fiduciary with respect to an employee benefit plan is prohibited from engaging in certain types of activities. ERISA Section 406 (b) prohibits a fiduciary from (1) dealing with plan assets in its own interest or for its own account; (2) acting in any transaction involving the plan on behalf of a party whose interests are adverse to the interests of the plan; and (3) receiving any consideration for its own personal account from any party dealing with such plan in connection with a transaction involving the assets of the plan. The provision generally limit transaction between fiduciaries (such as the trustees or plan sponsor) and the plan.

However, it is not appreciated generally that if the property management agreement regarding a plan asset permits substantial discretion to be delegated, in fact or in practice, to the property manager in connection with the operation and management of the property, then the property manager might under certain circumstances be deemed to be a fiduciary to the plan. One result is that a fiduciary property manager may not under any circumstances engage in affiliate transactions in connection with management of the property.

Circumstances which affect whether a property manager may be deemed to be a fiduciary are illustrated by one administrative exemption granted by the Secretary of Labor relating to, among other things, property managers for pension plan real property, permitting the plan to enter into certain otherwise prohibited transactions with the property manager, which was a party-in-interest. One condition of the exemption was that the property manager does not have "discretionary authority, control, responsibility, or influence with respect to the management or disposition of the plan assets. . ." (Prohibited Transaction Exemption 78-19 (PTE 78-19)).

The position of the Labor Department as to when a property manager is a fiduciary is demonstrated by a letter recently issued by the Department of Labor. Relying on the specific condition in PTE 78-19, the Department issued the letter to an insurance company permitting the insurance company to purchase properties from a joint venturer with the company, which joint venturer also acted as a property manager of properties owned by the joint venture. The degree of control that the insurance company maintained over its co-venturer property manager is instructive and is described as follows by the Department of Labor:

> Generally, property managers are responsible for the leasing, physical maintenance and day-to-day operation of Account properties, and are compensated by means of a fee which normally is charged against the rentals generated by the managed property. [The insurance company], however, still remains responsible for the management of Account property managers. All Account properties are managed pursuant to annual budgets that are carefully scrutinized and approved by [the insurance company]. Any expenditure of funds that exceeds specified limits (typically between $1,000 and $10,000) must be specifically approved by [the insurance company] even if it has been included in a previously approved budget. Before a property manager may retain another party to perform any function in connection with an Account property, the property manager must comply with competitive bidding procedures established by [the insurance company]. All leases of Account properties must also be approved by [the insurance company].

The activities of property managers are also subject to surprise audits by [the insurance company]. [The insurance company] currently maintains a real estate staff of more than 300 persons throughout the United States, that is responsible for overseeing all properties owned by [the insurance company] (including those allocated to its general account) and the activities of Account property managers.

Without such control, it is not clear that the Labor Department would have issued the letter.

A property manager and pension plan owner cannot ignore the implications of ERISA; certain standard practices may need to be either proscribed or prohibited, and each party should carefully consider the nature of the property management arrangement, and restrictions and limitations that may be imposed by ERISA.

SUMMARY

The emergence of pension plans and institutional investment in real property have materially influenced those aspects of property management which have traditionally not been the subject of rigorous analysis and careful attention. This chapter has discussed property management arrangements that fiduciary owners must consider and that all owners may find to be advantageous.

Charles O. Thomas
Managing Partner
Arthur Young & Company
San Diego, California

Charles O. Thomas is the Managing Partner of the San Diego office of Arthur Young. He started with Arthur Young in 1956 and was the firm's Western Region Director of Taxes from 1973 to 1975. Mr. Thomas is Chairman of the firm's Real Estate Industry Committee. He graduated from the Harvard Business School of Advanced Management Program in 1975 and obtained his undergraduate degree from the University of Arkansas in 1956.

Barbara Ann Buklad
Arthur Young & Company
San Diego, California

Barbara Ann Buklad is a member of the tax staff of the San Diego office of Arthur Young. She has worked extensively with real estate partnerships. She received an MBA degree from the University of New Mexico and an AB degree from Vassar College.

Eric C. Green
Tax Manager
Arthur Young & Company
Dallas, Texas

Eric C. Green is a Tax Manager with the Dallas office of Arthur Young. He specializes in Real Estate Tax Planning. He is a graduate of Southern Methodist University with a BBA in Accounting.

CHAPTER 5

TAX ASPECTS OF
ASSET MANAGEMENT

INTRODUCTION

Real estate has long been a favorite tax shelter. This is primarily because real estate investments can generate significant tax losses, even while generating a positive cash flow or appreciating in overall value. Additionally, any gain on the sale of real estate can often be taxed at favorable capital gains rates. Real estate investments may be held in a variety of forms of ownership, making it possible for a number of small investors to pool their resources in one investment and for large investment funds or corporations to profitably use vast sums of capital. Thus, real estate investments may be accessible to a large number of investors of varying financial means.

Structuring real estate transactions and operations so that these owners and investors can benefit from favorable tax attributes can be complex. There are a number of factors affecting the tax treatment of the various aspects of real estate transactions. This chapter discusses some of them.

INVESTIGATION, START-UP, AND ORGANIZATIONAL COSTS

Before acquiring real estate, a prospective owner generally investigates the feasibility of a project. Substantial costs, including accounting fees and travel and other out-of-pocket expenses, may be incurred. The tax treatment of these costs, particularly in cases where the project under investigation is ultimately not acquired, has been a much litigated issue.

If investigation expenses are related to projects that would be considered investments, the deduction would be particularly uncertain. Such expenses are not deductible if related to a general search for investments or to an investigation of which, if any, project to invest in. Only the expenses a taxpayer incurs after he has decided to acquire a particular investment are deductible. These expenses are deductible whether the investment was successfully acquired or not.

If the project under investigation would form part of an existing trade or business, investigation expenses would generally be deductible, even if the taxpayer decided against adopting the project. However, in some cases, preliminary costs may be connected with a business that is still in the formation stages. Start-up costs incurred after business has begun are deductible, but if they are incurred before business activities have started, they are not deductible. These nondeductible costs may, however, be capitalized and amortized over a 60-month period beginning with the start of business, provided a timely election is made.

The difficulty is pinpointing when the business has begun. The Internal Revenue Service (IRS) and the taxpayer may have different viewpoints, and little legal precedent is available for guidance. If a taxpayer deducts these costs and they are later disallowed on the grounds that the business had not yet begun, the taxpayer would not be entitled to make a retroactive election to capitalize and amortize the costs. In fact, the deduction could be lost permanently. Taxpayers and their advisors should consider these risks in determining how to handle start-up costs.

A third type of expense frequently encountered at the onset of a real estate venture is organization costs. These costs include legal fees in drafting partnership or corporate documents, expenses of temporary directors, and incorporation and registration fees incurred in forming either a corporation or a partnership. These costs may not be deducted, but are capitalized and, provided a timely election is made, may be amortized over a 60-month period. Syndication fees and the costs of issuing and selling shares of stocks or partnership interests are neither deductible nor amortizable.

ALTERNATIVE VEHICLES FOR OWNERSHIP OF REAL ESTATE

The selection of the type of entity to use to acquire, hold, improve, and sell real estate is one of the most important tax decisions.

The tax advantages and disadvantages of utilizing each type of entity must be carefully evaluated. One way of quantifying the evaluation process is to compute the relative "tax savings" or "tax cost" for each alternative. This computation must be made for each period of time from acquisition through the time of sale or disposition of the real property. In some situations, changing the entity used at the appropriate time during the period of ownership may produce even greater tax savings.

The following paragraphs outline the principal types of entities which may be used together with some of the tax characteristics for each entity:

Sole Proprietorship

In a sole proprietorship, profits and losses are taxed at the individual owner's level. Losses can be used to offset individual's other income.

Corporation

A corporation is a separate entity that can choose any year-end and select its own accounting methods.

As a separate entity, it is taxed at graduated rates of up to 40% on the first $100,000 of taxable income and at 46% on its income in excess of $100,000. Capital gains are generally taxed at a flat 28%. Losses may only be used to offset income generated by the corporation.

Dividend distributions to a corporation's shareholders are generally taxed to the shareholders as ordinary income. Such distributions do not reduce the corporation's taxable income; therefore, double taxation occurs. Compensation to owners is deductible only to the extent it is reasonable in amount.

Loans from stockholders could be recharacterized by the IRS as capital contributions, if the IRS considers the corporation to be "thinly capitalized." The consequences of this characterization are onerous. Since both "interest" and "principal" payments could be considered dividends the corporation cannot deduct the "interest" payments and the stock-holders will generally be taxed on the repayment of the "principal."

S-Corporations

S-Corporations were formerly known as Subchapter-S Corporations. Undistributed and distributed profits are taxed at the shareholder's level. S-Corporation losses pass through to the shareholders. The total amount of S-Corp losses deducted by a shareholder may not exceed the shareholder's basis in his stock and in loans from the shareholder to the corporation. An S-Corp is typically used to pass start-up losses through to investors. If it is later desirable for the S-Corp to be taxed instead as a regular corporation, S-Corp status may be voluntarily terminated.

A corporation must meet a number of requirements to qualify for S-Corp status. If at any time these requirements are not met, S-Corp status will be involuntarily terminated.

As a separate entity, an S-Corp can choose its own accounting methods. Selection of the year-end, however, will generally be limited to a calendar year-end.

General or Limited Partnership

Undistributed and distributed profits are taxed at the partner level. Losses passing through to the partners reduce such partner's tax basis in his partnership interests. The tax basis of a partner's interest is increased by the share of liabilities for which the partner is personally liable and his pro-rata share of nonrecourse partnership debt. Losses exceeding a partner's tax basis cannot be deducted in that year by the partner. However, such losses may be deducted in future years if the partner's tax basis is increased.

Corporations may be limited partners and the general partner may also be a corporation subject to the partnership not being treated as an association taxable as a corporation.

ACCOUNTING METHOD

The accounting method the taxpayer uses to report taxable income will determine when his income and deductions are reported. If, by using a particular method, a taxpayer can postpone reporting income for a year, he will postpone paying taxes on that income and may use that tax savings interest-free for the entire year. Thus, it is important to choose an accounting method carefully.

There are two basic accounting methods: the cash method and the accrual method. Whichever method is chosen, it must be used consistently and it must, in the opinion of the IRS, clearly reflect income.

Under the cash method, income is generally reported when it is received and deductions are generally reported when paid. Income may be received in a form other than cash. For example, if a taxpayer receives property or services in lieu of rent, the value of such property or services would be reported as rental income in the tax period in which the property is received or the services are rendered. Also, income is reportable when it is constructively as well as actually received. Thus, if a tenant deposits rent with a landlord's relative, the rent is deemed received when it is deposited because it can be collected by the landlord at any time.

In contrast, income is reported under the accrual method when it is earned, regardless of when received. Deductions are reported when the liability for an expense becomes fixed and the amount can be reasonably determined. For example, under the accrual method, rental income is reported during the rental period even if the rent is received later. Interest on a loan would be deducted as time lapses, even if the interest is not paid until the end of the loan period.

There are numerous exceptions to these rules, some of which are commonly encountered by the real estate owner. Advance rent must be reported by the accrual taxpayer in the year it is received, even though it has not yet been earned. Neither prepaid interest nor prepaid rent is deductible by a cash basis taxpayer until the interest or rent has accrued.

In addition to these exceptions, the requirement that an accounting method clearly reflect income can modify the time for reporting certain items. Thus, a cash basis taxpayer may not be permitted to deduct large prepayments for goods and services to be received or rendered over several years. Also, special methods are available or may be required for reporting particular kinds of income and deductions, such as sales of inventory, income from long-term contracts, and installment sales.

The accrual method will accelerate deductions for many real estate operations. For example, if property taxes can be paid much later than the assessment date, an accrual taxpayer can deduct taxes before he actually pays them. The accrual taxpayer may also have an advantage under certain financing arrangements. For example, if interest or part of the interest on a loan is merely added to the loan balance instead of being paid, or if loan fees and interest are withheld from the loan proceeds, the accrual taxpayer can deduct these expenses as they accrue. The cash basis taxpayer must wait, however, until he actually repays the loan, interest, or fees.

The cash method is simpler to use, but may be advantageous to only a limited number of real estate ventures. If many operating expenses will be prepaid or if significant amounts of rental or interest income will not be received until after the income has been earned, the cash basis taxpayer may have an advantage. But, in the usual case, where interest costs are more substantial than other operating expenses that could be prepaid and where rental income is generally received as it is earned, the cash method may offer no advantage. Because the business's entire operation must be considered in choosing an accounting method, professional advice should be sought before this decision is made.

Once an accounting method is used to report taxable income, the same method must be used from then on unless the IRS changes or grants permission for the taxpayer to change his method. Books and records must be kept to substantiate the reporting of income and deductions according to the method used.

If a taxpayer has more than one trade or business and separate books are kept for the different businesses, then different accounting methods may be used for the different businesses. Also, different entities may use different methods. For example, a partnership or a corporation may use the accrual method while individual partners or shareholders use the cash method. This allows a great deal of flexibility in planning for tax deferral.

BASIS

The basis of an asset could be viewed as the federal income tax cost value assigned to the asset. This tax basis is important both in determining the amount of depreciation and cost recovery deductions and, later, in determining the amount of gain or loss on the sale, retirement, or other disposition of an asset.

How basis is initially calculated depends upon how the asset is acquired. This initially determined basis is later adjusted by adding the cost of capital improvements and by subtracting the amount of depreciation or cost recovery deductions allowable. It is this "adjusted basis" that is used to calculate gain or loss on the disposition of an asset.

Assets Acquired by Purchase

If an asset is purchased, its adjusted basis before any depreciation is its cost. Its cost is equal to the total of (1) the cash plus fair market value of other property paid to the seller, (2) any liabilities assumed by the buyer (or if the property is taken subject to any liabilities, the outstanding balance of those liabilities), (3) any expenses paid by the buyer in connection with the purchase, and (4) the costs of preparing the asset for its intended use.

Assets Acquired in a Tax-Free Exchange

Occasionally, real estate is acquired in a like-kind exchange. A like-kind exchange is a generally tax-free swap of properties. Under such circumstances, the adjusted basis of the newly-acquired property is the adjusted basis of the property given up with certain adjustments for liabilities assumed and relieved of in the transaction, cash paid or received, or non-like-kind property paid or received. Generally, the basis of property acquired in a tax-free exchange is lower than the basis of similar purchased property. Thus, the depreciation or recovery deductions will also be lower.

Assets Converted from Personal Use

Property that is originally used for personal purposes can be converted to business or investment use. The basis of such converted property is the lesser of the property's adjusted basis or the fair market value on the date of conversion.

Assets Acquired by Inheritance or Gift

The basis of inherited property is the fair market value of the property at the date of death or as reported on the decedent's estate tax return. For depreciation purposes, the basis of property acquired by gift is the same as the donor's basis of the property adjusted for gift tax paid.

Self-Constructed Assets

The basis of constructed assets is the total of construction costs that were capitalized. These include labor, materials, allocated overhead, and engineering and architectural fees. By election, interest, taxes, and other carrying charges can also be capitalized and added to basis, instead of being deducted.

Allocation of Basis in Lump-Sum Purchases

In the typical real estate purchase or other acquisition, a number of separate assets are acquired. For example, land, a building, personal property such as signs, carpeting, fixtures, and appliances may all be acquired in one real estate purchase. Land, because it does not have a limited life and is not subject to wear and tear, is not depreciable. The basis of personal property can be depreciated far more quickly than that of a building. Because of these differences, it is critical that the cost of real estate be properly allocated to each individual asset in the transaction. This allocation must be based on the relative fair market value of each asset. Thus, if the land represents 15% of the fair market value of the entire purchase, 15% of the purchase price will be allocated to the land.

Objective evidence supporting a taxpayer's allocation of the purchase price can be critical in upholding the allocation against IRS attack. Tax assessments that separate assessed values of land from those of improvements or independent appraisal reports may be supporting evidence. Written purchase contracts that establish separate values for each individual asset can also be beneficial, provided they are reasonable and based on arms length bargaining.

DISPOSITION OF REAL PROPERTY

The gain or loss on the sale of property equals the amount realized minus the adjusted basis of the property sold and any selling expenses. The amount realized is the sum of cash received, the net fair market value of property received, and the debt from which the taxpayer is relieved. The adjusted basis is the basis upon acquisition, increased by capital expenditures less aggregated depreciation (cost recovery) deductions.

Business Assets and Capital Assets

The gain realized on the sale will be taxed as a capital gain if the asset sold is a capital asset or if it had been used in a trade or business. However, to the extent of depreciation recaptured on the sale, a portion of the gain will be treated as ordinary income. Losses on selling capital assets are capital losses, while those on selling property used in a trade or business are ordinary losses.

Sales of real property held primarily for sale to customers in the ordinary course of business are not eligible for capital gain treatment. All gains are taxed as ordinary income and losses are ordinary deductions. This disparity in the treatment of sales of property held for investment and property held for sale makes the distinction between a real estate investor and a real estate dealer critical. Particularly when repeated sales of real estate are contemplated, the many court decisions surrounding this controversy should be studied.

Deferral Opportunities: Installment Sales and Like-Kind Exchange

The importance of timing the reporting of the gain on the disposition of real property has resulted in changes to the statutory tax law as well as in numerous court decisions. In some cases gain is not taxed in the year of sale but is deferred until a later tax period.

If at least one payment will not be received until after the tax year in which the sale occurs, gain is reportable on the installment method. This method spreads out the taxable gain over the period in which payments are received. The Installment Sales Revision Act of 1980 made many changes to installment reporting of gain and should be studied to insure proper tax planning.

Like-kind exchanges also afford opportunities for deferring gain. If real property is exchanged for other real property, recognition of gain or loss is usually deferred until the property received in the exchange is sold. Recent court decisions have had an important effect on like-kind exchanges. These decisions and other technical requirements must be carefully considered when a tax-free exchange is planned.

ACCELERATED COST RECOVERY SYSTEM (ACRS) AND DEPRECIATION

One of the main reasons real estate has proven to be an attractive tax shelter is the availability of depreciation deductions, or, as they are termed under the Accelerated Cost Recovery System (ACRS), cost recovery deductions. Generally, the cost of an asset that will be used for more than one year cannot be expensed in the year purchased. However, if a business or investment asset has a limited life, that is, if it is subject to wear, tear, obsolescence, or expiration, then its cost can be deducted over a period of years. That deduction, termed depreciation or recovery deduction, depending on the system used, can provide a substantial tax write-off even when the market value of the property is rising.

Depreciation

Assets placed in service before January 1, 1981 do not fall under ACRS. Instead, they are depreciated under methods and rules very similar to those used for financial accounting purposes. Basically, the cost or tax basis of the asset less its expected salvage value is deducted over the expected economic useful life of the asset. The depreciation method chosen determines what portion of an asset's basis can be deducted each year. For example, under the straight-line method, the depreciation deduction is the same for each year of service. This deduction equals the cost of the asset less its salvage value, divided by the number of years the asset is expected to be used. Under an accelerated method a larger portion of the asset's cost would be deducted in the first years an asset is used, while smaller deductions would be allowed in later years. There are a number of different accelerated methods such as declining balance and sum-of-the-years-digits, each of which has a particular formula for calculating depreciation.

ACRS

The Accelerated Cost Recovery System (ACRS), introduced for federal tax purposes in 1981, dramatically changed these rules for nearly all assets placed in service after December 31, 1980. Under ACRS, the deduction is termed a "recovery deduction" rather than depreciation. But the changes are far more substantial than changes in terminology. ACRS ignores the useful life of an asset in determining the period over which the basis of an asset can be deducted. Instead, ACRS establishes four main classes of depreciable property, each with a primary recovery period and two longer recovery periods that may be used at the taxpayer's option. ACRS also ignores salvage value. The entire basis of an asset may be deducted over its recovery period. The four main classes of recovery property and their recovery periods are listed below:

1.   15-Year Real Property.   Nearly all real property is 15-year real property. Recovery periods of 15, 35, or 45 years are also available.
2.   10-Year Property.   Only rarely does real property fall into this class. It includes certain types of public utility property, certain mobile homes, and theme park structures. Recovery periods of 10, 25, or 35 years are available.
3.   5-Year Property.   Nearly all machinery, equipment, furniture, fixtures, and other types of personal property falls into this class. A recovery period of either 5, 12, or 15 years may be used.
4.   3-Year Property.   Generally, personal property having a useful life of four years or less under IRS guidelines, such as automobiles, light-weight trucks, and certain special tools, qualify as 3-year property. Personal property used in research and experimentation would also qualify. The recovery periods available are 3, 5, or 12 years.

For many assets, the primary recovery periods under ACRS are significantly shorter than the useful lives might be. For example, buildings placed in service before January 1, 1981 are generally depreciated over useful lives of between 30 to 50 years. Yet the entire cost of a building qualifying under ACRS can be deducted over a recovery period of only 15 years.

There is a drawback to ACRS, however. Component depreciation, which is available for non-ACRS assets, may not be used for buildings under ACRS. Component depreciation involves allocating the total building cost into the costs of its components, for example, its electrical system, heating and air conditioning, plumbing, foundation, and shell. Each component is then depreciated over its own useful life. Because many components have a shorter useful life than the building shell, depreciation of the non-ACRS building could be accelerated through the use of component depreciation.

Fixtures and Personal Property

For buildings under ACRS, the entire building will be treated as one asset. However, the cost of tangible personal property within the building, such as carpets, drapes, appliances, and moveable partitions, are not considered part of the building. Generally, such property would fall in the five-year—not the 15-year—recovery class. Because of this shorter recovery period, and also because personal property may qualify for investment credit and a special election to expense the entire cost of the asset in one year, it is important to identify the cost of such personal property. This issue will be discussed in more detail in a later section.

Leasehold improvements may fall under special rules to be discussed in the leasing section of this chapter.

Once the class of recovery property has been identified and its basis determined, the recovery deduction each year can be determined relatively simply. For each class of property, there is a table showing the percentage of basis that may be recovered each year. The tables are based on an accelerated depreciation method so that higher deductions are available in the earlier years.

In the case of 15-year real property, there are two tables, one for most property (Table 5.1) and a faster one for low-income housing (Table 5.2). Either table bases the deduction on the number of months the property is in service during the first tax year. For example, if a building (15-year real property) is placed in service in the fourth month of the tax year, the fourth column of the table is used. In the first tax year, 9% of basis will be deducted, and in the second year, 11% of basis will be deducted.

In the case of personal property (Table 5.3), the deduction for the first year is the same regardless of how many months the property is in use. No deduction is allowed in the year the asset is sold.

Regardless of the class of property, if the tax period is shorter than twelve months, only a portion of the deduction is allowed. Thus, if the taxable period

TABLE 5.1

ACRS Cost Recovery Table for 15-Year Real Property.
Percentage of Basis Deducted Each Year.

Recovery Year	Month of First Year Property Is Placed In Service											
	1	2	3	4	5	6	7	8	9	10	11	12
1	12	11	10	9	8	7	6	5	4	3	2	1
2	10	10	11	11	11	11	11	11	11	11	11	12
3	9	9	9	9	10	10	10	10	10	10	10	10
4	8	8	8	8	8	8	9	9	9	9	9	9
5	7	7	7	7	7	7	8	8	8	8	8	8
6	6	6	6	6	7	7	7	7	7	7	7	7
7	6	6	6	6	6	6	6	6	6	6	6	6
8	6	6	6	6	6	6	5	6	6	6	6	6
9	6	6	6	6	5	6	5	5	5	6	6	6
10	5	6	5	6	5	5	5	5	5	5	6	5
11	5	5	5	5	5	5	5	5	5	5	5	5
12	5	5	5	5	5	5	5	5	5	5	5	5
13	5	5	5	5	5	5	5	5	5	5	5	5
14	5	5	5	5	5	5	5	5	5	5	5	5
15	5	5	5	5	5	5	5	5	5	5	5	5
16	—	—	1	1	2	2	3	3	4	4	4	5

is only nine months, 9/12ths of the applicable percentage will be used to determine the deduction.

Straight-Line Election Versus Use of ACRS Tables

Instead of using the ACRS tables, a taxpayer can use the straight-line method over the primary recovery period or one of the two longer periods available. For example, the owner of a building could either use the table to calculate his deduction or divide the basis of his building by either 15, 35, or 45 years and deduct that straight-line amount during each full year the building is in service. Different methods may be chosen for different pieces of real property. However, the same method must be used for all personal property within the same ACRS class placed in service in the same year.

Although real estate entrepreneurs generally benefit from accelerating deductions, the straight-line election for ACRS real property brings overall tax savings in many cases. First, use of the accelerated tables could increase income taxes of some taxpayers by subjecting them to the minimum or alternative minimum tax. These taxes are imposed on those claiming substantial amounts

TABLE 5.2

ACRS Cost Recovery Table for Low-Income Housing.
Percentage of Basis Deducted Each Year.

Recovery Year	Month of First Year Property Is Placed In Service											
	1	2	3	4	5	6	7	8	9	10	11	12
1	13	12	11	10	9	8	7	6	4	3	2	1
2	12	12	12	12	12	12	12	13	13	13	13	13
3	10	10	10	10	11	11	11	11	11	11	11	11
4	9	9	9	9	9	9	9	9	10	10	10	10
5	8	8	8	8	8	8	8	8	8	8	8	9
6	7	7	7	7	7	7	7	7	7	7	7	7
7	6	6	6	6	6	6	6	6	6	6	6	6
8	5	5	5	5	5	5	5	5	5	5	6	6
9	5	5	5	5	5	5	5	5	5	5	5	5
10	5	5	5	5	5	5	5	5	5	5	5	5
11	4	5	5	5	5	5	5	5	5	5	5	5
12	4	4	4	5	4	5	5	5	5	5	5	5
13	4	4	4	4	4	4	5	4	5	5	5	5
14	4	4	4	4	4	4	4	4	4	5	4	4
15	4	4	4	4	4	4	4	4	4	4	4	4
16	—	—	1	1	2	2	2	3	3	3	4	4

TABLE 5.3

ACRS Cost Recovery Table for Personal Property:
Percentage of Basis Deducted Each Year.

Recovery Year	Class of Property		
	3-Year	5-Year	10-Year
1	25	15	8
2	38	22	14
3	37	21	12
4		21	10
5		21	10
6			10
7			9
8			9
9			9
10			9

Note: For taxable periods of less than twelve months, the percentages in Tables 5.1, 5.2, and 5.3 must be prorated.

of certain tax deductions or exclusions considered to be preferential. Second, the gain on sale of the property will be taxed differently depending on whether the ACRS tables or the straight-line method was used. In many cases, using the straight-line election instead of the ACRS tables will substantially decrease the tax on sale of the property.

Recovery Deductions on Sale of Property

When property held for investment or used in a trade or business is sold at a gain, the gain may be eligible for favorable capital gain treatment. However, if depreciation or cost recovery deductions were taken on the property before it was sold, some of the depreciation may be recaptured and taxed at ordinary income rates. For example, if the total gain on property sold is $25,000, and $10,000 of previously taken cost recovery deductions are subject to recapture, $10,000 of the gain will be taxed at ordinary income rates, while only $15,000 will be eligible for favorable capital gain treatment.

How much of the recovery deductions previously taken on real property will be subject to recapture depends upon whether the property is residential or non-residential. In addition, the rules for corporate taxpayers differ slightly from those for non-corporate taxpayers.

Recapture Rules for Non-Corporate Taxpayers

Non-corporate taxpayers who have used the ACRS tables to recover the cost of non-residential real estate will recapture *all* recovery deductions to the extent of the gain from the sale. However, if they had used the straight-line election, they would not recapture any recovery deductions. For this reason, it is generally advisable for non-corporate taxpayers to use the straight-line method to recover the cost of non-residential real property.

For example, suppose an individual purchases non-residential real estate for $100,000, holds it for two years, and sells it for $120,000 (see Table 5.4). Had the accelerated tables, been used, a total of $22,000 in recovery deductions would have been taken. The owner's gain would be $42,000, the difference between the selling price and the adjusted basis. (Adjusted basis equals the original tax basis less total depreciation or recovery deductions.) In addition, all of the $22,000 of recovery deductions would be subject to recapture, and, in this case, taxed as ordinary income. The remaining $20,000 could qualify for treatment as capital gain, subject to the 60% capital gain deduction. Thus, the taxpayer's total taxable gain would be $30,000.

If the same individual made the straight-line election, he would have taken lower recovery deductions each year totalling only $13,334. Thus, the adjusted basis would have been $86,666 and the total gain only $33,334. None of the recovery deductions would be recaptured, and all of the gain could be reportable as capital gain. After the capital gain deduction is taken, the taxpayer's total taxable gain would be only $13,334. Thus, in this example, if the taxpayer

TABLE 5.4

Recapture of Recovery Deductions on Sale of Real Property: Non-Corporate Taxpayer.

	Non-Residential 15-Year Real Property		Residential Rental 15-Year Real Property	
	If ACRS table % used	If 15-year straight-line used	If ACRS table % used	If 15-Year straight-line used
Cost basis	$100,000	$100,000	$100,000	$100,000
Cost recovery deductions:				
Year 1 (assume property	12,000	6,667	12,000	6,667
Year 2 placed in service	10,000	6,667	10,000	6,667
in Jan. of Yr. 1)				
Total	22,000	13,334	22,000	13,334
Selling price	120,000	120,000	120,000	120,000
Adjusted basis, beginning of Year 3 (cost basis less total cost recovery deduction)	78,000	86,666	78,000	86,666
Total gain	$ 42,000	$ 33,334	$ 42,000	$ 33,334
Recapture (taxed at ordinary income rates)	$ 22,000	$ —	$ 8,666	$ —
Capital gain (or §1231 gain)	20,000	33,334	33,334	33,334
60% capital gain deduction	(12,000)	(20,000)	(20,000)	(20,000)
Taxable capital gain	8,000	13,334	13,334	13,334
Total taxable gain (recapture plus taxable capital gain)	$ 30,000	$ 13,334	$ 22,000	$ 13,334

Note: This example ignores the effect of the alternative minimum tax.

had used the ACRS tables instead of a straight-line election, his total cost recovery deductions would have been $8,666 higher, but his taxable gain on the sale of the property would have been $16,666 higher.

If the non-corporate taxpayer has used ACRS tables to recover the cost of residential rental real property, the only deductions subject to recapture would be those that exceeded the straight-line amount. If the straight-line method had been used, no deductions would be recaptured. Table 5.4 illustrates these tax consequences. In this case, the taxpayer would have probably benefitted from use of the ACRS tables. By using the tables, the taxpayer's deductions in the first two years would have been $8,666 higher, and his taxable gain in the beginning of the third year would have been $8,666 higher. Because his tax savings from the additional deductions would have benefitted him in the first two years, while his additional tax was not due until the third year, it would probably have been beneficial for the taxpayer to use the ACRS tables.

Recapture Rules for Corporate Taxpayers

Corporate taxpayers recapture slightly higher amounts of recovery deductions. In the case of non-residential real property, all recovery deductions are subject to recapture if the ACRS tables were used, but only 15% of the deductions would be subject to recapture if the straight-line method were used. In the case of residential rental real property, corporate taxpayers using accelerated ACRS tables will find that to the extent that their recovery deductions exceed 85% of the straight-line amounts, they will be subject to recapture. If they had used the straight-line method, 15% of the deductions would be subject to recapture.

Corporate taxpayers recovering the cost of non-residential property using the ACRS tables will find that all recovery deductions allowed are subject to recapture while corporations using the straight-line method will find only 15% of deductions are subject to recapture.

Table 5.5 illustrates these consequences in the case of a corporation having taxable income over $100,000. The ordinary income of such corporations is taxed at the highest corporate tax rate of 46% while capital gains are taxed at lower alternative tax rates of 28%. Results would differ if the taxable income of the corporation were lower, particularly if under $50,000.

Determining whether a corporate taxpayer should use the accelerated table or a straight-line method is complex and must be done on a case-by-case basis.

Anti-Churning Rules

To prevent taxpayers from gaining the benefits of the new ACRS rules for property owned or used prior to January 1, 1981, "anti-churning rules" prevent certain post-1980 acquisitions from qualifying as ACRS property. For example, if someone owned property in 1980 and transferred this property to a relative in 1981, the new owner could be barred from using ACRS, even though the property was placed in service after December 31, 1980. Anti-churning rules can also bar the use of ACRS for a portion of assets acquired in certain like-kind exchanges and other tax-free transactions.

REPAIRS AND IMPROVEMENTS

Repairs Versus Improvements

General maintenance, repair, and operating costs are expensed in the period they are paid or accrued. The cost of improvements to assets, however, must be capitalized and deducted either through depreciation or recovery deductions. Thus, it is important to distinguish capital improvements from maintenance and repairs. Generally, a cost will be considered a repair if it does not ap-

TABLE 5.5

Recapture of Recovery Deductions on Sale of Real Property: Corporate Taxpayer with Taxable Income Over $100,000.

	Non-Residential 15-Year Real Property		Residential Rental 15-Year Real Property	
	If ACRS table % used	If 15-year straight-line used	If ACRS table % used	If 15-Year straight-line used
Cost basis	$100,000	$100,000	$100,000	$100,000
Cost recovery deductions:				
Year 1 (assume property	12,000	6,667	12,000	6,667
Year 2 placed in service	10,000	6,667	10,000	6,667
in Jan. of Yr. 1)				
Total	22,000	13,334	22,000	13,334
Selling price	120,000	120,000	120,000	120,000
Adjusted basis, beginning of Year 3 (cost basis less total cost recovery deduction)	78,000	86,666	78,000	86,666
Total gain	$ 42,000	$ 33,334	$ 42,000	$ 33,334
Recapture (taxed at ordinary income rates) (assume corporation is in top marginal rate of 46%)	$ 22,000	$ 2,000	$ 10,666	$ 2,000
Capital gain (or §1231 gain) (taxed at alternative capital gains rate of 28%)	20,000	31,334	31,334	31,334
Total taxable gain:				
Amounts taxed at 46%	22,000	2,000	10,666	2,000
Amounts taxed at 28%	20,000	31,334	31,334	31,334
Total tax on sale	$ 15,720	$ 9,694	$ 13,680	$ 9,694

Note: This example assumes the corporation is in highest marginal tax bracket in order that the alternative capital gains tax will apply.
This example ignores any possible effect of the alternative minimum tax.

preciably prolong the life of the asset or materially add to its value. A cost that does prolong the life of the asset, or increases its value or functions will be an improvement. For example, patching a leak in a roof is a repair, but replacing the entire roof is an improvement. Furthermore, if a great many repairs are undertaken at once to refurbish a building, they may constitute a capital improvement, even though they might have been deductible expenses if carried out over a number of years.

Cost Recovery of Improvements

Substantial improvements, even if made to a non-ACRS building, will be considered a separate ACRS asset in the 15-year real property class. To be considered "substantial," improvement costs incurred in a 24-month period must equal at least 25% of the adjusted basis of the building. If improvements are not considered substantial, their cost is merely added to the cost of the existing building, thus increasing the basis used for depreciation or recovery deductions over the remaining recovery period. Thus, substantial improvements may be deducted over 15 years, while lesser improvements could be recovered more quickly. Because of the different time periods over which isolated repairs, substantial improvements, and other improvements may be deducted, it is important to plan the timing of repair and improvement programs.

Rehabilitation Credit

Another consideration in making improvements to older buildings is whether the improvements would qualify for a special rehabilitation credit. Rehabilitation of a commercial building that is at least 30 years old might qualify for a 15% credit while rehabilitation of a 40-year-old commercial building might qualify for a 20% credit. In either case, the basis of the property must be reduced by the amount of the credit. In the case of a residential or commercial certified historic structure a 25% credit might be available. The basis of a certified historic structure would be reduced by only one-half of the credit. Part of the rehabilitation credit may be recaptured if the rehabilitated building is not kept in service for a full five years.

A number of technical requirements must be met for a rehabilitation project to qualify for the credit. For example, expenditures must reach certain dollar amounts within specified time frames and a certain percentage of existing walls must remain intact. Because of the many technical requirements and because of the large tax credit at stake, it is imperative that plans for any rehabilitation of an older building be carefully reviewed by a competent tax advisor.

INVESTMENT CREDIT

The investment credit is a direct credit against tax liability. The amount of credit varies from 6 to 10% of qualifying depreciable property. The credit for 3-year ACRS property is 6% of its cost; the credit for 5- or 10-year property is 10%. However, the basis for depreciation purposes must be reduced by one-half of the credit allowed. Instead of this basis reduction, an election can be made to reduce the allowable credit by 2%.

Qualifying Property

Buildings and their structural components do not qualify for the credit. Neither does property used for residential units, except for coin-operated vending machines, washing machines, and dryers and property used by motels and hotels providing transient lodging. In addition, credits are not allowed on property used by governmental or non-profit units nor on property held outside the United States. In spite of these broad restrictions, investment credit is available for many types of property encountered in real estate ventures.

Tangible, personal property (except air conditioning and heating units) used for non-residential purposes does generally qualify. Thus, the cost of appliances, signs, carpeting, drapes, etc., that could be segregated from the cost of a non-residential building and classed as 5-year property for ACRS would qualify as investment credit property as well. Moreover, the cost of special flooring to support a heavy piece of equipment or special wiring for the equipment would be included in the cost of that equipment and would also qualify.

Real property other than buildings can qualify, but only if such property is used as an integral part of manufacturing, extraction, transportation, communications, electrical energy, gas, water, or sewage disposal services. Under these rules, fences used in cattle raising or logging roads would generally qualify (because they are integral parts of extraction activities), but fences around the farm worker's house or roads used by the loggers for commuting to and from work would not. Thus, in many cases, it is the particular use to which property is put, and not the type of property itself, that determines whether the property qualifies for investment credit.

Because real property can qualify only if used in certain activities and because components of buildings may not qualify under any circumstances, taxpayers have liberally interpreted what constitutes personal property. The ensuing court battles with the IRS have developed a number of factors to help distinguish personal from real property.

First, local law is not controlling. Thus, fixtures considered to be real property or improvements may be personal property for investment credit purposes. Second, mere attachment to land or a building does not make property an improvement or part of the building. Improvements are permanently attached, but personal property is removable, without damaging either the property or what it has been attached to. The argument that a particular item is personal property is strengthened if there are reasons the property may have to be removed, if it has been designed to be removable, or if it is expected to be removed.

Bases on such criteria, drywall partitions have been found to be non-qualifying structural components, while movable partitions have been found to qualify. Pole lights imbedded in concrete may be non-qualifying permanent improvements, but pole lights designed to be detachable from their bases have qualified as personal property. The list of possible qualifying items is endless—accoustical tiling, cabinets, security systems, vault doors, signs—but whether a particular item will qualify depends on how that particular item has been designed, installed, and used.

When large amounts of potential investment credit property may be involved in a project, for example in building a new plant or office building or constructing large scale tenant improvements, it may be worthwhile to enlist the services of a tax consultant and engineer well-versed in investment credit rules to audit the project. Such consultants can help identify and establish the cost of potentially qualifying items, and, if consulted early enough in the planning stages, may be able to suggest design and material changes that would enhance the likelihood that the property would qualify.

Limitations on Credit

The amount of investment credit that can be taken in any one tax year is limited. In no case can the amount of credit used exceed the tax liability. If the tax liability is higher than $25,000, the limit through the 1982 tax year is $25,000 plus 90% of the excess liability. Starting in 1983, the limit will reduce to $25,000 plus 85% of the tax liability exceeding $25,000. Additionally, the amount of used property that can qualify is limited to $125,000 per year. Unused credits may be carried back three tax years and carried forward fifteen years.

Recapture of Credit

If qualifying three-year recovery property is not held for the full three years, or if qualifying 5-, 10- or 15-year recovery property is not held for a full five years, all or a portion of the investment credit used may be recaptured and due as an additional tax. The following table gives the percentage of investment credit that must be recaptured:

	The recapture percentage is:	
If the Recovery Property Remains Qualifying Property	*For 15-Year 10-Year and 5-Year Property*	*For 3-Year Property*
At least 5 full years	0	0
Less than 5 years but at least 4 full years	20	0
Less than 4 years but at least 3 full years	40	0
Less than 3 years but at least 2 full years	60	33
Less than 2 years but at least 1 full year	80	66
Less than 1 full year	100	100

For example, if a full 10% credit had been taken on 5-year property that had been kept for only three and a half years, 40% of the credit would be recaptured.

ELECTION TO EXPENSE INVESTMENT CREDIT PROPERTY

The cost of property that qualifies for investment credit and that has been purchased for use in a trade or business may, by special election, be expensed in the year of purchase. In any given year, the dollar amount that can be expensed is limited as follows:

For Property Placed In Service In Taxable Years Beginning In	*Limit On Amount Expensed*
1983	$ 5,000
1984 and 1985	7,500
1986 and after	10,000

If the property is later sold or disposed of, the entire amount expensed is subject to recapture as ordinary income. Also, investment credit may not be taken on expensed property. Because of these drawbacks, it is not always advantageous to expense property under this election. The recovery period of the property, the marginal tax rate of the taxpayer, and the after-tax return a taxpayer could earn on any current tax savings will all affect which alternative is most advantageous.

ENERGY CREDIT

Another credit that could bring substantial tax savings to the real estate owner is the business energy credit. This credit of from 10 to 15% is available for investment in qualifying energy property such as alternative energy property, specially defined energy property, solar or wind property, recycling equipment, biomass energy property, and shale oil energy equipment. Detailed Treasury Department regulations specify the energy property that qualifies.

In addition to meeting the Treasury Department specifications, energy property must also be either ACRS property or property that is depreciable or amortizable. It also must be new, as opposed to used, property. Structural components of buildings can qualify for the credit. If property qualifies for both investment credit and the business energy credit, both credits may be taken. Like the regular investment credit, the energy credit is subject to recapture and will reduce the tax basis of qualifying property. Also, the sum of the investment and energy credits used cannot exceed the total tax in a given year.

MORTGAGE FINANCING

Mortgage financing can be an attractive means of acquiring funds to purchase or improve real estate or of taking advantage of the appreciation of property already owned to finance new projects. Loan proceeds are not taxable when received. Moreover, if property is purchased subject to a mortgage or if a mortgage secured by the property is assumed on purchase, the amount of the loan is included in the basis of the property. Thus, without generating taxable income, debt financing can increase depreciation or recovery deductions beyond the initial cash investment.

Refinancing appreciated property can be especially advantageous. Through refinancing, the owner can receive cash benefit from the appreciated value without recognizing taxable income or giving up ownership. Even if the loan secured by his property exceeds his basis in the property, the owner will not recognize taxable income, unless the secured property is transferred or sold.

Effect of Financing on Deduction of Real Estate Losses

Mortgage financing will not limit the deduction of real estate losses under the "at risk" limitations. At risk rules that generally prohibit investors from deducting losses financed through nonrecourse borrowing do not apply to the holding of real estate.

In the case of a partnership, mortgage financing might increase the portion of partnership losses that is deductible by the partners. Under partnership rules, a partner may not deduct partnership losses that exceed his basis in his partnership interest. Included in a partner's basis is his share of partnership liabilities. A general partner may include his pro rata share of all partnership liabilities, while a limited partner includes his pro rata share of all nonrecourse partnership liabilities. Thus, if the partnership incurs nonrecourse real estate debt, each limited or general partner may increase his basis—thereby increasing the limit on his deduction of partnership losses.

Shareholders in S-Corporations do not benefit in a similar fashion from mortgage financing. An S-Corp shareholder is also limited in the deduction of S-Corp losses. Losses that exceed the shareholder's basis in S-Corp stock plus the amounts he has personally loaned to the S-Corp may not be deducted. However, the shareholder may not include any share of the corporation's liabilities in his basis. A better alternative for the S-Corp shareholder might be to borrow the money personally and lend it to the corporation.

Tax Treatment of Interest and Other Costs of Borrowing

The many costs of borrowing, such as interest, service fees, loan commitment fees, and legal fees, will generally yield tax benefits. In many cases, however, the deduction of these costs is limited or postponed. The nature of the cost, as well as the type of property or project being financed determines the tax treatment of the cost.

Tax Treatment of Interest: CPIT, Investment Interest, and Prepaid Interest

Interest used to acquire or carry any property that yields tax-free income is not deductible. Otherwise, interest charges will eventually be deductible, although special rules and limitations may apply.

The deduction of interest on loans used to finance construction of a building or other real property improvement is generally deferred under the rules for construction period interest and taxes (CPIT). During the period beginning when construction starts to the time the constructed property is ready to be placed in service or held for sale, non-corporate taxpayers must capitalize construction period interest and taxes on all property except certain low-income housing. If construction was started in a fiscal year beginning after December 31, 1982, corporate taxpayers must also capitalize CPIT incurred on non-residential construction projects. Although a small portion of CPIT is deductible in the year paid or accrued, amortization of the capitalized portion does not begin until the construction period is over. The amortization period is generally 10 years.

Investment interest rules could also limit the interest deduction of non-corporate taxpayers. These restrictions generally limit the deduction of interest incurred to hold or acquire investment property to $10,000 plus the amount of net investment income and certain out-of-pocket expenses incurred on leased property. Real property would be considered investment property unless it is used in a trade or business or for personal purposes. Leased property will be considered investment property for this purpose if there is a guaranteed return on the property or if certain operating expenses (i.e., business expenses excluding depreciation, interest, rents and reimbursed amounts) total less than 15% of the rental income produced by the property. If in any given taxable year, investment interest exceeds allowable limits, the excess may be carried over and deducted in later years subject to these same limitations.

Other restrictions apply to prepaid interest, loan discounts, or interest deducted from loan proceeds. The accrual basis taxpayer can deduct such interest as it accrues over the term of the loan. For the cash basis taxpayer, the situation may be more complex. The cash basis taxpayer cannot deduct interest until it is paid. In addition, interest cannot be deducted before it accrues (unless it is interest on the taxpayer's principal residence). Thus, if a cash basis taxpayer prepays interest, only the amount that actually accrues may be deducted. If the bank deducts interest from the loan proceeds or adds interest to the loan balance, a cash basis debtor will not be considered as having paid that interest.

Accordingly, he will not be entitled to a deduction until the interest has been both repaid *and* accrued. For this purpose, the repayment of loan principal will be applied toward any unpaid interest before it is applied to other unpaid loan proceeds. For example, suppose that a bank deducts $1,000 from the proceeds of a loan to a cash basis taxpayer. At the end of the year, the taxpayer has repaid $500 of the loan principal. At that time, he is considered as having paid $500 of interest. If only $250 of this interest had actually accrued, he could deduct only $250. If, however, $600 interest had accrued by the end of the year, the entire $500 he paid could be deducted. The remaining $100 of accrued interest cannot be deducted until an additional $100 of principal is repaid.

Loan Acquisition Costs, Service Costs, Commitment Fees

Other fees may be charged by lenders for their services or by those helping to arrange financing. These service fees are distinguished from interest because their tax treatment differs. In general, service fees are capitalized and deducted ratably over the term of the loan. They are not subject to CPIT or investment interest restrictions.

"Points" charged on a loan could be additional interest or they could be a service charge expressed as a percentage of the loan amount. Loan documents should specify what type of charge they are. Other charges associated with obtaining financing, such as legal fees or surveying costs required by the lender, are treated in the same manner as service charges and must be capitalized and deducted over the term of the loan. Loan commitment fees, according to the current position of the IRS, are amortizable over the term of any loan that results from the commitment.

Allocation of Payments Into Principal and Interest

It is also important for the loan agreement to specify how loan payments would be allocated between principal and interest. Interest would be taxable income to the lender and a tax deduction to the borrower. Principal repayments are neither taxable income to the lender not a tax deduction to the borrower. If a loan agreement is bona fide and made at arms length, its allocation formula should be honored for tax purposes.

LEASING

Leasing real estate can be attractive to both landlord and tenant for tax as well as business reasons. An investor-owner can use rent payments to provide operating funds. Although this rent is taxable income, the combined tax benefits of depreciation or ACRS deductions, as well as deductible operating and interest expenses could more than offset the tax on rental income. The business whose plant requirements may change within the near future or which needs to conserve capital for operations may find plant ownership impractical. Such businesses may find that a leasing arrangement, under which they make deductible rent payments, is a less expensive, more flexible means of acquiring a physical plant.

Tax consequences are an important factor both in the property owner's decision on whether to lease or sell his property and in the property user's decision on whether to lease or buy the property he needs. Once a decision to lease has been made, care must be taken to insure that the terms of the lease reflect the desired tax effects. It is especially important to insure that a lease will be honored as such for tax purposes. As will be discussed later in this section, a lease agreement having too many characteristics of a sale, could be treated as a conditional sale for tax purposes.

Security Deposits and Advance Rent

Lease arrangements often require tenants to pay security deposits or prepay several months rent. Because these two types of payments are treated differently for tax purposes, they must be carefully distinguished and accounted for.

Security deposits are neither deductible by the tenant not taxable income to the landlord. This treatment holds as long as the landlord is obligated to return the deposit to the tenant. Once the deposit is forfeited by the tenant, for example, if the deposit is applied to delinquent rent, the deposit becomes taxable income to the landlord and a deductible rent payment to the tenant.

Advance rent is treated differently from security deposits. Landlords, whether cash basis or accrual taxpayers, report income from advance rent when they receive it. The tenant, however, may not be entitled to an immediate deduction. Ordinarily, neither cash basis nor accrual taxpayers may deduct rent prepayments until the period for which the rent applies. Some courts, however, have permitted cash basis tenants to deduct prepayments attributable to rental periods that will lapse within 11 months of the end of the taxable year.

Lease Acquisition Costs

Tenants may also pay bonuses, legal fees, lease purchase costs, or similar costs in acquiring a lease. These costs are not currently deductible, but must be capitalized and amortized over the term of the lease including, in some cases, any renewal periods. Sometimes, a tenant may acquire a lease together with other rights, such as a purchase option, or it may purchase an improved leasehold from another lessee. In these cases, the cost should be reasonably allocated among the lease, improvements, and purchase option. While the lease acquisition cost will be amortized over the remaining life of the lease, the option cost would be capitalized until the option is either exercised (when it would be added to the cost of the property acquired), or it expires (when it would be treated as either a capital or ordinary loss, depending upon the nature of the option property expensed). Any cost allocable to improvements should be deducted either through ACRS or depreciation, or if the lease term is shorter than the recovery period or useful life, amortized over the lease term.

Landlords can also incur costs such as commission expenses or legal fees in acquiring and negotiating a lease. In some cases, the landlord will incur costs in negotiating leases that do not materialize. Legal fees and other similar costs incurred in unsuccessful lease negotiations should be itemized separately from successful lease acquisition costs. While the costs associated with unsuccessful negotiations are deductible currently, successful lease acquisition costs must be capitalized and amortized over the lease term.

Lease Cancellation Payments

Should a tenant pay the landlord to cancel the lease, the tenant will usually be allowed a current business deduction for the payment. However, if the purpose of cancellation is to obtain a new lease on the same premises, the cancellation payment would be considered a lease acquisition cost, amortizable over the term of the new lease. In either case, the cancellation payment would be taxable income to the landlord.

In some cases a landlord might make lease cancellation payments to the tenant. If this is because the landlord wants to enter into a new lease on the same premises, that payment would be a lease acquisition cost amortizable over the new lease term. If not, the payment would be amortizable over the remaining term of the cancelled lease. In either case, the tenant receiving the payment would treat it as proceeds from the sale of a lease. Generally, any gain from the sale would receive capital gain treatment.

Leasehold Improvements

Either the landlord or the tenant may construct leasehold improvements. Whoever bears the risk for such improvements, usually whoever pays for them, will be entitled to depreciation. For example, if the tenant constructs the improvements at his own expense, he would be entitled to depreciate them. However, if the construction was done in return for free rent, their cost would be considered rent—a deductible business expense to the tenant and taxable income to the landlord. The landlord would then be entitled to depreciation. If the tenant were granted an allowance for leasehold improvements, that is, if the landlord agreed to pay for a certain portion of the tenant's cost in constructing improvements, the landlord would generally be entitled to deduct depreciation of the improvements he paid for.

Improvements constructed by and depreciable by the tenant may be amortized over the term of the lease (generally including renewal periods) if the lease term is shorter than the recovery period or useful life that would otherwise be used. However, if a lease is between related parties, this shorter amortization period is not available. The cost of improvements would be deducted over the normal recovery period.

Improvements constructed by a tenant at his own expense (unless they are considered rent) are not taxable income to the landlord, even if the landlord has a reversionary interest in them. Neither will such tenant-constructed improvements alter a landlord's basis in the property.

Improvements constructed by the landlord would fall under the general rules for building improvements. If they are 15-year ACRS property, their costs will either be added to the cost of the building or recovered as a separate improvement depending on how extensive the improvements are (see the earlier discussion of depreciation). If the property is not ACRS property, it will be depreciated over its useful life. If the improvements were so tailor-made for a particular tenant that they will have to be dismantled before the premises are leased to another tenant, the useful life of the improvement would generally not be longer than the remaining lease term.

Investment and Energy Credits on Leased Property

Leased property can qualify for the investment and energy credits. In most cases, however, non-corporate lessors are barred from taking the credits on property they lease. Only if a non-corporate lessor constructed the property in his trade or business or if the term of the lease (including optional renewal periods) is less than one-half the property's useful life and the operating expenses (i.e., expenses excluding interest, taxes and depreciation) of the first year exceed 15% of the rent from the property, will the non-corporate lessor be entitled to the investment or energy credits.

Lessors may choose to pass these credits on to the lessee. For example, if a non-corporate lessor is barred from using the credit himself, he could elect to pass it through to the lessee, possibly using this pass-through as a lease bargaining point.

Leases Treated as Sales

Purchase options contained within lease agreements also raise the question of whether the lease will be treated as a sale for tax purposes. If the lease term is unusually long in relation to the expected life of the property, or if rental payments are higher than what a normal market rent would be, if a bargain purchase option is contained in the lease agreement, or if equity is transferred through the lease terms, there is a chance that the "lease" will be ignored and that the transaction will instead be treated as a deferred payment or conditionals sales agreement.

Treating such a lease agreement as a purchase will have substantial tax consequences. A lessee could find that he is making installment purchase payments instead of paying deductible rent. Part of these payments might be deductible as interest, but part would represent non-deductible principal payments. Depreciation or cost recovery deductions would be allowed on the imputed purchase price of depreciable improvements, but not on the portion of the purchase price allocated to the land.

In such a situation, the landlord, too, would find a change in tax treatment. Instead of treating the entire payment as taxable rental income, the landlord/seller would treat part of each payment as interest income and part as principal repayment. If the sale was being reported on the installment basis (which would be available in most cases), part of this principal repayment would be taxable gain while part would be a tax-free recovery of the basis. If the landlord elected not to use the installment method, the entire gain would be reported in the first year of the lease, and subsequent principal repayments would be tax-free. In addition to these tax consequences, depreciation, recovery deductions, and investment credit would not be allowed to the landlord/seller.

There is no general rule as to whether it is preferable for a lease agreement to be treated either as a lease or a sale. But, because of the great differences in tax treatment, it is important that each particular case be analyzed, and a determination made as to whether lease or deferred payment treatment is preferable. The lease agreement and other factors surrounding the arrangement should be planned to support the most beneficial alternative.

Sale-Leasebacks

In a sale-leaseback, the owner-user of a property sells the property and then leases it back from the purchaser. The former owner is then in the tax position of a tenant and will substitute deductible rent payments for depreciation and other deductions associated with ownership. The gain from the sale of the business property would be taxed as capital gain, subject to depreciation recapture rules. If the sale is structured and reported as an installment sale, the taxable gain could be spread out as payments are received from the buyer.

The buyer-landlord in a sales-leaseback transaction receives (1) the various tax benefits of property ownership and (2) the insurance of a tenant without incurring additional commission expenses.

Sale-leasebacks can be arranged among related parties. For example, shareholders in a corporation desiring depreciation deductions to lower their individual tax liabilities may buy the corporation's plant and then lease it back to the corporation. However, since related party transactions are always subject to particular scrutiny, care should be taken that the transaction is executed on an arms-length basis. In addition, there is no tax deduction for losses on sales between certain related parties and the gain on sales of depreciable property between certain related parties is treated as ordinary income instead of capital gain. Sale-leaseback transactions will be carefully scrutinized by the IRS to insure that there is substance to them. If the transaction does not qualify as a sale-leaseback, then it will be treated as a financing arrangement. Even more so than other leases, the terms of a sale-leaseback should be planned with the assistance of a tax advisor.

Equity-Sharing Arrangements

Because of high interest rates, record construction costs, and a competitive leasing market, many lessors are generating tax losses in excess of what they can currently use. Such lessors may be able to attract tenants by offering to share with them the tax benefits of ownership.

This could be accomplished by the lessor transferring the property to a specially created limited partnership. The owner-lessor could assume the role of general partner and manager. Selected tenants could be offered limited partnership interests. The partnership agreement could call for a special allocation of items affecting the tax liability of partners. Recovery deductions, investment credits, operating losses, and other items that could reduce current tax liabilities might be allocated to the limited partners alone. Then, capital gain on the ultimate sale of the project might be allocated to the limited partners only to the extent of their capital investments plus the sum of the deductions previously allocated to them. Any excess gain might be allocated to the general partner alone. In this matter, tax benefits that would not be currently usable by the owner could be passed to tenants, while most of the economic value of appreciation would remain with the owner. Variations in this type of equity-sharing arrangement could meet particular needs of the tenant and landlord.

SUMMARY

This chapter has outlined some of the many tax issues involved in acquiring, managing, and selling real estate. Because of the numerous tax aspects involved, planning real estate transactions to best manage tax consequences is critical. Moreover, because tax law is constantly changing, existing plans must be continually reviewed and updated. Such careful attention to tax consequences is an integral part of effective real estate management.

CRAIG A. ROSS
Marketing Vice President
Dennison Monarch Systems, Inc.
New Windsor, New York

Craig A. Ross is the Marketing Vice President for Dennison Monarch Systems, Inc., a subsidiary of Dennison Manufacturing Company. He has researched and designed several One-Write record keeping systems for Real Estate Managers. He earned his BS in Business Administration from Montclair State College, and his MBA from Wayne State University in Detroit.

WARREN V. MUSSER
Vice Chairman
Safeguard Business Systems, Inc.
King of Prussia, Pennsylvania

Warren V. Musser is a graduate of Lehigh University with a BS in Industrial Engineering. Mr. Musser is Vice Chairman of Safeguard Business Systems, Inc. and a Director. Safeguard Business Systems, Inc. is the world's leading supplier of information systems to the small business market with over 700,000 customers. Safeguard Business Systems, Inc. provides manual and data processing systems.

CHAPTER 6

RECORD KEEPING AND FINANCIAL REPORTING FOR EFFECTIVE PROPERTY MANAGEMENT

INTRODUCTION

The heart of sound property management lies in efficient, accurate, and thorough record keeping procedures and systems. Virtually all property management functions revolve around the data that is collected at the individual property locations. It is important to focus on determining the exact property management source data records needed and the most effective methods to organize the data collection procedures. Properly collected source data can be readily converted into meaningful management information—ultimately resulting in sound and profitable property management.

Real estate investors will find that a working knowledge of record keeping procedures will help in selecting a property manager and an accounting firm specializing in property management. Familiarity with record keeping procedures will facilitate discussions of how the property manager and the accounting firm plan to capture source data, handle various problems, control cash, and pay your income.

Investors intending to manage the property themselves or property managers will find the following record keeping information valuable in setting up and maximizing the efficiency of their procedures. The importance of generating accurate records cannot be overstressed. Equally important, however, is to establish procedures that are not all encompassing and do not take time away from other critical management functions.

A good record keeping system establishes a well-defined audit trail. All income and expenses should be traceable to the source with no means of conducting any off-the-books or unrecorded transactions. A well-established audit trail is valuable in assuring that the investment has the maximum protection available.

This chapter discusses why records are so important, what records should be maintained, alternative methods of maintaining the records, and how to convert these records into information that will benefit property management activities.

THE IMPORTANCE OF GOOD RECORDS

The reasons for maintaining good property management records can be placed in four broad categories:

1. Financial control.
2. Tax reporting.
3. Management control.
4. Legal requirements.

The above elements are equally important and work in harmony to produce well-managed properties. A deficiency in any of the areas will adversely impact the overall management process. Interestingly, the root of all the categories is the source documents and how accurately and thoroughly they are captured.

Financial Control Overview

Precise records are the backbone of effective financial control. Accurate recording of income and expense disbursements allows reliable budgeting, timely comparison of budget to actual expenses, responsive corrective action toward unfavorable budget variances, and future budgeting. These actions, in turn, allow for determining cash requirements in advance and lead to good cash management. Problem properties can be quickly identified and either corrected or sold. Close control over subcontracted maintenance and petty cash can add significantly to the total control process.

Accurate financial records are also beneficial in obtaining additional lines of credit. Bankers and other lending institution managers look favorably on well-maintained and documented financial records because they can accurately assess and respond to your financial position.

Tax Reporting Overview

Accurate and complete records will assist the investor's accountant in preparing financial statements. An audit trail will be available to document each and every available deduction. An accurate breakdown of all the income items will be provided so they can be properly categorized. Good records will save a lot of your own and your accountant's time since everything will be documented and records will not have to be recreated. This is especially important in the event of a tax audit.

If the investment is being used as a tax shelter, good record keeping is a must to provide the necessary back-up documentation. Again, should any regulatory body raise questions, the necessary back-up records will be easily available.

Management Control Overview

Accurate and complete records should provide managers with key information to effectively manage their properties. The necessary data to perform analyses on occupancy rates, maintenance cost per unit, delinquent rents, and the like, should be at their fingertips at any time during a given period. This allows establishment of a property plan based on fact rather than conjecture. The investor's various properties can be compared, rent or policy changes can be made to compensate for problem areas, and the value of the property can be accurately determined. Management with a plan means that each and every step is deliberate; the desired objectives for the profitability and growth can be achieved. Managing without a plan can destroy the entire investment and make life miserable for the tenants occupying the property. Successful planning starts with accurate input records.

Legal Requirements Overview

The various states and municipalities have set down several guidelines concerning landlord/tenant relationships. It is beyond the scope of this chapter to discuss each specific case, but most of the guidelines have a requirement for sound record keeping. Good records are often the determining factor in settling eviction disputes, possession problems, and negligence cases.

It is important to know the local legal requirements and assure that the record keeping system you establish captures all the required information. Many states require that all third-party funds be held in a separate trust account. Payment of interest on security deposits is another area that varies widely. The rule of thumb to follow is to establish the records necessary to back-up your individual position.

THE BASIC RECORD KEEPING SYSTEMS

There are six basic areas of record keeping encountered by property managers:

1. Rent collections.
2. Property expense disbursements.
3. Maintenance control.
4. Petty cash control.
5. Payroll.
6. General operating account.

Depending on the size of the firm, all or some of the above systems may be required. Discuss your requirements with your accountant and systems consultant to ensure that the proper systems for your needs are set up.

Rent Collections

There are three major ways that rents are collected: (1) in person on-site (usually in cash); (2) upon presentation of itemized bill; and (3) via fixed monthly rental payments.

Rentals with fixed payments that include utilities and services are the easiest to collect since the amount is always the same. The tenant knows exactly how much is due and can make the correct remittance. There are many apartment complex situations where the actual charges for utilities and services are billed or collected with the rent. It is important to keep track of the various amounts collected. First, the tenant should be provided with an itemized bill or receipt. Second, many of the charges can be treated as a recovery of costs and need not be reflected as income.

In person on-site collections are often delegated to an on-site manager with significant amounts of cash changing hands. It becomes increasingly important that the receipting system possess the controls to assure that all cash collected is properly accounted for.

The primary document of rent receipting is the rent roll, which is frequently called the rental journal. The rent roll is a monthly document that should include the following items.

1. Property identification.
2. Date collected.

3. Tenant's name.
4. Monthly rental charge.
5. Time period covered.
6. Miscellaneous charges or assessments.
7. Total amount received.
8. Balance due (if any).

The rent roll should also show the total amount of available rental income. The difference between the total collected and the total available is the non-occupied units and the delinquent tenants. These two classes should be identified since they will provide key management information for future analysis. The rent roll document should be given to the accountant so accurate financial reports can be prepared.

In addition to the rent roll, a tenant ledger card should be maintained by individual unit. This tenant ledger should include the exact same information as the rent roll, with the exception that it will only contain the data for that particular unit. This will enable determination of whether a specific tenant's rent is current or how far they are in arrears. It also provides a good payment history in the event eviction procedures are necessary. Most tenant ledgers allow room at the top for key information regarding the tenant, such as employer name and phone number, next of kin or emergency notification procedures, and serial numbers of key appliances and equipment in the unit.

In multiple unit properties where rent is frequently collected in cash, it is reasonable to expect that a tenant will want a receipt as proof of payment. The receipt should contain the same information that appears on the rent roll, that is, name, date, and itemized individual amounts. It should also show the name under which your property management firm is operating. In addition, space should be provided for the receipt to be signed by the person physically receiving the payment. In extremely small situations, such as duplexes or quadplexes, the receipting can be done with stock stationary receipt books and forms stamped with the name of your company. For good cash control, it is advisable to provide receipts for all payments, even those made by check.

As the number of units and different types of charges increase, these tasks become burdensome. A solution to this problem is what is generally known as a "one-write" system. One-write systems utilize specially treated carbon strips on the back of receipts and no carbon required (NCR) paper for the ledgers and journals. As noted earlier, the exact same data is recorded on the receipt, the tenant ledger, and the rent roll. With a one-write system, the information is automatically recorded on both the pre-aligned ledger and rent roll positioned below it, thus eliminating the need to recopy the same information two additional times. It also assures that all the entries are correct since they are all identical. By pre-numbering the receipts, an effective audit trail is built into the system. All sequentially-numbered receipts must be accounted for. Reconciliation of the ledgers to the rent roll is accomplished via a simple proving calculation. An illustration of a one-write system for property expense disbursements is shown in Figure 6.1.

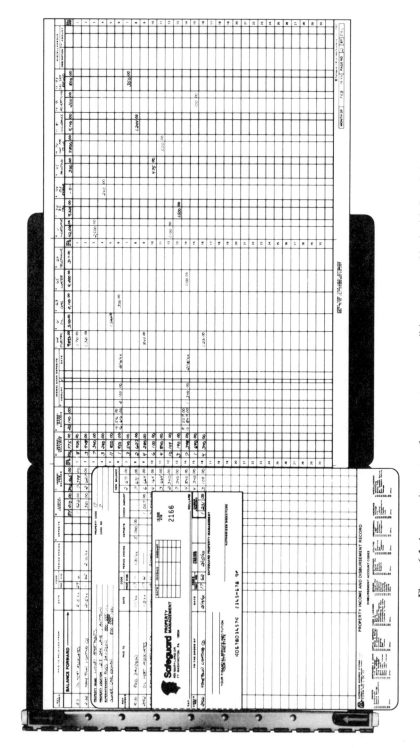

Figure 6.1 A one-write system for property expense disbursements. "Used with Permission. Copywrited Safeguard Business Systems, Inc., Ft. Washington, PA."

One-write systems are flexible in that the receipt can be easily modified to become the rent bill, thus creating a one-write billing system. It will still create a tenant ledger and rent roll. When payment is received it is simply noted on the ledger and journal. Receipting systems are also available for rentals with fixed monthly payments.

As the property management firm continues to grow, it can become impractical to handle billings and collections on a manual basis. Two alternatives are available at this juncture: (1) batch billing service; and (2) in-house micro computer.

Batch billing services receive data input forms from the property manager and proceed to generate and mail the appropriate bills. Often, payment is made to a lockbox and the payment credited while the computer is on-line. These same service bureaus can produce some of the financial management reports that will be discussed further along in this chapter.

Property managers should carefully examine their particular needs and examine all of the alternatives. The main focus should be on generating the necessary records to properly and efficiently manage the property.

Property Expense Disbursements

One certainty of property management is that expenses will be incurred and have to be paid. It is common practice to maintain several properties out of a single trust account (see Chapter 4). Therefore, it becomes important to assure that individual property expenses are properly recorded and applied toward the correct property.

Most property managers will not track expenses to the individual unit level unless the expenses are directly attributable to that unit, for example, appliance repair or repainting. Expenses such as utility bills, mortgage payments, and so forth, are usually applied to the entire property and allocated on a square footage or other equitable basis.

A disbursements journal containing the following data should be maintained:

1. Payee.
2. Date.
3. Period covered.
4. Type of expense.
5. Amount of expense.
6. Property applied against.
7. Distribution columns for classification by type of expense, for example, utilities, mortgage, insurance, repairs.

Careful attention paid to capturing the above data will simplify the future preparation of the financial statements. These items should be recorded as soon as the disbursement check is made and not necessarily left to memory for future entry. The odds favor that a mistake will occur.

A Property Ledger should be maintained when multiple properties are being handled from one trust account. The property ledger should show the same data in the disbursements journal except that it will only show those expenses for that property. One can easily examine the cards and determine which properties have costs that are out of line with the others. Sound management decisions will result.

The payment process starts with the receipt of a bill or statement and the physical writing of a check. Interestingly, the same information that appears on the property ledger and disbursements journal appears on the check. The check has the name of the property management company, the bank name, and other key bank information printed on it. An authorizing signature block is also provided. Checks should be sequentially numbered. This number should be noted on the ledger, journal, and the invoice being paid. This establishes the audit trail mentioned previously. Figure 6.1 shows a typical one-write disbursement system that is well-suited for the average sized property manager. Like the rent receipt, the check has a specialized carbon strip on the back. As the check is written, the information automatically transfers to the property ledger and the disbursements journal. By copying the check number onto the check the proper audit trail is once again established.

The ledger card in the illustrated system can also be used to record property income. This way, all transactions on behalf of an individual client can be captured on one card. Space should be provided on the ledger card to record the amount of the security deposit being held in trust. (The total of all security deposits for all the units should be established and the trust account never allowed to fall below this minimum.) The ledger card showing income and disbursements can be photocopied and sent to the absentee owner as a statement of transactions on behalf of their account.

Maintenance Control

Overview. Maintenance control is an area that is usually looked upon as not being controllable via simple record keeping. However, contrary to that belief, it is one of the areas most easily managed by following simple record keeping procedures. Failure to control the maintenance function can result in rapidly escalating costs, tenant dissatisfaction, and less than maximum return on investment. Properly maintained maintenance records allow for:

1. Cost reductions and improved operating efficiency.
2. Improved scheduling and prioritizing.
3. Improved use of material, labor and inventory.
4. Proper control over maintenance employees.
5. Improved tenant relations.
6. Reduced number of maintenance related complaints.
7. Improved occupancy rates.
8. Reduced injury liability exposure.

9. Maintaining and increasing property values.
10. Improving return on investment.

Property managers must determine the most efficient method of delivering the required maintenance to their units. Some of the available alternatives include on-site maintenance departments, centralized maintenance serving several complexes, and subcontracted maintenance.

Recording Maintenance Data.   Regardless of the method selected, accurate recording of the maintenance requested and the actual maintenance performed is required. A journal should be maintained in chronological order giving the following information:

1. Name of the person making the request.
2. The unit or property identification number.
3. A summary of the maintenance requested.
4. The exact time and date the request was received.
5. Date work was completed.
6. Cost of any repair made after the work was completed.

The journal should give an at-a-glance summary of the total maintenance performed plus the maintenance still remaining to be done. This further simplifies the process of prioritizing and scheduling the work. It also allows for overall analysis of the total maintenance performed so costs can be properly controlled.

A ledger card should be maintained by individual unit and/or property. This ledger, usually called a maintenance record, should contain the following information:

1. Name of the person making the request.
2. The unit or property identification number.
3. A summary of the maintenance requested.
4. The exact time and date the request was received.
5. The date the work was completed.
6. The cost of the repair.

Capturing this data by unit allows immediate identification of problem units where costs are running higher than the norm. It also allows determination of whether the problem is caused by the equipment or the tenant. With backup documentation, the tenant can be tactfully notified of the problem. If the tenant is unresponsive, the necessary backup exists to take the appropriate eviction action.

Maintenance records should also be maintained on common spaces such as hallways, on equipment such as boilers and air conditioners, and the grounds. This is important if all maintenance costs are to be traced back to their source.

Handling Requests For Maintenance.   When a request for maintenance is received, a work order should be prepared. The work order should contain the information on the maintenance record along with a detailed description of the work to be performed. Many tenants have trouble articulating the nature of their problem. It is good practice at this point to request permission to enter the unit. This will avoid any misunderstanding between the landlord and the tenant. In many parts of the country permission to enter is required. A well-designed work order will show the agreed to time the service is to be performed and will serve as the authorization for the maintenance worker to enter the unit.

The work order should provide ample space to enter a detailed description of the actual work performed, including labor, material, and any specific problems that arose. A job status section indicating an anticipated completion date is also helpful, as is a section for the estimated costs of the repairs. A common practice in the industry is to use multi-part work orders and leave a completed copy behind for the tenant. This allows the tenant to see the cost of the repair and gives the repair a higher perceived value. Some states are requiring this documentation to be left in the apartment after entry.

A sample one-write maintenance control system is shown in Figure 6.2. As with the previous systems, the same information is being recorded several times resulting in unnecessary recopying of numbers. The topmost form, titled Maintenance Request and Work Order, is a three-part, no-carbon-required form which captures the data discussed. A copy can be provided to the tenant, the on-site manager, and the property management company. The maintenance record and journal are automatically posted as the work order is prepared. There are several excellent maintenance control systems available in the marketplace.

Since the maintenance control function involves answering the phone, recording the problem, immediately resolving emergencies, and the many alternative methods available to solve the problem, it does not readily adapt itself to computerization. Large property management companies find that accurate one-write input complements their computerized systems by providing precise cost information.

Preventive Maintenance.   Another maintenance function that deserves consideration is preventive maintenance. Scheduled maintenance often saves a great deal of money that would be spent on emergency repairs and also keeps the property values at the desired level. Preventive maintenance can easily be integrated into the maintenance control system described above.

A schedule should be developed which outlines regularly occurring events such as cleaning burners, oiling blowers, changing filters, lubricating equipment. Regular inspections, such as weighing fire extinguishers, testing smoke detectors and electrical ground fault circuits should also be developed.

Preventive maintenance is best accomplished with a tickler system incorporating a perpetual calender index tray. Slips can be made up in advance

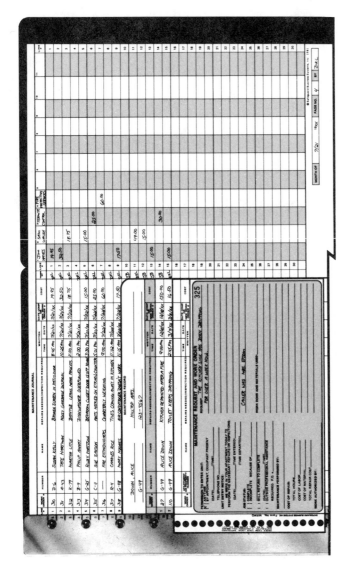

Figure 6.2 A one-write system for maintenance control. "Used with Permission. Copywrited Safeguard Business Systems, Inc., Ft. Washington, PA."

showing the equipment to be maintained and/or the inspection required and giving an exact description of what needs to be done. In the case of an inspection, the slip should also show who needs to be notified.

These cards should be filed under the date they are to be performed. Each day the file is checked, and when a card appears the maintenance manager knows what needs to be done. A work order can then be originated and recorded into the maintenance system. This is a simple, yet money-saving, procedure.

Petty Cash Control

Cash control can be a serious problem, especially if it is maintained at a location other than the property management office. A good petty cash system should provide a numbered voucher containing the following information:

1. Detailed description of what the payment is for or to whom payment is being made.
2. Date.
3. Initials of the person making the payment.
4. Amount of the payment.
5. Signature of the person receiving the payment.

This same information, along with the voucher number, should be recorded on a control journal. All vouchers, including voided ones, should be accounted for. The system should be flexible enough to handle short-term advances as well as cash returns. Vouchers should be used for both disbursements and returns since they will establish the needed audit trail. Whenever a receipt is available, it should be attached to the voucher. Reimbursement of the petty cash fund should only be made when the properly filled out vouchers are presented.

There are several manual and one-write systems available for the overall control of petty cash.

Payroll

Depending on the size of the property management company and maintenance departments, payroll can become a time-consuming process. There are several alternatives available for handling payroll:

1. Manually.
2. One-write system.
3. Batch processing service.
4. In-house computer.

A good payroll system must include, at the minimum, payroll checks, earnings statements, employee earnings records, and a payroll register. These should include the following information:

1. Employee name.
2. Date of check.
3. Pay period covered.
4. Itemization of earnings (regular time, overtime, bonus, etc.).
5. Itemization of deductions (FIT, FICA, local taxes, insurance, etc.).
6. Net pay.

Provisions should be made to total this information on a quarterly basis so IRS Form 941 can be prepared and submitted on a timely basis. At year end, the information will be required for the preparation of the employee W-2 statements and any additional state and local taxes. An accountant should be consulted about any detailed reporting requirements for your specific tax location.

General Account

The final area of key financial record keeping is that of a general disbursements account. This account includes all the property management company disbursements that do not fall within the trust account guidelines. Expenses paid out of this account may include rent, utilities, office supplies, and other miscellaneous items.

In smaller operations, this account can frequently be combined with the payroll account, further simplifying the record keeping function. The general account should include a disbursements journal capturing the following:

1. Check number.
2. Payee name.
3. Date.
4. Description of payment.
5. Amount of check.
6. Distribution to proper expense category.

Distribution to proper expense category is the process of entering the check amount directly to the appropriate expense category, usually identified by a "chart of accounts" number. Charts of accounts will be discussed in the following section.

Record Keeping Recap

The records that must be maintained for effective property management have been highlighted above. However, setting up a good record keeping system is only the beginning. One must exercise discipline to be sure that the systems are properly installed and are continually used. This will assure an ongoing flow of key financial data. An accountant or financial advisor should be consulted to assure that all needed information is being recorded. The astute property manager captures only the information needed and does not waste time on unnecessary items.

ORGANIZING THE RECORDED DATA

The data that has been collected thus far must be converted into usable management information. It is only after this conversion takes place that the managerial benefits discussed earlier can be achieved. The critical bridge between data and financial reports is the "general ledger." The account balance in the general ledger controls the balance sheet, income statement, comparative statements, and other financial reports. It is advisable to discuss general ledger requirements with an accountant or financial advisor well-versed on property management.

General Ledger

Every financial transaction that occurs is posted to a general ledger account. Property managers should have available a "chart of accounts." This is a listing of code numbers identifying the accounts making up the general ledger. A typical property management chart of accounts is shown in Figures 6.3 and 6.4.

There are several significant breakdowns in the sample charts. First, the accounts are broken into two separate categories: balance sheet accounts (Figure 6.3) and statement of earnings account (Figure 6.4). There are the following further classifications within the balance sheet accounts:

1. Current Assets (100 series).
2. Fixed Assets (200 series).
3. Other Assets (200 series).
4. Current Liabilities (300 series).
5. Long term debt (300 series).
6. Capital and equity accounts (400 series).

Similar accounts all begin with the same number so they can be easily identified and posting errors minimized. The statement of earnings accounts contain the following classifications:

1. Income (500 series).
2. Costs (700 series). In property management situations, there will usually be no cost section generated as no product is being produced; rather a service is being provided.

3. Operating Expenses (800 series).
4. Earnings (900 series).

It is beneficial to code as many of the above items as possible at the time they are recorded onto the source document. It is much easier to note the nature of an expense when the check is being written as opposed to trying to remember it several days later. In most general ledgers, provisions are made for a reference number (check number, receipt number, etc.) and a description. This enhances the established audit trail by accurately maintaining the original records.

There are several methods of maintaining a general ledger: manually; batch data processing; and in-house computer.

Account #	Title	Account #	Title
100	ASSETS	333-01	FEDERAL INCOME TAX WITHHELD
101	CURRENT ASSETS	333-02	FICA TAX WITHHELD
102	PETTY CASH	333-03	STATE INCOME TAX WITHHELD
104	CASH	333-04	CITY INCOME TAX WITHHELD
121	ACCOUNTS RECEIVABLE	333-05	STATE DISABILITY PAY
129	TOTAL	333-06	STATE UNEMPLOYMENT PAY
130	PROVISION FOR BAD DEBTS	333-07	FEDERAL UNEMPLOYMENT PAYABLE
160-01	PREPAID INSURANCE	333	PAYROLL TAXES PAYABLE
160-02	PREPAID TAXES	338-01	ACCRUED PAYROLL
160-03	PREPAID OTHER	338-02	ACCRUED RETIREMENT PLAN
160	PREPAID EXPENSES	338-03	OTHER ACCRUED EXPENSES
179	TOTAL CURRENT ASSETS	338	ACCRUED EXPENSES
180	INVESTMENTS	354	INCOME TAXES PAYABLE
190	TOTAL INVESTMENTS	369	TOTAL CURRENT LIABILITIES
		370	OTHER LIABILITIES
200	FIXED ASSETS	379	TOTAL OTHER LIABILITIES
201	LAND		
205	BUILDINGS	380	LONG-TERM DEBT
206	ACCUMULATED DEPRECIATION	381	MORTGAGES PAYABLE
207	MACHINERY AND EQUIPMENT	396	TOTAL
208	ACCUMULATED DEPRECIATION	397	LESS CURRENT MATURITIES
209	FURNITURE AND FIXTURES	398	TOTAL LONG-TERM DEBT
210	ACCUMULATED DEPRECIATION	399	TOTAL LIABILITIES
211	AUTOMOBILES		
212	ACCUMULATED DEPRECIATION	400	DEFERRED INCOME
271	LEASEHOLD IMPROVEMENTS	409	TOTAL DEFERRED INCOME
272	ACCUMULATED AMORTIZATION	410	STOCKHOLDERS' EQUITY
279	TOTAL FIXED ASSETS	413	COMMON STOCK
280	OTHER ASSETS	420	RETAINED EARNINGS
283	REFUNDABLE DEPOSITS	426	SUSPENSE
298	TOTAL OTHER ASSETS	428	TOTAL STOCKHOLDERS' EQUITY
299	TOTAL ASSETS	429	TOTAL LIABILITY AND EQUITY
		430	CAPITAL
300	LIABILITIES	431	DRAWINGS
301	CURRENT LIABILITIES	432	CURRENT EARNINGS, PERCENT ____
302	NOTES PAYABLE	433	CAPITAL
310	CURRENT MATURITIES	497	SUSPENSE
313	ACCOUNTS PAYABLE	498	TOTAL CAPITAL
315	SECURITY DEPOSITS PAYABLE	499	TOTAL LIABILITY AND CAPITAL

Figure 6.3 Typical property management chart of accounts. Balance sheet items. Example courtesy of Safeguard Business Systems, Inc., Ft. Washington, PA.

Account #	Title	Account #	Title
500	INCOME	847	OFFICE SUPPLIES
501	RENTAL	859	POSTAGE
502	CONDOMINIUM INCOME	863	BANK CHARGES
503	PROPERTY MANAGEMENT FEES	871	CONTRIBUTIONS
504	LAUNDRY	873	TELEPHONE
505	VENDING COMMISSIONS	875	TRAVEL AND ENTERTAINMENT
506	SWIMMING POOL FEES	877	AUTOMOBILE
507	MISCELLANEOUS	879	LICENSES
515	OTHER	881	OTHER TAXES
516	TOTAL FEES	883	LEGAL AND ACCOUNTING
517	REFUNDS	885	INTEREST
518	NET FEES	887	DEPRECIATION-OTHER
525	COMMISSION INCOME	889	AMORTIZATION
549	TOTAL INCOME	895	MISCELLANEOUS
		897	TOTAL OPERATING EXPENSE
700	COST OF SALES	898	TOTAL EXPENSES
749	GROSS PROFIT	899	EARNINGS FROM OPERATIONS
750			
799		900	OTHER INCOME
		939	TOTAL OTHER INCOME
800	OPERATING EXPENSE	940	OTHER EXPENSE
801	MANAGER SALARIES	979	TOTAL OTHER EXPENSE
803	CLERICAL SALARIES		
805	MAINTENANCE SALARIES	980	EARNINGS BEFORE TAXES
813	PAYROLL TAXES	981	CORPORATE INCOME TAXES
817	EMPLOYEE BENEFITS	982	NET EARNINGS
816	DEPRECIATION-BUILDINGS	983	ADD
827	MAINTENANCE AND REPAIRS	984	RETAINED EARNINGS-BEGIN
829	UTILITIES	989	TOTAL
831	PROPERTY TAXES	990	SUBTRACT
835	LIABILITY INSURANCE	995	SUSPENSE
837	OTHER INSURANCE	996	TOTAL
841	EQUIPMENT RENTAL	997	RETAINED EARNINGS-ENDING
843	ADVERTISING	998	SUSPENSE
845	DUES AND SUBSCRIPTIONS	999	NET EARNINGS

Figure 6.4 Typical property management chart of accounts. Income statement items. Example courtesy of Safeguard Business Systems, Inc., Ft. Washington, PA.

The manual method involves recording simultaneous debits and credits onto the books. In the case of small properties, this presents no problems and can easily be performed under the direction of an accountant.

Batch data processing via a service bureau saves a great deal of time for the following reasons:

1. Inputs can be made directly from source documents (e.g. duplicate journals, check stubs, etc.).
2. The batch service can maintain a cumulative general ledger.
3. The service can automatically generate the desired financial statements and reports.

A great number of closing and adjusting entries are necessary to balance the books, so most service bureaus prefer to process via an accountant unless the property manager is thoroughly familiar with all accounting procedures. There are many national and local service bureaus that offer this type of processing. Remember that the output is only as good as the accuracy of the input.

The last alternative, the in-house computer, is used by many large property management concerns today. The various software packages available vary considerably in their capability, but all utilize a chart of accounts with accurate input documentation. When considering an in-house computer be sure to determine how the audit trail is established and maintained. Be sure that it will fit current needs and has expansion capabilities to meet your future needs.

Currently there are several fine software packages on the market, with the promise of several new and expanded packages to be developed over the next few years.

FINANCIAL REPORTS

Statement of Earnings

One of the most important reports for property managers is the statement of earnings. This statement shows how much money is made or lost on a specific property or group of properties. A sample property management income statement is shown in Figure 6.5. The income statement should show the following:

1. Total income (clearly broken down by type of income).
2. Total costs and expenses (clearly broken down by type of cost or expense).
3. Net earnings.

These statements should show the current period total plus the year-to-date totals. If several properties are on a consolidated statement, a breakdown of the income or expense by individual property would be desirable. Comparative statements showing the current year actual to prior year actual and/or the current year actual to current year budget should also be developed. These are all necessary for a proper evaluation of your properties. When problems are identified, further detailed reports, such as departmental breakdowns, can be generated if the accurate input records are being maintained.

Balance Sheet

The balance sheet is important in that it shows the net worth and financial strength of the properties managed as of a given point of time. Simply stated, it is a periodic analysis of balance sheet general ledger accounts. The balance sheet will show assets, liabilities, and owners equity.

The assets will always equal the liabilities plus owners equity if the general ledger has been maintained with 100% accuracy and all closing and adjusting

	FROM April 01, 19xx TO April 30, 19xx	Percent	Year To Date	Percent
INCOME				
Potential Rent	42,000	102.4	168,000	102.4
Less Vacancies	2,400	5.9	9,600	5.9
Less Adjustments	100	0.2	400	0.2
RENTAL INCOME	39,500	96.3	158,000	96.3
OTHER INCOME				
Late Charges	150	0.4	600	0.4
Laundry Income	350	0.9	1,400	0.9
Swimming Pool Fees	1,000	2.4	4,000	2.4
TOTAL OTHER INCOME	1,500	3.7	6,000	3.7
TOTAL INCOME	41,000	100.0	164,000	100.0
OPERATING EXPENSES				
Utilities and Services				
Gas & Electric	7,000	17.1	28,000	17.1
Water & Sewer	800	2.0	3,200	2.0
Trash Removal	500	1.2	2,000	1.2
Total Utilities & Services	8,300	20.3	33,200	20.3
REPAIRS & MAINTENANCE				
Building	3,000	7.3	12,000	7.3
Equipment	1,000	2.4	4,000	2.4
Grounds	300	0.7	1,200	0.7
Pool	500	1.2	2,000	1.2
Supplies	400	1.0	1,600	1.0
TOTAL REPAIRS & MAINTENANCE	5,200	12.7	20.800	12.7
MISCELLANEOUS OPERATING EXPENSE				
Real Estate Taxes	4,000	9.8	16,000	9.8
Insurance	1,600	3.9	6,400	3.9
Advertising	400	1.0	1,600	1.0
TOTAL MISC. EXPENSES	6,000	14.6	24,000	14.6
TOTAL OPERATING EXPENSES	19,500	47.6	78,000	47.6
EARNINGS FROM OPERATIONS	21,500	52.4	86,000	52.4
OTHER EXPENSES				
Depreciation	9,000	22.0	36,000	22.0
Interest 1st Mortgage	3,500	8.5	14,000	8.5
Interest 2nd Mortgage	300	0.7	1,200	0.7
TOTAL OTHER EXPENSES	12,800	31.2	51,200	31.2
NET EARNINGS	8,700	21.2	34,800	21.2

Figure 6.5 Example property management statement of earnings. Example courtesy of Safeguard Business Systems, Inc., Ft. Washington, PA.

entries properly made. It is standard procedure to generate a trial balance to see if any errors exist and then go back and make the necessary adjustments. When several properties are managed together, supporting schedules may be necessary to give the desired detail.

SUMMARY

This chapter has given an overview of the need and benefits of accurate record keeping. It has also highlighted the key reports most beneficial to effective management. Use this as a guide to set up the system and procedures that are most suitable to your particular situation. Feel free to discuss that situation with specialists such as accountants, financial advisors, systems specialists, attorneys, bankers, and absentee owners. Clearly defined needs will enable you to keep the necessary records to manage effectively with the minimum amount of time and effort. Following this simple advice will allow the flexibility to truly manage your property in a professional manner. The net result should be increased income, controlled expenses, and increasing equity.

JOHN B. STETSON, IV, R.A., *Vice President*
Day & Zimmerman Construction
Services Division
MDC Systems Corp.
Philadelphia, Pennsylvania

John B. Stetson is a registered architect with more than 20 years of experience in the management of design and construction projects. In addition to leading architect-engineer design teams for a wide range of real estate developments, his experience includes services as the Director of General Services for an international airline, and Manager Technical Staff for a facilities development and management task force consulting to Real Estate Branch of the U.S. Postal Service. In his present Day & Zimmerman position, Mr. Stetson is responsible for major project management assignments, including, most recently, the preparation of a comprehensive program execution plan for a $5 billion overseas development program covering more than 200 square miles. He holds a Master of Architecture degree from Yale University, is a member of the Project Management Institute and Construction Specifications Institute, and is a construction arbitration panelist for the American Arbitration Association.

CHAPTER 7

THE USE OF
THE ARCHITECT,
ENGINEER, AND
LANDSCAPE ARCHITECT

INTRODUCTION

Modern real estate management, whether of residential, retail, service, industrial, or general office facilities, is continually confronted with the need to accommodate change in the day-to-day functions associated with property operations and in the physical character of the property being managed. Retaining existing tenants, attracting new tenants, and simultaneously controlling costs and rent increases without damaging the cash flow are fundamental pressures that force managers to recognize the value of physical change in their property as a principal means of responding to entrepreneurial challenge.

Architects, engineers, and landscape architects become intimately involved in the process of making physical changes to real estate, as the primary design professionals involved with construction. The success of this aspect of real estate management requires that the property manager and the architect/ engineer (A/E) team approach this collaboration with a mutual understanding of their respective roles and the contributions each is expected to make. This chapter addresses the nature of these relationships from the perspective of the principal design professionals.

THE A/E TEAM

A/E Defined

A wide variety of technical disciplines are involved in changes to commercial property. Those which the property manager will be primarily involved with are architecture, structural engineering, mechanical engineering (including heating, ventilating, air conditioning, and plumbing), electrical engineering, and landscape architecture. These will be discussed in this chapter. Interior design, another major discipline, will be addressed in another chapter.

Other specialized areas of expertise that may be needed include elevator and escalator engineering, graphics, lighting, acoustics, and food service design. Generally, however, the property manager expects specialized requirements such as these to be provided through one of the primary disciplines.

The principal management objective of the property manager must be that of retaining an effective A/E team to effectuate the property changes envisioned. Achieving this objective involves careful selection of consultants.

A/E Assignments

In broad terms A/E assignments fall into one of two categories: (1) feasibility studies or (2) design and construction assignments. Each involves the same technical disciplines but have a distinct focus. Feasibility studies address problem definition, alternative potential solutions, and optimum courses of action. Design and construction assignments involve execution of the work.

Feasibility Studies

A/E feasibility studies can range from simple analyses of alternative partition plans for subdividing rental space to preparation of alternatives for refurbishing an entire structure which would involve all technical disciplines such as, for example, a renovation study for a mixed use high-rise structure that might include retail, office, and residential components. Of critical importance in such instances is the skill and experience of the A/E team in diagnosing the condition of the existing structure and in developing assessments of salvageable building systems. The assessment must be accurate in functional and cost terms and with respect to the proposed investor's property objectives, which the A/E may be translating into several alternative concepts for final evaluation. Frequently such studies have an interactive nature in that these objectives may well shift as alternative A/E studies are developed and more attractive financial potentials emerge.

Although the final pro forma will be influenced significantly by the A/E team, the A/Es contribution is only one of many information components required to reach effective real estate capital investment decisions. Knowledgeable A/Es and property managers both recognize the importance of many other factors such as legal, marketing, and financing considerations in such decisions as well as the pitfalls of an inadequate background evaluation of the problems and costs of effecting change to existing structures.

Too often, the A/E has been thought to guide the development of feasibility studies toward the need for maximum change. A specific kind of A/E study that often is directed toward determining the minimal amount of change needed is the study of a property being purchased or otherwise taken over by a new property management. In such instances, the prospective new owner may use the A/E more to help verify the condition and value of the existing property than to assess the cost of change. In other instances, the diagnosis may call for the removal of previously completed, but misdirected, improvements in order to restore lost value to the property.

Design and Construction Services

The second major role for the A/E team follows the decision to effectuate a given alternative. This normally involves the design and construction functions associated with property development. However, unlike new projects, renovation to existing property carries added considerations with respect to integrating changes into existing structures. Frequently, this requires careful coordination at both the design and construction phase to insure maintenance of full operating services for building occupants while changes are being implemented. A special problem facing the A/E and property manager here is insuring maintenance of seldom-used, easily overlooked safety systems such as emergency stairs or electrical generators. Significant liability can accrue to all parties involved if these systems are "out of service" or "being worked on" when they are needed most.

Even when safety and legal considerations are not involved, occupant inconvenience and disruption can become a major concern which the A/E must address. For example, in the recent renovation of the principal entrance to a center city high-rise office structure, which involved an extensive rearrangement of the three escalators required for normal use by the building's occupants, extreme care had to be taken both in design and in structuring the construction work packages to maintain operation of two escalators (one up, one down) while the third was being altered. Special planning considerations included arranging in advance for standby emergency service during this work in case of escalator failure, and training security personnel to operate a single escalator by hand control in the event of escalator failure.

The following three specific aspects of property change to commercial real estate that will enhance its financial value and performance must be considered: *imagery*, *functional utility*, and *operating costs*. Although each can be considered separately, any one change will likely impact all of these aspects. Further, the *marketplace* factor in determining change effectiveness must not be overlooked. The personal preference of the A/E, no matter how well intended, cannot take precedence over the objective assessment of the user's preferences.

IMAGERY

Imagery Concept

Imagery, an intangible and admittedly subjective concept, is the total impact of a property's aesthetic qualities combined with the retained perception of these qualities by the user. Image change and its effect upon public perception is often a matter of paramount importance to both the property manager and the A/E. Because it is so subjective, this aspect of change is difficult to evaluate in terms of cost effectiveness. Imagery change is even more difficult to evaluate in instances where a change is desired simply for change's sake, perhaps to provide a new marketing approach, as opposed to a change resulting from an inherent deficiency in the property. Here, the designer, usually the architect, often acts arbitrarily and with unpredictable and on occasion counterproductive results.

Loss in value of a property asset can arise if an existing positive market image is not identified and change to this positive image is introduced by the A/E. Change to the image of an existing property in purely aesthetic terms is not enough. Property managers and design professionals must be able to correlate imagery analysis with the entrepreneurial aspects inherent in property management. Fortunately, with today's prevalent and heightened interest in the preservation and adaptive reuse of existing structures (largely generated by farsighted property managers working with responsive designers), this area of potential conflict between the property manager's interests and the designer's aesthetic instincts has lessened.

Elements Involved in Imagery

Since the concept of property image involves all of the aesthetic qualities of the property, the full range of sensory and environmental elements become involved as, for example, the visual aspects of building design such as the facade, space arrangement, the choice and use of appropriate material in terms of color and texture, graphics, and signage. All of these elements contribute to imagery. In addition, a tactile sense of materials, acoustics, ease and convenience of layout and access, a sense of spaciousness, and even of smell, will have an impact on the overall image of a property. Furnishings and landscaping are other important facets of property image.

High-Impact Focus

Achieving change in property image within budget constraints often requires focusing on specific high-impact areas and elements. These, in turn, may vary among properties of a similar nature depending on specific market intentions. For example, in the modernization of older, urban residential buildings, one property manager may want to reduce individual unit size to create more units at a moderate price, while another manager may want to consolidate into fewer larger units at a higher market range. In the former situation, aesthetic design emphasis might be placed on the entry and principal living or public space of the unit. In the latter situation, where space is not at a premium, a relatively higher percentage of the renovation budget might be allocated to creating individual luxury bathrooms—the most private space within the units. While equally valid, the disparity in approach here highlights the need for an effective understanding between the property manager and the A/E team. It also illustrates another important factor that the A/E must recognize, namely, that the contemporary property manager usually has a well-developed concept of the kind of change needed for his market. The A/E should respect this.

A critical aspect of the property image is the approach—that is, achieving "curb appeal." Entrances, lobbies, and principal public circulation spaces are areas of high imagery impact, particularly for retail and office properties. Residential properties, on the other hand, often involve a contrasting emphasis where the property approach, exterior, and public circulation spaces are developed in a deliberately neutral manner to increase their sense of privacy. Specific imagery is then focused on the specialized unit spaces.

Use of Landscaping in Imagery

Landscape design as a major contributing component of property imagery has emerged over the past decade, particularly in commercial real estate. Today, the landscape architect is no longer an after-the-fact participant in property design whose function is limited to providing screening for problem areas. The need to analyze and understand basic site conditions and the unique opportunities for positive change in existing or planned site utilization, often places the landscape architect in the lead position as the first design professional with whom the property manager must be involved. In some instances, such as suburban residential or industrial park developments where site landscaping can be the controlling element, the landscape architect may be designated as the lead professional with a mandate to retain architects and engineers as subconsultants. This is a complete reversal of traditional working relationships.

One demographic factor behind this contemporary development is the increased pressure on owners to consider the use of sites formerly bypassed. These are sites which, as a result of urban growth, have become superior locations for commercial, residential, and recreational development. Such sites might include inner city railyards, port facilities, and abandoned suburban quarries. While these sites often require extraordinary efforts to become viable (as for example in the case of the railyard where soil nutrition and drainage characteristics might have to be reestablished), these sites clearly possess unique characteristics and offer a high potential for successful renewal. Identification of the potential benefits (as well as burdens) of renewing this type of property is most important to the concept of property management.

Although exterior landscape consideration is associated with new development, it can apply equally to the on-going management of existing property. Creative exterior landscaping can be a major means of developing curb appeal and distinctive approach.

Frequently, opportunities exist for relatively economical change in the curb appeal aspects of existing property due to years of landscape maintenance neglect. Conversion of former estate mansions into multiple unit condominiums is common. Here, retention of existing exterior character is of critical importance in the development of market appeal. Moreover, creating both new, multiple-unit approaches as well as parking areas with minimal disturbance to the existing environment is equally important to the property manager and the landscape architect.

Interior Landscaping.   The rapid emergence of interior landscaping has been most dramatic. It is frequently a significant factor in the design and resultant imagery of contemporary real estate projects.

The development of the atrium as a primary architectural concept (best illustrated by the highly publicized hotel atriums created in the 1970s and, to a lesser degree, the office landscape approach to interior design), has brought the landscape architect inside the building as a design participant. The development of the heavily landscaped interior mall in shopping centers is another example of this trend, which is being applied increasingly to smaller facilities such as medical centers. The interior mall concept today is being applied both to redeveloped properties and to new projects. The recently completed restoration of Philadelphia's historic Bourse Building, formerly a stock exchange and office building and now a small retail shopping center, included integrating a new skylighted central space populated with large-scaled plant materials.

The integration of large amounts of plant material, decorative boulders and running water into interior space has had impact on many of the mechanical engineers' concerns pertaining to building environmental systems and controls. Occasionally, structural engineers may have to be consulted. The result is increased need for collaboration among landscape architects, building systems engineers, and interior designers.

Landscape Service Firms.   Another result of the increased use of plant material, often of exotic variety and of massive size, has been the development of full-service interior landscaping firms offering long-term maintenance services, including guarantees which assure replacement of plant materials that fail. Such services can relieve the property manager with respect to maintenance and care of plant material—a not-so-insignificant concern. In addition, the guarantee assures the property manager and the design professional that the investment in this property image as well as the overall aesthetic enhancement of the property will remain relatively as planned.

FUNCTIONAL UTILITY

The second basic facet of the property change concept is that of effecting physical change for the purpose of creating new use or improving upon existing functional utility of a property. This type of change can be large and dramatic, as when it is interrelated with overall imagery change. It can also be small in scale and impact. In either event, it can still exert an important influence on the property manager's rental return and overall cash flow.

Change in Property Use

Change in basic property use generally involves a major or dramatic property change. These projects are often similar to the development of a totally new project from a scale of effort and quantity of investment viewpoint. The Bourse

Building project referred to previously is an example of adaptive reuse of space and structural elements intended for one kind of commercial activity transformed into another kind of activity. Even more dramatic, adaptive reuse is demonstrated in the recasting of strategically located warehouses and factories into apartments, cooperatives, or condominiums. This is an increasingly popular reuse resulting from transportation shifts that have made facilities in many larger cities obsolete for their originally intended function. San Francisco's highly publicized Ghirardelli Square exemplifies reuse involving these obsolete structures. Here, the Square was developed into interior and exterior shopping malls.

Another reuse development is occurring as a result of demographic change: school facilities that are being closed as the school population declines are being adapted for other uses. These facilities, usually ideally located for residential-related use and often in a relatively new condition or in a high level of repair, represent significant property management challenges to institutional owners and investors because of the strong community (and legal) reaction to change and the strong concerns of almost any proposed reuse.

Existing Use Improvements

Making existing use improvements involves the modernization of property space and building systems in order to increase their effectiveness and utility without making basic use alterations. These changes are smaller scale changes in functional utility. They are usually made in response to competitive pressure on existing (or replacement) tenants. Shifting from manual to automatic elevators, adding remotely monitored security systems, modernizing residential bath and kitchen fixtures, or even incorporating new electrical and heating, ventilating, and air conditioning (HVAC) systems, exemplify this type of change.

These assignments often have a higher potential for failure than larger, more dramatic renovations, for they often tend to be incidental to other work the A/E is performing for the property manager and sometimes they do not receive adequate management attention. In addition, the amount of investment involved may be too small to warrant the level of initial investigation required to accurately anticipate construction complications and costs. Finally, the beneficial impact of these small changes is often misjudged and turns out to be inadequate, particularly if they are undertaken on a piecemeal basis.

OPERATING AND MAINTENANCE COST

The preceding development of the first two facets of property change, those involving property image and functional utility, addressed the property manager's concern with maintaining or improving the income portion of the cash flow equation. Property change also can be oriented to reducing operating and maintenance costs.

Maintenance

Changes made to improve operating costs that do not simultaneously affect the property's image or utility for its occupants are rare. Typically, they involve building maintenance systems or service functions. One example of such a change might be the provision of centralized automatic trash compaction equipment in order to reduce the frequency of trash handling by the operating staff. Another example could involve consideration of alternative window systems based on cleaning requirements. One system might include fixed windows at lower installation costs, and the use of exterior cleaning scaffolds; another could involve pivoting windows requiring higher investment costs, but permitting cleaning from the interior. Considerations pertaining to insurance and financial costs further complicate these trade-offs.

Generally, changes made for imagery or utilitarian reasons involve operating costs. In material selection, the A/E must consider cleaning, repair, and maintenance requirements. Equipment modernization such as elevator or HVAC system replacement provides an opportunity to reduce operating costs as well as to improve imagery and utility.

Energy Conservation

Now a major design consideration in every building project, energy conservation is an important factor in property change decision, requiring the contribution of both the architect and the engineer. Traditionally, property managers have been able to pass through energy costs either by the use of separate metering or by a lease clause permitting energy-use cost adjustments. Accordingly, they have been reluctant to invest in capital improvements to achieve operating benefits from energy conservation. Faced with the continuing pressures of fuel costs, governmental influences, and increased tenant concern, building managers share with the A/E an interest in new solutions that achieve reduction in energy consumption. This is true for both existing property and new development. Energy economies can be contributed to by improvements in building envelope tightness and insulation, better control of heating and air conditioning systems, and more efficient lighting systems. In older buildings, lighting systems often can be replaced with contemporary low-energy fixtures which result in improved lighting characteristics and reduced energy consumption.

Property managers as well as A/E firms need to stay aware of governmental energy conservation action that may affect property change decisions. In 1979, the federal government, with the general backing of leading design profession associations including the American Institute of Architects (AIA) and the American Society of Heating and Refrigeration Engineers (ASHRAE), endorsed and promulgated the "ASHRAE 90 Standards" for building energy use. Moreover, the federal government has created tax incentives designed to encourage investment leading to reduced energy consumption.

Similar actions have been taken or are being planned at the state level. For example, Pennsylvania enacted a Building Energy Conservation Act (Pennsylvania Act 222) in 1980. Although primarily directed at defining energy conservation standards for new construction, the Act also applies to new portions of major renovation projects unless they fall within specific exceptions.

EFFECTIVE DOLLAR USAGE

Change of any type is always related to financial cash-flow objectives. Effective dollar usage is of major consequence to the property manager and must be equally important to the A/E.

The concept of effective dollar usage can be compared with the concept of government sponsored value engineering. The objective of value engineering is the determination of maximum cost-to-benefit ratios in alternative methods of accomplishing the same function. Similarly, as indicated in the discussion of trade-offs to achieve operating cost reductions, the property manager expects the A/E team to develop alternative solutions and cost projections for accomplishing identified changes. In doing so, the manager is relying heavily on the A/E's cost-estimating skills and on his integrity with respect to not "loading the deck" in favor of an aesthetically preferred solution.

When analyzing capital investments, the property manager is faced with problems similar to those the A/E faces in preparing cost estimates. The manager must be responsible for the revenue flow assumptions that will result if proposed changes are executed as well as external factors such as future interest and inflation rates. Errors in these assumptions can be as catastrophic as those resulting if the A/E cost estimates for physical work are erroneous. Ideally, the property manager and the A/E should combine resources in order to determine optimum budget allocations.

Cost Estimates

Given the importance of the proposed capital costs to a project's overall economic analysis, property managers must be aware of the detail and accuracy of cost estimates.

Initial concept estimates will often be prepared on a parameter basis, that is, $X per-square-foot of area, and may vary by 30% from the final cost. Experienced estimators will tend to use high unit rates at this stage in anticipation of project scope change or growth in work required.

Estimates prepared at the design development stage, when more specific data relating to the quantity and quality of the work and the principal building systems is known, may vary plus or minus 20%. Generally, these estimates represent the maximum level of detail available when final choices among the various alternatives are made, since it is not practical to carry multiple schemes through detailed design.

The final stage is having detailed estimates prepared on the basis of specifications and fully detailed construction documents. Here, the manager can check the soundness of the project and provide a basis for evaluating and negotiating contractor prices. Given the volatile marketplace conditions under which an A/E must predict costs to be incurred in the future, detailed construction estimates should be allowed a range of plus or minus 10% and appropriate contingency allowances made in the overall pro forma.

Complicating estimate accuracy is the fact that work involving renovation to existing property is often performed on a crash basis through the use of private funds and often construction contracts are negotiated directly. Renovation often involves extensive unknown or hidden conditions and work must be performed on a time-and-materials basis. These factors make consistent estimating results one of the greatest challenge for the A/E. When renovation is planned, property managers must be sensitive to the high risk of cost estimating and the degree these estimates can effect project evaluation. Failure to do so can lead to unexpected and expensive problems.

Another factor involved in structuring the project budget is consideration of the long-term plans for the property in question. If the property is to be sold in the near future, emphasis may shift from material or equipment having longer-life characteristics at higher costs to reducing overall cost by making expenditures on other elements which can have a greater immediate impact. Landscaping would be an example. Conversely, if the property manager anticipates holding the property, a larger investment in long-life and reduced maintenance elements may be more appropriate. In the final analysis, if the A/E and property manager have achieved an effective collaboration in managing these factors, the project budget will contain an effective investment plan.

While cost estimates have been defined in relation to fixed points in the development process, estimating itself can be a valuable A/E component when applied on a continuing basis. Seasoned estimators normally have specified discipline expertise, such as architectural, electrical, mechanical, and the like, that will enable them to offer alternative design suggestions and assist in controlling costs throughout the design phase. Property managers familiar with the benefit of continuing cost analysis throughout the estimating and design function carefully examine this aspect of an A/E's credentials in their selection process.

Construction Control

Effective dollar usage requires strong control during construction. In situations in which time and material contracts are required, the progress of the work must be monitored closely to maintain an awareness of cost commitment and more importantly, to detect emerging conditions requiring correction.

The A/E role during construction varies from project to project. However, certain minimum requirements normally remain constant, such as certifying the contractor's payment requests, approving shop drawings and material samples, making reasonable design clarifications, preparing change orders, and periodic observation of the work for general conformance with the drawings and specifications. In all construction phase activities, the A/E is involved in review and approval action and in decisions affecting dollar commitment in relation to value received.

Particular care must be exercised that contractor progress payments are properly managed. Allowing excessive front-end loading of progress payment schedules or overpayment of progress payments can seriously affect the owner's leverage for gaining final completion of the work, especially if a significant punch-list of defects requiring correction exists. When payment retainage has not been adequately withheld, a contractor might be sufficiently whole. Final work in such a situation is often processed indifferently. This can lead to serious disruption problems for the property manager and his tenants.

SPECIAL RESTORATION/MODERNIZATION CONSIDERATIONS

Restoration and modernization of older, often historic structures has become a frequent type of project in which the A/E and property manager collaborate. Until recently, projects of this type remained within the domain of special interest groups. While these properties had need for management, they seldom were subject to the entrepreneurial review aspects of investment real estate. They were usually renovated and operated by non-profit organizations using grant financing from public or private sources. Today, historic properties increasingly are involved in commercial investment and the property manager as well as the A/E must recognize the opportunities and constraints involved.

An existing physical character with strong aesthetic and emotional values which, in the aggregate, merits preservation is a principal asset that is inherent in a historic structure. These property characteristics can be of major marketing value. For the designer, these attributes can be a challenge, for he must balance the desire to preserve historic aesthetics with functional and cost requirements.

A historic structure generally requires adaptation to a new type of use. This use often involves considerable internal space rearrangement requiring modification to portions of the building. Small entrance ways, undersized lobbies, poor column spacing, and inadequate and/or poorly placed windows are typical of such elements. The success of the project in architectural and financial terms depends on how effectively such modifications are accomplished. In one recent renovation of a large, turn-of-the-century hotel into luxury condominiums, these conflicts were minimal because the principal aspects to be preserved, the exteriors and public entry level spaces, could be maintained in their original configurations while the upper floors were being modernized and rearranged.

In other instances, small-scale, heavily partitioned interiors often found in older structures are incompatible with contemporary use and image of desired space, and the A/E and property manager must elect to preserve only the exterior character. This will retain the value of the identity of the existing property while allowing internal design freedom. Often, the image impact of this identity can be heightened by contrasting a highly contemporary interior with the restored facade. Approaches of this type are frequently used in historic townhouse restoration.

Facade Grants from Designer's Viewpoint

Historic facade grants or easements involve the donation to a nonprofit organization (often a historical society) of the right to alter the facade of a qualifying building. This donation is made in exchange for tax benefits to the donor. This financial incentive has been created to foster preservation of the public exterior of historic structures, particularly when a desired cumulative effect pertaining to a number of structures depends on historical preservation by individual owners. While this serves a valuable purpose, the facade grant can be a constraining force to the designer for it imposes an unusually high degree of limitation even on minor facade adjustments. Thus, using facade grants when converting historic residential structures to commercial use can cause severe limitations on the development of display windows, identification signs, and graphics. On the other hand, the presence of restrictive covenants assures the property manager and A/E that preservation of the structure will not be unduly effected by an inappropriate renovation in the area.

Building Systems

The successful introduction of modern building systems is a critical dimension in renovating historic structures. Perhaps the most difficult situations are imposed by the introduction of new vertical circulation systems (elevators, escalators, new stairs, etc.), which may be required where occupancy changes are made. New heating, ventilating, and air conditioning systems require extensive air ducts and grilles, and toilet room modernization requires piping. The introduction of these elements frequently interferes with efforts to maximize historic features and details.

A closely related consideration, which can be severe, is the necessity of compliancy with local building codes and/or general safety standards. Since most structures being restored predate current code adoption, the A/E is challenged to find unobtrusive ways to introduce safety features such as fire suppression systems (sprinklers) and/or fire-protected stairways and exits.

The conversion of large estate residences into luxury market condominiums involves careful A/E design and coordination of every building system component in order to take maximum advantage of the quality and character of the original exterior and interior construction. The financial viability of projects in this market depends on success in both building preservation and in the introduction of completely modern systems and conveniences.

Site Limitations

Generally, properties being adapted for commercial real estate purposes which have historic preservation aspects are located in crowded, heavily built portions of a city. These properties often impose severe limitations on vehicular access. This, in turn, impinges on effective property development in terms of user access and parking, and imposes difficult property access conditions for janitorial services and truck delivery. Although property adaptation for increased vehicular use is common in most property management situations, it is particularly taxing in situations involving historic properties, since the general scale and space demands for vehicles is incompatible with those of the older structure which the A/E is attempting to preserve.

Construction

Historic building restoration projects often involve numerous specialty contractors and craftsmen. An important A/E task concerns locating appropriate specialists and assisting the owner in evaluating their suitability, availability, and cost. Such evaluation is especially important since specialists are always in high demand, and their failure to perform on time can impede other areas of a project's development.

Being able to effectively perform these assessments requires that the A/E have a superior level of skill in the special work involved. Background experience and familiarity with historic restoration can be most important in A/E selection for projects of this type.

SELECTING THE A/E TEAM

A discussion of the roles and relationship between the property manager and his technical design consultants must involve selection criteria. The identification of an A/E team well suited for a given assignment is critical.

Being selected for new assignments is a life-or-death concern to all professional service firms. Purchasers of such services all too often make selections on an ad hoc or friendship network basis as opposed to viewing this activity with an appropriate sense of importance. For the firm so selected, the assignment can prove to be counterproductive if the assignment emerges as a misassignment due to inadequate preliminary considerations by both parties.

While careful selection screening cannot substitute for the direct knowledge and sense of confidence which results from prior project collaboration, property managers today are making A/E selections on the basis of detailed, often highly demanding evaluations. They are correct in doing so.

Understanding the Property Manager's Perspective

The bottom line in selection evaluation is the final assessment of the fit that can result in a solid working relationship between a property manager and the A/E team. Although many criteria can be evaluated, the overriding requirement is that the A/E possess a comprehensive awareness of the property manager's approach and entrepreneurial objectives. In turn, this requires understanding of the development process and constraints.

The A/E can be expected to bring the design creativity and building technology skills associated with his profession to the project. However, another aspect of the A/E's role is the proper perception and understanding of the uniquely stringent limitations placed on his exercise of design by the financial and marketplace considerations of the investment. The A/E must be receptive to the fact that property managers often apply their increased sophistication in physical environmental design to the development of programmatic elements such as space requirement, design criteria relating to desired image, and even building systems criteria. Although initial functions such as these are usually envisioned by the A/E as integral aspects of his professional design role, he should recognize this reality prior to accepting the assignment.

Time factors imposed in commercial real estate development are an integral part of financial and marketplace considerations. The property manager's overriding concern is to meet a tightly scheduled target date for commencement of the revenue flow and to avoid the negative consequences resulting from failure to meet a lease commencement date. Property managers and A/Es who have worked together on shopping mall projects know the tensions surrounding the opening day milestone and appreciate its importance.

Type of Firm

Since the property manager determines the nature of the A/E team's organization, the manager should recognize the potential variations in team composition in relationship to the required services. The manager must assess carefully his own capabilities and tailor his requirements accordingly. In instances where the nature of the work involves extensive coordination among the various technical disciplines, such as in a wholesale modernization of a high-rise structure, the project manager will benefit from the single point of responsibility provided by the full or comprehensive service firm.

Conversely, a highly experienced real estate developer may want to stay personally active and wish to exercise a high level of direct control. This experienced developer might, therefore, contract with multiple firms each offering a limited range of services. This frequently happens in situations where a unique capability appropriate to the project exists as, for example, in historic landmark restorations where specialized expertise is needed. Here, property managers must make a high degree of direct commitment of their time and energy since no one professional firm will act in a leadership capacity.

A compromise variation occurs when the property manager selects one firm, usually the architect, to provide the required services through the use of subconsultants hired by the architect. Many successful A/E ventures are performed in this manner. Here the property manager obtains the same single point of responsibility that a comprehensive services firm offers. However, this form of delivery has the potential for design coordination problems among the subconsultant disciplines and a higher potential for inaccurate estimating due to decentralization. Advocates of this form of A/E team argue that since each of the firms will be a specialist, the overall level of performance will be higher. In practice where real estate projects need close coordination and control of time and dollars, particularly when extensive renovation is involved, property managers tend to favor the high level of accountability inherent in dealing with a single comprehensive service firm.

In rare instances, firms will emphasize a particular expertise in one phase of project work and participate either as subcontractors or on a joint venture basis with a firm that offers complimentary phase expertise. Thus, architects who have achieved a reputation for planning and overall aesthetic design creativity may offer their services in combination with a second architectural firm which has detailing, building systems design, and construction expertise. A further variation on this theme occurs when the design architect is engaged for a remote project and forms an association with a local architect, usually for the actual construction administration tasks. Care must be taken in these dual-service arrangements that the firms and project individuals can collaborate effectively.

Prior Experience

Another principal selection factor is the degree of prior experience in the type of project under consideration. Several aspects are involved in evaluating prior experience. One important consideration involves the distinction between new development and renovation. Most A/E firms will have had experience in new work in which the architect or engineer starts with a "blank sheet" and is, in this sense, in complete control. Renovation work, however, is continually constrained by preexisting construction which often remains hidden and therefore unknown. Sound planning and design judgments in this environment depend, in large measure, on prior experience with similar conditions. This is highly significant in cost estimating where the existing conditions can have a major impact and where adequate existing cost records or standards from which to start are rare. In these instances, the ingrained expertise of the estimator is of major importance.

Historic structures undergoing simultaneous restoration and modernization present an exaggerated instance in which prior experience is critical. Finding ways to introduce new plumbing or air conditioning systems into a space or through walls without affecting their external appearance is a trial-and-error process in which improved methods are developed project by project. Similarly, with respect to restoration construction, which often required hand-finished moldings, decorative plaster trim, hand-crafted glass, custom wood paneling and other specialty work, experience in detailing and prior exposure to sources of expertise and the costs involved will be of substantial benefit.

Another facet of prior experience involves the nature of the property use intended. Architectural firms may develop particular strengths by virtue of accumulated experience in facilities for specific occupancies such as commercial, residential, educational, health care, or industrial. Such background experience may be of significant value to the property manager, especially if he or his company is entering a new real estate market. Conversely, situations can exist in which totally new design solutions are desired, leading the property manager to seek a firm which has a reputation for design creativity, but not a specialist in the kind of facility desired.

An additional factor can be the nature of the structure itself. High-rise urban buildings have design considerations in terms of image and identity, and with respect to building systems, such as vertical transportation and fire safety, which are distinct from those of low-rise structures. The most qualified A/E for one type may not be as well qualified for the other.

Many of these contrasts can be illustrated by comparing two similar projects encompassing the renovation of existing structures for offices. The first involves a major department store's current plan to adapt a single-level, contemporary retail store located on a former golf course to a leased office facility. In addition to the straightforward building modification, for which accurate existing construction documents are available, extensive site utilization planning is involved. By contrast, several years ago the former Federal Reserve Bank building located in central Philadelphia, a high-rise structure built early in this century, was studied for conversion to leased office space. The exterior facade, ground and top floors included unique architectural treatments which were to be restored; all building systems were to be modernized, and numerous building code violations were to be corrected. On the other hand, no site work was required.

Many of the skills, disciplines, and experience appropriate to one of these renovation assignments would not be required on the other. Therefore, an A/E firm well-suited for one of these might not be qualified for the second, even though the same owner, an office space developer, may have been involved and might otherwise have preferred to deal with one firm.

Construction Phase Administration Capability

An important selection factor can be the need for a higher than normal level of A/E services in the administration of the actual construction. Although many

A/Es are prepared to provide the standard AIA level of such services, not all have the desire or capability of providing the extended amounts of field support involved in larger projects, especially if extensive renovation and/or restoration is involved. In such instances, a full-time project representative with supporting personnel may be needed. Where time and material contracts are involved, material quantity and field force records should be kept. Occasionally, projects will involve multiple prime contracts or construction trade specialists for separate phases of the work, in which case owners will then be obligated to perform the overall scheduling and coordination tasks otherwise performed by the general contractor. In these instances, the property manager may require extended construction phase A/E services and must consider this in the A/E evaluation and selection process.

Project Delivery Track Record

In addition to measuring the A/E's fit in terms of real estate development awareness and relevant experience, the A/E's track record in specific control aspects associated with project delivery must be of prime importance to the real estate manager. Performance in controlling prior projects is a strong indication of an A/E's management strengths and internal quality control. Construction phase change order activity, in terms of numbers, dollar value, and nature, often provides an indication of the degree of thoroughness exercised in design and construction document preparation. Examination of planned-versus-actual cost and schedule data for recent projects is also a key indicator of A/E performance. Occasionally, property managers will extend their track record analysis to include an inspection of one or more of the A/E's past projects to see first-hand how the A/E's work has withstood the test of time in terms of user acceptance and physical appearance.

Proposed Project Personnel

The ability of the A/E team and property manager to achieve an effective working relationship is as dependent on human chemistry as on the firm's professional qualifications. The presence of positive face-to-face relationships among the A/E team members and the owner's representatives is significant in determining a project's results. In short, the successful use of A/E services involves a high degree of interactive skills among the people involved.

For this reason, A/E selection reviews and interviews should include the A/E's key project personnel—those individuals with whom the property manager can expect to work on a daily basis. In considering larger firms whose principals are seldom able to allocate significant amounts of time to any one project, experienced property managers will want to know who will be responsible for their assignment and be assured that an effective working relationship will be likely to develop with them.

This factor can be of even greater importance if the selection of a particular firm is based on specific skills and capabilities demonstrated in past projects. In such instances, the property manager may want to be sure that the A/E staff members responsible for the success of those projects will be available to contribute their expertise to his project.

SUMMARY

No rules conveniently define the relationship of the property manager to the architects, engineers, and landscape architects whose services he must use to effect physical change in the property he manages. Rather, there are numerous possible roles and functions out of which the relationship will be formed. Ultimately, it will be determined by the manager's level of participation, the capabilities and personality of the A/E team he selects, and the specific requirements of the project on which the property manager and A/E collaborate.

Awareness of the entrepreneurial forces in real estate investment is critical to the success of such collaboration. While improvement in the man-made environment is a legitimate objective in its own right, from the property manager's perspective the A/E work will be most strenuously measured by the cash-flow results of the property changes made, whether in imagery, functional utility, or operating costs. If the underlying financial objectives are clearly comprehended and respected, the A/E team's skills in effecting property change will be properly focused in terms of the real estate developer's marketplace perception.

Through the selection process, the property manager can exert maximum influence on the use of the A/E team. By carefully determining that the A/E possesses the requisite understanding of commercial property objectives, has experience and skills appropriate to his project, and will be compatible in the working relationship he envisions, the property manager will have established a strong probability that optimum use of the A/E team will be realized.

KAREN DAROFF
President
Daroff Design Inc.
Philadelphia, Pennsylvania

Karen Daroff, President and Principal in Charge of Design, founded Daroff Design Inc. (DDI) in 1973. The organization, billing over $2 million annually, is a flexible, multi-disciplinary firm comprised of three interlocking groups of professionals: DDI Interiors, DDI Graphics, and DDI Architects, PC. DDI works with developers and other professionals in the design of offices and other commercial facilities, and in the areas of tenant planning, interior architectural renovation, and adaptive reuse. A graduate of Moore College of Art, Philadelphia, Ms. Daroff holds a BFA in Interior Design. She serves on the Board of the Greater Philadelphia Chamber of Commerce and is a member of the Executive Committee of the Mayor's Small Business Advisory Council.

BARBARA MERLE GILMORE
Director of Marketing
Daroff Design Inc.
Philadelphia, Pennsylvania

Barbara Merle Gilmore, Director of Marketing for DDI, joined the Philadelphia-based design firm after several years as an internal management consultant for a Fortune 100 consumer products firm. Ms. Gilmore supports DDI clients interested in financial and operational efficiencies of interior space planning and design. Ms. Gilmore received an MBA from the Wharton School, University of Pennsylvania, and a BFA from Carnegie-Mellon University. She has completed additional studies at Harvard University.

CHAPTER 8

THE USE OF THE INTERIOR DESIGNER— FROM THE FINANCIAL STANDPOINT

INTRODUCTION

The work of the interior design professional has evolved from the traditional job of choosing furniture, wall colors, materials, and window coverings to include consultation on all financial, functional, and aesthetic aspects of the interior space. Expertise is provided on such diverse subjects as life cycle cost analyses, property feasibility studies, and recommendations that will heighten a facility's physical and psychological comfort, as well as increase employee productivity through devices such as interior and exterior orientation systems and human factors engineering—"ergonomics in the workplace."

Interior design professionals have become an essential part of the corporate management consulting establishment. They have the expertise to affect positively the corporate earnings profile and the bottom line—just as financial, strategic planning, and market research consultants do. The mission of interior design professionals is to provide their clients with an efficient, economical, and productive environment that happens to be attractive and pleasant as well.

The current economic climate has forced building owners to investigate potential savings that would increase their return on investment. Therefore, costs saved by design professionals are important contributions to the investment and operating economics that office professionals demand and that help make worthwhile projects possible.

There are several reasons for the increased responsibility of the interior design profession. However, the following statement from a recent Harvard Real Estate study captures one of the most important: ". . . the buildings and land owned by companies that are not primarily in the real estate business, [now] typically accounts for twenty-five percent (25%) or more of a firm's total assets."* The interior designer has developed tools to meet the demand for more fiscally sound treatment of these corporate assets.

Investors demand and design professionals are looking for (1) a greater return on investment in buildings, real estate, and other fixed assets, and (2) a reduction in long-term operating expenses associated with those assets. In addition to long-term advantages such as cost savings, the use of an interior designer by an owner-occupant or developer has two more obvious advantages: immediate access to expertise not readily available to the client in-house and a check-and-balance system, a source of independent thought, for ongoing project control.

SHORT-TERM OWNER-USER BENEFITS

Developers and owner-occupants want to complete their projects quickly and within their projected budgets. The industry calls this "fast-tracking." Pressure to fast-track increased tremendously as construction costs, interest rates, and inflation skyrocketed in the late 1970s. Successful and efficient fast-tracking, whether in ordering furniture or equipment or in the design process itself, requires knowledge and experience. The use of an experienced interior designer eliminates the learning period necessary for those inexperienced in space planning and interior design. The result is a project that is professionally executed and satisfactorily completed to specification, on budget, and on time.

In addition to rapid project completion, another special sensitivity of build-

---

*Harvard Real Estate, Inc., *Corporate Real Estate Asset Management in the United States* (Cambridge, Mass.: the President and Fellows of Harvard College, 1981), p. iv.

ing tenants is the amount of occupied space required. The professional space planner is trained to quickly produce a design that can efficiently, and without sacrifice, reduce the required square footage or maximize the use of available space. Whether space costs $18 per square foot or more per year to rent or $100 per square foot to construct, the corporate visibility of required space and its associated cost places a large part of the burden of reducing space costs on the design firm. Through creative, knowledgeable design and through the use of new component systems discussed later in this chapter, planners can often reduce space requirements by 7 to 10%.

Use of an interior design firm in conjunction with an architect affords the owner-developer the advantage of a check-and-balance system of project operations and cost control. The architect and interior designer work as a team. Each, with his independent training and approach, is responsible for assessing the work of the other team members and for assessing the impact of that work on his own. This dialectic approach assures the owner that no one facet, phase, or expenditure of the building outweighs in importance any other. The building's external appearance cannot become a monument to the owner to the detriment of the occupants and tenants, nor can it become an over-designed interior environment requiring prohibitively expensive engineering to support misplaced design features. The dialectic approach gives the owner, developer, or facilities manager a check-and-balance on costs. It provides second opinions without second guessing.

LONG-TERM OWNER-USER BENEFITS

To reiterate, the owner-occupant or facilities manager calls upon the interior designer to provide an expertise, usually unavailable in-house, that will result in short-term and long-term financial benefit. In turn, whether the job calls for maintenance of an existing facility through updating and renovation, construction of a new facility for corporate use, or construction of a new office building for speculation, the aware professional interior designer-architect now responds from two positions of responsibility: technical and economic.

In view of the longer term economic benefits, the key concept is that of the time value of money. Briefly, present value theory is the assumption that the value of a dollar today can be calculated through introduction of (1) an assigned inflation factor and (2) the opportunity cost of that dollar into the equation. Present value represents the velocity of money or the discounted cash flow of a capital budget. With the present value method, all cash flows are discounted to the present value using the required rate of return.

The compounded value of a dollar to the owner 10 years in the future can be contrasted with the value of the current dollar. Inversely, the value of a future dollar can be deflated to compare it to a current dollar. In this manner, a value may be assigned to decisions in equal terms—apples-to-apples (versus apples to oranges).

By way of illustration, the following comparison can be made to the cost over time and to the value of Decision A versus Decision B:

Cash Flow for Year X (for all years)

Sum of $(1 + i)^n$ where n is the number of years in the future and i is the annual discount rate*

In the following illustration, Project A is preferred because the net present value is larger at the chosen discount rate. Even though the total benefit is the same for the two projects, Project A gives more benefits in the early years. Because a dollar in year one is worth more than a dollar in year six, investors want their dollar returns early. (Just as a bird in the hand is worth two in the bush, a dollar today is worth more than a dollar tomorrow.) The concept of the time value of money helps anyone to compare different forecasts of benefits or to analyze alternatives and to choose the one that is preferable.

Investment Example

Year	Project A	Project B	Comment
0	$(10,000)	$(10,000)	Project costs
1	2,500	2,000	Project benefit
2	2,500	2,000	benefit
3	2,500	2,000	benefit
4	2,500	2,000	benefit
5	2,500	2,000	benefit
6	1,500	2,000	benefit
7	1,500	2,000	benefit
8	1,500	2,000	benefit
9	1,500	2,000	benefit
10	1,500	2,000	benefit
Total costs and benefits	$ 10,000	$ 10,000	
Net present value at 15% discount rate	$ 880	$ 38	

Not all facilities owners and managers are in the position, or have the time, to take advantage of or to respond to all the pertinent economic issues in the purest sense. However, the theory behind the analysis of these issues has been tested and proven. Therefore, it must be given serious consideration before embarking on any major facility changes.

---

*In a more sophisticated analysis, the discount rate is adjusted from year to year, reflecting different projections of year-to-year economic and financial conditions by the investment analysis team.

FINANCIAL PERSPECTIVE ON DESIGN DECISIONS

Of sobering responsibility are the available real estate options and individual building schemes presented to the interior designer. Interior designers are often asked to examine available facility options for clients before the interior design issues are addressed. For many companies, the real estate decision is one of renting office or commercial space at the best rate, with the lowest occupancy taxes, operating costs, and escalation clauses. For others, it involves investing in a project just under development. For a third group, it is the analysis of the pros and cons of becoming an owner-occupant. In each case, issues of cost, efficiency, life cycle expense over the term of the lease or mortgage, and tax implications all come to bear in the decision-making process.

Economic Recovery Tax Act of 1981

The Economic Recovery Tax Act of 1981 (ERTA) due to Accelerated Cost Recovery Systems (ACRS) has served to expand the role of the interior designer. Before the enactment of ERTA, developers and owners allocated their building investment dollars into separate categories based upon the poorly defined theory of useful life. For instance, in the case of a building elevator, the developer, prior to ERTA, would define the elevator as several components of a line item budget: the shaft was granted a useful life of 30 to 40 years, like that of a building; the cab and riggings were given a useful life of 10 to 15 years; the electrical connections and motor were assigned a useful life of 7 to 10 years; and the interior decor of the cab, which had to be refurbished every several years, had its useful life assigned accordingly. The developer separated out the costs of these components and accounted for them independently as he set his depreciation schedule.

Depreciation is the accounting method used to write down the investment in an asset by charging the expense of the asset being depreciated over its useful life against the gross income. If the component outlives its depreciation schedule, as most do with reasonable maintenance, the owner continues to use an asset which has no book value. The goal of the owner is usually to write off as much as possible, as quickly as possible, in order to reduce the tax burden on earnings and investments.

ERTA has not removed the concept of useful life from the depreciation criteria, but it has further refined that concept by defining a clearer version of accounting for the building as a whole and by postulating a shorter depreciation period. ERTA has widened the potential role of the interior designer from the viewpoint of economic responsibility by assisting the owner-developer to allocate parts of the building as Personal Property Tax Items or by making other parts eligible for ACRS and related investment tax credits. The interior designer is the only member of the professional team educated in all aspects of the use of factory-made components eligible as 1245 items.

The new system has three major advantages: (1) the investor recoups in tax dollars up to 50% of his initial outlay for the items; (2) the system permits faster freeing of dollars for other investments; and (3) it allows more leverage in lease negotiations for occupants of rented space.

Accelerated Cost Recovery

The new tax code reduces the time in which certain office components, systems, and equipment can be depreciated to five years from the previous 8 to 10 years. In fact, the process is most frequently known as Accelerated Cost Recovery (ACRS).

In general, the useful life of a building has now been set at 15 years. This means that at least one-fifteenth of the building investment can be written off against current income each year for 15 years.

As of this writing, Congress is reviewing the ACR system with indications that the 15 year formula may be extended.

Personal Property Items

As stated earlier, the building investment may be structured so that a significant portion of that investment is in what is known as "1245 Tangible Personal Property Items." Tangible Personal Property Items are depreciated much more quickly; the interior designer is educated and experienced in specifying these more quickly depreciated items. Usually made in a factory, 1245 interior component items have details that do not damage the building when they are installed or removed. Eligible component items may include: office furniture systems, moveable partition walls, flat wire for data, signal, and power transmission, carpet tiles, furniture, lighting integrated into that furniture, and component lighting systems. Examples of interior items *not* considered personal property items are full-height architectural walls, under-floor raceways and electrical wiring, glue-down broadloom carpeting and other permanent floor fixtures, and ceiling mounted lighting.

Definition of Project Responsibilities

Under the new code, when creating an elevator in a building, for example, the developer easily may make and document the depreciation through his allocation of the procurement responsibility. If the building owner gets a bill for $150,000 from the general contractor for one elevator, he must obtain an itemized bill from that general contractor to avoid the use of the one-fifteenth write-off formula for the total amount.

However, if he gets one bill of $100,000 from the general contractor for the elevator and another bill for $50,000 from an interior designer or his designated contractor for the 1245 tangible personal property components of that elevator (cab finishes, carpet, graphics, etc.), then two allocations are most clearly established. The second group can be depreciated over five years.

In a more detailed explanation, construction cost increases for the highly-skilled field jobs usually associated with a first class office interior exceed by far the Consumer Price Index rates, due in part to limited skilled workers. Factory controls and production methods seem to be able to produce high quality interior components at less cost in less time with fewer punch list error corrections than field construction of the same components (e.g., doors, architectural woodwork, factory prefinished partitions, ceiling systems, wiring systems, and workstations). The new tax code grants tax credits and fast depreciation to factory-built components of an interior development, but it specifically no longer allows the prior practice of component allocations for depreciation.

Before ERTA took effect, the developer could make his own list of components which were part of the building and allocate them into various years of depreciation (i.e., use them as tax write-offs based upon the concept of useful life). Under ERTA, if the construction includes certain components as part of an overall lump-sum contract, it may be more difficult to allocate either the components themselves or the fees and other soft costs associated with these components unless the allocation is clearly documented.

Use of Interior Component Systems

For these reasons, interior design professionals are assuming a greater role in the construction process, while the interiors contract industry (which produces factory-made furniture and equipment for commercial interiors) is taking substantial work from the field construction industry. Moreover, since factory-made items come with fixed, factory-assigned sizes and dimensions, the inter-relationship of these items with the building's semi-variable sizes and dimensions becomes a major interior design consideration.

For clarity in tax reporting regarding the source and use of these components, the owner-developer might make the responsibility allocations prior to the architect establishing his scope of services, prior to the financial development package, and prior to the program analysis of the project. Based upon the above set of issues, a budget allocation of various components can be made and cast into three lots: (1) the building and its infrastructure (Base Building); (2) the interior furniture, furnishings, and equipment (Interior Items); and (3) specialized equipment and the base building interior components on which the finishes are applied (Interior Component Items).

The base building items are clearly associated with the architectural and engineering professional activities. The furniture, furnishings, and equipment are clearly associated with the interior design professional services. The specialized equipment and base building interior components would, before the benefits of ERTA, have been part of the architect's drawings and specifications but today are in transition from the architect's boards and contractor's work to the factory and the interior designer's specification documents.

CASE STUDY: THE ACME IMPORT AND MARKETING CORPORATION (AIMCO)

The following case study illustrates the professional consulting role in providing the above considerations in a pro-and-con analysis of the construction of an owner-occupied corporate headquarters building. This analysis compares the traditional drywall system to the component system solution with accorded tax benefits. In study of this comparison, the facilities manager may want to keep in mind that total use of component systems may not always be to the advantage of every owner-occupant, but that this analysis may be applied in part or in whole.

The purpose of this case is to show the advantage of a system interior over traditional architectural interior as documented and analyzed by an interior design professional. Therefore, special emphasis is given to line items which are likely to vary with the decision to create a system interior.

The effects of the decision to assign the base building to the project architect while assigning the programming and tenant work letter components to the interior designer (in addition to the traditional assignment of the furniture, furnishings, and equipment [FF&E] components of the project) should be noted. This case study was made available through the courtesy of James E. Rappoport, AIA, a New York businessman and real estate economics consultant. Mr. Rappoport has a career-long association with the contract furniture industry and with state-of-the-art design innovations. He currently consults on tax and asset management issues for several Fortune 500 corporations and is a management consultant to Daroff Design Inc.

AIMCO is planning to build a mid-rise, owner-occupied corporate headquarters building in the Mid-Atlantic states. Based upon the discussed allocation, the facility budget can be cast into three areas: (1) Base Building Architecture; (2) Interior Items; and (3) Interior Component Items. The following set of requirements has been made for the proposed AIMCO Corporate Headquarters Development Project:

1. The total building (gross) area will be 88,000 square feet.
2. The overall project budget, set in contract-year 1984 dollars should not exceed $15,000,000.
3. Parking will be on grade, not within the building.
4. The program will not include a mainframe computer facility.
5. The finished building will be consistent with a high quality standard as exemplified by AIMCO business practices.

As a result of recent experiences on similar projects in the Mid-Atlantic region, a base building allocation of approximately $67 per square foot for a headquarters project is foreseen. The base building is the building without interior components. This is at the low end of the range of possible costs and is about at the average for companies of the size and resources of AIMCO. Using a 10% per annum rate of inflation for construction costs, and a projected contract date of one and one-half years hence, this allocation inflates to approximately $78 per square foot.

For the sake of size and scale comparisons, the following assumptions for office and workstation requirements have been made:

	Quantity	Size Each	Total Sq Ft	Linear Ft @ Window		Unit Cost	Extension
Private Offices							
Senior executive	1	625	625	50 each	50	$15,000	$ 15,000
Executive VPs	3	400	1,200	40	120	8,000	24,000
Division managers	12	240	2,880	20	240	6,000	72,000
Section managers	70	150	10,500	12	840	5,000	350,000
Total all offices	86		15,205		1,250		$ 461,000
Total supervisors	40	100	4,000	internal views		3,500	$ 140,000
Workstations							
Technical	22	90	1,980			$ 3,000	$ 66,000
Executive secretary	25	90	2,250			3,000	75,000
Secretary	47	50	2,350			2,400	112,800
Clerks	50	60	3,000			2,000	100,000
Entry clerks	50	40	2,000			1,400	70,000
Total Workstations	194		11,580				$ 423,800
Total program	320		30,875 sq ft	1,250 ft			$1,024,800
Related files and storage			5,000				
Special spaces, conference rooms, etc.			10,000				
Circulation between workstations			14,000				
Circulation between groups and lobbies			12,215				
Net to gross areas, mechanical, etc.			16,000				
Total gross building area			88,000 sq ft sq ft				

Notes: Furniture, fixtures, and accessories are priced here (only) in current dollars.
The building should provide 1,250 linear feet of window wall for the private offices shown and window wall or atrium exposure for the open plan workstations.

Based upon the office and workstation assumptions, a typical scenario or line item budget for the facility can be created:

Line Items	Base Building Architecture	Interiors Items	Interior Components	Totals	Details*
General carpet area		$ 140,000		$ 140,000	2
Special carpet areas		90,000		90,000	2
Tile and stone lobby finishes			$ 25,000	$ 25,000	
Executive office furniture		461,000		461,000	3
Workstations		564,000		564,000	
Filing and storage		80,000		80,000	4
Lobby and lounge furniture		60,000		60,000	
Meeting rooms furniture		40,000		40,000	3
Coffee facilities		15,000		15,000	
Mail distribution equip.	$110,000			110,000	

Line Items	Base Building Architecture	Interiors Items	Interior Components	Totals	Details*
Central file, library		30,000		30,000	1
Window treatment(s)		35,000		35,000	
Fabric and vinyl wall coverings		100,000		100,000	6
Paint		100,000		100,000	6
Elevator and lobby finishes		40,000		40,000	
Other special finishes			12,000	12,000	
Coat closets		10,000		10,000	
Accessories package(s)		30,000		30,000	
Security systems			40,000	40,000	
Garden and patio furniture		5,000		5,000	
Sound System and PA equip.			40,000	40,000	
Lighting controls			10,000	10,000	
Audiovisual and TV equip.			20,000	20,000	
Telephone communications equip.			350,000	350,000	
Tack boards, chalkboards, etc.		20,000		20,000	7
Trash compactor	40,000			40,000	
Mailroom equip. (not machines)		20,000		20,000	
Time clocks & systems			20,000	20,000	
Plants and planters (interior)		25,000		25,000	
Nurses' station		20,000		20,000	
Display equip. in lobby		15,000		15,000	
Lighting for same		15,000		15,000	
Kitchen equip.	30,000			30,000	
Dining room furniture		45,000		45,000	
Dining room smallwares (china)		10,000		10,000	
Major meeting room		25,000		25,000	
Guard station		5,000		5,000	
Classroom seating and tables		40,000		40,000	
Classroom storage and teacher's wall		20,000		20,000	9
Ceiling system			270,000	270,000	10
Wall system			200,000	200,000	11
Doors and hardware			100,000	100,000	12
Millwork			60,000	60,000	13
Ambient lighting			250,000	250,000	14
Task lighting		80,000		80,000	
Workstation wiring hookups			40,000	40,000	15
Totals	$180,000	$2,140,000	$1,437,000	$3,757,000	

*Details coincide with expanded budget details in next section.

With these basic line items, the remaining estimates for the project can be derived:

Line Items	Base Building Architecture	Interiors Items	Interior Components	Totals
Totals from above	$ 180,000	$2,140,000	$1,437,000	$ 3,757,000
Add local sales tax and delivery	10,000	260,000	130,000	400,000
Add contingencies	15,000	300,000	200,000	515,000
Add 10% per annum inflation factor to mid Year Two	19,000	380,000	250,000	649,000
Totals in mid Year Two dollars	$ 224,000	$3,080,000	$2,017,000	$ 5,321,000
Base building budget @ $78/sq ft	6,900,000			6,900,000
Site improvements	1,000,000			1,000,000
Art, signage and special items		260,000		260,000
Architectural and interior fees	402,000	167,000	101,000	670,000
Site acquisition	1,000,000			
Total budget allocations	$9,526,000	$3,507,000	$2,118,000	$15,151,000

Life Cycle Cost Analysis

The purpose of life cycle cost analysis is to identify the lowest net present value construction alternative. Alternatives arise from selecting a traditional construction approach versus a component alternative. In theory, a fully integrated and factory-produced interior system should:

1. Require less architectural space for a given user program.
2. Install in less time, granting earlier move-in dates (i.e., fast-track).
3. Cost the same or less to buy and install the first time.
4. Cost less to operate over time.
5. Cost less to maintain or refinish over time.
6. Cost less to change or rearrange at some future time.
7. Take maximum financial advantage of accounting policies and the newest tax laws.

While a sophisticated analysis is required to identify and document precisely the expected savings associated with all of these design goals at once, they can be understood and examined individually. Experience shows that benefits of these kinds are the most significant for occupants. Therefore, they are the first that are considered in the life cycle cost analysis.

Additional information and assumptions include:

1. A 10% per annum inflation factor for operations and other cost increases.
2. Tax credits are at 10%.

3. Tax depreciation, using ACRS guidelines.
4. All savings are assumed to be taken as cost reductions, rather than to be invested in added quality or added features.
5. For simplicity, local tax treatment is the same for the two examples. (In practice, this assumption is valid.)

Since movable full height partitions and storage walls allow full reusage, they are recommended highly for growing operations (over fixed sheet-rock walls and fixed storage rooms). Because AIMCO plans substantial expansion over the next few years, the need to relocate 25% of the project's walls within the next five years is set as one of the life cycle assumptions. This ability to relocate will allow for changing work methods, automation, technological innovations, and variations in staff and office as the expansion occurs.

Finally, with new wiring systems, the technical ability to relocate offices and workstations without major electrical installation and reinstallation costs should be noted. The combination of wiring with snap-together fittings, within the office furniture systems and the use of so-called flat wire components to wire workstations at various locations, provides this needed economic and physical flexibility at substantial life cycle cost savings.

Line Items Studied	Architectural Solution	System Solution	Total Savings From Use of System
1.* By using storage walls and the layout of juxtaposed storage units as may be required on both sides of various walls, as much as 6% of gross building area can be saved. To be conservative, we will use 3%.			
3% of 88,000 sq ft = 2600 sq ft @$78/sq ft	$ 6,900,000	$ 6,660,000	$ 240,000
2.* Carpet costs can also be reduced; here we will use the total 6% savings.	230,000	216,000	14,000
3.* Reduction in office and meeting room storage units due to the proposed storage walls.	501,000	391,000	110,000
4.* Higher cost of the storage wall; floor-to-ceiling units.	80,000	100,000	(20,000)
5.* Central file and library storage cost reduction.	30,000	25,000	5,000
Reduction of storage space required for central file due to storage system; the facility can save approximately 1000 sq ft of (gross area.		(−78,000)	78,000
6. All paint and other finishes in the facility are reduced by the reduction in the amount of floor space at $78/sq ft	200,000	190,000	10,000
In addition, factory-applied finishes last longer and are easier to maintain.			

Line Items Studied	Architectural Solution	System Solution	Total Savings From Use of System
7.* Tack boards and chalkboards or white boards may not be required since factory-finished walls can be written on.	20,000		20,000
8. Other special storage items are provided in typical fashion in rooms, etc.			
9.* The training room and its storage requirements are less costly.	20,000	15,000	5,000
10.* To achieve a fully movable system, a modular ceiling system with troffers to hold the vertical elements is required. Such a system costs more to install than a typical ceiling.	270,000	300,000	(30,000)
11.* The wall system is also more costly to purchase than a sheet-rock wall, but there is less wall to install.	200,000	260,000	(60,000)
12.* Doors and hardware are less costly due to factory production.	100,000	95,000	5,000
13.* Most millwork is built into the storage walls.	60,000	40,000	20,000
14.* Lighting system costs less due to its inclusion within the system.	250,000	220,000	30,000
15.* Workstations and desk wiring with flat wire saves time and money.	60,000	40,000	20,000
Total	$ 8,921,000	$ 8,474,000	$ 447,000
Add taxes, delivery, contingencies and inflation	1,157,000	1,100,000	57,000
Add all other items which remain about the same in this study	5,073,000	4,978,000	95,000
Total base cost estimate allocations	$15,151,000	$14,552,000	$ 599,000

*Items marked * are 1245 Property which qualify for ITC and 5-year ACRS depreciation. The other items are fixed assets with 15-year write-offs.

It is likely that *fees* associated with items * marked will have the same five-year treatment, while fixed asset items and their associated fees have a 15-year write-off.

	Architectural Solution	System Solution	Total Savings From Use of System
Fees: are indicated above as 5% of project costs	$ 670,000	$ 645,000	$ 25,000
Fees associated with component items	167,000	283,000	(116,000)
Allocated chattels	3,339,000	5,665,000	(2,326,000)

These issues will be shown below in the life cycle cost to be important in the write-off analysis

Land acquisition	$ 1,000,000	$ 1,000,000	
Fixed assets and fees	10,575,000	7,604,000	$3,041,000
Chattel items and fees	3,506,000	5,948,000	(2,442,000)
Total all items	$15,151,000	$14,552,000	$ 599,000

Line Items Studied	Architectural Solution	System Solution	Total Savings From Use of System
Construction cost savings			$ 529,000
With this basis, 10% tax credit on the 5-year depreciable component items	350,600	594,800	244,200
First year write-off on these items (remember, we use 50%)	262,600	446,000	183,400
First year write-off on the 15-year fixed asset items	354,000	254,000	100,000
But, in addition, we estimate that we can move into the facility 4 months earlier due to the system approach with far fewer "wet trades." Assuming the present facility can be rented or sold 4 months earlier, we foresee a savings of			$ 133,000
Net savings after the 1st year			$1,259,600
In addition to the savings noted above, there are two other line items to add to the savings.			
These savings can be anticipated by interest earned on the $1,259,600: we assume a tax-free yield of 10%			125,000
Finally, there is approximately 3,600 sq ft less building to heat, power to maintain. If we assume an operating budget of $3 per sq ft we save approximately			10,800
Estimated savings after 1st year			$1,395,400
In the second year, the write-offs are	$ 912,000	$ 1,205,000	$ 293,000
Operational savings are			12,000
Continued use of the cash saved from year 1			139,000
Use of this year's savings			30,000
			$ 474,000
Added to the 1st year's savings			1,395,400
Total estimated savings after 2nd year			$1,869,400
During the 3rd year, the write-offs are	650,000	760,000	110,000
Operational savings are			13,000
Continued use of the cash saved			186,000
Use of this year's savings			12,000
Plus, in this year, we foresee some repainting of architectural elements	50,000		50,000
We also foresee a relocation of 15% of the partitions to make room for expansion and changes in management groups.			
The architectural walls must be removed and rebuilt	70,000		70,000
With some tax write-offs for the debris	(20,000)		(20,000)
The system walls are relocated with little in-house labor and no waste		5,000	(5,000)
			$ 416,000

Line Items Studied	Architectural Solution	System Solution	Total Savings From Use of System
Added to earlier savings			1,869,400
Total estimated savings after 3rd year			$ 2,285,000
During the 4th year, the write-offs are	655,000	760,000	$ 105,000
Operational savings are			15,000
Continued use of the case saved			228,500
Use of this year's savings			12,000
			$ 360,500
Added to earlier savings			2,285,000
			$ 2,645,500
During the 5th year, the write-offs are	655,000	760,000	105,000
Operational savings are			17,000
Continued use of the cash saved			264,000
Use of this year's savings			12,000
Additional painting costs	60,000		60,000
Relocation of 10% of the walls	45,000	5,000	40,000
			$ 498,000
Added to earlier savings			2,645,500
			$ 3,143,500

Case Study: Conclusion

It is clear that the savings derive from many sources and are cash savings as well as tax savings.

For years 5 to 10, the first line of savings becomes less useful since the five-year items have been written off. The operational savings and the use of the saved money are still important issues, as is the ability to respond quickly to needed changes in the operations. Both of the solutions afford greater savings than relocation of the structural elements found in the typical architectural solution.

Moreover, considering the down-side risk, such a facility could be easily made useful for most sub-tenants in a short period of time and with little capital expense.

TECHNICAL PERSPECTIVE ON DESIGN DECISIONS

A professional, technical perspective is not a luxury. It is a necessity to reduce maintenance and operating costs and, more important, to plan for the integration of technological developments that will occur during the life of the facility. This knowledge is rarely available to the developer or facilities manager in-house, because his employees do not have the experience to research the issues nor the time to establish the necessary physical sample library.

Differentiation between technical knowledge and the previously discussed financial and economic consulting responsibilities cannot be made in many cases, nor should it be. For instance, durability of the facility and the interior components encompasses both technical and economic issues. An example of the interior designer's response from a position of technical responsibility occurred during Daroff Design's work on a one million-square foot adminis-tration-conference-training center to house approximately 1,450 executives and support staff at move-in. Daroff Design was consulted to respond to the architect's preliminary design on interiors issues. The architect had designed the base building on a five-foot module, so that common elements, such as the columns, were five feet, or multiples of five feet, apart.

Given the office and workstation standards and the amount and types of furniture that the client required, it was found that the furniture could only be arranged so that individuals in the office would be forced to sit with their backs to the window wall. This situation would cause a visitor to squint at the occupant. It would cause the occupant to work in his own shadow and it would necessitate a light level high enough to eliminate that shadow. By recom-mending a change to a four-foot module, which would allow the desk to be placed perpendicular to the window wall, we were able to reduce the energy requirement by reducing the level of lighting required throughout the office part of the facility. The savings to the client was approximately $4 million over a 10-year life of the building. In addition, the client benefited from a pleasant outdoor view of the countryside, rather than of the interior wall.

Accommodating Current and Future Office Technologies

Integrating current technology into the workplace is not simply resolved by the add-on method. As David L. Armstrong, one of the persons instrumental in creating the Facility Management Institute, Ann Arbor, Michigan has said "The key for facilities management is that CRTs and other electronic equip-ment strengthen the ties among the physical environment, work processes, and workers . . . you must deal with people, process, and place as interdepen-dent."† Interior design professionals are specifically trained to integrate these issues.

Corporations cannot afford to increase rentable space by 10 to 15% (as some service providers forecast) for every task that may become automated. An essential part of the space programming for the technically-responsible de-signer must be to help redefine or analyze the individual jobs in question . . . to have a knowledge of the equipment which, in the future, may reduce the workspace required for the same, automated function.

Armstrong states, in fact, that working with these particular technical skills ". . . a workstation is redesigned around the job task and the CRT is inte-grated into work processes and the workstation, the workstation can be the

†David L. Armstrong, "CRT Impact in Office Design and Management," INTERIORS, August 1982, p. 12.

same size or slightly smaller than the space used for the *same non-automated function*."‡ Responsible designers with technical consulting skills extend that thought to all forms of office automation and telecommunications and provide clients with flexible facilities that will accommodate technological developments far into the future and for the life of their new facilities.

A concept now gaining favor for technical, financial, and psychological reasons is the "inside-out design." That is, the design responds to the needs of the user, both current and future. Owners can no longer afford monuments to their corporate image with limited building efficiency. Every 1,000 square feet of non-habitable space caused by poor planning or design inefficiencies, may cost the owner or tenant $250,000 over the course of a 10-year life cycle.

SUMMARY

In conclusion, the interior designer provides more than decorative services. The professional and responsible interior designer or architect is an integral part of the management and decision-making team at many major American corporations. Having the opportunity and expertise to positively structure up to 25% of corporate America's capital assets, the design professional provides a technical skill and financial analysis ability that is not found in combination outside of the interior design profession. By augmenting the value of the owner's capital facility investment through multiple cost savings, the mission of the designer has changed from designing the offices of corporate executives to that of functioning as a planning, financial, and economic consultant to those executives.

‡Ibid.

NEAL I. RODIN
President
Rodin Realty Investment Corporation
Philadelphia, Pennsylvania

Neal I. Rodin, the co-editor of this handbook, is President of Rodin Realty Investment Corporation, Rodin Enterprises Incorporated, and Rodin Management Incorporated, which companies are correspondent companies for Sun Life Insurance Company of America. Mr. Rodin is on the faculty of the New York Law Journal Program. His companies manage over one billion dollars in residential and commercial property. Mr. Rodin received his degree in Finance and Economics from Temple University.

CHAPTER 9

MANAGING AND TURNING AROUND TROUBLED PROPERTIES

INTRODUCTION

The primary function of the property manager is to insure that investment real estate produces the highest level of return for its investors without jeopardizing the security of the investment. Initially, the management team seeks to replace chaos with order and control. Successful programs have been established along four primary areas: educating the tenant, collecting the rents, insuring occupancy, and public relations and promotion.

Regardless of whether the property is commercial or residential, these four primary areas are essential starting points to the successful turnaround of all types of investment real estate.

EDUCATING THE TENANTS

When the new property management company takes over, there is a great deal of concern and apprehension on the part of that property's existing residents and staff. Residents are concerned about whether the changes made by the new management company will jeopardize their homes. It is always important to remember that a successful management program is one that is basically fair but firm.

Prior to the takeover of management, the property should be analyzed by your management team in order to make everyone aware of any particular problems inherent to the subject property. This should develop the beginning framework of a management plan. The management plan should attempt to achieve the owner's goals and objectives. Thus, it is important to review the owner's desires and specific requirements.

In some cases, the management agent will be taking over a situation of utter chaos. It is imperative in these instances that a set of rules and regulations be quickly established for the particular property. In other cases, only simple modification of the existing rules and regulations will be required. Once established, the new rules and regulations must be distributed to each individual resident. It is important to note that when the rules and regulations are being drafted for the subject property, the specific needs of that property and the locale of the area should be taken into consideration. Once the revised rules and regulations have been distributed to the residents, the property manager must be prepared to take steps to insure that these rules and regulations are followed. Sometimes, this may require filing for eviction after appropriate notice to the resident. The control of the property under the guidelines of the management plan is extremely important if the real estate investment is to be successful.

Curb Appeal

As part of the rules and regulations, specifics should be included as to trash, littering, and personal items. We define "curb appeal" as the overall cleanliness and well-kept appearance of the property. The residents must be educated not to leave their personal belongings outside. Examples of this include barbecue grills, bicycles, baby carriages, tables, chairs, and similar items. This is unappealing both to existing residents and new prospects visiting the property. The property should be neat and well-kept. In order for this to be accomplished, the residents must cooperate with management's guidelines. The curb appeal of the property is extremely important and will be further discussed in the section on insuring occupancy.

Pets

Another part of the revised rules and regulations should include policies as to pets. The consideration of whether a property is to allow pets must be heavily weighed with regard to the impact on the leasing of the available units and overall occupancy. Approximately 56% of the population are pet owners of some type. In most cases of turning around a troubled property with a great number of vacancies, it is not advisable to exclude 56% of the market by not allowing pets. It is a better policy to provide guidelines for the pets. Many management companies have devised methods of allowing certain pets within a property. Some of these guidelines are questionable. An example is one dog per unit, with the dog not to exceed 20 pounds. Does the management office weigh these dogs upon arrival? It is our understanding that in some cases this has been the practice. Other property managers take a photograph of the pet upon arrival. This photograph is then placed in a file. Should a dispute ever arise as to the pet that is allowed in the apartment, the picture is then retrieved and analyzed.

These solutions or controls are usually limited in nature. The weigh-in principle of a pet is usually not successful because, in most cases, what was once a small puppy grows into a large dog. The photograph technique can be used to insure that the only pet that is allowed in a particular unit is the one in the photograph. These controls omit one important fact: the chief concern is controlling the owner, not the pet. In most cases, pets are purely a reflection of poor owner habits and lack of training. Guidelines on pets should immediately be established within the rules and regulations, allowing that no pet shall run loose on the property and that all pets be leashed at all times. In addition, pet walking areas should be specific. In the specific case of cats and dogs, it may be necessary to charge either a one-time pet fee or additional security to insure against damage by the pet.

The important factor is to ensure that all pet owners presently on the property adhere to the guidelines of the property. If this is not done, the end result may be the loss of existing residents who simply move because the pets were not controlled.

Children

Children must also follow the guidelines established in the rules and regulations of the management company. The main problem that occurs with children is lack of supervision. It is beneficial if a property has designated play areas for the children. Children should never be allowed to play unsupervised in the recreational areas of the property such as the swimming pool, tennis court, or clubhouse.

As part of management, all members of the property staff should assist in insuring that pet owners and children abide by the rules and regulations of the property. Above all, if children or pets are discovered violating a rule, this should not be ignored but corrected immediately.

Problem Residents

In taking over a residential property, the management agent must sometimes deal with problem residents. Such residents normally have a total disregard for all rules and regulations. If the management company is to be effective in managing the property, it must insure that all residents abide by the rules and regulations. If a problem resident is allowed to violate the guidelines established by the management company, it will undermine the property manager's control of the property as well as disturb good residents. If the problem is not handled, these good residents will eventually leave the complex.

Initially upon takeover, it is important that the education of the resident be established from an organized management plan. In most cases, residents appreciate a complex that has specific guidelines to insure their quiet enjoyment of the property. Remember, this is their home.

COLLECTION OF RENTS

One of the basics of the industry has always been the prompt collection of outstanding rents. If residents have been allowed to drift into bad habits, in all probability the complex has a collection problem. In most cases, rents are due on the first of the month. However, a property may be taken over in which the rents are due at various times during the month. One of the initial steps should be an attempt to conform all of the rental due dates to the first of the month.

It can be determined rather quickly if the property is having a collection problem. By the sixth of the month, 95% of the rents at the property should have been collected. By the tenth of the month, 100% should be collected. If the property is not close to these percentages, action must be taken immediately. A delinquency list should be drawn up and all persons who are delinquent should be sent a notice giving a specific amount of time to bring their account current before proceeding with legal action. The amount of time will vary depending on the local laws of the property's municipality.

All delinquencies must be brought under control. This may mean proceeding with legal action and eviction against some of the non-paying tenants. Do not hesitate when considering legal action. This will also act as an example to other residents of your adherence to a strong collections procedure.

A high collection percentage produces good maintenance, better vendor relationships, less tenant turnover, more employee productivity, and an improvement in the all-important cash flow of the property.

Methods of Collection

The method for successful collection percentages is to diligently follow three principles: (1) proper leasing; (2) follow-up system; and (3) knowledge of laws (court proceedings and collection laws may vary from jurisdiction to jurisdiction).

The lease is extremely important in establishing good collection procedures. It gives specific guidelines of when the rent is due. In most leases, the rent is due on the first of the month and that is when it should be expected. Residents should also be made aware that they can pre-pay their rent, with or without discount, depending on company policy.

A suggested procedure for follow-up as to collections is detailed below:

1. Rent due on first of month.
2. On the sixth of the month, late notices must be delivered to all residents who did not pay rent by the fifth of the month.
3. On the tenth of the month, the residents must be called.
4. On the twelfth of the month, the residents who were not reached by phone must be visited.
5. On the fifteenth, a decision must be made as to whether to take legal action against the resident.

Our firm has taken the art of collecting rent one step further by establishing its own collection department. This department consists of two people whose sole job is to contact tenants and collect rent. These people are salaried employees who act in addition to the local management's collection efforts. On most properties, the manager has established a rapport with the residents. The collection department can be very hardnosed about collecting rents without jeopardizing the rapport that has been established by the management team.

Late Charges

It is important that late charges be addressed when reviewing delinquent accounts on problem properties. No management agent should strive to collect late fees as its principal aim. The management agent should attempt to collect the rental when due. It should be noted that in most cases the administrative cost of collecting late charges far outweigh the actual dollars and cents of the late charge. Additionally, the property has normal expenses which must be paid. Rentals must be collected when due in order to cover these expenses. The management agent must insure that all late charges, once posted, are collected. Late charges become an empty threat if not collected or waived month after month. It is important that late charges be mentioned in the lease. Late charges should also compound each month, so that if residents are delinquent a number of months, they are delinquent the same number of months in late fees. The management agent should not collect rent payments if the late charges have not been included in the payment. When filing with a court on a delinquent account, be sure to include late charges as well as appropriate legal fees as part of the monies due.

There are many ways to handle delinquencies on a property. Each property will vary as to the exact method that is the most successful. In some cases, a discount or bonus system to insure that payments are made when due can be used. This system is simple—all rents are increased, for example, by $20. The resident is then given a coupon book for 12 months. Each coupon allows the resident $20 off the rent if paid by the fifth of the month. The resident is then instructed to pay the lesser amount but to include the coupon when paying the rent. The effective rent of the property remains the same, and a system of reward rather than punishment has been instituted. This has been extremely successful in many complexes, but remember that what may work successfully on one property may be a total failure on another property.

Some time should be taken to address late notices in connection with the collection of rents. The late notice is a courtesy that is usually extended to a resident who has not paid rent on the due date. Some management operations allow a grace period of five days before rendering a late notice. Preferably, the late notice should be hand-delivered. In lieu of that, it may be slipped under the door or placed in the mail (certified). On occasion, it may be necessary to write a special letter to a tenant regarding payment of rent. Please bear in mind that a letter is not as effective as telephone contact or a personal visit. Having it in writing, however, provides excellent documentation for your files. The collection department concept can also be successful in providing excellent follow-up.

It has been found through experience that idle threats are unsuccessful. Never threaten anything in writing unless you intend to follow through. Use some form of communication to indicate charges that will be levied. The forms section of this handbook contains a copy of a standard late notice that is used on residential properties.

Resident Contact

The best method of contacting a resident regarding a delinquency is a personal visit. However, this is not always practical. A telephone call to a resident who has not paid his rent can also be an effective and useful tool. If the resident is contacted by phone, remember to ask why the rent is late. The answer will indicate whether this lateness will be a monthly occurrence or an isolated incident. In the phone call, refer to the part of the lease about the rent being due at a specific time. Residents are usually receptive when it is explained that the rent is due on the first day of the month as stated in the lease and that the complex would prefer to receive the rent on time rather than collect the late fees involved.

If the resident promises payment in a week, two weeks, or by the end of the month, then you should ask why the tenant is late. A specific time and day should be agreed upon for payment of the rent. At this point, a confirmation should also be made regarding the promptness of the next month's rent payment. It may be important to impress upon the residents that a legal action will be filed against them even though they have agreed to pay. The legal action should be pursued so that in case the resident backs out of the oral agreement no time has been lost in following through with litigation.

If you are not able to reach the resident by telephone or the resident does not respond to your notes, keep leaving notes and continue to call.

In addition, make sure that the person you are talking to over the telephone regarding the delinquency is the lessee and not a guest or a sub-lessee.

It is extremely important to have immediate follow-up on oral agreements with residents. If the resident has indicated that payment will be on the fifteenth of the month, a call should be placed on the sixteenth regarding the delinquency.

A basic rule to obtaining a good collection percentage is to adhere to a strict procedure and have consistent follow-up. The basic philosophy is to discover the real problem and why a specific resident is not paying rent. A course of action should be set and followed to an end result.

The image of the management company with regard to delinquencies and collections should be professional, yet firm and consistent. In most cases, residents appreciate knowing what is expected of them.

INSURING OCCUPANCY

In many cases, one of the causes of a property having fallen into a difficult period is a lack of leasing activity. One of the key elements to a successful property is an active and goal-oriented leasing campaign. A great deal of the financial problems can be handled at a residential property by improving the occupancy levels.

Market Analysis

It is necessary to know the market thoroughly prior to structuring the leasing campaign. This first requires an analysis of the property. Attempt to analyze the typical resident and define a resident profile: What type of resident is attracted to the property? Are you content with this type of resident? Review your leasing campaign and structure it toward the preferred type of resident. When analyzing the resident profile, be realistic. Do not over-shoot and attempt to attract a type of resident that is not suited to the property. For example, it is futile to seek families for a property that has a mix of studios and one-bedrooms. Families may give your complex a more secure and stable residency, but it is improper to assume that families can live in a one-bedroom unit.

Once the tenant profile is reviewed, a mix of the apartment community can be determined. At this point, it may be beneficial to sectionalize your property. This is done by selecting certain buildings or areas of the property which will be devoted to families, singles, or the elderly. There are great advantages in creating these areas. Each will become its own homogeneous community, which leads to happier, more satisfied residents and increased renewals.

Once the resident profile has been reviewed and analyzed, a review of the market is necessary. This requires a competitive market study of the surrounding area. The forms section of this handbook contains an example of a competitive market study done for a residential complex. It is important to realize that when a comparison is made of residential complexes in the area of the subject property, all specific amenities should be evaluated. It is important to know who pays utilities, which appliances are included in the apartment, what types of units the complexes have available, and any other information which you feel will be helpful in setting your rent structure.

In most cases, it is extremely helpful to chart the sizes of all units on the competitive market study and equate the monthly rental costs to a cost-per-square-foot basis. This will act as a common denominator for comparison. It will also help differentiate the large one-bedroom from the small one-bedroom apartment.

If leasing has been a problem, the rentals at the subject property should be competitive. In some instances it may even be necessary to roll back your rentals. If this approach is taken, it may be beneficial to tie this rollback to an advertising campaign. The idea of the competitive market analysis is to illustrate exactly what a prospective resident sees as to the availability of units. The goal of the analysis is to make your property more appealing on the basis of factual information.

Once the market analysis is completed, it should be reviewed in detail and compared to the subject property. The subject property's rents should be analyzed to find out where they fit within the strata of the competitive market.

Once rentals have been set on the subject property, the next important issue is the availability of unit. The vacancy list should be reviewed to learn if the vacancies are of one specific type or layout. If this is the case, specific marketing attention must be devoted to this type of unit.

In the majority of cases, when turning around a troubled property, the vacancies will be excessive at the property and the number of units available for immediate rental will be minimal. The term "ready units" refers to units which have been cleaned, painted, repaired, and are essentially ready for tenants. Ready units are the only ones that should be shown to prospects. In all probability, prospects will not rent a unit that is not clean or well-maintained. Most prospects do not have the imagination to envision what a unit will look like once it is completed.

A system should be established for the make-ready of the units that you have available. In most cases this can be done through the utilization of the on-site staff. The property staff should be scheduled to handle specific tasks on available units to insure that they are ready. A successful schedule of making units ready is as follows:

1. Trash out—remove all trash and debris from the unit.
2. Maintenance—have all maintenance completed in the unit.
3. Carpeting—either shampoo carpeting or replace where necessary.
4. Cleaning—clean the apartment.
5. Painting—paint the apartment.

The available units should be scheduled so that they are in various stages of completion. An ongoing make-ready program should be established. It is important to have units available as soon as possible. If the property has a great many available units, it may be necessary to hire outside contractors either to do the entire program or specific areas of the program. One week is a satisfactory turnaround time. Keep in mind that leasing activity will not be successful unless completed, available units are ready to be shown to prospects.

Once a number of ready units are available and a rental schedule has been set up, the condition and overall appearance of the property should be addressed.

Competitive Edge

It is important to the leasing campaign to establish a competitive edge for the property. It must be an appealing and inviting complex with units available to rent and hours of operation convenient to the prospects. The appearance of the property is what the prospect sees when driving up. If the property does not have good curb appeal—that is, if it is not clean, neat, orderly, and inviting to the prospect, in most cases the prospect will not even visit the leasing office.

Specific attention should be directed at the grounds to insure that grass has been cut, edging has been completed, and bushes have been trimmed or sculpted. The signs on the property should be uniform and professional. The property name should be clearly visible, as should the types of units available, and the telephone number and the hours of operation of the leasing information center. There should be additional signs indicating the route to the leasing center and enough of these signs to insure that the prospect will not become lost.

This is an opportunity to guide the prospect through the property. The most appealing route should be taken to the leasing center. All buildings along this route should be neat and in order. The grounds of the property should be picked a minimum of once a day. The property staff should be trained to either handle simple problems or report any problems to the management office so that corrective action may be taken.

As discussed previously, any personal property that has been left outside by residents, such as bicycles, baby carriages, barbecue grills, tables and chairs, should be picked up by the residents or cleared away by the management staff. The curb appeal of a property is extremely important in a successful leasing campaign.

Another area of concern is ample coverage in your leasing information center and hours of operation. This will vary in different parts of the country. In some areas of the Midwest and Northeast, very little leasing activity is done on Sunday. In areas of the South, Saturdays and Sundays are the main leasing days. On the West Coast, daily evening hours are usually very desirable for leasing. It all depends upon the specific area of the country. It is important to remember that when a leasing campaign is undertaken, every lease is important. If you are unsure about establishing additional hours, use a trial method. Whenever establishing new hours, test the market for a weekend or two, gauge the traffic flow, and adjust accordingly. For example, if the property in question has never had weekend hours, the hours from 10:00 A.M. to 3:00 P.M. on Saturday and from 12:00 noon to 5:00 P.M. on Sunday might be established on a trial basis. These hours can be adjusted according to the response. If one new lease is generated from the additional hours, those hours were worth-while.

In addition to generating new leases, it is important to realize the value of the residents already at the property. Each renewal generated of an existing resident, in essence, creates a new lease. It also saves the property the cost of make-ready for that unit, should it be put back on the market. This cost will vary depending upon area, use of in-house personnel or outside contractors, and type of unit. A program should be established to follow up on renewals. Residents should be contacted about 60 days prior to the expiration of their lease to encourage them to renew. A preferential rate schedule may be established for renewing residents (perhaps the market rate reduced by $5 per month for the renewal). This serves a dual purpose. It encourages the existing resident to renew by offering some preference over outside prospects while allowing the management company to test the outside market. If the market rate is accepted by the public, it can eventually be passed along to renewal residents with a higher market rate established later. The value of renewals to a troubled property cannot be overestimated.

Leasing Strategies

It is important, when establishing a leasing campaign, to review existing advertising and leasing strategies at the property. In advertising the available units, it is extremely important that the property at least have exposure with a minimal advertisement in the classified section of the newspaper. Display advertisements, from a leasing standpoint, can be costly and have questionable value. A management team may wish to test a display advertisement by reviewing its effectiveness with the prospects who visit the property.

When developing leasing strategies, attempt to develop new and unusual ideas. Property promotions such as on-site radio broadcasts, cocktail parties, pool parties, and other different ideas to generate interest in the property may work in a specific locale. Additionally, a resident referral system can usually gain additional leases. In most cases, the resident is given either a $50 referral fee, credit on their rent, or a small house plant. When residents are proud of their community and enjoy their property, the referral system is successful.

Rental concessions are also an excellent draw to prospects. Concessions should never lower the minimal competitive market rate the property should obtain. The rental concession can take many forms—it can be a direct concession to the rent, a decorating allowance, a moving allowance, or it can take any other form. Promotions involving small appliances such as televisions or stereos can be successful depending on the area. However, when a promotion of this type arises the control of the gift items can become a problem for management. This type of promotion should be done very cautiously.

PUBLIC RELATIONS AND PROMOTION

The image of the property is extremely important to a successful turnaround. In some cases, the property manager will want to change the image. Some changes will be evident through the establishment or modification of the rules and regulations, along with the obvious cleanup of the property.

In many instances, however, the property reputation is part of the property name. In these cases, the property must undergo a name change. In order to effectively change the name of the property, additional promotion must be utilized. A public relations firm may be necessary. In most instances, however, this is too costly for the apartment complex. The management team must often come up with innovative ideas in order to establish a new name for the property. Advertising in periodicals is one way to establish the new name. Billboards, bus advertising, bus benches, and radio spots are other effectively utilized alternatives. The promotion of the property should be geared toward the type of resident being sought. Troubled properties can be turned around by attracting a totally new type of resident. For example, a garden complex with transient residents, dangerous property, and drug-trafficking on the property grounds was cleared out and marketed as a complex for the elderly. Through successful promotions via community groups and religious organizations, the turnaround was extremely successful a very violent property became a well-maintained, well-managed complex for adults.

The image and reputation of the property is extremely important in the success of a leasing campaign. The proper public relations and promotion allows the property to attract the sought-after type of resident.

COMMERCIAL PROPERTY

Many of the primary functions in turning around a troubled property that were discussed in relation to residential investments also apply to commercial real estate. However, there are peculiarities to commercial properties that must be discussed.

The primary concern of a commercial tenant is doing business. This concern is equally evident at shopping centers, office buildings, and warehouses. In a shopping center, the retail customer is the most important element. If a tenant is not doing business, then the rental income of this center will eventually be affected. It is important that the management agent attempt to lease the shopping center to the appropriate tenant mix. Consideration should be given to tenants that are a definite draw of customers and those that do extensive advertising.

A distinction should be made in the initial review as to whether the shopping center has established itself as a retail center or a service center. A retail center will attract customers who are primarily going to shop, look, and buy. A service center is a center that a customer will go to for convenience and to acquire various services. An example of some types of tenants that may be found in a service center are a dry cleaners, hair stylists, meat market, library, camera shop, and health club. Although these tenants may be found in a retail center, there will be a greater number of this type in a service center. A customer profile should be prepared to help determine the type of center being reviewed and the best tenants that can be selected. This profile should include the type of shopper that shops at the center and what they shop for.

In some cases, it may be advisable to create a theme center. This is done not only with cosmetic improvement to denote such a theme, but also through merchant selection. An example of a merchant selection theme would be a discount shopping center or a fashion mart. It is important to establish a tenant mix that will attract customers. The greatest concern of a retailer in a shopping center is doing business.

An office building tenant also has the primary goal of doing business. However, the tenant does not usually seek to attract retail customers. In the great number of cases, the convenience and accessibility of the office building will play a major role. The majority of office building tenants desire space where their clients and customers can reach them with a minimum of inconvenience. In turning a troubled office building, the entire building must be analyzed for the prototype tenant. If the building is in a suburban location, ample convenient parking can be an important feature.

A selection of the type of tenant will be determined by an analysis of what will be the ideal tenant for the building. For example, a centrally located downtown office building convenient to municipal courts and city hall will attract attorneys and legal-related service entities. A suburban office building may lend itself to insurance companies. An office building across from a hospital will be attractive to medical and health-related offices.

The market area of the subject property must be analyzed in depth. The competition plays an important role in the success of a commercial property. The rental per square foot as well as estimated sales volumes are extremely important. The overall trend of the area should also be reviewed.

As in residential investment properties, curb appeal is an extremely important item. The property must attract customers as well as prospective tenants. Attention should not only be given to the regular maintenance items but also the specific items particular to the subject property. These special items will vary as to each property. Certain items that should always be reviewed are lighting, traffic flow, overall access, and condition of drives and parking lots.

A commercial property should always be reviewed as to additional, revenue-producing areas. In a shopping center, this may be out-parcels, a selection in the parking lot that will lend itself to development, or additional kiosks in a mall. In an office building, it may be the marketing of office space as storage.

The property manager, should attempt to maximize the income of the property.

It is important that the subject property be analyzed in depth to determine the character of the property and possible areas of improvement. A management plan should be structured that would not only include a physical review but leasing and marketing. Once the plan is structured it should be continually reevaluated. It is important that the plan be flexible enough to allow for change in order to maximize the improvements which can be obtained.

SUMMARY

The management agent can accomplish a successful turnaround of troubled properties by zeroing in on the specific deficiencies of the property. In many instances, this will require the review of the four primary functions: educating the tenant, collecting the rent, insuring occupancy, and public relations and promotion. In most cases, the owners' goals and objectives can be met through the establishment of positive operating policies, specific guidelines, and rules and regulations for the occupants of the property. Above all else, a management team should be professional, consistent, firm and fair.

PATRICK F. CARTON
Executive Vice President
Corroon & Black Co. of N.Y., Inc.
New York, New York

Patrick F. Carton is an Executive Vice President for Corroon & Black Company of New York, Inc. Mr. Carton has responsibility for Risk Management Services, New Account Production, Marketing, and Employee Benefits operations. During the past 25 years he has had extensive experience in client services including insurance program design and loss control for large national and international industrial corporations. A graduate of Iona College, New Rochelle, New York, with a degree in Business Administration, he obtained additional formal education at the College of Insurance and the Factory Mutual Training Center for Loss Control Management Association. He was a panel member for the American Paper Institute's seminar on property insurance. In addition, he has made presentations to chapter meetings of the Risk and Insurance Management Society, the Corporate Practice Institute of Wisconsin Bar Association, the American Management Association and is a co-author of The Business Insurance Handbook.

CHAPTER 10

EFFICIENT INSURANCE PROGRAMMING

RISK IDENTIFICATION AND CONTROL MECHANISMS

There is a universal feeling that the insurance mechanism is inefficient and the cost of insurance is expensive in relation to the value received. This feeling is particularly true for those companies which have had good loss experience.

Real estate management is a highly competitive business. Control of expenses is essential to successful management. Efficient insurance programs can accomplish the dual objectives of a properly designed insurance and benefits program that will protect the assets of the company and, at the same time, be cost efficient.

In developing the real estate management organizational structure, it is important to recognize that a member of the management team should be given the responsibility of identifying the various exposures to loss and given the authority to take those steps necessary in dealing most efficiently with the specific risk. The risk of loss is inherent in the ownership, maintenance, and use of all property; including real property, personal property, property under one's custody and control, improvements and betterments, and fixtures and supplies. In addition, there is concern about loss of income such as rents. Losses for which we are responsible, whether such responsibility is imposed upon us by contract, statue, or through adjudication of legal liability, must also be dealt with.

Risk identification requires a first hand knowledge of the properties involved, the management philosophy of the organization, and the operating personnel who can control the working environment and have daily contact with tenants, employees, and the public at large.

Once the risk has been identified, risk control mechanisms, including risk avoidance, loss control, and separation can then be brought into play. Risk avoidance, in its simplest terms, is removing the exposure to loss. An example of risk avoidance is the conscious decision either not to purchase a specific property or to sell the property since the risk of loss is greater than the economic gain. Risk reduction introduces the element of loss control and engineering and it is directed to those identified areas of real or potential loss. Utilization of the loss control facilities of an insurance carrier, an insurance broker or independent provider can have a material effect in reducing the frequency and/or severity of property losses and injury to employees and third parties. Separation simply means "not keeping all our eggs in one basket." A geographical spread of properties as opposed to concentration reduces the exposure to loss.

The transfer of risk is the last mechanism that may be used. For example, through the terms of a lease, the risk in whole or in part, can be transferred to the tenant.

Upon completion of the analysis of the exposure to loss and after the risk control techniques are applied, the business must determine which is the most cost-effective way to finance the losses that will occur. One option is to retain the losses within the business. The losses may be funded out of current operational income, paid for through reserves established for that purpose or financed through an established line of credit.

THE INSURANCE POLICY

The final option is the purchase of insurance, which transfers the risk. For many, the insurance policy loss financing technique is the most cost efficient. In arranging for an appropriate insurance policy, it is usually necessary to utilize the services of an insurance broker or agent. Technically, a broker represents the insured and an agent represents the insurance company. However, both can arrange for insurance and both have an obligation to perform to a high standard of professional conduct. In selecting an agent or broker both for new and in-place projects, consideration must be given to his or her ability to provide services and other facilities required by the insured, such as:

1. Placement, negotiation and review of all insurance contracts.
2. Assignment of a construction specialist to the development site for surveillance of Loss Control practices—and to assist the Owner's employee responsible for safety.
3. Verification of workers' compensation classifications and payrolls.
4. Preparation of an Insurance Guide, describing the insurance program.
5. Preparation of the forms necessary for reporting the data that must be acquired.
6. Supervision of all claims handling and establishment of procedures for prompt reporting.
7. Regular review of all claims, paid and pending, to determine their effect on premium costs, possible third party action, etc.
8. Collaboration with all parties involved with Loss Control, regarding services rendered and investigation of reported accidents involving personal injury and property damage.
9. Verification of all premium statements presented by the carrier to confirm accuracy of classifications assigned to specific operations, codes, rates and premiums.
10. Review of any retrospective rate adjustments for correct mathematics and for verification of individual claims that are the basis for any adjustment.
11. Review and verify loss experience reports from the insurance carrier(s), including analysis of major claims, confirmation of estimates of future payments-to-date, payments, and possible third party action.
12. Represent the owner in negotiating terms of final premium settlement based upon the actual loss experience.

THE OWNER-CONTROLLED INSURANCE PROGRAM FOR PROPERTY BEING BUILT

Rebuilding the cities of this country has presented new opportunities in the insurance management of the new properties being built.

It is possible to both develop substantial savings and improve the investment opportunity of a project from the very inception of construction. This involves bringing in the eventual owners and managers of the property at the inception of the project in an approach which is known as the "owner-controlled insurance program." The program encompasses four basic areas and includes risk management and cash flow considerations.

Casualty Insurance

Workers' compensation, employer's liability, and comprehensive general liability protection covering the project exposures is provided for owners, contractors, and subcontractors under the owner-controlled insurance program.

The primary insurance program is written with broad terms and conditions. The cost is developed under a "paid loss" retrospective rating plan. Minimum limits of $1 million combined per occurrence, for each named insured and $5 million per occurrence aggregate limit for all occurrences during the policy year should be provided. Excess coverage, in the form of a broad umbrella liability policy, would provide total insurance limits of $25 million to $100 million. The amount of insurance provided should be based upon proceived need and cost constraints.

Builders Risk Insurance

Builders risk insurance would consist of a manuscripted form covering "all risk" of physical loss or damage with limits adequate for exposures to loss on the job site, offsite, in storage, and in transit. Protection against design error may be included as part of the program of protection. The deductibles can be tailored to the size and exposure represented by the project. The program can be extended to include contractual exposures, direct and/or contingent coverage for business interruption, extra expense, and loss of rental income resulting from a time delay caused by an insured occurrence.

Safety and Claims Control

A program of safety and claims control can be implemented more effectively when it is provided by a single source. A strong loss prevention program can reduce the frequency and severity of losses. In addition, by consolidating claims handling, there is improved efficiency and reduced cost in handling claims. Under a conventional approach, claims handling procedures are beyond the control of the owner since multiple insurance carriers and other responsible parties may be involved in a single loss. This results in disputes as to who is responsible and the extent of such responsibility.

With a single source owner controlled program the owner has a direct voice in the payment of claims. The workers' compensation and general liability loss payments can be reduced with an aggressive approach to claims payment.

Subcontractors, who otherwise might qualify, are often unable to provide the insurance coverages required by the general contractor and/or the owner. The owner-controlled insurance program eliminates this problem with respect to the quality and limits of insurance coverages available to the subcontractor and contractor bidders.

Finally, with a single source providing improved loss control and claims handling, there are fewer disputes. The result is increased productivity by on-site personnel assigned to the project. They would monitor the contractors compliance with all procedures and obligations. The owners and managers receive regular reports on safety and claim payments control as mandated in the specifications.

Cost Reduction

The benefit of such a program is reduced insurance cost. Normally, the insurance charges in contractors' bids are subject to mark-up. The mark-up range is 5 to 15%. The use of an owner-controlled insurance program eliminates this extra charge. In addition, the insurance charges included in the contractor bid are based upon expected losses rather than actual losses. If loss experience is better than expected, the contractor will, for a specific job, receive a return premium or dividend from the insurance carrier. Under the owner-controlled insurance program, savings resulting from improved loss experience will go directly to the owner-manager. In addition, duplication of coverage and premium by the various parties is eliminated.

The owner-controlled insurance program cost is loss sensitive. The insured would have the cash flow advantage of spreading the loss cost portion of the program over an extended period of time coinciding with the payout of claims. In other words, the program can be structured so that the premium payments would be limited to the insurance carrier's charges for administrative services, excess insurance coverage, engineering service, and paid losses. The insured retains use of the funds associated with the unpaid losses and claim adjusting until payment is actually made. Generally, the premiums paid in the first year would be approximately one-third of the total "standard" premium.

When insurance charges are included in the contractor's bids, they become part of the construction project's cost and are capitalized. The tax deductibility of these insurance costs are realized as the project is depreciated; 10 to 30 years. The owner-controlled insurance program accelerates the expensing of insurance costs and provides additional cash flow benefits to insured.

A strong and consistent safety and loss prevention program has the effect of reducing the frequency and severity of compensation and general liability losses, thereby reducing the owner-controlled insurance program costs. By having a single source provide the loss prevention, there is no disagreement as to who is responsible for providing a safe place to work and the methods by which the responsibility will be enforced.

The owner-controlled insurance program also provides broader and more uniform insurance protection because the program is generally written on a manuscript form to provide the broadest insurance coverages. This coverage is customized for the project's exposure. Under the conventional approach each contractor and sub-contractor provides a certificate of insurance indicating the coverage afforded. Usually, there are insurance and risk management for operating properties.

INSURANCE AND RISK MANAGEMENT FOR OPERATING PROPERTIES

The foregoing portions of this chapter have developed the establishment of a risk management program, including a cost efficient method of covering the interests of the owner, contractor, subcontractors and other parties during construction. The following reviews the development of a program of insurance and risk management for operating properties. It includes:

1. Property insurance.
2. Comprehensive general liability.
3. Comprehensive automobile liability and physical damage.
4. Workers compensation and employers liability.
5. Crime coverage.
6. Umbrella liability.

The following is a summary of the elements of a program that should be considered in tailoring a program of insurance protection to suit individual company needs.

The Data Base

Accurate information is the foundation of a well-designed efficient program. As a guide, it is generally considered wise to maintain a data base of information covering the current year and the four years immediately preceding. This information should include the following:

1. Schedule of locations.
2. Payrolls segregated by state, and classification code.
3. Numerical employee count.
4. Property values by location divided into the following categories:
   real property;
   improvements and betterments;
   machinery and equipment;
   stock and supplies; and
   revenue (rents).
5. Claim information segregated by
   Type of policy; e.g. fire, boiler and machinery; workers compensation, general liability, automobile liability, and automobile physical damage;
   Date of loss;
   Amount of loss, amount paid, and amount reserved;
   Details of losses over $25,000;
   Amount of deductible, if any.

6. Resume of each insurance policy.
7. Schedule of vehicles by type of vehicle and garaging location.

Property Insurance

The conventional way to insure property is through a named peril contract which specifies the peril that must cause the loss, e.g., fire, before the policy will indemnify for such loss. Today the "all risk" approach has found good acceptance with both the insurance companies and insureds. The all risk property insurance approach should incorporate the following elements:

Property Insured: All real and personal property owned by the insured; also, property under their care, custody or control, including property of others for which the insured may be held liable.

Perils Insured: All risk of physical loss or damage including water damage, flood and earthquake.

Protection Provided Should Include:

1. Replacement cost—Eliminates the factor of depreciation in the settlement of a loss.
2. No coinsurance—The standard provision in most "fire" insurance policies which imposes a penalty on the insured in the event of a partial loss if the values insured do not represent a predetermined percentage of value of the property. This potential penalty can and should be eliminated.
3. Debris removal—Pays the specific cost of debris removal of insured property damaged by an insured peril.
4. Increased cost of construction—Normally, the insurance company is responsible for the repair or replacement of damaged property of a similar nature. However, if a local law or ordinance will not permit such reconstruction this clause will reimburse for the additional cost incurred solely related to compliance with a specific law or ordinance.
5. Notice of cancellation—The standard cancellation clause should be amended to a minimum of 60 days advance notice if the insurance company intends to cancel the contract before expiration.
6. Deductible—A single combined deductible should be incorporated in the contract to eliminate the work involved in small nuisance claims and gain premium credit. The deductible level selected would be based upon several factors including the amount of premium credit, the frequency of losses anticipated and the ability of the insured to absorb loss.
7. Loss of revenue—The principle source of revenue in real estate is rental income. The contract should include business interruption cov-

erage to reimburse for loss of rental income caused by an insured peril. If the lease agreements contain stipulations which permit the lease holder to terminate the lease and move from the premises this may require a negotiated extension of the insurance contract to adequately protect the landlord.

8. Newly acquired property—Covered automatically subject to notice to underwriters on an agreed basis, e.g., annually, when all values of property insured is reviewed and the premium is adjusted pro rata for the remaining term of the policy to reflect increases and/or decreases in insurable values.

9. Valuable papers and records coverage—Designed to pay for cost to reconstruct, if necessary, rather than the conventional approach which is based upon the cost to reproduce (copy).

10. Policy limits—A single combined limit representing the combined total of all the property insured, including the indirect coverages such as Business interruption, is available from some insurance companies. An acceptable alternative might be a single combined limit representing the total values exposed to one loss, e.g., a hurricane in the Gulf Coast area in which event the total values insured in the Gulf Coast would be used as the blanket policy limit.

Boiler and Machinery Insurance

An adjunct to property insurance is insurance on boilers, pressure vessels, air conditioning or refrigeration systems, and mechanical and electrical equipment that compensates the owner or operator for damages which results from an accident (breakdown) of such equipment.

Steam boilers and other equipment operating under pressure has the inherent capacity to explode, causing substantial loss. In addition, mechanical and electrical equipment, such as steam turbines, compressors, electric motors, transformers, and electric switch gear sometimes break down.

The recommended approach is to insure all such equipment on a blanket basis in a combined fire-boiler policy. If this is not feasible, a separate boiler and machinery policy with a joint loss agreement signed by both the fire and boiler and machinery underwriters is an option to be considered. The joint loss agreement is designed to speed payment to the insured when there is controversy between underwriters over which policy is liable for a particular claim. The combined fire-boiler policy provides the fire policy limits for boiler and machinery losses and eliminates the need to select limits. If a separate boiler and machinery contract is purchased it is recommended that a single combined limit be secured that equals or exceeds a loss represented by the object which could cause the greatest loss, e.g., the steam boiler.

Workers Compensation and Employers Liability

Insurance for job-related injuries to employees is provided by workers compensation insurance. Coverage A pays employees for benefits as required by state law for injuries suffered in the course of employment. In addition, under policy Coverage B Employers Liability, an insured is indemnified for all sums that he may be legally obligated to pay as damages due to bodily injury claims of employees not covered under policy Coverage A.

Extentions of coverage which should be considered are:

1. United States Longshoremen and Harbor Workers Act Endorsements which extend coverage to include employees and benefits payable under this Federal Act.
2. Broad Form All States Endorsement which extends the policy to include all states which recognize policies issued by commercial insurances companies (excludes so called monopolistic states which do not permit commercial insurance).
3. Voluntary Compensation Endorsement which extends coverage to all employees who are not covered by workmans compensation statutes but for whom the insured has agreed to provide coverage. This extension usually includes employer sponsored sports and recreational activities.
4. The Stop Gap Coverage Endorsement which extends employers liability coverage in monopolistic states, Canada and Puerto Rico.

Comprehensive General Liability Insurance

This coverage pays on behalf of the insured, up to the limits of the policy, sums which the insured is legally liable to pay to third parties as damages resulting from bodily injury or property damage.

Limits of liability should include at least $1 million combined single limit each occurrence as well as the annual aggregate that would be paid for all claims under the policy.

Coverage including extensions should include the following:

1. Contractual liability extending protection for liabilities assumed under contract.
2. Personal injury liability covering claims arising out of false arrest, libel or slander and similar offenses.
3. Premises medical payments which pays for medical costs for persons who are injured on the premises of the insured.
4. Host liquor law liability which insures against liability arising out of the giving or serving of alcoholic beverages at functions incidental to the insured's business.

5. Fire legal liability which affords protection for property damage to structures rented by the insured if the damage arises out of fire and is a result of the insured's negligence.

6. Incidental medical malpractice which provides protection for injuries arising out of the rendering or the failure to render medical, surgical, dental, x-ray or nursing services or treatment, including the furnishing or dispensing of drugs or medical supplies.

7. Assault and battery clause which extends coverage for intentional acts committed to protect persons or property.

8. Non-owned and hired automobile Coverage which includes protection for the use by any person, other than the insured, of a non-owned private passenger automobile in the business of the insured; also, the occasional use by an employee of a non-owned automobile in the insured's business.

Comprehensive Automobile Liability Insurance

Comprehensive automobile liability coverage pays for the legal liability of the insured resulting from bodily injury or property damage caused by an accident resulting from the ownership, maintenance, or use of automobiles. The policy may also include coverage for medical payments and automobile physical damage (collision and comprehensive fire and theft).

A typical program should include the limits of liability of at least $1 million for each occurrence and also the annual aggregate that would be paid for all claims under the liability section of the policy.

Coverage including extensions should include the following:

1. Hired and non-owned automobiles included under the definition of insured automobile. Personal injury protection and medical payments coverage should be included for these vehicles.

2. Drive other car coverage protects employees and family members who use company-owned or leased vehicles while they are using other vehicles which are not owned or leased.

3. Trailers should be included for coverage.

4. Temporary substitute vehicles coverage should be provided for employees who use a temporary substitute vehicle in place of a regularly assigned vehicle even if the vehicle is owned by the employee.

5. Vehicles hired by employees coverage is provided for employees who hire vehicles in the course of the insureds business.

6. Uninsured motorists insurance provides coverage for sums which the insured is entitled to recover as damages from the owner or operator of an uninsured vehicle.

7. Personal injury protection provides "no-fault" coverage in accordance with various statutory requirements.

Umbrella Liability Insurance

Umbrella liability insurance is designed to provide excess insurance (higher limits) in amounts of from $1 to $50 million or more over the insureds traditional liability insurance policies such as, general liability, automobile liability, and workers compensation. This insurance will provide liability coverage for situations that are not covered by these traditional policies such as, for example, advertisers liability and non-owned aircraft exposures. The usual deductible for this clause is $25,000.

Crime Insurance

A comprehensive blanket crime policy should provide the following protection:

1. Employee dishonesty coverage—This covers the loss of money and securities and other property through fraudulent or dishonest acts of employees.
2. Loss inside the premises—Covers loss of money and securities by destruction, disappearance or wrongful abstraction on the premises or on banking premises.
3. Loss outside the premises—Covers loss of money or securities by destruction, disappearance or wrongful abstraction while outside the premises and/or being conveyed by a messenger or armored vehicle company.
4. Depositors forgery—Covers loss from forged or altered checks, drafts and similar instruments. Amendments to the standard crime policy should include an extension which extend the definition of employees to include directors and trustees in handling funds or property of any employee welfare or pension benefit plan of the insured or trustee, officer or employee of the plan itself.

SUMMARY

The objective of this chapter has been to highlight the important and necessary forms of insurance protection and to comment on extensions of coverage that have specific application to real estate management.

As in any other area of business, size gives leverage and leverage provides options and alternative methods of structuring insurance programs and saving premium dollars. Attention to loss control principles can reduce losses over time and make the risk more attractive to underwriters. Size of risk and loss experience will dictate whether the insured should buy his insurance on a guaranteed cost plan (fixed cost) or on some retrospective rating plan where there is some potential to benefit from return premiums resulting from favorable experience.

HARLEY J. MULLINS
Executive Vice President
UIDC Management, Inc.
Chicago, Illinois

Harley J. Mullins, Executive Vice President, UIDC Management, Inc. and General Manager of the Urban Engineering division, has been involved with physical plant operations and property management for 28 years and energy management programs for 15 years. Mr. Mullins is an author of numerous articles on energy management and HVAC system operations and maintenance.

CHAPTER 11

REDUCING AND MAINTAINING ENERGY CONSUMPTION

INTRODUCTION

Today's building managers and owners are confronted with the problem of controlling ever-increasing costs of operating buildings. The major component of this escalation of costs is energy. Energy has increased in cost over 100% during the last 10 years making it imperative that efforts be made to reduce energy consumption within our buildings. This percentage of increase has far outweighed all other building operating costs. The prospects for the future show a 12½ to 15% per year increase in energy costs during the next decade.

The high cost of operation is affecting the marketability of office space throughout the country. Prospective tenants are also becoming sophisticated in their view of how building management controls the cost of operation—which they ultimately pay. When lease renewal time comes, existing tenants may very well look for space elsewhere if operating costs are high in their existing buildings. If a building gains a reputation for being a high cost building, new prospective tenants may not view that building as a viable alternative.

Trying to control energy, especially with the demands of tenants, is a problem in both new and existing buildings. In older buildings, the cost of modification cannot be passed on to the tenants under their present lease constraints. In new construction, energy conservation is a major concern of the developer and is taken into consideration in the building's design. A major constraint in new structures is the first cost connected with a more sophisticated energy management system. A balance of first cost and operating revenues must be achieved as an optimum.

As an example of the problems associated with existing structures, consider a change requiring a relatively small outlay in capital costs that will be recoverable within a one- to two-year period. It is easy to justify the expense on the marketability aspects of the building alone. Whether the costs can be passed on to the tenant in the form of escalated rent is another issue. Where retrofit modifications of the heating, ventilating, and air conditioning (HVAC) and/or electrical system are contemplated with paybacks of longer than two years, justification for this expense to the owner without recovery from the tenants is highly questionable. It is possible to approach the tenants on lease modification to pass on all or part of the costs for these major retrofit items. This will require a great deal of time and effort on the part of the building's management team, and the success of such a program is questionable.

Another approach may be to make lease modifications on all new leases so that additional future capital expenditures will be borne by the tenants who receive the benefits of these major retrofit items.

In new buildings, evaluation of various energy conservation approaches to the HVAC and electrical distribution system should be made by computer analysis using programs that are available to the consultant engineers. These evaluations will give the owning costs of various alternate skin, glass, HVAC, and electrical systems for the structure. One example of this analysis would bring out the lower operating costs achieved when utilizing a variable air volume system for the heating and cooling of the building. If this is taken a step further, to show the analysis of the use of demand control with a variable air volume system, it will be seen that the demand control becomes non-cost effective due to the effect on this more sophisticated modern system. A complete evaluation of all possible materials and systems can be made quickly through the use of this computer analysis.

A word of caution: When evaluating the results of these analysis programs, be sure that the data input by the engineers and architects associated with the building is accurate and precise. A mistake can be costly. For example, if the engineer used a lower-than-actual cost for electrical energy, electric heat may be chosen over gas, hot water, or municipal steam system heat. If the building owner is unaware that a low figure was used, and chose electric heat on the basis of the engineer's figures, the actual high cost of electrical power in operation will be a shock.

An essential part of a good energy management program is a comprehensive preventive maintenance and training program to upgrade the operating personnel to meet the technical needs of the sophisticated equipment and systems.

Without a good preventive maintenance program and training program, the staff's ability to maintain the high efficiency levels achieved during the initial phases of a good energy management program will be stymied. There are no short-cuts to this comprehensive program. To optimize the results, a great deal of effort must be put into both the development and maintenance of the management program.

This chapter will outline an energy management program for existing buildings that managers can institute to initially bring their energy consumption down and to maintain the levels of energy consumption over the life of the building. The latter part of this chapter will be devoted to the development and establishment of a comprehensive preventive maintenance program that will, if strictly adhered to, maximize the efficiency of operation of the mechanical-electrical systems within the building.

THE ENERGY MANAGEMENT PROGRAM

Many building owners and managers have asked this question: "Why do we need energy management and energy control when the tenants pay all pass-through costs and the owner only has the cost of installation of these systems with no return or benefit to them?" Maintaining and reducing operating expenses is viewed by the tenant as an owner-management responsibility under their lease commitments. Today's more sophisticated tenants are taking a dim view of building owners and managers who do not put every effort toward controlling the rising cost of energy. In today's competitive leasing market, which will continue during the remainder of the 1980s and 1990s, it is imperative that owners and managers understand the tenants strong need to control the costs of building operation.

In new buildings coming on-stream, major tenants leasing multiple floors are requiring cost containment constraints be included in the lease to make it mandatory for the managers to control energy consumption and other operating costs. Market pressures are dictating that the management team carefully review the installed systems with a view toward operating them at the most efficient levels. Sophisticated management is required more than ever before in the history of building operations.

The first step in this program is the establishment of an energy management team consisting of the building's chief engineer, an engineering consultant hired by the manager or owner, and a mechanical and electrical contractor who would assist in the implementation and the building manager. The first meeting of this group should establish each individual's role, how they will contribute to the team effort, and outline the program that will be used to reduce energy consumption within the structure. A timetable should also be established for completion of each phase within the program. Everyone should be aware of their time commitments to this effort.

The selection of the consultant engineer for this energy management team should be a careful, structured process. Criteria for selection should be established by the manager and include the following:

1.   A listing of the energy audits which the firm has engaged in.
2.   A resume on the principals of the firm, and particularly those people who will be working on the energy management team.
3.   Examples of one or two energy audits that the firm has produced in the past.
4.   After the firm has reviewed the specifications outlined by the management team, they should give an estimate of the time that it will take to perform the consulting work necessary.
5.   A time plus expense type contract should be shied away from unless it has a maximum price that will not be exceeded. It is recommended that a fixed sum cost is more appropriate for this type of work to protect the building from excess cost involved in this consulting work.

Large engineering firms, although well-equipped with talented people, should be closely scrutinized if their proposal is chosen. There must be assurances that the personnel committed to in the proposal remain on the energy management team until the job is completed. Many small energy management jobs are used for fillers by large engineering firms and the key personnel will be pulled off when another large design job is ready for production.

The energy management team within a building must first understand the energy consumers within their building. We are all aware that the cost of various utilities are increasing monthly, but the problem is finding out where this energy is actually being consumed. In any building operation, the major consumers of energy are lighting, the HVAC system, the elevator, and, finally, miscellaneous uses. The order and magnitude of their consumption as a percentage of the total bill is:

Lighting and receptacles   40–65%
HVAC   30–45%
Tenant Special Use   0–30%
Miscellaneous   05–15%

TABLE 11.1

Power Consumption by Function.

System	KWH Consumed	Percent of Total Use
Lighting	3,352,800	42.7
HVAC	2,248,800	28.6
General power	1,064,800	13.5
Computer	771,800	9.8
Food service	129,500	1.6
Miscellaneous	278,800	3.5
Total	7,846,500	100%

TABLE 11.2

Electrical Energy Use Breakdown by Building.

Building and Load Type	Demand Load KW	KWH Usage Annual	Percent of Building
Investment Building			
Lighting	525	2,362,500	40.0
General power[a]	400	1,105,270	18.8
HVAC[b]	1010	1,523,000	25.9
Restaurant[c]	33	129,500	2.2
Computer Room[c]	90	771,800	13.1
HQ Bldg.			
Lighting	125	562,500	40.5
General power[a]	84	238,330	17.2
HVAC[b]	361	586,600	42.3
Garage			
Lighting	105	427,800	75.4
HVAC	24	139,200	24.6
Facility total		7,846,500	

[a]General power included office equipment, elevators, escalators, and outlet receptacles.
[b]HVAC equipment includes air handling units, heating pumps, and refrigeration equipment.
[c]Separately metered items.

Other consuming devices, such as computers and office equipment, are not considered as consumptions controllable by the manager. These systems are installed and operated by the tenant, and the tenants bear the cost directly for these systems. Management can, however, lend assistance to the tenant in reducing their operating costs through energy conservation efforts which are instituted by the tenant.

The electrical energy consumed by these tenant systems may not be the only effect on the building. Consideration must be given to the heat generated by these tenant systems and how they affect the HVAC system in the building. The tenant using the system must bear the cost of the additional load imposed on the HVAC system. Additional allocation of cost is justified in many of these cases.

Now that the energy users have been found out, controls on their consumption of energy must also be established. In this discussion, the term "energy consumption" includes all forms of energy entering the building, including, but not limited to, electrical power, gas consumption, oil consumption, coal consumption, municipal steam systems, and municipal or central cooling systems. Solar heating systems and so-called free cooling systems either through strainer cycle or double-bundle condensers in the chillers are, in most cases, a net deduction in energy costs. An understanding of the sources of energy that are used within the subject building is imperative to the program outlined in this chapter.

OPERATING HOURS

With all of these systems, the hours of operation are a major contributing factor to their energy consumption. System start-up and shut-down schedules are

TABLE 11.3

Electrical Energy Cost Analysis.

		1977 Rate: $0.03127/KWH		1978 Rate: $0.035/KWH	
	System	KWH Used	1977 Cost ($)	Estimated 1978 Cost ($)	Percent of Total Cost
1.	Lighting	19,515,100	$ 611,347	$ 683,029	33.9
2.	HVAC[a]	12,821,900	401,669	448,767	22.3
3.	General power	2,317,300	72,593	81,106	4.0
4.	Computer[b]	18,170,500	569,224	635,968	31.6
5.	Food service	1,063,900	33,328	37,237	1.8
6.	Miscellaneous	3,666,300	114,853	128,321	6.4
Total		57,555,000	$1,803,014	$2,014,428	100.0

[a]Excluding computer areas.
[b]Includes HVAC for computer areas.

critically important to the control of energy consumption. Additional hours of operation over and above the normal requirement for these systems can easily add 20% to 30% on to the property's energy consumption. When a tenant requests excess hours of operation within the building, the minimum amount of equipment should be turned on and elevator usage should be controlled. The tenant should pay for these directly as a total recovery of costs (see Figure 11.1).

LIGHTING CONTROL

The largest consumer of energy in today's buildings is the lighting system. There are a variety of different approaches to the reduction and control of lighting usage. Some of the devices and systems on the market lend themselves more to retrofit than to new installation. They are cost effective and easily installed within existing buildings. Some of these systems are:

1. Reduced wattage fluorescent lamps which can be retrofitted into any building's fluorescent lighting system.

2. Total floor-by-floor or zone-by-zone lighting control that can take advantage of the amount of natural light in many offices on the exterior of the building and also control the janitorial cleaning lighting usage.

3. Retrofit type fixture lenses are also available that will increase the effective light and are generally used with reduced wattage lamps.

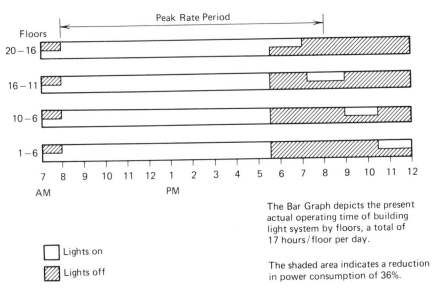

Figure 11.1 Proposed lighting operation hours schedule.

TABLE 11.4

Lighting Reduction Comparison Summary.

No.	System Description	Initial Cost	Watts—Two Lamps—and Ballast	Relative Light Output (%)	Annual Energy Cost Savings ($)	Time to Recover Initial Cost	Remarks
1.	Std. 75W lamps on standard ballast (base system)	$ 0	175	100	0	0	
2.	Energy savers 60W warm white lamps with standard ballast	1,875	140	88.9	92,810	0.24 month	Replace lamps during relamping
3.	Energy savers 60W light white lamps with standard ballast	5,935	140	95.2	92,810	0.77 month	Replace lamps during relamping
4.	Energy savers 60W warm white lamps with energy saving ballast	368,160	135	97.5	106,070	3.47 years	
5.	Energy savers 60W light white lamps with energy saving ballast	372,220	135	104.5	106,070	3.51 years	

Caution must be advised in the selection of some of the gimmick-type devices on the market. A consultant engineer can verify the effectiveness of some of these devices if their use is contemplated.

THE HVAC SYSTEM

For the purpose of this chapter, the HVAC system is defined to include:

1. All boilers, electric heat and steam converters, and the hot water or steam piping within the building.
2. The chill water plant and all associated pumps and cooling towers.
3. All supply return and exhaust fans associated with the building operations.
4. The air distribution system, all diffusers, variable air volume boxes, and return air systems.
5. The temperature control systems including dampers, control valves, thermostats, and any computerized control and/or monitoring systems.

It is essential to understand the scope of the HVAC system because of its high energy consumption as a percent of the total.

Air Volume Adjustments

The HVAC systems in older buildings distribute far more air than is needed for proper environmental control. The energy management program should place special emphasis on reducing the amount of ventilating air and also reduce the horsepower of the motors by motor replacement. In the past, load shedding and demand limiting were used in an effort to reduce the energy consumption within a building. The reduction of air quantities and motor sizes in the HVAC system will generate the same or greater returns without increasing the failure rate and high maintenance cost of the HVAC system.

As an example of the problems associated with load shedding and demand control, a major building in Denver installed a computerized load shedding and demand control system after evaluation of the estimated cost reductions associated with its use. After less than one year of operation, they found that the maintenance costs of the equipment had increased and that the cost of maintaining the computerized system offset the saving to the point where there was a net add of operating cost of approximately 15%. The measure was certainly not a cost effective approach to energy management.

When using the approach of reducing motor sizes and air quantities to reduce overall power consumption, a major hotel in Chicago achieved a 20 to 25% energy reduction immediately—with no increase in maintenance cost or effect on the environmental conditions within the building. This is a simple, cost-effective approach, but it does not use the high technology that is available today.

Architectural Modifications and Maintenance

The skin material and insulation, as well as the glass and roof insulation, used in a building are major contributing factors to the energy consumption for heating and cooling. The problem is that there is little or no opportunity for modification to produce energy reductions. The high cost of retrofitting these components eliminates their acceptability. Infiltration of outside air through caulking joints, window glazing, roof openings, door openings, etc. are increasing energy consumption. Reduction can be achieved through a program of inspection and repair of areas of infiltration, and a maintenance program can prevent any reoccurrence. This type of program is usually cost effective and the payback is usually fairly short. The other positive aspect of this program is that it can be done in conjunction with normal building skin maintenance programs.

The energy consumption of the heating system in buildings, whether it be electric or fossil fuel, is controlled by the building's external losses and ventilation air requirements. The insulation quality of the windows, skin, and roof materials along with the air infiltration will dictate how many BTUs of heating energy will be lost to the exterior environment.

Ventilation Air Adjustments

Internal ventilation requirements are normally building code and comfort related and are controlled by the HVAC systems outside air dampers. It should be noted that most outside air dampers have minimum stops to guarantee a fixed amount of ventilation at any time the HVAC system is operative. A major shortfall of these settings is that they are set by percentage of damper opening rather than by the minimum quantities of outside air necessary to meet the requirements. The minimum quantities of outside air should be accurately measured and the dampers reset to their new minimum position.

Today, there are a number of types of cooling systems that are presently installed in U.S. buildings. They vary from electric refrigeration to steam and hot water absorption systems with some having added features such as free cooling or ice storage.

The cooling system must relieve the heat generated from both internal and external sources. Internal heat gain is basically generated from office equipment and other appliances running within the building, lighting systems, and the people occupying the building. The external sources of heat are skin increases in temperature due to solar load, outside air temperature, and the requirement for ventilation air. Again, it is apparent that the ventilation air requirements and the accuracy of the set of the outside air dampers is important in controlling the energy consumption.

Demand control and equipment cycling, do nothing to relieve the internal or external heat gains within the building. During the off cycle of these programs, the heat builds up within the space and must be relieved through the only vehicle available, the cooling system. The energy necessary to remove the heat from the space or the entire building is still the same, and no reduction has been achieved relative to the cooling system. In cases where variable air volume systems are installed, the effect may be an increase in energy consumption due to the high air volume requirements when the system is restarted.

Internal heat gain will be reduced through the energy reduction recommendations associated with the lighting system. It must be remembered that for every watt consumed by an energy producing device, 3.416 BTUs is given off as heat. As lighting is the largest energy consumer, any reduction will also reduce the internal heat gain, and consequently the need for cooling, in the core of the building.

Free Cooling Systems

The use of so-called free cooling (strainer cycle) and ice storage systems are ways of reducing both energy demand and energy consumption within the building. Consideration of these systems must be evaluated by a knowledgeable consulting engineer who has had experience in this field. The cost of retrofitting the cooling system to accommodate these state-of-the-art systems is very high. The maintenance and operation of these systems requires a high degree of sophistication by the operating maintenance staff. It is doubtful that most buildings would have the sophisticated staff necessary to achieve the objectives. In addition, careful consideration has to be given to the water treatment systems to ensure the cleanliness of the heat exchangers so that the proper heat transfer can take place in both the chillers and the water to air coils which are part of the HVAC system. With the above-stated concerns in mind, it is recommended that careful evaluation be given to these systems. They produce large energy savings in many buildings throughout the country.

EXHAUST SYSTEMS

The building's exhaust system can be a large component of energy consumption. The system must be viewed as to its need and its effect on the entire building. In many cases, little can be done to reduce the requirements for such things as toilet exhaust, process load exhaust, stack considerations for boilers, and other toxic vapor exhaust requirements. There are some opportunities to reduce the amount of air requirements for exhaust systems. These are basically in kitchen exhaust requirements where new energy efficient hoods can be installed in place of more inefficient ones. Paybacks are of reasonable length. Most of these systems fall in the area of tenant responsibility, but they affect the entire operation of the building.

MISCELLANEOUS LOADS

There are numerous miscellaneous loads within the building operation. Some of these are water coolers, elevators, escalators, unit heaters for loading docks and some equipment rooms, electricity-driven water pumps, air compressors for temperature control systems, and security systems. These represent the smallest increment of power consumption within the building and are the most difficult to modify to effect energy reductions. In most cases, the cost of implementing any energy reduction efforts far outweigh the savings and could affect the tenants view of the building. The one exception to this is the control of escalator usage within the building. Escalators running on a continuous basis do consume tremendous amounts of energy. The scheduling of escalator operation during peak periods is advisable and cost effective.

People are an integral part of all of the factors on our list. People make decisions and select sites, systems and equipment. People also determine schedules for equipment and building utilization and often form habits that contribute to energy waste. Fortunately, people are also the most important ingredient in any energy management program. Informed and motivated, people will revise previous decisions and schedules and initiate action to eliminate energy waste in our buildings. The building manager and the operating staff must solicit the aid and cooperation of all people in the building, from the custodial contracting personnel to the occupants. Everyone must participate in the effort in order to maximize the result.

Understanding the energy consumers and what controls their consumption, the process of developing a good energy management system within the building can begin. It is extremely important that the building's owners and investors actively support the management team's efforts to reduce energy consumption within the building. The major tenants should also play an active role in this program so that less opposition is encountered during the investigative and implementation phases of the program.

THE CONSUMPTION ANALYSIS

A comprehensive analysis of the energy consumption within the structure must be taken. The emphasis of this procedure is not on the cost of energy, but on the consumption in units of energy. The basic energy unit that is normally used is BTU. All energy consumption can be reflected in BTU values.

A complete review of the utility bills for the previous three years must be accomplished, taking into consideration all electric utility, gas, and other fuel bills for the building during that period. If there are minimum demand billings during certain periods of time, they should be taken into consideration in reviewing energy consumption and energy reduction recommendations. If this information is unavailable from the building's accounting records, the local

TABLE 11.5

Typical Format; Electric Cost Summary.

Month	Total Cost[a] KWH ×10⁶	Total Cost[a] Cost ($)	Total Cost[a] $/KWH	Heating KWH ×10⁶	Heating Cost ($)	Heating $/KWH	Lighting KWH ×10⁶	Lighting Cost ($)	Lighting $/KWH	Air Conditioning KWH ×10⁶	Air Conditioning Cost ($)	Air Conditioning $/KWH	Air Conditioning Demand KW[b]	Air Conditioning Cost ($)	Air Conditioning $/KWH
Jan	3.270	156,420	.0469	.244	9,248	.0379	1.019	47,807	.0469	1.190	45,101	.0379	—	—	—
Feb	3.370	163,769	.0486	.245	9,530	.0389	1.049	50,272	.0479	1.221	47,497	.0389	—	—	—
Mar	3.267	158,669	.0486	.174	6,734	.0387	1.054	50,178	.0476	1.219	47,175	.0387	—	—	—
Apr	3.236	153,075	.0473	.099	3,772	.0381	.922	43,337	.0470	1.493	56,883	.0381	—	—	—
May	3.475	157,537	.0453	.091	3,349	.0368	.994	45,469	.0457	1.664	61,235	.0368	—	—	—
June	4.470	223,446	.0500	.026	895	.0344	1.024	50,669	.0495	2.682	92,261	.0344	6,628	35,725	5.39
July	4.373	232,534	.0532	.013	477	.0367	.954	49,874	.0523	2.667	97,879	.0367	6,086	39,072	6.42
Aug	4.222	234,359	.0555	.011	413	.0375	.952	50,440	.0530	2.584	96,900	.0375	6,398	41,075	6.42
Sept	3.852	222,477	.0578	.014	538	.0389	1.020	54,827	.0538	2.106	80,870	.0384	6,044	38,802	6.42
Oct	3.265	171,311	.0525	.044	1,703	.0387	1.037	51,275	.0494	1.416	54,799	.0387	—	—	—
Nov	3.134	167,974	.0536	.106	4,123	.0389	1.076	53,458	.0497	1.145	44,540	.0389	—	—	—
Dec	3.401	183,197	.0463	.250	10,025	.0401	1.127	57,276	.0452	1.153	46,235	.0401	—	—	—
Total	43.330[c] 100%		.0513 Avg.	1.317[c] 3%	50,807[c] 2%	.0386 Avg.	12.228[c] 28%	604,882 27%	.0495 Avg.	20.540[c] 47%	771,375 35%	.0376 Avg.	6,628 Max.	154,674 7%	6.16 Avg.

[a]Total Costs include all KWH charges, demand charges, taxes and additions.

[b]Includes demand charge on air conditioning metters only.

[c]Sum of the heating, lighting and air conditioning KWH do not equal the total KWH in Column No. 1. The difference is attributed to miscellaneous electrical use directly by the tenants.

199

TABLE 11.6

Typical Format; Heating Cost Summary.

Month	Total[a] Therms	Total[a] Cost $	$ Per[a] Therm	Therms H.W. Boilers	Garage Heating		Hotel Dom. Water Htg.	
					Therms	Cost $	Therms	Cost
January	111,883.24	45,199.24	0.404	105,576	72,003	29,089	33,573	13,563
February	98,937.18	39,001.46	0.394	96,692	73,486	28,953	23,206	9,143
March	69,244.74	29,323.15	0.423	77,876	56,849	24,047	21,027	8,894
April	34,614.25	14,946.41	0.432	32,489	20,793	8,982	11,696	5,053
May	74,679.45	31,508.13	0.422	29,686	13,359	5,637	16,327	6,890
June	14,227.00	6,065.28	0.426	14,313	8,158	3,415	6,155	2,622
July	10,834.25	4,646.32	0.429	11,447	-0-	-0-	11,447	4,911
August	10,967.50	5,006.42	0.456	12,258	-0-	-0-	12,258	5,590
September	21,406.10	9,488.73	0.443	10,097	-0-	-0-	10,097	4,473
October	33,835.25	15,494.75	0.458	27,960	6,710	3,073	21,250	9,732
November	681.62	324.63	0.476	31,096	15,548	7,400	15,548	7,400
December	89,144.25	41,681.62	0.468	72,039	23,052	10,788	48,987	22,926
Total	570,454.83	242,686.14	0.425	521,529	289,958	121,444	231,571	101,107

[a]Total therms and total costs are taken from Peoples Gas. Co. bills and used only to determine the average $ per therm in Column 4. This average $/therm is then used to calculate the garage heating and domestic hot water heating cost.

utility companies might be able to supply these records at a nominal fee (see Figure 11.2). In addition, many electrical utilities will supply a profile of electrical energy consumption during one-month period indicating each demand level for each demand interval during that period. The consultant engineer on the energy management team should know what is available from the local utility companies, as well as a viable allocation procedure.

The actual energy consumption of each piece of equipment and each system within the building should be determined. To do this, the engineering consultant and the chief engineer should take load tests of each component and each system. This will require each motor's amperage to be recorded, each fan system's cubic foot of air per minute (CFM) to be measured, each cooling and heating coil's capacity to be established, and an accurate calculation of other energy loads to be made. It is a time consuming effort, but one that is vital for accuracy. Once all components and systems have been analyzed and loads established, they should be compared with the original engineering data used in designing these systems if it is available. If the original data is unavailable, the consulting engineer should make calculations to determine efficiency of operation at the present level of consumption.

During this phase of the program, the building management team must also determine the hours of operation of the building as established by lease and by other constraints. Examples of such constraints include the lease requirements for excess hours usage of the building, the control of additional equipment installed by the tenant, and any limitations as to the use of this space. The investigation is valuable when the energy management team is reviewing the possible energy reduction recommendations established during the program.

All government regulations must be reviewed to see if there is any impact on either energy consumption in the building or modifications that may be presented by the team. These regulations include but are not limited to energy usage constraints, life safety considerations, health considerations, and ventilation requirements.

Most government regulations have grandfather clauses which exclude existing buildings. However, if major modifications are performed in the existing structures, the grandfather clause may become invalid and any new regulation may be applicable to the building.

THE ENERGY AUDIT

Once the consumption analysis is completed, the energy audit phase begins. For the best possible results and quickest action, this phase should be conducted in two parts.

Data Collection and Analysis Phase

The discovery phase has been completed in which all levels of consumption within the building have been established. Now, the highest consumers will be

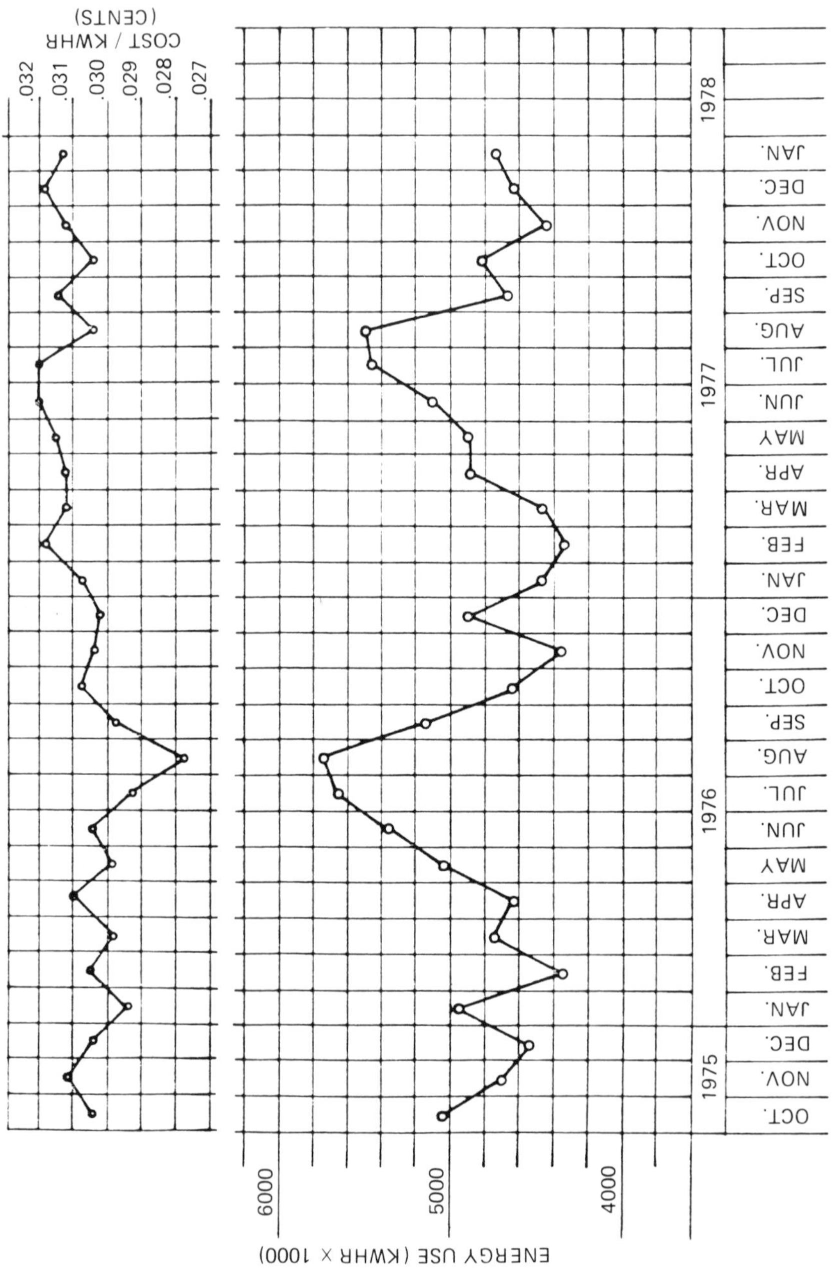

KWHR CONSUMPTION 1975 – 78

Figure 11.2 Typical building power consumption chart.

TABLE 11.7

Electrical Energy Use Breakdown by Building.

Building and Load Type	Demand Load KW	KWH Usage	Percent of Building Use
1. *Main Building*			
Lighting	1,064	5,180,300	57.1
General power[a]	380	988,700	10.9
HVAC[b]	690	2,898,500	32.0
2. *East Wing*			
Lighting	410	1,920,600	65.7
General power[a]	61	158,200	5.4
HVAC[b]	234	844,500	28.9
3. *West Wing*			
Lighting	278	1,348,300	71.2
General Power[a]	44	92,400	4.9
HVAC[b]	127	454,300	23.9
4. *Tower*			
Lighting	1,549	7,268,700	61.7
General power[a]	220	1,031,500	8.7
HVAC[b]	435	3,491,600	29.6
5. *Cafeteria and Training*			
Lighting	436	1,250,600	46.4
General power[a]	23	46,500	1.7
HVAC[b]	98	336,000	12.5
Food service	682	1,063,900	39.4
6. *Chiller*			
Lighting	5	43,800	1.0
Equipment[c]	2,111	4,159,700	99.0
7. *Boiler*			
Lighting	11	96,400	13.1
Equipment[d]	20	637,300	86.9
8. *Computer*			
Lighting	349	2,406,400	11.7
HVAC	986	5,990,600	29.1
Equipment	1,541	12,179,900	59.2
9. *Miscellaneous*[e]		3,666,300	
Facility Total	11,944	57,555,000	

[a]General Power includes office equipment, vending machines, elevators/escalators and vacuuming equipment.
[b]HVAC Systems include air handling units, supply and return air fans, and exhaust fans.
[c]Refrigeration equipment for central chiller plant.
[d]Boilers and accessories for central heating.
[e]Miscellaneous includes Parking Garage and Tunnel, telephone, communications, security, sound and photo developing equipment, electrical equipment system losses and Electric Company metering error.

identified as possible targets for energy reduction. The building design requirements and occupancy lease requirements have also been established so that they can be analyzed during the audit phase.

In the first part of the energy audit phase, a comprehensive review of all energy consuming systems should be taken from the data and evaluated. All of the quick fix items which have the least cost of implementation and the greatest amount of energy savings can be determined at this point.

Each energy consuming piece of equipment and/or system must be categorized showing the actual consumption of energy vs. the building environmental design requirements. These should be listed in an order of priority with the highest consuming systems or pieces of equipment listed first.

The consulting engineer's services are brought in to play here as the dominant role in this review. Once the existing systems are categorized and the levels of consumption have been established, he will take alternate systems into consideration. As part of the engineer's review and analysis, the chief engineer's input as to the operability of suggested modifications should be noted. He should also consult with the electrical contractor and the mechanical contractor to evaluate the practicality of any retrofit or modifications that must be done to the equipment or systems. The contractors should also be consulted to establish a budget for the implementation of the recommendations.

At this point a report should be generated listing all areas of energy reduction, estimated savings in both energy units and dollars, and the cost of implementation of each recommendation. This will, in turn, give an analysis of simple payback which should also be included. The report should go on to analyze those items which can be implemented having the quickest payback and the lowest capital dollars investment. This process will allow the quick fix items to be taken care of on an expeditious basis. Items requiring further investigation or a verification of costs from manufacturers and suppliers will fall into the second phase of the audit.

Engineering Review Phase

The second part of this energy audit requires the consultant engineer to take an in-depth view of the major capital cost recommendations and establish the magnitude of savings as well as a firm cost of implementation. Problems associated with implementation, including the effect they will have on the normal operation of the building, should be included. Tenant disruption during the implementation phase of many of the major retrofit recommendations is a vital consideration on whether that recommendation should be implemented.

Major retrofit items will be considered during this part of the audit. These include, but are not limited to, new roof insulation, new windows, major modification or replacement of the heating and/or cooling systems, the installation of a free cooling cycle within the cooling system, ice or chilled water storage systems, and major modifications to the temperature control system. All of these approaches have potentially high energy savings, but are high

TABLE 11.8

Energy Audit Report Summary.

HVAC Retrofit Cost, Savings and Payback

Item	Description	Page	Estimated Cost ($)	Estimated 1-Year Saving ($)	Estimated Payback (years)
1.	Perimeter radiation valves	31, 32	$ 45,000	$ 7,200	6.2
2.	VAV retrofit	33, 34, 35	105,000	80,000	2.0
3.	Duty cycling	36	25,900[a]	8,950	3.0[a]
4.	Duct modifications	37	10,000	2,800	3.5
5.	Multi-zone systems	37	2,000[a]	670	3.0[a]
6.	Auditorium club room chiller	38, 39	45,000	15,000	3.0
7.	East wing induction system	41	18,000	5,875	3.2
8.	East wing interior fans	42	42,000[a]	14,045	3.0[a]
9.	East wing O.A. dampers, fans	43	17,200[a]	5,750	3.0[a]
10.	West wing perimeter radiation	44	5,000	1,400	3.5
11.	West wing R.A. fans	44	7,200[a]	2,400	3.0[a]
12.	Tunnel htg. w/R.A.	45	17,000	4,900	3.5
13.	Tower fan cycling	46	19,200[a]	6,400	3.0[a]
14.	O.A. control modification	47	12,000[a]	4,000	3.0[a]
15.	Chiller optimization	50	5,000	3,600	1.5
16.	Condenser water control	51	10,500[a]	3,500	3.0[a]
17.	Boiler	53	12,000	7,000	1.7
18.	C & T control modification	55	6,000[a]	2,000	3.0[a]
19.	Computer area heat exchanger	59	40,000	36,000	1.2
20.	Start/stop optimization	60	115,800[a]	38,600	3.0[a]
21.	Enthalpy control	61	18,000[a]	6,000	3.0[a]
	Total		$577,800	$256,090	

[a]Indicates control item cost and payback which will be determined by the control system selected. A payback of three years or less is anticipated in each case.

capital intensive installations. If replacement of any of these components or systems are contemplated due to their deterioration and failure, this will greatly impact the priority which you should place upon their evaluation.

During this phase, the building manager should pay special attention to the engineer's assumptions of and the downside risk for both the management and the owner of the building. Operational personnel should be consulted and brought into this decision-making process.

At the end of this part of the energy audit, all of the recommendations, both to be implemented now and in the future, should be reviewed by the energy management team. The team should keep in mind all the information that was developed during the initial phases of this energy management program.

TABLE 11.9

Summary of Cost Impact and Recommendations.[a]

Item	Description	Page	Estimated Cost ($)	Estimated 1-Year Saving ($)	Estimated Payback
1.	Reduce ventilation Perimeter systems	7−8	None	$ 1,120	Immediate
2.	Reduce ventilation Interior systems	9−10	None	2,880	Immediate
3.	Reduce reheat and total circulated air	9−11	$22,000	27,500	.8 year
4.	Reduce lighting 35% 10 story building	16−19	35,000	45,800	8 year
5.	Automatic lighting control	20−21	20,000	9,500	2.1 years
6.	Automatic CO control for garage	24	7,500	2,600	2.9 years
	Total		$84,500	$89,400	1 year

[a]Details of alternatives are outlined in the body of this report.

TABLE 11.10

Energy Impact From Recommendations (Reductions).[a]

Description	Steam (1000 lbs.)	Demand (kW)	Consumption (kWh)	BTU (million)
Reduce ventilation		107	103,200	352
Reduce reheat and air circulation	2,417	186	409,600	3,815
Reduce lighting 35% in 10 story bldg.		364	1,262,000	4,307
Automatic lighting control			403,000	1,375
Garage CO control			126,900	433
Total	2,417	657	2,248,700	10,282

[a]This represents a reduction in energy consumption of 19.7%. Energy utilization index of 237,600 BTU/sq ft/yr is reduced to 190,836 BTU/sq ft/yr.

THE ENERGY CONSUMPTION MODEL

At the completion of the energy audit stage, a model of building energy consumption should be calculated by the consultant engineer in order to establish a base for monitoring the energy consumption of the building after all of the accepted recommendations are implemented. This is a important factor in establishing a target energy that will be maintained for the remainder of the life of the building (barring any modifications necessary in the building's use or occupancy).

It is impractical for all of the recommendations to be implemented at the same time. The quick fix items will be done in rapid order and the results will show energy reduction in a short span of time. The other recommendations, i.e., those requiring retrofit and/or major modification will take more time.

MONITORING AND CONTROLLING THE LEVEL OF CONSUMPTION

Now that an energy efficient building has been established, that efficiency must be maintained by monitoring and controlling the level of consumption modeled by the engineer during the latter part of the energy audit. The building management team must set up a system to monitor all energy consumption within the buildings and insure that those levels are maintained. If there is any variation in the levels of energy usage, the building management should take the necessary steps to bring them in line. This usually consists of a review of the monthly utility and fuel bills and, in some cases, breaking these bills down to

TABLE 11.11

Projection of Energy Reduction Cost Avoidance.

Energy	1979	1980	1981	1982	1983
	Without Energy Conservation				
25,464,000 lbs	$117,701	$125,940	$134,755	$144,187	$154,280
7,847,000 kW	258,877	276,998	296,387	317,134	339,333
Total	$376,578	$402,938	$431,142	$461,321	$493,613
	With Recommended Energy Conservation Implemented				
23,047,000 lbs	$106,529	$113,986	$121,965	$130,502	$139,638
5,598,300 kW	181,577	194,287	207,877	222,439	238,009
Total	$288,106	$308,273	$329,852	$352,941	$377,647
Cost avoidance	$ 89,400	$ 95,658	$102,354	$109,518	$117,184
Cumulative Total	$ 89,400	$185,058	$287,412	$396,930	$514,114

actual system consumptions. Note that this system should monitor energy consumption and not dollars of cost. Although energy consumption has been reduced, the cost of energy has not. Therefore, it is possible that the dollar expenditures will either continue increasing, although at a reduced rate, or be stable.

The operation and maintenance of all mechanical-electrical systems within the building are the key to successfully maintaining low levels of energy consumption within the building. To this end, it is important that the operating maintenance personnel:

1. Be in harmony with the program as it is established by the energy management team.
2. Be educated in operation and maintenance procedures which will maintain these lower levels of energy consumption.
3. Enlist the help of the tenants to assist in the maintaining of levels of energy consumption. The cost reduction can be the motivating force behind their cooperation.
4. Be directed to establish a comprehensive preventive maintenance program with management reports to monitor the progress of the key element in maintaining the energy consumption levels.

TABLE 11.12

Denver Building "A" Case Study.

Building A, Denver, Colorado – 700,000 sq ft – 34 floors
Rental office building
Major tenants: Banking, legal, accounting and oil exploration
30,000 sq ft EDP department
EUI 1975 = 168,000   EUI 1976 = 112,000 – 1980 = 87421
Operational changes:
1975 – Damper control revisions, elimination of preheat
1976 – 1980
    1. Equipment operating schedule
    2. Air balancing
    3. Closer equipment, lighting and custodial schedule
    4. Equipment maintenance
    5. Reset schedule, perimeter radiation
Energy reduction – 21.9%
Cost avoidance 1976 versus 1980 = 136.7%

TABLE 11.13

Building "A" Summary.

	BTU/ Sq Ft Year	Cost/ Sq Ft Year	Cost/ 1,000,000 BTU	Percent Reduction of Energy	Percent of Cost Change
1976	112,000	.5807	5.18	0	0
1977	104,000	.5917	5.74	7.14	10.81
1978	102,000	.7463	7.32	8.92	41.31
1979	103,000	.8788	8.53	8.03	64.67
1980	87,421	1.0723	12.26	21.95	136.68

TABLE 11.14

Denver Building "B" Case Study.

Building B, Denver, Colorado−500,000 sq ft−32 floors

Rental office building

Major tenants: Real estate, stock brokerage, legal, accounting and oil exploration

16,000 sq ft EDP area

10,000 sq ft food service areas

EUI 1977 = 288,000−1980 = 203,000

Operational changes:

1. Schedules
2. Lighting reduction and control
3. Air and water balance
4. Damper control revisions and maintenance
5. Cleaning water coils and piping
6. Combustion controls and adjustments
7. General equipment maintenance

Energy reduction−29.51%

Cost avoidance 1977 versus 1980 = 175%

TABLE 11.15

Building "B" Summary.

	BTU/ Sq Ft Year	Cost/ Sq Ft Year	Cost/ 1,000,000 BTU	Percent Reduction of Energy	Percent of Cost Change
1977	288,000	.8569	2.47	0	0
1978	268,000	1.0002	3.73	6.94	51.01
1979	246,000	1.1163	4.54	14.58	83.80
1980	203,000	1.3809	6.80	29.51	175.30

TABLE 11.16

Denver Building "C" Case Study.

Building C, Denver, Colorado — 900,000 sq ft — 42 floors

Rental office building

Major tenants: Stock brokerage, accountants, legal,
oil exploration

25,000 sq ft EDP areas

EUI 1979 = 78,000 — 1980 = 76,800

Operational changes:

    1. Minimal schedule changes

    2. Fine system tuning

    3. Equipment maintenance

Energy reduction = 1.5%

Cost avoidance = 43.6%

	BTU/ Sq Ft Year	Cost/ Sq Ft Year	Cost/ 1,000,000 BTU	Percent Reduction of Energy	Percent of Cost Change
1979	78,000	.6401	8.21	0	0
1980	76,000	.9192	11.97	1.5	43.6

TABLE 11.17

Milwaukee Building "D" Case Study.

Building D, Milwaukee, Wisconsin — 400,000 sq ft — 20 floors

Home insurance building

40,000 sq ft EDP department

EUI 1976 = 237,000 — 1980 = 190,000

Operational changes:

    1. Damper revision

    2. Reduced air circulation

    3. Eliminated preheat

    4. Air balancing

    5. Water balancing

    6. Reduced lighting

    7. Reduced schedules

        Custodial, lighting and equipment operation

Energy reduction = 19.38%

Cost avoidance 1976 versus 1980 = 116%

	BTU/ Sq Ft Year	Cost/ Sq Ft Year	Cost/ 1,000,000 BTU	Percent Reduction of Energy	Percent of Cost Change
1976	237,000	1.2774	5.39	0	0
1980	190,000	2.7586	11.64	19.83	115.95

TABLE 11.18

Chicago Building "E" Case Study.

Building E, Chicago, Illinois—1.2 Million sq ft—48 stories

Insurance company home office

80,000 sq ft EDP department

EUI 1979 = 174,000—1980 = 163,000

EDP 1979 = 742,000—1980 = 868,000

$$\frac{\text{EDP } 1979 = 742,000-1980 = 868,000}{\text{EUI}}$$

Operational changes:

    1. Equipment operating schedule

    2. Temperature control maintenance

    3. Elimination of preheat

    4. Lighting control

    5. Balancing of equipment air and water flow

Energy reduction = 6.32%

Cost avoidance = 26.98%

	BTU/ Sq Ft Year	Cost/ Sq Ft Year	Cost/ 1,000,000 BTU	Percent Reduction of Energy	Percent of Cost Change
1979	174,000	1.5717	9.03	0	0
1980	163,000	1.9582	12.01	6.32	26.98

THE PREVENTIVE MAINTENANCE PROGRAM

The heart of a sound energy management program and the maintenance of the energy levels within the building lies in a strong comprehensive preventive maintenance program established for that building. Preventive maintenance has been viewed as a way to reduce repair bills and maintain operating efficiency for years. But it has not necessarily been viewed as a way to control and maintain energy consumption. Preventive maintenance, unlike breakdown maintenance, which is at the opposite end of the spectrum, maintains the equipment as asset status within the building management program. Breakdown maintenance by its nature will cause service interruptions to the tenants which will detract from the leasing market's perception of the building.

A comprehensive preventive maintenance program anticipates normal wear of equipment and systems and takes continuous corrective action to maximize the efficiency of the equipment or systems while minimizing its deterioration. It is a planned control program of systematic inspections, adjustments, lubrication, replacement of components, plus performance testing and analysis. This sounds complicated—and it is. In addition, the cost of implementing this type of program is higher than normally anticipated in building operations. But the rewards are great and the reduction in operating costs due to premature replacement of equipment, failure of equipment, and low energy consumption are the rewards.

During the last part of the energy audit, a model of the building's energy consumption was established. This model took into consideration the components and systems that were modified and adjusted to become the new environmental system for the building. Each component was brought up to design standards or better, and each system was modified to perform at the new, high efficiency levels. This information is an integral part of the preventive maintenance program.

Some of the benefits of a comprehensive preventive maintenance program should be reviewed so that the costs versus the rewards can be evaluated.

1. Disruption of service is minimized when this program is established. This will mean fewer complaints by tenants and of course less energy consumption.

2. Repair costs are contained. Premature failure of equipment is all but eliminated.

3. Energy consumption is reduced as higher operating efficiencies have been achieved.

4. Systems and equipment life is extended. Reliability is enhanced. Replacement of assets are kept to a minimum.

5. With the scheduling that is necessary in this comprehensive program, labor productivity is improved which reduces the cost of overall building operations.

6. When repairs are necessary, they can be handled expeditiously by the well trained staff with the knowledge and data base that will enable them to repair the equipment quickly, reducing the effect on the overall building operations.

7. Management will have a better control of operating costs and with special emphasis on energy costs.

It is important to understand that the preventive maintenance program of this magnitude will not be successful unless the managers and owners are willing to put the full efforts of the management team behind it. The ingredients necessary to establish this program are: a total inventory of all systems equipment and devices; scheduling of routines; supervision and control of all aspects; and training and equipping of all operation maintenance personnel. The recordkeeping and monitoring of the results are management's tools to maintaining the established operating objectives.

Inventory Process

The first step in establishing this program is for the operating maintenance personnel to take a complete inventory of all equipment and systems including their location, basic manufacturing data, and other information developed during this phase (see Figure 11.3). Obtaining all operation and maintenance manuals for all equipment is a prerequisite. This includes performance curves and efficiency test sheets established for the particular building or for the equipment from the manufacturer. The performance specifications are a vital part of this comprehensive program and must be either procured from the manufacturer or established in the field by the consulting engineer and operating personnel (see Figure 11.4).

Now that the data has been compiled a series of questions that establish the basic constraints and requirements of the preventive maintenance program must be asked:

1. What are the parameters of the inspections, testing and servicing that are necessary on each piece of equipment and system?
2. What is the frequency of maintenance, servicing and testing necessary for each component piece of equipment and system?
3. How many labor hours are necessary to complete each task?
4. What are the intervals of maintenance, servicing and testing necessary?
5. What is the system and/or equiment used for?
6. At what period in time in the day or week can the system best be serviced?

Cataloguing Equipment and Systems

The next step in this process is to categorize equipment and systems as to their importance to the building's operation. If time or labor constraints are encountered, it may be necessary to eliminate some low priority equipment, such as minor exhaust fans or unit heaters servicing low priority areas, from this program. Evaluation of the cost of the preventive maintenance program vs. the replacement cost of the equipment is necessary in order to contain the cost of this program and improve the overall building operating efficiency.

Special consideration and high priority must be placed on the critical equipment associated with tenant and/or occupants environmental systems and business activities. For example, high priorities are placed on the HVAC system, elevators, and escalators.

All high priority items must take precedence over any other route in the scheduling phase. A major effort must be placed on supplying continuous service to the tenants so that their activities are not disrupted. Low priority

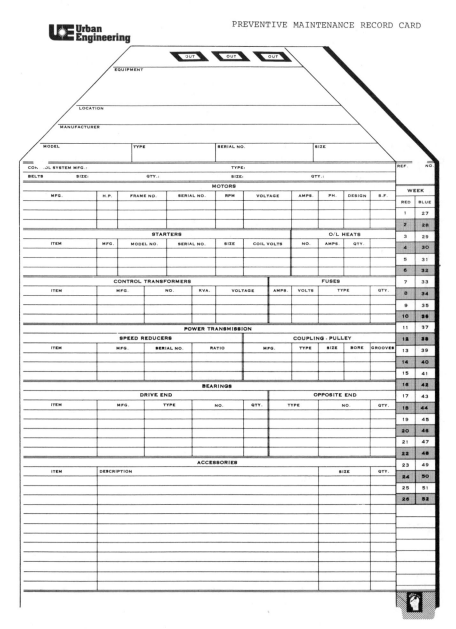

Figure 11.3 Preventive maintenance record card.

Urban Engineering

Gentlemen:

We have the responsibility at our _____
Division for the operation and maintenance of your equipment
installed at _____.

We have found that we are missing from files the data listed below.

May we prevail upon you to forward the checklisted information for
the following equipment.

Name_____ Size of Frame_____

Model No._____ Serial No._____

Voltage_____ Amperage_____

Other_____

Data Required_____

____Operating Instructions   ____Teardown Assembly, and Repair
                                       Instruction, Including Tolerance
____General Maintenance Data   Information

____Parts Catalog   ____Pump Curves

____Fan Curves   ____Design Shop Drawings

____Field Wiring Diagrams   ____As Built Drawings

____Electrical Schematics   ____Mech/Elect. Contact Design
                                       Drawings

Other_____

Please Forward To:

                                  Very truly yours,

PM-11 (6-80)

Figure 11.4 Operation and maintenance data.

items such as toilet exhaust systems, equipment room heating and exhaust systems, and other low impact systems can be taken care of during normal working hours with little if any disruption to the tenant's activities.

Cost Versus Reward

Some managers will be concerned by the cost of implementation and the effect of scheduling of the building staff when anticipating this kind of a program.

The start-up and implementation costs of the comprehensive program will affect the building operating costs for a period of one to two years. But, even during that period of time, a reduction in tenant complaints, reduced repair costs and overall increase in efficiency of equipment can be seen. In the long run, the protection of the asset and the maintenance of low operating costs in comparison with comparable buildings will show an economic return to the owners and enhance the marketability of the asset.

There are alternatives to using in-house staff to accomplish these objectives. Many of these activities can be contracted out to local service organizations which will have the necessary test equipment and special tools. Such organizations also have trained personnel—thus taking a big burden off many of the building managers who do not have the staff nor the need to have highly-trained personnel as permanent members of their staff.

Organizing and Scheduling

The organizing and scheduling of the preventive maintenance work is the next item on the agenda. A clear-cut separation of repair functions and preventive maintenance functions must be made at this point. In order for this program to be effective over the long term, it is imperative that preventive maintenance takes the highest of priorities and not be lowered to priority two or three. It is understood that many managers view this as contrary to the norm, but, in order for this program to be effective, it must be done.

All preventive maintenance work should be divided into routes. Each route should encompass an individual or group of specific forms of service, maintenance, or testing. A route should comprise, for example, only filter changing, lubrication, and belt servicing. The diagnostic testing and analysis should be performed as a separate function. By segregating this work, concentration by the operating maintenance personnel on the objectives of the particular route will be achieved. The equipment and systems will be more frequently inspected during a year's period. The amount of materials, service equipment, and instrumentation will be reduced on each particular route. It is difficult for an operating maintenance engineer to keep his hands clean to handle test equipment when he has just lubricated the equipment or changed filters. In larger operations, it also gives management the ability to assign the best qualified person for the specific job to be performed.

This outline program does not intend to isolate certain personnel on a full time basis performing preventive maintenance. In fact, it is better to utilize the entire staff at various times and for various routes so that they become more familiar with the overall preventive maintenance program. This also gives management a way to insure that the work is being accomplished by changing personnel so that one person cannot continue to do an ineffective job which could hurt the overall performance of the building. In smaller buildings and facilities without the opportunity to assign various personnel to these activities, management must take a closer look at the preventive maintenance activities.

Monitoring the Program

The work routes and personnel should be scheduled on the most efficient basis to achieve the objectives. A scheduling board should be developed to establish the frequency of the routes and some visual indication of work status (see Figure 11.5). In addition, a file system should be developed which includes all work activities for each route along with all pertinent data and machinery manuals that are required for that route. This is in addition to a complete individual machinery history record that should be kept on each piece of equipment and system. There are various suppliers of recordkeeping systems available—the one that best meets your needs should be employed.

Each route should include a written schedule of the work to be performed. The format should include space for the individual performing the work to

Figure 11.5 Personnel scheduling board.

check off each item and sign as to overall performance of the work. It has been found that when an individual signs off on a document, where others may be following up on the next scheduled route in that area, he will be less apt to perform below standard work (see Figure 11.6).

In allocating time for each task, time needed for the individual to inspect the equipment and reflect on the analysis and input information that is received on

Urban Engineering				
Route No._____Project No._____				
EQPT. No._____File No._____Page_____OF_____				

MAINT. CODE: VIS – visual inspection   CKP – check packing
                  ADJ – adjust linkages   ICP – inspect cap tube for
                  TSC – tighten set screws   chafing
                                            TOP – test, operate, observe
                                                proper action. Calibrate
                                                    and adjust as required.

CONDITION CODE:
        G – good, minor wear, deterioration
        F – fair, medium wear, deterioration
        P – poor, usable, replace next inspection
        N – new, replaced this inspection

DEVICE	MAINT. CODE	COND.	SET	REMARKS
Main air PRV				
Main damp switch pos.				
Summer/Winter Contr.				
Freeze Prot.Stat.				
Coil pump T. Stat				
Outside air stat				
Mixed air stat				
Return air stat				
Disch. air stat				
Low Limit stat				
Dan/night stat				
Heat valve & oper.				
Cool vale & oper				
F A damp. & oper				
Exh. air damp & oper				
Zone 1 stat				
Zone 1 valve/damper				
Zone 2 stat				
Zone 2 valve/damper				
Zone 3 stat				
Zone 3 damp/oper				
Zone 4 stat				
Zone 4 damp & oper				
Zone 5 stat				
Zone 5 damp & oper				
Zone 6 stat				
Zone 6 damp & oper				
Zone 7 stat				
Zone 7 damp & oper				

Note * Check & record all stat check points when all other work is completed
OUTSIDE AMBIENT CONDITION=Temp.Db   Wb
Week Scheduled_____Week Inspected_____Time Started_____

Completed_____Engr._____Reviewed by:_____
PM-5 (6-80)

Figure 11.6 Typical inspection form. A/C system control inspection.

Urban Engineering

TO:	DATE:
FROM:	SUBJECT: PREVENTIVE MAINT. CHECKLIST
	CENTER:_____

ITEM	YES	NO	REMARKS
Manual On Hand			
Read by Engineers			
Initialed by Engineers			
Equipment List Complete			
Equipment Numbered			
Control Board Complete			
Data Cards Complete			
Repair Record Cards Used			
Reference File Set Up			
Route Information Cards Comp			
Route File Set Up			
Route Sheets In Route Sub-File			
Tenant File Set Up			
Projected Overhaul Schedule			

Figure 11.7 PM program checklist.

the inspection must be taken into account. If any repair of equipment is necessary, it should be recorded with notification to the supervisor. The supervisor should schedule the repair at an appropriate time. The repair should not be handled by the individual performing the preventive maintenance route. If possible, repair work should be scheduled after the completion of the preventive maintenance route or assigned to another operating maintenance engineer.

Management Controls

The chief engineer or head mechanical person should oversee this entire program to insure that the mechanics are doing their job effectively. It is important for managers to spot-check various work activities from time to time to show management's dedication to the program as well as check to see how efficiently the job is being handled. During periodic staff meetings, which should be handled on a weekly or bi-monthly basis, the status of the preventive maintenance program as a whole should be reviewed. The efficiency of operation energy consumption of the building, labor utilization, and the number of tenant complaints will indicate how effective the preventive maintenance program is (see Figure 11.7).

Most preventive maintenance programs have flaws in them from the start. Be cognizant of this during the start-up phase of the program. Be aware of its short-falls and record them. It is important to give the program approximately a six- to nine-month period before making any major changes. Many times, what initially appears to be a flaw in the program will work its way out as the program stabilizes itself.

SUMMARY

Energy management is not a one-time, short-term program. It is a program that will affect a change in the management philosophy of your building. Care and dedication to the goals and objectives of this program are the keys to its success. The rewards are worth the cost and effort. Asset values will be enhanced making the building more valuable in future years.

GEORGE L. TUTT
Director Mid-West Region
office of the President
SBS Real Estate Communications
Corporation
McLean, Virginia

SBS Real Estate Communications Corporation is a provider of advanced communications services to the real estate community. Mr. Tutt was formerly a vice president of Urban Investment & Development Co. His background includes Financial, Accounting, and Information Systems Management, bringing experience both as user and provider of computer based systems. He holds a BA in Economics, an MSBA in Industrial Management. In 1982, he received an MBA from the University of Chicago's Executive Program.

JOHN SALERNO
President
Data Compass Corp.
New Hyde Park, New York

John Salerno earned the B.S. degree in Mathematics from Fordham University and was a Lieutenant in the U. S. Marine Corps. He has 21 years' experience in Data Processing and in 1969 he formed his present company, Data Compass Corporation. Real estate and cash management systems are his areas of specialization.

CHAPTER 12

THE USE OF
THE COMPUTER

INTRODUCTION

The 1980s offer new opportunities for incorporating use of the computer in real estate management. The cost of hardware has been driven to new lows via introduction of the versatile microcomputers and a concurrent continuing price performance improvement in all ranges of computers. Software (application and operating programs) has started to truly come of age with clear documentation, diverse systems featuring integration across functions, and sophisticated data bases. There has been a clearly focused effort to produce new user friendly software that reduces or eliminates the need for direct involvement of computer personnel in operation of the systems.

While automation will not turn an inadequate system into an adequate one or make an ineffective management effective, it presents an opportunity for a firm to take a fresh look at what is in place and what is needed. In fact, today there is essentially no lower limit in size or activity level to forestall use of a computer. It is becoming increasingly true that such systems are necessary for efficient management of resources. This is the future: it is the environment in which firms will conduct their business and compete with others.

DEVELOPING AND IMPLEMENTING AN AUTOMATED SYSTEM

To take advantage of the computer, there are essential steps in developing and implementing an "automated system." These may be viewed as distinct elements or as a continuum. They are:

1. Definition of needs.
2. Review of current system.
3. Evaluation of alternatives.
4. Conversion/implementation.

Definition of Needs

This is the foundation of the process of automation. It must provide a reasonable clear formal definition and understanding of the information needed to run the business. The ideal product of this step would be an "information system plan" for the firm that can only be assembled by those who understand all the facets of the business. In a larger firm, this typically is assembled by a project team in a formal structured process. In a smaller firm, one or more persons can assemble this plan, usually informally. This is an important step to assure that over time, the commitment of effort and funds expended will result in useful integrated systems rather than a series of unconnected and independently managed data sources. If this is not done, then it effectively is done by default. This idealistic statement must be tempered by reality. All needs will never be identified completely, and, given the changing nature of business, competition, and various federal, state, and local regulations, even identified requirements will change over time. However, the essence of the information plan remains: be sure the pieces of the system do relate one to another.

Given the diverse range of real estate managed, the types of management performed, and the variety of sophistication in management, we cannot identify the ideal system needs. Later in this chapter some key modules/systems that firms normally would require will be reviewed. The actual content and complexity of these modules varies widely for managers of rental homes, apartments, shopping centers, office buildings, industrial properties, etc . Some key points are to: determine where your managerial and clerical time is spent (the functions requiring the most time obviously offer the greatest opportunity for time-saving); and determine where tighter control of resources is needed. (Cash management and vacancy management are examples of two areas where great benefits can often be gained.)

There are a variety of management systems that either incorporate some of the system features described later or become links (specialized modules) to perform functions for a particular need. The key thing is to recognize that a master tenant system (in whatever form or forms it takes) provides the property owner-manager new opportunities in management by use of automation.

Having stated the need to clearly determine and state requirements, we can move forward to discussion of the next step.

Review of the Current Systems

Unless the firm is starting anew, it is important to recognize the need for this step and to complete it with care. It performs two functions. First, it is an affirmation that previously-defined needs have not overlooked some key things that you now have. Second, it is essential that the current system be understood to assure that a transition to a new system can be planned effectively and with the proper degree of caution. The later conversion/implementation phase is of great concern as you are leaving a known system and going to an unknown. The new and old systems should run parallel for a defined period to assure that the new system functions and that the new data can be relied upon. The old system is the only reasonable base to provide this benchmark, and understanding is key. If major problems are encountered, by continuing use of the old system, you can buy time that may be essential to the ultimate success of the implementation. Do not bypass this step in haste toward automation.

Evaluation of Alternatives

There are three choices that normally emerge from a review: (1) development and implementation of your own system; (2) use of a Service Bureau to provide the services; or (3) purchase software and implement the new system for yourself. The actual choice will be based on a variety of factors but there are some clear considerations the firm should be aware of. (Our later discussions of methods of providing computer service and software options will clarify some of these options.)

In weighing these alternatives, the selection or design of the software is the essential element. Do not compromise in any way that will limit the usefulness of the system. Automation can be an expensive, troublesome change. It is not something you should plan to repeat. With this in mind, consider the firm's growth and the need to be able to expand the system to meet future needs. Recognize that all new systems need not be implemented at once—in fact that would typically be a disaster—but that systems can be selectively implemented over a period of time, starting with those that will provide the greatest benefits. The choice of available software may be limited to that which will run on currently owned hardware, or it may be unrestrained if the hardware choice is open, or a Service Bureau will be used. Do not underestimate the costs and time of developing you own software and the risk of starting up an unproven system. The approach of doing your own is typically only warranted by the very large or specialized firm who can effectively do it or who has no reasonable alternative. Weighing the firm's needs against the options is a job for senior management. It is important that the needs be clearly understood and that the options be well examined. Management should recognize this as a business decision, one that is not inherently easy to implement and one that should not be clouded by over-expectations or a fascination with technology. The purpose of the firm is real estate management/ownership and the computer, and attendant automation, are only to facilitate and bring efficiency to this stewardship.

Conversion/Implementation

Planning is a byword for this process. It is nothing more than a plan and schedule to move from one system to another in a series of defined steps. It will provide specifics as to when to start, what each step is to be along the way, who will participate, how much time it will take, how verification of data is to be handled, and who carries responsibility. In a large company it is handled formally, while in a small one, it will be informal. Regardless of size, it warrants careful attention and should be a model of conservatism. Any acceptable plan must provide for contingencies based upon a variety of things that will go wrong. A successful implementation is not usually based on everything going perfectly, but rather on adequate handling of a variety of unforeseen problems.

Implementation, in fact, would appear to be somewhat of an art rather than a science.

Methods of Providing Computer Service

There are basically three types of computer processing methods:

1. Remote service bureau.
2. Time-sharing service bureau.
3. In-house computer.

Remote Service Bureau.   This is a service-type function that involves sending coded forms to a computer center where they are processed through the service bureau's property management software and the output or reports are returned to the customer. The service bureau's responsibility includes data entry, editing, processing, and customer support. The service bureau will normally assist the property manager in converting his data for this type of data processing. The initial two months of processing is the most difficult period for both the service bureau and the property manager. The response to customer needs together with the timeliness and accuracy of the service bureau usually determines the length of time the property manager continues the relationship. The property manager makes no investment in software or hardware and is free to discontinue the service with minimal notice. The cost for the service is usually based upon a fixed charge per tenant plus a transaction charge.

Time-Sharing Service Bureau.   (This service also referred to as "on-line computing services") requires a video terminal and printer connected to a host computer via a telephone and modem (a device which converts computer signals so that they may be transmitted). In a time-sharing network many users access the same computer simultaneously. The user is able to process most of his work on the terminal located at the property manager's office. Bulk-type printing and reporting are generally done at the time-sharing center with delivery to the customer. The property manager is charged a base fee for accessing certain programs, plus a connect charge based upon terminal usage and a storage charge for the amount of file data maintained by the host computer. Relationships of this type normally require the user to purchase or lease the terminal equipment and expend the time necessary to learn the proper use of the time-sharing firms property management software.

In-House Computer.   An in-house computer installation ranges from a small personal business microprocessor to a large scale mainframe computer. The property manager with his own computer is responsible for his own data entry and everyday processing. He uses property management programs developed by his own technical staff or purchased from a software firm. The software firm may have also sold him the computer hardware as part of a "turn-key installation." In many cases, the software firm will provide continuing support and software upgrades as they become available. The cost of the computer installation can range from a few thousand dollars for a simple microprocessor based system to several hundred thousand for the large scale systems.

Software Options

There are three ways of acquiring the software for a computer system.

Use Software at a Service Bureau.   This option will not be a custom system and is linked to the use of either remote or time-sharing service bureaus. It is designed to permit a variety of firms to utilize a central system using uniform software. The costs consist of a minimal monthly fee plus a charge based on usage. This permits a firm to predict their costs based on usage and to adjust to changes in business requirements immediately. The service bureau concept is based on economies of scale. The hardware and software can be utilized to a maximum degree and thus achieve economies for all users while providing a profit for the service company. The following advantages and disadvantages can be anticipated relative to choice of a service bureau:

Advantages:
Proven flexible operational systems.
Costs are predictable and fluctuate with volume.
Professional operation.
Well-documented systems.
Strong training and support.
Disadvantages:
Must run on bureau's schedule.
Modification either not available or expensive.
Dependency on outside agency for vital functions.

Develop and Operate Your Own System.   This second approach is a traditional approach that has been followed by many companies. It requires a particularly clear definition and understanding of what is needed, and a commitment to support and fund the development process overtime. It will provide a custom system that will tailor reports to match what you want, features to handle your unique business needs, and can be developed on hardware of your selection (which you may already have). In the past, this was the only viable way to provide a system since good software and support were atypical. It remains the most flexible way to support a business but also is essentially the most perilous. You can expect the following:

Advantages:

Complete flexibility to meet firm's needs.

Custom report formats.

Optimum operation based on specific needs.

Ability to alter system on request quickly.

Utilization of existing hardware.

Disadvantages:

Long lead time to design, program, test and implement.

Uncertain costs based on changing requirements, problems.

Lack of needed features based on inadequate definition or communication.

Purchase Software.   This last alternative is a blend of the other two. It is to purchase software and operate the system yourself. This is a middle ground that minimizes the exposure of development of a system but picks up exposure on operations. The relative merits of this choice can be assessed against the following:

Advantages:

Provides proven well documented system.

Costs are known (implementation excluded).

System is usually maintained by provider with appropriate updates and improvements.

Training and assistance are available from provider.

Disadvantages:

System will not operate optimally due to large variety of options for various users.

Choice of hardware may be limited.

Vendor may not keep system current as anticipated.

Most firms using computers or computer services do so primarily for the property management functions. After implementing basic accounting applications the trend is to use computers for leasing brokerage listings, financing and amortization schedules, and investment analysis. The method of computer processing over the past years has shifted from the batch type service bureau to time-sharing and remote computing and, more recently to in-house systems. The larger firms have been going with mainframe and mini-computers while the smaller firms tend to go with the microcomputer or small business computer. This shift has come about because of the need for timely accurate reporting, the increasing cost-effectiveness of an in-house system, and the availability of good property management software. There is general acceptance in all forms of business that the computer, more specifically the small business computer, can help the businessman or realtor in the everyday operation of his business.

The development and implementation of an automated system should be successful if these guidelines are followed, and the option appropriate to the firm's needs are selected.

AVOIDING PITFALLS

There are a number of pitfalls to be aware of in the process of bringing automation to the firm. The first is the natural resistance to change. This is one that will plague implementation until time proves the viability of the system. The second would be a tendency to sell the system as the perfect answer to all needs. This clearly cannot be and, in time, the system will be correctly viewed as a significant improvement bringing new flexibility but not all the answers. In addition, the introduction of automation will require a degree of regimentation not experienced before. Requirements like maintenance before posting, setting up accounts before using, special input for corrections, and dependency on outsiders or specialists, will bring frustration until personnel adjust to them. The extreme flexibility that existed before will depart due to the requirements of the system. Regardless of the flexibility of the system, some will perceive it as rigid because they can no longer get the exact report they got before, or get it on the same schedule. In extreme cases, people will demand information they thought the system would provide but, in fact, no provision was made for putting it in the system. In other cases, the system will offer more features than the users can possibly comprehend and some of the power of the system will be wasted, based on this lack of knowledge. The key to mitigating these problems is to have excellent training prior to, during, and following implementation.

Years of experience in automation suggests that these types of problems and related ones often reduce the benefits that the new systems can bring. However, particularly with use of the microcomputer, the actual users of the systems are developing an understanding of the systems and an appreciation for their function that almost assures an increased ratio of success. This encouraging sign would suggest that even those who have considered automation with skepticism should again review the opportunities with an open mind.

The computer is superb at basic recordkeeping. Its use develops a discipline that inherently is healthy for a firm. The basis for this is the "system" that determines what information is kept, what parameters it must fit, how it is organized, and then permits selective reporting. This data organization allows various data bases on various properties to be related. This relation or combination permits consolidated reporting, analysis, and comparisons. It typically permits growth at a nominal increase in staff and provides increasingly for automated linkages to lockbox services, banking information, and other service organizations. It is now commonplace for a firm's auditors to directly access the data base for audit purposes thus promoting the efficiency of the process and reducing the cost. Special care must be exercised in backing up the basic records and storing these copies off-site in recognition of the exposure to destruction either through fire, theft, or pressing a wrong key. An adequate system will provide for the needed security. It is interesting to note that computer records can be stored off-site while this is not a practical alternative for ordinary business records. In effect, considering all risks, computer records can even be more secure than manual records.

One should view automation of an office in a positive manner. It is achievable through careful planning, well proven, and offers enormous potential for improving the firm's operation. A positive flexible approach should overcome the normal pitfalls.

CURRENT USES OF COMPUTERS

The real estate business is one of the nation's largest and most important industries; yet, in terms of back office operations and the effective utilization of the new data processing tools, it is one of the least effectively run structures in the country. To be specific, these are some of the problems:

1. Records are so complex and subject to change that whole departments exist to provide proper reporting information.
2. Instant and complete information is not always available for management decisions.
3. Today's changing technology makes it economically impractical for some real estate firms to install an in-house computer system in one form or another without outside assistance.
4. Finally, federal and state regulations and law in real estate make reporting requirements complex and burdensome.

All these comments, in essence, serve to demonstrate the need for standardized information and recordkeeping. Little has been done to date because of the specialization of each participant in the real estate industry, coupled with a generally confined geographic interest. Now, because of high interest rates and rising operating costs it appears that information management relative to real estate is undergoing fundamental change.

Recordkeeping involves not only the information necessary for day-to-day operation of properties, but also the historical data necessary for legal purposes as well as projections of the future.

Records in property management fall into five general categories:

1. *Property Lease Data*
    All information generally found in lease abstracts.
    Apartment history/inventory detail in heavily-regulated properties.

2. *Billing/Lockbox*
   The account status of each tenant.

3. *Cash Status Data*
   The receipts and disbursements made.

4. *Accounts Payable*
   The account status and history of vendors.

5. *General Ledger*
   Past, present, and estimated future accounting date.

Given the diverse range of real estate managed, the types of management performed and the variety of sophistication in management, we cannot identify every recordkeeping function. We can only address some key modules/systems that firms normally require. The actual content and complexity of these modules varies widely for managers of rental homes, apartments, shopping centers, office buildings, industrial properties, etc.

Master Tenant System

This property lease data system is considered the core of property management. It contains the property name, address, the tenant information, including name, address, contact person, phone, apartment number/retail space number, square footage, lease begin date, lease expiration, security deposit, sales history where percentage rents are used, and other data pertinent to the property. This system must match the needs of the business as it is the repository of key data and permits integration of reporting. It is from this system that the bills are generated, cash flows are forecast, lease expiration reports are developed, mix of tenants is reviewed, and budgets are prepared. In contrast to the accounting systems which will be discussed later, this type of system is essentially a management database and automation has opened up new opportunities for the property manager or owner to review and manage his holdings. The more complete systems include extensive management reporting such as:

1. Monitoring lease expiration and lease options to determine requirements in the leasing area and provide information for negotiations. Provides capability to sort information in various ways to set priorities.
2. Generating renewal letters and/or renewal contracts automatically, based on pre-determined increase amounts.
3. Reports on occupancy to determine trends based on weighted average occupancy and the impact of rent adjustments, upgrading of property, and the effectiveness of property management.

4. Vacancy control, through lists of vacancies expiring leases estimated income list, and ability to pro-rate for mid-month occupancy.

5. Allocation of various expenses such as taxes, common area maintenance and insurance to tenants based upon terms of the lease. This may include calculation or charges based on rentable, occupied or fixed terms.

6. Budgeting information provided by manipulation of this system. Sales and/or rent forecasts can be based upon variable selection parameters. The forecasts can utilize historical trends, percent changes, and inflation projections. By providing the link to lease expiration and renewal, the current base becomes dynamic in the area of forecasting.

7. Sales monitoring in shopping centers to forecast income based on percentage rent. They maintain a history of tenant sales to project sales based on historical trends and to project more than one type of sale per tenant. This monitoring also provides the average sales per-square-foot to spot trends in determining leasing mix.

8. Landlord utilities billing where utilities are billable based on special terms such as space utilized, power consumed directly, etc. These systems provide the means to allocate and bill those amounts.

9. Communication with tenants, utilizing the capability to produce informational mailings and notices either to all tenants or those selected based on special parameters.

10. Specialized reports, such as HUD reports, may easily be generated from this system.

11. Improvement of cash control through identification of tenants who are already late payers.

Security Deposits

Although this is usually part of the master tenant system, it is occasionally found as a separate entity—particularly if it is provided as a service by the bank where the deposits are kept. The system should provide a record of deposits, refunds, and interest, with the apartment number and tenant name on each entry.

Apartment History

As rent regulations become increasingly complex, a detailed history of each rental space becomes necessary. Abstracts of all leases and renewals, records of improvements, and other reasons for charges, or base rent increases may be kept.

Billing/Lockbox

One of the most important innovations in Property Management recordkeeping in recent years has been the automation of lockbox collection. The impact on cash management is often dramatic. The procedure is as follows:

> A bank which supports the automated lockbox function will rent a post office box in the management firm's name, from which it will make collections daily.

The management firm's computer generates bills which it specially encodes with computer-readable scan lines on the stubs which represent the apartment numbers. These bills are automatically stuffed into envelopes and sent out to the tenants. The tenants mail their payments, together with the specially encoded stubs, to the lockbox.

The bank deposits the payments directly to the management firm's account. The bank's computer reads the data coded on the stubs and sends it, together with the amount received, back to the management firm's computer.

By the following morning, all payments are posted and each tenant account is up-to-date. Automatic interfaces usually are provided to the general ledger.

Accounts Receivable

With cash status data completely up-to-date, through the billing/lockbox system late charges can be immediately and automatically billed, providing increased incentive for on-time payments by tenants.

Overdue notices can be generated automatically, as can eviction or other legal documents for serious arrears. These documents can be selectively printed, based on a particular firm's criteria.

The ability to ascertain clearly what is overdue and provide for aggressive follow-up is essential to the property manager.

A good accounts receivable system should be able to separate other charges besides rent, such as parking, mail service, utilities, penalty fees, etc. Unpaid charges may be carried forward in one of two ways:

1. *Open-item billing*—Each payment is applied to specific charges, and, if any are unpaid at the end of the month, a bill is generated with the unpaid charges itemized.

2. *Balance-forward billing*—All payments are on-account, and if any charges remain unpaid at the end of the month, the next bill is generated with only a single balance forward shown.

The accounts receivable system usually posts to the general ledger system automatically.

Accounts Payable

This system provides for payment of bills. A complete system starts by validating an invoice against a master list of approved vendors. The invoice is then coded to one or more general ledger accounts. A check is automatically printed (and the cash disbursement posted) upon demand.

A well-integrated system provides edits against the general ledger chart of accounts to assure valid entry. In addition many systems feature a vendor history which accumulates payments by vendor, automatically checks to be sure that invoices have not been paid before, and cash requirements forecasting that permits managing payments based on outstanding invoices. Automatic check reconciliation with bank statements is also included in some systems and often is linked to bank data furnished on computer tape.

General Ledger

When billing and accounts payable are automated, a well-designed computer system should be able to generate the general ledger and the financial statements with little additional input. A great benefit in this area is that the computer can do double-entry bookkeeping in such a way as to keep the books always in balance, greatly reducing the time spent at the end of a financial period for closing the books. If the data is input on a timely basis, financial statements can be made up at any time during a period, as needed.

Depending on the degree of outside accounting help, it may be possible to negotiate accounting and/or auditing fees when data is presented in computerized form.

Financial statements can now be viewed in many different ways:

1. Current figures can be compared to last year's.
2. Current figures can be compared to a budget.
3. The same report can be produced at different levels.
4. Properties and/or corporations can be combined or subdivided at will.
5. Any report can be produced on a per-square-foot or per-building basis simply by having the computer divide each figure.
6. Partnership can show entire reports broken out by any percentages desired.

Cash-Flow Statements

If income and payments are automated, a record of the cash position of each property over a period of time is kept. Modern cash management techniques depend primarily on this type of recordkeeping. Many real estate managers have no idea of how much float they are generating in their checking accounts. Separate bank accounts are kept for each property or entity. Some computer systems pay for themselves in increased use of this money alone.

Budgeting

Usually in the same format as the general ledger or linked to it, budget data can be kept on a monthly or annual basis. Each monthly amount can vary, so that seasonal expenses (such as snow removal) can be estimated only for the months in which they can be expected to occur.

Each month the system can compare expenses to budget. This is done for current period and year-to-date, with variances expressed as dollars and/or percents.

Knowing the year-to-date variance from estimates, the system can project what the total variances for the year will be at current rates of income and expense. In addition, flexible budgeting linked to occupancy levels, heat requirements based on degree days and other such refinements, become reasonable with the help from a computer.

Fixed Assets/Inventory

This system may or may not be important to the property manager in its automated form. Inventories of appliances and other items can be tracked in great detail, including purchase dates, dollar costs, maintenance records, serial numbers, locations, depreciation, and other data. This allows management to control assets and their disposition, and is very useful in providing data for tax purposes. It also allows management to keep track of which brands need repair the most, and the expected life of each.

Payroll

The complexity of recordkeeping and reportmaking in this function makes it readily adaptable to computerization. A good payroll system will handle all payroll taxes, all deductions; all government forms and reports. It will also produce employer W-2 forms at calendar year-end.

This system should also provide data to be fed into a job cost system where this is a requirement for the property manager. This will be essential to track services provided to specific tenants as well as to properly allocate costs to operation of the property. Linkage should be provided to the general ledger.

Word Processing

All correspondence and other typing can be done in this system; it is particularly useful for long documents, as it eliminates the need to re-type each time a correction is made. The automation of the typing function is often integrated into the tenant system, so as to be able to send communications easily to selected tenants.

For example, a letter specifying renewal options can be typed in outline form. The computer can then be instructed to select all tenants whose leases are expiring in a given month, apply certain percentages for one-, two-, or three-year renewals, and type each letter to the appropriate tenant with his proper renewal amounts and security increases included.

COMPUTER MODELING

In the past, computer modeling was available only to those firms and individuals fortunate enough to have access to or own their own computer. Access was usually through small keyboard terminals and phone connections. The user would be one of many terminals connected to a large scale time-sharing computer. Computer modeling would be accomplished by entering basic data and then applying a set of assumptions to that data using various "what if"-type programs. Needless to say, the use of large main frame computers for computer modeling has been, and will continue to be, an expensive decision-making tool for property managers.

The advent of the microcomputer and small personal business computers has opened up the whole area of computer modeling in the 1980s. Automatic spreadsheet programs and business planners are already being used by a wide range of businesses. Even as forecasting is made more difficult by changing depreciation rules, creative financing methods, and increasingly complex tax rules, these powerful little machines are finding their place in the real estate community.

Projections of rent rolls, tax expense and increased energy costs are typical of the "what if" questions real estate operators will be asking in the 1980s. By projecting these varying expenses a realtor will be able to write tenant leases with realistic escalation clauses. By plugging in some basic assumptions against an accurate data base, realtors can determine whether to keep or sell a property.

The analysis of real estate using more advanced methods and modern personal business microcomputers will proliferate throughout the United States during this decade. This analysis will involve many more factors upon which decisions are made. No one individual can match the power and accuracy of the computer and produce the desired results within a time frame that makes the data analyzed useful. By projecting into future years, one can easily see the direct impact of inflation, the time value of money, taxes, and cash flow requirements.

Modeling can give immediate financial comparison of similar properties to determine which one would provide the best yield. By consolidating a pending acquisition with an existing portfolio, the real estate operator can determine the overall impact resulting from such an acquisition. Similarly, projecting the elimination of one or more troublesome properties may be accomplished by requesting an optimization of the yield from the portfolio. Computer modeling will provide important management information for realtors for the acquisition and operation of properties. An additional benefit from such modeling is the projection of percentage rents for commercial and shopping center operators.

Shopping center operators usually rent their properties by the square-foot plus a percentage of sales over a set dollar amount. This information is usually submitted monthly and sometimes annually and probably later than the realtor would like. Upon receipt of the sales data, the shopping center manager will issue a charge if the sales exceed the break point. By maintaining the reported sales information and some sophisticated use of computer modeling, a shopping center operator can project the annual sales of tenants and use this information as justification for billing a tenant an estimated projected monthly percentage rent charge. When actual sales data is received, the proper adjustment to the estimated charge may then be made. This is an example of using computer modeling not only to project future income and expenses, but actually to collect percentage rent charges and improve cash flow.

FUTURE USES OF COMPUTERS IN REAL ESTATE

The bounds of computer use are limited only by imagination. Some trends and uses we can foresee include:

Automatic Funds Transfer: For many years the banking community has been trying to implement the automatic payment of bills by its customers. This is finally becoming a reality, with automatic payment of rents as one of the priority items. There are great opportunities here for cash flow improvement and reduction of paperwork.

More Sophisticated Integration of Computer Processes: As the computer industry "grows up," systems become more powerful, and capable of doing many more functions without the need for intervention by an operator. There is increasing use of database systems that link information together to address the "what if" questions that are needed for sophisticated management. Telecommunications links operations and remote offices to answer inquiries and to support geographic expansion.

Lower Costs and Better Equipment: A general rule in computers is that it will always be cheaper to do it next year. Keep in mind that if it's cost-effective now you should do it now. Expect to trade-up to a newer system within a few years, just as you would a car. Your needs will expand and the requirements for support in your business will expand. Micro-computers are replacing mini-computers, while mini's grow to take over main frame functions.

Systems will be Easier to Use: There has been increasing emphasis on the machine man interface. Recent breakthroughs indicate remarkable advances are imminent. You can anticipate easier implementation with less training and resistance to new systems.

Integrated Software: As in the machine-man interface, developments are moving very fast. Computer graphics are advancing rapidly, providing easy preparation and presentation of material in graphic form complete with color. Documentation is improving and integration of applications means stable, reliable data bases across various applications.

SOFTWARE EVALUATION

The process of software evaluation, which was alluded to in our discussion of defining needs, reviewing current systems, and evaluating of alternatives will now be reviewed. The base for the process starts with the clear definition of requirements. These requirements should be ranked high to low—from "must have" to "would be nice to have." Having accomplished this, the next step would be to seek proposals from in-house staff, software vendors, and service bureaus. If this is to be very structured, a formal "request for proposal" (RFP) may be issued to which all respondents must reply by a specific date. An informal approach would be to ask interested parties to tell you what they can offer in the automated property management area.

How do you determine who to send RFP's to or whom to approach? It may be from general industry knowledge of who is progressive, a recommendation of your auditors, a review of service bureau offerings, hardware vendor's suggestions, your bank's recommendations, or other varied sources. It is such a broad field that the initial search should not be limited. Follow all reasonable leads. Look for company strength, number of systems installed, a list of users to contact, and in particular, those systems that appear to address your specific business needs. It is not uncommon to uncover a system that may not be on the market but one in which a company similar to yours would be pleased to recoup some of its investment. Do not overlook the candid information that can be gleaned from a series of phone calls. However, only a few systems will warrant formal presentations and indepth reviews. If you are wary, engage a professional consultant to assist but be aware of any biases. Given a variety of offerings, a consultant will typically opt for those he is intimately familar with. You may be precluded from a better system because your consultant does not really understand the options. While this is not unique to software selection, it is an inherent danger. Use your consultant as an advisor, not as the decision maker.

The next step would be to match the software item-by-item against your list of requirements. Have the vendor participate in this with your staff. Let him tell you how it functions, what data is in the system files, and what reports are available. If he says they do not have such a report but it would be easy to do, ask him to have it done so you can see it. If the system is to be developed internally, probe with the same intensity. It is more difficult since there is nothing operational to review and you are only dealing with conceptual systems. The more elaborate your requirements, the less likely you will be satisfied and the greater your cost will be. Be realistic, and work with basics. In any case, list your requirements and then provide a column for rating each system on how well it fulfills each of them. Eliminate any that fail on key issues. Take the two or three systems that then rate highest and evaluate them further on reputation, user feedback, ability of their personnel to work well with your staff, a viable implementation plan, documentation, training, expandability, and future support and improvements to system (new modules, new features, on-line capability, etc.). If it is for in-house operation, have estimated timings of runs, resources required, and costs from your staff. If run by a service bureau, these will be available automatically as part of their response. Remember, service bureau costs include the price of software amortization.

The decision should be relatively clear at this time. If not, probe further, and see if the top runners are willing to offer any special concessions that make their offer more attractive. Remember, you are usually only spending a small amount on the package itself, so dollar differences by themselves are not that meaningful. Conversion, implementation, training, and operation of the system over several years will easily offset most dollar differences. For a new system being developed, try to determine how good the estimates of time and cost may be; if it will be dependent on hiring new staff, find what other projects are being developed that will compete with it for resources, and what the track record is for other previously developed systems.

With major proven software, your chance of any major mistakes are minimal if you follow these procedures. Problems usually have to do with inadequate training, understanding, or operations rather than true system deficiencies. However, these problems are usually attributed to an inadequate system. For systems chosen under development, or planned for future development, the risks are high, but the pay-off may be high also. This is usually true where the application is unique or the approach to the application is very unusual. You must assess the risk-reward equation.

SUMMARY

Improvements in hardware have been followed by similar trends in software. These trends continue. As was pointed out initially, effective systems are necessary today for efficient management of resources. The real estate manager or owner should incorporate use of the computer if they have not done so, or continue its expansion where systems are in place.

FORMS APPENDICES

APPENDICES CONTENTS

work, cooperation, responsibility, initiative, quantity of work and dependability

Appendix 19.   Employment application

Appendix 20.   Fee register to keep record of cash application fee

Appendix 21.   Inspection report (apartment maintenance checklist) (move-in) to be signed by tenant and maintenance department at time of occupancy

Appendix 22.   Inspection report (move-out) indicating condition of vacated apartment and disposition of security deposit

Appendix 23.   Late notice to be sent by management company to tenant

Appendix 24.   Lease abstract review form (residential) summarizing major terms of the lease

Appendix 25.   Lease abstract review form (commercial) summarizing major terms of the lease

Appendix 26.   Lease addendum to be added as a rider to the original apartment lease

Appendix 27.   Lease addendum including notice of rent increase (usually sent with renewal)

Appendix 28.   Maintenance call-in sheet for tenant's requests for service

Appendix 29.   Move-in sheet for new tenants including amount of any pro-rated rent

Appendix 30.   Personnel action notice including personal data, salary, allowances, rate change (cause and amount), etc.

Appendix 31.   Petty cash reimbursement voucher and reconciliation of petty cash fund

Appendix 32.   Purchase confirmation showing list of invoices, description of item, location of use and amount

Appendix 33.   Rental information sheet giving manager particulars of individual complex

Appendix 34.   Credit bureau associates and rentcheck/telecheck notice to new tenants regarding credit reporting

Appendix 35.   Rent roll summarizing leases and rents

Appendix 36.   Security deposit agreement to be signed by tenants and management company

Appendix 37.   Tenant application including personal data, present and previous addresses and employment information of prospective tenants

Appendix 38.   Tenant card for record of amounts paid

Appendix 39.   Time card for employee's regular and overtime hours

Appendix 40.   Traffic sheet to keep record of interested tenants

APPENDIX 1.

BUILDING MANAGEMENT AGREEMENT

Regarding

_____[MAJOR OFFICE BUILDING]

Between

_____[OFFICE BUILDING OWNER]

And

_____[PROPERTY MANAGER]

TABLE OF CONTENTS

BUILDING MANAGEMENT AGREEMENT

        This Building Management Agreement (the "Agreement")
dated as of the _____ day of _____, 19__, by and
between _____, a
Pennsylvania _____ having an office
at _____, _____,
Pennsylvania _____ ("Owner")
and _____, a
Pennsylvania _____ located
at _____, _____,
Pennsylvania _____ ("Manager")

              W I T N E S S E T H:

        WHEREAS Owner owns or has the right to collect rents
from and manage that certain building presently known
as _____ and intended to be
constructed on premises located at _____, _____
as more specifically described in Schedule "A" attached hereto
and made a part hereof and desires to engage Manager to manage
the same;

        NOW THEREFORE, in consideration of the mutual covenants
hereinafter set forth and other good and valuable considerations
and intending to be legally bound hereby, the parties agree for
themselves and their successors and assigns as follows:

                  ARTICLE 1

                THE PROPERTY

        1.01 The Property. The property described and
identified in Schedule "A" is the real property to come under the
terms and conditions of this Agreement. As used in this
Agreement, Schedule "A" shall also mean the amended or revised
list of all properties which may from time to time be under the
management of Manager. Each Property listed on Schedule "A",
which may be amended in writing from time to time, is hereinafter
referred to as a or the Property," and more than one Property are
referred to as "Properties". No parcel of real property shall be
subject to the terms and conditions of this Agreement unless
specifically listed under Schedule "A".

                  ARTICLE 2

               COMMENCEMENT DATE

        2.01 Term of Agreement. Manager's appointment under
this Agreement shall begin as of the _____ day of _____,
19__, and unless terminated prior thereto in accordance with the
terms and provisions of Article 14 hereof shall remain in full
force and effect until _____, and shall continue
thereafter from month to month in full force and effect,
terminable upon fifteen (15) days written notice by Owner or
Manager.

ARTICLE 3

MANAGER'S RESPONSIBILITIES

3.01 <u>Management-Scope of Services</u>. Manager shall manage, operate, and maintain the Property listed on <u>Schedule "A"</u> in an efficient and satisfactory manner. Manager shall act in a fiduciary capacity with respect to the proper protection of and accounting for Owner's assets. In this capacity, Manager shall deal at arm's length with all third parties, and Manager shall serve Owner's interests at all times. The management scope of services to be performed by Manager with respect to the Property during the Design and Pre-opening and the Operating phases of the development and operation of the Property are set forth in <u>Schedule "B"</u>, attached hereto and made a part hereof. Such services shall be performed in accordance with the terms and conditions set forth in this agreement.

3.02 <u>Employees; Independent Contractor</u>. Manager shall have in its employ at all times a sufficient number of capable employees to enable it to properly, adequately, safely and economically manage, operate, and maintain the Property. Manager may upon Owner's prior written approval employ such persons through a subcontract provided that Manager remains fully liable for the performance and quality of the services to be performed hereunder. Manager may subcontract or otherwise delegate without Owner's prior approval, to its wholly owned subsidiary (ies) _____ and/or _____ any or all of Manager's services to be performed under this Agreement, provided that Manager shall remain fully liable to Owner for the performance and quality of such services and for such subsidiaries failure or default. All matters pertaining to the employment of such employees are the responsibility of Manager, which is in all respects the employer of such employees. Manager shall fully comply or cause to be complied with all applicable laws and regulations having to do with workers's compensation, social security, unemployment insurance, hours of labor, wages, working conditions, and other employer-employee related subjects. Manager represents that it and its subcontractors, if any, are and will continue to be Equal Opportunity Employers during the term of this Agreement. This Agreement is not one of agency by Manager for Owner but one with Manager engaged independently in the business of managing properties on its own behalf as an independent contractor. All employment arrangements are therefore solely Manager's concern, and Owner shall have no liability or responsibility with respect thereto.

3.03 <u>Schedule of Reimbursable Employees and Fees</u>. The Schedule of Reimbursable Employees and Fees relating to the Design and Pre-opening Phases and the Operating Phase, attached hereto as <u>Schedule "C"</u>, sets forth for the Property, subject to the terms and conditions of this Agreement with respect to (1) the employees employed "on-site" in the direct management, operating and maintenance of the Property, and (2) the "off-site" employees whose salaries shall be charged pro-rata to the Property for services rendered in connection with the management, operation and maintenance of the Property, (i) the number of such Employees, (ii) the titles and salaries of such Employees, (iii) whether or not such Employees shall be bonded, and (iv) the pro rata share of any salary therefore, if any, that shall be charged to the Property. Manager's employees, whose salaries may not be charged pro-rata as to the Property, include, without limitation, general management personnel, accountants and auditors.

3.04 <u>Compliance with Laws, Mortgages, etc</u>. Manager shall be responsible for full compliance with Federal, State and Municipal laws, ordinances, regulations and orders relative to the management, maintenance of the Property and with the rules, regulations or orders of the local Board of Fire Underwriters or other similar body. Manager shall promptly remedy any violation of any such law, ordinance, rule, regulation or order which comes to its attention.

Expenses incurred in remedying violations may be paid from the "Operating Account" (as such term is hereinafter defined) provided such expenses do not exceed the sum of _____ ($_____) Dollars in any one instance. In the event that (i) more than such amount is required, or (ii) the violation is one for which the Property title holder might be subject to a fine or penalty, Manager shall notify Owner on the next business day in order that prompt arrangements may be made to cure or remedy the violation.

Manager shall be responsible for full compliance with all terms and conditions contained in any ground lease, space lease, mortgage, deed of trust or other operating or security instruments affecting the Property, provided that Owner supplies to Manager copies of the instruments or documents affecting each Property. Manager shall not be required to make any payment on account thereof.

3.05 <u>Approved Budgets</u>. Manager shall prepare and submit to Owner a proposed "Operating Budget" and a proposed "Capital Budget" for the Manager's operation, repair and maintenance of Property for the forthcoming calendar year prepared on a monthly basis. Each proposed budget shall be delivered to Owner within thirty (30) days after the execution of this Agreement and each subsequent proposed budget no later than October 1 of each calendar year.

Owner will consider the proposed budgets and then will consult with Manager in the ensuing period prior to the commencement of the forthcoming calendar year in order to approve and agree on an "Approved Operating Budget" and an "Approved Capital Budget".

Manager agrees to use due diligence and to employ all reasonable efforts to ensure that the actual costs of maintaining and operating the Property shall not exceed either the Approved Operating Budget and the Approved Capital Budget pertaining thereto either in total or in any one accounting category. Manager shall secure Owner's prior written approval for any expenditure (except for utility costs) that, when added to other actual and budgeted expenditures, would cause total expenditures to exceed 105% of the annual budgeted amount in any one accounting category; provided, however, that in the event of any such written approval by Owner to the amount of any excess expenditure in any one accounting category, the excess expenditure amount approved by Owner shall not be taken into consideration thereafter in the determination of whether Owner's written approval shall thereafter be required in connection with other such excess expenditure.

During the calendar year, Manager agrees to inform Owner of any major increases in costs and expenses that were not foreseen during the budget preparation period and were not therefore reflected in either the Approved Operating Budget or Approved Capital Budget.

3.06 <u>Collection of Rents and Other Income</u>. Manager shall use diligent efforts to collect all rents (including additional rent or escalation billings resulting from tenant participation in increases in expenses, taxes and common area maintenance charges) and other charges which may become due at any time from any tenant or from others for services provided in connection with or for the use of the Property or any portion thereof. Manager shall collect and identify any income due Owner from miscellaneous services provided on the Property to tenants or the public including, but not limited to, parking income, tenant storage, and coin-operated machines of all types (e.g., vending machines, pay telephones, etc.). All moneys so collected shall be deposited promptly into the Operating Account. Manager shall not terminate any lease, lock out any tenant, or institute suit for rent or for use and occupancy or proceedings for recovery of possession, without the prior written approval of Owner. In connection with such suits or proceeding, only legal counsel designated in writing by Owner shall be retained. Expenses actually incurred by Manager in beinging such approved suit or proceeding will be paid from the operating Account. Manager shall not write off any income items without prior written approval of Owner.

3.07 <u>Repairs.</u> Manager shall attend to the making and supervision of all ordinary and extraordinary repairs, decorations and alterations. Except as otherwise previously budgeted and approved by Owner, no single expenditure made for these purposes shall exceed the sum of ($_____) Dollars without the prior written approval of Owner. Actual and reasonable expenses for material and labor for such purposes will be paid from the Operating Account. The prior agreement by Owner to the Propery's Annual Operating Budget does not override or negate Owner's right of approval with respect to individual expenditures exceeding the foregoing limitation. In an emergency Manager may, if in Manager's reasonable opinion such emergency requires immediate action, make expenditures for repairs in excess of such limit.

3.08 <u>Capital Expenditures</u>. The Approved Capital Budget shall not consitute an authorization for Manager to expend any money. Any capital expenditure in excess of _____ ($_____) Dollars, or if the total capital expenditures for the fiscal year exceed _____ ($_____) Dollars in the aggregate, all capital expenditures irrespective of the amount thereof, must be specifically authorized in writing by Owner. With respect to the purchase and installation of major items of new or replacement equipment (including, without limitation, elevators, heating or air conditioning equipment, incinerators, furniture and furnishings, rugs, carpets or other floor coverings, and other similar items), Manager shall recommend that Owner purchase these items when Manager believes such purchase or purchases to be necessary or desirable. Owner may arrange to purchase and install such items itself or may authorize Manager to do so subject to the supervision of consultant and Owner's Architect or other design or engineering consultant and Owner's specification requirements, either by memorandum or as an amendment to this Agreement, all new or replacement equipment exceeding ($_____) Dollars unless otherwise authorized in writing by Owner shall be awarded on the behalf of competitive bidding.

(a) When reasonably available or obtainable, a minimum of three (3) written bids shall be obtained for each purchase;

(b) Each bid will be solicited in a uniform form so that uniformity will exist in the bid quotes;

(c) Manager shall provide Owner with all bid responses accompanied by Manager's recommendations as to the most acceptable bid (if Manager advises acceptance of other than the lowest bidder, Manager shall adequately support, in writing, its recommendations); and

(d) Owner shall be free to accept or reject any and all bids.

Owner will communicate to Manager its acceptance of rejection of bids. Owner may pay for capital expenses from its own resources or may authorize payment by Manager out of the Operating Account.

3.09 Service Contracts. Manager shall not enter into any contract for cleaning, maintaining, repairing or servicing any Property or any of the consitituent parts of any Property without the prior written consent of Owner. As a condition to obtaining such consent, Manager shall supply Owner with a copy of the proposed contract and shall state to Owner the relationship, if any, between Manager (or the person or persons in control of Manager) and the party proposed to supply such goods or services, or both. Unless otherwise previously approved by Owner each service contract shall (i) have a term not in excess of one (1) year and (ii) require that the contractor provide evidence of satisfactory insurance coverage. Unless Owner specifically waives such requirements, either by memorandum or as an amendment to this Agreement, all service contracts with respect to the annual cost to Owner which will exceed _____ ($_____) Dollars shall be subject to bid under the procedure specified in Section 3.08. In the event that this Agreement (a) is terminated as to any specific Property under Section 14.01 hereof, or (b) expires on the date set forth in Section 2.01 hereof, Owner agrees to comply with all of Manager's obligations subsequent to (but not prior to) any such respective termination or expiration date under all service contracts approved by Owner, as aforesaid, as to any specific Property or any such termination under Section 14.01 or as to all Properties covered by this Agreement in the event that this Agreement expires under Section 2.01 hereof.

3.10 Taxes, Mortgages. Manager shall, if so requested, obtain and verify bills for real estate and personal property taxes, improvement assessments and other like charges which are or may become liens against each Property, and Manager shall recommend payment or appeal as its best judgment may decide. Manager shall forward such bills to Owner for payment by Owner in such time to permit Owner to take advantage of all discounts. Manager will participate and cooperate with Owner's counsel with respect to any and all Appeals or protests of Real Estate taxes or assessments affecting the Property. Manager shall not make any payments on account of any ground lease, mortgage, deed of trust or other security instrument, if any, affecting the Property.

3.11 _Leasing and Cross Default._ Owner intends to engage the services of a leasing agent to lease the Property and Manager agrees to cooperate with such leasing agent in furtherance of Owner's leasing program and to provide such leasing agent with such information as may be necessary to facilitate the performance of such services. In the event Manager or an affiliate of Manager is employed by Owner as leasing agent to lease the Property pursuant to a separate agreement, Manager's (or its affiliate's) failure to perform its obligations under such Leasing Agreement or any default by Manager (or its affiliate) may, at Owner's sole and absolute option, constitute a default under this Agreement.

3.12 _Advertising._ Manager shall not use Owner's name in any advertising or promotional material without Owner's express prior written approval in each instance. Manager's advertising and promotional materials shall be prepared in full compliance with Federal, State and Municipal laws, ordinances, regulations, and orders. The Approved Operating Budget for each Property shall contain an accounting category for the cost of (i) any advertising and (ii) the printing of any promotional materials for the Property approved by Owner in writing and not otherwise prepared by owner's leasing agent. Manager shall bear the sole cost and expense of all brochures, plans, advertising and promotional materials which list or discuss the Property together with other properties for which Manager acts as Manager or which constitute general advertising materials of Manager. All references to the Building in such general materials must have the prior written approval of Owner.

3.13 _Signs._ Subject to all applicable laws and regulations, an appropriate sign or signs indicating Management as Owner's "Manager" for each Property shall, at Owner's sole cost and expense, and subject to Owner's prior written approval, be placed in or about the lobby or entrances to the Property, the exterior of the Property and directory boards within the Property.

ARTICLE 4

INSURANCE

4.01 _Insurance._ Owner, at its expense, will obtain and keep in force adequate insurance against physical damage (e.g., fire with extended coverage endorsement, boiler and machinery, operation or maintenance of any of the Property and each other Property added to _Schedule "A"_ by amendment hereto. Manager will be covered as an additional insured in all liability insurance maintained with respect to Property and each other Property added to _Schedule "A"_. Owner shall save Manager harmless from any liability on account of loss, damage or injury actually insured against by Owner with respect to the Property, provided Manager:

(a)   notifies Owner on the next business day after Manager receives notice of any such loss, damage or injury;

(b)   takes no action (such as admission of liability) which might bar Owner from obtaining any protection afforded by any policy Owner may hold or which might prejudice Owner in Owner's defense to a claim based on such loss, damage or injury; and

(c)   agrees that Owner shall have the exculsive right, at Owner's option, to conduct the defense to any claim, demand or suit within limits prescribed by the policy or policies of insurance. Nothing herein shall be construed as indemnifying Manager against any error, omission or deliberate act of Manager or its agents, servants, employees, or contractors or indemnifying Manager against any error, omission or act for which insurance protection is not available; neither is the foregoing intended to affect the general requirement of this Agreement that the Property, and each other Property added to Schedule "A" by amendment hereto, shall be managed, leased, operated and maintained by Manager in a safe condition and in a proper and careful manner.

Manager shall furnish whatever information is requested by Owner for the purpose of establishing the placing of insurance coverages or surety bonds and shall aid and cooperate in every reasonable way with respect to such insurance and any loss thereunder. Owner shall include in the Standard Fire and Extended Coverage Policy of Insurance covering the property or the personal property, fixtures or equipment located thereon, and Manager shall include in any fire policies for Owner's furniture, furnishings or fixtures situated on the Property, appropriate clauses pursuant to which the respective insurance carriers shall waive all rights of subrogation with respect to losses payable under such policies and having obtained such clause or endorsement of waiver of subrogation or consent to a waiver of right of recovery, Owner hereby agrees that it will not make any claim against or seek to recover from Agent for any loss or damage to property of the type covered by such insurance.

4.02 Additional Insurance. Manager must furnish evidence of comprehensive crime insurance in amounts of not less than_____ ($_____) Dollars or such higher amount as may be routinely provided Manager to owners of other similar properties managed by Manager. Owner shall be named as an additional insured under such policy or policies. Owner will not reimburse Manager for Manager's cost of such insurance or for any and all coverages that Manager obtains for its own account.

ARTICLE 5

FINANCIAL REPORTING AND RECORDKEEPING

5.01 Books of Accounts. Manager, in the conduct of its responsibilities of Owner, shall maintain adequate and separate books and records for the Property and each other Property, if any, added to Schedule "A" by amendment hereto, the entries to which shall be supported by sufficient documentation or computer records to ascertain that said entries are properly and accurately recorded to the Account . for the Property or that for each other Property, if any, added to Schedule "A". Such books and records shall be maintained by Manager at the Property or at Manager's _____or at such other location as may be approved by Owner in writing. Manager shall ensure such control over accounting and financial transactions as is reasonably required to protect Owner's assets from error or fraudulent activity on the part of Manager's agents, servants, associates or employees. Losses arising from such instances are to be borne by Manager and shall include but not be limited to:

(a)   Theft of assets by Manager's agents, associates, servants, or employees;

(b)   Penalties, interest or loss of vendor discounts due to delay in payment of invoices, bills or other like charges (except where such penalties, interest or loss of vendor discounts are solely due to failure of Owner to provide sufficient funds in the Operating Account);

(c)   Overpayment or duplicate payment of invoice arising from either fraud or error;

(d)   Overpayment of labor costs arising from either fraud or error;

(e)   A sum equal to the value of any form of payment from purveyors to Manager's agents, servants, employees or associates arising from the purchase of goods or services for Owner's Properties; and

(f)   Unauthorized use of facilities by Manager's agents, associates, servants, or employees.

5.02   Account Classification. Manager shall adopt Owner's "Chart of Accounts" (a system of classification of accounting entries) or at Owner's request provide a means of classification which can be easily translated or conformed by Owner to Owner's requirements.

5.03   Financial Reports. Manager shall furnish reports of all transactions occurring from the 16th day of the prior month to the 15th day of the current month. These reports are to be received by Owner no later than ten (10) calendar days after the end of the above-described accounting period and much show, rounded to the nearest dollar, all collections, expenses, delinquencies, uncollectible items, vacancies and other matters pertaining to the management, operation and maintenance of Property during the month. The reports shall include the items listed on Schedule "D" annexed hereto and made a part hereof and shall also include a comparison of monthly and year-to-date actual income and expense with the monthly and year-to-date Approved Operating Budget for each Property. In addition, Manager shall render to Owner all unexpended funds (except for a reserve for contingencies which shall remain in the Operating Account in the amount of _____ ($_____) Dollars or disbursements have been made from the Operating Account in each Property's Operating Account as of the 15th of the reporting month. The remittance shall be gross of any Manager's fee payable under the terms and conditions of this Agreement.

5.04   Supporting Documentation. As additional support to the monthly financial statement, Manager shall provide copies of the following:

(a)   All bank statements, cancelled checks, if available, bank deposit slips, bank reconciliations and computer records,

(b)   Detailed cash receipts and disbursement listings,

(c)   Paid invoices, (d)   Detailed monthly rent roll showing prior month delinquencies and advances, current month charges and collections, and delinquencies and advances at the end of the current period,

(e)   Summaries of unpaid vendor changes, invoices or other known liabilities, exceeding _____ ($_____) Dollars or more than sixty (60) days overdue,

(f)   Supporting documentation for payroll, payroll taxes and employee benefits, and

(g)   Support for any adjusting entries.

5.05   Accounting Principles.   All financial statements and reports required by Owner will be prepared on a cash basis in accordance with general accepted accounting principles.

ARTICLE 6

OWNER'S RIGHT TO AUDIT

6.01   Audit by Owner.   Owner reserves the right for Owner's employees or others appointed by Owner to conduct examination, without notification, of the books and records maintained for owner by Manager and regardless of where the books and records are located.   Owner also reserves the right to perform any and all additional audit tests relating to Manager's activities either at the Property or at any office of the Manager, provided such audit tests are related to those activities performed by Manager for Owner and performed within a reasonable time following the transaction or period in question, but in no event more than five (5) years thereafter.

Should Owner's employees or appointees discover either weaknesses in internal control or errors in recordkeeping, Manager shall correct such discrepancies either upon discovery or within a reasonable period of time.   Manager shall promptly inform Owner in writing of the action to be taken to correct such audit discrepancies.

Any and all such audits conducted either by Owner's employees or appointees will be at the sole expense of Owner.

ARTICLE 7

BANK ACCOUNTS

7.01   Operating Account.   Manager shall deposit all rents and other funds collected from the operation of each Property, including any and all advance funds, in a bank approved by Owner in a special account ("Operating Account") for the Property in the following name:

_____
Office Building Operating Account

In the event that more than one Property is subject to this Agreement, the above name shall be amended by Owner to create a unique account name for each Property account.   Out of each account, Manager shall pay the operating expenses of the respective Property and any other payments relative to each Property as required by the terms of this Agreement.

Owner shall from time to time deposit sufficient sums in the Operating Account to permit Manager to pay the operating expenses for the Property in accordance with Article 8 hereof.

7.02 <u>Security Deposit Account</u>. Where law requires the tenant security deposits be separately maintained, a separate account (or separate interest-bearing account) will be opened by Manager at a bank approved by Owner. Such account shall be maintained in accordance with applicable law. The account will be used only for maintaining tenant security deposits and will be opened under the following name:

<u>Office Building Account-Security Deposits</u>

In case of more than one Property, separate security deposit account will be maintained for each Property, and the above name will be amended by Owner to create a unique name for each account. Manager will maintain detailed records of all security deposits deposited in each account, and such records will be open for inspection by Owner's employees or appointees. Manager shall obtain prior written approval of Owner prior to the return of such deposits to any particular tenent when the amount of such return, in any single instance, exceeds
($ _____) Dollars.

7.03 <u>Change of Banks</u>. Owner may from time to time direct Manager to change a depository bank or the depository arrangements.

ARTICLE 8

PAYMENTS OF EXPENSES

8.01 <u>Manager's Cost to be Reimbursed</u>. The following costs shall be paid out of the Operating Account:

(a) Costs of the gross salary and wages or pro rata share thereof, payroll taxes, insurance, workmen's compensation and other benefits of Manager's employees required to properly, adequately, safely and economically manage, lease, operate and maintain each Property subject to this Agreement, provided that such employees have been identified and enumerated on <u>Schedule "C"</u> of this Agreement relating to such Property.

(b) Cost of printed forms and supplies required for use at a or the Property.

8.02 <u>Costs Eligible for Payment from Operating Account</u>. Manager may pay the following expenses directly from the Operating Account subject to the conditions outlined in Article 3 of this Agreement:

(a) Cost to correct any violation of Federal, State and Municipal laws, ordinances, regulations and orders relative to the leasing, management, use, repair and maintenance of such Properties or relative to the rules, regulations or orders of the local Board of Fire Underwriters or other similar body, provided such cost is not the result of Manager's negligence and the making of all repairs.

(b) Actual and reasonable cost of operating expenses/decorations and alterations, provided such cost is not the result of Manager's negligence.

(c) Cost incurred by Manager resulting from an Owner-approved suit for the collection of rentals.

(d)   Cost of collection of delinquent rentals collected through an attorney or collection agency approved by Owner.

(e)   Cost of capital expenditures subject to the restrictions in Section 3.08 of this Agreement.   (f)Cost of printed checks for each bank account required by Owner.

(g)   Cost of cash register, adding machines and other equipment of such type and use (excluding any and all electronic data processing equipment of such type and use) (excluding any and all electronic data processing equipment) located at a Property and owned by Owner.

ARTICLE 9

MANAGER'S COSTS NOT TO BE REIMBURSED

9.01 Non-reimbursable Costs.   The following expenses or costs incurred by or on behalf of Manager in connection with the management leasing of any particular Property shall at the sole cost and expense of Manager and shall not be reimbursed by Owner.

(a)   Cost of gross salary and wages, payroll taxes, insurance, workmen's compensation and other benefits of Manager's office personnel not identified in the Schedule "C" relating to the Property.

(b)   Cost of general accounting and reporting services which are considered to be within the reasonable scope of Manager's responsibility to Owner.

(c)   Cost of forms, papers, ledgers and other supplies and equipment used in Manager's office at any location off the Property or Properties.

(d)   Cost of electronic data processing equipment or any pro rata charge thereon, whether or not located at a Property.

(e)   Cost of electronic data processing or any pro rata charge thereon, whether or not located at a Property.

(f)   Cost of all bonuses paid by Manager to Manager's agents, servants, employees or associates to and from each Property.

(g)   Cost of advance made to Manager's agents, servants, employees or associates, and the cost of travel by Manager's agents, servants, employees or associates to and from each Property.

(h)   Cost attributable to losses arising from negligence or fraud on the part of Manager's agents, servants, employees or associates.

(i)   Cost of comprehensive crime insurance (including bonding employees).

ARTICLE 10

INSUFFICIENT GROSS INCOME

10.01 Priorities. If at any time the gross income from
any particular Property shall not be sufficient to pay the bills
and charges which may be incurred with respect to such Property
or if such gross income is insufficient to pay the combined sum
of both bills and charges, then such items will be paid out of
the Operating Accounting in the following order of priority:

(a) First, bills and charges of third parties.

(b) Second, bills and charges, if any, incurred by
Manager for Manager's services provided to Owner.

10.02 Statement of Unpaid Items. After Manager has
paid, to the extent of available gross income, all bills and
charges based upon the ordered priorities set forth in Section
10.01, Manager shall submit to Owner a statement of all remaining
unpaid bills. Owner shall promptly provide sufficient moneys to
pay any such unpaid bills.

10.03 Segregation of Accounts. In each instance where
Manager manages several Properties for Owner, Manager shall
segregate the income and expenses of each Property so that gross
income from each Property will be applied only to the bills and
charges from that Property.

ARTICLE 11

SALE OF A PROPERTY

11.01 Manager Not A Sales Broker. In the event that
Owner desires to sell a Property through a real estate broker
while this Agreement is in effect, Owner shall have no obligation
whatsoever to contact Manager relative to acting as Owner's real
estate broker on such sale.

11.02 Cooperation with Sales Broker. If Owner executes
a listing agreement with a real estate broker for sale of any of
the Properties, Manager shall cooperate with such real estate
broker to the end that the respective activities of Manager and
the real estate broker may be carried on without friction and
without interference with or unnecessary inconvenience to tenants
and occupants of the Property. Manager will permit the real
estate broker to exhibit any particular Property during
reasonable business hours, provided the real estate broker has
secured the Manager's permission in advance. The ability to sell
any Property is important to Owner, and Manager agrees that the
failure on its part to extend cooperation to a real estate broker
desiring to show a Property is a default on its part under this
Agreement.

ARTICLE 12

COOPERATION

12.01 Cooperation. Should any claims, demands, suits
or other legal proceedings be made or instituted by any entity or
person against Owner of title holder of the Property which arise
out of any of the matters relating to this Agreement, Manager
shall give Owner all pertinent information and all reasonable
assistance in the defense or other disposition thereof.

ARTICLE 13

COMPENSTATION

13.01 Compensation. During the term of this Agreement
and any renewal thereof, the sole and only compensation payable
to Manager for all services to be performed and supplied by
Manager under the terms and conditions of this Agreement shall,
except as otherwise specifically set forth in this Agreement, be
as set forth in Schedule "B".

ARTICLE 14

TERMINATION

14.01 Termination as to Specific Property. This
Agreement shall terminate automatically as to any specific
Property on the date of the sale thereof by Owner. Owner shall
promptly give Manager written notice of any such termination.

14.02 Termination for Cause After Notice. In the event
that Owner at any time shall deem the performance of Manager
under this Agreement unsatisfactory by failure of Manager (i) to
fully perform the services required of Manager herein, or (ii) to
fully comply with all terms, conditions or covenants hereof,
(iii) or to fully perform services required of Manager or its
affiliate under the Exclusive Leasing Agency Agreement regarding
the Property of even date herewith or to fully comply with the
terms, conditions or covenants of Leasing Agent thereunder, Owner
shall notify Manager in writing of such failure, and, if the
conditions specified therein by Owner are not corrected to
Owner's satisfaction within thirty (30) days after receipt of
such notice (or such longer period of time as agreed to by Owner
in said notice) by Manager, then, in that event, Owner shall have
the right in Owner's sole discretion to immediately terminate
this Agreement by notice in writing to Manager.

14.03 Automatic Termination Without Notice. This
Agreement shall automatically terminate, without any further
action by Owner or any period of notice, immediately upon the
happening of any of the following events: (i) the dissolution of
termination of the corporate existence of Manager (except where
(i) Manager's parent company or (ii) a wholly owned subsidiary of
Manager succeeds to substantially all of Manager's part to
continue to do business); (ii) the termination or suspension of
Manager's real estate brokerage license; (iii) the insolvency of
Manager; (iv) the making of an assignment for the benefit of
creditors by Manager; (v) the filing by Manager of a petition in
bankruptcy, or for reorganization, or for the appointment of a
receiver; (vi) the filing of a petition in bankruptcy against
Manager; (vii) the appointment of a receiver or conservator or
other judicial representative for Manager; and (viii) the failure
of Manager to properly deal with any operating and security
deposit accounts concerning any Property.

14.04 Obligations and Rights After Termination or
Expiration. In the event that this Agreement is terminated as to
any specific Property under Section 14.01 hereof, Owner shall
within thirty (30) days pay Manager (i) the proportionate part of
the monthly fee for the current month (prorated to the date of
termination) under Section 13.01, provided that Manager is
entitled to receive said monthly fee for that Property under the
terms and conditions of this Agreement, and (ii) the
proportionate part of the Management Fee due for the current

month (pro rated to the date of termination) under Section 13.01 based on the Management Fee paid to Manager for the prior month, provided that Manager is entitled to receive said Management Fee for that Property under the terms and conditions of this Agreement.

In the event that this Agreement is terminated by Owner pursuant to the terms and conditions of Section 14.02 or Section 14.03 hereof, (a) Owner shall not be obligated to make any further payments to Manager (i) under Section 13.01 for the month during which this Agreement is terminated under said Section 14.02 or Section 14.03 hereof or any further month, or (ii), except as provided in this Section 14.04, under any other terms and conditions of this Agreement; and (b) this Agreement shall terminate and end and be of no further force and effect.

In the event that this Agreement expires on the expiration date set forth in Section 2.01 hereof without being theretofore duly renewed by Owner and Manager, Manager shall be entitled to receive the same type of payments or compensation as set forth in the first paragraph of this Section 14.04 (relative to the termination of this Agreement as to a specific Property), except that the payments or compensation shall apply to all Properties covered by this Agreement on said expiration date.

14.05 Final Accounting. Upon the termination or expiration of this Agreement (a) as to any specific Property or (b) in its entirety, for any reason, Manager shall deliver the following items to Owner within thirty (30) days after such termination or expiration date:

(a) A final accounting reflecting the balance of income and expenses on the specific Property or on each Property, as the case may be, as of the date of termination;

(b) Any balance of moneys of Owner or tenant security deposits, or both, held by Manager with respect to the specific Property or to each Property, as the case may be; and

(c) All records, contracts, leases, receipts for deposits, unpaid bills and other papers or documents which pertain to the specific Property or to each Property, as the case may be.

ARTICLE 15

SUBSIDIARIES AND AFFILIATES OF MANAGER

15.01 Contracts with Subsidiaries and Affiliates of Manager. Manager shall give Owner written notice of any contemplated contract or lease of any kind whatsoever with (i) any of Manager's subsidiary or affiliate corporations, if any, (ii) all persons, corporations or other entities, if any, controlling or affiliated with Manager, and (iii) all corporations or other entities, if any, owned or controlled by such controlling or affiliated persons, corporations or other entities, if any, in connection with any Property, and Manager agrees not to execute any such contract or lease without the prior written approval of Owner.

ARTICLE 16

NOTICES

16.01 <u>Notices</u>. All notices, demands, consents and reports provided for in this Agreement shall be in writing and shall be given to the Owner or the Manager at the addresses set forth below or at such other addresses as they individually may specify thereafter in writing:

_____
_____
_____
Attention:

and

_____
_____
_____
Attention:

and

_____
_____
_____
Attention:

and

AGENT:

_____
_____
_____
Attention:

and

_____
_____
_____
Attention:

and

_____
_____
_____
Attention:

and

_____
_____
_____
Attention:

Such notice or other communication may be mailed by United States registered or certified mail, return receipt requested, postage prepaid, and may be deposited in a United States Post Office or a depository for the receipt of mail regularly maintained by the post office. Such notices, demands, consents and reports may also be delivered by hand or by any other method or means permitted by law.

ARTICLE 17

GENERAL PROVISIONS

17.01 No Assignment. This Agreement and any and all of the rights and obligations hereunder shall not be assignable by Manager, except with the prior written approval of Owner. In the event of any such approval assignment of any or all of the rights and obligations of Manager under this Agreement, Manager shall remain fully liable for the performance of same unless expressly released therefrom by Owner.

17.02 Consents and Approvals. Owner's consents or approvals may be given only by representatives of Owner from time to time designated in writing by Owner or Owner's General Project Manager located at the addresses provided in or pursuant to Section 16.01 of this Agreement.

17.03 Pronouns. The pronouns used in this Agreement referring to Manager and Owner shall be understood and construed to apply whether Manager or Owner is respectively an individual, co-partnership, corporation or an individual or individuals doing business under a firm or trade name.

17.04 Headings. All headings herein are inserted only for convenience and ease of reference and are not to be considered in the construction or interpretation of any provisions of this Agreement.

17.05 State Law. This Agreement is made and executed in and shall be construed under the laws of the State of _____.

IN WITNESS WHEREOF, the parties hereto have executed this Building Management Agreement on the day and year first above written.

ATTEST: OWNER:

BY: BY:

BY:_____   BY:_____

                                 MANAGER:

                                 By:_____
                                    Title:_____

COMPARISON OF RATES FOR $1,000 OF
SINGLE-PREMIUM LIFE INSURANCE

	AGE			
	30	40	50	60
Group Paid-Up				
1. Up to 12/31/59	418.41	510.20	609.76	714.29
2. 1/1/60 to 6/30/68	320.51	411.52	520.83	636.94
3. 7/1/68 to Date	270.27	361.01	471.70	595.24
Individual Paid-Up (Non-Par)				
1. 6/1/47 to 4/30/58	445.49	539.81	648.01	760.69
2. 5/1/58 to 6/30/62	394.19	488.60	593.32	707.78
3. 7/1/62 to 12/31/67	341.56	432.57	542.14	661.37
4. 1/1/68 to 6/31/76	332.97	419.25	525.94	644.73
5. 7/1/76 to 2/14/81	303.01	396.52	511.04	637.53

TABLE "A"

APPENDIX 2.

Rodin Management, Incorporated

Agreement of Lease made this   day of   , 19   , between

RODIN MANAGEMENT, INCORPORATED, a corporation organized and existing under the laws of the Commonwealth of Pennsylvania, Authorized Agent for Lessor and

(hereinafter referred to as "Lessee").

Witnesseth: Lessor hereby demises and lets unto Lessee and Lessee hereby leases from Lessor, subject to all of the terms, conditions, provisions and covenants set forth herein, the certain premises described as follows:

together with all fixtures, equipment, improvements and appurtenances thereto attached as of the commencement of the term hereof (hereinafter referred to as "the Premises") in the building known as
(hereinafter referred to as "the Building," as further defined on Exhibit "A" hereof, in the County of
     State/Commonwealth of   for a term of
as herein defined.

Base Rent   **1.**   (a) The minimum annual rental for the term of this Lease shall be

annum ("Base Rent") payable in full without any set-off or deduction in equal monthly installments of   ($) per

($), which Lessee agrees to pay in advance of each month's occupancy or use of the Premises on or before the first day of each calendar month during the term of this Lease (except that Lessee shall pay the first monthly installment on the date of execution hereof), plus such Additional Rent (as hereinafter defined) and other charges as shall become due under any provision of this Lease all to be paid to Lessor at or such other place as Lessor may from time to time designate, in lawful money of the United States. Lessee does hereby covenant and agree promptly to pay the said Base Rent, Additional Rent and other charges herein described (all of which are collectively sometimes referred to herein as "rent") as and when the same shall become due without demand therefor, and without any set-off or deduction whatsoever, and to keep and perform, and to permit no violation of, each and every of the covenants, agreements, terms, provisions, and conditions herein contained on the part and on behalf of Lessee to be kept and performed.

Proration   (b) If the term of this Lease begins on a day other than the first day of a month, rent from such day until the first day of the following month shall be prorated (on the basis of the number of days during the first month) and shall be payable, in advance, on the first day of the term hereof.

No Waiver   (c) If Lessor, at any time or times, shall accept said rent or any other sum due to it hereunder after the same shall become due and payable, such acceptance shall not excuse delay upon subsequent occasions, or constitute, or be construed as, a waiver of any of Lessor's rights hereunder. No payment by Lessee or receipt by Lessor of a lesser amount than the rents and charges herein stipulated shall be deemed to be other than on account of the earliest stipulated rent, nor shall any endorsement or statement on any check or any letter accompanying any check or payment as rent be deemed an accord and satisfaction, and Lessor may accept such check or payment without prejudice to Lessor's right to recover the balance of such rent or pursue any other remedy in this Lease provided or otherwise available.

All Sums Due Considered As Rent   (d) All sums payable by Lessee under this Lease, whether or not stated to be rent or additional rent, shall be collectible by Lessor as additional rent, and in default in payment thereof Lessor shall have the same rights and remedies as for failure to pay rent without prejudice to any other right or remedy available therefor.

Default Under Other Leases   (e) If Lessee shall be in default in the payment of any rent or charges to Lessor pursuant to the terms of another lease with Lessor or with Lessor's predecessor in interest in this Lease, then, at Lessor's option, Lessor may terminate this Lease and or require that Lessee pay to Lessor immediately, or at such time as Lessor may designate, the full amounts due on account of said default(s) as a condition precedent to all of Lessee's rights hereunder.

with the use of any of the other areas of the Building by, or occasion discomfort, inconvenience or annoyance to, any of the other tenants or occupants of the Building.

(e) If any governmental license or permit or payment of such business, use, occupancy or similar tax shall be required for the proper and lawful conduct of Lessee's business or other activity carried on in the Premises, payment of such tax shall be Lessee's sole responsibility and if the failure to secure such license or permit would in any way affect Lessor, Lessee, at Lessee's sole cost and expense, shall duly procure and thereafter maintain such license or permit and submit a copy of same to Lessor, verified to be true and correct by Lessee. Lessee, at Lessee's sole cost and expense, shall, at all times, comply with the terms and conditions of each such license or permit.

(f) The statement in this Lease of the nature of the business to be conducted by Lessee in the demised Premises shall not be deemed or construed to constitute a representation or guaranty by Lessor that such business may be conducted in the Premises or is lawful or permissible under the statement or certificate of occupancy issued for the Building or is otherwise permitted by law.

Certain Meanings; Limitation of Liability   **4.**   (a) The term "office" or "offices" wherever used in this Lease shall not be construed to mean Premises used for residential purposes, as a store or stores, for the sale or display, at any time, of goods, wares or merchandise of any kind or as a restaurant, shop, booth, bootblack, or other stand, barber shop, or for other similar purposes or for the manufacturing of any commodity or the preparation or dispensing of food and beverages of any kind.

(b) The words "re-enter" and "re-entry" as used in this Lease are not restricted to their technical legal meaning.

Term

2. (a) The term of this Lease shall commence on the earlier of (1) the date upon which Lessee shall occupy or use the Premises or any part thereof, or (2) the date of ____________, 19____, and shall end on the earlier of (1) the date upon which this Lease may expire or be terminated pursuant to any of the provisions of this Lease or pursuant to law, or (2) the date of ____________, 19____.

Memorandum

(b) When the date of commencement of the term of this Lease is established, Lessor and Lessee shall promptly execute and acknowledge a memorandum setting forth the date of commencement, the Premises and the date of this Lease.

Renewal or Termination At End of Term

(c) It is hereby mutually agreed that either party hereto may determine this Lease at the end of said term by giving to the other party written notice thereof at least ninety (90) days prior thereto, but in default of such notice, this Lease shall continue upon the same terms and conditions in force immediately prior to the expiration of the term hereof as are herein contained for a further period of one year and so on from year to year unless or until terminated by either party hereto, giving the other at least ninety (90) days written notice for removal previous to expiration of the then current term; PROVIDED, however, that should this Lease be continued for a further period under the terms hereinabove mentioned or pursuant to Subparagraph (d) below, any allowances or concessions given Lessee on the rent or with respect to decorations or the like during the original term, shall not extend beyond such original term and further provided, that if the Lessor shall have given such written notice prior to the expiration of any term, of its intention to change the terms and conditions of this Lease, and Lessee shall not within fifteen days from such notice notify Lessor of Lessee's intention to vacate the demised Premises at the end of the then current term, Lessee shall be considered as Lessee under this Lease as modified by the terms and conditions mentioned in such notice for a further term as above provided, unless said notice shall fix a different term, in which event the term fixed in said notice shall apply.

Allowances or Concessions Not to Survive Original Term

Holdover Provisions

(d) If Lessee shall fail to surrender possession of the demised Premises and remove all of its property therefrom upon the termination of this Lease by expiration of the then current term or otherwise, Lessee shall pay Lessor (i) as agreed liquidated damages for such unlawful retention alone an amount equal to 200% of the rent payable by Lessee during the final month of the Lease term for each month or portion thereof, Lessee thus remains in possession said amount to be calculated on a monthly basis without any proration or apportionment, and (ii) all other damages, costs and expenses sustained by Lessor by reason of Lessee's unlawful retention of the demised Premises. In such event, Lessor may elect (a) to treat Lessee as a tenant at will or (b) to treat Lessee as a tenant for a further term of one year, or (c) at any time after such date upon which Lessee failed or refused to vacate, give the said Lessee ten days' written notice to vacate whereupon the Lessee expressly agrees to vacate said Premises at the expiration of the period specified in said notice.

For purposes of this Subparagraph, the word "rent" shall include base rent and all additional rent, including, without limitation, any amounts payable under applicable escalation clauses. Without limiting any rights and remedies of Lessor resulting by reason of the wrongful holding over of Lessee, or creating any right in Lessee to continue in possession of the demised Premises, all of Lessee's obligations with respect to the use, occupancy and maintenance of the demised Premises shall continue during such period of unlawful retention.

Rights and Obligations to Survive Original Term

(e) All powers, authorities, remedies and benefits granted to Lessor by this Lease may be exercised by Lessor and all obligations imposed upon Lessee by this Lease shall be performed by Lessee as fully during any extension of the original term of this Lease as during the original term itself.

Use of Premises

3. (a) The Premises shall be used for the following and no other purpose, namely:

Lessee shall not use the Premises or any part thereof, or permit the Premises or any part thereof to be used for any purpose other than the use hereinbefore specifically mentioned, subject, however, to all covenants, agreements, terms, provisions and conditions of this Lease. Lessee agrees that the use of the Premises or any portion thereof for any purpose other than the foregoing, except with Lessor's prior written consent, shall constitute a default under this Lease.

(b) Those portions, if any, of the Premises which on the building plans existing as of the date of commencement of this Lease or the plan(s) attached hereto are shown as water or wash closets and utility areas shall be used by Lessee only for the purposes for which they are designed.

(c) Lessee will not at any time use or occupy the Premises or any part thereof, or permit the Premises or any part thereof to be used or occupied, in violation of any use registration permit or statement or certificate of occupancy issued for the Building and/or the Premises.

(d) Lessee shall not use or permit the use of the Premises or any part thereof in any way which would violate any of the other covenants, agreements, terms, provisions and conditions of this Lease or for any unlawful purposes or in any unlawful manner and Lessee shall not suffer or permit the Premises or any part thereof to be used in any manner or anything to be done therein or suffer or permit anything to be brought into or kept in the Premises which, in the sole judgment of Lessor, shall in any way impair or tend to impair the character, reputation or appearance of the Building as a first-class office building, impair, interfere with or tend to impair or interfere with any of the Building services or the proper and economic heating, ventilating, cleaning, air conditioning or other servicing of the Building or the Premises, or impair or interfere with or tend to impair or interfere

(c) The term "business days" as used in this Lease shall exclude Saturdays, Sundays, and all days observed by the Federal Government as legal holidays.

(d) The term "Lessor" as used in this Lease means the fee owner of the Building or, if different, the party holding and exercising the right, as against all others (except space tenants of the Building) to possession of the entire Building. Lessor hereunder represents that it is the holder of such rights as of the date hereof. In the event of the voluntary or involuntary transfer of such ownership or right to a successor-in-interest of Lessor or, if for any reason Lessor becomes no longer entitled to receive the rental hereunder, the said Lessor shall be freed and relieved of all liability and obligation hereunder which shall thereafter accrue and Lessee shall look solely to such successor-in-interest for the performance of the covenants and obligations of the Lessor hereunder which shall thereafter accrue. The liability of Lessor and its successors-in-interest, under or with respect to this Lease, shall be strictly limited to and enforceable only out of its or their interest in the Building and Land, and shall not be enforceable out of any other assets. No mortgagee or ground lessor which shall succeed to the interest of Lessor hereunder (either in terms of ownership or possessory rights) shall: (i) be liable for any previous act or omission of a prior Lessor, (ii) be subject to any rental offsets or defenses against a prior Lessor, (iii) be bound by any amendment of this Lease made without its written consent, or by payment by Lessee of rent in advance in excess of one (1) month's rent, (iv) be liable for any security not actually received by it, or (v) be liable for any initial construction of the improvements to be made to the demised Premises.

Additional Rent

5. It is understood that the Base Rent specified in Paragraph 1 does not anticipate any increase in the amount of taxes on the Premises or Building or in the cost of operations and maintenance thereof. Therefore, in order that the rental payable throughout the term of this Lease shall reflect any such increase, the parties agree as follows:

Lessee's Proportionate Share

(a) The term "Lessee's Proportionate Share" shall be the ratio that the demised Premises (which for purposes of determining such proportionate share is hereby conclusively deemed to contain ________ square feet) bears to the total amount of rentable space in the Building (which is hereby conclusively deemed to contain ______ square feet). On the above basis Lessee's Proportionate Share is ______%. It is understood that the area termed "total amount of rentable space" does not include any garage, storage, basement or common areas and corridors.

No Adjustment in Stated Space

(b) The amount of rentable space in the Building specified above shall not be deemed to have changed by reason of the leasing of any space excluded therefrom or any sale or transfer of individual floors, suites or offices in the event that the Building is the subject of a conversion to condominium or similar form of ownership. In either event, the floor area of any such space shall continue to be included in or excluded from such total figure to the same extent it was originally included therein or excluded therefrom.

Base Year

(c) As used herein the "Base Year" shall be the calendar year prior to the calendar year in which the original term of this Lease commenced, i.e. 19____.

Tax and Operation and Maintenance Increases

(d) Lessee shall pay as Additional Rent each year during the term of this Lease and any extensions or renewals thereof "Lessee's Proportionate Share" of (i) the increase, if any, of the cost of operation and maintenance, as hereafter defined, of the land, Building and all appurtenances thereto, in excess of the cost thereof for the Base Year; and (ii) the real estate taxes, as hereafter defined, levied, assessed or imposed upon the land, Building and/or all appurtenances thereto in excess of the real estate taxes for the Base Year.

Costs of Operation and Maintenance

(e) Said costs of operation and maintenance shall include, but shall not be limited to: Water and sewer rents; any applicable sales, service and utility taxes upon any expenses itemized herein; heating, air conditioning, lighting, power, steam, fuel and all other utility costs; labor costs (including wages and salaries, payments to pension, welfare and similar funds, medical, life and other insurance, and all other "fringe" benefits, unemployment compensation insurance, payroll, social security and other employment related taxes incurred with respect to all persons performing services rendered in connection with the operation and maintenance of the land or Building including without limitation: elevator operators; elevator starters; window cleaners; porters; janitors; maids; miscellaneous handymen; watchmen; persons engaged in patrolling and protecting the land and Building; carpenters; engineers; firemen; mechanics; electricians; plumbers; building superintendent and assistants; building manager; and clerical and administrative personnel); the replacement cost of all necessary supplies, tools and equipment; the cost of uniforms and dry cleaning, window and sidewalk cleaning, painting, landscaping, ice and snow removal; management fees, including those payable to entities related to or affiliated with Lessor provided only that the same be commercially reasonable; premiums and other charges, including deductible amounts paid in connection with any claim incurred by Lessor with respect to all insurance relating to the land and Building and the operation and maintenance thereof, including, without limitation, fire and extended coverage insurance, including windstorm, hail, explosion, riot, rioting attending a strike, civil commotion, aircraft, vehicle and smoke insurance; public liability, elevator, workmen's compensation, boiler and machinery, rent, use and occupancy, and health, accident and group life insurance of all employees; costs incurred for operation, service, maintenance, inspection, repairs and alterations of the land and Building and the heating, air-conditioning, ventilating, plumbing, electrical and elevator systems of the Building (including separate contracts therefor) and the costs of labor materials, supplies and equipment used in connection with all of the aforesaid items; the cost of repainting, restoring, renovating or otherwise redecorating any part of the Building; Christmas decorations for the lobby and other public portions of the Building; dues paid to state or local associations representing landlords; the cost of licenses, permits and similar fees and charges related to operation, repair and maintenance of the Building, security expenditures; service contracts with independent contractors; consulting, attorney, accounting and other professional fees; costs for telephone, telegraph, postage, repair, replacement and maintenance of office equipment, copying, stationary, office supplies and similar costs related to operation of the Building managers' and superintendent's offices; advertising and leasing expenditures; any charges, fees or increases in interest in excess of the base percentage interest payable during the Base Year pursuant to any note, bond or mortgage secured by the land and/or Building of which the Premises is a part and all other items properly constituting direct operating and maintenance costs according to standard accounting practices as determined by accountants employed by Lessor, which determination shall be final.

Notwithstanding the foregoing, any expenditure relating to the operation or maintenance of the Building which amounts to $2,500.00 or less shall be deemed properly includable in such costs of operation and maintenance as herein defined regardless of whether or not it would be classed as a direct cost or expense item according to generally accepted accounting principles.

Adjustment of Base Year Costs (f) If after the Base Year, Lessor shall eliminate or reduce any costs as a result of the installation of labor or energy saving devices or by any other means, the corresponding items of cost shall be deducted from said costs of operation and maintenance for the Base Year in computing the Additional Rent payable hereunder.

Vacancy Adjustment (g) In determining the costs of operation and maintenance for the purpose of this Paragraph, either for the Base Year or for any subsequent year, (i) if less than 100% of the rentable space in the Building shall have been occupied by tenants and fully used by them, at any time during the year, costs of operation and maintenance shall be deemed to be increased to include an inputed cost for unoccupied portions of the Building in an amount with respect to each such area equal to the product of (A) One Dollar ($1.00), times (B) a fraction, the numerator of which is the number of days during such Year such portion of the Building was unoccupied and the denominator of which is 365, times (C) the rentable area of such unoccupied space in square feet. In the event that more than one such portion of rentable area shall be unoccupied on separate dates within a relevant year, then a separate computation, shall be made with respect to each such unoccupied portion, and the products of such computations shall be added together, and the total thereof shall be the amount of operating costs imputed to such unoccupied portions for such year, or (ii) if Lessor is not furnishing any

Service Adjustment particular work or service (the cost of which if performed by Lessor would constitute a cost of operation or maintenance) to a tenant who has undertaken to perform such work or service in lieu of the performance thereof by Lessor, the costs of operation and maintenance shall be deemed to be increased by an amount equal to the additional expense which would reasonably have been incurred during such period by Lessor if it had at its own expense furnished such work or service to such tenant.

Real Estate Taxes (h) For the purpose of this Paragraph, Real Estate taxes shall be deemed to be the aggregate amount of all taxes and assessments levied, assessed or imposed upon the land and/or Building of which the Premises is a part of any kind whatsoever, ordinary or extraordinary, foreseen or unforeseen, general or special, including but not limited to general real estate taxes, school taxes, assessments for improvements on or benefits to the property, vault taxes, and any other governmental charges levied, assessed or imposed in lieu of any such taxes. Real Estate Taxes shall also be deemed to include any new tax of a nature not presently in effect but which may be hereafter levied, assessed or imposed upon the Lessor or the land and/or Building of which the Premises is a part, if such tax shall be based upon or arise out of the ownership, use or operation of the demised Premises. For the purpose of computing Lessee's liability for such new type of tax, the demised Premises shall be deemed the sole property of Lessor.

(i) "Land Taxes" shall mean all taxes as defined in Subparagraph (h) above, levied, assessed or imposed only with respect to the land on which the Building of which the demised Premises is a part is erected.

(j) "Building Taxes" shall mean all taxes as defined in Sub-paragraph (h) above, levied, assessed or imposed only with respect to the Building of which the demised Premises is a part.

Effect of Partial Tax Abatement (k) In the event that the Building or land may qualify for and receive the benefits of any tax abatement program whereby real estate taxes attributable to either the land or Building (but not both) shall be wholly abated for a period of time during the term of this Lease or any extension or renewal thereof (the "Abatement Period") then for purposes of computing Lessee's liability for Additional Rent under this Paragraph during the Abatement Period the portion of such taxes attributable to either the Building or land (whichever is abated by such program) shall be deducted from the Base Year.

Adjustment of Base Year Real Estate Taxes (l) In the event that the amount of taxes levied, assessed or imposed upon either the Building or Land or both should be reduced by reason of appeal or contest of such tax or a reduction in the assessed value and or the applicable rate of tax, then, for purposes of computing Lessee's liability for additional rent under this Paragraph, the taxes levied, assessed or imposed upon the property in the Base Year shall be deemed to be reduced to the same extent.

Initial Assessment Determinative (m) For purposes of this Paragraph, any assessment upon which Lessee's share of Taxes is based shall be deemed to be the amount initially assessed until such time as an abatement, refund, rebate or increase, if any (retroactive or otherwise), shall be the last mentioned increased monthly installments of rent shall continue beyond the end of the twelve month period for which such payments were payable, any necessary adjustment will be made when the next succeeding index comparative statement is sent to Lessee.

(c) In no event shall the annual Base Rent for any lease year be less than the annual Base Rent paid by Lessee immediately preceding the commencement thereof.

(d) In the event the Index shall hereafter be converted to a different standard reference base or otherwise revised, the determination of the stated annual minimum rent shall be made with the use of such conversion factor, formula or table for converting the Index as may be published by the Bureau of Labor Statistics or, if said Bureau shall not publish the same, then with the use of such conversion factor, formula or table as may be published by Prentice Hall, Inc. or any other nationally recognized publisher of similar statistical information as Lessor may designate. In the event the Index shall cease to be published, then, for the purposes of this Lease, there shall be substituted for the Index such other substantially similar Index as Lessor may designate.

Additional Rent Payable on Demand **7.** (a) Lessee's liability for any charges specified as Additional Rent shall commence as of the date of this Lease and it shall pay such Additional Rent in full annually upon demand by Lessor if Lessor has not elected to require the payment of same in advance on an estimated monthly or other basis.

Disputes and Notice Requirements (b) The information set forth on each statement furnished to Lessee as provided in Paragraphs 5 or 6 hereof shall be deemed conclusively to have been accepted and approved by Lessee, unless, within ten (10) days after submission to Lessee, Lessee shall notify Lessor in writing that it disputes the correctness thereof specifying the basis for such assertion. However, notwithstanding any such dispute and the giving of such notice, Lessee shall continue to pay the Additional Rent in accordance with such statement within the periods provided therefor until such dispute shall be resolved. No dispute of any charges shall be made by Lessee until such statement shall have been received by it. Lessor agrees to promptly provide to Lessee, upon request, photostats of extracts from Lessor's books and records which are relevant to any items in dispute.

Lessee's Obligation To Survive Lease Term (c) Whenever any obligation for which Lessee or its successor is responsible under the terms of this Lease is not capable of calculation or billing prior to the expiration or other termination of the Lease, said obligation shall continue in full force and effect despite any expiration, termination, cancellation or other supersedence of the Lease unless released by specific reference in writing thereto, and the party or parties obligated therefor shall promptly make payment when due, failing which Lessor shall have all of the rights and remedies available under said Lease, which shall, for purposes of enforcing this obligation, remain in full force and effect until said obligation has been fulfilled.

Lessee Improvements **8.** (a) Lessee shall make no alterations, decorations, installations, additions or improvements in or to the Premises, including but not limited to electrical or plumbing installations, water coolers, heating, ventilating, air conditioning or cooling systems, units or parts thereof or other apparatus of like or other nature, without Lessor's prior written consent, and then only by such contractors or mechanics as are approved by Lessor who shall not, in Lessor's reasonable opinion, prejudice Lessor's relationship with its contractors, subcontractors or employees or disturb harmonious labor relations, and in accordance with such detailed plans, drawings, and specifications relating thereto which are to be submitted to and approved in writing by Lessor in advance of such work. All such work, alterations, decorations, installations, additions or improvements shall be done at Lessee's sole cost and expense and at such time and in such manner as Lessor may from time to time designate. All alterations, decorations, installations, additions or improvements upon the Premises made by either party, including all paneling, decorations, partitions, railings, mezzanine floors, galleries and the like, shall, unless Lessor elects otherwise (which election shall be made by giving a notice pursuant to the provisions hereinafter set forth not less than thirty (30) days prior to the expiration or other termination of this Lease or any renewal or extension thereof) become the property of Lessor, and shall remain upon and be surrendered with said Premises, as a part thereof at the end of the term or renewal term, as the case may be. In the event Lessor shall elect otherwise, then any or all such alterations, decorations, installations, additions or improvements made by Lessee upon the Premises as the Lessor shall select shall be removed and the Premises shall be restored to its original condition, at Lessee's sole cost and expense, at or prior to the expiration of the then current term.

Required Lien Waivers, Etc. (b) As a condition precedent to Lessor's consent to the making by Lessee of alterations, decorations, installations, additions or improvements to the Premises, Lessee agrees, prior to the commencement of any work or the delivery of any materials, to obtain and deliver to Lessor written and unconditioned waivers of mechanics' and materialmens' liens and all other liens upon the Building for all work, labor, and services to be performed and materials to be furnished by them in connection with such work, properly executed by all contractors, subcontractors, materialmen and laborers to become involved in such work. Lessee shall also provide Lessor with evidence of proper permits and certificates for contractor's public liability insurance, and workman's compensation prior to the commencement of any such work. Notwithstanding the foregoing, if any mechanic's or materialman's lien is filed against the Premises or the Building for work claimed to have been done for, or materials claimed to have been furnished to Lessee, it shall be discharged by Lessee within ten (10) days thereafter, at Lessee's expense, by filing the bond required by law, and Lessee shall at all times defend and save Lessor harmless of and from any and all liability, fees, costs and expenses arising from or relating to any such lien.

finally determined to be due, and upon such final determination, Lessor shall promptly notify Lessee of the amount, if any, due to Lessee or Lessor, as the case may be, as a result of the adjustment, and appropriate payment to Lessor or Lessee, as the case may be, shall thereafter be promptly made. In particular, but without limiting the foregoing, if Taxes are paid on the basis of the qualification of the Building or Land for a tax abatement program, but it is subsequently determined that the Building or Land was not entitled to the benefit of such program and a retroactive assessment is made, Lessee's share of Taxes shall be retroactively computed on the basis of the actual amount of taxes required to be paid in the absence of abatement.

Rent Tax

(n) If, during the term of this Lease or any renewal or extension thereof, any tax is imposed upon the privilege of renting or occupying the demised Premises or upon the amount of rentals collected therefor, Lessee will pay each month, as Additional Rent, a sum equal to such tax or charge that is imposed for such month, but nothing herein shall be taken to require Lessee to pay any estate, inheritance or franchise tax imposed upon Lessor.

Lessor Not Obligated To Appeal Taxes

(o) Lessor shall have no duty to Lessee to contest, appeal or otherwise challenge any Taxes. In the event of any reduction in Taxes by reason of legal or other action taken by Lessor in contest of same, there shall be added to and be deemed a part of the Taxes in question the amount of Lessor's legal and other costs and expenses in obtaining the reduction. In the event that Lessor elects to contest or appeal any tax, Lessor shall have complete direction and control of such appeal. Lessee agrees that it shall not file any separate appeal of any taxes relating to the property or seek any relief in addition to that which may be obtained by Lessor.

No Limitation on Lessor's Rights

(p) Nothing herein contained shall be construed to limit in any way Lessor's right to add personnel, make improvements to the Building, or make changes in the management, operation and maintenance of the Building which Lessor in its sole judgement may deem to be necessary or proper.

Estimated Advance Payments of Additional Rent

(q) Lessor shall have the right at any time or times during the term of this lease at its option to make a reasonable good faith estimate of all or part of the Additional Rent to become payable by Lessee to Lessor under the above provisions and to require that Lessee pay all or part of such Additional Rent as estimated by Lessor, in one or more installments as Lessor may elect, prior to the time that Lessor actually incurs the costs and expenses which are the basis for such Additional Rent, so that Lessor will have received the full amount of the estimated additional costs or expenses by the time that such sums are due and payable by Lessor. If Lessor shall so estimate all or part of such Additional Rent, then within ninety (90) days after the actual amount of such Additional Rent shall be determined (whether such 90 day period shall be prior to or after the expiration or termination of this Lease), Lessor shall deliver to Lessee a statement, certified by Lessor, of the actual amount of such Additional Rent payable by Lessee. If the statement reveals that any Additional Rent is still due Lessor, Lessee shall pay such deficiency to Lessor within seven (7) days after the receipt of such statement, notwithstanding the earlier termination or expiration of this Lease. If the statement reveals that Lessee has overpaid the amount of such additional rent, Lessor shall credit such overpayment against the next payment of Additional Rent becoming due; provided however, if the statement is delivered after the expiration or termination of the Lease and all sums due Lessor under the Lease have been paid in full, Lessor shall refund such overpayment to Lessee at that time.

Cost of Living Adjustment

6. (a) The Base Rent called for hereunder shall be subject to increase each year in accordance with the terms of this Paragraph. As used in this Paragraph:

(a) "Index" shall mean the "Consumer Price Index for Urban Wage Earners and Clerical Workers", using the year 1967 as a base of 100, specified for "All Items" relating to the "United States City Average" and issued by the Bureau of Labor Statistics of the United States Department of Labor.

(ii) "Base Index" shall mean the Index in effect in September of the calendar year prior to the calendar year in which the original term of this lease commenced.

(iii) "Anniversary Month" shall mean September of the calendar year succeeding the calendar year in which the original term of this Lease commenced and each successive September thereafter during the original term and any extensions or renewals thereof.

(iv) "Percentage Increase" shall mean the percentage equal to the fraction, the numerator of which shall be the Index in the Anniversary Month less the Base Index, and the denominator of which shall be the Base Index.

(b) If the index in an Anniversary Month shall exceed the Base Index, then the Base Rent payable for the ensuing twelve month period, and thereafter until a new index comparative statement is sent to Lessee shall be increased by the Percentage Increase. At any time after October 1st of the said ensuing twelve month period, Lessor shall send Lessee an index comparative statement setting forth (i) the Index in the Anniversary Month preceding the date of the statement, (ii) the Base Index, (iii) the Percentage Increase, and (iv) the increase in the Base Rent. On the first day of the calendar month ("current month") following the month in which the index comparative statement was sent (A) Lessee shall pay to Lessor a sum equal to 1/12th of said increase in Base Annual Rent multiplied by the number of calendar months of the Lease term than elapsed since said October 1st, and (B) thereafter, commencing with the current month and continuing monthly thereafter until a different index comparative statement is sent to Lessee, the monthly installments of rent shall be increased by an amount equal to 1/12th of said increase. In the event

Completion Bond Requirement

(c) No changes or alterations involving an estimated cost of more than $50,000.00 shall be undertaken until the Lessor shall have been furnished by Lessee, at the Lessee's sole expense, with a bond on which the Lessee shall be principal, and a surety company authorized to do business in the state in which the demised Premises are situate shall be surety, conditioned upon the completion of and payment in full for such changes or alterations within a reasonable time, subject, however, to delays occasioned by strikes, lockouts, acts of God, inability to obtain labor or materials, governmental restrictions, or similar causes beyond the control of Lessee, or Lessee shall have deposited with the Lessor a sum sufficient to pay the entire cost of any such change or alteration as estimated by the architect or engineer under whose supervision the work is to be conducted, under an agreement whereby Lessor shall from time to time pay out said sums upon the written request of Lessee, which shall be accompanied by a certificate of the architect or engineer in charge of the work, stating (1) that the sum requested is justly due to the contractors, subcontractors, material men, laborers, engineers, architects or other persons, firms or corporations rendering services or materials for such changes or alterations, or is justly required to reimburse Lessee for expenditures made by it in connection with such changes or alterations, and when added to all sums previously paid out by Lessor, does not exceed the value of the work done to the date of such certificate; and (2) that the remaining funds so deposited by Lessee with Lessor will be sufficient upon the completion of such work to pay for the same in full; and, upon submission of proof satisfactory to Lessor, that the work has been paid for in full, turn over to Lessee the balance of the funds so deposited by Lessee with Lessor. Lessee shall also furnish Lessor at the time of any such payment with an official search, or other evidence satisfactory to Lessor, that there has not been filed with respect to the demised Premises any mechanic's or other lien which has not been discharged of record, in respect of any work, labor, services or materials performed, furnished or supplied, or claimed to have been performed, furnished or supplied, in connection with any such work.

Supervision of Work

(d) All changes and alterations involving an estimated cost of more than $50,000.00 shall be conducted under the supervision of an architect or engineer who shall be reasonably satisfactory to the Lessor.

No Adverse Effect on Valuation

(e) All changes and alterations when completed shall be of such a character as not to reduce or otherwise adversely affect the value of the demised Premises, nor to reduce the rentable space therein.

Quality of Work

(f) All work done in connection with any change or alteration shall be done in a good and workmanlike manner and in compliance with the building and zoning laws of the place in which the demised Premises are located and with all laws, ordinances, orders, rules, regulations and requirements of all federal, state and municipal governments and the appropriate departments, commissions, boards and officers thereof, and in accordance with the orders, rules and regulations of the Board of Fire Underwriters where the demised Premises are situate or any other body exercising similar functions.

Lessee Responsible For Increased Taxes Due To Improvements

(g) Lessee agrees that it will be solely responsible for and will promptly pay to Lessor, upon demand, as Additional Rent hereunder, the full amount of any increase in the amount of real estate taxes assessed or imposed upon the Building or the Premises which is caused by the making of any alteration, decoration, installation, addition or improvement to the Premises. It is expressly understood and agreed that such payments are to be in addition to all payments for which Lessee may become liable under the provisions of Paragraph 5 hereof and may be estimated and collected in advance as provided therein.

Care of Premises

9. (a) Lessee shall take good care of the Premises and the fixtures and appurtenances therein and at its sole cost and expense make all repairs thereto as and when needed to preserve them in good working order and condition. All damage or injury to the Premises and to its fixtures, appurtenances and equipment or to the Building or to its fixtures, appurtenances and equipment caused by Lessee moving property in or out of the Premises or Building or by installation or removal of furniture, fixtures or other property, or resulting from heating, ventilating, or air conditioning units or systems, short circuits, flow or leakage of water, steam, illuminating gas, sewer gas, sewerage or odors or by frost or by bursting or leaking of pipes or plumbing works or gas, or from any other cause of any other kind of nature whatsoever due to any act, omission, or other cause of Lessee, its servants, employees, agents, visitors, invitees or licensees without regard to whether or not the same constitutes negligence, shall be repaired, restored or replaced promptly by Lessee at its sole cost and expense to the satisfaction of Lessor. All aforesaid repairs, restorations and replacements shall be comparable in quality and class to the original work or installation. If Lessee fails to make such repairs, restorations or replacements, same may be made by Lessor at the sole cost and expense of Lessee and the cost thereof shall be considered as Additional Rent and be paid by Lessee within five (5) days after rendition by Lessor of a bill or statement therefor.

Moving of Heavy Objects

(b) Lessee agrees that it shall not move any safe, heavy machinery, heavy equipment, freight, bulky matter, or fixture into or out of the Premises or Building without Lessor's prior written consent. If such safe, machinery, equipment, freight, bulky matter or fixture requires special handling, Lessee agrees to employ only persons holding a Master Rigger's License to do said work, and that all work in connection therewith shall comply with the Administrative Code or similar regulations of governmental body(ies) having or claiming jurisdiction to regulate such matters. Notwithstanding the giving of said consent by Lessor, Lessee agrees that it shall relieve, indemnify and defend Lessor for, and hold Lessor harmless and free from liability by reason of any loss of life, injury or damage to any person or property caused by or resulting from any such activity and for any damages or monies paid out by Lessor in settlement of any claims or judgements, as well as for all expenses and attorneys' fees incurred in connection therewith and all costs incurred in repairing any resulting damage to the Premises, Building or appurtenances.

Floor Loads

(c) Lessee shall not place a load upon any floor of the Premises exceeding the floor load per square foot area which such floor was designed to carry and which is allowed by law. Lessor reserves the right to prescribe the weight and position of all safes or other heavy objects which must be placed so as to distribute the weight.

Placement of Machinery and Equipment

(d) Business machines and mechanical equipment shall be placed and maintained by Lessee at Lessee's sole cost and expense in settings sufficient in Lessor's judgment to absorb and prevent vibration, noise and annoyance to others, or the spillage or leakage of fluids, oils or grease on the floors of the demised Premises.

No Allowance or Liability for Lessor Repairs

(e) Except as expressly provided elsewhere herein, there shall be no allowance to Lessee for a diminution of rental value and no liability on the part of Lessor by reason of inconvenience, annoyance or injury to business arising from any act or omission by Lessor, Lessee or others making any repairs, alterations, additions or improvements in or to any portion of the Building or Premises, or in or to fixtures, appurtenances, or equipment thereof, and no liability upon Lessor for failure of Lessor or others to make any repairs, alterations, additions or improvements in or to any portion of the Building or Premises, or in or to the fixtures, appurtenances or equipment thereof.

Vermin

(f) If the Premises be or become infested with vermin, Lessee shall at Lessee's sole cost and expense cause the same to be exterminated from time to time to the satisfaction of Lessor and shall employ such exterminators and such exterminating company or companies as shall be approved in advance by Lessor.

Plumbing

(g) The water and wash closets and other plumbing fixtures shall not be used for any purposes other than those for which they were designed or constructed and no sweepings, rubbish, rags, acids, corrosives or other substances of any kind whatsoever shall be deposited therein.

Window Cleaning

(h) Lessee will not clean, nor require, permit, suffer or allow any window in the Premises to be cleaned from the outside.

Efficiency of HVAC

(i) Lessee shall keep all windows and doors of the Premises closed when required to maximize the efficiency of the heating and air conditioning systems.

Fuel Conservation

(j) Lessee shall comply with all rules and regulations from time to time promulgated by Lessor to conserve fuel and/or energy.

Compliance With Laws

10. Lessee, at its sole cost and expense, shall immediately comply with all laws, orders and regulations of Federal, State, County and Municipal Authorities, and with any direction of any public officer or officers, pursuant to law, which shall impose any violation, order or duty upon Lessor or Lessee with respect to the Premises, or the use or occupation thereof.

Fire Prevention and Regulations

11. Lessee shall use every reasonable precaution against fire and shall not do or permit to be done any act or thing upon said Premises which will invalidate or be in conflict with fire or other insurance policies covering the Building or the Premises, and fixtures and property therein, and shall not do or permit to be done any act or thing upon said Premises which shall or might subject Lessor to any liability or responsibility for injury to any person or persons or to property by reason of any business or operation being carried on upon said Premises or for any other reason; and Lessee at its sole cost and expense shall immediately comply with all rules, orders, regulations or requirements of the Board of Fire Underwriters, or any other similar body, and shall not do or permit anything to be done in or upon said Premises, or bring or keep anything therein except as now or hereafter permitted by the Fire Department, Board of Fire Underwriters, Fire Insurance Rating Organization, or other authority having or claiming jurisdiction, and then only in such quantity and manner of storage as not to increase the rate for fire insurance applicable to the Building, or use the Premises in a manner which shall increase the rate of fire insurance on the Building, or on property located therein, over that in effect prior to this Lease. If by reason of failure of Lessee to comply with the provisions of this Article including, but not limited to the mere use to which Lessee puts the Premises, the fire insurance rate shall at the beginning of this Lease or at any time thereafter be higher than it otherwise would be, then Lessee shall reimburse Lessor for that part of all fire insurance premiums thereafter paid by Lessor which shall have been charged because of such failure or use by Lessee and shall make such reimbursement upon the first day of the month following such outlay by Lessor. In any action or proceeding wherein Lessor and Lessee are parties, a schedule or "make up" of rate for the Building or Premises issued by the Fire Insurance Exchange, or other body making fire insurance rates for said Premises shall be conclusive evidence of the facts therein stated and of the several items and charges in the fire insurance rate then applicable to said Premises. Lessee shall not bring or permit to be brought ot kept in or on the Premises, any corrosive, flammable, combustible or explosive fluid, material, chemical or substance, or cause or permit any odors of cooking or other processes or any unusual or other objectionable odors to emanate from the Premises. That the Premises are being used for the permitted purpose set forth hereinabove shall not relieve Lessee from the foregoing duties, obligations and expenses.

occupancy shall keep said meter and related apparatus in good working order and repair at its sole cost and expense; or

Estimated Usage

(b) Estimate the rate by which Lessee's use of such service exceeds the Building Average based upon a survey of the Premises (which survey shall be made at the expense of Lessee) and bill Lessee therefor.

Administrative Charge

(c) Any payment for additional charges which may be made under the provisions of this Paragraph shall include an administrative charge of 15% of the amount charged for such services, all of which shall be considered as Additional Rent hereunder and shall be collectible in advance in the same manner as provided in Paragraph 5 hereof.

Conversion to Automatic Elevators

14. If the Building supplies manually operated elevator service, Lessor may proceed with alterations necessary to substitute automatic control elevator service upon ten (10) days written notice to Lessee without in any way relieving Lessee from any of its obligations hereunder.

Discontinuance Change or Suspension of Services or Utilities

15. (a) Lessor reserves the right to change or suspend service of the heating, ventilating, air conditioning, elevator, plumbing, gas, and electric systems and other machinery when necessary, by reason of accident, or emergency, or for repairs, alterations, replacements or improvements, in the judgement of Lessor desirable or necessary to be made, until said repairs, alterations, replacements or improvements shall have been completed, and Lessor shall have no responsibility or liability for failure to supply any such service during said period or when prevented from so doing by war, civil commotion, strikes, accidents, casualties, or by any cause beyond Lessor's control, or by laws, orders or regulations of any Federal, State or Municipal Authority, or failure of coal, oil, gas, electricity, or other suitable fuel supply, or inability by exercise of reasonable diligence to obtain coal, oil, gas, electricity or other suitable fuel.

(b) Lessor may at any time and from time to time discontinue any service furnished by Lessor indefinitely and without cause, except those services which Lessor has specifically agreed to provide.

(c) Payment by Lessee of all charges designated as rent or Additional Rent hereunder shall be a condition precedent to Lessor's obligation to supply any service to the demised Premises. In the event of default in any such payment, Lessor may immediately and without notice discontinue any and/or all services supplied to the demised Premises without incurring any liability for any damage of any kind whatsoever which may thereby be occasioned to Lessee or its business. Any such discontinuance of service as a result of Lessee's default shall not be deemed to constitute an actual or constructive eviction of Lessee in whole or in part or relieve Lessee from any of its obligations hereunder.

Release of Liability

16. Lessee hereby releases and relieves Lessor, its agents, servants, and employees, from all liability in connection with any and all damage to or loss of property, loss of life, loss of profits, interruption of business or other injury or damage occurring to Lessee, its agents, servants, employees, invitees, visitors or any other person, firm, corporation or entity, in or about or arising out of the demised Premises and the Building of which the demised Premises are a part from any cause whatsoever and regardless of whether such loss and/or damage is caused by or results from the negligence of Lessor, its agents, servants, employees or any person or persons whatsoever, including but not limited to the following causes: (a) any fire, other casualty, accident, occurrence or condition in or upon the demised Premises or the Building of which the demised Premises are a part; (b) any defect in or failure of the plumbing, sprinkling, electrical, HVAC systems, mechanisms or equipment, or any other systems, mechanisms and equipment of the demised Premises and the Building of which the demised Premises are a part; (c) the exercise by Lessor of any rights under the terms and conditions of this Lease, (d) any acts or omissions of other tenants or occupants of the Building or of nearby buildings; (e) any acts or omissions of other persons; (f) broken glass; (g) contact with or the handling of electric lamps, equipment or wires; (h) latent or patent defects or dangerous conditions existing in the demised Premises or the Building of which the demised Premises are a part; (i) the breaking or disrepair of any installations or equipment; (j) the use, misuse, abuse or defects in all or any of the elevators, hatches, openings, stairways, railings, walkways and hallways of any kind whatsoever which may exist or hereafter be erected on or constructed on the demised Premises or the Building of which the demised Premises are a part; (k) explosion; (l) deterioration; (m) wind, lightning, storm or other act of God, public enemy, injunction, riot, strike, insurrection, war, court order or any order of any governmental authorities having or claiming jurisdiction over the demised Premises; (n) escape of steam or gas or leakage in any part or portion of the demised Premises or any part or portion of the Building of which the demised Premises are a part, or caused by water, oil, rain or snow which may leak into, issue or flow from any part of the said Premises, or the Building of which the demised Premises are a part, from the roof, subsurface areas, drains, tanks, pipes or plumbing work of the same, or from any other place or quarter; (o) falling plaster, fixtures, or other building materials; (p) the entrustment of property to building employees; (q) theft; and (r) any other cause whatsoever.

Indemnification of Lessor

17. Lessee agrees to indemnify, defend and save Lessor, its agents, servants and employees, harmless from and against any and all claims, actions, demands, expenses, costs, losses, damages, obligations, charges, liabilities, penalties, orders, and judgments which may be imposed upon, incurred by or asserted against Lessor, its agents, servants, or employees, by or on behalf of any person(s), firm(s), corporation(s) or any other entity(ies) in connection with any and all loss of life, personal injury, damage to or loss of property, or loss of interruption of business arising from (a) anything whatsoever done in or about or out of the demised Premises or the Building of which the demises Premises are a part, (b) the use, occupancy, condition or maintenance of the demised Premises; (c) any breach or default on the part of Lessee in the performance of any term, covenant, condition or agreement on the part of Lessee to be performed or complied with by Lessee pursuant to the terms, covenants, conditions and agreements of this Lease; (d) any act or omission of Lessee, its agents,

Services and Facilities Furnished

12. As long as Lessee is not in default under any of the covenants of this Lease, Lessor shall:

Elevators

(a) Provide necessary elevator facilities on business days, except such days as are or hereafter may be designated to be national holidays, from 8:00 A.M. to 6:00 P.M. and on Saturdays from 8:00 A.M. to 1:00 P.M. and have an elevator subject to call at all other times;

HVAC

(b) Furnish heat, ventilation and air conditioning ("HVAC") to the demised Premises, when and as required by law, on business days, except such days as are or hereafter may be designated to be national holidays, from 8:00 A.M. to 6:00 P.M. Heat, ventilation and air conditioning required by Lessee at other times shall be supplied upon reasonable prior notice, and shall be paid for by Lessee as Additional Rent, promptly upon billing, at such rates as Lessor shall establish therefor (such rates not to be in excess of one hundred twenty percent (120%) of Lessor's actual cost of labor and utilities);

HVAC Requirements In Excess Of Building Standard

(c) If, by reason of Lessee's installation of additional heat generating equipment such as, without limitation, computers and/or similar equipment or machinery, the Premises shall require additional HVAC services in excess of the Building standard for HVAC, Lessee agrees to pay Lessor for all costs related to the provision of such additional services including, without limitation, any alterations or modifications to the Building's HVAC systems which may be necessitated thereby. Any such additional charges shall be deemed to be Additional Rent hereunder and shall be collectible in advance in the same manner as provided for in Paragraph 5 hereof. In addition to the actual charges for such additional HVAC services, the additional rental therefor shall include an administrative fee payable to Lessor in the amount of 15% of the amount charged for such services;

Cleaning and Trash Removal

(d) At Lessor's expense, cause the Premises to be kept clean provided the same are kept in good order by Lessee. Extraordinary amounts of trash or refuse will be removed as required at Lessee's expense. If, however, it is agreed that the Premises are to be kept clean by Lessee, such cleaning shall be done at Lessee's sole cost and expense in a manner satisfactory to Lessor, and no one other than persons approved by Lessor shall be permitted to enter said Premises or the Building for such purpose. Lessee shall pay to the cost of removal of any of Lessee's refuse and rubbish from the Building. Bills for the same shall be rendered by Lessor to Lessee at such time as Lessor may elect and shall be due and payable when rendered, and the amount of such bills shall be deemed to be, and be paid as, Additional Rent.

Access

(e) Lessor shall furnish to Lessee's employees and agents access to the demised Premises during normal building hours, subject to compliance with such security measures as shall from time to time be in effect for the Building.

Directory

(f) Lessor shall maintain a directory of office tenants in the lobby area of the Building on which shall be listed the name of Lessee.

Water

(g) Lessor shall furnish hot and cold water for drinking, lavatory, toilet and ordinary cleaning purposes to be drawn from the bathrooms or other approved fixtures on each floor.

Gas and Electric

(h) Lessor shall furnish the demised Premises with a reasonable amount of gas and/or electric current, as Lessor may determine, for lighting and normal office use and for heating and air conditioning, and shall replace light bulbs and tubes, plus the labor cost for such replacement, shall be chargeable to Lessee and collectible as Additional Rent. Lessee shall not install or operate in the demised Premises any electrically operated equipment or other machinery, other than typewriters, adding machines, reproduction machines, and other machinery and equipment normally used in modern offices, without first obtaining the prior written consent of the Lessor. Lessor may condition such consent upon the payment by Lessee of Additional Rent as compensation for the additional consumption of electricity occasioned by the operation of said equipment or machinery. Lessor may require that special, high electricity installations of Lessee (such as computer or reproduction facilities) be separately sub-metered for electrical consumption as hereinafter provided at Lessee's cost.

Excessive Use of Utilities Or Services: Lessor's Options

13. Lessor reserves the right, in the event that it determines in its sole judgment that Lessee uses gas, electricity, HVAC, water, or any other utility or service furnished in an extravagant or unreasonable manner or for any purpose other than the normal purposes for which such is supplied or in an amount greater than the average of the other office tenants in the Building ("Building Average"), to at its sole option:

Metered Usage

(a) Require that Lessee install a gas, water and/or electric meter on the Premises by which to measure Lessee's consumption of any such service and pay Lessor for the amount used in excess of the Building Average. In such event, Lessee shall be solely responsible for the cost of such meter and the installation thereof and throughout the duration of its

servants, employees, invitees, licensees or visitors; (e) any accident, occurrence or happening whatsoever occurring in or about the demised Premises or the Building of which the demised Premises are a part; (f) any violation by Lessee, its agents, servants, employees, invitees, licensees or visitors of any law, ordinance or governmental order or regulation of any kind, or of any of the Rules and Regulations set forth on Exhibit B hereof (and as such Rules and Regulations may hereafter at any time or from time to time be modified, amended or added to); (g) the construction or installation (i) of any Lessee improvements, or (ii) of any alterations, decorations and improvements, to the demised Premises, and (h) any tax now or hereafter attributed to the execution or delivery of this Lease or any amendment thereof and (i) any cause provided for in Paragraph 16 hereof.

In the event that any action or proceeding is bought against Lessor, and (a) defend such action or proceeding upon written notice from Lessor by counsel selected by Lessor and (b) further indemnify, defend and save Lessor, its agents, servants and employees harmless from and against all costs, expenses, counsel fees, liabilities, orders and judgments incurred in or about any such action or proceeding including any monies paid out by Lessor in settlement of any claims or judgments.

Loss of Light and Air and Other Damages

18. Lessor shall not be liable for any injury or damage caused by operations in construction of any private, public or quasi-public work or for loss of light and air caused by the permanent or temporary closure, darkening or bricking up of any windows for any reason whatsoever, including without limitation, Lessor's own acts. In the event that said windows shall be closed, darkened or bricked up as aforesaid, it is expressly agreed that Lessee shall not be entitled to any compensation therefor nor to any abatement or diminution of the rental called for hereunder, nor shall the same release Lessee from its obligations under this Lease or be deemed to constitute an actual or constructive eviction in whole or in part.

Notice Of Fire, Etc.

19. Lessee agrees that it shall give Lessor immediate notice which shall be promptly confirmed in writing in case of any fire, loss or accident in the demised Premises or in the Building or of any discovered defects or dangerous conditions existing therein or in any machinery, fixtures, or equipment.

Destruction Of Premises By Fire Or Other Casualty

20. (a) If, during the term of this Lease, the Building is so injured by fire or other casualty that the demised Premises is rendered wholly unfit for occupancy and said demised Premises can not be repaired within sixty (60) days from the happening of such injury in the sole judgment of Lessor, or if any mortgagee of the Building shall not permit the application of adequate insurance proceeds for repair or restoration, or if the casualty is not included in the risks covered by Lessor's then current insurance policies, then, at Lessor's option exercisable by written notice to Lessee within thirty (30) days after Lessor is notified of the casualty and of the extent thereof, this Lease shall cease and determine as of the date of such injury with either party retaining any insurance proceeds received by them. In such event, Lessee shall pay the rent apportioned to the time of injury and shall immediately surrender the demised Premises to Lessor, who may enter upon and repossess the same. If such injury can be repaired within sixty (60) days thereafter in the sole judgment of Lessor, Lessor may enter and repair, and this Lease shall not be affected, except that the base rent payable by Lessee shall be apportioned based upon the percentage of the demised Premises which remains in sole judgment of Lessor as to such other portions of the Premises until five (5) days after Lessor gives written notice to Lessee that such repairs are substantially completed. If the said demised Premises shall be so slightly injured by fire or other casualty as aforesaid as not to be rendered unfit for occupancy, Lessor agrees that the same shall be repaired with reasonable promptness, in which case the rent accrued or accruing shall not be apportioned or suspended. Any insurance proceeds payable to Lessor or Lessee as a result of such occurrence shall be applied to the cost of any repairs. If the said demised Premises shall be injured by fire or other casualty occurring through the negligence of Lessee or those claiming under Lessee, or their employees respectively, then without prejudice to any other rights and remedies of Lessor and/or any rights of subrogation of Lessor's insurer, the Lessor may elect to repair the Premises at Lessee's sole cost and expense and there shall be no apportionment or abatement of the rent due hereunder. No penalty shall accrue and Lessor shall not be liable for any delay in making repairs under the provisions of this Paragraph which may arise due to insurance adjustment, labor problems or any other cause beyond Lessor's control. If any damage or destruction to the Premises is determined by Lessor to have been due to any negligence of Lessee or those claiming under Lessee, or their employees, respectively, all debris shall be removed from the Premises by and at the sole cost and expense of Lessee, without prejudice to or limitation of such other rights and remedies as Lessor may elect to assert. Lessee hereby expressly waives the benefit of any statute or law presently in force or which may hereafter be enacted which conflicts with the provisions of this Paragraph and agrees that the provisions of this Paragraph shall govern and control in lieu thereof.

Waiver of Subrogation

(b) Notwithstanding any other provision herein, Lessor and Lessee hereby release each other from liability for loss or damage to the property of the party granting such release, even if the loss or damage occurred through the negligence of such other party or its agents, servants, invitees or employees, providing that this release shall be effective only with respect to loss or damage (i) covered by insurance and (ii) occurring during such time as the relevant insurance policy of the party granting such release contains a clause to the effect that this release does not affect such policy or the right of the insured to recover thereunder. Each party will use its best efforts to obtain such a clause, but if an additional premium is charged therefor, the party benefitting therefrom, if it desires to have the waiver, will pay to the other the amount of such additional premium promptly upon being billed therefor.

Eminent Domain

21. (a) In the event that the Premises demised or any part thereof are taken or condemned for a public or quasi-public use, this Lease shall, as to that part so taken, terminate as of the date title or possession shall vest in the condemnor, and rent reserved shall abate proportionately to the square feet of leased space taken or condemned or shall cease if (i) the entire Premises demised be so taken or (ii) in the event of a partial taking if Lessor shall give Lessee notice, within thirty (30) days of Lessor's receipt of actual notice of such taking, of Lessor's election to terminate this Lease, which option is expressly reserved to Lessor. In the event of any total or partial taking, Lessee waives all claims as against Lessor and waives all claims for leasehold damages as against the condemning authority or party, and assigns all such claims for any loss or impairment of the value of its interest in the leasehold against the condemnor, if any, to Lessor. It is agreed that Lessee will make no claim by reason of the complete or partial taking of the demised Premises which would in any way reduce Lessor's award for such taking and it is further agreed that the Lessee shall not be entitled to any notice whatsoever from Lessor of the partial or complete termination of this Lease by reason of the aforesaid except as provided in subparagraph (a) (ii) hereof. The foregoing shall not, however, deprive Lessee of any separate award for moving expenses, business dislocation, damages or for any other award which would not reduce, directly or indirectly, the award otherwise payable to Lessor.

If all or any portion of the demised premises shall be taken by the exercise of the right of eminent domain for governmental occupancy for a limited period of time, this Lease shall not terminate and the Lessee shall continue to perform and observe all of its obligations hereunder as though such taking had not occurred except only to the extent that it may be prevented from so doing pursuant to the terms of the order of the authority which made the taking. In the event of such temporary taking, Lessee shall be entitled to receive the entire amount of any award made for such taking (whether paid by way of damages, rent or otherwise) unless the period of governmental occupancy extends beyond the expiration of the initial term of this Lease and there be no renewal thereof, or if this Lease be renewed, beyond the expiration of the last renewal term, in which case the award shall be apportioned between Lessor and Lessee as of the date of such termination. Lessee covenants that at the termination of any such governmental occupancy if during the term of this Lease or any renewal thereof, it will, at its sole cost and expense, restore the demised premises as nearly as may be reasonably possible to the condition in which the same was prior to such taking.

Condemnation For Unsafe Condition

(b) If the Premises herein demised, or any part thereof, or the Building of which the demised Premises are a part or any part thereof, are condemned or declared unsafe by any duly constituted authority having or claiming the power to make such condemnation or such declaration or are the subject of a violation notice or a notice by any such authority requiring repairs or construction, Lessor, at Lessor's sole election, may cancel and terminate this Lease, and in the event Lessor elects to so cancel and terminate this Lease, Lessee, upon notice from Lessor, shall immediately surrender said Premises to Lessor and this Lease shall terminate and the rent reserved shall be apportioned as of the date of such termination. In such event, Lessee waives all claims as against Lessor and as against the authority or party making said condemnation or declaring said Premises or any part thereof, or the Building of which the demised Premises are a part or any part thereof, unsafe, or giving the violation or other notice as aforesaid; and it is agreed that Lessee will make no claim by reason of the required surrender of said Premises.

Superior Lease

(c) In the event of the termination of any Lease held by Lessor's principal for the Premises of which the demised Premises form a part (whether by the Lessor of such Lease or by option exercised by Lessor's principal because of unsafe condition of the Building or Buildings of which the demised Premises form a part, or for any other reason) this Lease shall cease and terminate upon the same date that the Lease to Lessor's principal shall terminate, irrespective of whether or not any portion of the demised Premises is declared unsafe and or condemned. It is agreed that Lessee will make no claim either against Lessor herein or any other person or persons by reason of the aforesaid.

Vault Space, Etc.

22. No vaults, vault space or space not within the property line of the Building is leased hereunder, anything contained in or indicated on any sketch, blueprint or plan, or anything contained elsewhere in this Lease to the contrary notwithstanding. Lessor makes no representation as to the location of the property line of the Building. All vaults and vault space and all space not within the property line of the Building which Lessee may be permitted to use and or occupy is to be used and or occupied under a revocable license, and if such license be revoked, or if the amount of such space be diminished, taken or required by any Federal, State, or Municipal Authority or Public Utility, Lessor shall not be subject to any liability nor shall Lessee be thereby entitled to any compensation or diminution or abatement of rent. In no event shall such revocation, diminution or requisition be deemed to be a constructive or actual eviction of Lessee in whole or in part. Any fee or charge of municipal or other authorities for such vault shall be paid by Lessee.

payment of rent and the performance of any other terms of such subleases. Upon the curing of such default, such assignment shall become null and void. From and after such default and until the same is cured, any such subleases or subtenancies may not be cancelled or modified without the written consent of Lessor and any such cancellation or modification, shall create an immediate default hereunder.

Lessor's Right of Access and Other Reserved Rights

26. (a) Lessee shall permit Lessor to erect, use and maintain, pipes and conduits in and through the Premises. Lessor or Lessor's agents shall have the right to enter the Premises at all times to examine the same, to make appropriate surveys of Lessee's consumption of any services supplied, and to show them to, without limitation, prospective purchasers or lessees of the Building, and to make such decorations, repairs, alterations, improvements or additions as Lessor, in its sole judgement, may deem necessary or desirable. Further, it is agreed that Lessor shall be allowed to take all material into and upon said Premises that may be required therefor without the same constituting an actual or constructive eviction of Lessee in whole or in part. The rental due hereunder shall in no way abate while said decorations, repairs, alterations, improvements, or additions are being made, by reason of any loss or interruption of business of Lessee or otherwise.

(b) During the twelve months prior to the expiration of the term of this Lease, or any renewal term, Lessor may exhibit the Premises to prospective occupants and place upon said Premises the usual notices "To Let" or "For Sale", which notices Lessee shall permit to remain thereon without molestation or obstruction of any kind.

(c) If during the last month of the term, Lessee shall have removed all or substantially all of Lessee's property therefrom, Lessor may immediately enter and alter, renovate and re-decorate the Premises, without elimination or abatement of rent or incurring liability to Lessee for any compensation, and such acts shall have no effect upon this Lease. If Lessee shall not be personally present to open and permit an entry into said Premises, at any time, when for any reason an entry therein shall be necessary or permissible, Lessor or others acting on its behalf may enter the same by a master key, or may forcibly enter the same, without rendering Lessor or such persons liable in any way therefor and without in any manner affecting the obligations and covenants of this Lease.

(d) All locks shall be installed by Lessor at Lessee's sole cost and expense and Lessee shall furnish to Lessor, at Lessee's cost, a duplicate key(s) to all portions of the Premises. Nothing herein contained, however, shall be deemed or construed to impose upon Lessor any obligation, responsibility or liability whatsoever, for the care, supervision or repair, of the Premises or the Building or any part thereof other than as expressly herein provided.

(e) Lessor shall also have the right at any time, without the same constituting an actual or constructive eviction and without incurring any liability to Lessee therefor, to change the arrangement, appearance and or location of entrances or passageways, doors and doorways, and corridors, elevators, stairs, wash rooms, or other public parts or common areas of the Building and to change the name, number or designation by which the Building or Premises is commonly known.

Adjacent Excavation-Shoring

27. If an excavation shall be made upon land adjacent to the Premises, Lessee hereby grants a license to enter upon the Premises for the purpose of doing such work as Lessor shall deem necessary to preserve the walls or structure of the Building from injury or damage and to support the same by proper foundations and in such event, expressly waives and agrees not to make any claim for damages or indemnity against Lessor or for any diminution or abatement of rent.

New Code Requirements

28. If any existing code, statute, ordinance, regulation or the like pertaining to fire, safety, health, occupancy requirements or the like to which the Premises or the Building is subject shall be amended, or if any new code, statute, ordinance, regulation or the like pertaining to said matters shall be enacted, so as to require any alterations, additions or improvements to the Premises or the Building, Lessee shall pay to Lessor as Additional Rent upon demand each year, its proportionate share of the costs thereof including all amortizations, interest and other charges related to any such alterations, additions or improvements. Lessee's proportionate share shall be determined by multiplying the total amount of such costs by the percentage set forth in Paragraph 5(a) hereof. Any such Additional Rent may be estimated and collected in advance as provided in Paragraph 5 hereof.

Force Majeure

29. This Lease and the obligation of Lessee to pay all rental and other charges called for hereunder and perform all of the other covenants and agreements hereundertaken shall in no way be affected, impaired or excused because of Lessor's inability to fulfill any of its obligations under this Lease, to supply any service, to make any agreed upon repairs, additions, alterations or decorations or to supply any equipment or fixtures if such inability results from any cause whatsoever beyond Lessor's control including without limitation, war, civil commotion, strikes, or other acts of unions, suppliers, governmental bodies, agencies and or other third parties.

Lessee Negative Covenants

30. Lessee covenants and agrees that it will do none of the following things without obtaining the prior written consent of Lessor:

Subordination **23.** (a) This Lease is subject and subordinate to all ground or underlying leases and to all mortgages and other encumbrances which may now or hereafter affect such leases or the Premises or the Building, and to all renewals, modifications, consolidations, replacements and extensions thereof. This clause shall be self-operative and no further instrument of subordination shall be required by any mortgagee. Notwithstanding the foregoing, in confirmation of such subordination, Lessee shall execute promptly any certificate of estoppel, subordination, attornment or the like that Lessor may request. Lessee hereby irrevocably constitutes and appoints Lessor the Lessee's attorney-in-fact to execute any such certificates or certificates for and on behalf of Lessee.

(b) If Lessor is Lessee of the demised Premises or the Building of which the said Premises are a part, then Lessee agrees that Lessee takes possession as sub-tenant and agrees to be bound by the terms, conditions, covenants and agreements of the Lessor's tenancy whatever the same may be, and in case the Lessor's tenancy shall terminate either by expiration, forfeiture or otherwise, then this Lease shall thereupon immediately terminate, and Lessee hereby agrees thereupon to give immediate possession and Lessee further agrees to waive and hereby does waive, any and all claims for damages or otherwise, by reason of such other terms, conditions, covenants and agreements and their enforcement and for such termination.

(c) Anything herein contained to the contrary notwithstanding it is hereby expressly acknowledged and agreed that Lessor has the right to sell, lease, transfer or otherwise encumber in whole or in part, the Building of which the demised Premises is a portion and or the land upon which it is erected and or to apply for conversion of the Building to condominium or similar forms of ownership. Any such act shall in no way affect the obligations of Lessee hereunder nor entitle it to any abatement or diminution of any rental or other charges called for hereunder. Lessee specifically covenants that it will not seek to enjoin or otherwise interfere with or impede in any way, directly or indirectly, Lessor's exercise of such rights.

Assignment and Subletting **24.** Lessee, for itself, its heirs, distributees, executors, administrators, legal representatives, successors and assigns, expressly covenants that it shall not assign, mortgage or in any way encumber this Lease, nor sublease, underlet or suffer or permit the Premises or any part thereof to be used or occupied by anyone other than Lessee and its employees without the prior written consent of Lessor which shall not be unreasonably withheld. It will not be unreasonable for Lessor to withhold consent if the reputation, financial responsibility, or business of a proposed assignee or sub-lessee is unsatisfactory to Lessor, or if Lessor deems such business to not be consonant with that of other tenants or occupants in the Building, or if the intended use by the proposed assignee or sublease conflicts with any commitment made by Lessor to any other tenant or occupant in the Building.

Lessee's request for consent shall be in writing and contain the name, address, and description of the business of the proposed assignee or sub-lessee, its most recent financial statement and other evidence of financial responsibility, its intended use of demised Premises, and the terms and conditions of the proposed assignment or subletting.

Within thirty (30) days from receipt of such request, Lessor shall either: (a) grant or refuse consent; or (b) elect to require Lessee (i) to execute an assignment of lease or sublease of Lessee's interest hereunder to Lessor or its designee upon the same terms and conditions as are contained herein, together with an assignment of Lessee's interest as sublessor in any such proposed sublease, or (ii) if the request is for consent to a proposed assignment of this Lease, to terminate this Lease and the term hereof effective as of the last day of the third month following the month in which the request was received.

If Lessee is a corporation or a partnership and if control thereof is changed or transferred at any time during the term of this lease or any extension or renewal thereof, Lessor may, at its sole option, exercised at any time after receiving notice thereof, upon giving thirty (30) days written notice to Lessee declare such a change or transfer of control to be a breach of this Lease and may terminate this Lease and exercise all of its rights and remedies reserved hereunder or otherwise available to it.

Each assignee or sublessee hereunder shall assume and be deemed to have assumed this Lease and shall be and remain liable jointly and severally with Lessee for all payments and for the due performance of all terms, covenants, conditions and provisions herein contained on Lessee's part to be observed and performed. No assignment shall be binding upon Lessor unless the assignee shall deliver to Lessor an instrument in recordable form containing a covenant of assumption by the assignee, but the failure or refusal of assignee to execute the same shall not release assignee from its liability as set forth herein.

All the foregoing notwithstanding, Lessee shall not enter into any lease, sublease, license, concession or other agreement for the use, occupancy or utilization of the demised Premises or any portion thereof, which provides for a rental or other payment for such use, occupancy or utilization based in whole or in part on the income or profits derived by any person from the property leased, used, occupied or utilized (other than an amount based on a fixed percentage or percentages of receipts or sales). Any such purported lease, sublease, license, concession or other agreement shall be absolutely void and ineffective as a conveyance of any right or interest in the possession, use or occupancy of any part of the demised Premises.

Any consent by Lessor hereunder shall not constitute a waiver of strict future compliance by Lessee with the provisions of this Paragraph or a release of Lessee from the full performance by Lessee of any of the terms, covenants, provisions, or conditions in this Lease contained.

If this Lease be assigned, or if the Premises or any part thereof be sublet or underlet or occupied by anyone other than Lessee in violation of this covenant, Lessor may collect rent from the assignee, underlessee, sublessee or occupant, and apply the net amount collected to the rent herein reserved, but no such assignment, subleasing, underletting, occupancy or collection shall be deemed a waiver of this covenant, or the acceptance of the assignee, underlessee, sublessee or occupant as a lessee or in place of Lessee, or a release of Lessee from the further performance by Lessee of any covenants herein contained.

Assignment of Subleases **25.** If a default shall occur under the terms of this agreement, Lessee hereby assigns to Lessor all subleases and subtenancies now or hereafter to be made of the demised Premises or any parts thereof, as well as all rents or other sums of money which may hereafter become due and payable thereunder to Lessee, and all security at any time deposited for the

(a) Keep upon or attach to the Premises any goods or chattels acquired under a conditional sale, security agreement or other secured transaction title to which is reserved in some other person, and Lessee hereby agrees that all goods, property and chattels to be used or kept or to be attached upon the Premises demised herein, shall be owned by Lessee or leased by Lessee, provided, however, that no such leased goods or chattels shall be leased with the understanding that they shall be exempt from levy for rent and other charges herein reserved as rent.

(b) Remove, attempt to remove or manifest in the reasonable opinion of Lessor an intention to remove Lessee's goods or property from or out of the demised Premises other than in the ordinary course of business, without having first paid Lessor all rent which may become due during the entire term of this Lease.

(c) Vacate or desert said Premises during the term of this Lease, or permit the same to be empty and unoccupied.

(d) Conduct any public sale or auction of any kind.

(e) Manufacture any commodity, or prepare or dispense any foods or beverages in the demised premises.

(f) Transfer all or a majority of its beneficial ownership interests.

If any consent by Lessor, is given in any one instance pursuant to this paragraph, such consent shall not in any way be construed to relieve Lessee from its obligation to obtain the express prior written consent of Lessor to any further acts listed herein.

Default **31.** Any other provisions in this Lease notwithstanding, it shall be an Event of Default under this Lease if (a) Lessee fails to pay any installment of Fixed Rent, Additional Rent or other sum payable by Lessee hereunder when due and such failure continues for a period of five (5) days after notice by or on behalf of Lessor, provided, however, Lessor need not give any such notice, and Lessee shall not be entitled to any such period of grace, more than twice in any 12 month period; (b) Lessee vacates the demised Premises, or uses or occupies the demised Premisees otherwise than permitted hereunder, or assigns or sublets, or purports to assign or sublet, the demised Premises or any part thereof otherwise than in the manner and upon the conditions set forth in Paragraph 24 hereof; (c) Lessee fails to observe or perform any other covenant or agreement of Lessee for more than five (5) days and such additional time, if any, as is reasonably necessary to cure such failure provided that Lessee, within said five (5) day period shall have commenced and thereafter proceed with reasonable diligence and in good faith to remedy or cure such default; (d) Without Lessor's prior written consent, Lessee removes or attempts to remove or manifests an intention to remove any or all of its property from the demised Premises otherwise than in the ordinary and usual course of business; (e) Lessee makes any assignment for the benefit of or calls a meeting of its creditors, or if Lessee seeks or makes any composition or arrangement with its creditors; Lessee commits an act of bankruptcy or files a petition or commences any proceeding under any bankruptcy or insolvency law; a petition is filed or any proceeding is commenced against Lessee under any bankruptcy or insolvency law; Lessee is adjudicated a bankrupt; Lessee by any act indicates its consent to, approval of or acquiescence in, or a court approves, a petition filed or proceeding commenced against Lessee under any bankruptcy or insolvency law; a receiver or other official is appointed for Lessee for a substantial part of Lessee's assets or for Lessee's interests in this Lease; any attachment or execution against a substantial part of Lessee's assets or of Lessee's interests in this Lease is made; a substantial part of Lessee's assets or of Lessee's interest in this Lease is taken by legal process in any action against Lessee; or (f) Any of the foregoing occur as to any guarantor or surety of Lessee's performance under this Lease, or such guarantor or surety defaults on any provision under its guaranty or suretyship agreement.

Lessor's Remedies **32.** (a) If an Event of Default hereunder shall have happened Lessor may, at its option:

(i) declare to be immediately due and payable and sue for and recover, all unpaid Base Rent for the unexpired balance period of the term of this Lease (and also all Additional Rent as the amount(s) of same can be determined) as if by the terms of this Lease the same were payable in advance, together with all legal fees and other expenses incurred by Lessor in connection with the enforcement of any of Lessor's rights and remedies hereunder, and or

(ii) distrain, collect or bring action for such Base Rent and Additional Rent as being rent in arrears, or may enter judgment therefor in an amicable action as herein elsewhere provided for in case of rent in arrears, or may file a Proof of Claim in any bankruptcy or insolvency proceeding for such Base Rent and Additional Rent, or institute any other proceedings, whether similar or dissimilar to the foregoing, to enforce payment thereof, and or

(iii) terminate the Lease Term by giving written notice thereof and, upon the giving of such notice, the Lease Term and the estate hereby granted shall expire and terminate with the same force and effect as though the date of such notice was the date hereinbefore fixed for the expiration of the Lease Term, and all rights of Lessee hereunder shall expire and terminate, but Lessee shall remain liable as hereinafter provided, and or

(iv) exercise any other rights and remedies available to Lessor at law or in equity.

Re-entry and Distraint **33.** In the event of any default in any of the agreements, covenants and conditions of this Lease on the part of the Lessee, Lessor, or any one acting on Lessor's behalf, at Lessor's option:

(a) May without notice or demand enter the demised Premises, breaking open locked doors if necessary to effect entrance, without liability to action for prosecution or damages for such entry or for the manner thereof, for the purpose of distraining or levying to the extent legally permissible and for any other purposes, and to the extent legally permissible take possession of and sell all goods and chattels at auction, on five days' notice served in person on Lessee, or left on the Premises, and pay said Lessor out of the proceeds; and Lessee hereby releases and discharges Lessor, and its agents, from all claims, actions, suits, damages and penalties, for or by reason or on account of any entry, distraint, levy, appraisement or sale; and/or

(b) May enter the Premises, breaking open locked doors if necessary to effect entrance without liability to action for prosecutions or damages for such entry or for the manner thereof, and without demand, to the extent legally permissible, proceed by distress and sale of the goods there found to pay the rent and/or other charges herein payable as rent, and all costs and officer's commissions, including watchmen's wages and sums payable to Lessor, and further including a sum equal to 5% of the amount of the levy as commissions to the constable or other persons making the levy, shall be paid by Lessee, and in such case all costs, officer's commissions, and other charges shall immediately attach and become part of the claim of Lessor. Lessee, to the extent legally permissible, hereby expressly waives in favor of Lessor the benefit of all laws now made or which may hereafter be made regarding any limitation as to the goods upon which, or the time within which, distress is to be made after removal of goods, and further relieves Lessor of the obligation of proving or identifying such goods, it being the purpose and intent of this provision that all goods of Lessee, whether upon the demised Premises or not, shall be liable to distress for rent. Lessee, to the extent legally permissible, waives in favor of Lessor all rights under any statute and law, and all supplements and amendments thereto that have been or may hereafter be enacted, and authorizes the sale of any goods distrained for rent at any time after five days from the said distraint without any appraisement and/or condemnation thereof.

Lessee further waives the right to issue a Writ of Replevin under any Rule of Civil Procedure and the Laws of the State in which the demised Premises herein or such property or goods so distrained or levied upon are located, or under any other law previously enacted and now in force, or which may be hereafter enacted, for the recovery of any articles, household goods, furniture, etc., seized under a distress for rent or levy upon an execution for rent, damages or otherwise; all waivers hereinbefore mentioned are hereby extended to apply to any such action; and/or

Bank Accounts

(c) May immediately attach and/or garnish any funds in any bank accounts which are maintained by Lessee and immediately apply such funds to the full extent of the liability Lessee has incurred by reason of such default as provided for herein including all additional charges agreed to be paid in the event of such default. Lessee expressly waives the benefit of any laws, existing or which may hereafter be enacted, which may limit or prohibit such attachment and/or garnishment it being the intent and purpose of this provision that all funds in such accounts shall be liable to collection for such default. Lessee hereby expressly directs and empowers any Bank in which such accounts are maintained to pay to Lessor or its Authorized Agent such sums from said accounts as are stated to be due and owing to Lessor hereunder upon presentation of a copy of this Lease verified to be true and correct and an affidavit of Lessor or its Authorized Agent setting forth the nature of the default and the amount due and owing to Lessor as a result of such default. Lessee hereby expressly releases and discharges said Bank and its officers, directors and employees from all claims, actions, suits, damages and penalties for or by reason of or on account of the payment of any funds from Lessee's accounts as provided for hereunder. Lessee further releases and discharges Lessor and all persons acting on its behalf from all claims, actions, suits, damages and penalties for or by reason or on account of the exercise of its rights hereunder, provided only that Lessor shall be responsible to refund any sums which after collection may be determined to be in excess of Lessee's liability for such default; and/or

Reletting of Premises

(d) May, as agent of Lessee, re-let the demised Premises or any part or parts thereof to such person or persons as may in Lessor's sole discretion seem best for any unexpired portion of the term hereof, and receive the rent therefor, and Lessee shall be liable for any loss of rent for the balance of the then current term and for all expenses incurred in such reletting or the making of alterations in connection therewith. Lessor shall have no duty or obligation to mitigate Lessee's liability for damages hereunder and Lessor shall in no event be responsible or liable for any failure to re-let the demised Premises or any part thereof, or for any failure to collect any rent due upon a reletting.

Confession of Judgment for Money

34. If rent and/or charges hereby reserved as rent shall remain unpaid on any day when the same ought to be paid, Lessee hereby empowers any Prothonotary, clerk or attorney of any Court of Record to appear for Lessee in any and all actions which may be bought for rent and/or charges, payments, costs and expenses reserved as rent, or agreed to be paid by Lessee, and to sign for Lessee an agreement for entering in any Competent Court an amicable action or actions for the recovery of rent or other charges or expenses, and in said suits or in said amicable action or actions to confess judgment against Lessee for all or any part of the rent specified in this Lease and then unpaid including, at Lessor's option, the rent for the entire unexpired balance of the term of this Lease, and/or other charges, payments, costs and expenses reserved as rent or agreed to be paid by Lessee, and for interest and costs together with an attorney's commission of 5%. Such authority shall not be exhausted by one exercise thereof, but judgment may be confessed as aforesaid from time to time as often as any of said rent and/or charges reserved as rent shall fall due or be in arrears, and such powers may be exercised during the term hereof, and/or after the expiration of the original term, and/or during or after any extension or renewal of this Lease.

Inability to Tender Possession

43. If the Lessor shall be unable to give possession of the Premises on the date of the commencement of the term hereof by reason of the fact that the Premises are located in a building being constructed and which has not been sufficiently completed to make the Premises ready for occupancy or by reason of the fact that a certificate of occupancy has not been procured or for any other reason, Lessor shall not be subject to any liability for the failure to give possession on said date. Under such circumstances the rent reserved and convenanted to be paid herein shall not commence until the possession of the Premises is given or the Premises are available for occupancy by Lessee, and no such failure to give possession on the date of commencement of the term shall in any way affect the validity of this Lease or the obligations of Lessee hereunder, nor shall same be construed in any way to extend the term of this Lease. If the Building in which the Premises are located is not in course of construction, and Lessor is unable to give possession of the Premises on the date of the commencement of the term hereof by reason of the holding over or retention of possession of any tenant, tenants or occupants or for any other reason, or if repairs, improvements or decorations of the Premises or of the Building are not completed, no abatement or diminution of any rent to be paid hereunder shall be allowed to Lessee nor shall the validity of the Lease be impaired under such circumstances. If permission is given to Lessee to enter into possession of the Premises or to occupy premises other than the demised Premises prior to the date specified as the commencement of the term of this Lease, Lessee covenants and agrees that such occupancy shall be deemed to be under all the terms, covenants, conditions and provisions of this Lease, including but not limited to the covenants to pay rent.

Quiet Enjoyment

44. Lessor covenants and agrees with Lessee that, conditioned upon Lessee paying the Base Rent and Additional Rent and observing and performing all the terms, covenants and conditions on Lessee's part to be observed and performed, Lessee may peaceably and quietly enjoy the Premises hereby demised, subject, nevertheless, to the terms and conditions of this Lease and to the terms and conditions of all ground leases, underlying leases, mortgages and other encumbrances hereinbefore mentioned.

Surrender of Premises

45. Upon the expiration or other termination of the term of this Lease, and/or any extension or renewal term thereof, Lessee shall quit and surrender to Lessor the Premises, broom clean, in good order and condition, ordinary wear excepted, and shall immediately remove all property located on the Premises with the exception of attached furniture, furnishings and other fixtures. Lessee's obligation to observe or perform this covenant shall survive the expiration or other termination of the term of this Lease.

Security Deposit

46. Lessee has deposited with Lessor the sum of $________ as security for the faithful performance and observance by Lessee of the terms, covenants, provisions, and conditions of this Lease. It is agreed that Lessee shall not be entitled to and shall make no claim for any interest on such deposit. Nor shall the holding of such deposit by Lessor be construed as establishing a trust or any other relationship between the parties other than that of debtor and creditor.

It is agreed that in the event Lessee defaults in respect of any of the terms, covenants, provisions and conditions of this Lease, including, but not limited to, the payment of Base Rent and Additional Rent, Lessor may use, apply or retain the whole or any part of the security as deposited to the extent required for the payment of any Base Rent and Additional Rent or any other sum as to which Lessee is in default or for any sum which Lessor may expend or may be required to expend by reason of Lessee's default in respect of any of the terms, covenants and conditions of this Lease, including but not limited to, any damages or deficiency in the reletting of the Premises, whether such damages or deficiency accured before or after re-entry pursuant to summary proceedings or otherwise by Lessor.

In the event that Lessee shall fully and faithfully comply with all of the terms, provisions, covenants and conditions of this Lease, the security shall be returned to Lessee within 30 days after the date fixed as the end of the Lease or any extension or renewal thereof and after delivery of entire possession of the Premises in good condition to Lessor.

In the event of a sale of the land and Building or leasing of the Building, Lessor shall have the right to transfer the security to the vendee or lessee, and Lessor shall thereupon be automatically released by Lessee from all liability for the return of such security, and Lessee agrees to look solely to such new lessor for the return of said security; and it is agreed that the provisions hereof shall apply to every transfer or assignment of the security to a new lessor.

Lessee further covenants that it will not assign or encumber the monies deposited herein as security, and that neither Lessor nor its successors or assigns shall be bound by any such assignment, encumbrance, attempted assignment or attempted encumbrance. In the event that the monthly rental shall be increased hereunder for any reason including without limitation increases in taxes, operating and maintainance costs or for any other charges as may be imposed hereunder Lessee agrees that it will, upon demand, provide Lessor with such additional security as Lessor may deem appropriate to cover such additional obligations.

Lessee expressly waives the benefit of all laws presently in force or which hereafter may be enacted which conflict in any way with the provisions of this paragraph and agrees that the provisions set forth herein shall conclusively govern in lieu thereof.

Confession of Judgment for Possession

35. When this Lease shall be determined by term, covenant, or condition broken, either during the original term of this Lease or any renewal or extension hereof, and also when and as soon as the term hereby created or any extension thereof shall have expired, it shall be lawful for and Lessee hereby empowers any attorney as attorney for Lessee to file an agreement for entering in any Competent Court an amicable action in ejectment against Lessee and all persons claiming under Lessee for the recovery by Lessor of possession of the herein demised Premises,for which this Lease shall be his sufficient warrant, whereupon, if Lessor so desires, a writ of execution or possession may issue forthwith, without any prior writ or proceedings whatsoever; and provided that, if for any reason after such action have been commenced the same shall be determined and the possession of the Premises hereby demised remain in or be restored to Lessee, Lessor shall have the right upon any subsequent default or defaults, or upon the termination of this Lease as hereinbefore set forth, to bring one or more amicable action or actions as hereinbefore set forth to recover possession of the said premises.

Copy of Lease Sufficient Warrant

36. In any amicable action of ejectment and or for rent in arrears, Lessor shall first cause to be filed in such action an affidavit made by it or someone acting for it setting forth the facts necessary to authorize the entry of judgment, of which facts such affidavit shall be conclusive evidence and if a true copy of this Lease (and of the truth of the copy such affidavit shall sufficient evidence) be filed in such action, it shall not be necessary to file the original as a warrant of attorney, any rule of Court, custom or practice to the contrary notwithstanding.

Finality of Judgment and Waivers

37. Lessee expressly agrees that any judgment, order or decree entered against Lessee by or in any Court by virtue of the powers of attorney contained in this Lease, or otherwise, shall be final, and that Lessee will not take an appeal, certiorari, writ of error, exception or objection to the same, or file a motion or rule to strike off or open or to stay execution of the same, and releases to Lessor and to any and all attorneys who may appear for Lessee all errors in the said proceedings, and all liability therefor. Lessee expressly waives the benefits of all laws, now or hereafter in force, exempting any goods on the demised premises or elsewhere from distraint, levy or sale in any legal proceeding taken by the Lessor to enforce any rights under this Lease. Lessee further waives the right of inquisition on any real estate that may be levied upon to collect any amount which may become due under the terms and conditions of this Lease, and does hereby voluntarily condemn the same and authorizes the Prothonotary or clerk to enter a writ of execution or other process. If proceedings shall be commenced by Lessor to recover possession under any statute or law, either at the end of the term or sooner termination of this lease, or for nonpayment of rent or any other reason, Lessee specifically waives the right to any notice required by such statute, and agrees that five days' notice shall be sufficient in either or any such case.

Waiver of Trial by Jury

38. It is mutually agreed by and between Lessor and Lessee that the respective parties hereto shall and they hereby do waive trial by jury in any action, proceeding or counterclaim brought by either of the parties hereto against the other on any matters whatsoever arising out of or in any way connected with this Lease, the relationship of Lessor and Lessee, Lessee's use or occupancy of the Premises, and/or any claim of injury or damage, and any emergency statutory or any other statutory remedy. It is further mutually agreed that in the event Lessor commences any summary or other proceeding for non-payment of rent or ejectment, Lessee will not interpose any counterclaim of whatever nature or description in any such proceeding.

Interest on Late Payments

39. Any rent (including charges collectible as Additional Rent, overdue for a period of more than ten (10) days shall bear interest at the rate of 4% per annum above the prime lending rate then in effect as charged by First Pennsylvania Bank, Philadelphia, Pennsylvania to its most credit-worthy commercial customers on 90 day unsecured loans (or the highest rate allowed by law, if other than such stated rate) until paid, such interest shall be considered Additional Rent and shall be payable on demand.

Lessor's Right to Perform Lessee's Obligation

40. If Lessee shall default in the performance of any covenant required to be performed by it under this Lease, Lessor may perform the same for and at the expense of Lessee, after first giving notice to Lessee of its intention to do so. If Lessor or Owner at any time is compelled to pay, or elects to pay, any sum of money, or to do any act which will require the payment of any sum of money, by reason of the failure of Lessee to comply with any provisions hereof, or if Lessor is compelled to incur any expense, including reasonable counsel fees, in instituting, prosecuting or defending against any action or proceeding instituted by reason of any default of Lessee hereunder, the amount of such payments or expenses shall be paid by Lessee to Lessor as additional rent on the next day following such payment or the incurring of such expenses upon which a regular monthly rental payment is due, together with interest thereon at the rate set forth in Paragraph 39 hereof (or the highest rate allowed by law, if other than such stated rate).

Rights of Assignees of Lessor

41. The right to enter judgment against Lessee and to enforce all of the other provisions of this Lease hereinabove provided for may be exercised by any assignee of Lessor's right, title and interest in this Lease in his, her, its or their own name, notwithstanding the fact that any or all assignments of the said right, title, and interest may not be executed and/or witnessed in accordance with the provisions or requirements of any statute or law, and all supplements and amendments thereto that have been or may hereafter be enacted, and Lessee hereby expressly waives the requirements of any and all such laws regulating the manner and/or form in which such assignments shall be executed and witnessed.

All Remedies Cumulative and Concurrent

42. All of the remedies hereinbefore given to Lessor and all rights and remedies given to it by law and equity shall be cumulative and concurrent. No determination of this Lease or the taking or recovering of the Premises shall deprive Lessor of any of its remedies or actions against Lessee for rent and sums due at the time or which, under the terms hereof, would in the future become due as if there had been no determination; nor shall the bringing of any action for rent or breach of covenant, nor the resort to any other remedy herein provided for the recovery of rent, be construed as a waiver of the right to obtain possession of the Premises.

No Right To Renewal Or Extension

47. If there be any agreement between Lessor and Lessee providing for the cancellation of this Lease upon certain provisions or contingencies, and or an agreement for the renewal hereof at the expiration of the term first above mentioned, the right to such renewal or the execution of a renewal agreement between Lessor and Lessee prior to the expiration of such first mentioned term shall not be considered an extension thereof or a vested right in Lessee to such further term so as to prevent Lessor from cancelling this Lease and any such extension thereof during the remainder of the original term hereby granted. Such privilege, if and when so exercised by Lessor, shall cancel and terminate this Lease and any such renewal or extension. Any right herein contained on the part of Lessor to cancel this Lease shall continue during any extension or renewal hereof. Any option on the part of Lessee herein contained for an extension or renewal hereof shall not be deemed to give lessee any option for a further extension beyond the first renewal or extended term.

No Waiver

48. No act or forebearance by Lessor or Lessor's agents during the term hereby demised shall be deemed an acceptance or a surrender of the Premises, and no agreement purporting to accept such surrender shall be valid unless in writing and signed by Lessor. The delivery of keys to any employee of Lessor or of Lessor's agents shall not operate as a termination of the Lease or a surrender of the Premises. In the event that Lessee at any time desires to have Lessor sublet the Premises for Lessee's account, Lessor or Lessor's agents are authorized to receive said keys for such purposes with the express understanding that such act shall not release Lessee from any of its obligations under this Lease, and Lessee hereby relieves Lessor of any liability for loss of or damage to any of Lessee's effects suffered in connection with any such subletting. The failure of Lessor to seek redress for violation of, or to insist upon the strict performance of, any term, covenant or condition of this Lease, or any of the Rules and Regulations set forth or hereafter adopted by Lessor, shall not prevent a subsequent act, which would have originally constituted a violation from having all the force and effect of an original violation. The receipt by Lessor of any rent with knowledge of the breach of any covenant of this Lease shall not be deemed a waiver of such breach. The failure of Lessor to enforce any of the Rules and Regulations set forth, or hereafter adopted, against Lessee and/or any other occupant in the building shall not be deemed a waiver of any such Rules and Regulations. No provision of this Lease shall be deemed to have been waived by Lessor, unless such waiver be in writing signed by Lessor.

Requested Modifications

49. If, in connection with obtaining, continuing or renewing financing for which the Building, Land or the demised Premises or any interest therein represents collateral in whole or in part, a banking, insurance or other lender shall request reasonable modifications of this Lease as a condition of such financing, Lessee will not unreasonably withhold, delay or defer its consent thereto, provided that such modifications do not increase the monetary obligations of Lessee hereunder or adversely affect to a material degree the Lessee's leasehold interest hereby created.

Required Insurance

50. Lessee shall at all times during the period in which it has any occupancy rights in the demised Premises, maintain in full force and effect comprehensive public liability insurance, naming Lessor and its managing agent as additional insureds, covering injury to persons in amounts at least equal to $500,000 per accident, and damage to property of at least $250,000, occurring in or about the demised Premises. Lessee shall lodge with Lessor duplicate originals or certificates of such insurance at or prior to the date Lessee shall make any entry into the demised Premises, together with evidence of paid up permiums, and shall lodge with Lessor renewals thereof at least fifteen (15) days prior to expiration. All such policies of insurance shall provide that they shall not be cancelled or amended without at least twenty (20) days prior written notice to Lessor and said managing agent.

Notices

51. Except as otherwise in this Lease provided, a bill, statement, notice or communication which Lessor may desire or be required to give to Lessee, shall be deemed sufficiently given or rendered if, in writing, delivered to Lessee personally or sent by registered mail addressed to Lessee at the Premises or at the last known residence address or business address of Lessee or left at the Premises addressed to Lessee, and the time of the rendition of such bill or statement and of the giving of such notice or communication shall be deemed to be the time when the same is delivered to Lessee, mailed, or left at the Premises as herein provided. Any notice by Lessee to Lessor must be served by registered mail, return receipt requested, addressed to Lessor at the address first hereinabove given or at such other address as Lessor shall hereafter designate by written notice.

Parties Bound

52. The covenants, conditions and agreements contained in this Lease shall bind and inure to the benefit of Lessor and Lessee and their respective heirs, distributees, executors, administrators, successors, and except as otherwise provided in this Lease, their assigns. If there shall be more than one Lessee, they shall all be bound jointly and severally by the terms, covenants and agreements herein, and the word "Lessee" shall be deemed and taken to mean each and every person or party mentioned as a Lessee herein, be the same one or more; and if there shall be more than one Lessee, any notice required or permitted by the terms of this lease may be given by or to any one thereof; and shall have the same force and effect as if given by or to all thereof.

Conduct Of Lessee

53. This lease is granted upon the express condition that Lessee and/or the occupants of the Premises herein demised, shall not conduct themselves in a manner which Lessor in its sole opinion may deem improper or objectionable.

Compliance With Rules and Regulations

54. Lessee and its servants, employees, agents, visitors, invitees and licensees shall observe faithfully, and comply strictly with the Rules and Regulations and such other and further Rules and Regulations as Lessor or Lessor's agents in their sole judgment may from time to time adopt. Notice of any additional rules or regulations shall be given in such manner as Lessor may elect. Nothing contained in this Lease shall be construed to impose upon Lessor any duty or obligation to enforce the Rules and Regulations or terms, covenants or conditions in any other lease, as against any other tenant or occupant and Lessor shall not be liable to Lessee for violation of the same by any other tenant or occupant, its servants, employees, agents, visitors, invitees or licensees.

Right To Relocate Tenants and Terminate Certain Leases

55. Lessor shall have the sole right to relocate any tenant to comparable space in the Building. Lessor shall have the further right to cancel without penalty or liability to Lessee any lease of one thousand square feet or less upon giving the Lessee ninety (90) days prior written notice.

Submission Of Lease Not An Option to Lessee.

56. Submission of this Lease for examination does not constitute a reservation of, or option for, the Premises. This Lease shall not be binding upon the Lessor until executed by Lessor or Lessor's Authorized Agent, and an executed copy of the Lease is sent to Lessee.

Condition Of Premises

57. Lessee hereby acknowledges that Lessee has examined the demised Premises and that they are in good and tenantable condition, and it is agreed that Lessee's entering to possession of the demised Premises shall be an acknowledgment by Lessee that the said Premises are in good and tenantable condition at the beginning of the term hereof. Lessor has let the demised Premises in their present condition and without any representation on the part of Lessor, its officers, employees, servants and/or agents as to the Building, Premises or land on which they are erected except as herein expressly set forth, and no rights, easements, or licenses are acquired by Lessee, by implication or otherwise except those, if any, expressly set forth in the provisions of this Lease. Lessee has agreed to accept the Premises "as is" and it is understood and agreed that Lessor is under no duty to make repairs or alterations at the time of letting, unless specifically set forth elsewhere herein, or at any time thereafter. No contract entered into or that may be subsequently entered into by Lessee, relative to any alterations, additions or improvements, shall in any way affect the payment of the rent at the time specified in this Lease.

Real Estate Brokers

58. Lessee warrants and represents that it dealt with no Real Estate Broker in the negotiation of this Lease, and Lessor in executing this Lease is relying upon such representation. Lessee expressly agrees to be responsible for and to relieve, indemnify and defend Lessor from any claims by any finder or broker which may be made in connection herewith.

Recording Prohibited

59. Neither this Lease nor any memorandum, affidavit or other writing with respect thereto, shall be recorded by Lessee or by anyone acting through, under or on behalf of Lessee, and the recording thereof in violation of this provision shall make this Lease null and void at Lessor's election.

Severability

60. If any term, provision or condition contained in this Lease shall, to any extent, be invalid or unenforceable, the remainder of this Lease, or the application of such term, provision or condition to persons or circumstances other than those in respect of which it is invalid or unenforceable shall not be affected thereby, and each and every other term, provision and condition of this Lease shall be valid and enforceable to the fullest extent permitted by law.

Grammatical Changes

61. The necessary grammatical changes required to make the provisions hereof apply either to corporations or partnerships or individuals, men or women, as the case may require, shall in all cases be assumed as though in each case fully expressed.

Captions

62. The captions or marginal notations to paragraphs in this Lease are inserted solely for convenience, are not part of this Lease and shall not be considered or given any effect in construing the provisions hereof.

Removal and Abandonment Of Property

63. Any and all property which may be removed from the demised Premises by Lessor may be handled, removed, stored or otherwise disposed of by Lessor at the sole risk and expense of Lessee, and Lessor shall in no event be responsible for the preservation or safe-keeping thereof. Lessee shall pay to Lessor upon demand, any and all expenses incurred in such removal and all storage charges against said property so long as the same shall be in Lessor's possession or under Lessor's control. If any property shall remain in said Premises or in the possession of Lessor and shall not be removed by Lessee within a period of ten (10) days from the time the Premises are either abandoned by Lessee or repossessed by Lessor under the terms of this Lease, said property shall conclusively be deemed to have been forever abandoned by Lessee.

Estoppel Statement

64. Lessee shall from time to time, within ten (10) days after request by Lessor, execute, acknowledge and deliver to Lessor a statement, which may be relied upon by Lessor or any proposed assignee of Lessor's interest in this Lease or any existing or proposed purchaser, mortgagee or ground lessor, certifying that this Lease is unmodified and in full force and effect (or that the same is in full force and effect as modified, listing the instruments of modification), the dates to which all rent and other charges have been paid, and whether or not, to the best of Lessee's knowledge, there exists any default in the performance of any covenant, agreement, term, provision or condition contained in this Lease or whether Lessee has any claims or demands against Lessor (and, if so, the default, claim and/or demand shall be specified).

Apportionment Or Proration

65. Whenever any provision for apportionment of rent or for proration of time is specified in this Lease such apportionment or proration shall be made on a per diem basis using a base year of 360 days unless some other basis is specified.

Governing Law

66. Interpretation of this Lease shall be governed by the law of the State/Commonwealth in which the Premises is located.

Entire Agreement

67. This Lease and the Rules and Regulations and riders, if any, attached hereto contains the entire agreement between the parties and there are no promises, agreements, conditions or understandings between Lessor and Lessee, either oral or written, other than as herein set forth. Any agreement hereafter made shall be ineffective to change, modify, discharge or effect an abandonment of this Lease in whole or in part unless such agreement is in writing, and is signed by Lessor.

In Witness Whereof and intending to be legally bound hereby the parties hereto have set their respective hands and seals and/or caused these presents to be executed by their duly authorized officers the day and year above first written.

Witness:

INDIVIDUAL LESSEE

Signature _____ [Seal]

Signature _____ [Seal]

PARTNERSHIP LESSEE

Name of Partnership _____

Witness:

By: _____ [Seal]

By: _____ [Seal]

By: _____ [Seal]

By: _____ [Seal]

By: _____ [Seal]

By: _____ [Seal]

(ALL OF THE PARTNERS)

CORPORATE LESSEE:

(Corporate Seal)   Name of Corporation

Attest:

                                                  By:

                                                  Title:

                                                  RODIN MANAGEMENT INC.,
                    (Corporate Seal)   LESSOR'S AUTHORIZED AGENT

                                                  By:

—————————————————————   Title:

LESSEE ACKNOWLEDGEMENT

CORPORATE LESSEE   INDIVIDUAL, PARTNERSHIP LESSEE
STATE/COMMONWEALTH OF   )   STATE/COMMONWEALTH OF   )
COUNTY OF   ) ss: COUNTY OF   ) ss:
)   )

    On this   day of   , 19   , before me   On the   day of   , 19   , before me,

the undersigned officer, personally appeared   the undersigned officer, personally appeared
known to me (or satisfactorily proven) to be the
              which is the Lessee under the foregoing instru-   known to me (or satisfactorily proven) to be the person
ment, and being duly sworn, did depose and say that he resides in   whose name   subscribed to the foregoing instrument, and being duly sworn
                                                        did depose and say that he executed the same as LESSEE for the purposes there-
that he is the   of   in contained.
the corporation described in and which executed the foregoing instrument as the
LESSEE for the purposes therein contained; that he knows the seal of said corpor-   IN WITNESS WHEREOF, I have hereunto set my hand and official seal.
ation; that the seal affixed to said instrument is such corporate seal; that it was so
affixed by the order of the Board of Directors of said corporation, and that he
signed his name thereto by like order.

    IN WITNESS WHEREOF, I have hereunto set my hand and official seal.
                                                                          NOTARY PUBLIC

                    NOTARY PUBLIC

EXHIBIT "B"
RULES AND REGULATIONS

Referred to in the Foregoing Lease, and Forming a Part Thereof

1. The sidewalks, halls, passages, elevators and stairways shall not be obstructed by any of the tenants, nor used by them for any other purpose than for ingress and egress to and from their respective offices, nor shall they be used as a waiting or lounging place for tenants, tenants' employees or those having business with tenants. The halls, passages, elevators, stairways and roofs are not for the use of the general public, and Lessor retains in all cases the right to control and prevent access to any part of said building, or of any adjoining building, of all persons whose presence, in the judgment of Lessor or Lessor's employees, will be prejudicial to the safety, character, reputation or interests of the building and its occupants. In case of invasion, mob, riot, public excitement or other commotion, Lessor reserves the right to prevent access to the building during the continuance of the same by closing the doors or otherwise, for the safety of tenants and the protection of property in said building. During other than business hours, access to the building may also be refused, unless the person seeking admission is known by the watchman in charge to have the right to enter demised premises therein or is properly identified and the production of a key to such demised premises may in addition be required, provided that Lessor shall in no case be liable for damages for the admission or exclusion of any person from said building.

2. The floors, walls, partitions, skylights, windows, doors and transoms that reflect or admit light into passage-ways, or into any place in said building, shall not be covered or obstructed by any of the tenants. The wash-rooms, water-closets, sinks, and other water apparatus shall not be used for any purposes other than those for which they were constructed and no sweeping, rubbish, rags, ashes, chemicals, or refuse from electric batteries or other unsuitable substance, shall be thrown or placed therein. Any damage resulting from such misuse or abuse shall be borne and immediately paid by the tenant by whom or by whose employees it shall have been caused.

3. Nothing shall be placed by tenants or their employees on the outside of the building, or on the windows, window-sills or projections.

4. No sign, advertisement or notice shall be inscribed, painted or affixed on any part of the outside, or inside of said building, unless of such character, color, size and material, and in such place, as shall be first designated by Lessor by endorsement hereon. A sign painter authorized by Lessor will do such work at tenants' expense.

5. No additional locks or bolts of any kind shall be placed upon any of the doors or windows by any tenant, nor shall any changes be made in existing locks or the mechanism thereof. Each tenant must upon surrendering possession at the termination of the foregoing lease deliver to Lessor all keys of said demised premises, and of water-closets and wash-rooms appurtenant thereto, and leave the windows and doors in the demised premises in like condition as at the date of said lease.

6. Lessor retains in all cases the right to prescribe the method and manner in which any merchandise, furniture, iron safe or heavy or bulky object shall be brought in or taken out of the said building, and the hours at which the same shall be done, and further retains the right to limit and prescribe the weight, size and proper position thereof, and all damage done to the building by the bringing in or taking out thereof, or by reason of the presence thereof in the building, shall be made good and immediately paid by the tenant by, through or under whom the said damage may have been done. No iron safe or other heavy or bulky object shall be brought into the building or removed therefrom, except by experienced safe men, movers or riggers, authorized in writing by Lessor. Tenants shall notify the Building Superintendent of the weight or size of the safe, or other such heavy or bulky object, and arrange with him as to time, method and manner for receiving or delivering the same.

7. In order that the leased premises may be kept in a good state of preservation and cleanliness, each tenant shall, during the continuance of the lease, permit Lessor's employees take care of and clean said leased premises. No tenant shall employ any person or persons other than Lessor's employees for such purpose, it being understood and agreed that Lessor shall be in no way responsible for any damage done to the furniture or other effects of tenants or others by any of Lessor's employees, or any other person or for any loss of property from leased premises, however occurring. Tenants will see each day that the windows are closed, the lights turned out and the doors securely locked before leaving the building. Tenants desiring windows shades or awnings, or desiring to be served with ice or towels or other supplies, upon application to Lessor, will be given the name of the person, firm or company authorized to furnish the same at tenants' expense, no others to be employed by tenants for such purpose, nor for caring for shades or awnings. Shades and awnings shall be of the material, style, form and color adopted by Lessor for the building, and no tenant shall put up any that do not conform to such standard.

8. No space in the Building shall be used by tenants or others for manufacturing, for the storage of merchandise, for the sale of merchandise, goods or property of any kind at auction or for an employment agency, or for securing employees other than to be employed on the demised premises, or for the payment or salaries or wages to employees or persons not actually employed in the building, nor for any other purpose except that specified in the application of the tenant.

9. Tenants, their employees, or others, shall not make or commit any improper noises or disturbances of any kind in the building, smoke in the elevators, mark or defile the elevators, water-closets, wash-rooms, or the walls, windows, doors or any other part of the building, nor interfere in any way with other tenants or those having business in the building. Tenants shall be liable for all damage to the building done by their employees.

10. No carpet, rug or other article shall be hung or shaken out of any window, and nothing shall be thrown by the tenants or tenants' employees nor be allowed by them to drop, out of the windows or doors, or down the passages or skylights of the building; and no tenant shall sweep or throw, or permit to be swept or thrown from the leased premises, any dirt or other substance into any of the corridors or halls, elevators or stairways of said building, or into any of the light-shafts or ventilators thereof, or upon any adjoining building or roof.

11. No bicycles, vehicles or animals of any kind shall be brought into or kept in or about the premises.

12. If tenants desire to introduce signaling, telegraphic, telephonic or other wires and instruments, Lessor will direct the electricians as to where and how the same are to be placed, and without such direction, no placing, boring or cutting of wires will be permitted. Lessor retains in all cases the right to require the placing and using of such electrical protecting devices to prevent the transmission of excessive currents of electricity into or through the building, and require the changing of wires and of their placing and arrangements underground or otherwise as Lessor may direct, and further, to require compliance on the part of all using or seeking access to such wires with such rules as Lessor may establish relating thereto, and in the event of noncompliance by tenants or by those furnishing service or by using such wires or by others with the directions, requirements or rules, Lessor shall have the right to immediately cut, displace and prevent the use of such wires. Notice requiring such changing of wires and their replacing and rearrangement shall take effect immediately. All wires used by tenants must be clearly tagged at the distributing boards and junction-boxes and elsewhere in the building, with the number of the office to which said wires lead, and the purpose for which said wires respectively are used, together with the name of the company operating same.

13. A directory in a conspicuous place on the first floor, with the names of tenants, will be provided by Lessor.

14. Tenants shall not keep or use or allow to be used on the demised premises any article having an offensive odor, nor any ether, naphtha, phosphorus, bensole, gasoline, benzine, petroleum or any product thereof, crude or refined earth or coal oils, flashlight powder, or other explosive, kerosene, camphene, burning fluid or other illuminating material, except gas, electric light or candles.

15. No tenant and no employees of any tenant shall go upon the roofs of said building or any adjoining building, without the written consent of Lessor.

16. Furniture, bulky packages and freight will be received in the building, and shall be removed therefrom 7:30 to 9:00 A.M. and 4:30 to 6:00 P.M., and the same shall not be taken to or from the demised premises except by elevator, and during said hours, unless otherwise ordered by Lessor in writing. Lessor reserves the right but shall not be obligated to inspect all freight to be brought into the building and to exclude from the building all freight which violates any of these Rules and Regulations or the lease of which these Rules and Regulations are a part. Tenants shall notify the Building Superintendent in advance of the dates they plan to move in or out of the Building and arrange with him the times for such activity in order to minimize inconvenience to other occupants of the building. Each tenant shall provide Lessor with a list of all furniture, trade fixtures, equipment and similar articles to be removed from the Building and the list must be approved at the office of the Building Superintendent before building employees shall permit any article to be removed.

17. There shall not be used in any space, or in the public halls of the building, either by any tenant or by jobbers or others, in the delivery or receipt of merchandise, any hand trucks, except those equipped with rubber tires and side guards.

18. Unless expressly permitted by Lessor, no tenant shall place or allow anything to be against or near the glass of partitions or doors of said premises, or be unsightly from halls, corridors, or exterior of the Building. No show cases or other articles shall be put in front of or affixed to any part of the exterior of the building, nor placed in the halls, corridors or vestibules without the prior written consent of Lessor.

19. Unless expressly permitted by Lessor, all doors to said premises are to be kept closed at all times except when in actual use for entrance to or exit from said premises.

20. The leased premises shall not be used for lodging or sleeping purposes, and no cooking of food shall be done therein.

21. Neither hotplates nor vending machines may be installed or used in the premises without the prior written consent of Lessor.

22. The delivery of towels, ice, water, food, beverages, newspapers and other supplies will be permitted only under the direction, control and supervision of Lessor.

23. Lessor shall have the right to prohibit any advertising by any tenant which, in Lessor's opinion, tends to impair the reputation of the building or its desirability as a first class office building, and immediately upon notice by Lessor such tenant shall discontinue such advertising.

24. Canvassing, soliciting and peddling in the building is prohibited and Lessee will immediately report any such activity and will cooperate with Lessor in preventing the same.

25. Without Lessor's written consent, nothing shall be fastened to, nor shall holes be drilled or nails or screws driven into walls or partitions; nor shall walls or partitions be painted, papered or otherwise covered or moved in any way or marked or broken; nor shall any connection be made to electric wires for running fans or motors or other apparatus, devices or equipment nor shall machinery of any kind other than customary small business machines be allowed in the premises; nor shall tenants use any other method of heating, air conditioning or air cooling than that provided by Lessor. Telephones, switchboards and telephone wiring and equipment shall be placed only where designated by Lessor. No varnish, stain, paint, linoleum, oil-cloth, rubber, or other air-tight covering shall be laid or put upon the floors. No mechanics, other than those employed by Lessor, shall be allowed to work in or about the building without the written consent of Lessor first having been obtained.

26. The requirements of any tenant will be attended to only upon application at the office of the Building Superintendant. Building employees shall not perform any work or do anything outside of their regular duties unless under special instructions from the office of Lessor.

27. Lessor reserves the right to rescind, suspend or modify any rules or regulations and to make such other rules or regulations as, in Lessor's judgment, may from time to time be needed for the safety, care, maintenance, operation and cleanliness of the building, or for the preservation of good order therein. Notice of any action by Lessor referred to in this paragraph, when given to Lessee, shall have the same force and effect as if originally made a part of the foregoing lease.

28. These rules and regulations are not intended to give Lessee any rights or claims in the event that Lessor does not enforce any of them against other tenants or if Lessor does not have the right to enforce them against any other tenants, and such non-enforcement will not constitute a waiver as to Lessee.

APPROVE BY INITIALING

....

Lessee Lessor or Agent

OWNER-ORIENTED OFFICE BUILDING LEASE

AGREEMENT OF LEASE made as of this ＿＿ day of ＿＿＿ , 19＿＿ (hereinafter referred to as the "Lease") between a limited partnership (hereinafter referred to as "Landlord") and ＿＿＿＿＿＿＿＿＿＿＿

whose present address is ＿＿＿＿＿＿＿＿＿＿＿＿＿＿＿
(hereinafter referred to as "Tenant")

WITNESSETH:

Landlord hereby leases to Tenant, and Tenant hereby accepts from Landlord, the premises (hereinafter referred to as the "Premises") containing approximately ＿＿＿ square feet of Rentable Area (hereinafter defined) and designated on the plan attached hereto as Exhibit A in the building known as ＿＿＿ (hereinafter referred to as the "Building") located on land, the legal description of which is set forth on Exhibit A-1 which is attached hereto and made a part hereof and which is hereinafter referred to as the "Land", subject to the convenants, terms, provisions and conditions of this Lease. *Tenant shall have, as appurtenant to the Premises, rights to use in common, subject to reasonable rules of general applicability to tenants of the Building from time to time made by Landlord of which Tenant is given notice: (a) the common lobbies, corridors, stairways, elevators and loading platform of the Building, and the pipes, ducts, conduits, wires and appurtenant meters and equipment serving the Premises in common with others, (b) common walkways and driveways necessary for access to the Building, and (c) if the Premises include less than the entire rentable floor area of any floor, the common toilets, corridors and elevator lobby of such floor.*
In consideration thereof, Landlord and Tenant covenant and agree as follows:

1. Term. The term of this Lease (hereinafter referred to as the "Term") shall commence on the ＿＿ day of ＿＿＿ 19 ＿ (hereinafter referred to as the "Commencement Date") and ending on the ___ day of _____ 19 __ (hereinafter referred to as the "Termination Date"), unless sooner terminated as provided herein.

2. *Possession.* Landlord and Tenant shall be deemed to have entered into the work letter ("Work Letter") which is attached hereto, marked Exhibit B and made a part hereof, upon the execution of this Lease. In the event the Premises shall not be completed and ready for occupancy on the Commencement Date or in the event Landlord is unable to deliver possession on such date by reason of the holding over or retention of possession by any tenant or occupant, this Lease shall nevertheless continue in force and effect, but Rent (as hereinafter defined) shall abate until the Premises are ready for occupancy or until the Landlord is able to deliver possession, as the case may be, and Landlord shall have no other liability whatsoever on account hereof; provided, however, there shall be no abatement of Rent if the Premises are not ready for occupancy because of failure to complete the installation of special equipment, fixtures or materials ordered by Tenant, or because of any delays resulting from Tenant's failure to promptly submit plans in accordance with the Work Letter attached hereto as Exhibit B or resulting from changes or additions to Tenant's plans after the initial submission thereof. The Premises shall not be deemed incomplete or not ready for occupancy if only insubstantial details of construction, decoration or mechanical adjustments remain to be done. The determination of Landlord's architect or interior space planner for the Building shall be final and conclusive as to whether the Premises are completed and ready for occupancy.

If Tenant shall take possession of the Premises or any part thereof prior to the Commencement Date (which Tenant may not do without Landlord's prior written consent), all of the covenants and conditions of this Lease shall be binding upon the parties hereto with respect to such whole or part of the Premises as if the Commencement Date had been fixed as the date when Tenant took possession of such whole or part of the Premises and Tenant shall pay Rent for the period of such occupancy prior to the Commencement Date at the rate of the annual Base Rent set forth in Paragraph 3 hereof prorated for such period of occupancy and, if less than the whole Premises are occupied, for the proportionate area of the total Premises so occupied.

Under no circumstances shall the occurrence of any of the events described in this Paragraph 2 be deemed to accelerate or defer the Termination Date.

3. *Base Rent.*

A. *Amount of Base Rent.* Tenant shall pay to Landlord or Landlord's agent at the Office of the Building, One Logan Square, Philadelphia, Pennsylvania, or at such other place as Landlord may from time to time designate in writing, in coin or currency which, at the time or payment, is legal tender for private or public debts in the United States of America, rent in an amount equal to one-twelfth of the product obtained by multiplying _____ Dollars ($ ___) by the number of square feet of Rentable Area included in the Premises payable in advance on or before the first day of each and every month during the Term, without any set-off or deduction whatsoever, except that Tenant shall pay the first full monthly installment at the time of execution of this Lease. If the term commences other than on the first day of a month or ends other than on the last day of the month, the Rent for such month shall be prorated. The prorated Rent for the portion of the month in which the Term commences shall be paid on the first day of the first full month of the Term.

B. *Definitions.*   As used in the Paragraph 3 and elsewhere in this Lease the terms:

(i) "Gross Floor Area" for *each* floor in the Building shall mean the area contained within the exterior walls surrounding said floor measured from the exterior surface of the exterior wall (or the outside edge of the floor slab if the slab does not extend to the exterior wall) at a point five feet above floor level. Gross Floor Area includes the full area of shafts and other openings in the floor.

(ii) "Common Area" for *each* floor in the Building shall mean area within all common facilities which are a fixed part of the plan of said floor including toilet rooms, janitor's closets, fan rooms, freight vestibules, electrical and communications closets, elevator lobbies and corridors which serve more than one tenant, central mechanical loading storage and maintenance facilities.

(iii) "Usable Area" for *each* floor in the Building shall mean the space actually available for the discretionary use of the tenants for the accommodation of their personnel and equipment.

(iv) "Rentable Area" for *each* floor in the Building shall mean the Gross Floor Area of the floor less a) the thickness of the outside wall or one-half of the thickness of the perimeter glass walls where windows represent 50% or more of the wall, and b) all shafts passing through said floor. The area of the shaft passing through the floor shall include the full thickness of walls surrounding the shafts. Shafts and shaft enclosing walls to be deducted from Gross Floor Area to arrive at Rentable Area shall include elevator shafts, mechanical shafts, plumbing chases where they extend from floor to ceiling and exit stairways.

(v) "Rentable Area of the Building" shall mean the sum of the Rentable Area of all floors in the Building but not including the central building lobby and central mechanical rooms or building service areas, such as loading and receiving areas, building shafts, maintenance, central storage or building employee offices, locker or toilet facilities.

(vi) "Loss Factor" shall mean for *each* floor in the Building the Rentable Area of said floor divided by the Usable Area of said floor.

(vii) "Rentable Area for the Premises" shall mean the Usable Area of the Premises multiplied by the Loss Factor for the floor on which the Premises are located. The Rentable Area is subject to adjustment throughout the Term based upon charges in the Loss Factor. Upon notice from

Landlord to Tenant of said adjustment this Lease shall be deemed amended to incorporate the revised Rentable Area as of the date of said notice.

4. Additional Rent.   In addition to paying the Base Rent specified in Section 3 hereof, Tenant shall pay as "Additional Rent" the amounts determined as hereinafter set forth. The Base Rent and the Additional Rent are sometimes herein collectively referred to as the "Rent". All amounts due under this paragraph as Additional Rent shall be payable for the same periods and in the same manner, time and place as the Base Rent. Without limitation on other obligations of Tenant which shall survive the expiration of the Term, the obligations of Tenant to pay the Additional Rent provided for in this Paragraph 4 shall survive the expiration of the Term. For any partial Calendar Year, Tenant shall be obligated to pay only a pro rata share of the Additional Rent, based on the number of the days of the Term falling within such Calendar Year.

A. *Definitions.*   As used in this Paragraph 4, the terms:

(i) "Base Year" shall mean the calendar year 19 ____ .

(ii) "Calendar Year" shall mean each calendar year in which any part of the Term falls, through and including the year in which the Term expires.

(iii) "Consumer Price Index" shall mean the United States Department of Labor, Bureau of Labor Statistics, Consumer Price Index for Urban Wage Earners and Clerical Workers (Philadelphia Area Only).

(iv) "Tenant's Proportionate Share" shall mean the percentage calculated by dividing the Rentable Area contained in the Premises by 95% of the Rentable Area of the Building.

(v) "Taxes" shall mean all real estate taxes and assessments, special or otherwise, levied or assessed upon or with respect to the Land and/or Building and ad valorem taxes for any personal property used in connection therewith. Should the Commonwealth of Pennsylvania, or any political subdivision thereof, or any other governmental authority having jurisidiction over the Land and/or the Building, (a) impose a tax, assessment, charge or fee, which Landlord shall be required to pay, wholly or partially in substitution for *or as a supplement to* such real estate taxes and ad valorem personal property taxes, or (b) impose an income or franchise tax or a tax on rents wholly or partially in substitution for or as a supplement to a tax levied against the Land and/or the Building and/or the personal property used in connection with the Land or Building, all such taxes, assessments, fees or charges (hereinafter defined as "In Lieu Taxes") shall be deemed to constitute Taxes hereunder. "Taxes" shall include all fees and costs, including attorneys' fees, appraisals and consultants; fees, incurred by Landlord in seeking to obtain a reduction of, or a limit on the increase in, any Taxes, regardless of whether any reduction or limitation is obtained. Except as hereinabove provided with regard to In Lieu Taxes, taxes shall not include any inheritance, estate, succession, transfer, gift, franchise, net income or capital stock tax.

(vi) "Operating Expenses" shall mean all expenses, costs and disbursements (other than Taxes) of every kind and nature (determined for the applicable Calendar Year on an accrual basis) paid or incurred by Landlord in connection with the ownership, management, operation, maintenance and repair of the Land and Building, except the following:

(a) Costs of Alterations of any tenant's premises;

(b) Principal or interest payments on loans secured by mortgages or trust deeds on the Building and/or on the Land;

(c) Costs of capital improvements, except that Operating Expenses shall include (a) the cost during the Term, as reasonably amortized by Landlord with interest at the rate of 12% on the unamortized amount, of any capital improvement completed after the Base Year which, in Landlord's reasonable opinion, will have the effect of reducing any component cost included within Operating Expenses; and (b) the cost during the Term, as reasonably amortized by Landlord with interest at the rate of 12% on the unamortized amount, of any capital improvements which are necessary to keep the Land and Building in compliance with all governmental rules and regulations applicable from time to time thereto; and

(d) Leasing commissions for space in the Building.

B. *Expense Adjustment.* Tenant shall pay to Landlord or Landlord's agent as Rent, in addition to the Base Rent required by Paragraph 3 hereof, an amount ("Expense Adjustment Amount") equal to Tenant's Proportionate Share of the amount by which the Operating Expenses (subject to adjustment pursuant to Paragraph 4C hereof) incurred with respect to each Calendar Year exceeds the product of (i) $3.90 and (ii) the Rentable Area of the Building ("Base Operating Expense"); provided, however, commencing with the first Calendar Year following the Calendar Year in which Tenant first copies the Premises, in determining the amount of Operating Expenses for any Calendar Year, if less than ninety-five percent (95%) of the Building's rentable area shall have been occupied by tenant(s) at any time during any such Calendar Year, Operating Expenses shall be determined for such Calendar Year to be an amount equal to the like expenses which would normally be expected to be incurred had such occupancy been ninety-five percent (95%) throughout such Calendar Year. The Expense Adjustment Amount with respect to each Calendar Year shall be paid in monthly installments, in an amount estimated from time to time by Landlord and communicated by written notice to Tenant. Landlord shall cause to be kept books and records showing Operating Expenses in accordance with generally accepted accounting principles. Following the close of each Calendar Year, Landlord shall cause the amount of the Expense Adjustment Amount for such Calendar Year to be computed based on Operating Expenses for such Calendar Year for the Building and Landlord shall deliver to Tenant a statement of such amount and Tenant shall pay any deficiency to Landlord as shown by such statement within thirty (30) days after receipt of such statement. If the total of the estimated monthly installments paid by Tenant during any Calendar Year exceed the actual Expense Adjustment Amount due from Tenant for such Calendar Year, at Landlord's option such excess shall be either credited against payments next due hereunder or refunded by Landlord, provided Tenant is not then in default hereunder.

C.   *Adjustment For Services Not Rendered by Landlord.* Tenant acknowledges that Landlord's projection of the floor amount of Operating Expenses stated in subparagraph 4B hereof is based upon the assumption that Landlord will be providing substantially similar services to all tenants in the Building. If this assumption is not in fact correct, that is, if Landlord is not furnishing any particular work or service (the cost of which, if performed by Landlord, would be included in Operating Expenses) to a tenant who has undertaken to perform such work or service in lieu of the performance thereof by Landlord, Operating Expenses shall be deemed for the purposes of this Paragraph to be increased by an amount equal to the additional Operating Expenses which would reasonably have been incurred during such period by Landlord if it had at its own expense furnished such work or service to such tenant.

D.   *Consumer Price Index Adjustment.*   In the event that the twelve (12) month average of the Consumer Price Index for the Base Year shall be less than the twelve (12) month average of the Consumer Price Index for any subsequent Calendar Year, Tenant shall pay to Landlord or Landlord's agent as Additional Rent with respect to such subsequent Calendar Year an amount (the "CPI Adjustment") equal to the product of (i) the amount equal to the Base Rent multiplied by thirty-five percent (35%) and (ii) the percentage by which the average Consumer Price Index for such subsequent Calendar Year exceeds the average Consumer Price Index for the Base Year.

The CPI Adjustment with respect to each Calendar Year shall be paid in monthly installments in advance on the first day of each and every calendar month during such Calendar Year in an amount estimated by Landlord from time to time and communicated to Tenant by written notice. After the expiration of a Calendar Year, Landlord shall furnish Tenant a statement showing (i) the average Consumer Price Index for the Base Year, (ii) the average Consumer Price Index for the applicable Calendar Year, (iii) the amount of the CPI Adjustment to be paid to Landlord, for such Calendar Year, (iv) the total of the estimated monthly installments paid to Landlord during such Calendar Year, and (v) the amount of any excess or deficiency with respect to such Calendar Year. Tenant shall pay any deficiency to Landlord as shown by such statement within thirty (30) days after receipt of such statement. If the total of the estimated monthly installments paid by Tenant during any Calendar Year exceeds the actual CPI Adjustment due from Tenant for such Calendar Year, at Landlord's option, such excess shall either be credited against payments next due hereunder or refunded by

Landlord, provided Tenant is not then in default hereunder. Delay in computation of the CPI Adjustment shall not be deemed a default hereunder or a waiver of Landlord's right to collect the CPI Adjustment.

If the manner in which the Consumer Price Index as determined by the Department of Labor shall be substantially revised, or if the 1967 average shall no longer by used as an index of 100, an adjustment shall be made in such revised index which would have obtained if the Consumer Price Index had not been so revised or if said average was still in use. If the Consumer Price Index shall become unavailable to the public because publication is discontinued, or otherwise, Landlord will substitute therefor a comparable index based upon changes in the cost of living or purchasing power of the consumer dollar published by any other governmental agency or, if no such index shall then be available, a comparable index published by a major bank or other financial institution or by a university or a recognized financial publication.

E.   *Tax Adjustment.*   Tenant shall pay to Landlord or Landlord's agent as Rent, in addition to Base Rent required by Paragraph 3 hereof, an amount ("Tax Adjustment Amount") equal to Tenant's proportionate share of the amount by which the Taxes *paid* with respect to each Calendar Year exceeds the product of (i) $1.60 and (ii) the Rentable Area of the Building ("Base Tax"). The Tax Adjustment Amount with respect to each Calendar Year shall be paid in monthly installments, in an amount estimated from time to time by Landlord and communicated by written notice to Tenant. Following the close of each Calendar Year, Landlord shall cause the amount of the Tax Adjustment Amount for such Calendar Year to be computed based on Taxes for such Calendar Year and Landlord shall deliver to Tenant a statement of such amount and Tenant shall pay any deficiency to Landlord as shown by such statement within thirty (30) days after receipt of such statement. If the total of the estimated monthly installments paid by Tenant during any Calendar Year exceed the actual Tax Adjustment amount due from Tenant for such Calendar Year, at Landlord's option such excess shall be either credited against payments next due hereunder or refunded by Landlord, provided Tenant is not then in default hereunder. The amount of any refund of Taxes received by Landlord shall be credited against Taxes for the year in which such refund is received. In determining the amount of Taxes for any year, the amount of special assessments to be included shall be limited to the amount of the installment (plus any interest payable thereon) of such special assessment required to be paid during such year if the Landlord had elected to have such special assessment paid over the maximum period of time permitted by law. All references to Taxes "for" a particular year shall be deemed to refer to Taxes paid during such year without regard to when such Taxes are assessed or levied.

F.   *Delay in Computation.*   Delay in computation of the Expense Adjustment Amount, the CPI Adjustment or Tax Adjustment Amount shall not be deemed a default hereunder or a waiver of Landlord's right to collect any of such amounts.

G. *No Credit.*   Tenant shall not be entitled to any rebate or credit in the event either Taxes, Operating Expenses or the Consumer Price Index for any Calendar Year is lower than any previous Calendar Year as to the Consumer Price Index or the floor amounts set forth in this Paragraph as to Taxes or Operating Expenses.

5. *Use of Premises.*   Tenant shall use and occupy the Premises solely as an office for _____

_____ and for no other purpose.

6. *Condition of Premises.*   Subject to the Work Letter, the Tenant's taking possession of the Premises or any portion thereof shall be conclusive evidence that the Premises or any such portion was in good order and satisfactory condition when the Tenant took possession. Tenant shall be responsible for any items of damage to the Premises caused by Tenant or its agents, employees, independent contractors or suppliers. No promise of the Landlord to alter, remodel or improve the Premises or the Building and no representation by Landlord or its agents respecting the condition of the Premises or the Building have been made to Tenant or relied upon by Tenant other than as may be contained in this Lease or in any written amendment hereto signed by Landlord and Tenant.

7. *Services.*

A. *List of Services.*   Landlord shall provide the following services on all days during the Term, except Sundays and holidays, unless otherwise stated:

(i) Subject to all governmental rules, regulations and guidelines applicable thereto, heating and air conditioning when necessary for normal comfort in the Premises, from Monday through Friday, during the period from 8 a.m. to 6 p.m. and on Saturday during the period from 8 a.m. to 1 p.m. Tenant will pay for all heating and air conditioning requested and furnished prior to or following such hours or required due to special heat-producing equipment installed by Tenant at rates to be established from time to time by Landlord.

(ii) Adequate electrical wiring and facilities for standard building lighting fixtures provided by Landlord and for Tenant's incidental uses, provided that (a) the connected electrical load of the incidental use equipment does not exceed an average of one watt per square foot of the Premises and (b) the electricity so furnished for incidental uses will be at a nominal 120 volts and no electrical circuit for the supply of such incidental use will have a current capacity exceeding 20 amperes. If Tenant's requirements for electricity for incidental uses are in excess of those set forth in the preceding sentence, the Landlord reserves the right to (i) require Tenant to install the conduit, wiring and other equipment necessary to supply electricity for such excess incidental use requirements at the Tenant's expense by arrangement with the appropriate approved local utility and (ii) estimate the additional charge for such excess use and shall bill Tenant and Tenant shall pay, on a monthly basis, the estimated additional charge; or at Tenant's option, Tenant shall install at its expense separate metering for such excess use and pay the cost therefor to the appropriate utility company. Tenant shall bear the cost of replacement of lamps, starters and ballasts for lighting fixtures.

(iii)   City water from the regular Building outlets for drinking, lavatory and toilet purposes.

(iv)   Janitorial services Monday through Friday in and about the Premises and window washing services pursuant to the specification set forth on Exhibit E which is attached hereto and made a part hereof.

(v)   Adequate automatic passenger elevator service at all times.

(vi)   Freight elevator services subject to scheduling by Landlord.

B.   *Interruption of Services.*   Tenant agrees that Landlord shall not be liable for damages (by abatement of Rent or otherwise) for failure to furnish or delay in furnishing any service, or for any diminution in the quality or quantity thereof, when such failure or delay or diminution is occasioned, in whole or in part, by repairs, renewals, or improvements, by any strike, lockout or other labor trouble, by inability to secure electricity, gas, water, or other fuel at the Building after reasonable effort to do so, by any accident or casualty whatsoever, by act or default of Tenant or other parties, or by any other cause beyond Landlord's reasonable control; and such failures or delays or diminution shall never be deemed to constitute an eviction or disturbance of the Tenant's use and possession of the Premises or relieve the Tenant from paying Rent or performing any of its obligations under this Lease.

C.   *Charges for Services.*   Charges for any service for which Tenant is required to pay from time to time hereunder including but not limited to hoisting services or after hours heating or air conditioning shall be due and payable at the same time as the installment of Rent with which they are billed, or if billed separately, shall be due and payable within ten (10) days after such billing. If Tenant shall fail to make payment for any such services, Landlord may, with notice to Tenant, discontinue any or all of such services and such discontinuance shall not be deemed to constitute an eviction or disturbance of the Tenant's use and possession of the Premises or relieve Tenant from paying Rent or performing any of its other obligations under this Lease.

8.   *Repairs.*   Tenant will, at Tenant's own expense, keep the Premises in good order, repair and condition at all times during the Term, and Tenant shall promptly and adequately repair all damage to the Premises and replace or repair all damaged or broken fixtures and appurtenances, under the supervision and subject to the approval of the Landlord, and within any reasonable period of time specified by the Landlord. If the Tenant does not do so,

Landlord may, but need not, make such repairs and replacements, and Tenant shall pay Landlord the cost thereof, including a percentage of the cost thereof (to be uniformly established for the Building) sufficient to reimburse Landlord for all overhead, general conditions, fees and other costs or expenses arising from Landlord's involvement with such repairs and replacements forthwith upon being billed for same. Landlord may, but shall not be required to, enter the Premises at all reasonable times to make such repairs, alterations, improvements and additions to the Premises or to the Building or to any equipment located in the Building as Landlord shall desire or deem necessary or as Landlord may be required to do by governmental or quasi-governmental authority or court order or decree.

9. *Additions and Alterations.*   Tenant shall not, without the prior written consent of Landlord, make any alterations, improvements or additions to the Premises. Landlord's refusal to give said consent shall be conclusive. If Landlord consents to said alterations, improvements or additions, it may impose such conditions with respect thereto as Landlord deems appropriate, including, without limitation, requiring Tenant to furnish Landlord with security for the payment of all costs to be incurred in connection with such work, a lien waiver from Tenant's general contractor, insurance against liabilities which may arise out of such work and plans, specifications and permits necessary for such work. The work necessary to make any alterations, improvements or additions to the Premises, whether prior to or subsequent to the Commencement Date, shall be done at Tenant's expense by employees of or contractors hired by Landlord except to the extent Landlord gives its prior written consent to Tenant's hiring contractors. Tenant shall promptly pay to Landlord or the Tenant's contractors, as the case may be, when due, the cost of all such work and of all repairs to the Building required by reason thereof. Tenant shall also pay to Landlord a percentage of the cost of such work (such percentage to be established on a uniform basis for the Building) sufficient to reimburse Landlord for all overhead, general conditions, fees and other costs and expenses arising from Landlord's involvement with such work. Upon completion of such work Tenant shall deliver to Landlord, if payment is made directly to contractors, evidence of payment, contractor's affidavits and full and final waivers of all liens for labor, services or materials. Tenant shall defend and hold Landlord harmless from all costs, damages, liens and expenses related to such work. All work done by Tenant or its contractors pursuant to Paragraphs 8 or 9 shall be done in a first-class workmanlike manner using only good grades of materials and shall comply with all insurance requirements and all applicable laws and ordinances and rules and regulations of governmental departments or agencies.

All alterations, improvements and additions to the Premises, whether temporary or permanent in character, made or paid for by Landlord or Tenant, shall without compensation to Tenant become Landlord's property at the termination of this Lease by lapse of time or otherwise and shall, unless

Landlord requests their removal (in which case Tenant shall remove the same as provided in Paragraph 17), be relinquished to Landlord in good condition, ordinary wear excepted.

10. Covenant Against Liens. Tenant has no authority or power to cause or permit any lien or encumbrance of any kind whatsoever, whether created by act of Tenant, operation of law or otherwise, to attach to or be placed upon Landlord's title or interest in the Land, Building or Premises, and any and all liens and encumbrances created by Tenant shall attach to Tenant's interest only. Tenant Convenants and agrees not to suffer or permit any lien of mechanics or material men or others to be placed against the Land, Building or the Premises with respect to work or services claimed to have been performed for or materials claimed to have been furnished to Tenant or the Premises, and, in case of any such lien attaching or notice of any lien, Tenant covenants and agrees to cause it to be immediately released and removed of record. In the event that such lien is not immediately released and removed, Landlord, at its sole option, may take all action necessary to release and remove such lien (without any duty to investigate the validity thereof) and Tenant shall promptly upon notice reimburse Landlord for all sums, costs and expenses (including reasonable attorney's fees) incurred by Landlord in connection with such lien.

11. Insurance.

A. *Waiver of Subrogation.* Landlord and Tenant each hereby waive any and every claim for recovery from the other for any and all loss of or damage to the Building or Premises or to the contents thereof, which loss or damage is covered by valid and collectible physical damage insurance policies, to the extent that such loss or damage is recoverable under said insurance policies. Inasmuch as this mutual waiver will preclude the assignment of any such claim by subrogation (or otherwise) to an insurance company (or any other person), Landlord and Tenant each agree to give to each insurance company which has issued, or in the future may issue, to its policies of physical damage insurance, written notice of the terms of this mutual waiver, and to have said insurance policies properly endorsed, if necessary, to prevent the invalidation of said insurance coverage by reason of said waiver.

B. *Coverage.* Tenant shall purchase and maintain insurance during the entire Term for the benefit of Tenant and Landlord (as their interests may appear) with terms, coverages and in companies satisfactory to Landlord, and with such increases in limits as Landlord may from time to time request, but initially Tenant shall maintain the following coverages in the following amounts:

(i) Comprehensive General Liability Insurance covering the Tenant and Landlord, Landlord's beneficiary and Landlord's Management Agent for claims of bodily injury, personal injury and property damage arising out of Tenant's operations, assumed liabilities or use of the Premises, for limits of liability not less than:

Bodily Injury Liability	$3,000,000 each occurrence
	$3,000,000 annual aggregate
Personal Injury Liability	$3,000,000 annual aggregate
	0% Insured's participation
Property Damage Liability	$1,000,000 each occurrence
	$1,000,000 annual aggregate

(ii)   Comprehensive Automobile Insurance covering all owned, non-owned and hired automobiles of Tenant including the loading and unloading of any automobile with limits of liability not less than:

Bodily Injury Liability	$3,000,000 each person
	$3,000,000 each accident
Property Damage Liability	$1,000,000 each accident

(iii)   Physical Damage Insurance covering all additions, improvements and alterations to the Premises which are beyond the building standard Tenant improvements provided by Landlord and all office furniture, trade fixtures, office equipment, merchandise and all other items of Tenant's property on the Premises. Such insurance shall be written on an "all risks" of physical loss or damage basis, for the full replacement cost value of the covered items and in amounts that meet any coinsurance clauses of the policies of insurance.

Tenant shall, prior to the commencement of the Term, furnish to Landlord certificates evidencing such coverage, which certificates shall state that such insurance coverage may not be changed or cancelled without at lease ten days' prior written notice to Landlord and Tenant and shall name Landlord as an additional insured. Any policies purchased by Tenant shall contain a clause pursuant to which the insurance carrier waives all rights of subrogation against the Landlord with respect to losses payable under such policies.

Landlord agrees to keep in force and effect a risk-financing program, which may be either insured or self-insured, on the Building against fire, vandalism, and malicious mischief, sprinkler leakage and such other risks as may be included in extended coverage insurance from time to time available in an amount not less than the greater of 100% of the full insurable replacement value of the Building or the amount sufficient to prevent Landlord from becoming a co-insurer under the terms of any applicable policies. Any policies purchased pursuant to said program shall contain a replacement cost endorsement and a clause pursuant to which the insurance carriers waive all rights of subrogation against the Tenant with respect to losses payable under such policies.

C.   *Avoid Action Increasing Rates.*   Tenant shall comply with all applicable laws and ordinances, all orders and decrees of court and all requirements of other governmental or quasi-governmental authorities, and shall not, directly or indirectly, make any use of the Premises which may thereby be prohibited or be dangerous to person or property or which may jeopardize any insurance coverage or may increase the cost of insurance or require additional insurance coverage. If by reason of the failure of Tenant to comply with the provisions of this Paragraph 11C, any insurance coverage is jeopardized or insurance premiums are increased, Landlord shall have the option either to terminate this Lease or to require Tenant to make immediate payment of the increased insurance premium.

12.   Fire or Casualty.   Paragraph 8 hereof notwithstanding, if the Premises or the Building (including machinery or equipment used in its operation) shall be damaged by fire or other casualty (except fires or other casualties resulting from Tenant's fault or neglect) and if such damage does not render all or a substantial portion (*for the purposes of this Paragraph 12, a substantial portion shall mean a portion which requires more than 90 days for repair and restoration*) of the Premises or Building untenantable, then Landlord shall repair and restore the same with reasonable promptness, subject to reasonable delays for insurance adjustments and delays caused by matters beyond Landlord's reasonable control. If any such damage renders all or a substantial portion of the Premises or Building untenantable, Landlord shall have the right to terminate this Lease as of the date of such damage (with appropriate prorations of Rent being made for Tenant's possession subsequent to the date of such damage of those tenantable portions of the Premises) upon giving written notice to the Tenant at any time within one hundred twenty days after the date of such damage. Landlord shall have no liability to Tenant, and Tenant shall not be entitled to terminate this Lease by virtue of any delays in completion of such repairs and restoration. Rent, however, shall abate on those portions of the Premises as are, from time to time, untenantable as a result of such damage. In the event the Building is damaged by fire or other casualty resulting from Tenant's failure or neglect, Landlord shall have no obligation to repair or restore the Building or any part thereof and Tenant shall not be released from any of its obligations hereunder including, without limitation, its duty to repair the Premises and its liability to Landlord for damages caused by such fire or other casualty. Tenant hereby acknowledges that Landlord is under no obligation to insure Landlord's interest in the Premises or the Building.

Notwithstanding anything to the contrary herein set forth, Landlord shall have no duty pursuant to this Paragraph 12 to repair or restore any portion of the alterations, additions or improvements in the Premises or the decorations thereto except to the extent that such alterations, additions, improvements and decorations were provided by Landlord, at Landlord's cost, at the beginning of the Term. If Tenant desires any other or additional repairs or restoration and if Landlord consents thereto, the same shall be done at Tenant's expense subject to all of the provisions of Paragraph 8 hereof. Tenant acknowledges that Landlord shall be entitled to the full proceeds of any insurance coverage, whether carried by Landlord or Tenant, for damage to alterations, additions, improvements or decorations provided by Landlord either directly or through an allowance to Tenant.

13.   Waiver of Claims – Indemnification.   To the extent not prohibited by law, Landlord and its partners, agents, servants and employees shall not be liable for any damage either to person or property or resulting from the loss of use thereof sustained by Tenant or by other persons claiming through Tenant due to the Building or any part thereof or any appurtenances thereof becoming out of repair, or due to the happening or any accident or event in or about the Building, or due to any act or neglect of any tenant or occupant of the Building, including the Premises, or of any other person. This provision shall apply particularly, but not exclusively, to damage caused by gas, electricity, snow, frost, steam, sewage, sewer gas or odors, fire, water or by the bursting or leaking of pipes, faucets, sprinklers, plumbing fixtures and windows, and shall apply without distinction as to the person whose act or neglect was responsible for the damage and whether the damage was due to any of the causes specifically enumerated above or to some other cause of an entirely different kind. Tenant further agrees that all personal property upon the Premises, or upon loading docks, receiving and holding areas, or freight elevators of the Building, shall be at the risk of Tenant only, and that Landlord shall not be liable for any loss or damage thereto or theft thereof. Without limitation of any other provisions thereof, Tenant agrees to defend, protect, indemnify and save harmless Landlord from and against all liability to third parties arising out of the acts of Tenants and its servants, agents, employees, contractors, suppliers, workers and invitees.

14.   Nonwaiver.   No waiver of any provision of this Lease shall be implied by any failure of Landlord to enforce any remedy on account of the violation of such provision, even if such violation be continued or repeated subsequently, and no express waiver shall affect any provision other than the one specified in such waiver and that one only for the time and in the manner specifically stated. No receipt of moneys by Landlord from Tenant after the termination of this Lease shall in any way alter the length of the Term or of Tenant's right of possession hereunder or after the giving of any notice shall reinstate, continue or extend the Term or affect any notice given Tenant prior to the receipt of such moneys, it being agreed that after the service of notice or the commencement of a suit or after final judgement for possession of the Premises, Landlord may receive and collect any Rent due, and the payment of said Rent shall not waive or affect said notice, suit or judgement.

15.   Condemnation.   If the Land or the Building or any portion thereof shall be taken or condemned by any competent authority for any public or quasi-public use or purpose (a "taking"), or if the configuration of any street adjacent to the Building is changed by any competent authority and such taking or change in configuration makes it necessary or desirable to remodel or reconstruct the Building, Landlord shall have the right, exercisable at its sole discretion, to cancel this Lease upon not less than ninety (90) days' notice prior to the date of cancellation designated in the notice. No money or other consideration shall be payable by Landlord to Tenant for the right of cancellation and Tenant shall have no right to share in the condemnation award or in any judgement for damages caused by such taking or change in configuration; provided, however, this provision shall not prelude Tenant from claiming special *damages such as* moving expenses so long as such claim does not serve to reduce Landlord's award.

16.   Assignment and Subletting.   Tenant shall not, without the prior written consent of Landlord, (i) assign, convey or mortgage this Lease or any interest hereunder; (ii) suffer to occur or permit to exist any assignment of this Lease, or any lien upon Tenant's interest, involuntarily or by operation of law; (iii) sublet the Premises or any part thereof, or (iv) permit the use of the Premises by any parties other than Tenant and its employees. Any such action on the part of Tenant shall be void and of no effect. Landlord's consent to any assignment, subletting or transfer or Landlord's election to accept any assignee, subtenant or transferee as the tenant hereunder and to collect rent from such assignee, subtenant or transferee shall not release Tenant or any subsequent tenant from any convenant or obligation under this Lease. Landlord's consent to any assignment, subletting or transfer shall not constitute a waiver of Landlord's right to withhold its consent to any future assignment, subletting, or transfer.

At least ninety (90) days prior to any proposed subletting or assignment, Tenant shall submit to Landlord a statement seeking Landlord's consent and containing the name and address of the proposed subtenant or assignee, the terms of the proposed sublease or assignment and such financial and other information with respect to the proposed subtenant as Landlord reasonably may request. Landlord shall indicate its consent or non-consent within sixty (60) days of its receipt of said statement.

In addition to withholding its consent, Landlord shall have the additional right to terminate this Lease as to that portion of the Premises which Tenant seeks to assign or sublet, whether by requesting Landlord's consent thereto or otherwise. Landlord may exercise such right to terminate by giving written notice to Tenant at any time prior to Landlord's written consent to such assignment or sublease. In the event that Landlord exercises such right to terminate, Landlord shall be entitled to recover possession of such portion of the Premises on the later of (i) the proposed date for possession by such assignee or subtenant, or (ii) ninety (90) days after the date of Landlord's notice of termination to Tenant *and Landlord shall have the further right to re-configure the remaining portion of the Premises for the purpose of maintaining access thereto.*

In the event that Landlord fails to exercise its termination right and its right to withhold its consent as set forth in the preceding Paragraph 16, and in the event that Landlord consents to any assignment or sublease of any portion of the Premises, as a condition of Landlord's consent, if Landlord so elects to consent, Tenant shall pay to Landlord ninety percent (90%) of all profit derived by Tenant from such assignment or sublease. Tenant shall furnish Landlord with a sworn statement, certified by an independent certified public accountant, setting forth in detail the computation of profit (which computation shall be based upon generally accepted accounting principles), and Landlord, or its representatives, shall have access to the books, records and papers of Tenant in relation thereto, and to make copies thereof. Any rent in excess of that paid by Tenant hereunder realized by reason of such assignment or sublease shall be deemed an item of such profit. If a part of the consideration for such assignment shall be payable other than in cash, the payment to Landlord shall be payable in accordance with the foregoing percentage of the cash and other non-cash considerations in such form as is satisfactory to Landlord. Such percentage of Tenant's profits shall be paid to Landlord promptly by Tenant upon Tenant's receipt from time to time of periodic payments from such assignee or subtenant or at such other time as Tenant shall realize its profits from such assignment or sublease.

17.   Surrender of Possession.   Upon the expiration of the Term or upon the termination of Tenant's right of possession, whether by lapse of time or otherwise, Tenant shall forthwith surrender the Premises to Landlord in good order, repair and condition, ordinary wear excepted, and shall, if Landlord so requires, restore the Premises to the condition existing at the beginning of the Term. Any interest of Tenant in the alterations, improvements and additions to the Premises made or paid for by Landlord or Tenant shall, without compensation to Tenant, become Landlord's property at the termination of this Lease by lapse of time or otherwise and such alterations, improvements and additions shall be relinquished to Landlord in good condition, ordinary wear excepted. Upon the termination of the Term or of Tenant's right of possession, Tenant shall remove office furniture, trade fixtures, office equipment and all other items of Tenant's property on the Premises. Tenant shall pay to Landlord upon demand the cost of repairing any damage to the Premises and to the Building caused by any such removal. If Tenant shall fail or refuse to remove any such property from the Premises, Tenant shall be conclusively presumed to have abandoned the same, and title thereto shall thereupon pass to Landlord without any cost either by setoff, credit, allowance or otherwise, the Landlord may at its option accept the title to such property or at Tenant's expense may (i) remove the same or any part thereof in any manner that Landlord shall choose, (ii) repair any damage to the Premises caused by such removal, and (iii) store, destroy or otherwise dispose of the same without incurring liability to Tenant or any other person.

18.   Holding Over.   Tenant shall pay to Landlord an amount as Rent equal to 200% of one-twelfth the Base Rent and 200% of one-twelfth the Additional Rent paid by Tenant during the previous Calendar Year herein provided during each month or portion thereof for which Tenant shall retain possession of the Premises or any part thereof after the termination of the Term or of Tenant's right of possession, whether by lapse of time or otherwise, and also shall pay all damages sustained by Landlord, whether direct or consequential, on account thereof. At the option of Landlord, expressed in a written notice to Tenant and not otherwise, such holding over shall constitute a renewal of this Lease for a period of one year at such Base Rent and Additional Rent as would be applicable for such year, and for purposes of determining the Additional Rent for any renewal period the original Base Year shall remain as the Base Year. The provisions of this Paragraph 18 shall not be deemed to limit or constitute a waiver of any other rights or remedies of Landlord provided herein or at law.

19.   *Estoppel Certificate.*   Tenant agrees, that, from time to time upon not less than ten days' prior request by Landlord, the Tenant, or Tenant's duly authorized representative having knowledge of the following facts, will deliver to Landlord a *certificate* in writing certifying (i) that this Lease is unmodified and in full force and effect (or if there have been modifications, that the Lease as modified is in full force and effect); (ii) the dates to which Rent and other charges have been paid; (iii) that the Landlord is not in default under any provision of this Lease, or, if in default, the nature thereof in detail and (iv) such further matters as are set forth on the form of estoppel certificate attached hereto as Exhibit C and made a part hereof, it being intended that any such statement may be relied upon by any prospective assignee of any tenant of the Building, any mortgages or prospective mortgagees thereof, or any prospective assignee of any mortgage thereof or any purchaser of the Building or an interest therein. Tenant shall execute and deliver whatever other instruments may be reasonably required for such purposes, and in the event Tenant fails so to do within ten (10) days after demand in writing, Tenant shall be considered in default under this Lease.

20.   *Subordination.*   This Lease is subject and subordinate to all present and future ground or underlying leases of the Land and to the lien of any mortgages or trust deeds, now or hereafter in force against the Land and Building, or either, and to all renewals, extensions, modifications, consolidations and replacements thereof, and to all advances made or hereafter to be made upon the security of such mortgages or trust deeds, unless the holders of such mortgages or trust deeds, or the lessors under such ground lease or underlying leases require in writing that this Lease shall be superior thereto. Tenant covenants and agrees in the event any proceedings are brought for the foreclosure of any such mortgage, to attorn, without any deductions or setoffs whatsoever, to the purchaser upon any such foreclosure sale if so requested to do so by such purchaser, and to recognize such purchaser as the lessor under this Lease. Tenant shall at Landlord's request execute such further instruments or assurances as Landlord may reasonably deem necessary to evidence or confirm the subordination or superiority of this Lease to any such mortgages, trust deeds, ground leases or underlying leases. Tenant hereby irrevocably

authorizes Landlord to execute and deliver in the name of Tenant any such instrument or instruments if Tenant fails to do so, provided that such shall in no way relieve Tenant from the obligation of executing such instruments of subordination or superiority.

21. Certain Rights Reserved by Landlord. Landlord shall have the following rights, each of which Landlord may exercise without notice to Tenant and without liability to Tenant for damage or injury to property, person or business on account of the exercise thereof, and the exercise of any such rights shall not be deemed to constitute an eviction or disturbance of Tenant's use or possession of the Premises and shall not give rise to any claim for setoff or abatement of rent and any other claim:

   (i)   To change the Building's name or street address.

   (ii)   To install, affix and maintain any and all signs on the exterior and on the interior of the Building.

   (iii)   To decorate or to make repairs, alterations, additions, or improvements, whether structural or otherwise (including alterations in the configuration of the Common Area), in and about the Building, or any part thereof, and for such purposes to enter upon the Premises, and during the continuance of any of said work, to temporarily close doors, entryways, public space and corridors in the Building and to interrupt or temporarily suspend services or use of facilities, all without affecting any of Tenant's obligations hereunder, so long as the Premises are reasonably accessible and usable.

   (iv)   To furnish door keys for the entry door(s) in the Premises at the commencement of the Lease and to retain at all times, and to use in appropriate instances, keys to all doors within and into the Premises. Tenant agrees to purchase only from Landlord or Landlord's designee additional duplicate keys as required, to change no locks, and to affix no locks on doors without the prior written consent of the Landlord. Notwithstanding the provisions for Landlord's access to Premises, Tenant relieves and releases the Landlord of all responsibility arising out of theft, robbery and pilferage. Upon the expiration of the Term or of Lessee's right to possession, Tenant shall return all keys to Landlord and shall disclose to Landlord the combination of any safes, cabinets or vaults left in the Premises.

   (v)   To designate and approve all window coverings used in the Building.

   (vi)   To approve the weight, size and location of safes, vaults and other heavy equipment and articles in and about the Premises and the Building so as not to exceed the live load per square foot designated by the structural engineers for the Building, and to require all such items and furniture and similar items to be moved into or out of the Building and Premises only as such times and in such manner as Landlord shall direct in writing. Tenant shall not install or operate machinery or any mechanical devices of a nature not directly related to Tenant's ordinary use of the Premises without the prior written consent of Landlord. Tenant's movements of property into or out of the Building or Premises and within the Building are entirely at the risk and responsibility of Tenant, and Landlord reserves the right to require permits before allowing any property to be moved into or out of the Building or Premises.

(vii)   To establish controls for the purpose of regulating all property and packages, both personal and otherwise, to be moved into or out of the Building and Premises and all persons using the Building after normal office hours.

(viii)   To regulate delivery and service of supplies in order to insure the cleanliness and security of the Premises and to avoid congestion of the loading docks, receiving areas and freight elevators.

(ix)   To show the Premises to prospective tenants at reasonable hours during the last twelve months of the Term and, if vacated or abandoned, to show the Premises at any time and to prepare the Premises for re-occupancy.

(x)   To erect, use and maintain pipes, ducts, wiring and conduits, and appurtenances thereto, in and through the Premises at reasonable locations.

(xi)   To enter the Premises at any reasonable time to inspect the Premises.

(xii)   To grant to any person or to reserve unto itself the exclusive right to conduct any business or render any service in the Building. If Landlord elects to make available to tenants in the Building any services or supplies, or arranges a master contract therefore, Tenant agrees to obtain its requirements, if any, therefore from Landlord or under any such contact, provided that the charges therefore are reasonable.

22.   *Rules and Regulations.*   Tenant agrees to observe the rules and regulations for the Building attached hereto as Exhibit D and made a part hereof. Landlord shall have the right from time to time to prescribe additional rules and regulations which, in its judgement, may be desirable for the use, entry, operation and management of the Premises and Building, each of which rules and regulations and any amendments thereto shall become a part of this Lease without further action of the parties. Tenant shall comply with all such rules and regulations; provided, however, that such rules and regulations shall not substantially diminish any right or privilege herein expressly granted to Tenant.

23.   *Landlord's Remedies.*   If default shall be made in the payment of the Rent or any installment thereof or in the payment of any other sum required to be paid by Tenant under this Lease or under the terms of any other agreement between Landlord and Tenant and such default shall continue for five (5) days after written notice to Tenant, or if default shall be made in the observance or performance of any of the other covenants or conditions in this Lease which

Tenant is required to observe and perform and such default shall continue for ten (10) days after written notice to Tenant, or if a default involves a hazardous condition and is not cured by Tenant immediately upon written notice to Tenant, or if the interest of Tenant in this Lease shall be levied on under execution or other legal process, or if any voluntary petition in bankruptcy or for corporate reorganization or any similar relief shall be filed by Tenant, or if any involuntary petition in bankruptcy shall be filed against Tenant, under any federal or state bankruptcy or insolvency act and shall not have been dismissed within thirty days from the filing thereof, or if a receiver shall be appointed for Tenant or any of the property of Tenant by any court and such receiver shall not have been dismissed within thirty days from the date of his appointment, or if Tenant shall make an assignment for the benefit of creditors, or if Tenant shall admit in writing Tenant's inability to meet Tenant's debts as they mature, or if Tenant shall cease to occupy the Premises for a period of seven days during the Term, then Landlord may treat the occurrence of any one or more of the foregoing events as a breach of this Lease, and thereupon at its option may, without notice or demand of any kind to Tenant or any other person, have any one or more of the following described remedies in addition to all other rights and remedies provided at law or in equity or elsewhere herein:

(i)   Landlord may terminate this Lease and the Term created hereby, in which event Landlord may forthwith repossess the Premises and be entitled to recover forthwith, in addition to any other sums or damages for which Tenant may be liable to Landlord, as liquidated damages a sum of money equal to the excess of the value of the Rent provided to be paid by Tenant for the balance of the Term over the fair market rental value of the Premises, after deduction of all anticipated expenses of reletting, for said period. Should the fair market rental value of the Premises, after deduction of all anticipated expenses of reletting, for the balance of the Term exceed the value of the Rent provided to be paid by Tenant for the balance of the Term, Landlord shall have no obligation to pay to Tenant the excess or any part thereof or to credit such excess or any part thereof against any other sums or damages for which Tenant may be liable to Landlord.

(ii)   Landlord may terminate Tenant's right of possession and may repossess the Premises by a forcible entry and detainer suit or by taking peaceful possession or otherwise, without terminating this Lease, in which event Landlord may, but shall be under no obligation to, relet the same or a portion thereof for the account of Tenant, for such rent and upon such terms as shall be satisfactory to Landlord. For the purpose of such reletting, Landlord is authorized to decorate, repair, remodel or alter the Premises or a portion thereof. If Landlord shall fail to relet the Premises, Tenant shall pay to Landlord a sum equal to the amount of the Rent reserved in this Lease for the balance of the Term. If the Premises are relet and a sufficient sum shall not be realized from such reletting after paying all of the costs and expenses of all decoration, repairs, remodeling, alterations and additions and the expenses of such reletting and of the collection of the rent accruing therefrom to satisfy the Rent provided for in this Lease, Tenant shall satisfy and pay the same upon demand therefor from time to time. Tenant shall not be entitled to any rents received by Landlord in excess of the Rent provided for in this Lease. Tenant agrees that Landlord may file suit to recover any sums falling due under the terms of this Paragraph 23 from time to time and that no suit or recovery of any portion due Landlord hereunder shall be any defense to any subsequent action brought for any amount not theretofore reduce to judgment in favor of Landlord.

(iii)   Landlord, without thereby waiving such default, may perform the same for the account and at the expense of Tenant, without notice in a case of emergency or in case of correction of a dangerous or hazardous condition, and in any other case if such default continues after 10 days from the date of the giving by Landlord to Tenant of written notice of intention so to do. Bills for any expense incurred by Landlord in connection with any such performance by Landlord for the account of Tenant, and shall be due and payable in accordance with the terms of said bills, and if not paid when due, the amounts thereof shall immediately become due and payable as Additional Rent under this Lease.

(iv)   Tenant further waives the right to any notices to quit as may be specified in the Landlord and Tenant Act of Pennsylvania, Act of April 6, 1951, as amended,and agrees that five (5) days' notice shall be sufficient in any case where a longer period may be statutorily specified.

(v)   Upon termination of Tenant's right of possession of the Premises it shall be lawful for any attorney as attorney for Tenant to file an agreement for entering in any competent Court an amicable action and judgment in ejectment against Tenant and all persons claiming under Tenant for the recovery by Landlord of possession of the Premises, for which this Lease shall be his sufficient warrant, whereupon, if Landlord so desires, a writ of Execution or of Possession may issue forthwith, without any prior writ or proceedings whatsoever, and provided that if for any reason after such action shall have been commenced the same shall be determined and the possession of the Premises remain in or be restored to Tenant, Landlord shall have the right upon any subsequent default or defaults, or upon the termination of this Lease as hereinbefore set forth, to bring one or more amicable action or actions as hereinbefore set forth to recover possession of the Premises.

(vi)   Tenant hereby empowers any Prothonotary, Clerk of Court or attorney of any Court of Record to appear for Tenant in any and all actions which may be brought for Rent and/or the charges, payments, costs and expenses agreed to be paid by the Tenant hereunder and/or to sign for Tenant an agreement for entering in any competent Court an amicable action or actions for the recovery of Rent or other charges, payments, costs and expenses, and in said suits or in said amicable action or actions to confess judgment against Tenant for all or any part of the Rent specified in this Lease and then unpaid including, at Landlord's option, the Rent for the entire unexpired balance of the Term of this Lease, and/or other charges, payments, costs and expenses agreed to be paid by the Tenant, and for interest and costs together with an attorney's commission of 5%. Such authority shall not be exhausted by one exercise thereof, but judgment may be confessed as aforesaid from time to time as often as any of said Rent and/or other charges, payments costs and expenses shall fall due or be in arrears, and such powers may be exercised as well after the expiration of the original Term and/or during any extension or renewal of this Lease.

(vii)   In any amicable action of ejectment and/or for Rent in arrears, Landlord shall first cause to be filed in such action an affidavit made by Landlord's authorized representative setting forth the facts necessary to authorize the entry of judgment, of which facts such affidavit shall be conclusive evidence, and if a true copy of this Lease (and of the truth of the copy such affidavit shall be sufficient evidence) be filed in such action, it shall not be necessary to file the original as a warrant of attorney, any rule of Court, custom or practice to the contrary notwithstanding.

(viii)   In the event of any default as above set forth, the Landlord or anyone acting on Landlord's behalf, at Landlord's option:

(a)   may without notice or demand enter the Premises, breaking open locked doors if necessary to effect entrance, without liability to action for prosecution or damages for such entry or for the manner thereof, for the purpose of distraining or levying and for any other purposes, and take possession of and sell all goods and chattels at auction, on three days' notice served in person on the Tenant or left on the Premises and pay the said Landlord out of proceeds, and even if the rent be not due and unpaid, should the Tenant at any time remove or attempt to remove goods and chattels from the Premises without leaving enough thereon to meet the next periodical payment, Tenant authorizes the Landlord to follow for a period of ninety days after such removal, take possession of and sell at auction upon like notice, sufficient of such goods to meet the proportion of Rent accrued at the time of such removal; and the Tenant hereby releases and discharges the Landlord, and its agents from all claims, action, suits, damages, and penalties, for or by reason or on account of any entry distraint, levy, appraisement or sale; and/or

(b)   may enter the Premises and without demand proceed by distress and sale of the goods there found to levy the Rent and/or other charges herein payable as Rent, and all costs and officers' commissions, including watchmen's wages and sums chargeable to Landlord, and further including a sum equal to 5% of the amount of the levy as commissions to the constable or other person making the levy shall be paid by the Tenant, and in such case all costs, officers' commission and other charges shall immediately attach and become part of the claim of Landlord for Rent, and any tender of Rent without said costs, commission and charges made after the issue of a warrant of distress shall not be sufficient to satisfy the claim of the Landlord. Tenant hereby expressly waives in favor of Landlord the benefit of all laws now made or which may hereafter be made regarding any limitation as to the goods upon which, or the time within which, distress is to be made after removal of goods, and further relieves the Landlord of the obligations of providing or identifying such goods, it being the purpose and intent of this provision that all goods of Tenant, whether upon the Premises or not, shall be liable to distress for Rent. Tenant waives in favor of Landlord all rights under the Act of Assembly of April 6, 1951, P.L. 69, and all supplements and amendments thereto that have been or may hereafter be passed and authorizes the sale of any goods distrained for Rent at any time after five days from said distraint without any appraisement and/or condemnation thereof.

(c)   The Tenant further waives the right to issue a Writ of Replevin under any law previously enacted and now in force or which may hereafter be enacted for the recovery of any articles, household goods, furniture, etc., seized under a distress for rent or levy upon an execution for rent damages or otherwise; all waivers hereinbefore mentioned are hereby extended to apply to any such act.

24.   Expenses of Enforcement.   The Tenant shall pay upon demand all Landlord's costs, charges and expenses including the fees and out-of-pocket expenses of counsel, agents and others retained by Landlord incurred in enforcing the Tenant's obligations hereunder or incurred by the Landlord in any litigation, negotiation or transaction in which the Tenant causes the Landlord without the Landlord's fault to become involved or concerned.

25.   Covenant of Quiet Enjoyment.   The Landlord covenants that the Tenant, on paying the Rent, charges for services and other payments herein reserved and on keeping, observing and performing all the other terms, covenants, conditions, provisions and agreements herein contained on the part of the Tenant to be kept, observed and performed, shall, during the Term, peaceably and quietly have, hold and enjoy the Premises subject to the terms, covenants, conditions, provisions and agreements hereof.

26.   Security Deposit.   Tenant hereby deposits with Landlord the sum of _____
_____ DOLLARS ($ _____), (hereinafter referred to as "Collateral"), as security for the prompt, full and faithful performance by Tenant of each and every provision of this Lease and of all obligations of Tenant hereunder. No interest shall be paid to Tenant on the Collateral.

If Tenant fails to perform any of its obligations hereunder, Landlord may use, apply or retain the whole or any part of the Collateral for the payment of

(i) any Rent or other sums of money which Tenant may not have paid when due, (ii) any sum expended by Landlord on Tenant's behalf in accordance with the provisions of this Lease, and/or (iii) any sum which Landlord may expend or be required to expend by reason of Tenant's default, including, without limitation, any damage or deficiency in or from the reletting of the Premises as provided in Paragraph 23. The use, application or retention of the Collateral, or any portion thereof, by Landlord shall not prevent Landlord from exercising any other right or remedy provided by this Lease or by law (it being intended that Landlord shall not first be required to proceed against the Collateral) and shall not operate as a limitation on any recovery to which Landlord may otherwise be entitled. If any portion of the Collateral is used, applied or retained by Landlord for the purposes set forth above, Tenant agrees, within ten days after the written demand therefore is made by Landlord, to deposit cash with the Landlord in an amount sufficient to restore the Collateral to its original amount.

If Tenant shall fully and faithfully comply with all of the provisions of this Lease, the Collateral, or any balance thereof, shall be returned to Tenant without interest after the expiration of the Term or upon any later date after which Tenant has vacated the Premises. In the absence of evidence satisfactory to Landlord of any permitted assignment of the right to receive the Collateral, or of the remaining balance thereof, Landlord may return the same to the original Tenant, regardless of one or more assignments of Tenant's interest in this Lease or the Collateral. In such event, upon the return of the Collateral, or the remaining balance thereof to the original Tenant, Landlord shall be completely relieved of liability under this Paragraph 26 or otherwise with respect to the Collateral.

Tenant acknowledges that Landlord has the right to transfer or mortgage its interest in the Land and the Building and in this Lease and Tenant agrees that in the event of any such transfer or mortgage, Landlord shall have the right to transfer or assign the Collateral to the transferee or mortgagee. Upon, and only upon, written acknowledgement of transferee's or mortgagee's receipt of such Collateral, Landlord shall thereby be released by Tenant from all liability or obligation for the return of such Collateral and Tenant shall look solely to such transferee or mortgagee for the return of the Collateral.

The Collateral shall not be mortgaged, assigned or encumbered in any manner whatsoever by Tenant without the prior written consent of Landlord.

27.   Real Estate Broker.   The Tenant represents that the Tenant has dealt with (and only with) _____

_____

as broker in connection with this Lease, and that insofar as the Tenant knows, no other broker negotiated this Lease or is entitled to any commission in connection therewith. Tenant agrees to indemnify, defend and hold Landlord and its beneficaries, employees, agents, their officers and partners, harmless from and against any claims made by any broker or finder other than the broker named above for a commission or fee in connection with this Lease, provided that Landlord has not in fact retained such broker or finder.

28.   Miscellaneous.

A.   *Rights Cumulative.*   All rights and remedies of Landlord under this Lease shall be cumulative and none shall exclude any other rights and remedies allowed by law.

B.   *Interest.*   All payments becoming due under this Lease and remaining unpaid when due shall bear interest until paid at the rate of the greater of (i) ten percent per annum or (ii) two percent per annum above the prime rate of interest changed from time to time by the *Philadelphia National Bank* (but in no event at a rate which is more than the highest rate which is at the time lawful in the Commonwealth of Pennsylvania).

C.   *Terms.*   The necessary grammatical changes required to make the provisions hereof apply either to corporations or partnerships or individuals, men or women, as the case may require, shall in all cases be assumed as though in each case fully expressed.

D.   *Binding Effect.*   Each of the provisions of this Lease shall extend to and shall, as the case may require, bind or inure to the benefit not only of the Landlord and of Tenant, but also of their respective successors or assigns, provided this clause shall not permit any assignment by Tenant contrary to the provisions of Paragraph 16 hereof.

E.   *Lease Contains All Terms.*   All of the representations and obligations of Landlord are contained herein and in the Work Letter, and no modification, waiver or amendment of this Lease or of any of its conditions or provisions shall be binding upon the Landlord unless in writing signed by Landlord or by a duly authorized agent of Landlord empowered by a written authority signed by Landlord.

F.   *Delivery for Examination.*   Submission of the form of the Lease for examination shall not bind Landlord in any manner, and no Lease or obligations of the Landlord shall arise until this instrument is signed by both Landlord and Tenant and delivery is made to each.

G.   *No Air Rights.*   No rights to any view or to light or air over any property, whether belonging to Landlord or any other person, are granted to Tenant by this Lease.

H.   *Modification of Lease.*   If any lender requires, as a condition to its lending funds the repayment of which is to be secured by a mortgage or trust deed on the Land and Building or either, that certain modifications be made to this Lease, which modifications will not require Tenant to pay any additional amounts or otherwise change materially the rights or obligations of Tenant hereunder, Tenant shall, upon Landlord's request, execute appropriate instruments effecting such modifications.

I.   *Substitution of Other Premises.*   At any time hereafter, Landlord may (upon thirty (30) days' prior notice) substitute for the Premises other premises in the Building (herein referred to as the "New Premises") provided that the New Premises shall be usable for Tenant's purpose; and if Tenant is already in occupancy of the Premises, then in addition Landlord shall pay the expenses of Tenant's moving from the Premises to the New Premises and for improving the New Premises so that they are substantially similar to the Premises. Such move shall be made during evenings, weekends or otherwise so as to incur the least inconvenience to Tenant.

J.   *Transfer of Landlord's Interest.*   Tenant acknowledges that Landlord has the right to transfer its interest in the Land and Building and in this Lease, and Tenant agrees that in the event of any such transfer Landlord shall automatically be released from all liability under this Lease and Tenant agrees to look solely to such transferee for the performance of Landlord's obligations hereunder after the data of transfer. Tenant further acknowledges that Landlord may assign its interest in this Lease to a mortgage lender as additional security and agrees that such an assignment shall not release Landlord from its obligations hereunder and that Tenant shall continue to look to Landlord for the performance of its obligations hereunder.

K.   *Landlord's Title.*   Landlord's title is and always shall be paramount to the title of Tenant. Nothing herein contained shall empower Tenant to do any act which can, shall or may encumber the title of Landlord.

L.   *Prohibition Against Recording.*   Neither this Lease, nor any memorandum, affidavit or other writing with respect thereto, shall be recorded by Tenant or by anyone acting through, under or on behalf of Tenant, and the recording thereof in violation of this provision shall make this Lease null and void at Landlord's election.

M.   *Captions.*   The captions of Paragraphs and subparagraphs are for convenience only and shall not be deemed to limit, construe, affect or alter the meaning of such Paragraphs or subparagraphs.

N.   *Convenants and Conditions.*   All of the covenants of Tenant hereunder shall be deemed and construed to be "conditions", if Landlord so elects, as well as "covenants" as though the words specifically expressing or importing covenants and conditions were used in each separate instance.

O.   *Relationship of Parties.*   Nothing contained in this Lease shall be deemed or construed by the parties hereto or by any third party to create the relationship of principal and agent, partnership, joint venturer or any association between Landlord and Tenant, it being expressly understood and agreed that neither the method of computation of Rent nor any act of the parties hereto shall be deemed to create any relationship between Landlord and Tenant other than the relationship of landlord and tenant.

P.   *Application of Payments.*   Landlord shall have the right to apply payments received from Tenant pursuant to this Lease (regardless of Tenant's designation of such payments) to satisfy any obligations of Tenant hereunder, in such order and amounts, as Landlord, in its sole discretion, may elect.

Q. *Time of Essence.*   Time is of the essence of this Lease and each of its provisions.

R. *Governing Law.*   Interpretation of this Lease shall be governed by the law of the state in which the Premises is located.

S. *Partial Invalidity.*   If any term, provision or condition contained in this Lease shall, to any extent, be invalid or unenforceable, the remainder of this Lease (or the application of such term, provision or condition to persons or circumstances other than those in respect of which it is invalid or un-enforceable) shall not be affected thereby, and each and every other term, provision and condition of this Lease shall be valid and enforceable to the fullest extent possible permitted by law.

29.   Notices.   All notices to be given under this Lease shall be in writing and deposited in the United States mail, certified or registered mail, with return receipt requested, postage prepaid, addressed as follows:

If to Landlord:

or to such other person or such other address designated by notice sent by Landlord to Tenant.

If to Tenant:

And after occupancy of the Premises by Tenant, at the Premises, or to such other address as is designated by Tenant in a notice to Landlord.

Notice by mail shall be deemed to have been given when deposited in the United States mail as aforesaid.

In witness whereof, Landlord and Tenant have caused this Lease to be executed the day and date first above written.

TENANT: LANDLORD:

By:

By _____   By _____
Its _____   Its _____

TENANT-ORIENTED OFFICE BUILDING LEASE

Lease

AGREEMENT OF LEASE made as of this day of _____, 19__ (the "Lease") between a _____ ("Landlord") and _____ ("Tenant");

WITNESSETH

Landlord hereby leases to Tenant, and Tenant hereby accepts from Landlord, the premises designated on the plan attached hereto as Exhibit B containing approximately 200,000 square feet of Rentable Area (as defined in Exhibit D hereto [the "Rentable Area"]), and commonly described as Floors through both inclusive (the "Initial Premises"), and that space in the basement (the "Storage Space") containing approximately square feet designated on the plan attached hereto as a part of Exhibit B hereto, both in the building to be constructed hereafter and to be known as or such other designation as Landlord may from time to time select (hereinafter referred to as the "Building"), located on land in the legal description of which is set forth on Exhibit A hereto (the "Land"), subject to the covenants, terms, provisions and conditions of this Lease. Landlord shall have the right prior to the Commencement Date (hereinafter defined) to change the configuration of, and Rentable Area for, the Initial Premises and/or Storage Space, provided that Landlord shall use reasonable efforts not to increase or decrease the Rentable Area of the Initial Premises or the Storage Space by more than two (2%) percent. If Landlord so changes such configuration and/or Rentable Area, Landlord shall notify Tenant promptly of such change.

In consideration thereof, Landlord and Tenant covenant and agree as follows:

1. Term.

A. *Initial Term.* The initial term of this Lease (the "Initial Term") shall commence on the Commencement Date and shall end on the last day of the fifteenth (15th) Lease Year (hereinafter defined) following the Commencement Date unless extended or sooner terminated as provided herein. As used herein the term "Commencement Date" shall mean the date which is the first to occur of (i) the date on which Tenant first occupies the Initial Premises, or any portion thereof, other than for the sole purpose of installing Tenant finish work or equipment and (ii) the date which is thirty (30) days after the Substantial Completion Date, as defined in the work letter which constitutes Exhibit C to this Lease ("Work Letter"). As soon as the Commencement Date has been determined, a confirmation thereof will be signed by Landlord and Tenant setting forth the actual Commencement Date, the date on which the first Lease Year commences and the Expiration Date of the Initial Term of this Lease and certifying that Tenant is in occupancy on a full rent-paying basis and that this Lease is in full force and effect.

B. *Renewal Terms.* Subject to the rights of Landlord hereinafter set forth, Tenant shall have the option to extend the Initial Term for seven (7) consecutive periods of five (5) years each (each such period being herein called a "Renewal Term"). Subject to the proviso at the end of this sentence and to the rights of Landlord to cancel such exercise as hereinafter set forth, each such option shall, automatically and conclusively, be deemed exercised by Tenant without any notice to Landlord whatsoever, provided that, except under the circumstances set forth in the last sentence of this Paragraph B, Tenant shall have the right to elect not to exercise any such option with respect to a Renewal Term by so notifying Landlord, in writing, on or before the date (the "Renewal Option Date") which is two (2) years prior to the date on which such Renewal Term is to commence. In the event that an option to extend shall be deemed exercised by Tenant as hereinabove provided and if on or before thirty (30) days after the Renewal Option Date with respect to such option (i) an Event of Default (hereinafter defined) has occurred and is continuing hereunder, or (ii) Tenant is not occupying pursuant to the terms of this Lease at least one hundred thousand (100,000) square feet of Rentable Area in the Building, Landlord shall have the right, without limitation of any other of Landlord's rights or remedies hereunder or at law or in equity, to cancel the exercise by Tenant of such option to extend. Such right shall be exercised, if Landlord so elects, in a written notice to Tenant given on or before the expiration of the aforesaid thirty (30) day period. In such event, the Term hereof shall not be so extended by the applicable Renewal Term. In the event that Tenant shall elect not to exercise, or Landlord shall cancel the exercise by Tenant of, any one of the aforesaid options, Tenant shall have no further right to extend the Term hereof. In addition to the foregoing, Tenant shall automatically and conclusively be deemed to have exercised its option to extend for the next Renewal Term upon the exercise by Tenant of its right to lease Additional Space (as hereinafter in Paragraph 3 defined) if such Renewal Term is required so that the remaining Term (hereinafter defined) of this Lease, commencing with the Addition Date (hereinafter defined) for such Additional Space (without regard to any acceleration or deferral by Landlord as provided in Paragraph 2(i) below) will be not less than five (5) years.

C. *Certain Definitions.* As used herein, the following terms shall have the following meanings:

(i) "Term" shall mean and include the Initial Term and each Renewal Term with respect to which Tenant has exercised (and Landlord has not cancelled) its option as hereinabove provided.

(ii) "Termination Date" shall mean the date on which the Term ends.

(iii) "Premises" shall, as of any time, mean and include the Initial Premises, the Storage Space and all Additional Space with respect to which Tenant has exercised (and Landlord has not cancelled) its option in accordance with Paragraph 2 below.

(iv) "Lease Year" shall mean each period of twelve (12) consecutive calendar months included within the Term hereof. The first Lease Year shall commence on the first day of the first calendar month next succeeding the Commencement Date and each subsequent Lease Year shall commence on the anniversary thereof, provided, however, that the first Lease Year shall also include the calendar month, or part thereof, in which the Commencement Date occurs.

2. *Additional Space.* Subject to the rights of Landlord hereinafter set forth, Tenant shall have the option during the Term hereof to lease additional space in the Building, subject to and in accordance with the terms hereof (each such space individually, or all such space, collectively, as the context may require, being herein called the "Additional Space"), as follows:

Option Number	Lease Year at end of which Additional Space is added to the Premises (the date, with respect to each Additional Space, on which it may be added to the Premises being herein called the "Addition Date")	Rentable Area of Additional Space	Location of Additional Space
1	5th year	sq ft	westerly half of floor
2	8th year	sq ft	easterly half of floor
3	10th year	sq ft	westerly half of floor

4	13th year	sq ft	easterly half of floor
5	15th year	sq ft	floor
6	23rd year	sq ft	floor
7	30th year	sq ft	floor
8	38th year	sq ft	floor

Each of the options hereinabove set forth shall be, automatically and conclusively, deemed exercised by Tenant without any notice to Landlord whatsoever, provided that Tenant shall have the right to elect not to exercise such option with respect to any particular Additional Space by so notifying Landlord, in writing, on or before the date (the "Additional Space Date") which is eighteen (18) months prior to the Addition Date for such Additional Space and provided further that Landlord shall have the right to cancel such exercise on the terms hereinafter set forth. Each Additional Space shall be leased by Tenant from the Addition Date for such space through the Termination Date.

Without limitation of the other terms and provisions hereof, Tenant's rights with respect to leasing the Additional Space are further subject to the following terms and provisions:

(i) Landlord shall have the right to accelerate or defer the Addition Date for any Additional Space by a period of not more than six (6) months by so notifying Tenant, in writing, at least one (1) year prior to the stated Addition Date for such Additional Space, which notice shall specify such new Addition Date for such Additional Space.

(ii) Landlord shall further have the right to change the configuration of (without creating any enclave, without eliminating direct access from the elevators of the Building and without materially reducing the northerly boundaries of such Additional Space), and Rentable Area for, any Additional Space by so notifying Tenant, in writing, at least six (6) months prior to the stated Addition Date for such Additional Space, which notice shall be accompanied by a floor plan showing the new configuration for such Additional Space and the basis upon which the Rentable Area, as changed, has been determined. Landlord shall not increase or decrease the Rentable Area of any Additional Space by more than two (2%) percent.

(iii) If Tenant shall exercise any of the aforesaid options and if on or before thirty (30) days after the Additional Space Date for such option, (A) the net worth of Tenant at such time (determined in accordance with generally accepted accounting principles on the accrual basis of accounting) is less than twice the aggregate annual rental obligation of Tenant hereunder with respect to the Premises for the preceding calendar year (without regard to any Adjustments [hereinafter defined]), (B) Tenant is at such time not occupying at least one hundred thousand (100,000) square feet of Rentable

Area in the Building, or (C) an Event of Default has occurred and is continuing hereunder; Landlord shall have the right to cancel any such exercise of an option for Additional Space by Tenant. Such right shall be exercised, if Landlord so elects, in a written notice to Tenant given on or before the expiration of said thirty (30) day period. In such event the Additional Space subject to said option shall not be added to the Premises (and the Term shall not be extended by any Renewal Term which was deemed exercised by Tenant in connection therewith).

(iv)   Except as hereinafter provided with respect to options 5, 6, and 7, in the event that Tenant shall elect not to exercise, or Landlord shall cancel any exercise by Tenant of, any of the aforesaid options for Additional Space then, each such time, Tenant shall forfeit the right to exercise the then last remaining option for Additional Space hereunder (including any second options provided for herein with respect to options 5, 6 and 7). With respect to options 5, 6, and 7 (as first options), if Tenant shall elect not to exercise any one or more of said options within the respective time periods specified above, then provided that Tenant had the right to exercise any such option at the applicable Additional Space Date and Landlord could not have cancelled such election as hereinabove set forth, Tenant shall not forfeit its right to exercise the then last remaining option (including second options) and shall also be afforded a second option, subject to the terms and conditions hereinabove set forth with respect to the original options, to add the Additional Space covered by such second option to the Premises as follows:

Second Option Number	Addition Date for such Second Option
5	End of 25th Lease Year
6	End of 33rd Lease Year
7	End of 40th Lease Year

With respect to the 5th, 6th and 7th options hereunder (as first options), Tenant shall only forfeit its right to exercise the then last remaining option (including second options) hereunder if either (A) Landlord cancels an election by Tenant to exercise any such option (as a first option) or (B) Tenant has elected not to exercise such option (as a first option), but Landlord would have had a right to cancel such an exercise had it been made by Tenant as provided in clause (iii) above. Without limitation of the foregoing, if Tenant elects not to exercise any second option granted to Tenant hereunder with respect to the 5th, 6th and 7th options or Landlord cancels such an election with respect to such second option pursuant to clause (iii) above, then Tenant shall forfeit its right to exercise the then last remaining option, including second options, hereunder.

3.   Acceptance and Possession of Premises.   The Landlord shall commence and substantially complete the construction of the Building (other than

Tenant finish work) as provided in the Work Letter. The Landlord shall further install in the Initial Premises those items and perform the work set forth in the Work Letter, all at Tenant's sole cost and expense. If construction of the Building and Initial Premises is not substantially completed as provided in the Work Letter on or before _____, subject, however, to delays on account of Force Majeure as provided in Paragraph 27U hereof, this Lease shall nevertheless remain in full force and effect and Landlord shall pay to Tenant Tenant's actual direct damages for the period from said date, as the same may be extended, to the date on which the Commencement Date occurs which damages shall in no event include consequential or special damages; provided, however, there shall be no such payment by Landlord with respect to any period after said date (as the same may be extended) during which the Initial Premises were not so completed because of the occurrence at any time of any one or more of Tenant's Acts (as defined in the Work Letter).

At such time as the Initial Premises and Building are substantially completed, Landlord and Tenant shall execute an instrument confirming the number of square feet of Rentable Area in the Initial Premises and Storage Space and the number of square feet of Rentable Area in the Building (excluding Storage Space).

Any Additional Space will be accepted by Tenant in "as is" condition; provided, however, that if Tenant is the first occupant of such Additional Space and such Additional Space has not theretofore been improved, Tenant shall be given an allowance for the cost of building standard tenant finish work as the same is described in Section II C of the Work Letter.

4.   Rent.

A.   *Base Rent.*   Tenant shall pay to Landlord or Landlord's agent at the Building Management Office, or at such other place as Landlord may from time to time designate in writing, in coin or currency which, at the time of payment, is legal tender for private or public debts in the United States of America, rent (the "Base Rent") for each Lease Year in an amount equal to the sum of (i) the product obtained by multiplying the applicable dollar amount per square foot for such Lease Year set forth below by the number of square feet of Rentable Area included in the Initial Premises, (ii) the product obtained by multiplying the applicable dollar amount per square foot for such Lease Year as set forth below by the number of square feet of Rentable Area in the Storage Space, plus (iii) the product obtained by multiplying the applicable dollar amount per square foot for such Lease Year as set forth below by the number of square feet of Rentable Area included in any Additional Space then occupied by Tenant. One-twelfth (1/12) of such aggregate Base Rent shall be payable in advance on or before the first (1st) day of each and every month during the Term, without any setoff or deduction whatsoever, except as hereinafter in Paragraph B set forth. Tenant shall further pay to Landlord Base Rent for the month in which the Commencement Date occurs at the rate set forth below the amount of which Base Rent shall be appropriately prorated and shall be paid to Landlord on the Commencement Date. If the Term ends other than on the last day of the month, the Base Rent for such month shall be prorated. If any Additional Space is added to the Premises other than on the first day of a Lease Year, the portion of the Base Rent allocable to such Additional Space shall be prorated and if such Additional Space is added to the Premises other than on the first day of the month the portion of the Base Rent allocable to such month shall be prorated and shall be paid on the first day of the next succeeding month.

The dollar amount per square foot of Rentable Area payable with respect to the Premises is as follows:

INITIAL PREMISES

Lease Years	*Amount*
1 through 5 (including the month in which Commencement Date occurs)	$
6 through 9	$
11 through 15	$
Renewal Terms	To be agreed upon based on estimated fair market rental value as of the commencement of the applicable Renewal Term determined as hereinafter set forth.

ADDITIONAL SPACE

Option	*Amount*
Space Covered By Options 1 through 3 as shown in Paragraph 2 during Initial Term	$
Space Covered By Options 1 through 3 during Renewal Terms	To be agreed upon based on estimated fair market rental values as of commencement of applicable Renewal Term determined as hereinafter set forth.

Space Covered By Options 4 through 8 (including any second options as to 5, 6 and 7)	To be agreed upon for the period from the Addition Date for such space (including the Addition Date for any second option) through the end of the current Term based on estimated fair market rental values determined as hereinafter set forth as of the applicable Addition Date; and for any Renewal Term added to the Term at the time that such option is exercised or thereafter as of the commencement date of the applicable Renewal Term.

STORAGE SPACE

Initial Term	$ per square foot
Renewal Terms	To be agreed upon based on estimated fair market rental value determined as hereinafter set forth as of commencement of Renewal Term.

If Landlord and Tenant cannot, at least one hundred eighty (180) days before the last date (the "Decision Date") for Tenant to indicate its intention not to extend the Term of this Lease for any Renewal Term or not to add any Additional Space to the Initial Premises, agree on the applicable fair market rental value as of the commencement of the applicable Renewal Term or as of the applicable Addition Date, as the case may be, each will forthwith appoint and pay for an expert in first class office and storage space rental values in and at least one hundred twenty (120) days prior to the Decision Date the two (2) experts will agree on such fair market rental values. If such experts cannot agree on such fair market rental values by said date, such experts will at least one hundred five (105) days prior to the Decision Date select a third expert in first class office and storage space rental values in (the cost of such expert to be equally divided between Landlord and Tenant) and the third expert shall be instructed to determine (and advise the Landlord and Tenant of such determination) such fair market rental value at least ninety (90) days prior to the Decision Date. If such third expert is not selected at least one hundred five (105) days prior to the Decision Date, or if such third expert does not advise Landlord and Tenant of its determination at least ninety (90) days prior to the Decision Date, either Landlord or Tenant may request the Court of the City to appoint a special master to hear and determine the fair market rental value for such office and/or storage space as of the dates and for the periods specified above and the decision of such special master shall be retroactive if rendered after the date any fair market rental value is required to have been established. The determination of fair market rental value, whether made by the aforesaid two (2) experts or by said third expert or by said special master, shall be final and binding on Landlord and Tenant. Tenant shall continue to be obligated to indicate its intention not to extend the Term of this Lease for any Renewal Term or not to add Additional Space to the Initial Premises within the time periods specified in Paragraphs 1B and 2 hereof, respectively, whether or not any determination as to fair market rental value has been rendered at such time. In the event that the applicable fair market rental value has not been determined as of the commencement of any Renewal Term, Tenant shall until such determination is made continue paying Base Rent for the Initial Premises, Storage Area and any Renewal Space then part of the Premises at the rate in effect for such space for the Lease Year immediately preceding the commencement of such Renewal Term. In the event that the applicable fair market rental value has not been determined as of the Addition Date for any Additional Space, Tenant shall until such determination is made pay Base Rent therefor at the rate in effect for the Additional Space last added to the Premises or if there has been none, at the rate then in effect for the Initial Premises.

In determining such fair market rental value the aforesaid experts or special master, as the case may be, shall determine same by giving their best estimates as to what such fair market rental value will be with respect to the space in question as of the dates specified above. For purposes of determining such fair market rental value the experts shall consider rental values for areas similar in size, configuration, location, quality, age and service to the size, configuration, location, quality, age and service of the space in question, net of (i) leasing and renewal leasing commissions, which commissions shall in any event be not less than two and one-half (2-1/2%) percent of full rental values including Tenant's proportionate share of Operating Expenses (hereinafter defined) and real estate taxes; (ii) Operating Expenses; (iii) Tenant's proportionate share of real estate taxes; and (iv) special tenant improvements, if any, with Operating Expenses and real estate taxes to be the Operating Expenses and real estate taxes for the most recent year prior to the Decision Date.

B.   *Adjustments.*   Tenant shall be entitled to the following adjustments to Base Rent:

(i)   Tenant shall receive a credit against Base Rent hereunder in an aggregate amount equal to Dollars, which credit may be applied against the first payments of Base Rent otherwise becoming due hereunder.

(ii)   From and after the date (the "Rent Adjustment Date") which is the later of (i) January 1, or (ii) if the Substantial Completion Date is delayed beyond January 1, on account of events or circumstances constituting "Force Majeure" delays as provided in Paragraph 27U hereof, the first day of the twenty-fourth (24th) full calendar month after such Substantial Completion Date, Tenant shall be entitled to adjustments to the Base Rent, said adjustments to be subject to, and determined in accordance with, the following terms and conditions:

(a)   As used herein, the following terms shall have the following meanings:

(i)   *"Base Adjustment" for any quarterly or calendar year period shall mean an aggregate amount equal to _____ times the numbers of full calendar months in such period.*

(ii)   "Deferred Base Adjustment" for any quarterly or Calendar Year period shall mean the excess, if any (but not more than the Base Adjustment for such period), of the Base Adjustment for such period over the Net Cash Flow (hereinafter defined) for such period.

(iii)   "Additional Adjustment" for any quarterly or Calendar Year period shall mean:

(A)   With respect to any such period within the period commencing on the Rent Adjustment Date and terminating on the last day of the Calendar Year in which the first Renewal Term commences, an amount equal to five (5%) percent of the "Excess Net Cash Flow" (hereinafter defined) for such period; and

(B)   With respect to any such period within the period commencing on the first day of the Calendar Year next succeeding the Calendar Year in which the first Renewal Term commences and terminating on the Termination Date, an amount equal to seven (7%) percent of the Excess Net Cash Flow for such period; and

(C)   With respect to the Calendar Year in which the first Renewal Term commences, an amount equal to the product of (x) two (2%) percent of the Excess Net Cash Flow for such period, times (y) a fraction, the numerator of which is the number of days from the first day of the first Renewal Term to and including December 31st of the Calendar Year in which the Renewal Term commences and the denominator of which is 365.

(iv) "Total Building Costs", as of any date, shall mean an amount equal to (without duplication, however, of any amounts included by Landlord in Operating Expenses) (a) all costs (hard and soft) and expenses, direct and indirect (other than interest costs except as otherwise herein expressly included), of the acquisition, development, construction and marketing of the Building (including, without limitation, all costs and expenses for off-site improvements reasonably allocable to the Office Building and for on-site improvements reasonably allocable to the Office Building and Dollars for the cost of the Land), plus (b) all fees payable on any financing obtained with respect to the development, construction and operation of the Building and interest on each item of costs and expenses (other than Land) constituting a part of Total Building Costs from the date paid through the end of the Construction Period (hereinafter defined) at the rate of interest from time to time payable by the Landlord on its construction financing relating to the Building but not in excess of fifty (50) basis points over the base lending rate of in effect from time to time, plus (c) from the expiration of the Construction Period and thereafter all operating losses (excluding depreciation but including in determining such losses, Assumed Debt Service, hereinafter defined) from the Building, plus (d) all capital expenditures with respect to the Building incurred at any time after the Substantial Completion Date, and less (e) casualty insurance or condemnation proceeds applied to the reconstruction of the Building and less (f) for all periods prior to the Rent Adjustment Date any Net Cash Flow. To the extent that any of such costs and expenses were incurred in connection with the balance of the project that Landlord is undertaking as part of an overall development in which the Building is included (the "Project"), Landlord shall allocate such costs and expenses, in good faith, on a reasonable basis and at Tenant's request shall furnish Tenant with an explanation of the basis for such allocation, in form and detail reasonably satisfactory to Tenant. Prior to the Substantial Completion Date, Landlord shall not finance (pursuant to any loan secured by an interest in the Building) more than one hundred (100%) percent of the aggregate amount of Total Building Costs, less the amounts thereof allocable to the Land.

(v) "Assumed Debt Service" for any quarterly period shall mean an amount equal to the sum of (A) the Interest Factor (hereinafter defined) for such period multiplied by eighty-five (85%) percent of Total Building Costs as of the close of such period, plus (B) the Amortization Component (hereinafter defined) for such year in effect for such period. "Assumed Debt Service" for any annual period shall mean an amount equal to (C) the Interest Factor for such period, multiplied by eighty-five (85%) percent of an amount equal to the quotient obtained by dividing the sum of the Total Building Costs as of the end of each of the calendar quarters in such period by four, plus (D) the Amortization Component for such year.

(vi)   "Interest Factor" for any Calendar Year (and each quarter thereof) shall mean:

Except as provided below in the next two sentences of this paragraph, an annual rate of interest equal to the quotient (expressed as a percentage) of (x) the sum of (i) all interest (contingent, fixed, floating or other) paid with respect to such year on indebtedness ("Indebtedness") secured by the Building plus (ii) all distributions made with respect to such year to third parties (other than and their respective subsidiaries) in connection with actual capital contributions made by such third parties to the Landlord divided by (y) the sum of the daily average for such year of the outstanding balance of the Indebtedness and of all capital actually contributed by such third parties to the Landlord. During any period in which there is no financing arrangement in effect (whether Indebtedness or equity contributions to the Landlord by third parties) the Interest Factor for such period shall be agreed upon by the Landlord and Tenant for Indebtedness in an amount equal to eighty-five (85%) percent of Total Building Costs as of such time, based upon fair market rates in effect as of the commencement of such period and, if Landlord and Tenant cannot so agree, the Interest Factor for such period shall be determined by commercial arbitration as hereinafter provided. So long as the initial financing which the Landlord proposes to obtain from is in effect, the Interest Factor shall not exceed seventy-five (75) basis points over the base lending rate of in effect from time to time and Tenant shall not have the right to dispute the Interest Factor to the extent that it is based upon such Morgan financing.

If Tenant, in its good faith and reasonable judgment, believes that the Interest Factor is inflated on account of any of the "financing arrangements" hereinafter described, Tenant may dispute the Interest Factor (or the applicable portion thereof as hereinafter set forth) to the extent that it is based upon such financing arrangement and may require arbitration of the dispute in under the commercial arbitration rules of the American Arbitration Association. Tenant may so dispute (a) the portion of the Interest Factor which is based upon any Indebtedness furnished by and their respective subsidiaries, (b) the portion of the Interest Factor which is based upon any single financing arrangement if the same is for an amount in excess of eighty-five (85%) percent of the Total Building Costs and (c) the portion of the Interest Factor which is based upon any additional financing arrangement (obtained when any financing arrangement is then in place) which, when added to the financing then in place, results in aggregate financing arrangements in excess of eighty-five

(85%) percent of Total Building Costs. In any such event or in the event of a dispute as to the applicable Interest Factor for any period when no financing arrangement is in effect, the interest for Indebtedness (including contingent, fixed, floating and other) or the formula upon which amounts to be distributed to parties (other than and their respective subsidiaries) providing equity financing to the Landlord will be determined, or both, as the case may be, that would be necessary to obtain a financing arrangement of the type in question for an amount equal to eighty-five (85%) percent of the cost of the Total Building Costs (or, if the arrangement in question is of the type described in (a) above for the amount of such Indebtedness) from a third party other than or any of their respective subsidiaries shall be determined by such arbitration.

Once any financing arrangement (whether Indebtedness or equity, or both) is in place and has been accepted by Tenant or once the interest amount to be included in the Interest Factor on account thereof has been determined through arbitration, such financing arrangement shall not be subject to further arbitration. Tenant shall notify the Landlord, in writing, of its desire to arbitrate any financing arrangement as hereinabove set forth within thirty (30) days after the Landlord notifies Tenant of such financing arrangement. A failure by Tenant to send such notice shall constitute acceptance thereof. Pending completion of any such arbitration, Net Cash Flow shall be determined without regard to the pendency of such dispute. If such arbitration results in a revision of the Interest Factor, such revision shall be retroactive to the date of the event which gave rise to the dispute and the amount due to either Landlord or Tenant on account of such revision shall bear interest from such date at an annual rate equal to two (2%) percent plus the base lending rate of in effect from time to time. As used herein, the term financing arrangement shall mean and include any financing of the Land and/or Building consisting of Indebtedness or capital contributions to the Landlord by third parties, or both.

(vii)   The Amortization Component for any year (or quarterly period thereof) shall mean a number determined as follows:

The Amortization Component shall be zero prior to the time that the Landlord is required to make regular payments according to a standard amortization schedule on account of the principal portion of financing with respect to the Building. Thereafter, the Amortization Component shall change each time there is a refinancing of the Building. Subject to the foregoing, the Amortization Component for each year shall be the amount of principal amortization specified for such year by an amortization table for a loan equal to eighty-five (85%) percent of the Total Building Costs, as such costs are determined as of the date of the most recent of such refinancings, with such table to be computed on the basis of level monthly payments of principal and interest over a term equal to the greater of (x) the number of years in the period from the effective date of such refinancing through the thirty-fifth (35th) anniversary of the first refinancing and (y) the length of the actual schedule of amortization (as distinguished from the term of the loan or the period from its inception to its maturity) of such refinancing, and with interest equal to thirteen (13%) percent per annum.

(viii)   "Net Cash Flow" for any quarterly or annual period shall mean the excess of (A) the sum of (i) all cash receipts, including, without limitation, base rents and additional rents from the Building for such period and (ii) reimbursements of Operating Expenses and Taxes, from the operation of the Building for such period plus the amount of Adjustments actually deducted by Tenant from its Base Rent payments during such period pursuant to this Paragraph 4B, over (B) the sum of all Operating Expenses for such period, the Assumed Debt Service for such period and the amount of Taxes allocable to such period.

(ix)   "Excess Net Cash Flow" for any quarterly or annual period shall mean the excess, if any, of the Net Cash Flow for such period over the sum of all Base Adjustments for such period plus the amount of Deferred Base Adjustments which Tenant becomes entitled to deduct on account of the Net Cash Flow for such period as provided in Paragraph (b) below.

(x)   "Adjustments" shall mean and include the credit provided for under Paragraph 43(i) hereof, the Base Adjustments (including Deferred Base Adjustments) and the Additional Adjustments.

(xi)   "Construction Period" shall mean the period prior to the Rent Adjustment Date.

(b)   Subject to the other terms and conditions hereof, Tenant shall be entitled to deduct the Base Adjustment for any quarterly period from the Base Rent payable by it in subsequent quarterly periods to the extent of the Net Cash Flow for such current period. Any Deferred Base Adjustments (that is, Base Adjustment amounts not deductible by Tenant pursuant to the preceding sentence) shall be accumulated, without interest, and at such time as the Net Cash Flow for any subsequent period exceeds the Base Adjustment for such subsequent period, then Tenant shall be entitled to deduct an amount of such Deferred Base Adjustment not exceeding such excess from the Base Rent payable by Tenant in subsequent periods.

(c)   Additionally, Tenant shall be entitled to deduct the Additional Adjustment, if any, for any period from the Base Rent payable by it in subsequent periods.

(d)   Landlord shall, within thirty (30) days following the close of each quarter in each Calendar Year, prepare and furnish to Tenant a statement (the "Quarterly Statement") for such quarter showing (i) Total Building Costs as of the close of such quarter, (ii) all cash receipts from the Building for such quarter, (iii) all Operating Expenses, Taxes and Assumed Debt Service attributable to such quarter, (iv) Net Cash Flow and Excess Net Cash Flow for such quarter, (v) the portion of the Base Adjustment for such quarter which Tenant is entitled to deduct from its next payments of Base Rent and the portion thereof, if any, constituting "Deferred Base Adjustment", (vi) as of the close of such quarter, all Deferred Base Adjustments which Tenant may in the future become entitled to deduct from Base Rent, (vii) the amount of any Deferred Base Adjustments which Tenant is entitled to deduct from its next quarterly payments of Base Rent and (viii) the amount, if any, of the Additional Adjustment which Tenant is entitled to deduct from its next quarterly payments of Base Rent.

(e)   Within ninety (90) days following the close of each Calendar Year Landlord shall prepare or cause to be prepared and delivered to Tenant a year-end statement (the "Annual Statement") for such Calendar Year showing with respect thereto (i) Total Building Costs as of the close of each quarter in such Calendar Year, (ii) all cash receipts from the operation of the Building for such Calendar Year, (iii) all Operating Expenses, Taxes and Assumed Debt Service for such Calendar Year, (iv) Net Cash Flow and Excess Net Cash Flow for such Calendar Year, (v) the portion of the aggregate Base Adjustment for such Calendar Year which Tenant was entitled to deduct from payments of Base Rent and the portion thereof, if any, constituting Deferred Base Adjustment, (vi) as of the close of such Calendar Year, all Deferred Base Adjustments which Tenant may in the future become entitled to deduct from Base Rent, (vii) any Deferred Base Adjustments from prior years which Tenant, in such Calendar Year, became entitled to deduct from Base Rent and (viii) the amount, if any, of the Additional Adjustment for such Calendar Year. If such Annual Statement reflects that the aggregate Adjustments which Tenant was entitled to deduct for such Calendar Year exceed the amount shown in the Quarterly Statements, Tenant shall have the right to deduct such excess from the next payments of Base Rent coming due hereunder. If such Annual Statement shows that the aggregate Adjustments which Tenant was entitled to deduct for such Calendar Year is less than that shown in the Quarterly Statements, then to the extent such excess Adjustments were actually deducted by Tenant from its Base Rent payments, Tenant shall pay such excess Adjustments to Landlord concurrently with the next monthly payment of Base Rent hereunder.

(f)   Tenant shall have the right within thirty (30) days following the receipt of any of the aforesaid statements, at its expense, to cause a review to be made of any of the Quarterly Statements or Annual

Statements delivered by Landlord to Tenant hereunder and Landlord shall provide Tenant access to its books and records to the extent they are required for such review for such purpose at reasonable times during business hours. If upon such review of any Statement Tenant disputes any of the amounts reflected therein, the amounts not in dispute shall be deducted and/or paid as herein provided and the dispute shall forthwith be settled by a firm of independent certified public accountants selected by Tenant and Landlord. Determination of such firm shall be binding upon Tenant and Landlord and appropriate adjustments shall be made at the time of such determination. The fees of such firm shall be paid by Tenant unless Landlord's determination as to the Adjustments for which Tenant was entitled to a deduction was understated by more than ten (10%) percent.

(g)   The Additional Adjustment for the Calendar Year in which the Rent Adjustment Date occurs and for the Calendar Year in which the Term ends shall be appropriately prorated by multiplying the Additional Adjustment that would have been available for each such Calendar Year, based on the assumption that an entire Lease Year was included within such Calendar Year and that Tenant was entitled to a Base Adjustment for each month included in such Calendar Year, by a fraction, the numerator of which is the number of days in such Calendar Year during the Term and after the Rent Adjustment Date and the denominator of which is 365.

(h)   Tenant further agrees that provided its rights to the Adjustments provided for herein remain cumulative and are not further deferred or extinguished by such amendments, Tenant shall make such amendments to the provisions of this Paragraph 4B as Landlord's mortgagee or mortgagees may reasonably request.

(i)   Tenant's rights to a deduction for the Adjustments provided for above are subject to the following conditions being satisfied for each of the periods in question:

(i)   No payment of Rent or Additional Rent or any other amount due Landlord hereunder shall be more than ten (10) days past due (whether or not notice thereof has been given by Landlord hereunder);

(ii)   Without limitation of (i) above, no Event of Default shall exist and be continuing hereunder; and

(iii)   Tenant shall be occupying at least one hundred thousand (100,000) square feet of Rentable Area in the Building.

5.   *Additional Rent.*   In addition to paying the Base Rent specified in Paragraph 4 hereof, Tenant shall pay for each Calendar Year in the Term hereof, the "Expense Amount" and "Tax Amount" (as hereinafter defined) determined as hereinafter set forth (said amounts being hereinafter called the

"Additional Rent"). The Base Rent and the Additional Rent and any amounts payable by Tenant under Paragraph 8 hereof and elsewhere herein are sometimes herein individually and collectively referred to as the "Rent". All amounts due under this Paragraph 5 as Additional Rent shall be payable in the same manner and place as the Base Rent. Without limitation of the other obligations of Tenant which shall survive the expiration of the Term, the obligations of Tenant to pay the Additional Rent provided for in this Paragraph 5 shall survive the expiration of the Term. The Additional Rent for the calendar month in which the Commencement Date occurs shall be prorated based upon the number of days from the Commencement Date to the end of such calendar month. If the first or last Lease Years (including in the first Lease Year the month in which the Commencement Date occurs) are partial Calendar Years, Tenant shall be obligated to pay only a pro rata share of the Additional Rent, based on the number of days of the Term falling within such Calendar Year. Additionally, if any Additional Space is added to the Premises other than on the first day of a Calendar Year, the portion of the Additional Rent allocable to such Additional Space for such Calendar Year shall be prorated based on the number of days falling within such Calendar Year from the actual Addition Date (giving effect to any acceleration or deferral) for such Additional Space.

A. *Definitions.*   As used in this Paragraph 5, the terms:

(i)   "Calendar Year" shall mean each calendar year in which any part of the Term falls, through and including the year in which the Term expires.

(ii)   Subject to the prorations provided for above, "Tenant's Proportionate Share" for each Calendar Year shall mean a fraction, the numerator of which shall be the Rentable Area in the Premises (excluding Storage Space) as of the last day of such Calendar Year and the denominator of which shall be the aggregate Rentable Area in the Building (excluding Storage Space).

(iii)   "Taxes" shall mean all real estate taxes and assessments, special or otherwise, levied or assessed upon or with respect to the Land and/or Building and ad valorem taxes for any personal property used in connection therewith. Should the State of Pennsylvania, or any political subdivision thereof, or any other governmental authority having jurisdiction over the Land and/or the Building, (a) impose a tax, assessment, charge or fee, which Landlord shall be required to pay, wholly or partially, in substitution for such real estate taxes and ad valorem personal property taxes, or either, or (b) impose an income or franchise tax or a tax on rents, wholly or partially, in substitution for or as a supplement to a tax levied against the Land and/or the Building and/or the personal property used in connection with the Land or Building, all such taxes, assessments, fees or charges (hereinafter defined as "In Lieu Taxes") shall be deemed to constitute Taxes hereunder. If any taxes are calculated on a graduated method, Landlord shall calculate Landlord's tax liability with respect to the Land and/or Building by excluding the portion of any taxes and assessments levied or made against any land other than the Land and any structure or building other than the Building. "Taxes" shall also include all fees and costs, including, without limitation, attorneys' fees and costs, incurred by Landlord in seeking to obtain a reduction of, or a limit on the increase in, any Taxes, regardless of whether any reduction or limitation is obtained. Except as hereinabove provided with regard to In Lieu Taxes, Taxes shall not include any inheritance, estate, succession, transfer, gift, excise, franchise, merchantile license, business privilege, income or profits or capital stock or other net worth tax.

(iv) "Operating Expenses" shall mean all expenses, costs and disbursements (other than taxes [including Taxes] and Landlord's partnership administrative expenses) of every kind and nature (determined for the applicable Calendar Year on an accrual basis) paid or incurred by Landlord in connection with the ownership, management, operation, maintenance, janitorial services and repair of the Land and Building, except the following:

(a) Costs of alterations of any tenant's premises;

(b) Principal or interest payments on loans secured by mortgages or trust deeds on the Building and/or on the Land;

(c) Amounts deposited in Working Capital Accounts until such amounts are actually expended for items constituting Operating Expenses hereunder;

(d) Depreciation;

(e) Costs of capital improvements, including any cost for replacement of building elevators and systems except that Operating Expenses shall include (i) the cost, as reasonably amortized by Landlord with interest at the rate of ten (10%) percent on the unamortized amount, of any capital improvement completed after the Commencement Date (and not originally contemplated by the plans for the Building as such plans are described in Schedule 1 to the Work Letter) which, in the reasonable opinion of Landlord, is intended and is likely to have the effect of reducing materially and promptly any component cost included within Operating Expenses; and (ii) the cost of any capital improvements which are necessary to keep the Land and Building in compliance with governmental rules and regulations applicable from time to time thereto;

(f) Real Estate brokers' leasing commissions and management fees paid to Landlord or its affiliates in excess of management fees which would be payable to outside third parties at current market rates in the Philadelphia area; and

(g) Any reserve for payment of non-recurring expenses (other than the type of reserves provided for in Landlord's proforma of);

(h) The cost of providing to any other tenant's Rentable Area in the Building electrical energy for lighting and convenience power, provided that all other expenses in connection with providing such electrical energy including electrical utility charges for common areas and central building services common to all tenants shall be included; and

(i) The cost of providing to any other tenant's Rentable Area in the Building maintenance or repair services, other than standard janitorial services, the cost of all standard janitorial services to be included in Operating Expenses.

In the event that the Building is not at least eighty-five (85%) percent occupied during any Calendar Year prior to _____, for purposes of determining the Additional Rent hereunder, Operating Expenses shall be equitably adjusted to reflect the amount that Operating Expenses would have been, in the reasonable estimate of Landlord, if the Building were eighty-five (85%) percent occupied in such year.

In the event that Landlord shall furnish to any other tenant a greater level of service, heating, air-conditioning or convenience electrical power than that furnished to Tenant under Paragraph 8 hereof, the costs incurred by Landlord in connection with such excess services shall not be an Operating Expense hereunder and for the purposes of Paragraph 4B hereof, except as hereinafter provided, the receipts or benefits received by Landlord in connection therewith shall not reduce Operating Expenses or be included in determining Net Cash Flow; provided, however, that if such receipts exceed the cost of such excess services, then the amount of such excess shall not reduce Operating Expenses but shall be included in determining Net Cash Flow.

Landlord shall make available to Tenant Landlord's staff to perform repair or maintenance or other services (other than standard janitorial services). Landlord shall charge Tenant for such services in accordance with Landlord's schedule of charges uniformly applied to the Building or any other facility serviced by such staff.

(v) If costs and expenses constituting Operating Expenses or Taxes cover the Building and any other portion of the Project, Landlord shall allocate such costs and/or taxes on a reasonable good faith basis and shall furnish Tenant with a statement indicating the basis for such allocations, in form and detail reasonably satisfactory to Tenant.

B. *Expense Amount.* Tenant shall pay to Landlord or Landlord's agent as Rent in addition to the Base Rent required by Paragraph 4 hereof and all other amounts required to be paid by Tenant hereunder, an amount ("Expense Amount") equal to Tenant's Proportionate Share of the Operating Expenses incurred with respect to each Calendar Year, subject to prorations hereinabove set forth. The Expense Amount with respect to each Calendar Year shall be paid in monthly installments, in an amount estimated from time to time by Landlord and communicated by written notice to Tenant (it being agreed that the aggregate Expense Amount for the Calendar Year in which the Term commences shall be estimated by Landlord on a reasonable good faith basis and the Expense Amount for each subsequent Calendar Year shall be generally based upon the Expense Amount for the preceding Calendar Year with such increases thereto at the lower of (for each item contained therein) the inflation rate for the preceding Calendar Year or the actual known prospective increases to such item as Landlord reasonably deems appropriate). The monthly Expense Amount payable by Tenant hereunder with respect to a particular Calendar Year shall be adjusted at such time as any Additional Space is added to the Premises in such Calendar Year and the proportion of the Expense Amount allocable to such Additional Space for the month in which it is added to the Premises shall be paid with the next monthly payment of the Expense Amount due hereunder. Landlord shall cause to be kept books and records showing Operating Expenses in accordance with generally accepted accounting principles. Following the close of each calendar quarter (other than the last) of each Calendar Year and of each Calendar Year, Landlord shall cause the actual amount of the Expense Amount for such quarter or Calendar Year, as the case may be, to be computed based on actual Operating Expenses for such quarter or Calendar Year, as the case may be, for the Building and Landlord shall deliver to Tenant a statement of such amount and Tenant shall pay any deficiency to Landlord as shown by such statement within thirty (30) days after receipt of such statement. If the total of the estimated monthly installments paid by Tenant during any quarter or Calendar Year exceeds the actual Expense Amount due from Tenant with respect thereto, at Landlord's option, such excess shall be either credited against payments next due hereunder or refunded by Landlord, provided no payment of Rent, Additional Rent or any other amount due Landlord hereunder is past due for more than ten (10) days (whether or not Landlord has given Tenant notice thereof) and, without limitation of the foregoing, no Event of Default has occurred and is continuing hereunder. Delay in computation of the Expense Amount shall not be deemed a default hereunder or a waiver of Landlord's right to collect the Expense Amount.

C. *Tax Adjustment.* Tenant shall pay to Landlord or Landlord's agent as Rent, in addition to Base Rent required by Paragraph 4 hereof and all other amounts required to be paid by Tenant hereunder, an amount ("Tax Amount") equal to Tenant's Proportionate Share of the Taxes payable with respect to each Calendar Year. The Tax Amount with respect to each Calendar Year shall be paid by Tenant to Landlord within ten (10) days after receipt by Tenant of a written request by Landlord therefor, which request shall be accompanied by a copy of the tax bill for such period and Landlord shall pay such tax bill within ten (10) days after receipt from Tenant of the Tax Amount with respect to such bill. If Landlord is required, whether pursuant to the financing on the Land and Building or otherwise, to maintain a tax escrow, such Tax Amount shall be paid by Tenant to Landlord in monthly installments, in an amount estimated from time to time by Landlord (such estimate to be based on the amount which Landlord reasonably determines will be payable by it for such Calendar Year into such escrow) and communicated by written notice to Tenant. At all times during the term, Landlord shall use its best efforts to avoid being required to maintain a tax escrow. The Tax Amount payable by Tenant hereunder with respect to a particular Calendar Year shall be adjusted at such time as any Additional Space is added to the Premises in such Calendar Year and, if the Tax Amount is being paid monthly, the proportion of the Tax Amount allocable to the Additional Space for the month in which it is added to the Premises shall be paid with the next monthly payment of the Tax Amount due hereunder. If the Tax Amount is paid in monthly installments as hereinabove provided, following the close of each Calendar Year, Landlord shall cause the amount of the Tax Amount for such Calendar Year to be computed based on Taxes for such Calendar Year and Landlord shall deliver to Tenant a statement of such amount and Tenant shall pay any deficiency to Landlord as shown by such statement within thirty (30) days after receipt of such statement or if the total of the estimated monthly installments paid by Tenant during any Calendar Year exceed the actual Tax Amount due from Tenant for such Calendar Year, at Landlord's option, such excess shall be either credited against payments next due hereunder or refunded by Landlord, provided no payment of Rent, Additional Rent or any other amount due Landlord hereunder is past due for more than ten (10) days (whether or not Landlord has given Tenant notice thereof) and, without limitation of the foregoing, no Event of Default has occurred and is continuing hereunder. In determining the amount of Taxes for any Calendar Year, the amount of special assessments to be included shall be limited to the amount of the installment (plus any interest payable thereon) of such special assessment required to be paid during such Calendar Year if the Landlord had elected to have such special assessment paid over the maximum period of time permitted by law. Delay in computation of the Tax Amount shall not be deemed a default hereunder or a waiver of Landlord's right to collect the Tax Adjustment Amount.

D.   If Landlord shall receive any refund on account of any component Operating Expenses or Taxes, Landlord shall treat such refund as a reduction of Operating Expense or Taxes, as the case may be, in the period in which such refund is actually received.

E.   Landlord represents that Landlord has applied for full real estate tax abatement status for the Project under the Philadelphia Five-Year Real Estate Tax Abatement Program.

6.   *Use of Premises.*   Tenant shall use and occupy the Premises solely as an office for the practice of law and for no other purpose. Without limitation of any other term or provision hereof, during the Initial Term hereof, Tenant

shall at all times continue to occupy for its own use at least one hundred thousand (100,000) square feet of Rentable Area. Subject to the foregoing and to the provisions of Paragraph 17 hereof, if a portion of the Premises is sublet by Tenant as provided in said Paragraph 17, said sublet portion may be used as office space for any lawful purpose consistent with the terms of this Lease, including Exhibit F hereto.

7. *Condition of Premises.* Except with respect to (i) items listed by Tenant after an inspection of the Premises on a preliminary or final punch list delivered to Landlord pursuant to the Work Letter, (ii) latent defects in Tenant's Improvements (as defined in the Work Letter) discovered within one (1) year after the Commencement Date and (iii) latent defects in the Base Building (as defined in the Work Letter), Tenant's first occupying the Initial Premises, or any portion thereof, other than for the sole purpose of installing Tenant finish work or equipment shall be conclusive evidence as between Tenant and Landlord that the Premises, or any such portion, were in good order and satisfactory condition when the Tenant first occupied such space. Landlord will assign to Tenant all warranties and guarantees obtained by Landlord (Landlord hereby agreeing to obtain all customary guarantees and warranties, which shall, except with respect to items of equipment and other personal property, be for a period of at least one [1] year from the completion of the Work or supplying of materials covered thereby) with respect to work performed or materials supplied for Tenant's Improvements on or to the Premises by or at the direction of Landlord and Tenant will look solely to such guarantees and warranties to secure the correction of any defective work (including latent defects) relating to Tenant's Improvements. Tenant shall be responsible for any items of damage to the Premises caused by Tenant or its employees, agents, independent contractors or suppliers. No promise of the Landlord to alter, remodel or improve the Premises or the Building and no representation by Landlord or its agents respecting the condition of the Premises or the Building have been made to Tenant or relied upon by Tenant other than as may be contained in this Lease or in any written amendment hereto signed by Landlord and Tenant.

8. *Services.*

A. *List of Services.* Landlord shall provide the following services on all days during the Term, except Sundays and the holidays listed on Exhibit G hereto, unless otherwise stated:

(i) Heating and air-conditioning from Monday through Friday, during the period from 8:00 A.M. to 6:00 P.M. and on Saturday during the period from 8:00 A.M. to 1:00 P.M. Subject to compliance with any laws or regulations hereinafter enacted affecting same, including, without limitation, thermostat and interior temperature control regulations, Tenant's air-conditioning specification for interior temperature conditions for the season for which cooling is required to offset heat gains through the outside surface of the Building shall be 75 degrees Fahrenheit, plus or minus two

(2°) degrees. There will be no charge to Tenant for normal Building heating services beyond the specified hours. Tenant shall pay Landlord for air-conditioning requested and furnished prior to or following such specified hours, the amount charged therefor to be equal to Landlord's incremental, out-of-pocket operating cost of furnishing such air-conditioning. Air-conditioning equipment will permit selectivity by individual floors.

(ii)   Adequate electrical wiring and facilities for standard building lighting fixtures provided by Landlord and for Tenant's incidental uses, provided that (a) the maximum demand electrical load of the lighting and incidental use equipment does not exceed an average of 2.5 watts per square foot on any floor of the Premises and (b) the electricity furnished for incidental convenience uses will be at a normal 120 volts and no electrical circuit for the supply of such incidental use will have a current capacity exceeding 15 amperes. If Tenant's requirements for electricity for lighting and incidental uses will be in excess of those set forth in the preceding sentence, the Landlord reserves the right to require Tenant to install the conduit, wiring and other equipment necessary to supply electricity for such excess lighting and incidental use requirements at the Tenant's expense by arrangement with Philadelphia Electric Company. Tenant shall bear the cost of replacement of all lamps, tubes, ballasts and starters for lighting fixtures after the initial installation thereof.

(iii)   City water from the regular Building outlets for drinking, lavatory (including hot and cold water) and toilet purposes.

(iv)   Janitorial services Monday through Friday in and about the Premises according to the Schedule of Janitorial and Window Cleaning Services for the Building attached hereto as Exhibit E.

(v)   Window washing of all inside and outside windows in the Premises in accordance with Exhibit E.

(vi)   Adequate automatic passenger elevator service at all times, including Sundays and holidays.

(vii)   Freight elevator services subject to scheduling by Landlord.

(viii)   A Tenant directory in the lobby of the Building.

(ix)   Such building security service as Landlord reasonably deems appropriate.

B.   Landlord shall equip each floor of the Office Building so that it can be separately metered for consumption of electricity for tenant lighting and convenience power. Tenant shall pay for the installation of the meters and for the use of all electrical service to the Premises, or any portion thereof, as recorded by the electrical meters therein. Tenant shall be billed by Landlord for any such service (the cost thereof to be determined as aforesaid) and Tenant agrees to pay as Additional Rent each bill promptly in accordance with its terms.

If the Premises, or any portion thereof, is not separately metered for any reason, Tenant shall pay Landlord as Additional Rent, in monthly installments at the time prescribed for monthly installments of Base Rent, an amount, as estimated by Landlord from time to time, which Tenant would pay for any such electricity if the same were separately metered to the Premises, or any portion thereof, such amount to be determined in accordance with an engineer's projection of electrical consumption.

Landlord will monitor electric usage by other tenants in the Office Building and will take demand factors into account when charging any other tenant for electricity consumed for lighting and convenience power.

C. *Liability for Damages.* Tenant agrees that Landlord shall not be liable for damages (by abatement of rent or otherwise) for failure to furnish or delay in furnishing any service, or for any diminution in the quality or quantity thereof, when such failure or delay or diminution is occasioned, in whole or in part, by repairs, renewals, or improvements, by any strike, lockout or other labor trouble, by inability to secure electricity, gas, water or other fuel at the Building after reasonable effort so to do, by any accident or casualty whatsoever, by act or default of Tenant or other parties, or by any other cause beyond Landlord's reasonable control; and such failures or delays or diminution shall never be deemed to constitute an eviction or disturbance of the Tenant's use and possession of the Premises or relieve the Tenant from paying rent or performing any of its obligations under this Lease.

D. *Charges for Services.*   Charges for any services for which Tenant is required to pay from time to time hereunder, including, but not limited to, after-hours freight elevator services or after hours air-conditioning shall be due and payable at the same time as the installment of Base Rent with which they are billed, or if billed separately, shall be due and payable within fifteen (15) business days after such billing. If Tenant shall fail to make payment for any such services, Landlord may, with notice to Tenant, discontinue any or all of such services and such discontinuance shall not be deemed to constitute an eviction or disturbance of the Tenant's use and possession of the Premises or relieve Tenant from paying rent or performing any of its other obligations under this Lease.

9. *Repairs.*   Landlord will provide to Tenant's Premises all Janitorial Services as required pursuant to Exhibit E hereto, it being understood that the cost thereof (and the cost of providing such services to all other tenant space in the Building) is included in Operating Expenses hereunder. Except for the foregoing Janitorial Services and the provisions of Paragraph 27B hereof with respect to painting and recarpeting, Tenant will, at Tenant's own expense, keep the Premises in good order, repair and condition at all times during the Term, and Tenant shall promptly and adequately repair all damage to the Premises and replace or repair all damaged or broken fixtures and appurtenances, under the supervision and subject to the approval of the Landlord, and within any reasonable period of time specified by the Landlord. If the Tenant does not do so, Landlord may, but need not, make such repairs and replacements, and Tenant shall pay Landlord, forthwith upon being billed for same,

the cost thereof, including a percentage of the cost thereof (to be uniformly established for the Building) sufficient to reimburse Landlord for all overhead, general conditions, fees and other costs or expenses arising from Landlord's involvement with such repairs and replacements. Subject to the requirements of Paragraph 22(xi) hereby relating to conditions to Landlord's entry into the Premises, which conditions shall be applicable except in cases of emergency, Landlord may, but shall not be required to, enter the Premises at all reasonable times to make such repairs, alterations, improvements and additions to the Premises or to the Building or to any equipment located in the Building as may be required of Landlord hereunder or under the Work Letter or as Landlord shall desire or deem necessary or as Landlord may be required to do by governmental or quasi-governmental authority or court order or decree.

At all times during the Term, Landlord will keep all common areas, other than tenant space, in the Building in good order, repair and condition for a first-class office building.

10.   Additions and Alterations.   Except for Tenant Work covered by the Work Letter, Tenant shall not, without the prior written consent of Landlord, make any alterations, improvements or additions to the Premises; provided that, except as to structural alterations, improvements or additions and those prohibited by the Rules and Regulations attached hereto as Exhibit F, such consent shall not be unreasonably withheld. Subject to the foregoing, Landlord's refusal to give said consent shall be conclusive. If Landlord consents to said alterations, improvements or additions, it may impose such conditions with respect thereto as Landlord reasonably deems appropriate, including, without limitation, requiring Tenant to furnish Landlord with security for the payment of all costs to be incurred in connection with such work, insurance against all liabilities which may arise out of such work and plans, specifications and permits necessary for such work. The work necessary to make any alterations, improvements or additions to the Premises shall be done at Tenant's expense by employees of or contractors hired by Landlord, except to the extent Landlord gives its prior written consent to Tenant's hiring employees or contractors, which consent shall not be unreasonably withheld. Tenant shall promptly pay to Landlord or the Tenant's contractors, as the case may be, when due, the cost of all such work and of all repairs to the Building required by reason thereof. Tenant shall also pay to Landlord a percentage of the cost of such work (such percentage to be established on a uniform basis for the Building) sufficient to reimburse Landlord for all overhead, general conditions, fees and other costs and expenses arising from Landlord's involvement with such work. Upon completion of such work Tenant shall deliver to Landlord, if payment is made directly to contractors, evidence of payment, contractors' affidavits and full and final waivers of all liens for labor, services or materials. Tenant shall defend and hold Landlord and the Land and Building harmless from all costs, damages, liens and expenses related to such work. All work done by Tenant or its contractors pursuant to Paragraphs 9 or 10 shall be done in a first-class workmanlike manner using only good grades of materials and shall comply with all insurance requirements and all applicable laws and ordinances and rules and regulations of governmental departments or agencies.

All alterations, improvements and additions to the Premises, whether temporary or permanent in character, made or paid for by Landlord or Tenant shall without compensation to Tenant become Landlord's property at the termination of this Lease by lapse of time or otherwise and shall, unless Landlord requests their removal (in which case Tenant shall remove the same as provided in Paragraph 18), be relinquished to Landlord in good condition, ordinary wear and damage by insured casualty excepted.

11. Covenant Against Liens.   Tenant has no authority or power to cause or permit any lien or encumbrance of any kind whatsoever, whether created by act of Tenant, operation of law or otherwise, to attach to or be placed upon Landlord's title or interest in the Land, Building or Premises, and any and all liens and encumbrances created by Tenant shall attach to Tenant's interest only. Without modifying Tenant's right to arrange leasehold financing as provided for in Paragraph 17 hereof, Tenant covenants and agrees not to suffer or permit any lien of mechanics or materialmen or others to be placed against the Land, Building or the Premises with respect to work or services claimed to have been performed for or materials claimed to have been furnished to Tenant or the Premises, and, in case of any such lien attaching, Tenant covenants and agrees to either bond over the same, the amount of such bond and the issuer thereof to be satisfactory to Landlord, or to cause it to be immediately released and removed of record. In the event that such lien is not immediately bonded over or released or removed of record, Landlord, at its sole option, may take all action necessary to release and remove such lien (without any duty to investigate the validity thereof) and Tenant shall promptly upon notice remiburse Landlord for all sums, costs and expenses (including reasonable attorneys' fees) incurred by Landlord in connection with such lien.

12. Insurance.
A. *Risk of Loss.*   By this section, Landlord and Tenant intend that the risk of loss or damage to the Premises, the Building and Tenant's furniture, fixtures, equipment, improvements and betterments be borne by responsible insurance carriers to the extent herein provided, and Landlord and Tenant hereby agree to look solely to, and to seek recovery only from, the insurance carriers covering such losses in the event of a loss of a type described below to the extent that such coverage is agreed to be provided hereunder. For this purpose, any applicable deductible amount shall be treated as though it were recoverable under such policies. Landlord and Tenant agree that applicable portions of all monies collected from such insurance shall be used toward the full compliance of the obligations of Landlord and Tenant under this Lease in connection with damage resulting from fire or other casualty, subject to reasonable requirements imposed by Landlord's mortgagee or mortgagees, which at the time hold liens on the

Land and/or the Building, with respect to restoration of the Building. Landlord and Tenant each agrees to have all fire and extended coverage and other property damage insurance which it carries with respect to the Building or Premises or to the Property located in the Premises endorsed with a clause which reads substantially as follows: "This insurance shall not be invalidated should the insured waive in writing prior to a loss any or all rights of recovery against any party for loss occurring to the property described herein." Landlord and Tenant each hereby waives all claims for recovery from the other for any loss or damage to the Building or Premises or to the contents thereof which is insured hereunder.

B. *Coverage.* Tenant shall carry insurance with respect to the Premises during the entire Term insuring Tenant and Landlord (as their interest may appear) with terms, coverages and in companies satisfactory to Landlord, and with such increases in limits as Landlord may from time to time request, but initially Tenant shall maintain the following coverages in the following amounts:

(i)   In case of personal injury to or death of any person or persons, not less than One Million ($1,000,000.00) Dollars for each occurrence of injury or death to a person and Three Million ($3,000,000.00) Dollars for each coverage involving personal injury or death to persons, and, in case of property damage, not less than One Million ($1,000,000.00) Dollars for any one occurrence; and

(ii)   Physical damage insurance on all office furniture, drapes, fixtures, office equipment, merchandise and all other items of Tenant's property on the Premises. Said coverage shall be written on an "all risks" of physical loss or damage basis, in an amount not less than the full (100%) replacement cost value of such items and on a form or in amounts not subject to any coinsurance penalty. It is understood that a portion of such insurance may provide for deductibles under such policies in amounts reasonably deemed appropriate by Tenant.

Tenant shall, prior to the commencement of the Term, furnish to Landlord certificates evidencing such coverage, including renewals thereof, which certificates shall state that such insurance coverage may not be changed or cancelled without at least ten (10) days' prior written notice to Landlord and Tenant and shall name Landlord as an additional insured.

Additionally, Landlord shall purchase and maintain, at Tenant's sole cost and expense, physical damage insurance on the additions, improvements and alterations to the Premises considered real property. Such insurance shall cover Landlord and Tenant and shall be written on an "all risks" of physical loss or damage basis, in an amount not less than the full (100%) replacement cost of such items reported to Landlord and updated periodically by Tenant, and on a form or in amounts not subject to coinsurance penalty. In the event the value of the insured items reported to Landlord by Tenant are not sufficient to satisfy the coinsurance provisions of the insurance policy or are not sufficient to replace the damaged property, Tenant shall bear such penalty or reimburse Landlord for any difference between amount collected from insurance and amount expended for repair or replacement of damaged property. It is understood that a portion of such insurance may provide for deductibles thereunder in amounts reasonably satisfactory to Landlord and Tenant. Tenant shall pay to Landlord the entire cost of such insurance and all renewals thereof within ten (10) days of receipt of a demand therefor from Landlord. Landlord and Tenant shall be named as named insureds on such policy. Landlord shall furnish Tenant with certificates of insurance evidencing such coverage, including renewals thereof.

Landlord shall purchase and maintain physical damage insurance on the Building. Such coverage shall be written on an "all risks" of physical loss or damage basis, in an amount not less than the full (100%) replacement cost value of the Building and on a form or in amounts not subject to any coinsurance penalty. It is understood that a portion of such insurance may be subject to deductibles in amounts deemed reasonable by Landlord. All proceeds of all loss adjustments shall be payable directly and solely to Landlord, its assigns or mortgagees and Tenant shall have no interest therein or rights with respect thereto. Landlord shall furnish Tenant certificates evidencing such coverage, including renewals thereof.

Landlord shall also keep in full force and effect insurance with respect to accidents occurring on or about the common areas of the Building affording coverage in the case of personal injury to or death of any person or persons, not less than One Million ($1,000,000.00) Dollars for each occurrence of injury or death to one person and Three Million ($3,000,000.00) Dollars for each coverage involving personal injury or death to more than one person and affording coverage of not less than One Million ($1,000,000.00) Dollars in the case of property damage in any one occurrence.

C. *Avoid Action Increasing Rates.*   Tenant shall, in the use and maintenance of the Premises, comply with all applicable laws and ordinances, all orders and decrees of court and all requirements of other governmental or quasi-governmental authorities, and shall not, directly or indirectly, make any use of the Premises which may thereby be prohibited or be dangerous to person or property or which may jeopardize any insurance coverage or may increase the cost of insurance or require additional insurance coverage. If by reason of failure of Tenant to comply with the provisions of this Paragraph 12C, any insurance coverage is jeopardized or insurance premiums are increased, Landlord shall have the option either to terminate this Lease or to require Tenant to make immediate payment of the increased insurance premium. Notwithstanding the foregoing or any Rules or Regulations of the Building to the contrary, Tenant is hereby granted the privilege to operate a printing-duplicating department and a cafeteria for partners, employees and business invitees and subtenants.

13. Fire or Casualty. Paragraph 9 hereof notwithstanding, if the Premises or the Building (including machinery or equipment used in its operation) shall be damaged by fire or other casualty insured against hereunder then, subject to the provisions of the next succeeding paragraph, Landlord shall repair and restore the same with reasonable promptness, subject to reasonable delays for insurance adjustments and delays caused by matters beyond Landlord's reasonable control; provided that to the extent the cost of repairing or restoring the Premises exceeds the insurance proceeds available therefor, such expenses shall be at the sole cost and expense of Tenant. According to such customary procedures for the disbursement of insurance proceeds as Tenant's Mortgagee may reasonable require, all insurance proceeds under the policies of insurance covering such loss to the Premises shall be made available to Landlord for the restoration thereof. Landlord shall have no liability to Tenant, and Tenant shall not be entitled to terminate this Lease, by virtue of any delays in completion of such repairs and restoration. Base Rent and Additional Rent, however, shall abate on those portions of the Premises as are, from time to time, untenantable as a result of such damage. If Landlord fails to repair or restore with reasonable promptness, subject to reasonable delays as aforesaid, Tenant may use the proceeds of Tenant's insurance to repair and restore the Premises.

Notwithstanding the foregoing, if at any time during the last five (5) years of the current Term hereof any such damage renders all or a substantial portion of the Premises or Building untenantable, then Landlord shall have the right to terminate this Lease by so notifying Tenant, in writing, not later than one hundred twenty (120) days after the occurrence of such event, such termination to take effect as of the date specified in said notice (with appropriate prorations of Base Rent being made for Tenant's possession of any portion of the Premises rendered untenantable subsequent to the date of such damage); provided, however, that except in the case of such damage occurring in the last Renewal Term hereof, Landlord will nevertheless repair and restore the Building and Premises even if the damage thereto occurs in the last five (5) years of the Term if Tenant notifies Landlord, in writing (such notice to be given within thirty [30] days of receipt of the aforesaid notice from Landlord), that it elects to extend the Term for the next Renewal Term hereunder.

14. Waiver of Claims—Indemnification. To the extent not prohibited by law, Landlord and its partners, agents, servants and employees shall not be liable for any damage either to person or property or resulting from the loss of use thereof sustained by Tenant or by other persons claiming by, through or under Tenant due to the Building, or any part thereof, or any appurtenances thereto becoming out of repair, or due to the happening of any accident or event in or about the Building or Premises, or due to any act or neglect of any tenant or occupant of the Building or of any other person; provided that the foregoing provision shall not deny Tenant of the benefit of any insurance carried by Landlord covering any of the foregoing damages or claims arising on account of accidents or events occurring in or about the common areas of the

Building (but specifically excluding the Premises and any other space leased to tenants). This provision shall apply particularly, but not exclusively, to damage caused by gas, electricity, snow, frost, steam, sewage, sewer gas or odors, fire, water or by the bursting or leaking of pipes, faucets, sprinklers, plumbing fixtures and windows, and shall apply without distinction as to the person whose act or neglect was responsible for damage and whether the damage was due to any of the causes specifically enumerated above or to some other cause of any entirely different kind. The foregoing is intended to be a release of the liability of Landlord and its partners and is not intended to be, nor shall it be construed as, an indemnification by Tenant for the third party claims described above except as otherwise expressly included herein. At all times after Tenant first occupies the Premises for the purpose of installing therein Tenant's office equipment, furniture, fixtures and furnishings, Tenant further agrees that all personal property upon the Premises, or upon loading docks, receiving and holding areas, or freight elevators of the Building, shall be at the risk of Tenant only, and that Landlord shall not be liable for any loss or damage thereto or theft thereof. Without limitation of the any other provisions thereof, Tenant agrees to defend, protect, indemnify and save harmless Landlord from and against all liability to Landlord and third parties (whether damage to person or property) arising out of the acts of Tenant and its servants, agents, employees, contractors, suppliers, workmen and invitees or arising out of any accident or event occurring in or about the Premises.

15. Non-Waiver. No waiver of any provision of this Lease shall be implied by any failure of Landlord to enforce any remedy on account of the violation of such provision, even if such violation be continued or repeated subsequently, and no express waiver shall affect any provision other than the one specified in such waiver and that one only for the time and in the manner specifically stated. No receipt of monies by Landlord from Tenant after the termination of this Lease shall in any way alter the length of the Term or of Tenant's right of possession hereunder or after the giving of any notice shall reinstate, continue or extend the Term or affect any notice given Tenant prior to the receipt of such monies, it being agreed that after the service of notice or the commencement of a suit or after final judgment for possession of the Premises, Landlord may receive and collect any rent due, and the payment of said rent shall not waive or affect said notice, suit or judgment.

16. Condemnation. If the Land or the Building or any portion thereof (other than any insignificant portion thereof) shall be taken or condemned by any competent authority for any public or quasi-public use or purpose (a "taking"), or if the configuration of any street adjacent to the Building is changed by any competent authority and such taking or change in configuration makes it necessary or desirable, in Landlord's reasonable judgment, to remodel in any material respect or reconstruct the Building, then Landlord shall have the right, exercisable at its sole discretion, to cancel this Lease, at the same time as Landlord cancels all other leases in the Building or Tenant shall have the right, exercisable at its sole discretion to cancel this Lease, upon not less than thirty (30) days' notice prior to the date of cancellation designated in the notice, which notice, to be effective, must be given within ninety (90) days of any such taking or change in configuration. No money or other consideration shall be payable by Landlord to Tenant for the right of cancellation and, except as hereinafter provided, Tenant shall have no right to share in the condemnation award or in any judgment for damages caused by such taking or change in configuration; provided that Tenant shall have the right to pursue its own claim as to the value of its leasehold improvements or to pursue its own claim by joining with Landlord, if procedurally required, in pursuing the same (provided that such joinder shall not create any right of Landlord in and to all or any portion of such claim) and obtaining an apportionment of damages for the value of its leasehold improvements only.

17. *Assignment and Subletting.*

A.   Tenant shall have the right to sublet a portion or portions of the Premises to subtenants of quality, reasonably approved by Landlord, provided that Tenant shall give Landlord written notice of any such subletting at least ninety (90) days prior to the date on which any such subtenant is to take possession of the portion of the Premises to be sublet (which notice shall in any event disclose the name of the proposed subtenant, the portion of the Premises to be sublet and the rent to be paid therefor), Tenant shall remain primarily liable hereunder and Tenant shall continue to occupy, for its own use, at least one hundred thousand (100,000) square feet of Rentable Area. In such event Landlord shall be entitled to receive ninety (90%) percent of any excess (the "Excess Rents") of the Rent and additional rent (that is payments for Taxes and Operating Expenses) paid by such subtenant over the Rent (as the same may be adjusted by the Adjustments) and Additional Rent paid by Tenant. Tenant shall, however, be entitled to receive a separate reasonable charge for leasing furniture to subtenants. In the event that Tenant sublets the Premises in accordance with the foregoing, Tenant shall furnish Landlord with a sworn certification, setting forth in detail the computation of Excess Rents and Landlord, or its representatives, shall have access to the books, records and papers of Tenant in relation thereto, and the right to make copies thereof.

B.   Tenant shall have the right to finance all or a major portion of its costs in connection with the improvements to be made to the Initial Premises and to grant a leasehold mortgage on its interest hereunder in connection therewith provided that Landlord is furnished with prior written notice of Tenant's intention to secure such financing and true and complete copies of all documents executed in connection therewith and provided further that such instruments make all proceeds of insurance available to Tenant and Landlord for rebuilding as provided herein and give Landlord the right to cure any default by the Tenant thereunder.

C.   Except as otherwise provided above, Tenant shall not, without the prior written consent of Landlord, (w) assign, convey or mortgage this Lease or any interest hereunder, (x) suffer to occur or permit to exist any assignment of this Lease, or any lien upon Tenant's interest, involuntarily or by operation of law, (y) sublet the Premises or any part thereof, or (z) permit the use of the Premises by any parties other than Tenant and its employees. Except as hereinabove provided, any such action on the part of Tenant shall be void and of no effect. Landlord's consent to any assignment, subletting or transfer or Landlord's election to accept any assignee, subtenant or transferee as the Tenant hereunder and to collect rent from such assignee, subtenant or transferee shall not release Tenant or any subsequent Tenant from any covenant or obligation under this Lease. Landlord's consent to any assignment, subletting or transfer shall not constitute a waiver of Landlord's right to withhold its consent to any future assignment, subletting or transfer.

Except for subleases permitted under Paragraph A above, in addition to withholding its consent, Landlord shall have the additional right to terminate this Lease as to that portion of the Premises which Tenant seeks to assign or sublet, whether by requesting Landlord's consent thereto or otherwise. Landlord may exercise such right to terminate by giving written notice to Tenant at any time prior to Landlord's written consent to such assignment or sublease. In the event that Landlord exercises such right to terminate, Landlord shall be entitled to recover possession of such portion of the Premises on the latter of (A) the proposed date for possession by such assignee or subtenant or (B) ninety (90) days after the date of Landlord's notice of termination to Tenant.

18. *Surrender of Possession.*   Upon the expiration of the Term or upon the termination of Tenant's right of possession, whether by lapse of time or otherwise, at the option of Landlord as herein provided, Tenant shall forthwith surrender the Premises to Landlord in the order, repair and condition required to be maintained by Tenant hereunder. Any interest of Tenant in the alterations, improvements and additions to the Premises made or paid for by Landlord or Tenant shall, without compensation to Tenant, except as hereinafter provided, become Landlord's property at the termination of this Lease by lapse of time or otherwise and such alterations, improvements and additions shall be relinquished to Landlord in the condition, order and repair required to be maintained by Tenant hereunder. Prior to the termination of the Term or of Tenant's right of possession, Tenant shall remove office furniture, trade fixtures, office equipment, custom cabinetry and paneling and all other items of Tenant's property on the Premises. Tenant shall pay to Landlord upon demand the cost of repairing any damage to the Premises and to the Building caused by any such removal. If Tenant shall fail or refuse to remove any such property from the Premises, Tenant shall be conclusively presumed to have abandoned the same, and title thereto shall thereupon pass to Landlord without any cost either by set-off, credit, allowance or otherwise, and Landlord may at its option accept the title to such property or at Tenant's expense may (i) remove the same or any part thereof in any manner that Landlord shall choose, (ii) repair any damage to the Premises caused by such removal and (iii) store, destroy or otherwise dispose of the same without incurring liability to Tenant or any other person.

At the termination of this Lease solely on account of lapse of time (that is, at the stated expiration of the Term) and provided Tenant, immediately prior to such termination is occupying for its own use at least one hundred thousand (100,000) square feet of Rentable Area in the Building, Landlord shall pay to Tenant the following amounts:

Upon Expiration of Lease at End of Lease Year	*Amount to be Paid by Landlord, its Successors and Assigns*
15	
20	
25	
30	
35	
40	
45	
50	

19.   Holding Over.   Tenant shall pay to Landlord an amount as Rent (and without any Adjustments whatsoever) equal to two hundred (200%) percent of one-twelfth (1/12) of the Base Rent and two hundred (200%) percent of one-twelfth (1/12) of the Additional Rent required to be paid by Tenant during the previous Lease Year (without regard to any Adjustments taken in such Lease Year) as herein provided for each month or portion thereof for which Tenant shall retain possession of the Premises, or any part thereof, after the termination of the Term or of Tenant's right of possession, whether by lapse of time or otherwise, and also shall pay all damages sustained by Landlord, whether direct or consequential, on account thereof. At the option of Landlord, expressed in a written notice to Tenant and not otherwise, such holding over shall constitute a renewal of this Lease for a period of one (1) year at such Base Rent and Additional Rent as would be applicable for such year, but without any Adjustments to Base Rent whatsoever. The provisions of this Paragraph 19 shall not be deemed to limit or constitute a waiver of any other rights or remedies of Landlord provided herein or at law. If Landlord shall fail to make the payment required by Paragraph 18 hereof and Tenant shall retain possession of the Premises, or any portion thereof, after the termination of the Term, then Tenant shall pay to Landlord monthly an amount as rent equal to one hundred (100%) percent of one-twelfth (1/12) of the Rent and Additional Rent required to be paid by Tenant during the previous lease year (as the same had been adjusted by any Adjustments which Tenant was entitled to in such Lease Year) and shall continue to pay such rent until Landlord shall have made the payment required by Paragraph 18.

20.   Estoppel Certificate.   Each of Landlord and Tenant agrees that, from time to time upon not less than ten (10) days' prior request from the other, it will deliver to the other a statement in writing certifying (i) that this Lease is unmodified and in full force and effect (or if there have been modifications, that the Lease as modified is in full force and effect); (ii) the dates to which Rent and other charges have been paid; (iii) the amount of any Adjustments which Tenant is then entitled to take and the amount of any Deferred Adjustments; (iv) that, to the best of such party's knowledge, the other party is not in default under any provision of this Lease, or, if in default, the nature thereof in detail, (v) the expiration date of the Lease, (vi) whether any option for Additional Space has been exercised and whether any such option has been forfeited, and (vii) such further matters as such other party may reasonably request, it being intended that any such statement may be relied upon by any mortgagees or prospective mortgagees of the Building, or of Tenant's Premises, any prospective assignee of any mortgagee or any prospective purchaser of the Building or any permitted subtenant of Tenant.

21. Subordination.   Except as hereinafter provided, this Lease is intended to be senior and superior to any leases of the Land and to the lien of any mortgages on the Building and the Land. Provided that Tenant receives Non-Disturbance Agreements, in form and substance reasonably satisfactory to Tenant, from any mortgagee or ground lessor who desires Tenant to subordinate to a mortgage (or trust deed) or ground lease providing that so long as Tenant is not in default hereunder, no default in the performance by Landlord of its obligations under the mortgage (or trust deed) held by such mortgagee or under the ground lease, as the case may be, nor any foreclosure thereof or any exercise of rights thereunder, shall extinguish this Lease or adversely affect the rights of Tenant hereunder, including its right to Adjustments; Tenant agrees that this shall then be subject and subordinate to such mortgage (or trust) or ground lease and to all renewals, extensions, modifications, consolidations and replacements of any of the foregoing and to all made or hereafter to be made upon the security thereof. Tenant covenants and agrees that in the event any proceedings are brought for the foreclosure or other enforcement of any such mortgage (or trust deeds, to attorn, without any deductions or set-offs whatsoever (except for any Adjustments to which Tenant is then entitled) on account of defaults by the Landlord occurring prior to the conclusion of such foreclosure or other enforcement proceedings, to the purchaser upon any such foreclosure sale if so requested to do so by such purchaser and to recognize such purchaser as the lessor under this Lease. Tenant shall at Landlord's request execute such further instruments or assurances as Landlord may reasonably deem necessary to evidence or confirm the subordination or superiority of this Lease to any such mortgages (or trust deeds) or ground leases as hereinabove provided.

22. Certain Rights Reserved by Landlord.   Landlord shall have the following rights, each of which Landlord may exercise without notice to Tenant and without liability to Tenant for damage or injury to property, person or business on account of the exercise thereof, and the exercise of any such rights shall not be deemed to constitute an eviction or disturbance of Tenant's use or possession of the Premises and shall not give rise to any claim for set-off or abatement of rent or any other claim provided that Landlord agrees that in the exercise of such rights it shall not do or cause to be done anything which is, in any material respect, inconsistent with the operation of the Building as a first-class office building:

(i)   To change the Building's street address, if required by the U.S. Postal Service;

(ii)   To install, affix and maintain any and all signs on the exterior and on the interior of the Building; provided that such signs will comply with the sign criteria, if any, for the Building from time to time established by Landlord;

(iii)   To decorate or to make repairs, alterations, additions or improvements, whether structural or otherwise, in and about the Building, or any part thereof, and for such purposes to enter upon the Premises, and during the continuance of any of said work, to close temporarily doors, entryways, public space and corridors in the Building and to interrupt or temporarily suspend services or use of facilities, all without affecting any of Tenant's obligations hereunder, so long as the Premises are reasonably accessible and usable;

(iv)   To furnish door keys for the entry door(s) in the Premises at the commencement of the Lease and to retain at all times, and to use in appropriate instances, keys to all doors within and into the Premises. Tenant agrees to purchase only from Landlord (at Landlord's cost) or Landlord's designee additional duplicate keys as required, to change no locks, and not to affix locks on doors without the prior written consent of the Landlord. Notwithstanding the provisions for Landlord's access to Premises, Tenant relieves and releases the Landlord of all responsibility arising out of theft, robbery and pilferage. Upon the expiration of the Term or otherwise upon Tenant's right to possession, Tenant shall return all keys to Landlord and shall disclose to Landlord the combination of any safes, cabinets or vaults left in the Premises;

(v)   To designate and approve all window coverings used in the Building;

(vi)   To approve the weight, size and location of safes, vaults and other heavy equipment and articles in and about the Premises and Building so as not to exceed the live load per square foot designated by the structural engineers for the Building, and to require all such items and furniture and similar items to be moved into or out of the Building and Premises only at such times and in such manner as Landlord shall direct in writing. Tenant shall not install or operate machinery or any mechanical devices of a nature not directly related to Tenant's ordinary use of the Premises without the prior written consent of Landlord. Tenant's movements of property into or out of the Building or Premises and within the Building are entirely at the risk and responsibility of Tenant, and Landlord reserves the right to require permits before allowing any property to be moved into or out of the Building or Premises;

(vii)   To from time to time establish uniform controls for all tenants in the Building for the purpose of regulating all property and packages, both personal and otherwise, to be moved into or out of the Building and Premises and all persons using the Building after normal office hours;

(viii)   To regulate delivery and service of supplies in order to insure the cleanliness and security of the Premises and to avoid congestion of the loading docks, receiving areas and freight elevators;

(ix)   To show the Premises to prospective tenants at reasonable hours during the last eighteen (18) months of the Term and, if vacated or abandoned, to show the Premises at any time and to prepare the Premises for re-occupancy;

(x)   To erect, use and maintain pipes, ducts, wiring and conduits, and appurtenances thereto, in and through the walls and floors within the Premises at reasonable locations; provided that Landlord agrees to use reasonable efforts to perform such work in a manner which will minimize the interference with the business being conducted by Tenant within the Premises;

(xi)   To enter the Premises at reasonable times during business hours or after business hours upon reasonable prior notice to Tenant to inspect the Premises; it being understood that Tenant may elect to have a representative of Tenant present at such inspection to protect against the disclosure of confidential materials kept within the Premises; and

(xii)   To grant to any person or to reserve unto itself the exclusive right to conduct any business or render any service in the Building. If Landlord elects to make available to tenants in the Building any service or supplies in connection with the construction, operation or maintenance of the Building, including, without limitation, in connection with Janitorial Services, or arranges a master contract therefor, Tenant agrees to obtain its requirements, if any, therefor from Landlord or under any such contract, provided that the charges therefor are reasonable.

23.   Rules and Regulations.   Tenant agrees to observe the rules and regulations (as the same may from time to time be amended by Landlord) for the use, signs, occupancy and hours of operation of the Building attached hereto as Exhibit F and made a part hereof, which rules and regulations Landlord agrees will be uniformly applicable to all tenants in the Building. Landlord shall have the right from time to time to prescribe additional rules and regulations which, in its judgment, may be desirable for the use, signs, occupancy, entry, operation and management of the Premises and Building in a manner equivalent to other first-class office buildings in Philadelphia, each of which rules and regulations and any amendments thereto shall become a part of this Lease without any further action of the parties hereto and shall be uniformly applied to all Building tenants. Tenant shall comply with all such rules and regulations; provided, however, that such rules and regulations shall not substantially diminish any right or privilege herein expressly granted to Tenant.

24. Default; Landlord's Remedies. If (i) default shall be made in the payment of the Rent or any installment thereof or in the payment of any other sum required to be paid by Tenant under this Lease or under the terms of any other agreement between Landlord and Tenant and such default shall continue for five (5) days in the case of payment of Base Rent or ten (10) days in the case of any other payment hereunder after written notice of such default is delivered to Tenant, or (ii) default shall be made in the observance or performance of any of the other covenants or conditions in this Lease which Tenant is required to observe and perform and such default shall continue for thirty (30) days after written notice thereof is delivered to Tenant or if such default is of a nature that it cannot, with due diligence, be corrected within said thirty (30) day period, and if Tenant shall fail to commence to cure such default within said thirty (30) day period and thereafter diligently and continuously do so and in any event shall fail to cure said default within ninety (90) days after such notice, or, (iii) a default involving a hazardous condition shall occur and is not cured by Tenant immediately upon notice (oral or written) to Tenant or (iv) the interest of Tenant in this Lease shall be levied on under execution or other legal process, or (v) any voluntary petition in bankruptcy or for corporate reorganization or any similar relief shall be filed by Tenant, or (vi) any involuntary petition in bankruptcy shall be filed against Tenant under any federal or state bankruptcy or insolvency act and shall not have been dismissed within thirty (30) days from the filing thereof, or (vii) a receiver shall be appointed for Tenant or any of the property of Tenant by any court and such receiver shall not have been dismissed within thirty (30) days from the date of his appointment, or (viii) Tenant shall make an assignment for the benefit of creditors, or shall admit in writing its inability to meet Tenant's debts as they mature, or (ix) during the Initial Term, Tenant shall abandon or vacate more than one hundred thousand (100,000) square feet of Rentable Area in the Premises for a period in excess of thirty (30) days, then Landlord may treat the occurrence of any one or more of the foregoing events as an Event of Default under and breach of this Lease, and thereupon at its option may, with or without notice or demand of any kind to Tenant or any other person, have any one or more of the following described remedies in addition to all other rights and remedies provided at law or in equity or elsewhere herein:

(i)   Landlord may terminate this Lease and the Term created hereby in which event Landlord may forthwith repossess the Premises and be entitled to recover forthwith, in addition to any other sums or damages for which Tenant may be liable to Landlord, as liquidated damages, a sum of money equal to the excess of the value of the Rent provided to be paid by Tenant (without Adjustments) for the balance of the Term over the fair market value of the Premises, after deduction of all anticipated expenses of reletting, for said period and any other sum of money and damages owed by Tenant to Landlord. Should the fair market rental value of the Premises for the balance of the Term exceed the value of the rent provided to be paid by Tenant for the balance of the Term, Landlord shall have no obligation to pay to Tenant the excess or any part thereof or to credit such excess or any part thereof against any other sums or damages for which Tenant may be liable to Landlord.

(ii)   Landlord may terminate Tenant's right of possession and may repossess the Premises by a forcible entry or by taking peaceful possession or otherwise, without terminating this Lease, in which event Landlord may, but shall be under no obligation to, relet the same or a portion thereof for the account of Tenant, for such rent and upon such terms as shall be satisfactory to Landlord. For the purpose of such reletting, Landlord is authorized to decorate, repair, remodel or alter the Premises or a portion thereof. If Landlord shall fail to relet the Premises, Tenant shall pay to Landlord as liquidated damages a sum equal to the amount of the Rent (without Adjustments) reserved in this Lease for the balance of the Term. If the Premises are relet and a sufficient sum shall not be realized from such reletting after paying all of the costs and expenses of all decoration, repairs, remodeling, alterations and additions and the expenses of such reletting and of the collection of the rent accruing therefrom to satisfy the Rent provided for in this Lease (without Adjustments), Tenant shall satisfy and pay the same upon demand therefor from time to time. Tenant shall not be entitled to any rents received by Landlord in excess of the Rent provided for in this Lease. Without limitation of any other right or remedy of Landlord hereunder, Tenant agrees that Landlord may file suit to recover any sums falling due under the terms of this Paragraph 24 from time to time and that no suit or recovery of any portion due Landlord hereunder shall be any defense to any subsequent action brought for any amount not theretofore reduced to judgment in favor of Landlord.

(iii)   If proceedings shall be commenced by Landlord to recover possession under the Acts of Assembly, either at the end of the Term or upon the occurrence of any Event of Default, Tenant expressly waives all rights to notice in excess of five (5) days required by any Act of Assembly, including the Act of December 14, 1863, the Act of April 3, 1830 and/or the Act of April 6, 1951, and agrees that in either or any such case five (5) days' notice shall be sufficient. Without limitation of the foregoing, the Tenant hereby waives any and all demands, notices of intention and notices of action or proceedings which may be required by law to be given or taken prior to any entry or re-entry by summary proceedings, ejectment or otherwise, by Landlord, except as hereinbefore expressly provided with respect to the five (5) days' notice and provided further that this shall not be construed as a waiver by Tenant of any other notices to which this Lease expressly provides Tenant is entitled.

Notwithstanding the foregoing, Landlord agrees that it shall give to any first mortgagee (provided it receives written notice of the address of such mortgagee) of Tenant's leasehold interest hereunder (provided Tenant has complied with Paragraph 17 hereof) a copy of any notice to Tenant of any default by Tenant hereunder and that such mortagee shall have the right, in the same time period granted to Tenant hereunder, to cure any default by Tenant, provided, however, that if such default is of a nature that it can only be cured by such mortgagee's taking possession of the Leased Premises, then, provided that (and for so long as) the mortgagee shall pay Base Rent, Additional Rent, including Tenant's proportionate share of Operating Expenses and Taxes and all other amounts due from Tenant to Landlord hereunder as and when the same are due and payable and shall commit to Lender to cure any other default promptly upon completing a foreclosure on Tenant's leasehold estate, and provided further that such mortgagee proceeds with diligence to foreclosure Tenant's leasehold estate, Landlord shall not terminate the Lease pending such foreclosure. At such time as such mortgagee or another purchaser shall purchase the Premises in any judicial sale or accept an absolute assignment of the Lease in lieu of foreclosure, such mortgagee or purchaser and Landlord shall enter into a new lease on the same terms and conditions as in this Lease contained except that the provisions of Paragraphs 1B, 2, 4B, 18 and 29 shall be deleted therefrom. Failure to give such notice shall not, as to Tenant, invalidate the effect of any such notice to Tenant.

25.   Expenses of Enforcement.   The Tenant shall pay, upon demand, all Landlord's costs, charges and expenses, including the fees and out-of-pocket expenses of counsel, agents and others retained by Landlord incurred in successfully enforcing the Tenant's obligations hereunder or incurred by the Landlord in any litigation, negotiation or transaction in which the Landlord, without the Landlord's fault, becomes involved or concerned on account of its being the Landlord under this Lease. The Landlord shall pay, upon demand, all Tenant's costs, charges and expenses, including the fees and out-of-pocket expenses of counsel, agents and others retained by Tenant incurred in successfully enforcing the Landlord's obligations hereunder or incurred by the Tenant in any litigation, negotiation or transaction in which the Tenant, without the Tenant's fault, becomes involved or concerned on account of its being the Tenant under this Lease.

26.   Covenant of Quiet Enjoyment.   Subject to the provisions of Paragraph 16 dealing with condemnation, the Landlord covenants that the Tenant, on paying the rent, charges for services and other payments herein reserved and on keeping, observing and performing all the other terms, covenants, conditions, provisions and agreements herein contained on the part of the

Tenant to be kept, observed and performed, shall, during the Term, peaceably and quietly have, hold and enjoy the Premises subject to the terms, covenants, conditions, provisions and agreements hereof. Landlord represents that it owns the Land in fee simple absolute, free and clear of all liens and encumbrances, except as listed on Exhibit A.

27. *Miscellaneous.*

A.   The Tenant represents that the Tenant has not dealt with any broker in connection with this Lease other than, the fees of which shall be paid by Tenant, and that insofar as the Tenant knows, no other broker negotiated this Lease or is entitled to any compensation or commission in connection therewith. Tenant agrees to indemnify, defend and hold Landlord and its beneficiaries, employees, agents, their officers and partners, harmless from and against any claims made by and by any other broker or finder for a commission or fee in connection with this Lease, provided that Landlord has not in fact retained such other broker or finder. Landlord agrees to indemnify, defend and hold Tenant and its beneficiaries, employees, agents and their officers and partners harmless from any claims made by any broker or finder (other than, the fees of which will be paid by Tenant) retained by Landlord.

B.   Provided that Tenant is not in default hereunder and at the time such services, allowances or reimbursements are required Tenant occupies not less than one hundred thousand (100,000) square feet of Rentable Area in the Building and provided further that at such time there remains not less than five (5) years in the Term of the Lease, Landlord will cause all painted walls within the Initial Premises or any Renewal Space to be repainted at the end of every five (5) year period after such space is first occupied by Tenant, such repainting to consist of a coat of paint on each painted wall in the Premises in a color similar to the existing one and in a paint compatible with that then on such walls and will give Tenant an allowance of Dollars per square foot of Rentable Area in such space for new carpet installation at the end of every ten (10) year period after such space is first occupied by Tenant, such allowance to be paid to Tenant upon receipt by Landlord of an invoice for the carpet to be installed. If Tenant, at its election, paints or installs carpeting in the applicable space at a time which is not more than two (2) years prior to the end of the applicable five (5) or ten (10) year period, respectively, Landlord will reimburse Tenant for the cost of so doing against delivery by Tenant of invoices and such other evidence of payment as Landlord may require provided that Landlord's obligation shall be limited as to repainting to the amount it would have cost Landlord to do same as hereinabove provided and as to carpeting to the amount of the allowance for carpeting which Landlord would be required to afford Tenant at the end of the applicable period and provided further that Landlord shall be satisfied that the conditions set forth in the first sentence above are and will be satisfied. Such reimbursement by Landlord shall be applied as a dollar-for-dollar credit against Landlord's obligation to repaint or give an allowance for carpeting at the end of the applicable period.

C.   Tenant will furnish to Landlord financial statements and information expressly required by this Lease as Landlord may from time to time request and in any event will furnish to Landlord, within ninety (90) days of the close of Tenant's fiscal year, year-end financial statements of Tenant, prepared by Tenant's firm of independent certified public accountants and certified by the Managing Partner of Tenant.

D.   All rights and remedies of Landlord under this Lease shall be cumulative and none shall exclude any other rights and remedies allowed by law.

E.   Except as stated to the contrary in Paragraph 4B(vi) of this Lease, all payments becoming due under this Lease from either Landlord or Tenant and remaining unpaid more than five (5) days after the date when due shall bear interest beginning the sixth (6th) day after such due date until paid at the rate of the greater of (i) ten (10%) percent per annum or (ii) two (2%) percent per annum above the prime rate of interest announced from time to time by The Bank of _____ (but in no event at a rate which is more than the highest rate which is at the time lawful in the State of Pennsylvania).

F.   The necessary grammatical changes required to make the provisions hereof apply either to corporations or partnerships or individuals, men or women, as the case may require, shall in all cases be assumed as though in each case fully expressed.

G.   Each of the provisions of this Lease shall extend to and shall, as the case may require, bind or inure to the benefit not only of the Landlord and of Tenant, but also of their respective successors and assigns, provided this clause shall not permit any assignment by Tenant contrary to the provisions of Paragraph 17 hereof and provided further that the rights and benefits granted to Tenant under Paragraphs 1B, 2, 4B, 18 and 29 hereof shall be and are personal to Tenant and shall not run for the benefit of any mortgagee, assignee, subtenant or other successor in interest of Tenant.

H.   All of the representations and obligations of Landlord are contained herein and in the Work Letter, and no modification, waiver or amendment of this Lease or of any of its conditions or provisions shall be binding upon the Landlord unless in writing signed by Landlord or by a duly authorized agent of Landlord empowered by a written authority signed by Landlord. This Lease supersedes that certain Letter of Intent dated between Landlord and Tenant.

I.   Submission of the form of the Lease for examination shall not bind Landlord in any manner, and no lease or obligations of the Landlord shall arise until this instrument is signed by both Landlord and Tenant and delivery is made to each.

J. No rights to any view or to light or air over any property, whether belonging to Landlord or any other person are granted to Tenant by this Lease; provided that Landlord will not after the Commencement Date, without Tenant's prior written consent, which consent shall not be unreasonably withheld, construct any improvements as part of the Project which will obstruct the view from the Premises.

K. No partner of Tenant shall be personally liable with respect to any obligation of Tenant to Landlord under this Lease. Landlord agrees to enforce the obligations of this Lease only against the partnership assets of the Tenant.

L. Tenant acknowledges that Landlord has the right to transfer its interest in the Land and Building and in this Lease, and Tenant agrees that in the event of any such transfer Landlord shall automatically be released from all liability under this Lease arising on account of events, circumstances or obligations first occurring or which are to be performed from and after the date of such transfer and Tenant agrees to look solely to such transferee for the performance of Landlord's obligations hereunder after the date of transfer. Tenant further acknowledges that Landlord may assign its interest in this Lease to a mortgage lender as additional security and agrees that such an assignment shall not release Landlord from its obligations hereunder and that, until such mortgagee shall obtain possession and control of the Building, Tenant shall continue to look solely to Landlord and Landlord shall remain liable for the performance of its obligations hereunder.

M. Nothing herein contained shall empower Tenant to do any act which can, shall or may encumber the title of Landlord.

N. Neither this Lease, nor any memorandum, affidavit or other writing with respect thereto, shall be recorded by Tenant or by anyone acting through, under or on behalf of Tenant, without the written consent and approval of Landlord and the recording thereof in violation of this provision shall make this Lease null and void at Landlord's election. If Tenant requests, Landlord and Tenant shall execute and record (at Tenant's expense) a memorandum of this Lease, in form and content satisfactory to Landlord.

O. The captions of Paragraphs and subparagraphs are for convenience only and shall not be deemed to limit, construe, affect or alter the meaning of such Paragraphs or subparagraphs.

P. Nothing contained in this Lease shall be deemed or construed by the parties hereto or by any third party to create the relationship of principal and agent, partnership, joint venturer or any association between Landlord and Tenant, it being expressly understood and agreed that neither the method of computation of Rent nor any act of the parties hereto shall be deemed to create any relationship between Landlord and Tenant other than the relationships of landlord and tenant.

Q. Landlord shall have the right to apply payments received from Tenant pursuant to this Lease to satisfy any obligations of Tenant hereunder, in such order and amounts, as Landlord, in its sole discretion, may elect unless Tenant shall specifically designate such payment as being in satisfaction of a particular obligation of Tenant hereunder.

R. Subject to the provisions of Paragraph U below, time is of the essence of this Lease and each of its provisions.

S. Interpretation of this Lease shall be governed by the law of the State in which the Premises is located.

T. If any term, provision, or condition contained in this Lease shall, to any extent, be invalid or unenforceable, the remainder of this Lease (or the application of such term, provision or condition to persons or circumstances other than those in respect of which it is invalid or unenforceable) shall not be affected thereby, and each and every other term, provision and condition of this Lease shall be valid and enforceable to the fullest extent possible permitted by law.

U. Except as hereinafter expressly provided, the performance by any party hereto of any of its obligations hereunder shall be excused or delayed by the number of days of any Force Majeure Delay or Delays occurring with respect to such performance. As used herein, Force Majeure Delays shall be deemed to mean and include delays caused by strikes, lockouts, inability to obtain materials and/or labor, unusually inclement weather, casualty, war, acts of God or any other causes (other than inability to obtain financing) beyond the control of the party whose performance is required hereunder. It is expressly understood that the timely payment of Rent, Additional Rent and any other sums required to be paid by Tenant hereunder shall in no event be excused on account of the occurrence of a Force Majeure Delay.

28. Notices. All notices to be given under this Lease shall be in writing and delivered personally or deposited in the United States mail, certified or registered mail with return receipt requested, postage prepaid, addressed as follows:

If to Landlord:

with a copy to:

or to such other person or such other address designated by notice sent by Landlord or Tenant.

If to Tenant prior to the time it is in possession of any portion of the Premises at:

and after occupancy of the Premises by Tenant, at the Premises.

Except as stated to the contrary in Paragraph 24 of this Lease, notice by mail shall be deemed to have been given when deposited in the United States mail as aforesaid.

IN WITNESS WHEREOF, the undersigned have caused this Lease to be executed by their duly authorized representatives as of the day and year first above written.

TENANT: LANDLORD:

LEASE FORM CONTAINING EXPANSION OPTIONS AND RIGHT OF FIRST REFUSAL TO OBTAIN ADDITIONAL SPACE IN BUILDING

The Building Lease Dated

ARTICLE I.

Reference Data

1.1 Subjects Referred To.   Each reference in this Lease to any of the following subjects shall be construed to incorporate the data stated for that subject in this Article:

LANDLORD:

LANDLORD'S CONSTRUCTION REPRESENTATIVE:

TENANT:

TENANT'S CONSTRUCTION REPRESENTATIVE:

TENANT'S SPACE:

RENTABLE FLOOR AREA OF TENANT'S SPACE:

TOTAL RENTABLE FLOOR AREA OF THE BUILDING:

INITIAL TERM:

OPTIONS TO EXTEND:

SCHEDULED TERM COMMENCEMENT DATE:

ANNUAL FIXED RENT:

PERMITTED USES:

PUBLIC LIABILITY INSURANCE:
  BODILY INJURY:
  PROPERTY DAMAGE:

1.2   Exhibits.   These are incorporated as a part of this Lease:

EXHIBIT A—Description of Lot
EXHIBIT B—Plans Showing Tenant's Space
EXHIBIT C—Tenant Plan Requirements
EXHIBIT D—Building Standard Tenant Improvements
EXHIBIT E—Landlord's Services
EXHIBIT F—Subordination Agreement.

1.3   Table of Articles and Sections

ARTICLE VI—CASUALTY AND TAKING   372

ARTICLE VII—DEFAULT   373

ARTICLE VIII—MISCELLANEOUS   375

ARTICLE IX—RIGHTS OF MORTGAGEE   378

ARTICLE II

Premises, Term and Rent

2.1   Landlord hereby leases to Tenant and Tenant hereby hires from Landlord Tenant's Space in the Building, excluding exterior faces of exterior walls, the common stairways and stairwells, elevators and elevator wells, fan rooms, electric and telephone closets, janitor closets, freight elevator vestibules, and pipes, ducts, conduits, wires and appurtenant fixtures serving exclusively or in common other parts of the Building, and if Tenant's Space includes less than the entire rentable area of any floor, excluding the common corridors, elevator lobby and toilets located on such floor. Tenant's Space with such exclusions is hereinafter referred to as "the Premises." The term "Building" means the building erected on the Lot by Landlord, and the term "Lot" means all, and also any part of, the land described in Exhibit A plus any additions thereto resulting from the change of any abutting street line. "Property" means the Building and Lot.

2.2   Tenant shall have, as appurtenant to the Premises, rights to use in common, subject to reasonable rules of general applicability to tenants of the Building from time to time made by Landlord of which Tenant is given notice: (a) the common lobbies, corridors, stairways, elevators and loading platform of the Building, and the pipes, ducts, conduits, wires and appurtenant meters and equipment serving the Premises in common with others, (b) common walkways and driveways necessary for access to the Building, and (c) if the Premises include less than the entire rentable floor area of any floor, the common toilets, corridors and elevator lobby of such floor.

2.3   Landlord reserves the right from time to time, without unreasonable interference with Tenant's use: (a) to install, use, maintain, repair, replace and relocate for service to the Premises and other parts of the Building, or either, pipes, ducts, conduits, wires and appurtenant fixtures, wherever located in the Premises or Building, and (b) to alter or relocate any other common facility, provided that substitutions are substantially equivalent or better. Installations, replacements and relocations referred to in clause (a) above shall be located so far as practicable in the central core area of the Building, above ceiling surfaces, below floor surfaces or within perimeter walls of the Premises.

2.4   Tenant shall have and hold the Premises for a period commencing on the earlier of (a) that date on which the Premises are ready for occupancy as in Section 3.2 provided, or (b) that date on which Tenant commences occupancy of any portion of the Premises for the Permitted Uses, and continuing for the Term unless sooner terminated as provided in Section 6.1 or Article VII.

Tenant is hereby given two separate options to extend the Initial Term of this Lease upon the terms, covenants, conditions and provisions contained in this Lease, except as otherwise expressly provided, for periods of five years each to follow consecutively upon the Initial Term, provided that, at the time each such option to extend is exercised, this Lease shall be in effect. Such options shall be exercisable by written notice from Tenant to Landlord given not less than one year prior to the expiration date of the Initial Term, or the expiration date of the first extension thereof, as the case may be. The word "Term" refers as of any particular time to the Initial Term and also to any extension thereof with respect to which Tenant has, as of that time, exercised its extension option set forth in this Section 2.4.

In the event Tenant and Landlord are unable to agree on the Annual Fixed Rent for any extension of the Initial Term, i.e., are unable to agree upon the rental rate for comparable office space in comparable Class A buildings in Philadelphia at the latest date Tenant could exercise the option to extend, the Annual Fixed Rent shall be determined as follows.

At any time on or after the commencement of the extension of the Initial Term, either party may give notice to the other in writing that it desires to determine the Annual Fixed Rent pursuant to this Section 2.4 and at that time shall designate in writing a person to act as its appraiser for the purposes of establishing the Annual Fixed Rent. The party giving notice is hereinafter referred to as the "first party" and the party receiving the notice is hereinafter referred to as the "second party." Within ten (10) days after receipt of the first party's notice, the second party shall designate in writing a person to act as the second appraiser. If the second party fails to designate an appraiser within such ten (10) day period, the determination of Annual Fixed Rent by the first party's appraiser shall be the Annual Fixed Rent. The two appraisers desig- nated by the first and second parties, respectively, shall meet promptly to determine the Annual Fixed Rent. If within thirty (30) days following the designation of the second party's appraiser, the appraisers are unable to agree upon the Annual Fixed Rent, the appraisers shall designate in writing within ten (10) days thereafter a third appraiser. If the appraisers fail to designate the third appraiser in a timely manner, the appraisers or either party shall request the President of the Philadelphia Chapter of the American Institute of Real Estate Appraisers or its successor organization to designate the third appraiser. Each appraiser designated shall be a member of the American Institute of Real Estate Appraisers or a successor body exercising similar functions, shall have at least ten (10) years active experience as a real estate appraiser in the appraisal of property similar to the Building and shall never have been an employee of either Landlord, Tenant or the respective parents, subsidiaries or affiliates. If within thirty (30) days following the designation of the third appraiser the appraisers are unable to agree on the Annual Fixed Rent, the determination of the Annual Fixed Rent by the third appraiser shall be conclusive. Each party shall be responsible for the fees and expenses of the appraiser it designates; the fees and expenses of the third appraiser shall be borne equally by the first and second parties. Until the Annual Fixed Rent is determined pursuant to this Section 2.4, Tenant shall pay Rent at the rental rate in effect immediately prior to the extension of the Term and the appropriate payment shall be made by Tenant to Landlord or Landlord to Tenant, as the case may be, after the

Annual Fixed Rent has been determined pursuant to this Section 2.4.

2.5 Tenant shall pay, without notice or demand, monthly installments of 1/12 of the Annual Fixed Rent (sometimes hereinafter referred to as "fixed rent") in advance for each full calendar month of the Term, and the corresponding fraction of said 1/12 for any fraction of a calendar month at the beginning or end of the Term. If prior to the end of the calendar year the schedule of electric utility rates (including any fuel rate adjustments) charged by the public utility company serving the Building shall have changed from such rates effective with respect to November, effective as of the date of such change and thereafter during the balance of the Term the Annual Fixed Rent shall be increased or decreased by $.0089 per square foot for each 1% of change in such rates; and such adjustments in rent shall be made monthly in arrears during the period prior to the end of the calendar year after notice from Landlord of the amount of the adjustment.

2.6 If with respect to any full calendar year or fraction of a calendar year falling within the Term the items listed in the statement referred to below in this Section 2.6 for a full calendar year exceed, or for any such fraction of a calendar year exceed the corresponding fraction of then, on or before the thirtieth day following receipt by Tenant of the certified statement referred to below in this Section 2.6, Tenant shall pay to Landlord, as Additional Rent, the proportion of such excess which Rentable Floor Area of Tenant's Space bears to Total Rentable Floor Area of the Building. Not later than 90 days after the items listed in the statement hereinafter referred to are determinable for the first such calendar year or fraction thereof and for each succeeding calendar year or fraction thereof during the Term, Landlord shall render Tenant a statement in reasonable detail certified by a representative of Landlord showing for the preceding year or fraction thereof, as the case may be: real estate taxes on the Building and Lot; expenses of any proceedings for abatement of taxes and assessments with respect to the first or any subsequent calendar year or fraction of a calendar year; and abatements and refunds of any such taxes and assessments.

The term "real estate taxes" shall mean all taxes and special assessments of every kind and nature assessed by any governmental authority on the Lot or the Building which Landlord shall become obligated to pay because of or in connection with the ownership, leasing and operation of the Lot or Building, subject to the following:

(i) the amount of special taxes or special assessments to be included shall be limited to the amount of the installment (plus any interest, other than penalty interest, payable thereon) of such special tax or special assessment required to be paid during the year in respect of which such taxes are being determined;

(ii) there shall be excluded from such taxes all income taxes, excess profit taxes, excise taxes, franchise taxes, estate, succession, inheritance and transfer taxes; provided, however, that if at any time during the Term the present system of ad valorem taxation of real property shall be changed so that in lieu of the whole or any part of the ad valorem tax on real property, there shall be assessed on Landlord a capital levy or other tax on the gross rents received with respect to the Lot or Building, or a federal, state, county, municipal, or other local income, franchise, excise or similar tax, assessment, levy or charge (distinct from any now in effect) measured by or based, in whole or in part, upon any such gross rents, then any and all of such taxes, assessments, levies or charges to the extent so measured or based, shall be deemed to be included within the term "real estate tax" but only to the extent that the same would be payable if the Lot and Building were the only property of Landlord; (iii) there shall be excluded from such taxes any Use and Occupancy Tax which Landlord may be required by law to collect from Tenant for payment to any governmental authority, which Tenant shall pay separately to Landlord upon demand as additional rent if and to the extent Landlord is required by law to pay such tax to any such governmental authority; and (iv) there shall be excluded from such taxes all real estate taxes allocable to (A) additional buildings hereafter constructed on the Lot, (b) increases to the size of the Building, and (c) improvements hereafter made to the Building other than those made (a) to the Premises, (b) to the common areas and facilities Tenant has the right to use pursuant to Section 2.2, or (c) to other tenant areas in the Building in preparation for initial occupancy by a tenant.

Upon the request of tenants in the Building occupying fifteen percent (15%) or more the total rentable floor area thereof, Landlord shall contest, by appropriate proceedings, the amount or validity in whole or in part, of real estate taxes assessed against the Lot and Building. The institution or pendency of such proceedings shall not be deemed to postpone or defer Tenant's obligation to pay additional rent under this Section 2.6.

Upon receipt by Landlord of any abatements, reductions or refunds on account of real estate taxes for which Tenant made a payment to Landlord pursuant to this Section 2.6, Landlord shall pay to Tenant the proportion of such abatement reduction or refund which Rentable Floor Area of Tenant's space bears to Total Rentable Floor Area of the Building.

2.7   If with respect to any calendar year falling within the Term or fraction of a Calendar Year falling within the Term at the end thereof, Landlord's Operating Expenses Allocable to the Premises as hereinafter defined for a full calendar year exceed Landlord's Operating Expenses Allocable to the Premises for the 1976 Calendar Year, or for any such fraction of a Calendar Year exceed the corresponding fraction of Landlord's Operating Expenses Allocable to the Premises for the 1976 Calendar Year, then, subject to the provisions of the last two paragraphs of this Section 2.7, Tenant shall pay to Landlord, as Additional Rent, the amount of such excess. Such payments shall be made at the times and in the manner hereinafter provided in this Section 2.7. Not later than 90 days after the end of the first such Calendar Year or fraction thereof ending December 31 and of each succeeding Calendar Year during the Term, Landlord shall render Tenant a statement in reasonable detail and according to usual accounting practices certified by a representative of Landlord, showing for the preceding Calendar Year or fraction thereof, as the case may be: the operating expenses for the Building and Lot excluding the items of expense referred to in Section 2.6 hereof and costs of special services rendered to tenants (including Tenant) for which a special charge is made, but including, without limitation: premiums for insurance carried with respect to the Property (including insurance against loss in case of fire or casualty of monthly installments of fixed rent and any Additional Rent which may be due under this Lease and other leases of space in the Building for not more than 12 months in the case of both Fixed Rent and Additional Rent and, if there be any first mortgage of the Property, including such insurance as may be required by the holder of such first mortgage); compensation and all fringe benefits, workmen's compensation insurance premiums and payroll taxes paid to, for or with respect to all persons up to and including the level of Building manager engaged in the operating, maintaining, or cleaning of the Building or Lot; steam, water, sewer, electric, gas, oil and telephone charges not separately chargeable to tenants; cost of building and cleaning supplies and equipment; cost of maintenance, cleaning and repairs (other than repairs not properly chargeable against income or reimbursed from contractors under guaranties); cost of snow removal and care of landscaping; payments under service contracts with independent contractors; management fees at reasonable rates consistent with the type of occupancy and the service rendered; and all other reasonable and necessary expenses paid in connection with the operation, cleaning and maintenance of the Building and Lot and properly chargeable against income and not as capital expenditures in accordance with generally accepted accounting principles. The phrase "Landlord's Operating Expenses Allocable to the Premises" means the same proportion of the operating expenses for the Building and Lot for the items covered by the foregoing statement as Rentable Floor Area of Tenant's Space bears to the Total Rentable Floor Area of the Building, except that in case of services which are not rendered to all areas on a comparable basis, the proportion allocable to the Premises shall be the same proportion which Rentable Floor Area of Tenant's Space to which such service is rendered bears to the total rentable floor area in the Building to which such service is so rendered.

Commencing with the first day of the first month following the delivery to Tenant of the statement referred to above with respect to the first full Calendar Year of the Term and on the first day of each month thereafter, subject to the provisions of the last two paragraphs of this Section 2.7, Tenant shall pay to Landlord, on account toward Tenant's share of increases in operating costs anticipated for the then current year, one-twelfth of the total amount which Tenant was required to pay to Landlord with respect to the preceding year as shown on the most recent annual statement of operating costs delivered to Tenant. The statements to be rendered to Tenant referred to above shall also show for the preceding year or fraction thereof, as the case may be, the amounts of operating costs already paid by Tenant as additional rent, and the amount of operating costs remaining due from, or overpaid by, Tenant for the year or other period covered by the statement. Within 30 days after the date of delivery of such statement Tenant shall pay to Landlord, or Landlord shall pay to Tenant, as the case may be, the balance of the amounts, if any, required to be paid pursuant to the above provisions of this Section 2.7, except that Landlord may, at its option, credit any amounts due from it to Tenant as above provided against any sums then due from Tenant to Landlord under this Lease.

Notwithstanding anything in this Section 2.7 to the contrary, Tenant shall not be required to pay on account of increases in Operating Expenses Allocable to the Premises (other than for increases in the cost of electricity, steam and water, which shall be governed by the preceding paragraphs of this Section 2.7) during the first sixty months of the Term, Additional Rent in excess of an aggregate for said five years of Tenant's obligations with respect to additional rent on account of increases in Operating Expenses Allocable to the Premises for the balance of the Term after said fifth Calendar Year shall be governed by the preceding paragraphs of this Section 2.7.

Notwithstanding anything in this Section 2.7 to the contrary, if the Building is not 95% occupied by tenants for the entire Calendar Year 1976, Landlord's Operating Expenses for the Calendar Year 1976 shall be Landlord's actual operating expenses as appropriately increased to the amount of operating expenses that Landlord would have incurred had the Building been 95% occupied by tenants for the entire Calendar Year 1976.

2.8 Landlord shall have the right from time to time to change the periods of accounting under Sections 2.6 and 2.7 above, or either of them, to any other annual period than a Calendar Year, and upon any such change, all items referred to in said Sections 2.6 and 2.7 shall be appropriately apportioned. In all statements rendered under Sections 2.6 and 2.7, amounts for periods partially within and partially without the accounting periods shall be appropriately apportioned, and any items which are not determinable at the time of a statement shall be included therein on the basis of Landlord's estimate and with respect thereto Landlord shall render promptly after determination a supplemental statement and appropriate adjustment shall be made according thereto. All statements shall be prepared on an accrual basis of accounting.

Landlord shall make available upon Tenant's request from time to time all of Landlord's books and records containing information in connection with the computation of the increase or decrease in Annual Fixed Rent pursuant to Section 2.5, the additional rent paid by Tenant for its share of increase in real estate taxes pursuant to Section 2.6, and the additional rent paid by Tenant for increases in Landlord's Operating Expenses allocable to the Premises pursuant to Section 2.7.

2.9 Except as otherwise specifically provided herein, any sum, amount, item or charge designated or considered as additional rent in this Lease shall be paid by Tenant to Landlord on the first day of the month following the date on which Landlord notifies Tenant of the amount payable, or on the tenth day after the giving of such notice, whichever shall be later. Any such notice shall specify in reasonable detail the basis of such Additional Rent. Fixed rent and

Additional Rent shall be paid by Tenant to Landlord without offset or deduction, except as otherwise specifically provided in this Lease.

2.10   Tenant shall have the right and options to include in the Premises (a) contiguous space comprising approximately 50% of the remainder of the 16th floor (and designated as "Five-Year Space" on Exhibit B) for a period commencing five years after the earlier of (i) September 1, 1976 and (ii) the commencement date of the last lease which when added to the space covered by prior leases, if any, covers all of such contiguous space, and continuing for the balance of the Term remaining hereunder; and (b) the balance of the space on the 16th floor not designated on Exhibit B pursuant to subclause (a) hereof, for a period commencing on the tenth anniversary of the commencement date of this Lease and continuing for the balance of the Term remaining hereunder. Provided the Lease is then in full force and effect, such options shall be exercisable by notice from Tenant to Landlord given (i) in the case of subclause (a), not later than one year prior to the end of the five year period referred to in said subclause (a) (notice of the beginning of which period shall be given by Landlord to Tenant); and (ii) in the case of subclause (b), not later than one year prior to the tenth anniversary of the commencement date of this Lease. If Tenant exercises any or all of said options, the fixed rent for such included space shall be the rental rate of comparable office space in comparable Class A buildings in at the latest date Tenant could exercise the respective option and the Annual Fixed Rent shall be increased accordingly, and all other terms of this Lease shall be applicable to such included space, including without limitation the provisions of Sections 2.6 and 2.7, except as set forth in the following sentence.

Such included space shall be delivered to Tenant unoccupied and in the same condition as it would be in for a tenant then executing a lease with Landlord for such office space, with the same allowance to Tenant for leasehold improvements as Landlord would allow another tenant then executing a lease with Landlord for such office space.

In the event Tenant and Landlord are unable to agree on the increase in the Annual Fixed Rent, i.e., are unable to agree upon the rate for comparable office space in comparable Class A buildings in at the latest date Tenant could exercise the respective option, the increase in the Annual Fixed Rent shall be determined as follows.

At any time after the exercise of the option, either party may give notice to the other in writing that it desires to determine the increase in the Annual Fixed Rent pursuant to this Section 2.10 and at that time shall designate in writing a person to act as its appraiser for the purposes of establishing the increase in the Annual Fixed Rent. The party giving notice is hereinafter referred to as the "first party" and the party receiving the notice is hereinafter referred to as the "second party." Within ten (10) days after receipt of the first party's notice, the second party shall designate in writing a person to act as the second appraiser. If the second party fails to designate an appraiser within such ten (10) day period, the determination of the increase in Annual Fixed Rent by the first party's appraiser shall be the increase in Annual Fixed Rent. The two appraisers designated by the first and second parties, respectively, shall meet promptly to determine the increase in the Annual Fixed Rent. If within thirty (30) days following the designation of the second party's appraiser, the appraisers are unable to agree upon the Annual Fixed Rent, the appraiser shall designate in writing within ten (10) days thereafter a third appraiser. If the appraisers fail to designate the third appraiser in a timely manner, the appraisers or either party shall request the President of the Chapter of the American Institute of Real Estate Appraisers or its successor organization to designate the third appraiser. Each appraiser designated shall be a member of the American Institute of Real Estate Appraisers or a successor body exercising similar functions, shall have at least ten (10) years' active experience as a real estate appraiser in the appraisal of property similar to the Building and shall never have been an employee of either Landlord, Tenant or any of their respective parents, subsidiaries or affiliates. If within thirty (30) days following the designation of the third appraiser the appraisers are unable to agree on the increase in the Annual Fixed Rent, the determination of the increase in the Annual Fixed Rent by the third appraiser shall be conclusive. Each party shall be responsible for the fees and expenses of the appraiser it designates; the fees and expenses of the third appraiser shall be borne equally by the first and second parties. Until the increase in Annual Fixed Rent is determined pursuant to this Section 2.10, Tenant shall pay fixed rent for the included space at the Annual Fixed Rental rate in effect with respect to Tenant's Space immediately prior to the inclusion of the additional space and the appropriate payment shall be made by Tenant to Landlord or Landlord to Tenant, as the case may be, after the increase in the Annual Fixed Rent has been determined pursuant to this Section 2.10.

2.11   Tenant shall have a right of first refusal with respect to any leasing by Landlord (which means the right to enter into a lease with Landlord) of the space covered by the option described in subclause (a) of Section 2.10 during the Post-Exercise Period (as hereinafter defined) related to such option and of the space covered by the option described in subclause (b) of Section 2.10 during the Post-Exercise Period related to such option, in each case on the same terms offered to third parties. The Post-Exercise Period with respect to each of subclauses (a) and (b) shall refer to the six-month period following the last date by which Tenant may give written notice of its exercise of the option pursuant to Section 2.10. During the period commencing with the 15th anniversary of the commencement of the Term and ending with the 16th anniversary thereof (hereinafter referred to as the "Fifteenth Lease Year"), Tenant shall have a right of first refusal with respect to any leasing by Landlord of space on the (if not already included in the Premises) floor, provided that this right of refusal shall relate to a maximum of square feet and shall terminate upon Tenant's exercise thereof with respect to an aggregate of square feet.

During said Post-Exercise Periods and Fifteenth Lease Year Landlord shall notify Tenant in writing of its intention to lease the applicable space together with an offer to Tenant to lease such space, and unless Landlord shall have received Tenant's written acceptance of the offer and the terms proposed within 10 days thereafter, Landlord may make the proposed lease to a third party on the proposed terms or terms not substantially more favorable to the third party. In the event that Tenant accepts Landlord's offer and the proposed terms, the parties shall enter into a new lease with respect to the space described in the offer on the proposed terms, but the parties agree that the casualty and default clauses in such new lease shall be the same as those clauses in this Lease. Tenant shall not be entitled to accept an offer by Landlord hereunder unless the principal purpose for which it intends to obtain the space being offered is for its own use and occupancy.

The foregoing right of first refusal is subject to the following:

1.   It shall not apply to any renewal or extension of an existing lease with any present tenant in the Building nor to a new lease with such tenant of the same space or the same space plus additional space in the Building.

2.   In the event Tenant declines to accept an offer under the preceding paragraph, Landlord's lease to a third party may contain an expansion option or right of first refusal (which shall have priority over Tenant's right of first refusal) whether or not an expansion option or right of first refusal was contained in the offer by Landlord to Tenant.

The foregoing rights of first refusal shall continue only so long as Tenant is the tenant under this Lease. Tenant's exercise of one right of first refusal shall not exhaust the other rights of first refusal set forth above. Tenant's failure to exercise a right of first refusal shall terminate that right of first refusal unless Landlord shall fail to enter into a lease with the proposed third party and shall thereafter offer the same space to the proposed third party or another party on terms more favorable to that party than the terms originally offered to Tenant, in which case Tenant shall have a right of first refusal with respect to such new offer by Landlord.

ARTICLE III

Construction

3.1   Tenant agrees to deliver to Landlord no later than sufficient plans and information prepared at Tenant's expense to enable Landlord to determine the cost of improvements desired by Tenant in the Premises (herein called Pricing Plans) and no later than a detailed floor plan layout together with working drawings and written instructions all prepared at Tenant's expense (herein called Tenant's Plans) containing at least the information detailed in Exhibit C and reflecting the partitions and improvements desired by Tenant in the Premises. Tenant shall reimburse Landlord, as additional rent, for all costs of construction work and material and for engineering services furnished in completing the Premises to the extent the cost thereof exceeds the cost of

Building Standard Tenant Improvements set forth in Exhibit D and the cost of engineering services appropriate to such Building Standard Tenant Improvements, said excess cost to be hereinafter referred to as "Tenant Plan Excess Costs." During said construction work Landlord may, on or about the first day of each month, deliver to Tenant a statement showing that proportion of Tenant Plan Excess Costs allocable to the previous month's work. Tenant shall pay to Landlord as additional rent 90% of the amount specified in each such statement within ten days after receipt of such statement. Final payment by Tenant to Landlord shall be made upon the later of the date the Premises are deemed ready for occupancy pursuant to Section 3.2, or 10 days after receipt of a final statement delivered to Tenant by Landlord specifying the amount of final payment. Such final payment shall be deemed to be Additional Rent under this Lease.

Time is of the essence in connection with delivery of Pricing Plans and Tenant's Plans to Landlord.

3.2   Landlord agrees to use due diligence to complete the work described in Exhibit D and Tenant's Plans on or before the Scheduled Term Commencement Date. Landlord shall not be required to install any improvements which are not in conformity with the plans and specifications for the Building or which are not approved by Landlord's architect. In case of delays due to governmental regulation, unusual scarcity of or inability to obtain labor or materials, labor difficulties, casualty or other causes reasonably beyond Landlord's control, the Scheduled Term Commencement Date shall be extended for the period of such delays. Landlord agrees to notify Tenant as soon as possible if it appears to Landlord that the Premises will not be available for Tenant's occupancy on the original Scheduled Term Commencement Date or any extension thereof. The Premises shall be deemed ready for occupancy on the latest of (a) the date estimated for such readiness in a notice delivered to Tenant at least 30 days before such date, or (b) the date on which the work described in Exhibit D and Tenant's Plans, together with the common facilities for access and service to the Premises, has been completed except for items of work and adjustment of equipment and fixtures which can be completed after occupancy has been taken without causing substantial interference with Tenant's use of the Premises (i.e., so-called "punch list" items), or (c) the date on which Tenant receives a registered architect's or engineer's certificate of the completion in accordance with clause (b) of this sentence. Landlord shall complete as soon as conditions practically permit all items and work excepted by said clause (b) and Tenant shall not use the Premises in such manner as will increase the cost of completion. Landlord shall permit Tenant access for installing furnishings in portions of the Premises when it can be done without material interference with remaining work.

Each day of delay in delivery of Tenant's plans beyond the date specified in Section 3.1 shall conclusively be deemed to cause an equivalent day of delay by Landlord in substantially completing the work to be done by Landlord pursuant to this Section 3.2.

Tenant agrees that no delay by it, or anyone employed by it, in performing work to prepare the Premises for occupancy shall delay commencement of the Term or the obligation to pay rent, regardless of the reason for such delay or whether or not it is within the control of Tenant or any such employee.

3.3   This Section 3.3 shall apply before and during the Term. Tenant shall not make alterations and additions to Tenant's Space except in accordance with plans and specifications therefor first approved by Landlord. Landlord shall not be deemed unreasonable for withholding approval of any alterations or additions which (a) involve or might affect any structural or exterior element of the Building, any area or element outside of the Premises, or any facility serving any area of the Building outside of the Premises, or (b) will delay completion of the Premises or Building, or (c) will require unusual expense to readapt the Premises to normal office use on Lease termination or increase the cost of construction or of insurance or taxes on the Building or of the services called for by Section 4.1 unless Tenant first gives assurance acceptable to Landlord for payment of such increased cost and that such readaptation will be made prior to such termination without expense to Landlord. All alterations and additions shown on Tenant Plans shall be part of the Building. All alterations and additions not shown on Tenant Plans shall be part of the Building unless and until either Landlord or Tenant shall specify the same for removal pursuant to Section 5.2. All of Tenant's alterations and additions and installation of furnishings shall be coordinated with any work being performed by Landlord and in such manner as to maintain harmonious labor relations and not to damage the Building or Lot or interfere with Building construction or operation and, except for installation of furnishings, shall be performed by Landlord's general contractor or by contractors or workmen first approved by Landlord. Except for work by Landlord's general contractor, Tenant before its work is started shall: secure all licenses and permits necessary therefor; deliver to Landlord a statement of the names of all its contractors and subcontractors and the estimated cost of all labor and material to be furnished by them and security satisfactory to Landlord protecting Landlord against liens arising out of the furnishing of such labor and material; and cause each contractor to carry workmen's compensation insurance in statutory amounts covering all the contractor's and subcontractor's employees and comprehensive public liability insurance with such limits as Landlord may reasonably require, but in no event less than $300,000–$500,000, and property damage insurance with limits of not less than $100,000, (all such insurance to be written in companies approved by Landlord and insuring Landlord and Tenant as well as the contractors) and to deliver to Landlord certificates of all such insurance. Tenant agrees to pay promptly when due the entire cost of any work done on the Premises by Tenant, its agents, employees, or independent contractors, and not to cause or permit any liens for labor or materials performed or furnished in connection therewith to attach to the Premises and immediately to discharge any such liens which may so attach. Tenant shall pay, as additional rent, 100% of any increase in real estate taxes on the Building which shall, at any time after commencement of the Term, result from any alteration, addition or improvement to the Premises made by Tenant.

3.4   All construction work required or permitted by this Lease shall be done in a good and workmanlike manner and in compliance with all applicable laws and all lawful ordinances, regulations and orders of governmental authority and insurers of the Building. Each party may inspect the work of the other at reasonable times and shall promptly give notice of observed defects. Each party authorizes the other to rely in connection with design and construction upon approval and other actions on the party's behalf by an Construction Representative of the party named in Article I or any person hereafter designated in substitution or addition by notice to the party relying. Except as otherwise provided in Article IV, the work required of Landlord pursuant to this Article III shall be deemed approved by Tenant when Tenant commences occupancy of the Premises for the Permitted Uses, except for items which are then uncompleted or do not conform to the drawings and specifications referred to in Section 3.1 and as to which, in either case, Tenant shall have given notice to Landlord not later than sixty (60) days after Tenant commences occupancy of the Premises for the Permitted Uses.

ARTICLE IV

Landlord's Covenants; Interruptions and Delays

4.1   Landlord covenants.

4.1.1   to furnish services, utilities, facilities and supplies set forth in Exhibit E equal in quality to those customarily provided by landlords in high quality buildings in Philadelphia;

4.1.2   to furnish, at Tenant's expense, reasonable additional Building operation services which are usual and customary in similar office buildings in Philadelphia upon reasonable advance request of Tenant at reasonable and equitable rates from time to time established by Landlord;

4.1.3   except as otherwise provided in Article VI to make such repairs to all of the structural elements of the Building (including without limitation the roof, exterior walls and glass therein and floor slabs) and to common areas and facilities and equipment as may be necessary to keep them in serviceable condition;

4.1.4   to provide and install, at Tenant's expense, letters or numerals on doors in the Premises to identify Tenant's official name and Building address; all such letters and numerals shall be in the building standard graphics and no others shall be used or permitted on the Premises;

4.1.5   to provide during the Term the right to park 20 cars in the parking facility located in the Building (each such right to park a car being herein referred to as a "Parking Right," it being understood that said Parking Rights shall not give Tenant the right to particular designated spaces) for additional rent for the first 12 months of the Term of and for the balance of the Term thereafter at the prevailing rate charged by Landlord to other tenants in the Building from time to time, said fee to be adjusted annually. Tenant shall have the options to obtain two additional Parking Rights for each period commencing on the fifth, tenth and fifteenth anniversaries, respectively, of the commencement of the Term and continuing for the balance of the Term remaining hereunder. Such option shall be exercisable by notice in writing from Tenant to Landlord given not later than one year prior to the fifth, tenth or fifteenth anniversary of the commencement of the Term, as the case may be. If Tenant exercises such option, the fee for such additional Parking Rights shall be the then prevailing rate charged by Landlord to other tenants of the Building and thereafter said rates shall be adjusted annually to conform to changes in the prevailing rate from time to time;

4.1.6   that Tenant on paying the rent and performing the tenant obligations in this Lease shall peacefully and quietly have, hold and enjoy the Premises, subject to all of the terms and provisions hereof;

4.1.7   Landlord shall not unreasonably withhold its consent to the installation of vending machines in the Premises provided (i) if Landlord selects a vending machine contractor for the Building, Tenant shall utilize such contractor's services if such services are competitively priced with those offered by Tenant's contractor; (ii) any vending machine contractor selected by Tenant shall be subject to such reasonable rules and regulations as Landlord may promulgate to insure the operation of the Building as a first class office building; and (iii) Landlord shall approve a contract entered into between Tenant and its vending machine contractor which shall provide, inter alia, that same may be terminated on 30 days' notice in the event Landlord in its reasonable judgment deems such vending machine operation detrimental to the operation of the Building as a first class office building;

4.1.8   to defend with counsel, first approved by Tenant, save harmless and indemnify Tenant from any liability for injury, loss, accident or damage to any person or property, and from claims, actions, proceedings and expenses and costs in connection therewith (including without limitation reasonable counsel fees) arising from (A) the omission, fault, willful act, negligence or other misconduct of Landlord or (B) the failure of Landlord to perform and discharge its covenants and obligations under this Lease; to maintain in responsible companies qualified to do business, and in good standing, in Pennsylvania public liability insurance covering the Building insuring the Landlord with limits as are customarily carried in Philadelphia with respect to similar properties and, upon request of Tenant, to produce evidence of such insurance;

4.1.9   that Landlord shall not enforce its Rules and Regulations for the Building in a discriminatory manner;

4.1.10 to advise Tenant in writing of all mortgagees of Landlord's interest in the Property or any part thereof;

4.1.11 that Tenant shall have the right to acquire and keep upon the Premises furniture, furnishings, machinery and equipment under any arrangement pursuant to which the title thereto or a lien thereon is reserved in a person or entity other than Landlord or Tenant. Landlord shall execute in recordable form from time to time, upon request of Tenant or such third person or entity, any and all waivers and other instruments that may be necessary to enable Tenant to acquire any such furniture, furnishings, machinery and equipment pursuant to such an arrangement, and Landlord shall use its best efforts to obtain the execution of such instruments by any mortgagee, lienholder or encumbrancer of the Property, the Building or any part thereof evidencing the waiver of such mortgagee's, lienholder's or encumbrancer's interest in any of said furniture, furnishings, machinery and equipment that is required by the owner, seller, or lienor thereof; provided, however, that in no event may any such acquisition or retention cause or effect any lien upon or against the Building or Property;

4.1.12 that whenever Landlord's approval or consent is required under this Lease, it will not be unreasonably withheld;

4.1.13 and warrants that Landlord holds fee simple title to the Property as of the date of this Lease unrestricted by any agreement or encumbrance that prohibits or restricts its entry or performance of this Lease; and

4.1.14 to pay all reasonable costs, counsel and other fees incurred by Tenant in connection with the successful enforcement by Tenant of any obligations of Landlord under this Lease.

4.2 Interruptions and Delays in Services and Repairs, etc.

Landlord shall not be liable to Tenant for any compensation or reduction of rent by reason of inconvenience or annoyance or for loss of business arising from the necessity of Landlord or its agents entering the Premises for any of the purposes in this Lease authorized, or for repairing the Premises or any portion of the Building however the necessity may occur. In case Landlord is prevented or delayed from making any repairs, alterations or improvements, or furnishing any services or performing any other covenant or duty to be performed on Landlord's part, by reason of any cause reasonably beyond Landlord's control, including without limitation the causes set forth in Section 3.2 hereof as being reasonably beyond Landlord's control, Landlord shall not be liable to Tenant therefor, nor, except as expressly otherwise provided in Section 6.1, shall Tenant be entitled to any abatement or reduction of rent by reason thereof, nor shall the same give rise to a claim in Tenant's favor that such failure constitutes actual or constructive, total or partial, eviction from the Premises.

Landlord reserves the right to stop any service or utility system when necessary by reason of accident or emergency, or until necessary repairs have been completed; provided, however, that in each instance of stoppage, Landlord shall exercise reasonable diligence to eliminate the cause thereof. Except in case of emergency repairs Landlord will give Tenant reasonable advance notice of any contemplated stoppage and will use reasonable efforts to avoid unnecessary inconvenience to Tenant by reason thereof.

ARTICLE V

Tenant's Covenants

Tenant covenants during the Term and such further time as Tenant occupies any part of the Premises:

5.1   to pay when due all fixed rent and additional rent and all charges for utility services rendered to the Premises and service inspections therefor (except as otherwise provided in Exhibit E) and, as further additional rent, all charges for additional services rendered pursuant to Section 4.1.2;

5.2   except as otherwise provided in Article VI and Section 4.1.3, to keep the Premises in good order, repair and condition, reasonable wear and tear and damage by construction defect only excepted, and all glass in interior windows and doors (including any entrance doors) of the Premises whole and in good condition with glass of the same quality as that injured or broken, damage by casualty only excepted, and at the expiration or termination of this Lease peaceably to yield up the Premises and all alterations and additions thereto in good order, repair and condition, reasonable wear and tear and damage by casualty or construction defect excepted, first removing all goods and effects of Tenant and, to the extent specified by Landlord or Tenant by notice to the other given at least thirty days before such expiration or termination (except that in case of termination pursuant to Section 6.1, such notice shall be given within five days after notice of termination), all alterations and additions made by Tenant not shown on Tenant Plans, and repairing any damage caused by such removal and restoring the Premises and leaving them clean and neat;

5.3   continuously from the commencement of the Term to use and occupy the Premises for the Permitted Uses, and not to injure or deface the Premises, Building or Lot, nor to permit in the Premises any auction sale, vending machine (except pursuant to subsection 4.1.7), or inflamable fluids or chemicals, or nuisance, or the emission from the Premises of any objectionable noise or odor, nor to use or devote the Premises or any part thereof for any purpose other than the Permitted Uses, nor any use thereof which is inconsistent with the maintenance of the Building as an office building of the first class in the quality of its maintenance, use and occupancy, or which is improper, offensive, contrary to law or ordinance or liable to invalidate or increase the premiums for any insurance on the building or its contents or liable to render necessary any alteration or addition to the Building;

5.4   not to obstruct in any manner any portion of the Building not hereby leased or any portion thereof or of the Lot used by Tenant in common with others; not without prior consent of Landlord to permit the painting or placing of any curtains, blinds, shades, awnings, aerials or flagpoles, or the like, visible from outside the Premises; and to comply with all reasonable Rules and Regulations now or hereafter made by Landlord, of which Tenant has been given notice, for the care and use of the Building and Lot and their facilities and approaches; Landlord shall not be liable to Tenant for the failure of other occupants of the Building to conform to such Rules and Regulations;

5.5   to keep the Premises equipped with all safety appliances required by law or ordinance or any other regulation of any public authority because of any use made by Tenant other than normal office use, and to procure all licenses and permits so required because of such use and, if requested by Landlord, to do any work so required because of such use, it being understood that the foregoing provisions shall not be construed to broaden in any way Tenant's Permitted Uses;

5.6   not without prior consent of Landlord to assign, mortgage, pledge or otherwise transfer this Lease or to make any sublease, or to permit occupancy of the Premises of any part thereof by anyone other than Tenant; any assignment or sublease made without such consent shall be void; as additional rent, Tenant shall reimburse Landlord promptly for reasonable legal and other expense incurred by Landlord in connection with any request by Tenant for consent to assignment or subletting; no assignment or subletting shall affect the continuing primary liability of Tenant (which, following assignment, shall be joint and several with the assignee); and no consent to any of the foregoing in a specific instance shall operate as a waver in any subsequent instance;

5.7   to defend with counsel first approved by Landlord, save harmless, and indemnify Landlord from any liability for injury, loss, accident or damage to any person or property, and from any claims, actions, proceedings and expenses and costs in connection therewith (including without limitation reasonable counsel fees), (i) arising from (a) the omission, fault, willful act, negligence or other misconduct of Tenant or (b) from any use made or thing done or occurring on the Premises not due to the omission, fault, willful act, negligence or other misconduct of Landlord, or (ii) resulting from the failure of Tenant to perform and discharge its covenants and obligations under this Lease, to maintain in responsible companies qualified to do business, and in good standing, in Pennsylvania public liability insurance covering the Premises insuring Landlord as well as Tenant with limits which shall, at the commencement of the Term, be at least equal to those stated in Section 1.1 and from time to time during the Term shall be for such higher limits, if any, as are customarily carried in Philadelphia with respect to similar properties, and workmen's compensation insurance with statutory limits covering all of Tenant's employees working in the Premises, and to deposit promptly with Landlord certificates for such insurance, and all renewals thereof, bearing the endorsement that the policies will not be cancelled until after 10 days' written notice to Landlord;

5.8   that all of the furnishings, fixtures, equipment, effects and property of every kind, nature and description of Tenant and of all persons claiming by, through or under Tenant which, during the continuance of this Lease or any occupancy of the Premises by Tenant or anyone claiming under Tenant, may be on the Premises or elsewhere in the Building or on the Lot, shall as between Landlord and Tenant be at the sole risk and hazard of Tenant, and if the whole or any part thereof shall be destroyed or damaged by fire, water or otherwise, or by the leakage or bursting of water pipes, steam pipes, or other pipes, by theft or from any other cause, no part of said loss or damage is to be charged to or to be borne by Landlord, except that Landlord shall in no event be indemnified or held harmless or exonerated from any liability to Tenant or to any other person, for any injury, loss, damage or liability caused by the negligence of Landlord or its agents, employees or independent contractors;

5.9   to permit Landlord and its agents: to examine the Premises at reasonable times and, if Landlord shall so elect, to make any repairs or replacements Landlord may deem necessary; to remove, at Tenant's expense, any alterations, additions, signs, curtains, blinds, shades, awnings, aerials, flagpoles, or the like not consented to in writing; and to show the Premises to prospective tenants during the twelve months preceding expiration of the Term and to prospective purchasers and mortgagees at all reasonable times;

5.10   not to place a load upon the Premises exceeding an average rate of 100 pounds of live load per square foot of floor area (partitions shall be considered as part of the live load); and not to move any safe, vault or other heavy equipment in, about or out of the Premises except in such manner and at such time as Landlord shall in each instance authorize; Tenant's business machines and mechanical equipment which cause vibration or noise that may be transmitted to the Building structure or to any other space in the Building shall be so installed, maintained and used by Tenant as to eliminate such vibration or noise;

5.11   to pay promptly when due all taxes which may be imposed upon personal property (including, without limitation, fixtures and equipment) in the Premises to whomever assessed; and

5.12   as additional rent, to pay all reasonable costs, counsel and other fees incurred by Landlord in connection with the successful enforcement by Landlord of any obligations of Tenant under this Lease;

ARTICLE VI

Casualty and Taking

6.1   In case during the Term all or any substantial part of the Premises, the Building, or the Lot are damaged materially by fire or other casualty, or by action of public or other authority in consequence thereof, or are taken by eminent domain or Landlord receives compensable damage by reason of anything lawfully done in pursuance of public or other authority, this Lease shall terminate at Landlord's election, which may be made notwithstanding Landlord's entire interest may have been divested, by notice given to Tenant within 90 days after the election to terminate arises specifying the effective date of termination. The effective date of termination specified by Landlord shall not be less than 15 nor more than 30 days after the date of notice of such termination. There shall be an equitable abatement of rent from the date of damage or taking to the date of termination. Unless terminated pursuant to the foregoing provisions, this Lease shall remain in full force and effect following any such damage or taking, subject, however, to the following provisions. If in any such case the Premises are rendered unfit for use and occupation or there is a partial permanent taking and this Lease is not so terminated, Landlord shall use due diligence (following the expiration of the period in which Landlord may terminate this Lease pursuant to the foregoing provisions of this Section 6.1) to put the Premises, or in case of taking what may remain thereof (excluding in case of both casualty and taking any items installed or paid for by Tenant which Tenant may be required to remove pursuant to Section 5.2), into proper condition for use and occupation and a just proportion of the fixed rent and additional rent according to the nature and extent of the injury shall be abated until the Premises or such remainder shall have been put by Landlord in such condition; and in case of a taking which permanently reduces the area of the Premises, a just proportion of the fixed rent and additional rent shall be abated for the remainder of the Term. In case of a taking which permanently reduces the area of the Premises by more than 20%, Tenant shall have the right to terminate this Lease within ninety days after Landlord notifies Tenant of the taking.

6.2   Landlord reserves to itself any and all right to receive awards made for damages to the Premises and building and Lot and the leasehold hereby created, or any one or more of them, accruing by reason of exercise of eminent domain or by reason of anything lawfully done in pursuance of public or other authority. Tenant hereby releases and assigns to Landlord all Tenant's rights to such awards, and covenants to deliver such further assignments and assurances thereof as Landlord may from time to time request, hereby irrevocably designating and appointing Landlord as its attorney-in-fact to execute and deliver in Tenant's name and behalf all such further assignments thereof. Nothing in this Section 6.2 shall limit Tenant's right to claim against the condemning authority for any amounts of special damages (such as, without limitation, awards for personal property and moving expenses) that do not reduce the award payable to Landlord.

6.3   In the event of any taking of the Premises or any part thereof for temporary use, (i) this Lease shall be and remain unaffected thereby and rent shall not abate, and (ii) Tenant shall be entitled to receive for itself such portion or portions of any award made for such use with respect to the period of the taking which is within the Term, provided that if such taking shall remain in force at the expiration or earlier termination of this Lease, Tenant shall then pay to Landlord a sum equal to the reasonable cost of performing Tenant's obligations under Section 5.2 with respect to surrender of the Premises and upon such payment shall be excused from such obligations.

ARTICLE VII

Default

7.1   If any default by Tenant continues after notice, in case of fixed rent or additional rent for more than ten days, or in any other case for more than 30 days and such additional time, if any, as is reasonably necessary to cure the default if the default is of such a nature that it cannot reasonably be cured in 30 days; or if Tenant makes any assignment for the benefit of creditors, commits any act of bankruptcy or files a petition under any bankruptcy or insolvency law; or if such a petition is filed against Tenant and is not dismissed within 90 days; or if a receiver or similar officer becomes entitled to Tenant's leasehold hereunder and it is not returned to Tenant within 90 days; or if such leasehold is taken on execution or other process of law in any action against Tenant; then in any such case, whether or not the Term shall have begun, Landlord may immediately, or at any time while such default exists and without further notice and with or without process of law (forcibly, if necessary) enter into and upon the Premises or mail a notice of termination addressed to Tenant at the Premises, and repossess the same as of Landlord's former estate and expel Tenant and those claiming through or under Tenant and remove its and their effects (forcibly, if necessary) without being deemed guilty of any manner of trespass and without prejudice to any remedies which might otherwise be used for arrears of rent or preceding breach of covenent, and upon such entry or mailing as aforesaid this Lease shall terminate, but Tenant shall remain liable as hereinafter provided. Tenant hereby waives all statutory rights of redemption, if any, to the extent such rights may be lawfully waived and agrees that Landlord, without notice to Tenant, may store Tenant's effects, and those of any person claiming through or under Tenant at the expense and risk of Tenant, and, if Landlord so elects, may sell such effects at public auction or private sale following at least ten (10) days' notice to Tenant and apply the net proceeds to the payment of all sums due to Landlord from Tenant if any, and pay over the balance, if any, to Tenant.

7.2   In the event that this Lease is terminated under any of the provisions contained in Section 7.1 or shall be otherwise terminated for breach of any obligation of Tenant, Tenant covenants to pay forthwith to Landlord, as compensation, the excess of the total rent reserved for the residue of the Term over the rental value of the Premises for said residue of the Term, discounted to its present value at the rate of ten percent (10%) per annum. In calculating the rent reserved there shall be included, in addition to the fixed rent and all additional rent, the value of all other considerations agreed to be paid or performed by Tenant for said residue. Tenant further covenants as an additional and cumulative obligation after any such termination to pay punctually to Landlord all the sums and perform all the obligations which Tenant covenants in this Lease to pay and to perform in the same manner and to the same extent and at the same time as if this Lease had not been terminated. In calculating the amounts to be paid by Tenant under the next foregoing covenant Tenant shall be credited with any amount paid to Landlord as compensation as in this Section 7.2 provided and also with the net proceeds of any rent obtained by Landlord by reletting the Premises, after deducting all Landlord's expenses in connection with such reletting, including, without limitation, all repossession costs, brokerage commissions, fees for legal services and expenses of preparing the Premises for such reletting, it being agreed by Tenant that Landlord may (i) relet the Premises or any part or parts thereof, for a term or terms which may at Landlord's option be equal to or less than or exceed the period which would otherwise have constituted the balance of the Term and may grant such concessions and free rent as Landlord in its sole judgment considers advisable or necessary to relet the same and (ii) make such alterations, repairs and decorations in the Premises as Landlord in its sole judgment considers advisable or necessary to relet the same, and no action of Landlord in accordance with the foregoing or failure to relet or to collect rent under reletting shall operate or be construed to release or reduce Tenant's liability as aforesaid.

In lieu of any other damages or indemnity and in lieu of full recovery by Landlord of all sums payable under all the foregoing provisions of this Section 7.2, Landlord may by written notice to Tenant, at any time after this Lease is terminated under any of the provisions contained in Section 7.1 or is otherwise terminated for breach of any obligation of Tenant and before such full recovery, elect to recover, and Tenant shall thereupon pay, as liquidated damages, an amount equal to the aggregate of (i) the fixed rent and additional rent accrued (whether or not paid in whole or in part) under Sections 2.5, 2.6 and 2.7 in the 12 months ended next prior to such termination plus (ii) the amount of fixed rent and additional rent of any kind accrued and unpaid at the time of termination, less (iii) the amount of any recovery by Landlord under the foregoing provisions of this Section 7.2 up to the time of payment of such liquidated damages. If Landlord elects to recover, and does recover, liquidated damages from Tenant pursuant to this paragraph: Landlord shall repay to Tenant amounts of rent collected by Landlord with respect to the Premises during the one year period following lease termination up to the net amount received by Landlord from Tenant pursuant to clauses (i) and (iii) above; and Landlord shall use commercially reasonable efforts to relet the Premises for and during such period.

Nothing contained in this Lease shall limit or prejudice the right of Landlord to prove for and obtain in proceedings for backruptcy, insolvency or like proceedings by reason of the termination of this Lease, an amount equal to the maximum allowed by any statute or rule of law in effect at the time when, and governing the proceedings in which, the damages are to be proved, whether or not the amount be greater, equal to, or less than the amount of the loss or damages referred to above.

ARTICLE VIII

Miscellaneous

8.1   The "Rentable Floor Area" shall refer to (i) in the case of each floor all of which is included in the Premises, all area within the inside finish of the permanent building walls (measured from the plane of the interior surface of glass extended in a straight line through columns located between windows) of the Building less all the area constituting Service Areas of such floor (measured to the midpoint of the walls separating such area from the Premises), but including all the Common Areas on each such floor, and (ii) in case of the Premises other than floors referred to in clause (i), all area or areas on the particular floor measured from the inside finish of the permanent building walls of the Building to the midpoint of the walls separating such Premises from the areas leased by or held for lease to others or from areas constituting Common Areas or Service Areas but including a proportionate share of the Common Areas on such floor based on the ratio of Tenant's Rentable Area on such floor to the total Rentable Area of such floor, excluding however, in such ratio all Common Areas and Service Areas on such floor. No deductions shall be made in determining Rentable Area on account of columns or projections necessary to the Building as shown on Exhibit B. "Service Areas" shall refer to areas on the particular floor occupied by building stairs, fire towers, elevator shafts, flues, vents, stacks, pipe shafts and vertical ducts. "Common Areas" shall refer to areas on the particular floor occupied by elevator lobbies, corridors accessible to others than Tenant, the common toilets, janitor closets and mechanical rooms. If the Rentable Floor Area of Tenant's Space and of the Building do not reflect "as built" drawings, the data set forth in Section 1.1 shall be appropriately adjusted.

8.2   The titles of the Articles are for convenience only and not to be considered in construing this Lease. Tenant agrees not to record this Lease, but upon request of either party both parties shall execute and deliver a memorandum of this Lease in form appropriate for recording or registration, and if this Lease is terminated before the Term expires, an instrument in such form acknowledging the date of termination. Whenever any notice, approval, consent, request or election is given or made pursuant to this Lease it shall be in writing. Communications and payments shall be addressed if to Landlord at Landlord's Original Address or at such other address as may have been specified by prior notice to Tenant, and if to Tenant, at Tenant's Original Address or at such other place as may have been specified by prior notice to Landlord. Any communication so addressed shall be deemed duly served if mailed by registered or certified mail, return receipt requested. If Landlord by notice to Tenant at any time designates some other person to receive payments or notices, all payments or notices thereafter by Tenant shall be paid or given to the agent designated until notice to the contrary is received by Tenant from Landlord. The obligations of this Lease shall run with the land, and this Lease shall be binding upon and inure to the benefit of the parties hereto and their respective successors and assigns, except that only the original Landlord named herein shall be liable for obligations accruing before the beginning of the Term, and thereafter the original Landlord named herein and each successive owner of the Premises shall be liable only for obligations accruing during the period of its ownership. The obligations of Landlord shall be binding upon Landlord's trust estate, but not upon any trustee or beneficiary of the trust individually.

8.3   The failure of Landlord or of Tenant to seek redress for violation of, or to insist upon strict performance of, any covenant or condition of this Lease, or, with respect to such failure of Landlord, any of the Rules and Regulations referred to in Section 5.4, whether heretofore or hereafter adopted by Landlord, shall not be deemed a waiver of such violation nor prevent a subsequent act, which would have originally constituted a violation, from having all the force and effect of an original violation, nor shall the failure of Landlord to enforce any of said Rules and Regulations against any other tenant of the Building be deemed a waiver of any such Rules or Regulations. The receipt by Landlord of fixed rent or additional rent with knowledge of the breach of any covenant of this Lease shall not be deemed a waiver of such breach. No provision of this Lease shall be deemed to have been waived by Landlord, or by Tenant, unless such waiver be in writing signed by the party to be charged. No consent or waiver, express or implied, by Landlord or Tenant to or of any breach of any agreement or duty shall be construed as a waiver of consent to or of any other breach of the same or any other agreement or duty.

8.4   No acceptance by Landlord of a lesser sum than the fixed rent and additional rent then due shall be deemed to be other than on account of the earliest installment of such rent due, nor shall any endorsement or statement on any check or any letter accompanying any check or payment as rent be deemed an accord and satisfaction, and Landlord may accept such check or payment without prejudice to Landlord's right to recover the balance of such installment or pursue any other remedy in this Lease provided. The delivery of keys to any employee of Landlord or to Landlord's agent or any employee thereof shall not operate as a termination of this Lease or a surrender of the Premises.

8.5   The specific remedies to which Landlord may resort under the terms of this Lease are cumulative and are not intended to be exclusive of any other remedies or means of redress to which it may be lawfully entitled in case of any breach or threatened breach by Tenant of any provisions of this Lease. In addition to the other remedies provided in this Lease, Landlord shall be entitled to the restraint by injunction of the violation or attempted or threatened violation of any of the covenants, conditions or provisions of this Lease or to a decree compelling specific performance of any such covenants, conditions or provisions.

8.6   If any term of this Lease, or the application thereof to any person or circumstances, shall to any extent be invalid or unenforceable, the remainder of this Lease, or the application of such term to persons or circumstances other than those as to which it is invalid or unenforceable, shall not be affected thereby, and each term of this Lease shall be valid and enforceable to the fullest extent permitted by law.

8.7   If Tenant shall at any time default in the performance of any obligation under this Lease, Landlord shall have the right after the expiration of the grace period provided in Section 7.1 (except in case of emergency), but shall not be obligated, to enter upon the Premises and to perform such obligation notwithstanding the fact that no specific provision for such substituted performance by Landlord is made in this Lease with respect to such default. In performing such obligation, Landlord may make any payment of money or perform any other act. All sums so paid by Landlord (together with interest at the rate of 8% per annum) and all necessary incidental costs and expenses in connection with the performance of any such act by Landlord shall be deemed to be additional rent under this Lease and shall be payable to Landlord immediately on demand. Landlord may exercise the foregoing rights without waiving any other of its rights or releasing Tenant from any of its obligations under this Lease.

8.8   Tenant agrees from time to time, upon not less than fifteen days' prior written request by Landlord, to execute, acknowledge and deliver to Landlord a statement in writing certifying that this Lease is unmodified and in full force and effect and that Tenant has no defenses, offsets or counterclaims against its obligations to pay the fixed rent and additional rent and to perform its other covenants under this Lease and that there are no uncured defaults of Landlord or Tenant under this Lease (or, if there have been any modifications that the same is in full force and effect as modified and stating the modifications and, if there are any defenses, offsets, counterclaims, or defaults, setting them forth in reasonable detail), and the dates to which the fixed rent, additional rent and other charges have been paid. Any such statement delivered pursuant to this Section 8.8 may be relied upon by any prospective purchaser or mortgagee of the Premises or any prospective assignee of any mortgage of the Premises.

8.9   Any insurance carried by either party with respect to the Building or Premises or Property therein or occurrences thereon shall, if it can be so written without additional premium or with an additional premium which the other party agrees to pay, include a clause or endorsement denying to the insurer rights of subrogation against the other party to the extent rights have been waived by the insured prior to occurrence of injury or loss. Each party, notwithstanding any provisions of this Lease to the contrary, hereby waives any rights of recovery against the other for injury or loss due to hazards covered by such insurance to the extent of the indemnification received thereunder.

8.10   This Lease contains all of the agreements of the parties with respect to the subject matter thereof and supersedes all prior dealings between them with respect to such subject matter.

8.11   Tenant warrants that it has had no dealings with any broker or agent other than Jackson-Cross Co. and Cabot, Cabot & Forbes Co. in connection with this Lease and covenants to defend with counsel approved by Landlord, hold harmless and indemnify Landlord from and against any and all cost, expense or liability for any compensation, commissions and charges claimed by any broker or agent other than Jackson-Cross Co. and Cabot, Cabot & Forbes Co. with respect to Tenant's dealings in connection with this Lease or the negotiation thereof.

8.12   The submission of this Lease or a summary of some or all of its provisions for examination does not constitute a reservation of or option for the Premises or an offer to lease.

ARTICLE IX

Rights of Mortgagee

9.1   Tenant will agree to the subordination to this Lease of the first mortgage on the Premises subject to, and in accordance with, the form of agreement attached hereto as Exhibit F which shall be in recordable form and may be recorded at the election of either party. The word "mortgagee" as used in this Lease shall include the holder for the time being whenever the context permits.

9.2   No assignment of this Lease and no agreement to make or accept any surrender, termination or cancellation of this Lease and no agreement to modify so as to reduce the rent, change the Term, or otherwise materially change the rights of Landlord under this Lease, or to relieve Tenant of any obligations or liability under this Lease, shall be valid unless consented to by Landlord's mortgagees of record of which Landlord has notified Tenant pursuant to Section 4.1.10, if any. No fixed rent, additional rent, or any other charge shall be paid more than ten days prior to the due date thereof and payments made in violation of this provision shall (except to the extent that such payments are actually received by a mortgagee) be a nullity as against any mortgagee and Tenant shall be liable for the amount of such payments to such mortgagee.

9.3   No act or failure to act on the part of Landlord which would entitle Tenant under the terms of this Lease, or by law, to be relieved of Tenant's obligations hereunder or to terminate this Lease, shall result in a release or termination of such obligations or a termination of this Lease unless (i) Tenant shall have first given written notice of Landlord's act or failure to act to Landlord's mortgagees of record of which Landlord has notified Tenant pursuant to Section 4.1.10, if any, specifying the act or failure to act on the part of

Landlord which could or would give basis to Tenant's rights; and (ii) such mortgagees, after receipt of such notice, have failed or refused to correct or cure the condition complained of within a reasonable time thereafter; but nothing contained in this Section 9.3 shall be deemed to impose any obligation on any such mortgagees to correct or cure any such condition. "Reasonable time" as used above means and includes a reasonable time to obtain possession of the mortgaged premises if the mortgagee elects to do so and a reasonable time to correct or cure the condition if such condition is determined to exist.

9.4   Tenant agrees on request of Landlord to execute and deliver from time to time any agreement which may reasonably be deemed necessary to implement the provisions of this Article IX.

EXECUTED as a sealed instrument in two or more counterparts on the day and year first above written.

LANDLORD

TENANT

APPENDIX 6.

SAMPLE EXHIBITS OF OFFICE LEASE

Method of Floor Measurement for Office Buildings

GENERAL

Architectural plans when available are to be used.

Tenant special installations including, but not limited to, private elevators, stairs, special flues, dumbwaiter shafts and special air conditioning facilities are included within the rentable area of such tenant.

In determining whether a floor is, and in computing the aggregate rentable area of, a single tenancy floor, any special installation on said floor of another tenant shall be disregarded.

In computing the aggregate rentable area of any multiple occupancy floor, any special installation of a tenant who is not a tenant of any other part of such floor shall be disregarded.

SINGLE TENANCY FLOORS

Three steps are to be followed to determine the rentable area:

1A. Compute gross area
2B. Deduct certain areas
3C. Add applicable share of areas to be apportioned (see paragraph 3C).

1A. Gross Area. The gross area of a floor shall be the entire area within the exterior walls. If the exterior wall consists in whole or in part of windows, fixed clear glass, or other transparent material, the measurement shall be taken to the inside of the glass or other transparent material. If it consists solely of a non-transparent material, the measurement shall be taken to the inside surface of the outer masonry building wall.

2B.   Deductions from Gross Area.   The following non-rentable Building areas with their finished enclosing walls are to be deducted:

1. Public elevator shafts and elevator machine rooms
2. Public stairs
3. Fire tower and fire tower court
4. Areas within the gross area which are to be apportioned (see below paragraph 3C).

(Note: If a base Building area to be deducted and a base Building area that is rentable have a common wall, the thickness of the wall is to be equally divided; e.g., if an elevator shaft is adjacent to a telephone closet, the elevator shaft and half of the finished dividing wall are to be deducted.)

3C.   Areas to be Apportioned.

1.   Air conditioning facilities: All air conditioned floors and other areas throughout and within the Building (exclusive of tenant's special air conditioning facilities) including their finished enclosing walls containing equipment or enclosing pipes, ducts, or shafts serving the facilities are to be apportioned to the areas they serve.

2.   Whenever the height of an air conditioning facility room or floor above the grade floor shall exceed the average story height in the Building by more than 25%, then the area of such room or floor shall be determined by multiplying the floor area by the percentage that the height of the room or floor exceeds the average story height, and adding the area so determined to the area of the room or floor.

3.   The lobby area of the Building.

MULTIPLE OCCUPANCY FLOORS

The total of the rentable areas for two or more tenants on a floor shall be the rentable area for that floor as computed in the manner for single tenancy floors, except that public corridors of the floor shall be included.

Three steps are to be followed:

1. Compute the net area for such floor.
2. Compute the net area for each tenant.
3. To determine the rentable area for any tenant, multiply the rentable area of such floor by a fraction whose numerator is the net area for such tenant and whose denominator is the net area for such floor.

1.   Net Area For Any Floor.   The net area shall be the gross area as described for single tenancy floors less the entire core areas (including the finished enclosing walls thereof but excluding any part of the core rented to a tenant) and corridors (excluding the enclosing walls thereof).

2. *Net Area for Each Tenant.* Exterior walls are to be measured as described in procedure for gross area. Demising walls between tenants are to be equally divided. Corridor walls to the finished corridor side are to be included in the net area of each tenant.

STORES

1. The rentable area of a store shall be computed by measuring from the Building line in the case of street frontages, and from the inside surface of other outer Building walls to the finished surface of the corridor side of corridor partition and from the center of the partitions that separate the premises from adjoining rentable area.

2. No deductions shall be made for columns and projections necessary to the Building.

3. Rentable area of a store shall include all area within the outside walls, less Building stairs, fire towers, elevator shafts, flues, vents, stacks, pipe shafts, vertical ducts with their enclosing walls if serving more than one tenant.

4. Private stairs, private elevators, toilets, air conditioning facilities, janitors' closets, slop sinks, electrical closets and telephone closets, with their enclosing walls exclusively serving only that store, shall be included in rentable area. When air conditioning facilities serve more than one tenant area, they shall be apportioned in the same manner as that used for single tenancy floors.

5. Whereas a store fronts on a plaza or arcade which is intended for use by the general public and is not for the exclusive use of the store tenants, its customers, etc., the area of the plaza or arcade shall not be included in determining the rentable area of the store.

BASEMENTS

1. If the rentable area extends beyond the Building line under the sidewalk, the rentable area shall be computed by measuring from the finished surface of the retaining wall to the finished surface of the corridor side of corridor partition or other permanent partition, and from the center of the partitions that separate the premises from adjoining rentable area, provided such partitions are not bearing walls.

2. If the rentable area is entirely inside the Building line, the rentable area shall be computed by measuring from the inside surface of the outer building wall to the finished surface of corridor side of corridor partition or to other permanent partition and from the center of the partitions that separate the

premises from adjoining rentable area, provided such partitions are not bearing walls.

3.   No deductions shall be made for column projections or footings necessary to the Building.

4.   Rentable area of a basement shall include all area within the outside walls, less building stairs, fire towers, elevator shafts, flues, vents, stacks, pipe shafts, and vertical ducts, with their enclosing walls serving more than one tenant.

5.   Private stairs, private elevators, toilets, air conditioning facilities, janitors' closets, slop sinks, electrical closets and telephone closets, with their enclosing walls, exclusively serving only the tenant, shall be included in the rentable area.

6.   Where air conditioning facilities serve more than one tenant area, they shall be apportioned in the same manner as that used for single tenancy floors.

MEMORANDUM OF WORK AND INSTALLMENTS TO BE INITIALLY PERFORMED AND FURNISHED IN THE PREMISES

1.   Tenant, at Tenant's expense, shall prepare a final plan or final set of plans (which final plan or final set of plans, as the case may be, is hereinafter and in the foregoing annexed Lease called the "Final Plan") which shall contain complete information and dimensions necessary for the construction and finishing of the premises and for the engineering in connection therewith. The Final Plan shall be submitted by Tenant to Landlord on or before the following date(s):

A.   on or before October 4, 1978 for so much of the Final Plan as it pertains to the location and extent of floor loading in excess of building standard, and the location of all penetrations of floor slabs;

B.   on or before October 4, 1978 for (a) special air-conditioning requirements (including location and general description of requirements thereof and complete occupancy schedule, (b) location and description of special plumbing requirements and (c) estimated total electrical load, including loads for both lighting and electrical equipment;

C.   on or before May 1, 1979 for (a) dimensioned drawings showing partition locations and type, (b) dimensioned drawings showing door locations, size and type, (c) drawings showing hardware schedule and (d) dimensioned drawings showing reflected ceiling plans;

D.   on or before May 1, 1979 for (a) dimensioned drawings showing location of electrical outlets and telephone outlets (b) dimensioned drawings showing specific plumbing locations, including plans and sections and (c) dimensioned drawings showing ceiling heights and ceiling materials; and

E.   on or before May 1, 1979 for (a) dimensioned drawings showing non-structural architectural detailing, including cabinetwork and (b) drawings showing floor covering, paint colors, finishes and wall coverings.

2.   In accordance with the Final Plan, Landlord, at Landlord's expense, except as otherwise expressly specified in this Exhibit C and in the foregoing Lease, will make and complete in and to the premises the following work and installations, all of which shall be of material, manufacture, design, capacity, finish and color of the building standard adopted by Landlord for the Building:

Gypsum Board and Plastered Partitions

1.1   Furnish and install gypsum board and stud partitions. Such gypsum board and stud partitions shall have 2½″ metal studs with layer of ⅝″ gypsum board on both sides and shall be spackled and taped for painting. Such gypsum board partition shall be erected from finished floor to underside of hung ceiling above in a quantity not to exceed 1 linear foot of partition per 15 square feet of useable area. Of the aforesaid partition, if called for on Final Plan, 15% shall be erected from finished floor to the underside of slab above and such partition shall have 2½″ metal stud and 1 layer of ⅝″ gypsum board to slab above, 1 layer of ⅝″ gypsum board to 6 inches above hung ceiling, with batt insulation to 6 inches above hung ceiling and shall be spackled and taped for painting.

Doors, Bucks and Hardware

2.1   Furnish and erect doors and door bucks for all partitions called for in Section 1.1. Such bucks will be 16 gauge rolled steel and shall be reinforced to receive hardware. Doors shall be paint grade birch veneer, hollow core, 3′ × 7″. There shall not be more than one such door for each 25 linear feet of partition. Of the quantity of doors noted in preceding sentence, 5% of such doors, if called for on Final Plan, may be stain grade teak, walnut or oak solid core, 3′ × 8′4″ high.

2.2   Each 3′ × 7′ hollow core door shall be provided with one pair of ball bedring butts and a heavy duty latch set, Schlage tulip design with satin aluminum finish or equal, as selected by Landlord. Each solid core door shall be provided with two pair of ball bearing butts.

2.3   Furnish and install heavy duty lock sets wherever required by Building Code, and if indicated on the Final Plan not more than 5% of doors shall be provided with a heavy duty lock set. Such lock set shall be Schlage, or equal, as selected by Landlord, and have a satin aluminum finish. Furnish and install on not more than 5% of doors, if indicated on the Final Plan, surface mounted door closer. Such door closer shall be LCN #4040 or equal, as selected by Landlord.

2.4   On doors not provided with closers, a wall or floor stop shall be furnished.

Sound Baffles

3.1   Sound baffles shall be furnished and installed within peripheral air-conditioning enclosures where dividing partitions abut the peripheral enclosures.

Ceilings

4.1   Furnish and install a mechanically suspended exposed Tee Bar ceiling system in the premises having 60" × 60" modular runners with exposed bottom surface utilizing acoustical tile of natural fissured mineral fiber.

4.2   Ceiling heights to be generally 8'6" (except for top floor of Building which ceiling height to be generally 9'6").

Floor Coverings

5.1   Furnish and install ⅛" vinyl asbestos tile, color to be selected by Tenant from Landlord sample card on the uncarpeted sections of the floor of the premises. The expression "uncarpeted sections" shall not be deemed to include those areas in which rugs and/or carpets are used or are initially planned to be used.

5.2   Furnish and install black or brown base, straight or cove, as designated by Tenant.

5.3   Tenant shall furnish and install carpeting and Landlord will give Tenant a credit for such carpeting in the amount of Fifty Thousand ($50,000) Dollars, which credit shall be applied by Tenant against the fixed rent.

Distribution System

6.1   Furnish and install an underfloor cellular system including header ducts, boots and connections. Said cellular system shall be a triple duct system (cells to be 3" in depth) with one cell activated for normal electrical wiring and one cell activated for normal low-tension wiring and one unactivated cell. The spacing of the activted cells will generally be on 5' centers, subject, however, to the necessity to conform to Building conditions. The Building will contain wires, risers, conduits, feeders and switchboards necessary to furnish any room or area of the premises with electrical energy in an amount equal to 5 watts at 265/460 volts per square foot of useable floor area in the premises, of which 2 watts of the aforesaid 5 watts shall be 208/120 volts.

Lighting

7.1   Furnish and install a reasonable number of recessed fluorescent lighting fixtures in the premises. Such fixtures shall be 20″ × 60″ in size and designed to contain four 40-watt lamps with rapid start ballasts; each such fixture shall have an acrylic diffuser. Such lighting fixtures shall be an air return fixture. Such fixtures shall be mounted individually or end to end, as indicated on the Final Plan. The expression "reasonable number" shall mean not more than one such lighting fixture to every 90 square feet of useable floor area in the premises. The expression "lighting fixtures" shall be deemed to include lamps.

Receptacles, Outlets and Switches

8.1   Furnish and install a reasonable number of electrical devices, consisting of ceiling outlets, quiet-type switches and receptacles. The expression "reasonable number" shall mean (i) an adequate quantity of ceiling outlets and switches for the lighting fixtures specified in Section 7.1 hereof, and (ii) not more than one receptacle to every 125 square feet of useable floor area in the premises. Such receptacles shall be located in the partitions at the building standard mounting height or in the peripheral air-conditioning enclosures at the prefabricated knockout locations or on the floor directly above such cells of the cellular system as are activated for such receptacle use.

Telephone Installations

9.1   Furnish and install a reasonable number of telephone outlets, for normal _____ Telephone Company installations in the City of _____ . The expression "reasonable number" shall mean not more than one telephone outlet to every 200 square feet of uscable floor area in the premises. Such telephone outlets shall be located in the partitions at the building standard mounting height or on the floor directly above such cells of the cellular system as are activated for low-tension use. the expression "telephone outlets" does not include (i) any wiring of any type of (ii) outlets and conduit for separate intercommunications systems, call directors, or any similar installation.

Drinking Fountains

10.1   Provide two drinking fountains per floor as specified and as located on the "Base Building Architect's Plan".

Venetian Blinds

11.1   Furnish and install narrow slat venetian blinds for all windows of the premises; color to be Landlord's Building standard color.

Heating, Ventilating and Air-Conditioning

12.1   Furnish and install a heating, ventilating and air-conditioning system that shall provide interior conditions of 78 degrees F. dry bulb and 50% relative humidity when outside conditions are 95 degree F. dry bulb and 75 degrees F. wet bulb and 68 degrees F. inside when outside temperatures are not less than 5 degrees F. The air-conditioning system will include a perimeter system to be controlled by one thermostat for each heat pump unit (approximately one unit for each 10 linear feet of perimeter). The perimeter system is designed to provide air-conditioning for the first 15 feet of the premises inside the perimeter wall. The interior space will be conditioned by two packaged interior units per floor supplying low pressure air zoned each half floor and distributed through the ceiling distribution system. The air-conditioning system will provide fresh air in a quantity of not less than .10 cubic feet per minute per sq. ft. of useable floor area through the interior distribution system. The above conditions will be maintained provided that in any given room or area of the premises, the occupancy does not exceed one person for each 100 sq. ft. of useable floor area and total electric load does not exceed four watts per sq. ft. of useable floor area for all purposes, including lighting and power. One supply diffuser shall be furnished by Landlord for every 400 square feet of useable floor area in the interior of the premises and 300 square feet of useable floor area on the perimeter. Any change in location or number of building standard peripheral system units and supply diffusers shall be at the expense of Tenant.

Painting

13.1   Paint such walls, partitions, columns, peripheral air-conditioning enclosures, doors, door-bucks and metal trim as are building standard. Such painting, in the case of non-metal surfaces, shall consist of one coat of primer and two finish coats of flat or semi-gloss paint (at Tenant's option) and a stippled finish and, in the case of metal surfaces, shall consist of an enamel undercoat and an enamel finish coat. Colors shall be selected by Tenant from 12 standard pre-mixed colors with not more than two color selections in any room or open area.

Miscellaneous

14.1   Furnish and perform all engineering in connection with the work and installations to be performed by Landlord referred to in Sections 1.1 through 13.1 inclusive, of this Exhibit C (such work and installations are collectively hereinafter called "Landlord's Work). Such engineering shall include the development and preparation of the final engineering drawings (including mechanical (HVAC), plumbing, electrical and structural) needed for Landlord's Work. Such engineering drawings shall be submitted to Tenant for

Tenant's approval, which approval shall not be unreasonably withheld or delayed, it being expressly agreed by Tenant that if any such engineering drawing is not approved or disapproved within 10 working days after the submission of same by Landlord, such engineering drawing shall be deemed to have been approved by Tenant. In the event Tenant disapproves any such engineering drawing, Tenant shall specify in detail the basis for such disapproval.

3. Landlord, at Landlord's expense, will file with the appropriate governmental authorities all plans and specifications in connection with Landlord's Work and procure from such authorities all necessary approvals relating thereto. Landlord will procure from such authorities, after approval of the aforesaid plans and specifications, all necessary permits.

4. A. The term "Work Cost" as used in this Exhibit C shall mean the estimated actual cost (including the cost of applicable insurance premiums and the cost of additional engineering, if any, required by reason of different new material or Tenant's Finish Work as particularly set forth in Article V of this Exhibit C (the term "Tenant's Finish Work" is defined in Article V of this Exhibit C) to Landlord of furnishing and installing such different new materials or such Tenant's Finish Work, plus 21% of such actual cost (including the cost of applicable insurance premiums and the cost of any such additional engineering).

B. The term "Landlord's Cost" as used in this Exhibit C shall mean the estimated actual cost (including the cost of applicable insurance premiums) to Landlord of furnishing and installing Landlord's building standard materials thereby replaced.

C. The term "usable floor area" or "useable square feet" shall mean all floor areas of the premises from the inside of the glass line of the exterior walls of the Building excluding, however, all the core areas and the pre-rated areas outside of the premises.

5. Tenant may select different new materials (except venetian blinds) in place of building standard materials which would otherwise be initially furnished and installed by Landlord under the provisions of this Exhibit C and the foregoing Lease, provided such selection is indicated on the Final Plan and approved by Landlord. If Tenant shall make any such selection, or if different new materials are required because of any situation created by Tenant (by reason of subleasing or any other similar or dissimilar cause) wherein the Building Code prohibits the use of Landlord's building standard materials, and if the Work Cost of such different new materials shall exceed the Landlord's Cost of Landlord's building standard materials thereby replaced, Tenant shall pay to Landlord, as hereinafter provided, the difference between the Work Cost of such different new materials and the Landlord's Cost of Landlord's building standard materials thereby replaced. Tenant may also indicate on the Final Plan additional work and additional materials (subject to approval by Landlord) to be furnished and installed by Landlord at Tenant's expense (such

additional work and materials are collectively hereinafter called "Tenant's Finish Work") and Tenant shall pay to Landlord, as hereinafter provided, the Work Cost of Tenant's Finish Work. No such different new materials shall be furnished and installed in replacement for any of Landlord's building standard materials nor shall any Tenant's Finish Work be furnished and installed until Landlord shall have advised Tenant in writing of, and Landlord and Tenant shall have agreed in writing on, the Work Cost of such different new materials and the Landlord's Cost of such replaced Landlord's building standard materials, or the Work Cost of the Tenant's Finish Work, as the case may be. All amounts payable by Tenant to Landlord pursuant to this Exhibit C shall be paid by Tenant promptly after the rendering of bills therefor by Landlord to Tenant, it being understood and agreed that such bills may be rendered during the progress of the performance of the Work and/or the furnishing and/or installation of the materials to which such bills relate. All such amounts payable by Tenant as described in this Article V shall be deemed to be Additional Rent under the Lease and collectible as additional rent pursuant to the Lease and in default of payment thereof, Landlord shall (in addition to all other remedies) have the same rights as in the event of default of payment of Additional Rent under the Lease. Any such different new materials and any Tenant's Finish Work shall, upon installation, become the property of Landlord and shall be surrendered by Tenant to Landlord at the end or other expiration of the term of the Lease. There shall be no cash credits. Credit shall be granted to the Tenant for the omission of the Landlord's building standard materials where replacement in kind is made. Unit credit amounts shall be established and accepted by both Tenant and Landlord prior to the beginning of any work within the Premises. Such credit amounts may be deducted from any amounts payable by Tenant to Landlord for the Work Cost of Tenant's Finish Work.

6.   Tenant shall have the right to have its own contractors do work at the premises, provided that such Tenant's contractors do not interfere with Landlord's Work or the scheduling of Landlord's Work. Tenant shall provide to Landlord Workmen's Compensation and public liability insurance and property damage insurance, all in amounts and with companies and on forms satisfactory to Landlord and such insurance shall be maintained at all times by Tenant's contractors engaged in the performance of such Tenant work and before proceeding with such Tenant work, certificates of such insurance shall be delivered to Landlord. Tenant shall have the right to schedule access to the Building and the use of assigned elevators for movement of materials and personnel prior to Tenant's occupancy of the Premises.

Rules and Regulations

1.   The sidewalks, driveways, entrances, passages, courts, plazas, elevators, vestibules, stairways, corridors or halls shall not be obstructed or encumbered by any tenant or used for any purpose other than ingress and egress

to and from the Premises and Tenant shall not permit any of its employees, agents or invitees to congregate in any of said areas. No door mat of any kind whatsoever shall be placed or left in any public hall or outside any entry door of the Premises.

2. No awnings or other projections shall be attached to the outside walls of the Building. No curtains, blinds, shades or screens shall be attached to or hung in, or used in connection with, any window or door of the premises, without the prior written consent of Landlord. Such curtains, blinds, shades or screens must be of a quality, type, design and color, and attached in the manner, approved by Landlord.

3. No sign, insignia, advertisement, object, notice or other letter shall be exhibited, inscribed, painted or affixed by any tenant on any part of the outside or inside of the premises or the Building without the prior written consent of Landlord. In the event of the violation of the foregoing by any tenant, Landlord may remove the same without any liability, and may charge the expense incurred in such removal to the tenant or tenants violating this rule. Interior signs and lettering on doors and directory table shall, if and when approved by Landlord, be inscribed, painted or affixed for each tenant by Landlord at the expense of such tenant, and shall be of a size, color and style acceptable to Landlord.

4. The sashes, sash doors, skylights, windows, and doors that reflect or admit light and air into the halls, passageways or other public places in the Building shall not be covered or obstructed by any tenant, nor shall any bottles, parcels, or other articles be placed on the window sills or peripheral air conditioning enclosures.

5. No showcases or other articles shall be put in front of or affixed to any part of the exterior of the Building, nor placed in the halls, corridors or vestibules.

6. The water and wash closets and other plumbing fixtures shall not be used for any purposes other than those for which they were designed or constructed, and no sweepings, rubbish, rags, acids or other substances shall be thrown or deposited therein. All damages resulting from any misuse of the fixtures shall be borne by the tenant who, or whose servants, employees, agents visitors or licensees, shall have caused the same. Any cuspidors or containers or receptacles used as such in the Premises, or for garbage or similar refuse, shall be emptied, cared for and cleaned by and at the expense of Tenant.

7. No tenant shall mark, paint, drill into, or in any way deface, any part of the Premises or the Building. No boring, cutting or stringing of wires shall be permitted, except with the prior written consent of Landlord, and as Landlord may direct.

8. No bicycles, vehicles, animals, fish or birds of any kind shall be brought into or kept in or about the Premises.

9. No noise, including but not limited to, music or the playing of musical instruments, recordings, radio or television, which, in the judgment of Land-

lord, might disturb other tenants in the Building, shall be made or permitted by any tenant. Nothing shall be done or permitted in the Premises by any tenant which would impair or interfere with the use or enjoyment by any other tenant of any other space in the Building.

10.   No tenant, nor any tenant's servants, employees, agents, visitors or licensees, shall at any time bring or keep upon the premises any inflammable, combustible or explosive fluid, chemical or substance.

11.   Additional locks or bolts of any kind which shall not be operable by the Grand Master Key for the Building shall not be placed upon any of the doors or windows by any tenant, nor shall any changes be made in locks or the mechanism thereof which shall make such locks inoperable by said Grand Master Key. Each tenant shall, upon the termination of its tenancy, turn over to Landlord all keys of stores, offices and toilet rooms, either furnished to, or otherwise procured by, such tenant, and in the event of the loss of any keys furnished by Landlord, such tenant shall pay to Landlord the cost thereof.

12.   All removals, or the carrying in or out of any safes, freight, furniture, packages, boxes, crates or any other object or matter of any description must take place during such hours and in such elevators as Landlord or its Agent may determine from time to time. Landlord reserves the right to inspect all objects and matter to be brought into the Building and to exclude from the Building all objects and matter which violate any of these Rules and Regulations or the Lease of which these Rules and Regulations are a part. Landlord may require any person leaving the Building with any package or other object or matter to submit a pass, listing such package or object or matter, from the tenant from whose premises the package or object or matter is being removed, but the establishment and enforcement of such requirement shall not impose any responsibility on Landlord for the protection of any tenant against the removal of property from the premises of such tenant. Landlord shall in no way be liable to any tenant for damages or loss arising from the admission, exclusion or ejection of any person to or from the Premises or the Building under the provisions of this Rule 12 or of Rule 16 hereof.

13.   Tenant shall not occupy or permit any portion of the Premises to be occupied as an office for a public stenographer or public typist, or for the possession, storage, manufacture, or sale of liquor, narcotics, dope, tobacco in any form, or as a barber, beauty or manicure shop, or as an employment bureau. Tenant shall not engage or pay any employees on the Premises, except those actually working for Tenant on the Premises, nor advertise for laborers giving an address at the Premises. Tenant shall not use the Premises or any part thereof, or permit the Premises or any advertise for laborers giving an address at the Premises. Tenant shall not use the Premises or any part thereof, or permit the Premises or any part thereof to be used, for manufacturing, or for the sale at auction, of merchandise, goods or property of any kind.

14.   No tenant shall obtain, purchase or accept for use in the Premises ice, drinking water, food, coffee cart, beverage, towel, barbering, boot blacking,

cleaning, floor polishing or other similar services from any persons not authorized by Landlord in writing to furnish such services. Such services shall be
furnished only at such hours, in such places within the Premises, and under
such regulations, as may be fixed by Landlord.

15.   Landlord shall have the right to prohibit any advertising or identifying
sign by any tenant which, in Landlord's judgment, tends to impair the reputation of the Building or its desirability as a building for offices, and upon written
notice from Landlord, such tenant shall refrain from or discontinue such
advertising or identifying sign.

16.   Landlord reserves the right to exclude from the Building during hours
other than Business Hours (as defined in the foregoing Lease) all persons
connected with or calling upon Tenant who do not present a pass to the
Building signed by Tenant. Tenant shall furnish Landlord with a facsimile of
such pass. All persons entering and/or leaving the Building during hours other
than Business Hours may be required to sign a register. Tenant shall be
responsible for all persons whom it issues any such pass and shall be liable to
Landlord for all acts or omissions of such persons.

17.   Tenant, before closing and leaving the Premises at any time, shall see
that all operable windows are closed and all lights are turned out. All entrance
doors in the premises shall be left locked by Tenant when the Premises are not
in use. Entrance doors shall not be left open at any time.

18.   The Premises shall not be used for lodging or sleeping or for any
immoral or illegal purpose.

19.   The requirements of tenants will be attended to only upon application
at the office of the Building. Employees of Landlord shall not perform any
work or do anything outside of their regular duties, unless under special
instructions from Landlord.

20.   Canvassing, soliciting and peddling in the Building are prohibited and
each tenant shall cooperate to prevent the same.

21.   There shall not be used in any space, or in the public halls of the
Building, either by any tenant or by any others, in the moving or delivery or
receipt of safes, freight, furniture, packages, boxes, crates, paper, office material, or any other matter or thing, any hand trucks except those equipped with
rubber tires, side guards and such other safeguards as Landlord shall require.

22.   Tenant shall not cause or permit any odors of cooking or other processes or any unusual or objectionable odors to emanate from the Premises
which would annoy other tenants or create a public or private nuisance. No
cooking shall be done in the premises except as is expressly permitted in the
foregoing Lease.

23.   Landlord reserves the right to rescind, alter or waive any rule or
regulation at any time prescribed for the Building when, in its judgment, it
deems it necessary or desirable for the reputation, safety, care or appearance of
the Building, or the preservation of good order therein, or the operation or

maintenance of the Building, or the equipment thereof, or the comfort of tenants or others in the Building. No rescision, alteration or waiver of any rule or regulation in favor of one tenant shall operate as a rescision, alteration or waiver in favor of any other tenant.

Cleaning Specifications

ENTRANCE LOBBY

The entrance lobby is to be kept neat and clean at all times and the following minimum cleaning operations shall be maintained to attain this effect.

1. Wash floors nightly and scrub floors as necessary.
2. Dust walls and wash walls as necessary.
3. Wipe down all metal surfaces nightly and polish once per week.
4. High dust and wash if necessary all electrical and air conditioning ceiling fixtures as necessary.
5. Dust mail depository nightly.
6. Wash all rubber mats and clean wool or nylon runners as necessary.
7. Clean cigarette urns and screen sand as necessary.
8. Clean entrance door glass as necessary.

ELEVATORS AND ESCALATORS

1. Vacuum clean carpets in elevator cabs and spot clean as necessary.
2. Shampoo rugs at least twice per month.
3. Clean saddles, doors and frames of elevators at lobby nightly.
4. Clean door saddles and frames on floors above lobby and vacuum dirt from door tracks as necessary.
5. Clean escalators as necessary.
6. Clean lights in elevator cab as often as necessary.
7. Clean metal and sides of elevator cab nightly.
8. Clean elevator pits as necessary (elevator mechanic).

GENERAL OFFICE AREA

Nightly

1. Damp mop all stone ceramic tile, terrazzo and other types of unwaxed flooring.
2. Sweep all vinyl asbestos, asphalt, rubber and similar types of flooring using an approved chemically treated cloth.

3. Carpet sweep all carpeted areas four nights—vacuum clean one night each week.

4. Hand dust and wipe clean with damp or chemically treated cloth all furniture, file cabinets, fixtures, window sills, and convector enclosure tops.

5. Dust all telephones.

6. Dust all chair, rails, trim, etc.

7. Empty and clean all waste receptacles and remove wastepaper and waste materials to a designated area.

8. Empty and wipe clean all ash trays and screen all sand urns.

9. Wash clean all water coolers.

10. Clean all glass furniture tops.

11. Remove finger marks and dust doors of elevator hatchways.

12. This cleaning and additional cleaning operations shall be scheduled so that a minimum number of lights are to be left on at all times. Upon completion of the cleaning all lights are to be turned off. All entrance doors are to be kept locked during this entire operation.

Periodic

1. Hand dust all door louvers and other ventilating louvers within reach as necessary.

2. Dust all baseboards as necessary.

3. Remove fingermarks from all painted surfaces near light switches, entrance doors, etc., as necessary.

4. Wipe clean all bright work weekly.

5. Dust all picture frames; charts and similar hangings quarterly which were not reached in nightly cleaning.

6. Dust all vertical surfaces such as walls, partitions, doors and other surfaces not reached in nightly cleaning.

7. Dust exterior of lighting fixtures once per year.

8. Dust all venetian blinds quarterly and report any broken tapes, cords, etc., to supervisor.

9. Dust quarterly all air conditioning louvers, grills, etc., not reached in nightly cleaning.

TOILETS

Nightly

1. Wash all floors.

2. Wash all mirrors and powder shelves.

3. Wash all bright work.
4. Wash all plumbing fixtures.
5. Wash and disinfect all toilet seats, both sides.
6. Scour, wash and disinfect all basins, bowls, urinals throughout all toilets.
7. Empty paper towel receptacles and remove paper to designated area.
8. Fill toilet tissue holders (tissue to be furnished by owner).
9. Empty and clean sanitary disposal receptacles.
10. Remove fingermarks from painted surfaces.
11. Report all mechanical deficiencies, i.e., dripping faucets, etc., to building supervisor.
12. Matrons assigned to building will visit and inspect all ladies toilets and rest rooms during the day and keep same in neat and clean condition at all times.
13. Matrons will fill sanitary napkin dispenser with sanitary napkins furnished to the contractor and collect coins and turn proceeds over to duly authorized representative of the owner.

Other

1. Clean and wash all partitions once a week.
2. Scrub floors once each month.
3. Hand dust, clean and wash all tile walls once each month, more often if necessary.
4. High dusting to be done once each month which includes lights, walls and grills.
5. Wash toilet lighting fixtures as often as necessary.

PUBLIC AREAS

1. Police all public and private stairwells throughout the entire Building and keep in clean condition, and mop same as necessary.
2. Inspect and keep clean firehoses, extinguishers and similar equipment.
3. Dust all railings, etc., weekly and high dust quarterly.
4. Wash walls of public stairwells as necessary.
5. Wash all public corridors' flooring and wax as necessary. Public corridor shall mean elevator corridors on multiple tenant floors.

BUILDING SERVICE AREAS

1. Keep locker and slop sink rooms in a neat and orderly condition at all times.

2. Hose all sidewalks, ramps, loading dock, trucking area, etc., daily and scrub if necessary.

3. Dust all pipes, ducts, ventilating grills, air conditioning machines and other accessible equipment quarterly.

4. Keep loading dock area in neat clean condition at all times. Keep waste paper, cardboard and rubbish, etc., stored in area other than loading dock. Clean floors, walls, and doors, etc., as necessary.

EXTERIOR CLEANING

Maintain entire Building exterior including metal work, entrance doors, storefront trim and exterior window frames and mullions, clean standpipe and sprinkler siamese connections and hose bibs; in short, properly maintain the exterior of the building so that there is uniformity of color, brightness and cleanliness at all times.

WINDOW CLEANING

1. Clean all windows on the outside and inside from the 2nd floor to the roof once every 8 weeks. Window frames and associated metal to be wiped clean at same time.

2. Reasonable amount of partition glass throughout the Building interior to be cleaned as necessary.

3. Clean building entrance doors as necessary.

ROOFS AND SETBACKS

Clean roof and setback as often as necessary.

SIDEWALKS AND PROMENADE MALLS

1. Sweep sidewalks daily and hose all once per week, weather permitting.

2. Remove snow or ice as soon as possible on all sidewalks, plaza and loading docks.

3. Remove gum and foreign matter from sidewalks.

4. Scrub clean sidewalks and driveways as often as necessary.

PEST CONTROL

1. Render pest control services as necessary throughout all public space.
2. Service to be rendered by licensed board of health operator, with special emergency calls on request at no additional charge.

RELAMPING AND CLEANING OF FIXTURES IN PUBLIC AREAS

Contractor will provide all labor and material in all public and service areas at no expense to the owner for the following:

1. Electric light tubes and bulbs.
2. Electric light switches and ballasts.
3. Electric fuses and circuit breakers.
4. Clean lighting fixtures as often as necessary.

MORTGAGEE'S NON-DISTURBANCE AGREEMENT AND LESSEE'S AGREEMENT TO ATTORN

THIS AGREEMENT, made this ———— day of ———————— , 198——— , by and between ———————— TRUST COMPANY, a ———————— banking corporation (hereinafter referred to as "Mortgagee"), having its principal place of business at ————————————————, and ———————— ———————— (hereinafter referred to as "Lessee");

WITNESSETH

WHEREAS, Lessee has entered into a lease (the "Lease"), dated ————————————————, 19——— , between One Logan Square Associates, as landlord, and Lessee, as tenant, covering space (the "Demised Premises") in the building commonly known as ————————————————; and

WHEREAS, Mortgagee is the holder of a certain Mortgage and Security Agreement, dated ———————————————— , 19—— , which was recorded with the ———————————————————————— , which encumbers the building of which the Demised Premises form a part (hereinafter the "Mortgage"); and

WHEREAS, Mortgagee has requested that in the event Mortgagee should foreclose the Mortgage, Lessee attorn to Mortgagee or the purchaser (the "Purchaser") at the foreclosure or statutory sale, and Lessee has requested that in the event Mortgagee should foreclose the Mortgage, Mortgagee or the Purchaser not disturb Lessee's possessory rights in the Demised Premises; and

WHEREAS, Mortgagee and Lessee are willing to so agree on the terms and conditions hereinafter provided;

NOW, THEREFORE, in consideration of the foregoing and the mutual covenants contained herein, Mortgagee and Lessee hereby agree as follows:

1. The Lease and Lessee's rights thereunder are and shall at all times be subject and subordinate in all respects to the Mortgage and to any renewal(s),

modification(s), replacement(s) and/or extension(s) of the same and to any subsequent or supplemental mortgage(s) with which the Mortgage may be spread and/or consolidated.

2.   Provided the Lease is in full force and effect and Lessee complies with this Agreement and is not in default in the payment of rent or the performance of any of the other terms, conditions, covenants, or agreements on its part to be performed under the Lease, no foreclosure or other acquisition of the Demised Premises by Mortgagee or the Purchaser will disturb Lessee's possession under said Lease and the Lease will not be affected or cut off thereby, and notwithstanding any such foreclosure or other acquisition of the Demised Premises by Mortgagee or the Purchaser, the Lease will be continued and recognized as a direct lease from Mortgagee or the Purchaser, except that the Mortgagee, or any subsequent owner, shall not (a) be liable for any previous act or omission of landlord under the Lease, (b) be subject to any offset which shall theretofore have accrued to Lessee against landlord, (c) have any obligation with respect to any security deposited under the Lease unless such security has been physically delivered to Mortgagee, (d) be bound by any previous modification of the Lease or by any previous prepayment of rent or additional rent for a period greater than the current month, unless such modification or prepayment shall have been expressly approved in writing by the Mortgagee, or (e) have any personal liability under the Lease, its liability under the Lease to be limited to the extent of its interest in the real property of which the Demised Premises are a part.

3.   If Mortgagee elects to accept from the then mortgagor a deed in lieu of foreclosure, Lessee's right to receive or set off any monies or obligations owed or to be performed by the then landlord shall not be enforceable thereafter against Mortgagee or any subsequent owner.

4.   If Mortgagee or Purchaser or any successor in interest to either shall succeed to the right of the landlord under the Lease, whether through possession, surrender, assignment, judicial action, foreclosure or delivery of a deed in lieu of foreclosure or otherwise, Lessee shall at once attorn to and recognize the successor landlord as its landlord under the Lease. While the provisions of this Agreement shall be self-operative and no further instrument shall be necessary to effect the aforementioned continuation, attornment, recognition and subordination, nevertheless Lessee will upon request by Mortgagee, or any subsequent owner, execute and deliver a written agreement whereunder Lessee does confirm such continuation, attornment, recognition and subordination and affirm Lessee's obligations under the Lease and agree to pay all rentals and charges then due or to become due as they become due to Mortgagee or such subsequent owner.

5.   Lessee will not modify the Lease or offer or make prepayment of rent or additional rent for a period in excess of the current month without the express consent in writing of the Mortgagee.

6.   Nothing contained in this Agreement shall in any way impair or affect the lien created by the Mortgage.

7.   Lessee shall from time to time deliver such certificates as Lender shall request as to the continuance of the Lease in effect, as to payments of rent thereunder, and as to such related matters as Mortgagee shall request.

8.   Lessee certifies that there are no defaults on the part of landlord under the Lease known to Lessee, that the Lease in the form attached hereto as Exhibit A is a complete statement of the agreement of the parties thereto with respect to the leasing of the Demised Premises and that the Lease is in full force and effect. Lessee shall promptly notify Mortgagee of the occurrence of any default by landlord under the Lease or any event which with the giving of notice or passage of time, or both, could become a default. In the case of any default of landlord under the Lease which would entitle Lessee to cancel the Lease, Lessee agrees that notwithstanding any provision of the Lease no notice of cancellation thereof shall be effective unless Mortgagee has received the notice aforesaid and has failed within 30 days of the date thereof to cure the default, or, if the default cannot with reasonable diligence be cured by Mortgagee with 30 days, has failed within such 30-day period to commence to cure such default or thereafter fails to prosecute diligently the curing of such default.

9.   No modification, amendment, waiver or release of any provision of this Agreement or of any right, obligation, claim or cause of action arising hereunder shall be valid, or binding for any purpose whatsoever unless in writing and duly executed by the party against whom the same is sought to be asserted.

10.   Any notice required or permitted to be given hereunder by either party shall be deemed given if in writing and sent by registered or certified mail, postage prepaid (return receipt requested) as follows (or to such other address(es) [but not more than three (3) in the aggregate] as a party shall hereafter specify by notice):

To Lessee at:

To Mortgagee at:

with a copy to:

Any such notice mailed as aforesaid shall be effective upon receipt.

11.   This Agreement shall inure to the benefit of the parties hereto, their successors and assigns; provided, however, that the interest of Lessee under this Agreement may not be assigned or transferred.

IN WITNESS WHEREOF, the parties hereto have respectively signed and sealed this Agreement as of the day and year first above written.

_____ TRUST COMPANY

ATTEST:

By: _____

_____

ATTEST:

By: _____

_____

APPENDIX 8.

MANAGEMENT AGREEMENT

IN CONSIDERATION of the covenants herein contained, _____

_____

(hereinafter called "OWNER"), and _____Rodin Management Inc._____

_____

(hereinafter called "AGENT"), agree as follows:

    1. The OWNER hereby employs the AGENT exclusively to rent and manage the property (hereinafter called the "Premises") known as _____

_____

upon the terms and conditions hereinafter set forth, for a term of __2 years__ beginning on the _____day of _____, 19___, and ending on the _____day of_____, 19___, and thereafter for yearly periods from time to time, unless on or before __90__ days prior to the date last above mentioned or on or before __90__ days prior to the expiration of any such renewal period, either party hereto shall notify the other in writing that it elects to terminate this Agreement, in which case this Agreement shall be thereby terminated on said last mentioned date. (See also Paragraph 6.3 below.)

    2. THE AGENT AGREES:

    2.1 To accept the management of the Premises, to the extent, for the period, and upon the terms herein provided and agrees to furnish the services of its organization for the rental operation and management of the Premises.

    2.2 To render a monthly statement of receipts, disbursements, and charges to the following person(s) at the address(es) shown:

        Name   Address

_____

_____

    2.3 To (a) keep accurate and complete records of all payrolls and of all materials purchased or expenditures made in and concerning the premises.

        (b) deposit all rent and other sums collected from tenants in an account, separate from AGENT's funds.

        (c) account for security deposits made by all tenants.

In case the disbursements and charges shall be in excess of the receipts, the OWNER agrees to pay such excess promptly, but nothing herein contained shall obligate the AGENT to advance its own funds on behalf of the OWNER.

3. THE OWNER AGREES:

To give the AGENT the following authority and powers (all or any of which may be exercised in the name of the OWNER) and agrees to assume all expenses in connection therewith:

3.1 To advertise the Premises or any part thereof; to display signs thereon and to rent the same; to cause reference of prospective tenants to be investigated; to sign leases for terms not in excess of _____ year(s) and to renew and/or cancel the existing leases and prepare and execute the new leases without additional charge to the OWNER: provided, however, that the AGENT may collect from tenants all or any of the following: a late rent administrative charge, a non-negotiable check charge, credit report fee, a subleasing administrative charge and/or broker's commission and need not account for such charges and/or commission to the OWNER; to terminate tenancies and to sign and serve such notices as are deemed needful by the AGENT; to institute and prosecute actions to oust tenants and to recover possession of the Premises; to sue for and recover rent; and, when expedient, to settle, compromise, and release such actions or suits, or reinstate such tenancies. OWNER shall reimburse AGENT for all expenses of litigation including attorneys' fees, filing fees, and court costs which AGENT does not recover from tenants. AGENT may select the attorney of its choice to handle such litigation.

3.2 To hire, discharge, and pay all engineers, janitors, and other employees; to make or cause to be made all ordinary repairs and replacements necessary to preserve the Premises in its present condition and for the operating efficiency thereof and all alterations required to comply with lease requirements, and to do decorating on the Premises; to negotiate contracts for nonrecurring items not exceeding $ ___500.00___ and to enter into agreements for all necessary repairs, maintenance, minor alterations, and utility services; and to purchase supplies and pay all bills. AGENT shall secure the approval of the OWNER for any alterations or expenditures in excess of $ ___500.00___ for any one item, except monthly or recurring operating charges and emergency repairs in excess of the maximum, if, in the opinion of the AGENT, such repairs are necessary to protect the property from damage or to maintain services to the tenants as called for by their tenancy.

3.3 To collect rents and/or assessments and other items due or to become due and give receipts therefor.

3.4 To handle tenants' security deposits and to comply, on the OWNER's behalf, with applicable state or local laws concerning the AGENT's responsibility for security deposits and interest thereon, if any.

3.5 To execute and file all returns and other instruments and do and perform all acts required of the OWNER as an employer with respect to the Premises under the Federal Insurance Contribution Acts, the Federal Unemployment Tax Act, and Sub-title C of the Interal Revenue Code of 1954 with respect to wages paid by the AGENT on behalf of the OWNER and under any similar federal and state law now or here-after in force (and in connection therewith the OWNER agrees upon request to prompt-ly execute and deliver to the AGENT all necessary powers of attorny, notices of appointment, and the like).

3.6 The AGENT shall not be required to advance any monies for the care or management of said property, and the OWNER agrees to advance all monies nec-essary therefor. If the AGENT shall elect to advance any money in connection with the property, the OWNER agrees to reimburse the AGENT forthwith and hereby authorizes the AGENT to deduct such advances from any monies due the OWNER. The AGENT shall, upon instruction from the OWNER, impound reserves each month for the payment of real estate taxes, insurance, or any other special expenditure. In addition, the OWNER agrees to establizh a permanent Operating Reserve Account with the AGENT in the amount of $ 2,000.00 .

4. THE OWNER FURTHER AGREES

4.1 To indemnify, defend, and save the AGENT harmless from all suits in connection with the Premises and from liability for damage to property and injuries to or death of any employee or other person whomsoever, and to carry at his (its) own expense public liability, elevator liability (if elevators are part of the equipment of the Premises), and workmen's compensation insurance naming the OWNER and the AGENT and adequate to protect their interests and in form, substance, and amounts reasonably satisfactory to the AGENT, and to furnish to the AGENT certificates evidencing the existence of such insurance. Unless the OWNER shall provide such insurance and furnish such certificate within 30 days from the date of this Agreement, the AGENT may, but shall not be obligated to, place said insurance and charge the cost thereof to the account of the OWNER. All such insurance policies shall provide that the AGENT shall receive thirty (30) days' written notice prior to cancellation of the policy.

4.2 To hold AGENT harmless for all liabilities and debts of the premises and to pay all expenses incurred by the AGENT, including, but not limited to, reasonable attorneys' fees and AGENT's costs and time in connection with any claim, proceeding, or suit involving an alleged violation by the AGENT or the OWNER, or both, of any law pertaining to fair employment, fair credit reporting, environmental protection, rent control, taxes, or fair housing, including, but not limited to, any law prohibiting, or making illegal, discrimination on the basis of race, sex, creed, color, religion, national origin, or mental or physical handicap, provided, however, that the OWNER shall not be responsible to the AGENT for any such expenses in the event the AGENT is finally adjudicated to have personally, and not in a representative capacity, violated any such law. Nothing contained herein shall obligate the Agent to employ counsel to represent the OWNER in any such proceeding or suit, and the OWNER may elect to employ counsel to represent the OWNER in any such proceeding or suit. The OWNER also agrees to pay reasonable expenses (or an apportioned amount of such expenses where other employers of AGENT also benefit from the expenditure) incurred by the AGENT in obtaining legal advice regarding compliance with any law affecting the premises or activities related thereto.

4.3 To indemnify, defend, and save the AGENT harmless from all claims, investigations, and suits, or from actions or failures to act of the OWNER, with respect to any alleged or actual violation of state or federal laws. It is expressly agreed and understood that as between the OWNER and the AGENT, all persons employed in connection with the Premises are employees of the OWNER, not the AGENT. However, it shall be the responsibility of the AGENT to comply with all applicable state or federal labor laws. The OWNER's obligation under this paragraph 4.3 shall include the payment of all settlements, judgments, damages, liquidated damages, penalties, forfeitures, back pay awards, court costs, litigation expense, and attorney's fees.

4.4 To give adequate advance written notice to the AGENT if the OWNER desires that the AGENT make payment, out of the proceeds from the premises, of mortgage indebtedness, general taxes, special assessments, or fire, steam boiler, or any other insurance premiums. In no event shall the AGENT be required to advance its own money in payment of any such indebtedness, taxes, assessments, or premiums.

4.5 To bear the responsibility and sole expense to use an outside firm to do the complete calculations, audit and administration in the event of circumstances that creates extraordinary bookkeeping and accounting. For its supervision, AGENT shall receive a sum equal to 5% of all fees and expenses related to such circumstances. This clause refers to, without being limited to, filings for bankruptcy, property tax appeals, and rent control applications.

5. OWNER AND AGENT MUTUALLY AGREE:

To hold each other harmless for loss to the property to the extent that either party is reimbursed or indemnified by insurance coverage.

6. IT IS MUTUALLY AGREED THAT:

6.1 The OWNER expressly withholds from the AGENT any power or authority to make any structural changes in any building or to make any other major alterations or additions in or to any such building or equipment therein, or to incur any expense chargeable to the OWNER other than expenses related to exercising the express powers above vested in the AGENT without the prior written direction of the following person:

Name	Address

except such emergency repairs as may be required because of danger to life or property or which are immediately necessary for the preservation and safety of the Premises or the safety of the tenants and occupants thereof or are required to avoid the suspension of any necessary service to the Premises.

6.2 The AGENT does not assume and is given no responsibility for compliance of any building on the Premises or any equipment therein with the requirements of any statute, ordinance, law, or regulation of any governmental body or of any public authority or official thereof having jurisdiction, except to notify the OWNER promptly or forward to the OWNER promptly any complaints, warnings, notices, or summonses received by it relating to such matters. The OWNER represents that to the best of his (its) knowledge the Premises and such equipment comply with all such requirements and authorizes the AGENT to disclose the ownership of the Premises to any such officials and agrees to indemnify and hold harmless the

AGENT, its representatives, servants, and employees, of and from all loss, cost, expense, and liability whatsoever which may be imposed on them or any of them by reason of any present or future violation or alleged violation of such laws, ordinances, statutes, or regulations.

6.3 In the event it is alleged or charged that any building on the Premises or any equipment therein or any act or failure to act by the OWNER with respect to the Premises or the sale, rental, or other disposition thereof fails to comply with, or is in violation of, any of the requirements of any constitutional provision, statute, ordinance, law, or regulation of any governmental body or any order or ruling of any public authority or official thereof having or claiming to have jurisdication thereover, and the AGENT, in its sole and absolute discretion, considers that the action or position of the OWNER or registered managing agent with respect thereto may result in damage or liability to the AGENT, the AGENT shall have the right to cancel this Agreement at any time by written notice to the OWNER of its election so to do, which cancellation shall be effective upon the service of such notice. Such notice may be served personally or by registered mail, on or to the person named to receive the AGENT's monthly statement at the address designated for such person as provided in Paragraph 2.2 above, and if served by mail shall be deemed to have been served when deposited in the mails. Such cancellation shall not release the indemnities of the OWNER set forth in Paragraphs 4, 5 and 6.2 above and shall not terminate any liability or obligation of the OWNER to the AGENT for any payment, reimbursement, or other sum of money then due and payable to the AGENT hereunder.

7. This Agreement may be cancelled by OWNER before the termination date specified in paragraph I on not less than ____90____ days' prior written notice to the AGENT, provided that such notice is accompanied by payment to the AGENT of a cancellation fee in an amount equal to ____25____ % of the management fee that would accrue over the remainder of the stated term of the Agreement. For this purpose the monthly management fee for the remainder of the stated term shall be presumed to be the same as that of the last month prior to service of the notice of cancellation.

8. The OWNER shall pay or reimburse the AGENT for any sums of money due it under this Agreement for services for actions prior to termination, notwithstanding any termination of this Agreement. All provisions of this Agreement that require the OWNER to have insured or to defend, reimburse, or indemnify the AGENT (including, but not limited to, Paragraphs 4.1, 4.2, and 4.3) shall survive

any termination and, if AGENT is or becomes involved in any proceeding or litigation by reason of having been the OWNER's AGENT, such provisions shall apply as if this Agreement were still in effect. The parties understand and agree that the AGENT may withhold funds for thirty (30) days after the end of the month in which this Agreement is terminated to pay bills previously incurred but not yet invoiced and to close accounts.

9.1 FOR MANAGEMENT: Agent is to receive 6% of the monthly gross receipts or $2,500 whichever is higher in any given month. Gross receipts are all amounts received from the operation of the Premises, including, but not limited to rents, parking fees, deposits, fees and utility receipts.

9.2 Management is to receive the amount of $500 at execution of this Agreement to cover all set-up costs concerned with the take over of the property.

9.3 APARTMENT LEASING _____

_____

_____

_____

9.4 COMMERCIAL LEASING _____

_____

_____

_____

9.5 MODERNIZATION (REHABILITATION/CONSTRUCTIONS) _____

_____

_____

_____

9.6 FIRE RESTORATION _____

_____

_____

9.1 FOR MANAGEMENT: Agent is to receive an initial management fee of $1,800 per month until the time that construction starts. At that time, this fee will be increased for construction supervision by $500 per month for a total fee of $2,300 per month. The fee will then continue to be increased in $100 increments for every ten units that are completed by the contractor and turned over to Agent for leasing and management. The fee will continue to increase to a maximum of $6,000. Agent's monthly management fee will be the amount as previously described or 6% of the monthly gross collections whichever is greater in any given month.

9.2 Management is to receive the amount of $500 at execution of this Agreement to cover all set-up costs concerned with the take over of the property.

9.3 APARTMENT LEASING _____

_____

_____

_____

9.4 COMMERCIAL LEASING _____

_____

_____

_____

9.5 MODERNIZATION (REHABILITATION/CONSTRUCTIONS) _____

_____

_____

_____

9.6 FIRE RESTORATION _____

_____

_____

_____

9.1 FOR MANAGEMENT: Agent is to receive 4½% of the monthly gross receipts from the operation of the premises for the first six months of this Agreement. For the second six months of this Agreement, Agent is to receive a commission of 4% of the monthly gross receipts. Agent is to also receive a bonus during the second six month period for any given month of the second six month period where Agent collects 96% of gross possible lease rent, Agent is to receive an additional one-half percent for that month bringing the total commission to 4½%. In addition, if Agent collects 98% of gross possible lease rents Agent shall receive another one-half percent bringing the total commission for the month up to 5%. Gross receipts are all amounts received from the operation of the Premises, including, but not limited to, rents, parking fees, deposits, laundry

income, fees and utility receipts. Gross possible lease rent is the total of the

base rents for each individual unit whether occuppied or vacant.

9.2 Management is to receive the amount of $500.00 at execution of this

Agreement to cover all set-up costs concerned with the take over of the property.

9.3 APARTMENT LEASING_____

_____

_____

9.4 COMMERCIAL LEASING_____

_____

_____

9.5 MODERNIZATION (REHABILITATION/CONSTRUCTION)_____

_____

_____

9.6 FIRE RESTORATION_____

_____

_____

9.7 After transfer of ownership or cancellation of the Agent, if continued

liason with the management is necessary, it is understood that the management company

will be reimbursed on an hourly basis for the time that is necessary.

9.8 AS ADDITIONAL COMPENSATION FOR THE RECORDKEEPING REQUIRED

FOR MAINTAINING TENANTS' SECURITY DEPOSITS AND LAST MONTH RENT

DEPOSITS, all interest earned on said deposits except the interest which must be

paid to the tenant by law. In addition, owner will be charged $1.00 per Tenant per

month as computer fees.

10. OWNER hereby agrees that the office of RODIN ENTERPRISES, INC.

will have the exclusive sales listing of said Premises during the term of this AGREE-

MENT or any renewal thereof, and shall be paid a sales commission of six per cent

(6%) of the gross consideration for the sale of the Premises, provided said sale

is actually consummated.

11. The making, execution and delivery of this AGREEMENT by the parties

hereto have been induced by no representation, statements, warranties or agreements

other than those expressed herein. This AGREEMENT embodies the entire understand-

ing of the parties with respect to the subject matter hereof, and there are no further or other agreements or understandings, written or oral, in effect between the parties relating to the subject matter hereof, unless specifically referred to herein by reference.   This AGREEMENT or any part thereof may be amended or modified only by written instruction signed by the parties hereto.

12.   This AGREEMENT has been delivered in the Commonwealth of Pennsylvania and shall be governed by and construed in accordance with the laws of the Commonwealth of Pennsylvania.   Should any provision of this AGREEMENT be prohibited or invalid under such law, such provision shall be ineffective to the extent of such prohibition or invalidity without invalidating the remainder of such provision or the remaining provisions of this AGREEMENT.

This AGREEMENT shall be binding upon the successors and assigns of the AGENT and their heirs, administrators, executors, successors, and assigns of the OWNER.

IN WITNESS WHEREOF, the parties hereto have affixed or caused to be affixed their respective signatures this _____ day of _____ , 19____ .

WITNESSES: OWNER:

_____   _____

_____   _____

_____   _____

                                          AGENT:

                                          Firm: _____

_____   By: _____
Submitted by

CURRENT AD

Paper _____
Which Days _____

Project _____
Cost Per Week _____

Most newspapers use 34 characters per line. Write your ad in the spaces below using one space for every period, coma, etc.

CURRENT AD BILLING PROOF

Enter the Current Month in the top left box and then write the date of the days it appears across. Use this to check incoming ad bills.

AREA RENTAL ANALYSIS

Date: _____

Complex	Address	Phone #	Rental Amount				Heat Type O or T	Who Pays (O or T)				Pets	Child.	Ref.	D/W	W/D	G/D	Rug	Blinds	Pool	Misc.
			eff.	1 br.	2 br.	3 br.		Elec.	Gas	A/C											

Rodin Management, Inc.

CHECK REQUEST and AUTHORIZATION

(For use only when a request for a check is not accompanied by an approved invoice).

COMPLEX: NO.:   DATE   /   /

PAY TO THE ORDER OF: PRINT OR TYPE ALL INFORMATION   AMOUNT: $_____

    NAME   : _____

    ADDRESS: _____

    CITY   : _____ STATE: _____ ZIP: _____

REASON:

REQUESTED BY: APPROVED BY:

_____   _____
(Signature)   (Signature)

OFFICE USE ONLY

ACCOUNT TO BE CHARGED

_____ $____
_____ $____
_____ $____
_____ $____

CHECK PREPARED BY:

_____
(Signature)

STAMP

REMARKS:

CONTRACT AGREEMENT

Date _____

This is an agreement with _____ of _____
and _____ .
_____ will perform various services for _____
_____ as an outside contractor, on a "Per Job" basis.
_____ will maintain his/her own records and be responsible
for his/her own taxes and workmen's compensation insurance or liability insurance.
_____ will give _____ first
opportunity to perform all contract services that are needed for _____
_____ .

_____

(complex)

_____

DELINQUENTS

MONTH OF _____

DATE _____

NAME #	TOTAL DUE	COMMENTS

APPENDIX 14.

DEPOSIT WORKSHEET

DEPOSIT # _____

Key
A = B + C

DEPOSIT DATE _____

PREPARED BY _____

PROPERTY _____

Apartment Info.			A Prior month delinq.	A Lease rent	A Pre-paid coll.	A Fees	A Fees	A Late chgs.	B Total collected	T H	C Appl. of prepaid (P) rent	C Delinq. rents	C Delinq. elec.	Tenant allow.	PRC rate	Comments	New move in
Res. no.	Apt. no.	Resident name															
Page totals																	

DOCUMENT TRANSMITTAL FORM

PROPERTY: _____ NO.: _____ TRANS. NO.: _____

SUBMITTED BY: _____ DATE: __/__/__

		INVOICES			
Supplier	✔	Invoice			Office Use Only
		Date	Number	Amount	

Deposits			Miscellaneous
Date	✔	Amount	

VERIFIED BY: _____ DATE: __/__/__

EMPLOYEE JOB AND TIME FORM

Complex   Date

Job	Time In	Time Out	Job	Time In	Time Out	Job	Time In	Time Out	Job	Time In	Time Out	Job	Time In	Time Out

EMPLOYEE PERSONNEL RECORD

SIDE 1

YEAR _____

EMPLOYEE PERSONNEL RECORD

Personal data		Social security number
Name		___ . ___
Address		Date of birth ___/___/___
City	State	Zip Code	☐ Male ☐ Female ☐ Single ☐ Married
		No. dependents ___
Telephone No. ( )		E ☐ Caucasian ☐ Negro
Emergency contact	Tel. no.	E ☐ Oriental ☐ Sp/Am.
		O ☐ Other _____
Date of hire ___/___/___	Job Title	Dep't
Employment Status	☐ Full time ☐ Part time	☐ Permanent ☐ Temporary	☐ Exempt ☐ Non-exempt	☐ Non-union ☐ Union—Local no. ___
Salary	Regular rate of pay $___.___	☐ Hourly ☐ Weekly	☐ Daily ☐ Weekly ☐ Monthly	Overtime rate of pay $___.___ hourly	Hours
Allowances	Auto $___.___	☐ Daily ☐ Weekly ☐ Monthly	Other $___.___ Other $___.___	☐ Daily ☐ Weekly ☐ Monthly	Type

PERSONNEL ACTIVITY

Month	Salary Rate Change		Vacation Days			Sick Leave Days		
	Date	Amount	Earned	Taken	Balance	Earned	Taken	Balance
Balance								
January								
February								
March								
April								
May								
June								
July								
August								
September								
October								
November								
December								
Total								

Date of termination: /   /

Reason: _____

Comments: _____

YEAR ———

SIDE 2

EMPLOYEE
NAME ————————

SOCIAL
SECURITY NO. ————————

Activity Code (Circle—No Pay)

A — Absence — Excused	M — Military leave
B — Absence — Unexcused	S — Sick leave
F — Funeral leave	V — Vacation
H — Holiday	W — Leave of absence
J — Jury duty	
L — Lateness	

January

W/E	S	M	T	W	T	F	S

February

W/E	S	M	T	W	T	F	S

March

W/E	S	M	T	W	T	F	S

April								May								June							
W/E	S	M	T	W	T	F	S	W/E	S	M	T	W	T	F	S	W/E	S	M	T	W	T	F	S

July								August								September							
W/E	S	M	T	W	T	F	S	W/E	S	M	T	W	T	F	S	W/E	S	M	T	W	T	F	S

October								November								December							
W/E	S	M	T	W	T	F	S	W/E	S	M	T	W	T	F	S	W/E	S	M	T	W	T	F	S

APPENDIX 18.

EMPLOYEE PERFORMANCE RATING

NAME: _____

DEPARTMENT: _____

DATE OF RATING: _____

JOB CLASSIFICATION: _____

	5	4	3	2	1	RATINGS
JOB KNOWLEDGE	*How Well Does This Employee Understand The Requirements Of Job To Which Assigned:*					
	Thoroughly understand all aspects of job.	More than adequate knowledge of job.	Has sufficient knowledge to do job.	Insufficient Knowledge of some phases.	Continually needs instruction.	
QUALITY OF WORK	*How Accurate, Neat And Complete Is The Work:*					
	Consistently neat, accurate and thorough.	Careful worker seldom needs corrections.	Work is acceptable.	Occasionally Careless - needs checking.	Inaccurate and careless.	
CO-OPERATION	*Does This Employee Work Harmoniously And Effectively With Co-Workers And Supervision:*					
	Exceptionally willing and successful as a team worker.	Usually tactful and offers to assist others.	Gets along well enough, no problem.	Cooperation must be solicited, seldom volunteers.	Tends to be a trouble-maker.	
RESPONSIBILITY	*How Does This Employee Accept All The Responsibilities Of The Job:*					
	Accepts all responsibilities fully and meets emergencies.	Conscientiously tries to fulfill job responsibilities.	Accepts but does not seek responsibility.	Does some assigned tasks reluctantly.	Indifferent - avoids responsibilities.	
INITIATIVE	*How Well Does This Employee Begin An Assignment Without Direction And Recognize The Best Way Of Doing It:*					
	Self starter, makes practical suggestions.	Proceeds on assigned work voluntarily and readily accepts suggestions.	Does regular work without prompting.	Relies on others: needs help getting started.	Must usually be told exactly what to do.	
QUANTITY OF WORK	*How Much Satisfactory Work Is Consistently Turned Out By This Employee:*					
	Maintains unusually high out-put.	Usually does more than expected.	Does sufficient amount of work.	Inclined to be slow.	Inadequate turn-out of work.	
DEPENDABILITY	*How Faithful Is This Employee In Reporting To Work And Staying On The Job:*					
	Places company interests ahead of personal conveniences.	Punctual and does not waste company time.	Generally on the job as needed.	Some abuses - occasionally needs to be admonished.	Chronic abuses of working schedules.	
					TOTAL	

COMMENTS: _____

RATED BY: _____

DISCUSSED WITH EMPLOYEE BY: _____

Is any action being taken to help this employee improve his performance: _____ No _____ Yes - Specify: _____

Dept. Manager _____

APPENDIX 19.

FOR EMPLOYMENT

(Please Print Plainly)

PERSONAL

Date _____

Name_____ Social Security No_____
    Last   First   Middle

Present Address_____Telephone No_____
        No   Street   City   State   Zip

Are you legally eligible for employment in the U.S.A.?_____ Age if under 18 _____

What method of transportation will you use to get to work?_____

Position(s) applied for_____Rate of pay expected $_____ per week

Would you work Full-Time___Part-Time___Specify days and hours if part-time_____

Were you previously employed by us?____If yes, when?_____

If your application is considered favorably, on what date will you be available for
work? _____ 19_____.

Are there any other experiences, skills, or qualifications which you feel would especially
fit you for work with our organization? _____

RECORD OF EDUCATION

School	Name and Address of School	Course of Study	Years Completed	Graduate?	List Diploma or Degree
Elementary					
High					
College					
Other (specify)					

MILITARY SERVICE RECORD

Were you in U.S. Armed Forces? _____ If yes, what Branch? _____

Dates of duty:From_____ To_____Rank at discharge_____
           Month Day Year   Month Day Year

List duties in the service including special training _____

Have you taken any training under the G.I. Bill of Rights?_____If yes, what training did
you take? _____

PREVIOUS EMPLOYMENT

Name and Address of Company and Type of Business	From - To Mo./Yr. - Mo./Yr.	Describe the work you did	Weekly Starting Salary	Weekly Last Salary	Reason for Leaving	Name of Supervisor

Telephone No. _____

_____

Telephone No. _____

_____

Telephone No. _____

_____

May we contact the employers listed above? _____ If not, indicate by No which ones you do not wish us to contact _____

MAINTENANCE EXPERTISE

Plumbing _____   Carpentry _____   Boilers _____   Type _____
Painting _____   Roofing _____   A/C _____   Type _____
Glassing _____   Cement _____   Appliances _____   Type _____
Carpeting _____   Tile _____   Electric _____   Type _____

SECRETARIAL SKILLS

Typing: Manual _____ Electric _____ Speed _____ Shorthand _____ Speed _____

Dictaphone _____ QWIP _____ Word Processing _____ Filing _____

OFFICE SKILLS

Computer Experience _____ Keypunch _____
Adding Machine _____ P.B.X. _____ Copy Machine _____

PERSONAL REFERENCES
(Not Former Employers or Relatives)

Name and Occupation	Address	Phone Number

_____

_____

_____

PLEASE READ AND SIGN BELOW

The facts set forth in my application for employment are true and complete. I understand that if employed, false statements on this application shall be considered sufficient cause tor dismissal. You are hereby authorized to make any investigation ot my personal history and financial and credit record through any investigative or credit agencies or bureaus of your choice.

In making this application for employment I authorize you to make an investigative consumer report whereby information is obtained through personal interviews with my neighbors, friends, or others with whom I am acquainted. This inquiry, if made, may include information as to my character, general reputation, personal characteristics and mode of living. I understand that I have the right to make a written request within a reasonable period of time to receive additional, detailed information about the nature and scope of any such investigative report that is made.

_____
Signature of Applicant

To Applicant: READ THIS INTRODUCTION CAREFULLY BEFORE ANSWERING ANY QUESTIONS IN THIS BLOCKED-OFF AREA. The Civil Rights Act of 1964 prohibits discrimination in employment because of race, color, religion, sex or national origin. Federal law also prohibits discrimination on the basis of age with respect to certain individuals. The laws of most States also prohibit some or all of the above types of discrimination as well as some additional types such as discrimination based upon ancestry, marital status or physical or mental handicap or disability. DO NOT ANSWER ANY QUESTION CONTAINED IN THIS BLOCKED-OFF AREA UNLESS THE EMPLOYER HAS CHECKED THE BOX NEXT TO THE QUESTION, thereby indicating that for the position for which you are applying the requested information is needed for a legally permissible reason, including without limitation, national security requirements, a bona fide occupational qualification or business necessity.

__ How long have you lived at present address?_____

__ Previous address_____How long did you live there?_____
          No.   Street   City   State   Zip
__ Are you over the age of eighteen? _____If no, hire is subject to verification that you are of minimum age.

__ How do you wish to be addressed? Mr. __ Mrs. __ Miss __ Ms. __

__ Sex: M ___ F ___   __ Height: ____ft.____in.   __ Weight:_____ lbs.

__ Marital Status: Single __ Engaged __ Married __ Separated __ Divorced __ Widowed __

__ Date of Marriage _____   __ Number of dependents including yourself

__ Are you a citizen of the U.S.A? _____

__ What is your present Selective Service Classification _____

__ Indicate dates you attended school:

Elementary _____ High School _____ College _____
          From   To   From   To   From   To

Other (Specify type of school) _____
                                                    From   To

__ Have you ever been bonded? _____ If yes, on what jobs? _____

__ Have you ever been convicted of a crime, excluding misdemeanors and summary offenses, in the past ten years which has not been annulled or expunged or sealed by a court? _____ If yes, describe in full _____
_____

__ Do you have any physical condition which may limit your ability to perform the particular job for which you are applying? _____ If yes, describe such condition and explain how you can perform the job for which you are applying in spite of it. _____
_____
_____

__ Do you have any physical defects which preclude you from performing certain kinds of work? _____ If yes, describe such defects and specific work limitations. _____
_____

__ Have you had a major illness in the past 5 years? _____ If yes, describe _____
_____

__ Have you received compensation for injuries? _____ If yes, describe _____
_____

___ List any friends or relatives working for us, other than spouse _____

Name(s)

Employer may list other bona fide occupational questions on lines below:

_____

_____

APPLICANT - DO NOT WRITE ON THIS PAGE
FOR INTERVIEWER'S USE

Interviewer   Date   Comments

FOR TEST ADMINISTRATOR'S USE

Tests   Raw
Administered   Date   Score   Rating   Comments

REFERENCE CHECK

Position   Results of Reference Check

1

2

3

4

_____

APPENDIX 20.

FEE REGISTER

APPLICATION #	APT. #	NAME	PHONE #	APP. FEE	DATE	PICKED UP

APPENDIX 21.

APARTMENT MAINTENANCE CHECKLIST

BATHROOM

1. Toilet Flushes
   a) Refills properly _____
   b) Seal good _____

2. Sink
   a) Faucets washers good _____
   b) enamel touch-up _____
   c) trap not leaking _____

3. Mirror
   a) lights in mirror _____
   b) doors and cover _____
   c) fixture in place _____

4. Tub Area
   a) Enamel touch
   b) Shower head/seal _____
   c) Diverter okay _____
   d) water drains properly _____
   e) Tile grouted and eschutchen
      sealed _____
   f) shower rod/glass doors secure _____
   g) Soap, grab, towel bars in place _____
   h) Tile all secure _____

5. Water pressure and temperature okay _____

KITCHEN

1. Refrigerator working properly _____
   a) shelves and drawers in _____

2. Range
   a) burners working _____
   b) pilots lit _____

3. Sink Area
   a) check faucets for leaks _____
   b) clean screens on faucets _____
   c) check trap and disposal _____

4. All light fixtures and bulbs/covers _____

5. Cabinets - drawers/handles _____

6. Enamel touch up in sink _____

7. Condition of Floors _____

OTHER AREAS IN APARTMENT

1. Walls
   a) holes are spackled and
      ready for painting _____

2. Ceilings
   a) Tiles all in place-check
      for water stains _____

3. Windows
   a) all windows have thumb locks _____
   b) all are functional _____
   c) check sills and mulien for
      rotting _____

4. Floors okay _____

5. Doors
   a) Not scarred/marked _____
   b) locks functional/office has
      keys/mailbox key _____
   c) door jam okay _____

6. Heating and Cooling System okay
   a) Screens/filters and vents _____
   b) check all units in Apartments _____

7. Light Fixtures
   a) covers and bulbs _____

8. Receptacles
   a) covers _____
   b) working _____

9. Closets/Doors
   a) open and close properly _____
   b) floor guides
   c) rods

10. Interior doors
    a) hinges secure - open and
       close properly _____

11. Painting _____

_____
Tenant Signature

_____
Date

_____
Maintenance Signature

_____
Date

Inspection Report (Move Out)

RENTAL OFFICE

APT.
ADDRESS _____

THE FOLLOWING IS THE DISPOSITION OF
YOUR SECURITY DEPOSIT

DATE _____ COMPLEX _____

TO BE COMPLETED BY MAINTENANCE DEPT.

VACANT APT. REFURBISHING CHECK LIST CHARGEABLE ITEMS	ACCEPTABLE	UNACCEPTABLE	REFURBISHING EXPENSE ABOVE NORMAL	COMMENTS AND WORK TO BE PERFORMED NON-CHARGEABLE ITEMS
APPLIANCES				
1. Oven				
2. Refrigerator				
3. Dishwasher				
4. Washer				
5. Dryer				
6. Garbage disposal				
FLOORS				
7. Floors				
8. Ceramic				
9. Woodwork & doors				
10. Carpet				
11. Windows & screens				
12. Sliding glass door				
13. Hardware				
14. Painting				
15. Walls & ceilings				
16. Balcony or patio				
17. Kitchen cabinets				
18. Bathroom fixtures				
19. Medicine cabinets				
MISCELLANEOUS				
20. Trash removal				
21. Counter tops				
22. Elect. fixtures				
23. Keys returned				
24. Is Apt. generally clean				
25.				
26.				
27.				
28.				
29.				
30.				

INSPECTED BY _____

TOTAL DAMAGE DEDUCTIONS

DATE OF INSPECTION _____

TO BE COMPLETED BY RENTAL OFFICE

_____ Manager

_____ Lease Date

_____ Paid Last Month Rent

TO:

name _____

address _____

city _____ state _____

apt. no. transferred to _____

date apt. vacated _____

type of move out _____

reason for termination _____

AM'T OF SECURITY DPS.	$
TO BE DEDUCTED	AMOUNT
damage deductions	
late charges	
rent _____ unpaid month	
Fee for Prem. Term.	
legal fee	
TOTAL DEDUCTIONS	

AMOUNT   ☐ REFUNDED
TO BE   ☐ TRANSFERRED $
OR   ☐ DEFICIT

Your refund check in the amount of $_____ is enclosed. Check # _____ .

Please forward your check in the amount of $_____ within 5 days.

APPROVED BY _____

APPENDIX 23.

REGARDING YOUR RENT . . .

Per your lease agreement your rent is due the first of each month. For any rents not in our office by the fifth of the month, a $1.00 a day late charge will be added to your account.

If you continue to pay your rent late, we will have no choice but to ask you to move, or take the necessary action.

If your rent has already been paid, Thank You, and please disregard this notice.

Date _____

_____ Rent _____

_____

_____

Late Charges _____

Court Costs _____

Previous Bal. _____

Total Due _____

RODIN MANAGEMENT INCORPORATED
——————— *Property Management* ———————

1500 LAND TITLE BUILDING
PHILADELPHIA, PENNSYLVANIA 19110
(215) 563-7202

<u>LEASE ABSTRACT REVIEW FORM</u>

Date:_____

Property_____

Unit Leased_____

Tenant Name_____

Commencement Date_____

Term_____

Rent_____

	Yes	No
Rodin Management, Inc. Agent has been typed on the line where Landlord executes.	____	____
All areas on lease completed.	____	____
Witness Line Signed.	____	____
Tenant Signed Lease.	____	____
Tenant initialled Addendum.	____	____
Security Deposit Agreement completed and signed.	____	____
Credit check completed and attached.	____	____
Money order or certified check attached.	____	____
Lease, Security Agreement, Addendums, attached.	____	____

If you have responded No to any of the above, please comment on the back of this form.

Completed by:

_____

APPENDIX 25.

Property Name and Number_____

Document
Reference

Tenant Name: _____
Billing Address:_____
_____
_____
_____

I.D. Number   _____   Security Deposit $_____
Suite Number   _____   Gross Term Rent $_____
Square Footage   _____   Total T.I. and
Term of Lease   _____   Concessions   _____
Move-In Date   _____   Gross Rate PSF $_____
Commencement and   Net Rate PSF $_____
Expiration Date   _____

Type of Lease: (circle one)   New Lease   Renewal   Other _____

Tenant Use Clause:_____

Charges:	Monthly	Annual	Comments
a) Base Rent	_____	_____	_____
b) Electric	_____	_____	_____
c) Gas	_____	_____	_____
d) Steam	_____	_____	_____
e) Sewer & Water	_____	_____	_____
f) HVAC	_____	_____	_____
g) Tax Escalation	_____	_____	_____
h) Operating Esc.	_____	_____	_____
i) _____	_____	_____	_____
j) _____	_____	_____	_____
k) _____	_____	_____	_____
l) _____	_____	_____	_____
Total Rental	$_____	$_____	

Escalation:	Base Year	%	Remarks
Tax	_____	_____	_____
Operating	_____	_____	_____
Other _____	_____	_____	_____

Tenant Improvements: _____
_____
_____

Concessions, Abatements, Allowances or Takeover Agreements: _____
_____
_____
_____

Options: _____
_____
_____

Cancellation: _____
_____
_____

Special Items: _____
_____
_____

Remarks: _____
_____
_____
_____

Date of Abstract:_____   Prepared By:_____

433

LEASE ADDENDUM

This addendum is a rider to the lease dated _____ between
RODIN MANAGEMENT, INC. and _____
Address _____ Apt. _____

1. Lessee hereby agrees to pay a late charge of $1.00 per day for any rents not in the office of RODIN MANAGEMENT, INC. by the fifth day of the month. _____

2. Lessee is responsible for all _____ usage. _____

3. Lessee agrees to pay for any repairs to windows, screen doors, door locks and service of all clogged drains and fireplaces where damage was caused by the tenant. _____

4. Lessor is not responsible for repairs and/or replacement of the following if damage is done by the tenant. The following shall remain the property of the Lessor. (o/n/r = owner not responsible)

    A. Refrigerator _____ B. Range _____

    C. Rugs _____ D. Air Conditioner _____

    E. Garbage Disposal _____ F. Dishwasher _____

    G. Venetian Blinds _____ H. Washer _____

    I. Dryer _____

5. Lessee will not use the security deposit as the last month's rent. _____

6. If Lessee does not occupy the aforementioned apartment for twelve (12) consecutive months, the Lessee forfeits the entire security deposit. Apartment is to be occupied by Lessee only. _____

7. Lessee is responsible to keep their portion of the hallway and stairs clean. _____

8. The following are not permitted in the apartment:

    A. Children _____ B. Pets _____ C. Waterbeds _____

    D. Private Dishwasher _____ E. Private Washer & Dryer _____

    F. CB Equipment _____ G. Kerosene Heater _____

    H. Private Antennae _____ _____

9. Where parking is available, Lessee is granted one parking space only. Cars will towed at owner's expense. _____

10. The Lessor is not responsible for the loss or damage of any personal property belonging to the Lessee. It is recommended that the Lessee obtain apartment house or renters insurance. _____

11. Check Policy: For each check returned from the bank, there will be a $15.00 fee charged to the tenant. If this situation occurs twice, the office will no longer accept personal checks.   _____

12. Superintendent must have a copy of the apartment key.   _____

13. In the event that the local real estate taxes assessed against the complex, water & sewer charges, or the Lessor's cost of energy, i.e., fuel oil, electricity or natural gas, increases, the Lessor may require Lessee to pay a proportionate share of any such increases as additional rent. Such additional rent will be due and payable within thirty (30) days of written notice.   _____

14. Lessee is responsible for all court costs and landlord's attorney fees in the event that legal action has to be instituted for tenant's breach of lease.   _____

15. Where Lessor pays for all electric usage in the building, then Lessee shall pay an air conditioning fee of $_____ per month from May through October for each air conditioner in Lessee's apartment.   _____

16. Lessor is not responsible to maintain any fireplace that may be in the apartment.   _____

_____   _____

Witness   Seal

_____   _____

Date Signed   Seal

RODIN MANAGEMENT, INC.

LEASE ADDENDUM

RODIN MANAGEMENT, INC.

DATED _____

This addendum is an addition to your original lease agreement, by and between _____
_____ and _____ Apt. # _____

1. Lessee will pay $ _____ per month starting _____.
2. Lessee is responsible for all _____ usage.
3. The lease will be on a _____ to _____ with a _____( )
    day written notice required for cancellation or changes.
4. Lessee will pay a late charge of $1.00 per day for any rents not in the office of Rodin
    Management, Inc. by the fifth day of the month.
5. Lessee will pay for any repairs to windows, screens, doors, door locks, and service of all
    clogged drains and fireplaces during the term of this lease, where damage was caused by the
    tenant.
6. Where Lessor is responsible to provide the following, Lessor will not be responsible for the
    repairs to the following, if the damage is done by the tenant:

Refrigerator	Garbage Disposal	Range	Dryer
Air Conditioner	Dishwasher	Washer	Blinds/Shades

7. The following are not permitted in the apartment:

Pets	CB Equipment	Private Washer/Dryer	Waterbeds
Private Antennae	Kerosene Heater	Private Dishwasher	

8. Where parking is available, Lessee is granted one parking space only. Cars will be towed at
    owner's expense.
9. Lessor will not be responsible to make the pool available.
10. Lessor will not be responsible for the fireplace.
11. Lessee will not use the security deposit as the last month's rent.
12. Lessee is responsible to keep their portion of the hallway and stairs clean.
13. The Lessor is not responsible for the loss or damage of any personal property belonging
    to the Lessee. It is recommended that the Lessee obtain apartment house or renters
    insurance.

14. *CHECK POLICY:* For each check returned from the bank, there will be a $15.00 fee charged to the tenant. If this situation occurs twice, the office will no longer accept personal checks.

15. Superintendent must have a copy of the apartment key.

16. In the event that the local real estate taxes assessed against the complex, water & sewer charges, or the Lessor's cost of energy, i.e., fuel oil, electricity or natural gas, increases, the Lessor may require Lessee to pay a proportionate share of any such increases as additional rent. Such additional rent will be due and payable within thirty (30) days of written notice.

17. Lessee is responsible for all court costs and landlord's attorney fees in the event that legal action has to be instituted for tenant's breach of lease.

ALL CONDITIONS PREVIOUSLY CONTRACTED FOR IN YOUR ORIGINAL LEASE WILL BE IN EFFECT. IF YOU REMAIN IN THE APARTMENT, THE PRECEDING CONDITIONS WILL ALSO BE IN EFFECT.

APPENDIX 28.

MAINTENANCE CALL-IN SHEET FOR TENANT'S REQUESTS FOR SERVICE

Date	Name	Apt.	Phone	Key	Service Requested	Parts Used	Done

APPENDIX 29.

MOVE - INS

Tenant Name:_____   Date:_____

Apartment #:_____

Complex:_____

Tenant will begin paying rent in _____ in the amount
                                      (month)
of $_____.

Tenant will receive pro-rata credit in the amount of $_____

for _____.   Tenant is responsible for $_____ in
        (month)
_____.
    (month)

PAN-1 (4/81)

<u>PERSONNEL ACTION NOTICE</u>

COMPLEX:_____   ____NEW EMPLOYEE ____CHANGE TO EMPLOYEE

	PRINT OR TYPE ALL INFORMATION			
PERSONAL DATA	NAME			Social Security #
	ADDRESS		Zip Code	Effective Date
	CITY/STATE			/ /
EMPLOYMENT ___ New Hire ___ Rehire ___ L.O.A. _____	DATE OF BIRTH / /	TELEPHONE NO. ( )	___ Male ___ Female	R A C E ___ Caucasian ___ Negro ___ Orient ___ Span./Amer. ___ Other_____
	Full Time Part Time	Permanent Temporary	Exempt Non-Exempt	Non-Union Union - Local #
SALARY DATA	JOB TITLE			DEPARTMENT
	Regular Rate of Pay $. ___ Hourly ___ Weekly	Overtime Rate of Pay $. ___ Hourly ___ Weekly		Scheduled Hours ___ Daily ___ Weekly
ALLOWANCES	AUTO: $____.__ ___ Daily ___ Weekly ___ Monthly		OTHER: $____.__ ___ Daily ___ Weekly ___ Monthly	
RATE CHANGE ___Automatic ___Merit ___Position ___Promotion ___ _____	DATE OF HIRE / /	DATE OF LAST INCREASE / /	DATE OF NEXT REVIEW / /	
	New Rate of Pay $.	Hourly Weekly	Overtime Pay $.	Hourly Weekly
	Old Rate of Pay $.	Hourly Weekly	Overtime Pay $.	Hourly Weekly
	NEW JOB TITLE		OLD JOB TITLE	
DEPARTMENTAL TRANSFERS	DEPARTMENT			
	JOB TITLE			
	DEPT. MGR.			
SEPARATION ___Discharge ___L.O.A. ___Retire ___Resign ___ _____	EFF. DATE / / REHIRE? ___Yes ___No	REASON ___Unsatisfactory ___Excess Absenteeism ___Failure to Report ___Personal ___Illness ___Other_____ ___Normal ___Disability ___Other Employment ___Other_____ ___Other		
PAYROLL TAX WITHHOLDING	___ F.I.C.A. ___Federal Income (attach W-4 or W4E) ___ Local _____ ___ State_____ (Attach Non-Resident Certificate, if required)			
REMARKS				
SIGNATURES	DEP'T. MGR. Date	CONTROLLER Date	AUTHORIZED BY: Date	

PETTY CASH REIMBURSEMENT VOUCHER

COMPLEX: _____

DATE: ___ / ___ / ___

VOUCHER NO.: _____

SUBMITTED BY: _____

PERIOD: From _____ to _____

DATE	SUPPLIER	DESCRIPTION OF ITEMS PURCHASED	WHERE USED	AMOUNT OF PURCHASE	OFFICE USE ONLY

TOTAL EXPENDITURES

ATTACH ALL RECEIPTS

PREPARE RECONCILIATION - REVERSE SIDE

APPROVED BY: _____   DATE: ___ / ___ / ___

REVIEWED BY: _____   DATE: ___ / ___ / ___

RECONCILIATION OF PETTY CASH FUND

TOTAL PETTY CASH FUND TO ACCOUNT FOR	$ _____
DEDUCT: TOTAL EXPENDITURES PER VOUCHER	_____
BALANCE TO ACCOUNT FOR	$ _____
PETTY CASH ON HAND	_____
PETTY CASH FUND – SHORT or (OVER) – Explain	$ _____

SUBMITTED BY: _____   APPROVED BY: _____

PROPERTY: _____

No.: _____   DATE: __/__/__

PURCHASE CONFIRMATION

Use When Hardware Store
Invoices are Attached.

SUPPLIER: _____   STATEMENT NO.: _____

ADDRESS: _____   SUBMITTED BY: _____

CITY/STATE: _____ ZIP CODE _____   APPROVED BY: _____

INVOICE NO.	Q_TY	DESCRIPTION		WHERE USED	AMOUNT	RODIN MANAGEMENT ACCOUNT NO.
		DESCRIBE ITEM	ACCT. NAME			
			TOTAL AMOUNT OF PURCHASE			

RODIN MANAGEMENT INC. - 2/83

APPENDIX 33.

Rental Information

1. Apartment Rents

    1. Old Tenants Increased:

        A. efficiency _____

        B. 1 bedroom _____

        C. 2 bedroom _____

    2. New Tenants:

        A. Efficiency _____   (no. of) _____

        B. 1 bedroom _____   (no. of) _____

        C. 2 bedroom _____   (no. of) _____

Owner Supplies

    1. Refrigerator_____   2. Range_____   3. Rugs_____   4. Shades_____

    5. Air Conditioner_____   6. Garbage Disposal_____   7. Dishwasher_____

    8. Venetian Blinds_____   9. Washer_____   10. Dryer_____   11._____

3. Tenant Pays

    1. Rent_____   4.. Pool_____

    2. Electric_____   5. Kind of Heat_____

    3. Gas_____   6. _____

4. Apartment Allows

    1. Childern _____   3. _____

    2. Pets_____   4. _____

5. Leases

    1. one month's rent_____

    2. one month's _____

    3. last month's rent _____

RODIN MANAGEMENT INC.

Property Management

1500 LAND TITLE BUILDING   PHILADELPHIA, PA 19110   TELEPHONE (215) 563-7202

N O T I C E

Please be advised that this apartment complex is a member of
Credit Bureau Associates and RentCheck/TeleCheck. We use these
credit bureaus to screen our applicants thoroughly so that we
may obtain and maintain responsible and desirable residents in
our complex.

Also, if at any time you are delinquent in your rent or give us
a check which is returned for insufficient funds, this information
will be reported to the credit bureaus and could adversely affect
your credit.

LOS ANGELES • NEW YORK • NEW ORLEANS • FT. LAUDERDALE

RENT ROLL

PAGE _____ OF _____

MANAGING AGENT

MONTH _____

PROPERTY _____

KEY
1 = A
2 + A = B + C

| APARTMENT | | RENT CHANGE +/− | LEASE INFORMATION | | | (1) PRIOR MONTH DELINQ | (A) TOTAL CHG. ABLE RENT | CASH COLLECTIONS | | | | | (B) TOTAL COLLECTED | (C) APPL. OF PREPAID (P) RENT | (C) DELINQ. RENTS | (C) VACAN-CIES | (C) TENANT ALLOW | (C) EMP (E) AND MODEL (M) APTS | COMMENTS | SEC. HELD | LMR HELD | VACANCY VERIFICATION | |
NO.	RESIDENT TYPE		TERM	NOTICE	EXP.	LEASE RENT		(2) PRE. PAID COLL.	FEES	(2) FEES	(2) LATE CHGS.											IN OUT	EM PTY
PAGE TOTAL																							

SECURITY DEPOSIT AGREEMENT

1. Management agrees that, subject to the conditions listed below, and contained in the lease, this security deposit will be returned in full.

2. Undersigned agrees that this security deposit may not be applied as rent, and that the full monthly rent will be paid on or before the first day of every month including the last month of occupancy.

RELEASE OF THE SECURITY DEPOSIT IS SUBJECT TO THE FOLLOWING PROVISIONS:

Timely notice of intention to vacate apartment has been submitted, in writing, to the Management company.

No damage to property beyond fair wear and tear.

Entire apartment, including range, exhaust fan, refrigerator, bathroom, closets, cabinets, are clean. Refrigerator to be defrosted.

No stickers or scratches or holes on walls. All burned out light bulbs to be replaced.

No indentations or scratches in wood or resilent flooring caused by furniture.

No unpaid late charges or delinquent rents.

All keys are to be returned.

All debris and rubbish and discards placed in proper rubbish containers.

Forwarding address left with management.

Tenant must not have repainted any part of the apartment.

The costs of labor and materials for cleaning and repairs, and delinquent payments will be deducted from Security Deposit if the above provisions are not complied with. The Security Deposit will be refunded by a check mailed to the forwarding address, made payable to all persons signing the lease.

_____   _____
Tenant   Rodin Management Inc.

Number_____

RODIN MANAGEMENT INC.

Property Management

1500 LAND TITLE BUILDING PHILADELPHIA, PA 19110 TELEPHONE (215) 563-7202

TENANT APPLICATION

Date_____

Location_____

Apt. & Rent_____

Move In Date_____

Apt. Extras

Range_____ W/D_____
Refrig_____ Blinds_____
A/C_____ Rugs_____
D/W_____ Garb.Dis._____
Shades_____ Misc._____

LESSEE

Name (A)_____Age_____Soc.Sec.#_____

Name (B)_____Age_____Soc.Sec.#_____

Name of Children_____Ages_____

Credit Status (A) Good Fair Poor
                                    (Please Circle ONE)

Credit Status (B) Good Fair Poor

Phone where
we can reach
you

_____

ADDRESS

Present Address (A)_____Zip_____
Rent Paid To:_____How Long_____Ph#_____

Present Address (B)_____Zip_____
Rent Paid To:_____How Long_____Ph#_____

Previous Address:_____Zip_____
Rent Paid To:_____How Long_____Ph#_____

EMPLOYMENT

Employer (A)_____Address_____Zip_____
How Long_____Income_____Supervisor_____Position_____Ph#_____

Employer (B)_____Address_____Zip_____
How Long_____Income_____Supervisor_____Position_____Ph#_____

Previous Employer_____Address_____Zip_____
How Long_____Income_____Supervisor_____Position_____Ph#_____

Next of Kin:_____Address_____Ph#_____
Next of Kin:_____Address_____Ph#_____

I/We certify the foregoing information to be true and correct to the
best of my/our knowledge and belief. I/We understand and acknowledge
that an apartment is being considered for occupancy by me/us while a
credit report can be gotten and facts are verified. If I/We do not
execute a lease for any personal reason or false application information has been given, the fee in the amount of $_____will be forfeited.

Witness_____Applicant_____Dr.Lic.#_____

LOS ANGELES • NEW YORK • NEW ORLEANS • FT. LAUDERDALE

APPENDIX 38.

Tenant Card

LESSEE: _____ COMPLEX: _____ APT. # _____

_____ MOVE IN DATE: _____ TYPE _____

CO-SIGNER: _____ LEASE INFO.: _____/_____/_____ HUD PMT. _____

RES. PH # _____ BUS. PH # _____ SEC. & LMR. _____/_____ _____

BASE RENT DUE	MONTH RENT DUE	CHARGES				TOTAL PAID	R D	DATE PAID	CREDITS	
		L/C	C/C	MISC.					PRO RATE	MISC.
	JAN									
	FEB									
	MAR									
	APR									
	MAY									
	JUN									
	JUL									
	AUG									
	SEPT									
	OCT									
	NOV									
	DEC									
	JAN									
	FEB									
	MAR									
	APR									
	MAY									
	JUN									
	JUL									
	AUG									
	SEPT									
	OCT									
	NOV									
	DEC									

449

TIME CARD

EMPLOYEE NAME:_____

COMPLEX:_____

DATE	IN	OUT	OVERTIME IN	OUT	SPECIAL NOTES
TOTALS					

Payment Received $ Signature:

Adjustment Due: $

Adjustment Received $ Signature:

TRAFFIC SHEET

Name	PH	Date	Source	Visited	Comments

APPENDIX 41.

VACANCY FORM

OUT				IN			
Name	Date	Apt.		Name	Date	Size	Date Apt. will be ready

WEEKLY EXPENSE REPORT

FOR WEEK ENDED SUNDAY | MO | DAY | YR

1. Prepare this report on a Monday through Sunday basis only! (Do not split weeks.)
2. Attach receipts for all expenses except those indicated by an asterisk (*).
3. Record mileage in trip allowance section, multiply by authorized rate per mile and record dollar amount in mileage allowance box.

Expenses	Monday /	Tuesday /	Wednesday /	Thursday /	Friday /	Saturday /	Sunday /	C O D E	Totals
Food allowance								A	
Hotel								B	
Entertainment								C	
Auto rental								D	
Air-Rail								E	
Mileage allowance								F	
Tolls								G	
Parking								H	
Taxi and local fares								J	
Misc.								K	
Totals									

Cash items

Charge items												M	
Auto rental													
Air-Rail												N	
Totals													
Grand total													
Trip allow-ance:	From												
	To												
	Auto mileage												
Number in party													

		X
Advance		
Due company		Y
Due employee		Z

Explain misc. & entertainment expenses:

Purpose of trip:

Last name (print)	First	Title (print)	Social security no.

Signature | Dept. name | Complete only if check is to be mailed

Mailing address—No. & Street

Supervisor's approval (sign) | Home office use only | City | State | Zip Code

APPENDIX 43.

STATUS REPORT FOR WEEK ENDING_____

RODIN MANAGEMENT INC.

DEVELOPMENT_____

PREPARED BY_____

APARTMENT TYPE					4 WKS. AGO	3 WKS. AGO	2 WKS. AGO	1 WK. AGO	THIS WEEK
									No./%
1. TOTAL					- - - - - - - - - - - - - - - - -				
2. In Use (Rented)									/ %
3. Non-Revenue									/ %
4. Vacant/Ready	/	/	/	/	/	/	/	/	/
5. Applications									
6. Total Applications									
7. Notice to Vacate									
8. Renewal Notices Sent									
9. Move Ins (Actual)									
10. Move Outs (Actual)									
11. Phone Calls									
12. Visits									
13. Work Orders Requested									
14. Work Orders Completed									
15. Outstanding Work Orders									

16. Current Week's Deposit: Rent $_____ Sec. Dep. $_____ Other $_____

17. Cumulative Rent Deposited for Month Ending (___/25/___) $_____

18. a) Number of Delinquencies_____ b) Amount of Delinquent Rent $_____

19. Percentage of Rent Collected: 17 ÷ (17 + 18b) Indicate ONLY Prior to 25th of the Month   _____ %

COMMENTS: (Advertising, traffic, move outs, collections, delinquencies, maintenance, personnel, etc.)

_____

_____

_____

_____

_____

_____

_____

_____

_____

_____

PROPERTY SUPERVISOR

APPENDIX 44.

<u>WEEKLY INSPECTION REPORT</u>

RODIN MANAGEMENT INC.

DEVELOPMENT_____

PREPARED BY_____

DATE VISITED_____

OFFICE/MODELS	Condition of Each	GOOD	FAIR	POOR	COMMENTS
	Furniture	___	___	___	_____
	Floors	___	___	___	_____
	Windows	___	___	___	_____
	Gen. Appearance	___	___	___	_____
OUTSIDE AREA	Service Walks	___	___	___	_____
	Landscaping & Grass	___	___	___	_____
	Sidewalk	___	___	___	_____
	Trash Area	___	___	___	_____
	Parking Areas	___	___	___	_____
	Streets	___	___	___	_____
	Play Areas	___	___	___	_____
	Signs & Banners	___	___	___	_____
COMMUNITY AREAS	Gen. Appearance	___	___	___	_____
	Rest Rooms	___	___	___	_____
	Furniture	___	___	___	_____
	Floors	___	___	___	_____
	Windows	___	___	___	_____
COMMONS HALLS	Gen. Appearance	___	___	___	_____
SWIMMING POOL	Pool & Pool Area	___	___	___	_____
	Landscaping, Grass	___	___	___	_____
	Rest Rooms	___	___	___	_____
	Gen. Appearance	___	___	___	_____

OPERATIONS	YES	NO	COMMENTS
Vacancy Book Up-to-Date	___	___	_____
All Vacancies Walked	___	___	_____
All New Leases and Credit Checks Reviewed	___	___	_____
Applications Reviewed	___	___	_____
Tenant Cards Used Properly	___	___	_____
Deposits Reviewed	___	___	_____
Notices to Vacate Reviewed	___	___	_____
Work Orders Reviewed	___	___	_____
Payables Reviewed	___	___	_____
Petty Cash Reviewed	___	___	_____
Rent Roll Complete and Accurate	___	___	_____
Delinquency List Reviewed	___	___	_____
Property Advertising Reviewed	___	___	_____
Traffic Reviewed	___	___	_____

<u>SUGGESTIONS & RECOMMENDATIONS</u>

Cost Savings_____

Delinquencies_____

New Competition_____

Employees' Problems_____

Resident Problems_____

Maintenance Problems_____

Other_____
_____
_____

VICE-PRESIDENT

APPENDIX 45.

OFFICER INSPECTION REPORT

RODIN MANAGEMENT INC.

DEVELOPMENT_____

PREPARED BY_____

DATE VISITED_____

OFFICE/MODELS	Condition of Each	GOOD	FAIR	POOR	COMMENTS
	Furniture	____	____	____	_____
	Floors	____	____	____	_____
	Windows	____	____	____	_____
	Gen. Appearance	____	____	____	_____
OUTSIDE AREA	Service Walks	____	____	____	_____
	Landscaping & Grass	____	____	____	_____
	Sidewalk	____	____	____	_____
	Trash Area	____	____	____	_____
	Parking Areas	____	____	____	_____
	Streets	____	____	____	_____
	Play Areas	____	____	____	_____
	Signs & Banners	____	____	____	_____
COMMUNITY AREAS	Gen. Appearance	____	____	____	_____
	Rest Rooms	____	____	____	_____
	Furniture	____	____	____	_____
	Floors	____	____	____	_____
	Windows	____	____	____	_____
COMMONS HALLS	Gen. Appearance	____	____	____	_____
SWIMMING POOL	Pool & Pool Area	____	____	____	_____
	Landscaping, Grass	____	____	____	_____
	Rest Rooms	____	____	____	_____
	Gen. Appearance	____	____	____	_____

COMMENTS:

_____
_____
_____
_____
_____
_____
_____
_____
_____
_____
_____

ENERGY ACCOUNTING—FUEL OIL

FUEL OIL NO. _____   PROPANE _____

Base _____
Year 19__   Reported _____   Approved _____   Location _____
Primary fuel? _____   By _____   By _____
Facility size, ft² _____   Standby fuel? _____   Sheet _____ of _____ dated _____

1	2		3	4	5	6	7	8	9	10	11	12	13	14	15	16	17	18
Year 19__	Reading dates		Fuel used gallons × _____			$ Cost		$/Gallon		Degree days		Gallons/DD		% Gals per DD	Monthly sales	% of sales	Customer count	KWH customer
Month	From	To	Current	Base*	Difference	Current	Base	Current	Base	Current	Base	Current	Base					
Jan																		
Feb																		
Mar																		
1st q.																		
Apr																		
May																		
Jun																		
2nd q.																		
Jul																		
Aug																		
Sep																		
3rd q.																		
Oct																		
Nov																		
Dec																		
4th q.																		
Total																		

*Base—previous year

APPENDIX 47.

ENERGY ACCOUNTING—GAS

Base _____
Year _____
Firm? _____ Interruptable? _____
Facility size, ft² _____

Reported By _____
Approved By _____ Alternate fuel _____

Location _____
Sheet _____ of _____ dated _____

Column 1	2		3		4	5	6	7	8	9	10	11	12	13	14	15	16	17	18	19
	Reading dates		Total days		Gas used ft³ × Base year _____			$ Cost		$/MCF		Degree days		MCF/DD		% MCF per DD	Monthly sales	% of sales	Customer count	KWH customer
Year 19__ Month	From	To	Current	Base*	Current	Base year	Difference	Current	Base year	Current	Base	Current	Base	Current	Base					
Jan																				
Feb																				
Mar																				
1st q.																				
Apr																				
May																				
Jun																				
2nd q.																				
Jul																				
Aug																				
Sep																				
3rd q.																				
Oct																				
Nov																				
Dec																				
4th q.																				
Total																				

*Base—previous year

459

ENERGY ACCOUNTING—ELECTRICITY

Base year _____ Reported by _____ Approved by _____

Facility size, ft² _____

Location _____

Sheet _____ of _____ dated _____

Column 1	2 Reading dates		3 Total days		4 KWH used ×	5	6	7 $ Cost including demand charges	8	9 $/KWH including demand charges	10	11 Kilowatt demand	12	13 Comparison	14	15	16	17	18	19
Year 19__ Month	From	To	Current	Base*	Current	Base year	Difference	Current	Base year	Current	Base year	Current	Base	±% KWH	±% KW	±%$	Sales	% of sales	Customer count	KWH/ customer
Jan																				
Feb																				
Mar																				
1st q																				
Apr																				
May																				
Jun																				
2nd q																				
Jul																				
Aug																				
Sep																				
3rd q																				
Oct																				
Nov																				
Dec																				
4th q																				
Total																				

*Base—previous year

RECORD OF MONTHLY ENERGY USAGE

Year:	Min Max temp	Min Max humid	ELECTRICITY				GAS		FUEL OIL		WATER	
			Demand*		Usage							
			Cost	KW	Cost	KWH	Cost	Therms	Cost	Gals	Cost	Gals
Jan												
Feb												
Mar												
Apr												
May												
Jun												
Jul												
Aug												
Sep												
Oct												
Nov												
Dec												

Year: _____

	Min Max temp	Min Max humid	ELECTRICITY				GAS		FUEL OIL		WATER	
			Demand*		Usage							
			Cost	KW	Cost	KWH	Cost	Therms	Cost	Gals	Cost	Gals
Jan												
Feb												
Mar												
Apr												
May												
Jun												
Jul												
Aug												
Sep												
Oct												
Nov												
Dec												

*This is the GSD schedule. Usage is computed according to peak usage in any fifteen minute period.

APPENDIX 50.

BUILDING DATA – GENERAL INFORMATION

GROSS SQ. FT. _____

HEATED OR COOLED SQ. FT. _____

NUMBER OF FLOORS _____

TYPES OF USEAGE IN % OR SQ. FT. :

    OFFICES _____

    RETAIL _____

    STORAGE _____

    MECHANICAL EQUIPMENT _____

    LOBBIES OR MALLS (ENCLOSED) _____

    OTHER _____

    _____

    _____

OCCUPANCY

BUILDING USE AND OCCUPANCY :

WEEKDAYS: OCCUPIED BY: _____ PEOPLE FROM _____ TO _____ (HOURS)

    _____ _____ _____

    _____ _____ _____

    _____ _____ _____

    _____ _____ _____

SATURDAYS _____ _____ _____

SUNDAYS, HOLIDAYS _____ _____ _____

* (ACCOUNT FOR 24 HOURS A DAY, IF UNOCCUPIED, PUT IN ZERO)

INTERIOR LIGHTING

TOTAL AMOUNT OF INSTALLED LIGHTING:

    FLUORESCENT _____ KW

    INCANDESCENT _____ KW

HOURS/WEEK LIGHTED SPACE IS FULLY OCCUPIED *

    FLUORESCENT _____ HRS

    INCANDESCENT _____ HRS

HOURS/WEEK LIGHTS ARE "ON":

    FLUORESCENT _____ HRS

    INCANDESCENT _____ HRS

LIGHTS ARE ON DURING UNOCCUPIED HOURS BECAUSE OF:

    _____   JANITORS

    _____   OVERTIME

    _____   BOTH

    _____   OTHER

CHILLED WATER PLANT

ELECTRIC DRIVE CENTRIFUGAL CAPACITY: _____ TONS

STEAM TURBINE CENTRIFUGAL CAPACITY: _____ TONS

ABSORPTION MACHINE CAPACITY: _____ TONS

RECIPROCATING MACHINE CAPACITY. _____ TONS

---

    * DO NOT INCLUDE HOURS FOR JANITORIAL SERVICE
       OR CASUAL OVERTIME.

SPACE CONDITIONING EQUIPMENT AND SCHEDULES

TOTAL HP ALL AIR HANDLING FANS: _____ HP

TOTAL CFM HANDLED: _____ CFM

PERCENT OF OUTSIDE AIR: _____ CFM

TOTAL HOURS HVAC UNITS RUN EACH WEEK: _____ HRS

TOTAL HOURS PER WEEK SPACES SERVED ARE FULLY OCCUPIED: _____ HRS

TOTAL COOLING CAPACITY FOR HVAC UNITS HAVING INTERNAL REFRIGERATION
COMPRESSORS: _____

CHECK ONE: _____ KW   _____ BTU

_____ TONS

SPACE TEMPERATURE NORMALLY MAINTAINED DURING COOLING SEASON: _____ °F

HEATING SEASON DAYTIME TEMPERATURE (NORMAL SETTING) : _____ °F

IS THE TEMPERATURE SET BACK AT NIGHT DURING THE HEARING SEASON?

_____ YES   _____ NO

APPENDIX 51.

ENERGY HISTORY

YEAR OF ENERGY HISTORY: 19 ____

NUMBER OF MONTHS COVERED: _____ (MAX. 12 MONTHS)

ELECTRICITY

TOTAL AMOUNT USED: _____ KWH

TOTAL COST $ _____

WHAT % OF ABOVE ELECTRICAL COST IS DEMAND
CHARGES _____ %

NATURAL GAS

TOTAL AMOUNT USED: _____

(CHECK ONE)   CCF _____ THERMS _____

MCF _____

TOTAL COST: $ _____

OIL

TOTAL AMOUNT USED: _____ GALS.

TOTAL COST: $ _____

TYPE OF OIL: # _____

PURCHASED STEAM

TOTAL AMOUNT USED: _____

TOTAL COST: $ _____

PURCHASED CHILLED WATER

TOTAL AMOUNT USED: _____

(CHECK ONE)   MILLION BTU _____

TON/HRS _____

TOTAL COST $ _____

TOTAL COST OF FUEL OR PURCHASED ENERGY FOR HEATING ONLY:

$ _____

APPENDIX 52.

RESTAURANT DATA – GENERAL INFORMATION

GROSS SQUARE FEET _____

HEATED OR COOLED SQUARE FEET _____

NUMBER OF FLOORS _____

TYPES OF USAGE IN % OR SQUARE FEET

    CUSTOMER SERVICE   _____

    KITCHEN _____

    STORAGE _____

    MECHANIZAL EQUIPMENT _____

    MISCELLANEOUS _____

OCCUPANCY

RESTAURANT USE AND OCCUPANCY:	HOURS		CUSTOMER COUNT
WEEKDAYS:*	_____ TO	_____	_____
	_____ TO	_____	_____
	_____ TO	_____	_____
	_____ TO	_____	_____
	_____ TO	_____	_____
	_____ TO	_____	_____
SATURDAYS	_____ TO	_____	_____
SUNDAYS, HOLIDAYS	_____ TO	_____	_____

    * (ACCOUNT FOR 24 HOURS A DAY, IF UNOCCUPIED, PUT IN ZERO)

APPENDIX 53.

Name _____   Suite _____

Add. _____   PH # _____

CODES
A _____
B _____
C _____
D _____
E _____
F _____
Total Fixed _____

LEASE DATES _____ TERM _____
OPTIONS _____ SECURITY _____
ANNUAL RENT _____ SQ FT _____ RATE _____ PSF _____

BALANCE

MISC. CHARGES

FIXED EXPENSES

Month	Date	Paid Amount	Code	Balance	Comments	Date	Billed Amount	Paid Amount	Date	Billed Amount	Paid Amount	Other	Comments	Codes

Electric — Water Sewer

Month	Date	Paid Amount	Code	Balance	Comments	Electric			Water Sewer			Other	Comments	Codes	BALANCE
						Date	Billed Amount	Paid Amount	Date	Billed Amount	Paid Amount				

FIXED EXPENSES   MISC CHARGES

NOTES:

RODIN MANAGEMENT, INCORPORATED

INTEROFFICE MEMORANDUM

RODIN MANAGEMENT INC.
Property Management

VACANCY REPORT

Net Leasable Area:

Date:

Prepared By:

Suite   Square Footage

Vacant   _____   _____

Preleased   _____   _____

Net Available _____   _____

Comments:

NIGHT SIGN-IN SHEET FOR SECURITY

Date _____

Name	Room	In	Out	Name	Room	In	Out

COMMERCIAL LEASE ANALYSIS FORM

Date _____

Suite no.	Tenant name	Sq. ft.	Annual rent	Monthly rent	Other charges	Total monthly	Rate PSF	Base yr.	Bldg. %	Lease dates	Renewal	Comments

RODIN MANAGEMENT. INC.

DEPOSIT SUMMARY FORM

DEPOSIT # _____   DEPOSIT DATE _____

MANAGING AGENT _____   PROPERTY _____

Tenant	Base rent					Elec.	Misc.	Total	Comments
Totals									

COMMERCIAL TENANT FINISHING PROVISIONS FORM

PROPERTY: _____ RENT PER SQ. FT. _____

TENANT: _____ FINISHING COSTS _____

SUITE NO. _____ SQUARE FEET _____ PER SQ. FT. _____

Item	Description of work/materials	Quantity	Unit	Total
1. Carpet Shampoo Replacement				
2. Paint				
3. Wallcover				
4. Lighting fixtures				
5. Electrical outlets				
6. Tile Floor Ceiling				
7. Partitions Demolition Erection				
8. Doors				
9. Cleaning				
10. Other				

*****If cost of work and or materials is unknown, estimate by writing "EST" after the dollar amount. Attach all estimates. Date _____

Total cost: _____

By: _____

INDEX